GLOBAL  STUDIES

LATIN AMERICA

STAFF

Ian A. Nielsen   Publisher
Brenda S. Filley   Production Manager
Lisa M. Clyde   Developmental Editor
Charles Vitelli   Designer
Cheryl Greenleaf   Permissions Coordinator
Lisa Holmes-Doebrick   Administrative Coordinator
Shawn Callahan   Graphics Coordinator
Steve Shumaker   Graphics
Lara M. Johnson   Graphics
Libra Ann Cusack   Typesetting Supervisor
Juliana Arbo   Typesetter
Diane Barker   Editorial Assistant

GLOBAL  STUDIES

LATIN AMERICA

SIXTH EDITION

Dr. Paul Goodwin, Jr.
University of Connecticut, Storrs

The Dushkin Publishing Group, Inc., Sluice Dock, Guilford, Connecticut 06437

Latin America

OTHER BOOKS IN THE GLOBAL STUDIES SERIES

Africa
China
India and South Asia
Japan and the Pacific Rim
The Middle East
Russia, the Eurasian Republics,
   and Central/Eastern Europe
Western Europe

Library of Congress Cataloging in Publication Data
Main entry under title: Global studies: Latin America.
   1. Latin America—History. 2. Central America—History. 3. South America—History.
I. Title: Latin America. II. Goodwin, Paul, Jr., *comp.*
ISBN 1–56134–291–2   954   94–71536

©1994 by The Dushkin Publishing Group, Inc., Guilford, Connecticut 06437.

Global Studies® is a Registered Trademark of The Dushkin Publishing Group, Inc.

Sixth Edition

Printed in the United States of America

 Printed on recycled paper

Latin America

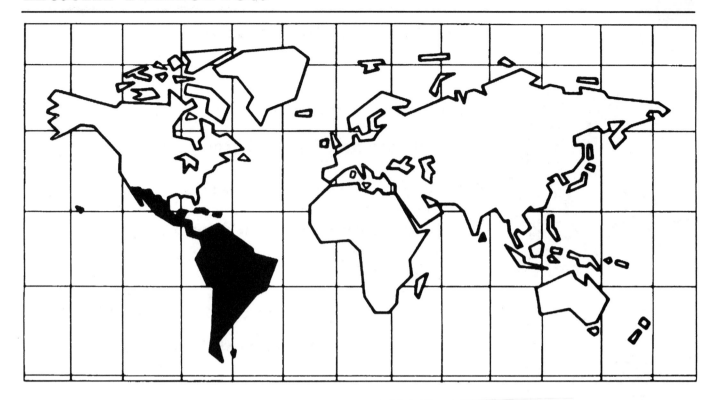

AUTHOR/EDITOR

Dr. Paul B. Goodwin, Jr.

The author/editor for *Global Studies: Latin America* is associate dean of Arts and Sciences at the University of Connecticut at Storrs. Dr. Goodwin has written, reviewed, and lectured extensively at universities all over the United States and in many other countries. His particular area of interest is modern Argentina and Anglo–Latin American relations. Dr. Goodwin's work with the Center for Latin American and Caribbean Studies has included running workshops and mini-courses designed to develop a better understanding of Latin America among educators throughout the United States.

SERIES CONSULTANT

H. Thomas Collins
Washington, D.C.

Contents

Global Studies: Latin America

Page 4

Page 12

Page 37

Page 62

Page 104

Mexico

5. **Can NAFTA Change Mexico?** Jorge G. Castañeda,   **164**
   Foreign Affairs, September/October 1993.
6. **The Revolution Continues,** *The Economist,* January 22, 1994.   **170**
7. **A New Chapter in Mexican Politics?** *World Press Review,*   **173**
   January 1994.
8. **Mexico's Environmental Future,** Steven E. Sanderson,   **175**
   Current History, February 1993.

Central America

9. **The Lost Decade: Central America Is Staggering Under Its**   **180**
   '80s Legacy, Douglas Farah, *Washington Post National
   Weekly Edition,* June 14–20, 1994.
10. **Can Central America Cope with Soaring Population?**   **183**
    Robert W. Fox, *USA Today Magazine (Society for the
    Advancement of Education),* September 1991.
11. **Central America's Latest War,** Yazmín Ross, *World Press*   **187**
    Review, May 1993.
12. **Even in Peace, the Armies Remain Entrenched,** Douglas   **189**
    Farah, *Washington Post National Weekly Edition,* June 14–20,
    1993.
13. **To NAFTA and EMU, a Child,** *The Economist,* July 17, 1993.   **193**
14. **Nicaragua: Sandinistas Still in the Driver's Seat,** Marvin   **195**
    Alisky, *USA Today Magazine (Society for the Advancement of
    Education),* January 1994.
15. **The Star System,** Berthold Riese, *The UNESCO Courier,*   **196**
    November 1993.

South America

16. **Pollution Is Growing Threat in Argentina,** Manuel Long,   **199**
    Latinamerica Press, September 16, 1993.
17. **"I Fight for Our Future,"** Hank Whittemore, *Parade,*   **200**
    April 12, 1992.
18. **The Sick Man of Latin America,** Joel Millman, *Forbes,*   **204**
    September 13, 1993.
19. **Healing Secrets in a Shaman's Forest,** Jimmy Wieskopf,   **207**
    Américas, July/August 1993.
20. **Indian Leader's Goal Is Land,** David Holmstrom, *Christian*   **210**
    Science Monitor, June 23, 1993.
21. **Kicking the Habit,** Steve Xydas, *Harvard International*   **212**
    Review, Summer 1993.

The Caribbean

22. **The Caribbean: Small Is Scary,** Aaron Segal, *Current*   **215**
    History, March 1991.
23. **Cuba Alone,** Johanna McGeary and Cathy Booth, *Time,*   **220**
    December 6, 1993.
24. **A Place Called Fear,** Bella Stumbo, *Vanity Fair,* February 1994.   **224**

Credits 235
Sources for Statistical Summaries 235
Glossary of Terms and Abbreviations 236
Bibliography 239
Index 241

Introduction

THE GLOBAL AGE

As we approach the end of the twentieth century, it is clear that the future we face will be considerably more international in nature than was ever believed possible in the past. Each day print and broadcast journalists make us aware that our world is becoming increasingly smaller and substantially more interdependent.

The energy crisis, world food shortages, nuclear proliferation, and the regional conflicts in Central America, the Middle East, and other areas that threaten to involve us all make it clear that the distinctions between domestic and foreign problems are all too often artificial—that many seemingly domestic problems no longer stop at national boundaries. As Rene Dubos, the 1969 Pulitzer Prize recipient, stated: "[I]t becomes obvious that each [of us] has two countries, [our] own and planet Earth." As global interdependence has become a reality, it has become vital for the citizens of this world to develop literacy in global matters.

THE GLOBAL STUDIES SERIES

It is the aim of the Global Studies series to help readers acquire a basic knowledge and understanding of the regions and countries in the world. Each volume provides a foundation of information—geographic, cultural, economic, political, historical, artistic, and religious—that allows readers better to understand the current and future problems within these countries and regions and to comprehend how events there might affect their own well-being. In short, these volumes provide background information necessary to respond to the realities of our global age.

Author/Editor
Each of the volumes in the Global Studies series is crafted under the careful direction of an author/editor—an expert in the area under study. The author/editors teach and conduct research and have traveled extensively through the regions about which they are writing.

The author/editor of *Global Studies: Latin America, Sixth Edition,* has written the umbrella regional essay introducing the area. He has also written the subregional essays and the country reports. In addition, he has been instrumental in the final selection of the world press articles.

Contents and Features
The Global Studies volumes are organized to provide concise information and current world press articles on the regions and countries within those areas under study.

Regional and Subregional Essays
Global Studies: Latin America, Sixth Edition, covers Mexico, Central America, South America, and the Caribbean. For each of these subregions, the author/editor has written

(United Nations/Yutaka Nagata)
The global age is making all countries and all peoples more interdependent.

an essay focusing on the geographical, cultural, sociopolitical, and economic differences and similarities of the countries and people in the region. The purpose of the *subregional essays* is to provide readers with an effective sense of the diversity of the area as well as an understanding of its common cultural and historical backgrounds. Accompanying each of the narratives is a full-page map showing the political boundaries of each of the countries within the subregion.

In addition to these subregional essays, the author provides a brief introductory narrative on Latin America. This *regional essay* examines a number of broad themes in an attempt to define what constitutes "Latin America."

Country Reports
Concise reports on the individual countries within the region follow each of the subregional essays. These reports are the heart of each Global Studies volume. *Global Studies: Latin America, Sixth Edition*, contains 33 *country reports*, including a Mexico report, 7 reports for Central America, 12 for South America, and 13 for the Caribbean region. The reports cover each *independent country* within the Latin American area.

The country reports are comprised of five standard elements. Each report contains a small, detailed map visually positioning the country among its neighboring states; a summary of statistical information; a current essay providing important historical, geographical, political, cultural, and economic information; a historical timeline offering a convenient visual survey of a few key historical events; and four graphic indicators, with summary statements about the country in terms of development, freedom, health/welfare, and achievements, at the end of each report.

All the country reports, regional and subregional essays, and graphic indicators have been updated to reflect the most current state of affairs in today's Latin American world. Since the first edition of *Global Studies: Latin America* was published, we have had a tremendous and positive response from both students and teachers alike. This important input is reflected in *Global Studies: Latin America, Sixth Edition.*

A Note on the Statistical Summaries

The statistical information provided for each country has been drawn from a wide range of sources (the most frequently referenced are listed on page 238). Every effort has been made to provide the most current and accurate information available. However, occasionally the information cited by these sources differs significantly; and, all too often, the only information available for some countries is quite dated. Aside from these difficulties, the statistical summary for each country is generally quite complete and reasonably current. (Care should be taken, however, in using these statistics—or, for that matter, any published statistics—in making hard comparisons among countries.) We have also included comparable statistics on Canada and the United States, which follow on the next two pages.

World Press Articles

Within each Global Studies volume is reprinted a number of articles carefully selected by our editorial staff and the author/editor from a broad range of international periodicals and newspapers. The articles have been chosen for currency, interest, and their differing perspectives on the subject countries and regions. There are 24 articles in *Global Studies: Latin America, Sixth Edition*—4 general articles, 4 articles pertaining to Mexico, 7 to Central America, 6 to South America, and 3 to the Caribbean.

The articles section is preceded by an *annotated table of contents* as well as a *topic guide*. The intent of the annotated table of contents is to offer a brief summary of each article, while the topic guide indicates the main theme(s) of each of the articles reprinted. Thus, readers desiring to focus on articles dealing with a particular theme, say, human rights, may refer to the topic guide to find those articles.

Glossary, Bibliography, Index

At the back of each Global Studies volume, readers will find a *glossary of terms and abbreviations*, which provides quick reference to the specialized vocabulary of the area under study and to the standard abbreviations (UN, OAS, GATT, etc.) used throughout the volume.

Following the glossary is a *bibliography*, which contains specific references for most of the literary works mentioned in the body of the text. The bibliography is organized into general reference volumes, national and regional histories, novels in translation, current events publications, and periodicals that provide regular coverage on Latin America.

The *index* at the end of the volume is an accurate reference to the contents of the volume. Readers seeking specific information and citations should consult this standard index.

Currency and Usefulness

Global Studies: Latin America, Sixth Edition, is intended to provide the most current and useful information available necessary to understand the events that are shaping the cultures of Latin America today.

We plan to issue this volume on a regular basis. The statistics will be updated, essays rewritten, country reports revised, and articles completely replaced as new information becomes available. In order to accomplish this task, we will turn to our author/editors, our advisory boards and—hopefully—to you, the users of this volume. Your comments are more than welcome. If you have an idea that you think will make the volume more useful; an article or bit of information that will make it more up to date; or a general comment on its organization, content, or features that you would like to share with us, please send it in for serious consideration for the next edition.

(United Nations photo)
Understanding the problems and lifestyles of other countries will help make us literate in global matters.

Canada

GEOGRAPHY

Area in Square Kilometers (Miles):
9,976,140 (3,850,790) (slightly larger
than the United States)
Capital (Population): Ottawa
(920.000)
Climate: from temperate in south to
subarctic and arctic in north

PEOPLE

Population
Total: 27,797,000
Annual Growth Rate: 1.28%
Rural/Urban Population Ratio: 23/77
Ethnic Makeup of Population: 40%
British Isles origin; 27% French
origin; 20% other European; 1.5%
indigenous Indian and Eskimo;
11.5% mixed
Languages: both English and French
are official

Health
Life Expectancy at Birth: 75 years
(male); 82 years (female)
Infant Mortality Rate (Ratio): 7/1,000
Average Caloric Intake: 127% of
FAO minimum
Physicians Available (Ratio): 1/449

Religion(s)
46% Roman Catholic; 16% United
Church; 10% Anglican; 28% others

Education
Adult Literacy Rate: 99%

COMMUNICATION

Telephones: 18,000,000
Newspapers: 96 in English; 11 in
French

TRANSPORTATION

Highways—Kilometers (Miles):
884,272 (549,133)
Railroads—Kilometers (Miles):
146,444 (90,942)
Usable Airfields: 1,142

GOVERNMENT

Type: confederation with
parliamentary democracy
Independence Date: July 1, 1867
Head of State: Queen Elizabeth II
Head of Government: Prime Minister
Jean Chrétien
Political Parties: Progressive
Conservative Party; Liberal Party;
New Democratic Party; Reform
Party; Bloc Québécois
Suffrage: universal at 18

MILITARY

Number of Armed Forces: 88,000
*Military Expenditures (% of Central
Government Expenditures):* 8.7%
Current Hostilities: none

ECONOMY

Currency ($U.S. Equivalent): 1.27
Canadian dollars = $1
Per Capita Income/GDP:
$19,600/$537.1 billion
Inflation Rate: 1.5%
Total Foreign Debt: $247 billion
Natural Resources: petroleum; natural
gas; fish; minerals; cement; forestry
products; fur
Agriculture: grains; livestock; dairy
products; potatoes; hogs; poultry and
eggs; tobacco
Industry: oil production and refining;
natural-gas development; fish
products; wood and paper products;
chemicals; transportation equipment

FOREIGN TRADE

Exports: $124 billion
Imports: $118 billion

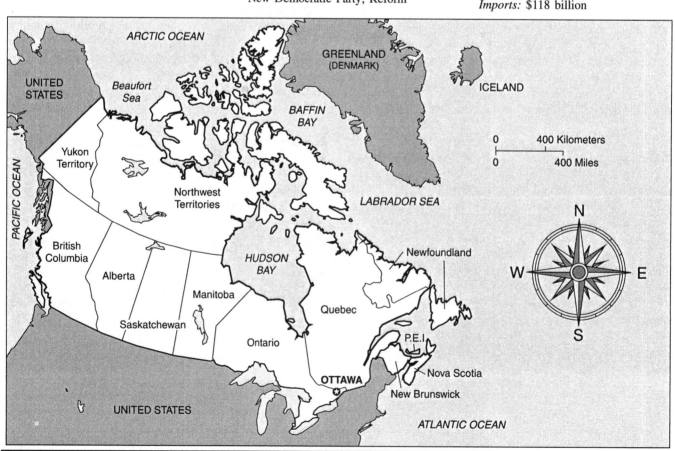

The United States

GEOGRAPHY

Area in Square Kilometers (Miles):
9,578,626 (3,618,770)
Capital (Population): Washington,
D.C. (606,900)
Climate: temperate

PEOPLE

Population
Total: 258,103,700
Annual Growth Rate: 1.02%
Rural/Urban Population Ratio: 26/74
Ethnic Makeup of Population: 80%
white; 12% black; 6% Hispanic; 2%
Asian, Pacific Islander, American
Indian, Eskimo, and Aleut
Languages: predominantly English; a
sizable Spanish-speaking minority

Health
Life Expectancy at Birth: 72 years
(male); 79 years (female)
Infant Mortality Rate (Ratio):
8.3/1,000
Average Caloric Intake: 138% of
FAO minimum
Physicians Available (Ratio): 1/404

Religion(s)
55% Protestant; 36% Roman
Catholic; 4% Jewish; 5% Muslim
and others

Education
Adult Literacy Rate: 97.9% (official)
(estimates vary widely)

COMMUNICATION

Telephones: 182,558,000
Newspapers: 1,679 dailies;
approximately 63,000,000 circulation

TRANSPORTATION

Highways—Kilometers (Miles):
7,599,250 (4,719,134)
Railroads—Kilometers (Miles):
270,312 (167,974)
Usable Airfields: 12,417

GOVERNMENT

Type: federal republic
Independence Date: July 4, 1776
Head of State: President William
("Bill") Jefferson Clinton
Political Parties: Democratic Party;
Republican Party; others of minor
political significance
Suffrage: universal at 18

MILITARY

Number of Armed Forces: 1,807,177
*Military Expenditures (% of Central
Government Expenditures):* 22.6%
Current Hostilities: none

ECONOMY

Per Capita Income/GDP:
$23,400/$5.95 trillion
Inflation Rate: 3%
Natural Resources: metallic and
nonmetallic minerals; petroleum;
arable land
Agriculture: food grains; feed crops;
oil-bearing crops; livestock; dairy
products
Industry: diversified in both capital-
and consumer-goods industries

FOREIGN TRADE

Exports: $442 billion
Imports: $544 billion

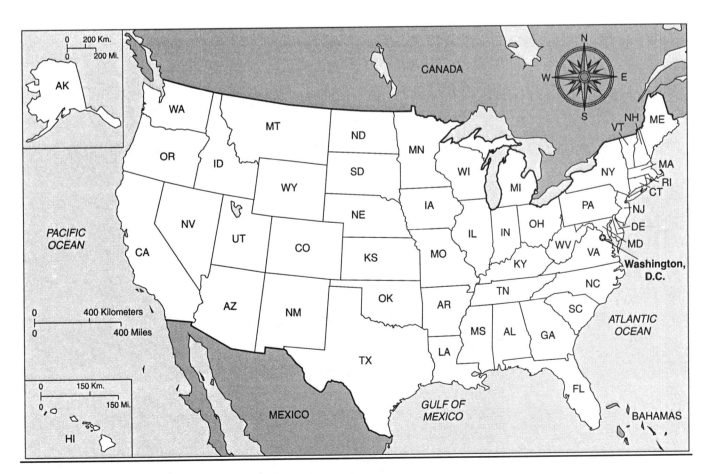

This map of the world highlights the Latin American and Caribbean countries that are discussed in this volume. We have included only independent countries of the Caribbean and exclude French departments, Dutch territories, British associate states, and United States possessions. All of the following essays are written from a cultural perspective in order to give the readers a sense of what life is like in these countries. The essays are designed to present the most current and useful information available. Other books in the Global Studies series cover different global areas and examine the current state of affairs of the countries within those regions.

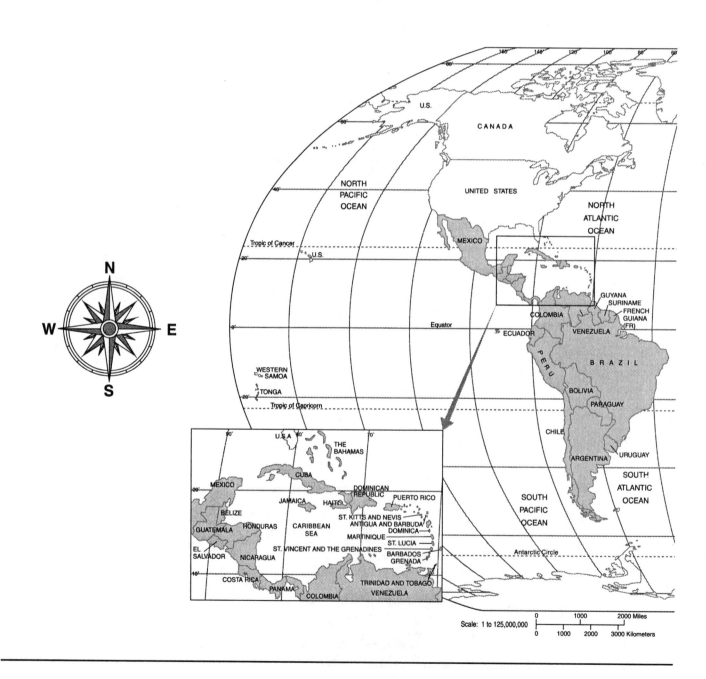

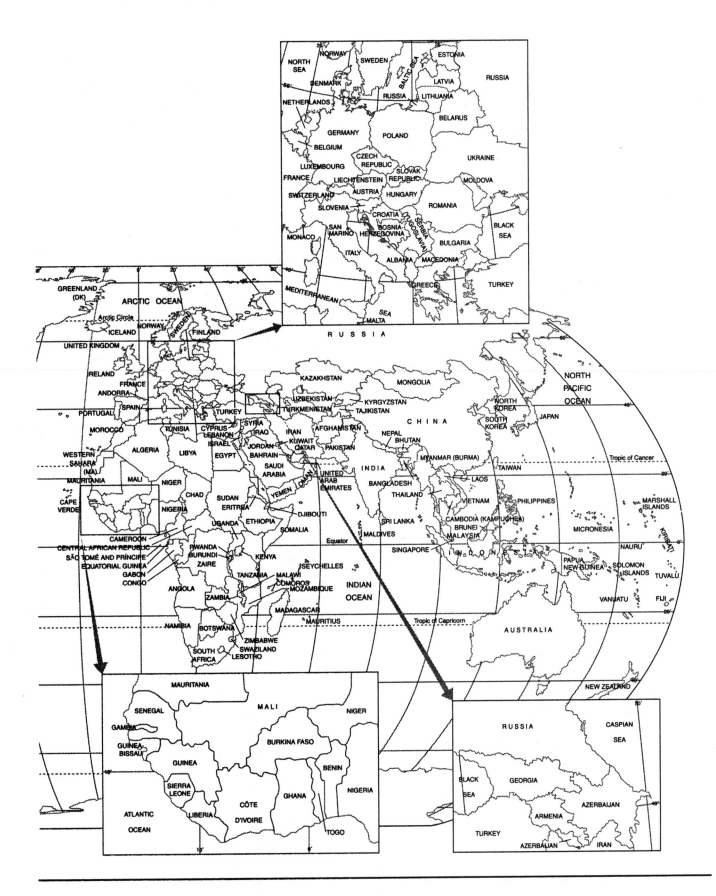

Latin America

Latin America: Myth and Reality

Much of the world still tends to view Latin Americans in terms of stereotypes. The popular image of the mustachioed *bandito* wearing a large sombrero and draped with cartridge belts has been replaced by the figure of the modern-day guerrilla. But the same essential image, of lawlessness and violence, persists. Another common stereotype is that of the lazy Latin American who constantly puts off things until *mañana* ("tomorrow"). The implied message here is that Latin Americans lack industry and do not know how to make the best use of their time. A third widespread image is that of the Latin lover and the cult of *machismo*.

Many of those outside the culture find it difficult to conceive of Latin America as a mixture of peoples and cultures, each one distinct from the others. Indeed, it was not so long ago that then–U.S. president Ronald Reagan, after a tour of the region, remarked with some surprise that all of the countries were "different." Stereotypes spring from ignorance and bias; images are not necessarily a reflection of reality. In the words of Spanish philosopher José Ortega y Gasset, "In politics and history, if one takes accepted statements at face value, one will be sadly misled."

THE LATIN AMERICAN REALITY

The reality of Latin America's multiplicity of cultures is, in a word, complexity. Europeans, Africans, and the indigenous people of Latin America have all contributed substantially to these cultures. If one sets aside non-Hispanic influences for a moment, is it possible to argue, as does historian Claudio Veliz, that "the Iberian [Spanish and Portuguese] inheritance is an essential part of our lives and customs; Brazil and Spanish America [*i.e.,* Spanish-speaking] have derived their personality from Iberia"? Many scholars would disagree. For example, political scientist Lawrence S. Graham argues that "what is clear is that generalizations about Latin American cultural unity are no longer tenable." And that "one of the effects of nationalism has been to . . . lead growing numbers of individuals within the region to identify with their own nation-state before they think in terms of a more amorphous land mass called Latin America."

Granted, Argentines speak of their Argentinity and Mexicans of their *mejicanidad.* It is true that there are profound differences that separate each of the nations of the region. But there exists a cultural bedrock that ties Latin America to Spain and Portugal, and even beyond—to the Roman Empire and the great cultures of the Mediterranean world. African influence, too, is substantial in many parts of the region. Latin America's Indians, of course, trace their roots to indigenous sources.

To understand the nature of Latin American culture, one must remember that there exist many exceptions to the generalizations; the cultural mold is not rigid. Much of what has happened in Latin America, including the evolution of its cultures, is because of a fortunate or unfortunate combination of various factors.

THE FAMILY

Let us first consider the Latin American family. The family unit has survived even Latin America's economic development and the pressures of modernization. Family ties are strong and dominant. These bonds are not confined to the nuclear family of father, mother, and children. The same close ties are found in the extended family (a network of second cousins, godparents, and close friends of blood relatives). In times of difficulty, the family can be counted on to help. It is a fortress against the misery of the outside world; it is the repository of dignity, honor, and respect.

AN URBAN CIVILIZATION

In a region where the interaction of networks of families is the rule and where frequent human contact is sought out,

(United Nations photo)

In Latin America, the family is an important element in the cultural context. These children, who live in a slum in Santiago, Chile, come from caring families.

it is not surprising to find that Latin Americans are, above all, an urban people. There are more cities of more than half a million people in Latin America than in the United States. This is considered unusual, for urbanization is usually associated with industrialization.

Latin American urban culture was not created by industrial growth; it actually pre-dated it. As soon as the opportunity presented itself, the Spanish conquerors of the New World, in Veliz's words, "founded cities in which to take refuge from the barbaric, harsh, uncivilized, and rural world outside.... For those men civilization was strictly and uniquely a function of well-ordered city life." The city, from the Spanish conquest until the present, has dominated the social and cultural horizon of Latin America. Opportunity is found in the city, not in the countryside. This cultural fact of life, in addition to economic motives, accounts for the continuing flow of population from rural to urban areas in Latin America.

A WORLD OF APPEARANCES

Because in their urban environment Latin Americans are in close contact with many people, appearances are important to them. There is a constant quest for prestige, dignity, status, and honor. People are forever trying to impress one another with their public worth. Hence, it is not unusual to see a blue-collar worker traveling to work dressed in a suit, briefcase in hand. It is not uncommon to see jungles of television antennas over shantytowns, although many are not connected to anything. It is a society, in the opinion of writer Octavio Paz, that hides behind masks. Latin Americans convey an impression of importance, no matter how menial their position. Glen Dealy, a political scientist, writes: "And those of the lower class who must wait on tables, wash cars, and do gardening for a living can help to gain back a measure of self-respect by having their shoes shined by someone else, buying a drink for a friend . . . , or concealing their occupation by wearing a tie to and from work."

MACHISMO

Closely related to appearances is machismo. Usually the term is understood solely, and mistakenly, in terms of virility—the image of the Latin lover, for example. But machismo also connotes generosity, dignity, and honor. Macho behavior, in many respects, is indulged in because of social convention; it is expected of men. Machismo is also one of those cultural traits that cuts through class lines, for the macho is admired regardless of his social position.

THE ROLE OF WOMEN

If the complex nature of machismo is misunderstood by those outside the culture, so too is the role of women. The commonly held stereotype is that Latin American women are submissive and that the culture is dominated by males. Again, appearances mask a far more complex reality, for Latin American cultures actually allow for strong female roles. Political scientist Evelyn Stevens has found that *marianismo,* the female counterpart of machismo, permeates all strata of Latin American society.

Marianismo is the cult of feminine spiritual superiority that "teaches that women are semi-divine, morally superior to and spiritually stronger than men." When Mexico's war for independence broke out in 1810, a religious symbol, the Virgin of Guadeloupe, was identified with the rebels and became a rallying point for the first stirrings of Mexican nationalism. Earlier in this century, it was not uncommon in Argentine textbooks to portray Eva Perón (1919–1952), the president's wife, in the image of the Virgin Mary, complete with a blue veil and halo. In less religious terms, one of Latin America's most popular novels, *Doña Barbara,* by Rómulo Gallegos, is the story of a female *caudillo* ("man on horseback") on the plains of Venezuela.

The Latin American woman dominates the family because of a deep-seated respect for motherhood. Personal identity is less of a problem for her because she retains her family name upon marriage and passes it on to her children. Women who have found employment outside the home are

(United Nations photo/Bernard P. Wolff)
The role of the native woman in Latin America has been defined by centuries of tradition. This woman is spinning wool, in Chimburaso, Ecuador, just as her ancestors did.

supposedly guaranteed the respect for motherhood, which is sacred. In any conflict between a woman's job and the needs of her family, the employer, by custom, must grant her a leave to tend to the family's needs. Recent historical scholarship also revealed that Latin American women have long enjoyed rights denied to women in other, more "advanced" parts of the world. For example, even in colonial days women were allowed to own property and to sign for mortgages in their own names. In the 1920s they won the right to vote in local elections in Yucatán, Mexico, and San Juan, Argentina.

Here again, though, appearances can be deceiving. Latin American constitutions in many instances guarantee equality of treatment, but reality is burdensome for women in many parts of the region. They do not have the same kinds of access to jobs that men enjoy, they seldom receive equal pay for equal work, and family life, at times, can be brutalizing.

WORK AND LEISURE

Work, leisure, and concepts of time in Latin America correspond to an entirely different cultural mind-set than in Northern Europe and North America. The essential difference was recently demonstrated in a North American television commercial for a wine, which portrayed two starry-eyed people giving the Spanish toast: *Salud, amor, y pesetas* ("Health, love, and money"). For a North American audience, the message was appropriate. But the full Spanish toast includes the tag line: *y el tiempo para gozarlos* ("and the time to enjoy them").

Leisure in Latin America is viewed as a perfectly rational goal. It has nothing to do with being lazy or indolent. Indeed, in *Ariel,* by writer José Enrique Rodo, leisure is described within the context of the culture: "To think, to dream, to admire—these are the ministrants that haunt my cell. The ancients ranked them under the word *otium,* well-employed leisure, which they deemed the highest use of being truly rational, liberty of thought emancipated of all ignoble chains. Such leisure meant that use of time which they opposed to mere economic activity as the expression of a higher life. Their concept of dignity was linked closely to this lofty conception of leisure." Work, by contrast, is often perceived as a necessary evil.

(United Nations photo/Jerry Frank)

Agriculture is the backbone of much of Latin America's cultures and economies. These workers are harvesting sugarcane on a plantation in the state of Pernambuco, Brazil.

CONCEPTS OF TIME

Latin American attitudes toward time also reveal the inner workings of the culture. Exasperated North American businesspeople have for years complained about the *mañana, mañana* attitude of Latin Americans. People always seem to come to appointments late; little appears to get done.

For the North American who believes that time is money, such behavior appears irrational. However, Glen Dealy, in his perceptive book *The Public Man,* argues that such behavior is perfectly rational. When a Latin American spends hours over lunch or over coffee in a cafe, he is not wasting time. For here, with his friends, he is with the source of his power. It is important to remember that networks of friends and families are the glue of Latin American society. "Without spending time in this fashion he would, in fact, soon have fewer friends. Additionally, he knows that to leave a cafe precipitously for an 'appointment' would signify to all that he must not keep someone else waiting—which further indicates his lack of importance. If he had power and position the other person would wait upon his arrival. It is the powerless who wait." Therefore, friends and power relationships are more important than rushing to keep an appointment. The North American who wants the "deal" will wait. In a sense, the North American is the client and the Latin American is the *patrón* (the "patron," or wielder of power).

Perceptions of time in Latin America also have a broader meaning. North American students who have been exposed to Latin American literature are almost always confused by the absence of a "logical," chronological development of the story. Time, for Latin Americans, tends to be circular rather than linear. That is, the past and the present are perceived as equally relevant—both are points on a circle. The past is as important as the present.

MYTH AND REALITY

The past that is exposed in works of literature as well as scholarly writings reflects wholly different attitudes toward what people from other cultures identify as reality. For example, in the Nobel Prize-winning writer Gabriél García Márquez's classic novel *One Hundred Years of Solitude,* which is a fictional history of the town of Macondo and its leading family, fantasy and tall tales abound. But García Márquez drew his inspiration from stories he heard on his grandmother's knee about Aracataca, Colombia, the real town in which he grew up. The point here is that the fanciful story of the town's origins constitute that town's memory of its past. The stories give the town a common heritage and memory.

The historical memory, from a North American or Northern European perspective, is faulty. From the Latin American perspective, however, it is the perception of the past that is important, regardless of its factual accuracy. Myth and reality, appearances and substance, merge.

POLITICAL CULTURE

The brief generalizations drawn here about Latin American society also apply to its political culture, which is essentially authoritarian and oriented toward power and power relationships. Ideology—be it liberalism, conservatism, or communism—is little more than window dressing. It is the means by which contenders for power can be separated. As Claudio Veliz has noted, regardless of the aims of revolutionary leaders, the great upheavals in Latin America in the twentieth century have without exception ended up by strengthening the political center, which is essentially authoritarian. This was true of the Mexican Revolution (1910), the Bolivian Revolution (1952), the Cuban Revolution (1958), and the Nicaraguan Revolution (1979).

Ideology has never been a decisive factor in the historical and social reality of Latin America. But charisma and the ability to lead are crucial ingredients. José Velasco Ibarra, five times the president of Ecuador in the twentieth century, once boasted: "Give me a balcony and I will be president!" He saw his personality, not his ideology, as the key to power.

In the realm of national and international relations, Latin America often appears to be in a constant state of turmoil and chaos. It seems that every day there is news that a regime has been ousted, border clashes have intensified, or guerrillas have taken over another section of a country. The conclusion that chaos reigns in Latin America is most often based on the visible political and social violence, not on the general nature of a country. Political violence is often local in nature, and the social fabric of the country is bound together by the social stability of the Latin American family. Again, there is the dualism of what appears to be and what is.

Much of this upheaval can be attributed to the division between the people of Mediterranean background and the native Indian population. Within a single country, there may be several hundred minority groups. The problems that arise from these intense internal differences, however, are not necessarily as detrimental as they might seem to someone outside the culture, because they contribute to the texture and color of Latin American culture.

SEEING BEHIND THE MASK

In order to grasp the essence of Latin America, one must ignore the stereotypes, appreciate appearances for what they are, and attempt to see behind the mask. Latin America must be appreciated as a culture in its own right, as an essentially Mediterranean variant of Western civilization.

A Latin American world view tends to be dualistic. The family constitutes the basic unit; here are found generosity, warmth, honor, and love. Beyond the walls of the home, in the world of business and politics, Latin Americans don their masks and enter "combat." It is a world of power relationships, of macho bravado, and of appearances. This dualism is deep-seated; scholars such as Richard Morse and Glen Dealy have traced its roots to the Middle Ages. For Latin Americans, one's activities are compartmentalized into those fitting for the City of God, which corresponds to religion, the home, and one's intimate circle of friends; and those appropriate for the City of Man, which is secular and often ruthless and corrupt. North Americans, who tend to measure their public and private lives by the same yardstick, often interpret Latin American dualism as hypocrisy. Nothing could be further from the truth.

For the Latin American, life exists on several planes, has purpose, and is perfectly rational. Indeed, one is tempted to suggest that many Latin American institutions—particularly the supportive network of families and friends—are more in tune with a world that can alienate and isolate than are our own. As you will see in the following reports, the social structure and cultural diversity of Latin America add greatly to its character and, paradoxically, to its stability.

Mexico (United Mexican States)

GEOGRAPHY

Area in Square Kilometers (Miles):
1,978,000 (764,000) (about 3 times the size of Texas)
Capital (Population): Mexico City (approximately 20,000,000)
Climate: varies from tropical to desert

PEOPLE

Population
Total: 92,381,000
Annual Growth Rate: 2.3%
Rural/Urban Population Ratio: 27/73
Ethnic Makeup of Population: 60% Mestizo; 30% Amerindian; 9% white; 1% others

Health
Life Expectancy at Birth: 69 years (male); 76 years (female)
Infant Mortality Rate (Ratio): 30/1,000
Average Caloric Intake: 121% of FAO minimum
Physicians Available (Ratio): 1/1,037

Religion(s)
97% Roman Catholic; 3% Protestant and others

Education
Adult Literacy Rate: 87%

COMMUNICATION

Telephones: 6,410,000
Newspapers: 308 dailies; 10,360,000 circulation

TRANSPORTATION

Highways—Kilometers (Miles):
238,006 (147,597)
Railroads—Kilometers (Miles): 24,500 (15,214)
Usable Airfields: 1,505

AMERICA'S FIRST COWBOY

When Hernán Cortéz claimed Mexico for the king of Spain, in 1519, by his side was his friend and fellow *conquistador* ("conqueror") Hernando Alonso. Eighty miles north of what is today Mexico City, Alonso established one of the first cattle ranches in Mexico and bred what may have been the first calves born in the Americas. Thus, Hernando Alonso may have been the first American cowboy.

GOVERNMENT

Type: federal republic
Independence Date: September 16, 1810
Head of State: President Carlos Salinas de Gortari
Political Parties: Institutionalized Revolutionary Party; National Action Party; Popular Socialist Party; Democratic Revolutionary Party; Cardenist Front for the National Reconstruction; Authentic Party of the Mexican Revolution
Suffrage: universal at 18

MILITARY

Number of Armed Forces: 148,500
Military Expenditures (% of Central Government Expenditures): 2.4%
Current Hostilities: none

ECONOMY

Currency ($ U.S. Equivalent): 3.11 pesos = $1 (floating rate)
Per Capita Income/GDP: $3,200/$289 billion
Inflation Rate: 18.8%
Total Foreign Debt: $98.4 billion
Natural Resources: petroleum; silver; copper; gold; lead; zinc; natural gas; timber
Agriculture: corn; beans; oilseeds; feed grains; fruit; cotton; coffee; sugarcane; winter vegetables
Industry: food processing; beverages; tobacco; chemicals; metals; petroleum products; mining; textiles; clothing

FOREIGN TRADE

Exports: $27.4 billion
Imports: $36.7 billion

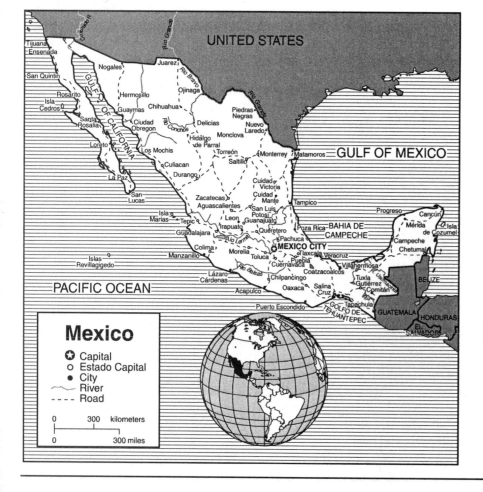

There is a story that Hernán Cortéz, the conqueror of the Aztec Empire in the sixteenth century, when asked to describe the landscape of New Spain (Mexico), took a piece of paper in his hands and crumpled it. The analogy is apt. Mexico is a tortured land of mountains and valleys, of deserts in the north and rain forests in the south. Geography has helped to create an intense regionalism in Mexico, and the existence of hundreds of *patrias chicas* ("little countries") has hindered national integration for decades. Much of Mexico's territory is vulnerable to earthquakes and volcanic activity. In 1943 a cornfield in one of Mexico's richest agricultural zones sprouted a volcano instead of maize. In 1982 a severe volcanic eruption in the south took several hundred lives, destroyed thousands of head of livestock, and buried crops under tons of ash. Thousands of people died when a series of earthquakes struck Mexico City in 1985.

It is a nation of climatic extremes. Needed rains often fall so hard that most of the water runs off before it can be absorbed by the soil. When the rains fail to materialize, crops die in the fields. The harsh face of the land, the unavailability of water, and erosion limit the agricultural potential of Mexico. Only 10 to 15 percent of Mexico's land can be planted with crops; but because of unpredictable weather or natural disasters, good harvests can be expected from only 6 to 8 percent of the land in any given year.

MEXICO CITY

Mexico's central region has the best cropland. It was here that the Aztecs built their capital city, the foundations of which lie beneath the current Mexican capital, Mexico City. Given their agricultural potential as well as its focus as the commercial and administrative center of the nation, Mexico City and the surrounding region have always supported a large population. For decades Mexico City has acted as a magnet for rural poor who have given up attempts to eke out a living from the soil. In the 1940s and 1950s, the city experienced a great population surge. In that era, however, it had the capacity to absorb the tens of thousands of migrants, and so a myth of plentiful money and employment was created. Even today that myth exercises a strong influence in the countryside and partially accounts for the tremendous growth of the city and its metropolitan area, now home to approximately 20 million people.

The size and location of Mexico City have spawned awesome problems. Because it lies in a valley surrounded by mountains, pollution is trapped. Mexico City has the worst smog in the Western Hemisphere. Traffic congestion is among the worst in the world. And essential services—including the provision of drinkable water, electricity, and sewers—have failed to keep pace with the city's growth.

Social and Cultural Changes

Dramatic social and cultural changes have accompanied Mexico's population growth. These are particularly evident in Mexico City, which daily becomes less Mexican and more cosmopolitan and international.

As Mexico City has become more worldly, English words have become increasingly common in everyday vocabulary. "Okay," "coffee break," and "happy hour" are some examples of English idioms that have slipped into popular usage. In urban centers quick lunches and coffee breaks have replaced the traditional large meal that was once served at noon. For most people the afternoon *siesta* ("nap") is a fondly remembered custom of bygone days.

Mass communication has had an incalculable impact on culture. Television commercials use, almost exclusively, models who are European or North American in appearance—preferably white, blue-eyed, and blonde. As if in defiance of the overwhelmingly Mestizo (mixed Indian and white) character of the population, Mexican newspapers and magazines carry advertisements for products guaranteed to lighten one's skin. Success has become associated with light skin. Another symbol of success is ownership of a television. Antennas cover rooftops even in the poorest urban slums. Acute observers might note, however, that many of the antennas are not connected to anything; the residents of many hovels merely want to convey the impression that they can afford one.

Television has also helped to educate the illiterate. Some Mexican soap operas, for instance, incorporate educational materials. On a given day, a show's characters may attend an adult-education class that stresses basic reading and writing skills. Both the television characters and the home-viewing audience sit in on the class. Literacy is portrayed as being essential to one's success and well-being. Mexican "soaps," or *telenovelas*, have a special focus on teenagers and problems common to adolescents. Solutions are advanced within a traditional cultural context and reaffirm the central role of the family.

Cultural Survival: Compadrazgo

Despite these obvious signs of change, distinct Mexican traditions and customs have not only survived Mexico's transformation but have also flourished because of it. The chaos of city life, the hundreds of thousands of migrants uprooted from rural settings, and the sense of isolation and alienation common to city dwellers the world over are in part eased by the Hispanic institution of *compadrazgo* ("co-godparenthood" or "sponsorship").

Compadrazgo is found at all levels of Mexican society, in both rural and urban areas. It is a device for building economic and social alliances that are more enduring than simple friendship. It has a religious dimension as well as a secular, or everyday, application. In addition to basic religious occasions (such as baptism, confirmation,

(United Nations photo/Claire Taplin)

Mexico City is now the world's largest city. More than 1,000 newcomers arrive daily. The city is little able to absorb them, as exemplified by this typical barrio in the foothills of the volcanic mountains surrounding Mexico City.

first communion, and marriage) Mexicans seek sponsors for minor religious occasions such as the blessing of a business or for events as common as a graduation or a boy's first haircut.

Anthropologist Robert V. Kemper observes that the institution of compadrazgo reaches across class lines and knits the various strands of Mexican society into a whole cloth. Compadrazgo performs many functions, including providing assistance from the more powerful to the less powerful and, reciprocally, providing homage from the less powerful to the more powerful. The most common choices for *compadres* are neighbors, relatives, fellow migrants, coworkers, and employers. A remarkably flexible institution, compadrazgo is perfectly compatible with the tensions and anxieties of urban life.

Yet even compadrazgo, a form of patron/client relationship, has its limitations. As Mexico City has sprawled across the landscape, a multitude of new neighborhoods have been created. Many are the result of well-planned land seizures, orchestrated by groups of people attracted by the promise of the city. Technically, such land seizures are illegal; and a primary goal of the *colonos*, or inhabitants of

these low-income communities, is legitimization and consequent community participation.

Beginning in the 1970s, colonos forcefully pushed their demands for legitimization through protest movements and demonstrations, some of which revealed a surprising degree of radicalization. In response the Mexican government adopted a two-track policy: It selectively repressed the best organized and most radical groups of colonos and tried to co-opt the remainder through negotiation. In the early 1980s, the government created Citizen Representation bodies, an official channel within Mexico City through which colonos could participate, within the system, in the articulation of their demands.

From the perspective of the colonos, the establishment of the citizen organizations afforded them an additional means to advance their demands for garbage collection; street-paving; provision of potable water; sewage removal; and, most critically, the regularization of land tenure—that is, legitimization. In the government's view, representation for the colonos served to win supporters for the Mexican political structure, particularly the rule of the official ruling party, at a time of outspoken challenge from other political sectors.

Citizens are encouraged to work within the system; potential dissidents are transformed through the process of co-optation into collaborators. In today's Mexico City, then, patronage and clientage have two faces: the traditional one of compadrazgo, the other a form of state paternalism that promotes community participation.

THE BORDER

Driven by poverty, unemployment, and underemployment, in the past few decades many Mexicans have chosen not Mexico City but the United States as the place to improve their lives. Mexican workers in the United States are not a new phenomenon. During World War II, the presidents of both nations agreed to allow Mexican workers, called *braceros*, to enter the United States as agricultural workers. They were strictly regulated. In contrast, the new wave of migrants is largely unregulated. Each year hundreds of thousands of undocumented Mexicans illegally cross the border in search of work. It has been estimated that, at any given time, between 4 million and 6 million Mexicans pursue an existence as illegal aliens in the United States.

While thousands of Mexicans are able to support families with the fruits of their labors, as undocumented workers they are not protected by the law. Many are callously exploited by those who smuggle them across the border as well as by employers in the United States. For the Mexican government, however, such mass emigration has been a blessing in disguise. Not only has it served as a kind of sociopolitical safety valve, but it has also resulted in an inflow of dollars sent home by the workers.

In recent years U.S. companies and the governments of Mexican states along the border have profited from the creation of assembly plants known as *maquiladoras*. Low wages and a docile labor force are attractive to employers, while Mexican government reaps the benefits of employment and tax dollars. Despite the appearance of prosperity along the border, it must be emphasized that chronic unemployment in other parts of Mexico ensures the misery of millions of Mexicans. How these realities will be affected by the implementation of the North American Free Trade Agreement (NAFTA) remains to be seen.

THE INDIAN "PROBLEM"

Over the course of this century, urbanization and racial mixing have changed the demographic face of Mexico. A government official once commented: "A country predominately Mestizo, where Indian and white are now minorities, Mexico preserves the festivity and ceremonialism of the Indian civilizations and the religiosity and legalism of the Spanish Empire." The quotation is revealing, for it clearly identifies the Indian as a marginal member of society, as an object of curiosity.

Mexico's Indians, as is the case with indigenous peoples in most of Latin America, are viewed as obstacles to national integration and economic progress. There exist in Mexico more than 200 distinct Indian tribes or ethnic groups, who speak more than 50 languages or dialects. In the view of "progressive" Mexicans, the "sociocultural fragmentation" caused by the diversity of languages fosters political misunderstanding, insecurity, and regional incomprehension. Indians suffer from widespread discrimination. Language is not the only barrier to their economic progress. For years they have endured the unequal practices of a ruling white and Mestizo elite. Indians may discover, for example, that they cannot expand a small industry, such as a furniture-making enterprise, because few financial institutions will lend a large amount of money to an Indian.

NATIONAL IDENTITY

Mexico's Mestizo face has had a profound impact on the attempts of intellectuals to understand the meaning of the term "Mexican." The question of national identity has always been an important theme in Mexican history; it became a particularly burning issue in the aftermath of the Revolution of 1910. Octavio Paz believes that most Mexicans have denied their origins: they do not want to be either Indian or Spaniard, but they also refuse to see themselves as a mixture of both. One result of this essential denial of one's ethnic roots is a collective inferiority complex. The Mexican, Paz writes, is insecure. To hide that insecurity, which stems from his "inferiority,"

(United Nations photo)

In many ways the Mexican people have two separate identities: one public and one private. This carved door by artist Diego Rivera, located in Chapingo, accurately depicts the dual identity that is so much a part of Mexican culture.

he wears a "mask." Machismo (the cult of manliness) is one example of such a mask. Aggressive behavior at a sporting event, while driving a car, or in relationships with women, in Paz's estimation, is reflective of a deep-seated identity crisis.

Perhaps an analogy can be drawn from Mexican domestic architecture. Traditional Mexican homes are surrounded by high, solid walls, often topped with shards of glass and devoid of windows looking out onto the street. From the outside these abodes appear cold and inhospitable. Once inside (once behind the mask), however, the Mexican home is warm and comfortable. Here, appearances are set aside and Mexicans can relax and be themselves. By contrast, homes in the United States have vast expanses of glass that allow every passerby to see within. That whole style of open architecture, at least for homes, is jolting for many Mexicans (as well as other Latin Americans).

THE FAILURE OF THE 1910 REVOLUTION

In addition to the elusive search for Mexican identity, one of Mexican intellectuals' favorite themes is the Revolution of 1910 and what they perceive as its shortcomings. That momentous struggle (1910–1917) cost more than 1 million lives, but it offered Mexico the promise of a new society, free from the abuses of past centuries. It began with a search for truth and honesty in government; it ended with an assertion of the dignity and equality of all men and women.

The goals of the 1910 Revolution were set forth in the Constitution of 1917, a remarkable document—not only in its own era but also today. Article 123, which concerns labor, includes the following provisions: an 8-hour workday and a general minimum wage, as well as a 6-week leave with pay for pregnant women before the approximate birth date and an additional 6-week leave with pay following the delivery of the child. During the nursing period, the mother must be given extra rest periods each day for nursing the baby. Equal wages must be paid for equal work, regardless of sex or nationality. Workers are entitled to a participation in the profits of an enterprise (*i.e.,* profit-sharing). Overtime work must carry double pay. Employers are responsible for and must pay appropriate compensation for injuries received by workers in the performance of their duties or for occupational diseases. In 1917 such provisions were viewed as astounding and revolutionary.

Unfulfilled Promises

Unfortunately, many of the goals of 1917 have yet to be achieved. A number of writers, frustrated by the slow pace of change, concluded long ago that the Mexican Revolution was dead. Leading thinkers and writers, such as the celebrated Carlos Fuentes, have bitterly criticized the failure of the Revolution to shape a more equitable society. Corruption, abuse of power, self-serving opportunism, and a general air of degeneration characterize Mexico today.

One of the failed goals of the Revolution, in the eyes of critics, was an agrarian-reform program that fell short of achieving a wholesale change of land ownership or even of raising the standard of living in rural areas. To be fair, however, over the years small-scale agriculture has sown the seeds of its own destruction. Plots of land that are barely adequate for subsistence farming have been further divided by peasant farmers anxious to satisfy the inheritance rights of their sons. More recently government price controls on grain and corn have driven many marginal producers out of the market and off their lands.

Land Reform: One Story

Juan Rulfo, a major figure in the history of postrevolutionary literature, captured the frustration of peasants who have "benefited" from agrarian reform. "But sir," the peasant complained to the government official overseeing the land reform, "the earth is all washed away and hard. We don't think the plow will cut into the earth . . . that's like a rock quarry. You'd have to make with a pick-axe to plant the seed, and even then you can't be sure that anything will come up. . . ." The official, cold and indifferent, responded: "You can state that in writing. And now you can go. You should be attacking the large-estate owners and not the government that is giving you the land."

More frequently, landowners have attacked peasants. During the past several years in Mexico, insistent peasant demands for a new allocation of lands have been the occasion of a number of human-rights abuses—some of a very serious character. Some impatient peasants who have occu-

(United Nations photo/Heidi Larson)
Mexican women won the right to vote in 1955. These women, at a political rally in Oaxaca, demonstrate their political consciousness.

pied lands in defiance of the law have been killed or have "disappeared." In one notorious case in 1982, 26 peasants were murdered in a dispute over land in the state of Puebla. The peasants, who claimed legal title to the land, were killed by mounted gunmen, reportedly hired by local ranchers. Political parties reacted to the massacre in characteristic fashion—all attempted to manipulate the event to their own advantage rather than to address the problem of land reform. Years later, in 1993, paramilitary bands and local police controlled by political bosses or landowners still routinely threatened and/or killed peasant activists.

The Promise of the Revolution

While critics of the 1910 Revolution are correct in identifying its failures, the Constitution of 1917 represents more than dashed hopes. The very radical nature of the document allows governments (should they desire) to pursue aggressive egalitarian policies and still be within the law. For example, when addressing Mexicans, public officials often invoke the Constitution—issues tend to become less controversial if they are placed within the broad context of 1917. When then-President Adolfo López Mateos declared in 1960 that his government would be "extremely leftist," he quickly added that his position would be "within the Constitution." In 1982, with the Mexican economy bordering on collapse, outgoing President José López Portillo nationalized the banks. The nationalization, allowable under the Constitution, was of little practical value; but it demonstrated to Mexicans that the government was serious about tackling economic problems and that the spirit of the Revolution of 1910 was still alive.

Women's Rights

Although the Constitution made reference to the equality of women in Mexican society, it was not until World War II that the women's-rights movement gathered strength. Women won the right to vote in 1955, and by the 1970s they had challenged laws and social customs that were prejudicial to women. Some women have served on presidential cabinets, and one woman became governor of the state of Colima. The most important victory for women occurred in 1974, when the Mexican Congress passed legislation that, in effect, asked Mexican men to grant women full equality in society—including jobs, salaries, and legal standing.

But attitudes are difficult to overcome with legislation, and much social behavior in Mexico still has a sexist orientation. Many Mexican men feel that there are male and female roles in society, regardless of law. Government, public corporations, private businesses, the Roman Catholic Church, and the armed forces represent important areas of male activity. The home, private religious rituals, and sec-

ondary service roles represent areas of female activity. One is clearly dominant, the other subordinate.

The Role of the Church

Under the Constitution of 1917, no religious organization is allowed to administer or teach in Mexico's primary, secondary, or normal (higher education) schools; nor may clergy participate in the education of workers or peasants. Yet between 1940 and 1979, private schools expanded to the point where they enrolled 1½ million of the country's 17 million pupils. Significantly, more than half of the private-school population attended Roman Catholic schools. Because they exist despite the fact that they are prohibited by law, the Catholic schools demonstrate the kinds of accommodation and flexibility that are possible in Mexico. It is in the best interests of the ruling party to satisfy as many interest groups as is possible, to achieve a certain societal balance.

From the perspective of politicians, the Roman Catholic Church in recent years has increasingly tilted the balance in the direction of social justice. Some Mexican bishops have been particularly outspoken on the issue, but when liberal or radical elements in the church embrace social change, they may cross into the jurisdiction of the state. Under the Constitution the state is responsible for improving the welfare of its people. Some committed clergy, however, believe that religion must play an active role in the transformation of society; it must not only have compassion for the poor but must also act to relieve poverty and eliminate injustice.

Mexican bishops in 1991 openly expressed their concern about the torture and mistreatment of prisoners, political persecution, corruption, discrimination against indigenous peoples, mistreatment of Central American refugees, and electoral fraud. In previous years the government would have reacted sharply against such charges emanating from the church. But in this case there was a significant rapprochement between the Roman Catholic Church and the state in Mexico. Begun by President Manuel de la Madrid and further elaborated by President Carlos Salinas de Gortari, the new relationship culminated in 1990 with the exchange of diplomatic representatives and Pope John Paul II's successful and popular visit to Mexico in May. Some critics interpreted the new policy vis-à-vis the church as another retreat from the goals of the Revolution. Others ascribed the move to pragmatic politics.

MEXICO'S STABILITY

The stability of the Mexican state, as has been suggested, depends on the ability of the ruling elite to maintain a state of relative equilibrium among the multiplicity of interests and demands in the nation. The whole political process is characterized by bargaining among elites with various views on politics, social injustice, economic policy, and the conduct of foreign relations.

It is the Institutionalized Revolutionary Party (PRI), in power since 1929, that sets policies and decides what is possible or desirable. All change is generated from above, from the president and presidential advisers. Although the Constitution provides for a federal system, power is effectively centralized. In the words of one authority, Mexico, with its one-party rule, is not a democracy but, rather, a "qualified authoritarianism." Indeed, the main role of the PRI in the political system is political domination, not power-sharing. Paternalistic and all-powerful, the state controls the bureaucracies that direct the labor unions, peasant organizations, student groups, and virtually every other dimension of organized society.

Politicians tend to be more interested in building their careers than in responding to the demands of their constituents. According to political scientist Peter Smith, Mexican politicians are forever bargaining with one another, seeking favors from their superiors, and communicating in a language of "exaggerated deference." They have learned how to maximize power and success within the existing political structure. By following the "rules of the game," they move ahead. The net result is a consensus at the upper echelons of power.

In the past few decades, that consensus has been undermined. One of the great successes of the Revolution of 1910 was the rise to middle-class status of millions of people. But the current economic crisis has alienated that upwardly mobile sector from the PRI. People have registered their dissatisfaction at the polls; in 1988, in fact, the official party finished second in Mexico City and other urban centers. In 1989 the PRI's unbroken winning streak of 60 years, facilitated by widespread electoral corruption, was broken in the state of Baja California del Norte, where the right-wing National Action Party (PAN) won the governorship.

Despite appearances Mexico remains a one-party democracy—or, as some critics have phrased it, a "selective democracy." Change is still engineered from the top down and is designed to preserve the hegemony of the PRI. To create an impression of broader participation in the workings of government, in the 1980s the authorities created an additional 200 seats in Congress. Half the new seats were reserved for minority parties. By 1990 the total number of seats in Mexico's Congress stood at 600. To channel discontent within the system, the registration of new political parties was fostered. (Electoral fraud, of course, would guarantee the PRI a comfortable majority in elections.)

Within the PRI, however, a new generation of leaders, typified by Carlos Salinas de Gortari, sees the need for political and economic change. Old-fashioned party and union bosses, on the other hand, see any change as threatening to their entrenched positions. Elections, to their way of think-

(United Nations photo/M. Tzovaras)

The Institutionalized Revolutionary Party (PRI) has been in power since 1929, which essentially has made Mexico a one-party government. Historically, the incumbent president carefully selects a PRI-sympathetic candidate to run as his successor, since the number of times one may hold the office is limited. Pictured above is President Carlos Salinas de Gortari, who must leave office in 1994. He chose Luis Donaldo Colosio as the next PRI candidate, but when Colosio was assassinated in March 1994, the PRI mantle passed on to Ernesto Zedillo Ponce de León.

ing, were never meant to allow anyone but PRI candidates to win. In the words of political scientist George Grayson, "the *carro completo* or clean sweep enables labor chieftains and peasant leaders to reward their loyalists." Reform, in such instances, is difficult but not impossible. Electoral results, even if rigged, could be used to foster change. Historically, the PRI could register its dissatisfaction with one of its own politicians by reducing the candidate's winning margin. This was a sign that if the politician did not shape up, then he or she was in danger of being ousted. Similarly, in the presidential elections of 1988, the PRI's poor showing gave Salinas all the justification he needed for reforming the party and for opening an unaccustomed dialogue with the opposition. In 1993 the PRI announced a broad range of proposals to reform the Mexican political process, in anticipation of elections in 1994. But in the southern state of Chiapas, the rhetoric of change failed to ease the reality of abuses perpetrated by local landowners against Mayan Indians. Rebellion broke out in January 1994. The Mayan insurgents were led by Subcommandant Marcos, an articulate and shrewd activist who quickly became a hero not only in Chiapas but also in much of the rest of Mexico, where he symbolized widespread dissatisfaction with the Salinas government. The Mayans were not intent on the destruction of the Mexican government but were insistent that their demands for justice be considered seriously. In an election year, a negotiated settlement seemed likely. Then, in March 1994, the PRI's presidential candidate, Luis Donaldo Colosio, was assassinated, further clouding Mexico's political future.

In other ways President Salinas behaved traditionally, essentially as a *patrón* to his people. This was apparent on a political working trip that he took through northern Mexico in 1989. Mexicans felt that such trips were, in the words of *New York Times* reporter Larry Rohter, "essential to the functioning of the country's political system, which invests the President with an aura of omnipotence and consequently demands that he appear to have a hand in every decision made in his name." The primacy of the executive branch in the Mexican political system convinces people that only the president has both the authority and the credibility to correct injustices and to get things done. In the words of one of Salinas's cabinet ministers, "This is a presidential system par excellence. People want to see the President and to hear things from his own mouth." People wanted to get close to him to deliver their letters and petitions.

ORGANIZED LABOR

Organized labor provides an excellent example of the ways in which power is wielded in Mexico and how social change occurs. Trade unions have the right to organize, negotiate, and strike. Most unions, however, are not independent of the government. The major portion of the labor movement is affiliated with the PRI through an umbrella organization known as the Confederation of Mexican Workers (CTM). The confederation, with a membership of 3½ million, is one of the PRI's most ardent supporters. Union bosses truck in large crowds for campaign rallies, help PRI candidates win impressive victory margins at election time, and secure from union members approval of government policies. Union bosses are well rewarded by the system they help to support. Most become moderately wealthy and acquire status and prestige. Fully one-third of Mexico's senators and congressional representatives, as well as an occasional governor, come from the ranks of union leadership.

Such a relationship must be reciprocal if it is to function properly. For years the CTM has used an impressive array of left-wing slogans to win gains for its members. It has projected an aura of radicalism when, in fact, it is not; the image is important to union members, however, for it gives them the feeling of independence from the government, and it gives a role to the true radicals in the movement.

Cracks have begun to appear in the foundation of union support for the government. The economic crisis has resulted in sharp cutbacks in government spending. Benefits and wage increases have fallen far behind the pace of inflation; layoffs and unemployment have led many union members to question the value of their special relationship with the government. Indeed, during the 1988 elections, the Mexican newspaper *El Norte* reported that Joaquín Hernández Galicia, the powerful leader of the Oil Workers' Union, was so upset with trends within the PRI that he directed his membership to vote for opposition candidates. Not surprisingly, President Salinas named a new leader to the Oil Workers' Union.

Independent unions outside the Confederation of Mexican Workers have capitalized on the crisis and increased their memberships. For the first time, these independent unions seem to possess sufficient power to challenge government policies. To negate the challenge from the independents, the CTM has invited them to join the larger organization. Incorporation of the dissidents into the system is seen as the only way in which the system's credibility can be maintained. It illustrates the state's power to neutralize opposing forces by absorbing them into its system. The demands of labor today are strong, and the government will have to make significant concessions. But if the system is preserved and dissidents are transformed into supporters of the state, the costs will be worthwhile.

ECONOMIC CRISIS

As has been suggested, the primary threat to the consensus politics of the PRI has come from the economic crisis that began to build in Mexico and other Latin American countries (notably Brazil, Venezuela, and Argentina) in the early 1980s. In the 1970s Mexico undertook economic policies designed to foster rapid and sustained industrial growth. Credit was readily available from international lending agencies and banks at low rates of interest. Initially the development plan seemed to work, and Mexico achieved impressive growth rates, in the range of 8 percent per year. The government, confident in its ability to pay back its debts from revenues generated by the vast deposits of petroleum beneath Mexico, recklessly expanded its economic infrastructure.

A glut on the petroleum market in late 1981 and 1982 led to falling prices for Mexican oil. Suddenly there was not enough money available to repay the interest on loans that were coming due, and the government had to borrow more money—at very high interest rates—to cover the unexpected shortfall. By the end of 1982, between 35 and 45 percent of Mexico's export earnings were devoured in interest payments on a debt of $80 billion. Before additional loans could be secured, foreign banks and lending organizations, such as the International Monetary Fund, demanded

			War with the United States; Mexico loses	The French take over the Mexican throne and install	Era of the dictator Porfirio	
Hernán Cortés lands at Vera Cruz **1519**	Destruction of the Aztec Empire **1521**	Mexico proclaims its independence of Spain **1810**	four-fifths of its territory **1846–1848**	Emperor Maximillian **1862–1867**	Díaz: modernization **1876–1910**	The Mexican Revolution **1910–1917**
●	●	●	●	●	●	●

that the Mexican government drastically reduce state spending. This demand translated into layoffs, inadequate funding for social-welfare programs, and a general austerity that devastated the poor and undermined the high standard of living of the middle class.

Although political reform was important to President Salinas, he clearly recognized that economic reform was of more compelling concern. Under Salinas the foreign debt was renegotiated and substantially reduced.

Petroleum exports, which generated 78 percent of Mexico's export dollars in 1978, now account for 35 percent. Tariffs on foreign imports have been cut and productivity encouraged, with the result that Mexico has increased the amount and variety of goods destined for export. The North American Free Trade Agreement among Mexico, the United States, and Canada is seen as essential if these advances are to continue and jobs are to be generated. Opposition politicians on the left generally oppose any free trade agreement, which they see as binding Mexico to the imperialist designs of the United States and giving the United States control over Mexican oil. In the meantime there has been a high social cost to economic reform: standards of living continue a downward spiral. Since 1983 wages have declined nearly 60 percent. The minimum wage for workers since 1982 has not been adequate to sustain a family above the poverty line.

Many of those workers will continue to make their way to the U.S. border, which remains accessible despite the passage of immigration-reform legislation and the uncertain promise of free trade with the colossus of the north. Others will be absorbed by the so-called informal sector, or underground economy. When walking in the streets of Mexico City, one quickly becomes aware that there exists an economy that is not recognized, licensed, regulated, or "protected" by the government. Yet in the 1980s this informal sector of the economy produced 25 to 35 percent of Mexico's gross domestic product (GDP) and served as a shield for millions of Mexicans who might otherwise have been reduced to destitution. According to George Grayson, "Extended families, which often have several members working and others hawking lottery tickets or shining shoes, establish a safety net for upward of one-third of the work force in a country where social security coverage is limited and unemployment compensation is nonexistent."

FOREIGN POLICY

The problems created by Mexico's economic policy have been balanced by a visibly successful foreign policy. His-

torically, Mexican foreign policy, which is noted for following an independent course of action, has been used by the government for domestic purposes. Former President Miguel de la Madrid identified revolutionary nationalism as the historical synthesis, or melding, of the Mexican people. History, he argued, taught Mexicans to be nationalist in order to resist external aggression, and history made Mexico revolutionary in order to enable it to transform unequal social and economic structures. These beliefs, when tied to the formulation of foreign policy, have fashioned policies with a definite leftist bias.

The country has been sympathetic to social change and has identified, at least in principle, with revolutionary causes all over the globe. The Mexican government opposed the economic and political isolation of Cuba that was so heartily endorsed by the United States. It supported the Marxist regime of Salvador Allende in Chile at a time when the United States was attempting to destabilize his government. Mexico was one of the first nations to break relations with then-President Anastasio Somoza of Nicaragua and to recognize the legitimacy of the struggle of the Sandinista guerrillas. In 1981 Mexico joined with France in recognizing the opposition front and guerrilla coalition in El Salvador. More recently Mexico, together with several other Latin American countries, urged a negotiated solution to the armed conflict in Central America.

Mexico's leftist foreign policy balances conservative domestic policies. A foreign policy identified with change and social justice has the effect of softening the impact of leftist demands in Mexico for land reform or political change. Mexicans, if displeased with government domestic policies, are soothed by a vigorous foreign policy that places Mexico in a leadership role, often in opposition to the United States. As is the case in virtually every aspect of Mexican life, there is a sense of balance.

FREEDOM OF THE PRESS

Freedom of the press, wholly unrestricted, could seriously undermine the consensus politics so laboriously constructed by the government. Not surprisingly, then, there are significant restraints on press freedom in Mexico. Journalists are expected to respect the privacy of individuals and not to disturb either the public peace or morals in their reporting. There is also an unwritten understanding between reporters and the government that indiscriminate, critical exposés of the personal lives of prominent officials are to be avoided. As part of the gov-

| Land distribution under President Cárdenas 1934–1940 | Nationalization of foreign petroleum companies 1938 | Women win the right to vote 1955 | The Olympic Games are held in Mexico City; riots and violence 1968 | Severe economic crisis; the peso is devalued; inflation soars; the foreign debt crisis escalates 1980s–1990s |

| Carlos Salinas de Gortari is elected president, succeeding Miguel de la Madrid | Presidential elections are scheduled for 1994; NAFTA is passed | PRI presidential candidate Luis Donaldo Colosio is assassinated; the PRI chooses Ernesto Zedillo Ponce de León as the substitute candidate |

ernment's campaign to eliminate corruption in government, a law was implemented in 1982 that made it a crime against the state to disclose government secrets. Journalists guilty of "disloyalty" are subject to stiff fines and/or jail terms.

The Mexican government can exert additional pressure on the nation's press because the state has traditionally controlled much of the supply of newsprint. The government made an effort in 1990 to improve freedom of the press when it decided to sell its controlling interest in the state-owned newsprint company, PIPSA. However, increased tariffs on imports of newsprint effectively raised prices by 20 percent. The net result was to leave PIPSA as the main supplier. The government, as the owner and operator of many key industries, also controls about half the advertising available to the press. Disapproved bank loans, electricity cut-offs, disruption in telephone service, fines for violation of health codes, and bribes have all been used by the government to bring newspapers or journalists into line. In 1984 the government, as part of its program of moral renovation, allowed more direct public criticism of its policies. True freedom of the press, however, remains an illusion in Mexico.

THE FUTURE

The key to Mexico's immediate future lies in the state of the nation's economy. Although the political and social systems are remarkably durable and resilient, rampant corruption, persistent inflation, high domestic interest rates, an overvalued peso, the foreign debt, austerity in state spending and associated reductions in social programs, and high unemployment and underemployment have significantly undermined the PRI's consensus politics. If the government complies with new election laws to reduce corruption, brings inflation under control, and can secure further loans abroad, and if the North American Free Trade Agreement lives up to expectations in terms of foreign exchange earnings and job creation, then Mexico will survive this latest challenge to its stability.

DEVELOPMENT

President Salinas's 5-year economic plan (1989–1994) included both economic and political goals: the defense of national sovereignty; the expansion of democracy; the recovery of the economy, with stability of prices; and a general improvement in the standard of living.

FREEDOM

Although the PRI has controlled Mexico's political life since 1929, opposition parties have made progress at the municipal and gubernatorial levels. Elections from 1983 to 1993 produced numerous charges of electoral fraud, despite the government's stated commitment to the principle of political pluralism.

HEALTH/WELFARE

Violence against women first became an issue of public policy when legislation was introduced in 1990 to amend the penal code with respect to sexual crimes. Among the provisions were specialized medical and social assistance for rape victims and penalties for sexual harassment.

ACHIEVEMENTS

Mexican authors and artists have won world acclaim. The works of novelists such as Carlos Fuentes, Mariano Azuela, and Juan Rulfo have been translated into many languages. The graphic-art styles of Posada and the mural art of Diego Rivera, José Clemente Orozco, and David Siqueiros are distinctively Mexican.

Central America

● Capital cities

Much of Central America has a common history. In 1821 the states of Guatemala, Honduras, El Salvador, Costa Rica, and Nicaragua declared themselves independent of Spain. In 1822 they joined the Empire of Mexico and in 1823 formed the United Provinces of Central America. This union lasted until 1838, when each member state severed its relations with the federation and went its own way. Since 1838 there have been more than 25 attempts to restore the union—but to no avail.

Central America: Lands in Turmoil

LIFE IN THE MOUTH OF THE VOLCANO

Sons of the Shaking Earth, a well-known study of Middle America by anthropologist Eric Wolf, captures in its title the critical interplay between people and the land in Central America. It asserts that the land is violent and that the inhabitants of the region live in an environment that is often shaken by natural disaster.

The dominant geographical feature of Central America is the impressive and forbidding range of volcanic mountains that runs from Mexico to Panama. These mountains have always been obstacles to communication, to the cultivation of the land, and to the national integration of the countries in which they lie. The volcanoes rest atop major fault lines; but some are dormant, others are active, and new ones have appeared periodically. Over the centuries eruptions and earthquakes have destroyed thousands of villages. Some have recovered but others remain buried beneath lava and ash. Nearly every Central American city has been destroyed at one time or another, and some, such as Managua, Nicaragua, have suffered repeated devastation.

An ancient Indian philosophy speaks of five great periods of time, each doomed to end in disaster. The fifth period, which is the time in which we now live, will terminate with a world-destroying earthquake. "Thus," writes Eric Wolf, "the people of Middle America live in the mouth of the volcano. Middle America . . . is one of the proving grounds of humanity." Earthquakes and eruptions are not the only natural disasters that plague the region. Between May and October of each year the rains fall heavily, and devastating floods are common. On the Caribbean coast, hurricanes often strike in the late summer and early autumn, threatening coastal cities and leveling crops. The constant threat of natural disaster has had a deep impact on Central Americans' views of life and development. Death and tragedy have conditioned the peoples' attitudes toward the present and the future.

GEOGRAPHY

The land is not only violent but also diverse. Central America, in political terms, consists of seven independent nations: Belize, Costa Rica, El Salvador, Guatemala, Honduras, Nicaragua, and Panama. With the exception of Costa Rica and Panama, where national borders coincide with geographical and human frontiers, political boundaries are artificial and were marked out in defiance of both the lay of the land and the cultural groupings of the region's peoples.

Geographically, Central America can be divided into four broad zones: Petén–Belize; the Caribbean coasts of Guatemala, Honduras, and Nicaragua; the Pacific volcanic region; and Costa Rica–Panama.

The northern Guatemalan territory of Petén and all of Belize are an extension of Mexico's Yucatán Peninsula. The

(United Nations photo/Sygma/J. P. Laffont)
The threat of earthquakes affects the lives of all Central Americans. Shown above is Guatemala City, Guatemala, after an earthquake.

region is heavily forested with stands of mahogany, cedar, and pine, which are a major source of revenue for Belize.

The Caribbean lowlands, steamy and disease-ridden, are sparsely settled. In Nicaragua, the inhabitants of the Caribbean coast include Miskito Indians and English-speaking blacks whose ancestors have lived in the area since the seventeenth century. Until recently the Hispanic population was small. Coastal Honduras presents a different picture. Because of heavy investments by foreign companies in the region's banana industry, it is a pocket of relative prosperity in the midst of a very poor country whose economy is based on agricultural production and textiles.

The Pacific volcanic highlands are the cultural heartland of Central America. Here, in highland valleys noted for their springlike climate, live more than 80 percent of the population of Central America; here are the largest cities. In cultural terms, the highlands are home to the whites, mixed bloods, Hispanicized Indians known as Ladinos, and pure-blooded Indians who descended from the Maya. These highland groups form a striking ethnic contrast to the more primitive Indians (such as the Miskito) and the mulattos and blacks of the coastlands. The entire country of El Salvador falls within this geographical zone and, unlike its neighbors, there is a uniformity to its land and its people.

The fourth region, divided between the nations of Costa Rica and Panama, constitutes a single geographical unit. Mountains form the spine of the isthmus. In Costa Rica, the Central Mesa, because of its climate, has attracted 70 percent of the nation's population.

CLIMATE AND CULTURE

The geographic and biological diversity of Central America—with its cool highlands and steaming lowlands, its incredible variety of microclimates and environments, its seemingly infinite types of flora and fauna, and its mineral wealth—has been a major factor in setting the course of the cultural history of Central America. Before the Spanish conquest, the environmental diversity favored the cultural cohesion of peoples. The products of one environmental niche could easily be exchanged for the products of another. In a sense, valley people and those living higher up in the mountains depended on one another. Here was one of the bases for the establishment of the advanced culture of the Maya.

The cultural history of Central America has focused on the densely populated highlands and Pacific plains—those areas most favorable for human occupation. Spaniards settled in the same regions, and centers of national life are located there today. But if geography has been a factor in bringing peoples together on a local level, it also has contributed to the formation of regional differences, loyalties, interests, and jealousies. Neither Mayan rulers nor Spanish bureaucrats could triumph over the natural obstacles presented by the region's harsh geography. The mountains and rain forests have mocked numerous attempts to create a single Central American state.

CULTURES IN CONFLICT

Although geography has interacted with culture, the contact between Indians and Spaniards since the sixteenth century has profoundly shaped the cultural face of today's Central America. According to historian Ralph Woodward, the religious traditions of the Indians, with Christianity imperfectly superimposed over them, "together with the violence of the Conquest and the centuries of slavery or serfdom which followed, left clear impressions on the personality and mentality of the Central American Indian."

To outsiders the Indians often appear docile and obedient to authority, but beneath this mask lie deeper emotions, including distrust and bitterness. The Indians' vision is usually local and oriented toward the village and family; they do not understand what it is to be a Guatemalan or Nicaraguan. When challenged, Indians have fought to defend their rights, and a long succession of rebellions from colo-

nial days until the present attests to their sense of what is just and what is not. The Indians, firmly tied to their traditional beliefs and values, have tried to resist modernization, despite government programs and policies designed to counter what urbanized whites perceive as backwardness and superstition.

Population growth, rather than government programs and policies, has had more of an impact on the region's Indian peoples and has already resulted in the recasting of cultural traditions. Peasant villages in much of Mesoamerica have traditionally organized their ritual life on the principle of *mayordomía,* or sponsorship. Waldemar Smith, an anthropologist who has explored the relationship between the fiesta system and economic change, has shown the impact of changing circumstances on traditional systems. In any Mesoamerican community in any given year, certain families are appointed *mayordomos,* or stewards, of the village saints; they are responsible for organizing and paying for the celebrations in their names. This responsibility ordinarily lasts for a year.

One of the outstanding features of the fiesta system is the phenomenal costs the designated family must bear. An individual might have to expend the equivalent of a year's earnings, or more, to act as a sponsor in a community *fiesta,* or ceremony. Psychological and social burdens must also be borne by the mayordomos, for they represent their community before its saints. Mayordomos, who in essence are priests for a year, are commonly expected to refrain from sexual activity for long durations as well as to devote much time to ritual forms. The office, while highly prestigious, can also be dangerous: Maya Indians, for example, believe that the saints use the weather as a weapon to punish transgressions, and extreme weather is often traced to ritual error or sins on the part of the mayordomo, who might on such occasions actually be jailed.

Since the late 1960s, the socioeconomic structure of much of the area heavily populated by Indians has changed, forcing changes in traditional cultural forms, including the fiesta system. Expansion of markets and educational opportunity, the absorption of much of the work force in seasonal plantation labor, more efficient transportation systems, and population growth have precipitated change. Traditional festivals in honor of a community's saints have significantly diminished in importance in a number of towns. Costs have been reduced or several families have been made responsible for fiesta sponsorship. This reflects not only modernization, but also crisis. Some communities have become too poor to support themselves, and the expensive fiestas have naturally suffered.

This increasing poverty is driven in part by population growth, which has exerted tremendous pressure on accessibility to land. Families that cannot be sustained on traditional lands must now seek seasonal wage labor on sugar, coffee, or cotton plantations. Others emigrate. The net result is a culture under siege. While traditional festivals may not vanish, they are surely in the process of change.

The Ladino World

Ladino, as a word, can be traced back to the Roman occupation of Spain. It referred to someone who had been "Latinized" and was therefore wise in the ways of the world. In Central America, the word has several meanings. In Guatemala, it refers to a person of mixed blood, or *Mestizo.* But in most of Central America, it refers to an Indian who has adopted white culture. The Ladinos are caught between two cultures, both of which initially rejected them. The Ladinos attempted to compensate for their lack of cultural roots and cultural identity by aggressively carving out a place in Central American society.

Acutely status-conscious, Ladinos contrast sharply with the Indians they physically resemble. Ladinos congregate in the larger towns and cities, speak Spanish, and seek a livelihood as shopkeepers or landowners. They compose the local elite in Guatemala, Nicaragua, Honduras, and El Salvador (El Salvador was almost entirely Ladinoized by the end of the nineteenth century), and they usually control re-

(United Nations photo)

Many people migrate from the poverty of rural life to the overburdened urban centers. It is beyond the capacity of many urban areas to support these migrants. The children pictured above have to get their water from a single, unsanitary tap.

gional politics. They are the most aggressive members of the community and are driven by the desire for self-advancement. Their vision is much broader than that of the Indian; they have a perspective that includes the capital city and the nation. The vast majority of the population speak Spanish; few villages retain the use of their original, native tongues.

The Elite

For the elite, who are culturally "white," the city dominates their social and cultural horizons. For them the world of the Indian is unimportant—save for the difficult questions of social integration and modernization. Businesspeople and bureaucrats, absentee landlords, and the professional class of doctors, lawyers, and engineers constitute an urban elite who are cosmopolitan and sophisticated. Wealth, status, and "good blood" are the keys to elite membership.

The Disadvantaged

The cities have also attracted the disadvantaged who have moved from poverty-stricken rural regions in search of economic opportunity. Many are self-employed as peddlers, small-scale traders, or independent craftspeople. Others seek low-paying, unskilled positions in industry, construction

(United Nations photo/Jerry Frank)

Central American Indians are firmly tied to their traditional beliefs and have strongly resisted the influence of European culture, as evidenced by this woman of the Cuna of Tubala Island in Panama.

work, and transportation. Most live on the edge of poverty and are the first to suffer in times of economic recession.

But in this harsh world there exist Hispanic institutions that help people of all classes to adjust. In each of the capital cities of Central America, lower-sector people seek help and sustenance from the more advantaged elements in society. They form economic and social alliances that are mutually beneficial. For example, a tradesman might approach a well-to-do merchant and seek advice, or perhaps a small loan. In return he can offer guaranteed service, a steady supply of crafts for the wholesaler, and a price that is right. It is a world built on mutual exchanges.

These networks, when they function, bind societies together and ease the alienation and isolation of the less advantaged inhabitants. Of course, networks that cut through class lines can effectively limit class action in pursuit of reforms; and in many instances, the networks do not exist or are exploitive.

POPULATION MOVEMENT

For years Central America's peoples have been peoples in motion. Many migrants who moved from rural areas into the cities were driven from the lands they once owned, either because of the expansion of landed estates at the expense of the smaller land holdings, population pressure, or division of the land into plots so small that subsistence farming was no longer possible. Others moved to the cities in search of a better life.

Population pressure on the land is most intense in El Salvador. No other Latin American state utilizes the whole of its territory to the extent that El Salvador does. Most of the land is still privately owned and is devoted to raising cotton and coffee crops for the export market or to cattle farming. There is not enough land to provide crops for a population that has grown at the most rapid rate in the Western Hemisphere. There are no empty lands left to occupy. Agrarian reform, even if successful, will still leave hundreds of thousands of peasants without land.

Many Salvadorans have moved to the capital city of San Salvador in search of employment. Others have crossed into neighboring countries. In the 1960s thousands moved to Honduras, where they settled on the land or were attracted to commerce and industry. By the end of that decade, more than 75 percent of all foreigners living in Honduras had crossed the border from El Salvador. Hondurans, increas-

(World Bank photo/Jaime Martin-Escobal)

Migration of rural people to urban centers has caused large numbers of squatters to take up residence in slums. The crowded conditions in urban El Salvador, as shown in this photograph, are typical of this phenomenon.

(United Nations photo/J. P. Laffont)

The problems incumbent with rapid population growth have put severe strains on many Central American nations. In Guatemala, government policy has driven Indians from ancestral villages to urbanized "resettlement" areas, such as the one pictured above.

ingly concerned by the growing presence of Salvadorans, acted to stem the flow and passed restrictive and discriminatory legislation against the immigrants. The tension, an ill-defined border, and festering animosity ultimately resulted in a brief war between Honduras and El Salvador in 1969.

Honduras, with a low population density of about 115 persons per square mile (as compared to El Salvador's 665), has attracted population not only from neighboring countries but also from the West Indies. Black migrants from the Antilles have been particularly attracted to the north coast, where they have been able to find employment on the banana plantations or in the light industry that has increasingly been established in the area. The presence of West Indians in moderate numbers has more sharply focused regional differences in Honduras. The coast, in many respects, is Caribbean in its peoples' identity and outlook; peoples of the highlands of the interior identify with the capital city of Tegucigalpa, which is Hispanic in culture.

THE REFUGEE PROBLEM

Contemporary turmoil in Central America has created yet another group of people on the move—refugees from the fighting in their own countries or from the persecution by extremists of the political left and right. Thousands of Salvadorans crowded into Honduras's western province. In the south, Miskito Indians, fleeing from Nicaragua's Sandinista government, crossed the Río Coco in large numbers. Additional thousands of armed Nicaraguan counterrevolutionaries camped along the border. Only in 1990–1991 did significant numbers of Salvadorans move back to their homeland. With the declared truce between Sandinistas and Contras and the election victory of Violeta Chamorro, Nicaraguan refugees were gradually repatriated. Guatemalan Indians sought refuge in southern Mexico, and Central Americans of all nationalities resettled in Costa Rica and Belize.

El Salvadorans, who began to emigrate to the United States in the 1960s, did so in much greater numbers with the onset of the El Salvadoran Civil War, which killed approximately 70,000 people and displaced about 25 percent of the nation's population. The Urban Institute, a Washington, D.C.–based research group, estimated in 1986 that at that time there were about three-quarters of a million El Salvadorans—of a total population of just over 5 million—living in the United States. Those emigrants became a major source of dollars for El Salvador; it is estimated that they now send home about $500 million a year. While those dollars have undoubtedly helped to keep the nation's economy above water, they have also generated, paradoxically, a good deal of anti-U.S. sentiment. Lindsey Gruson, a reporter for the *New York Times*, studied the impact of expatriate dollars in Intipuca, a town 100 miles southwest of the capital, and concluded that they had a profound impact on Intipueño culture. The influx of money was an incentive not to work, and townspeople said that the "free" dollars "perverted cherished values" and were "breaking up many families."

THE ROOTS OF VIOLENCE

Central America still feels the effects of civil war and violence. Armies, guerrillas, and terrorists of the political left and right exacted a high toll of human lives and property. The civil wars and guerrilla movements that spread violence to the region sprang from each of the societies in question.

A critical societal factor was (and remains) the emergence of a middle class in Central America. In some respects people of the middle class resemble the Mestizos or Ladinos, in that their wealth and position have placed them above the masses. But, like the Mestizos and Ladinos, they have been denied access to the upper reaches of power, which is the special preserve of the elite. Since World War II, it has been members of the middle class who have called for reform and a more equitable distribution of the national wealth. They have also attempted to forge alliances of opportunity with workers and peasants.

Nationalistic, assertive, restless, ambitious, and, to an extent, ruthless, people of the middle class (professionals, intellectuals, junior officers in the armed forces, office workers, businesspeople, teachers, students, and skilled workers) demand a greater voice in the political world. They want governments that are responsive to their interests and needs; and when governments have proven unresponsive or hostile, elements of the middle class have chosen confrontation. In the civil war that removed the Somoza family from power in Nicaragua in 1979, the middle class played a critical leadership role. Guerrilla leaders in El Salvador were middle class in terms of their social origins, and there is significant middle-class participation in the unrest in Guatemala. Indeed, in contrast to peasants and workers, Central America's middle class is among the most revolutionary groups in the region. Although middle-class people are well represented in antigovernment forces, they also resist changes that would tend to elevate those below them on the social scale. They are also significantly represented among right-wing groups, whose reputation for conservative views is accompanied by systematic terror.

Other societal factors also figure prominently in the violence in Central America. The rapid growth of population since the 1960s has severely strained each nation's resources. Many rural areas have become overpopulated, poor agricultural practices have caused extensive erosion, the amount of land available to subsistence farmers is inadequate, and poverty and misery are pervasive. These problems have combined to compel rural peoples to migrate to the cities or to whatever frontier lands are still available. In Guatemala, government policy has driven Indians from ancestral villages in the highlands to "resettlement" villages in the low-lying forested Petén to the north. Indians displaced in this manner have often, not surprisingly, joined guerrilla movements. They are not attracted to insurgency by the allure of socialist or communist ideology. They have simply responded to violence and the loss of their lands with violence against the governments that pursued such policies.

It is important to understand that the conflict in this region does not always pit landless or impoverished peasants against an unyielding elite. Some members of the elite see the need for change. Most peasants have not taken up arms, and the vast majority wish to be left in peace. Others who desire change may be found in the ranks of the military or within the hierarchy of the Roman Catholic Church. Reformers are drawn from all sectors of society. It is thus more appropriate to view the conflict in Central America as a civil war rather than a class struggle, as civil wars cut through the entire fabric of a nation.

ECONOMIC PROBLEMS

Central American economies, always fragile, have in recent years been plagued by a combination of vexing problems. Foreign debt, inflation, currency devaluations, recession, and in some instances U.S. and other outside interference have had deleterious effects on the standard of living in all the countries. Civil war, insurgency, corruption and mismanagement, and population growth have added fuel to the crisis—not only in the region's economies but also in their societies.

Civil war in El Salvador brought unprecedented death and destruction and was largely responsible for economic deterioration and a decline in per capita income of well over one-third from 1980 to 1992. Fully two-thirds of the working-age population are today either unemployed or underemployed. The struggle of the Sandinista government of Nicaragua against U.S.-sponsored rebels routinely consumed 60 percent of government spending; even with peace, much of the budget of the Chamorro regime is necessarily earmarked for economic recovery. In Guatemala, years of savage repression have not put an end to rural insurgency; meanwhile, real wages have declined; housing, land distribution, and unemployment remain unaddressed; and since 1987 the rate of violence has risen dramatically. U.S. efforts to force the ouster of Panamanian strongman Manuel Antonio Noriega through the application of economic sanctions probably harmed middle-class businesspeople in Panama more than Noriega.

Against this backdrop of economic malaise there have been some creative attempts to solve, or at least to confront, pressing problems. In 1987 the Costa Rican government proposed a series of debt-for-nature swaps to international conservation groups, such as the Nature Conservancy. The first of the transactions took place in 1988, when 4 organizations purchased more than $3 million of Costa Rica's foreign debt at 17 percent of face value. The plan called for the government to exchange with the organizations part of Costa Rica's external debt for government bonds. The conservation groups would then invest the earnings of the bonds in the management and protection of Costa Rican national parks. According to the National Wildlife Federation, while debt-for-nature swaps are not a cure-all for the Latin American debt crisis, at least the swaps can go some distance toward protecting natural resources and encouraging ecologically sound long-term economic development.

INTERNAL AND EXTERNAL DIMENSIONS OF CONFLICT

The continuing violence in much of Central America suggests that internal dynamics are perhaps more important than the overweening roles formerly ascribed to Havana, Moscow, and Washington. The removal of foreign "actors" from the stage lays bare the real reasons for violence: injustice, power, greed, revenge, and racial discrimination. Havana, Moscow, and Washington, among others, merely used Central American violence in pursuit of larger policy goals. And Central American governments and guerrilla groups were equally adept at using foreign powers to advance their own interests, be they revolutionary or reactionary.

Panama offers an interesting scenario. It, like the rest of Central America, is a poor nation consisting of subsistence farmers, rural laborers, urban workers, and unemployed and underemployed people dwelling in the shantytowns ringing the larger cities. For years the pressures for reform in Panama were skillfully rechanneled by the ruling elite toward the issue of the Panama Canal. Frustration and anger were deflected from the government, and an outdated social structure was attributed to the presence of a foreign power—the United States—in what Panamanians regarded as their territory.

Central America, in summary, is a region of diverse geography and is home to peoples of many cultures. It is a region of strong local loyalties; its problems are profound and perplexing. The violence of the land is matched by the violence of its peoples as they fight for something as noble as justice or human rights, or as ignoble as political power or self-promotion.

Belize

GEOGRAPHY

Area in Square Kilometers (Miles):
22,963 (8,866) (slightly larger than
Massachusetts)
Capital (Population): Belmopan
(5,280)
Climate: tropical

PEOPLE

Population
Total: 229,000
Annual Growth Rate: 3.0%
Rural/Urban Population Ratio: 48/52
Ethnic Makeup of Population: 40%
Creole; 33% Mestizo; 10% Mayan;
8% Garifuna; 2% East Indian; 7%
others

Health
Life Expectancy at Birth: 67 years
(male); 73 years (female)
Infant Mortality Rate (Ratio):
30/1,000
Average Caloric Intake: 111% of
FAO minimum
Physicians Available (Ratio): 1/2,097

BLACK CARIB CUSTOMS

With the nation's independence, the Black Caribs of Belize have
revived many of their old customs and beliefs in an effort to recover
their heritage. For the Black Caribs, the *uribagabaga*, or butterfly, is a
symbol of one's fortune. A black butterfly connotes bad news, an illness
in the family, or even death. On the other hand, brightly colored
butterflies, which abound in Belize, are omens of good news.

Religion(s)
62% Roman Catholic; 30%
Protestant; 8% others

Education
Adult Literacy Rate: 91%

COMMUNICATION

Telephones: 15,920
Newspapers: 4 weeklies

TRANSPORTATION

Highways—Kilometers (Miles): 2,710
(1,683)

Railroads—Kilometers (Miles): none
Usable Airfields: 34

GOVERNMENT

Type: parliamentary democracy
Independence Date: September 21,
1981
Head of State: Governor General
Dame Elmira Minita Gordon; Prime
Minister Manuel Esquivel (head of
government)
Political Parties: People's United
Party; United Democratic Party;
Belize Popular Party
Suffrage: universal at 18

MILITARY

Number of Armed Forces: Belize
Defense Force Air Wing, with RAF
Harrier detachment
*Military Expenditures (% of Central
Government Expenditures):* 3.3%
Current Hostilities: none

ECONOMY

Currency ($ U.S. Equivalent): 2
Belize dollars = $1 (fixed rate)
Per Capita Income/GDP:
$1,635/$373 million
Inflation Rate: 5%
Total Foreign Debt: $142 million
Natural Resources: arable land;
timber; fish
Agriculture: sugarcane; citrus fruits;
rice; beans; corn; cattle; bananas;
honey
Industry: sugar refining; clothing;
construction materials; rum
beverages; cigarettes

FOREIGN TRADE

Exports: $134 million
Imports: $194 million

Belize
- ★ Capital
- • City
- ∿ River
- - - - Road

0 — 150 kilometers
0 — 150 miles

A LITTLE BIT OF ENGLAND

Belize was settled in the late 1630s by English woodcutters, who also indulged in occasional piracy at the expense of the Spanish crown. The loggers were interested primarily in dye-woods, which, in the days before chemical dyes, were essential to British textile industries. The country's name is derived from Peter Wallace, a notorious buccaneer who, from his base there, haunted the coast in search of Spanish shipping. The natives shortened and mispronounced Wallace's name until he became known as Belize.

As a British colony (British Honduras), Belize enjoyed relative prosperity as an important *entrepôt,* or storage depot for merchandise, until the completion of the Panama Railway in 1855. With the opening of a rail route to the Pacific, commerce shifted south, away from Caribbean ports. Belize entered an economic tailspin (from which it has never entirely recovered). Colonial governments attempted to diversify the colony's agricultural base and to attract foreign immigration to develop the land. But, except for some Mexican settlers and a few former Confederate soldiers who came to the colony after the U.S. Civil War, the immigration policy failed. Economically depressed, its population exposed to the ravages of yellow fever, malaria, and dengue (a tropical fever), Belize was once described by British novelist Aldous Huxley in the following terms: "If the world had ends, Belize would be one of them."

Living conditions improved markedly by the 1950s, and the colony began to move toward independence of the United Kingdom. Although self-governing by 1964, Belize did not become fully independent until 1981 because of Guatemalan threats to invade what it even today considers a lost province, stolen by Great Britain. British policy calls for a termination of its military presence even though Guatemalan intentions toward Belize are ambivalent.

Culturally, Belize is English with Caribbean overtones. English common law is practiced in the courts, about 30 percent of the people are Protestants, and politics are patterned on the English parliamentary system. The people are primarily working-class poor and middle-class shopkeepers and merchants. There is no great difference between the well-to-do and the poor in Belize, and few people fall below the absolute poverty line.

Forty percent of the population are Creole (black and English mixture), 8 percent Garifuna (black and Indian mixture). The Garifuna originally inhabited the Caribbean island of St. Vincent. In the eighteenth century, they joined with native Indians in an uprising against the English authorities. As punishment, virtually all the Garifuna were deported to Belize.

Despite a pervasive myth of racial democracy in Belize, discrimination exists. Belize is not a harmonious multiethnic island in a sea of violence. For example, sociologist Bruce Ergood notes that it "is not uncommon to hear a light Creole bad mouth 'blacks,' even though both are considered Creole. This reflects a vestige of English colonial attitude summed up in the saying, 'Best to be white, less good to be mulatto, worst to be black. . . .' "

A shift in population occurred because of the turmoil in neighboring Central American states. For years well-educated English-speaking Creoles had been leaving Belize in search of better economic opportunities in other countries, but this was more than made up for by the inflow of perhaps as many as 40,000 Latin American refugees who fled the fighting in the region. Spanish is now the primary language of a significant percentage of the population, and some Belizeans are concerned about the "Hispanicization" of the country.

Women in Belize suffer discrimination that is rooted in the cultural, social, and economic structures of the society, even though the government promotes their participation in the nation's politics and development process. Great emphasis is placed on education (which is compulsory to age 16) and health care. Tropical diseases, once the primary cause of death in Belize, were brought under control by a government program of spraying. Health and nutritional awareness are emphasized in campaigns to encourage breastfeeding and the selection and preparation of meals using local produce.

DEVELOPMENT

Officials of the new Free Trade Zone of Central America (El Salvador, Guatemala, Honduras and Nicaragua) have expressed the hope that Panama and Belize will be eventual participants. With the Caribbean Community exploring the possibility of common economic policies with Central American governments, Belize's economic future seems promising.

FREEDOM

With the restructuring of Belize Broadcasting Network as an autonomous entity free of government control and its renaming as the Broadcasting Corporation of Belize, the radio media in the country became considerably more open.

HEALTH/WELFARE

Minimum ages for employment of children have been set at 14 for work in retail establishments and at 17 for work involving dangerous machinery. There is no across-the-board, nationwide minimum wage law because of the large number of self-employed agricultural and craft workers.

ACHIEVEMENTS

Recent digging by archaeologists uncovered several Mayan sites that have convinced scholars that indigenous civilization in the region was more extensive and refined than experts had previously believed.

Costa Rica (Republic of Costa Rica)

GEOGRAPHY

Area in Square Kilometers (Miles):
51,022 (19,700) (smaller than West
Virginia)
Capital (Population): San José
(890,400)
Climate: tropical and semitropical

PEOPLE

Population

Total: 3,187,000
Annual Growth Rate: 2.4%
Rural/Urban Population Ratio: 53/47
Ethnic Makeup of Population: 96%
white (including a few Mestizos); 2%
black; 1% Indian; 1% Chinese

Health

Life Expectancy at Birth: 75 years
(male); 79 years (female)
Infant Mortality Rate (Ratio):
12/1,000
Average Caloric Intake: 118% of
FAO minimum
Physicians Available (Ratio): 1/1,045

Religion(s)

95% Roman Catholic; 5% others

Education

Adult Literacy Rate: 93%

COMMUNICATION

Telephones: 292,000
Newspapers: 4 dailies

TRANSPORTATION

Highways—Kilometers (Miles):
35,000 (21,700)
Railroads—Kilometers (Miles): 828
(513)
Usable Airfields: 149

COSTA RICA: PROTECTING ITS NATURAL RESOURCE

Costa Rica, as well as being a model democracy, also leads Central
America in discouraging the soil-leaching deforestation that is ultimately so disastrous to agriculture. Costa Rica has 13 new national
parks and 6 biological reserves. In these parks some 2,000 native tree
species are protected—twice the number of species found in the continental United States. New species are constantly being discovered as
the lumber industry works virgin forest. To protect this important
national resource further, the government has tightly controlled the
number of permits it allows for the cutting and exporting of timber.

GOVERNMENT

Type: democratic republic
Independence Date: September 15,
1821
Head of State: President José María
Figueres Olsen
Political Parties: National Liberation
Party; Social Christian Union; New
Republic Movement; Progressive
Party; People's Party of Costa Rica;
Radical Democratic Party; Marxist
Popular Vanguard Party
Suffrage: universal and compulsory
at 18

MILITARY

Number of Armed Forces: about
4,700; army replaced by civil guard
in 1948
*Military Expenditures (% of Central
Government Expenditures):* 1.7%
Current Hostilities: none

ECONOMY

Currency ($ U.S. Equivalent): 136
colones = $1
Per Capita Income/GDP: $1,900/$5.9
billion
Inflation Rate: 12%
Total Foreign Debt: $4.5 billion
Natural Resources: hydroelectric
power
Agriculture: coffee; bananas;
sugarcane; rice; corn; cocoa;
livestock products
Industry: food processing; textiles
and clothing; construction materials;
fertilizer; tourism

FOREIGN TRADE

Exports: $1.5 billion
Imports: $1.8 billion

COSTA RICA: A DIFFERENT TRADITION?

Costa Rica has often been singled out as politically and socially unique in Latin America. It is true that the nation's historical development has not been as directly influenced by Spain as its neighbors' have, but this must not obscure the essential Hispanic character of the Costa Rican people and their institutions. Historian Ralph Woodward has observed that, historically, Costa Rica's "uniqueness was the product of her relative remoteness from the remainder of Central America, her slight economic importance to Spain, and her lack of a non-white subservient class and corresponding lack of a class of large landholders to exploit its labors." In 1900 Costa Rica had a higher percentage of farmers with small- and medium-range operations than any other Latin American country.

The nature of Costa Rica's economy allowed a wider participation in politics and fostered the development of political institutions dedicated to the equality of all people, which existed only in theory in other Latin American countries. Costa Rican politicians, since the late nineteenth century, have endorsed programs that have been largely middle class in content. The government has consistently demonstrated a commitment to the social welfare of its citizens.

AN INTEGRATED SOCIETY

Despite the recent atmosphere of crisis and disintegration in Central America, Costa Rica's durable democracy has avoided the twin evils of oppressive authoritarianism and class welfare. What might be construed as good luck is actually a reflection of Costa Rica's history. In social, racial, linguistic, and educational terms, Costa Rica is an integrated country without the fractures and cleavages that typify the rest of the region.

Despite its apparent singularity, Costa Rica is culturally an integral part of Latin America and embodies what is most positive about Hispanic political culture. The government has long played the role of benevolent patron to the majority of its citizens. Opposition and antagonism have historically been defused by a process of accommodation, mutual cooperation, and participation. In the early 1940s, for example, modernizers who wanted to create a dynamic capitalist economy took care to pacify the emerging labor movement with appropriate social legislation and benefits. Moreover, to assure that development did not sacrifice social welfare, the state assumed a traditional role with respect to the economy—that is, it took an active role in the production and distribution of income. After much discussion the Congress in 1993 authorized the privatization of the state-owned cement and fertilizer companies. In both cases, according to *Latin American Regional Reports,* "a 30% stake will be reserved for employees, 20% will be offered to private investors, and the remainder will be shared out between trade unions . . . and cooperatives." Tight controls remain on banking, insurance, oil-refining, and public utilities.

Women, who were granted the right to vote in the 1940s, have participated freely in Costa Rica's elections and have served as a vice president, minister of foreign commerce, and president of the Legislative Assembly. Although in broader terms the role of women is primarily domestic, they are legally unrestricted. Equal work, in general, is rewarded by equal pay for men and women. But women also hold, as a rule, lower-paying jobs.

POLITICS OF CONSENSUS

Political stability is assured by the politics of consensus. Deals and compacts are the order of the day among various competing elites. Political competition is open, and participation by labor and peasants is expanding. Election campaigns provide a forum to air differing viewpoints, to educate the voting public, and to keep politicians in touch with the population at large.

Costa Rica frequently has had strong, charismatic leaders who have been committed to social democracy and have rejected a brand of politics grounded in class differences. Democracy in Costa Rica has always reflected the paternalism and personalities of its presidents.

This tradition was again endorsed when José María Figueres Olsen won the presidential election on February 6, 1994. Figueres is the son of the founder of the modern Costa Rican democracy, and he has promised to return to a reduced version of the welfare state. He wants to help his country's poor and has called for "a prosperous nation, but one which shares its prosperity." On the other hand, the ugly campaign preceding the election raised disturbing questions about Figueres's character and reflected poorly on the Costa Rican political system.

(United Nations photo/Milton Grant)

The beauty of the Costa Rican mountains and forest is being sacrificed to "progress" as more and more of the land is being turned to money-making agricultural use.

The first Spanish
settlements in
Costa Rica
1522

Independence
of Spain
1821

Costa Rica is
part of the United
Provinces of
Central America
1823

Costa Rica's
independence as
a separate state
1838

Civil war;
reforms; abolition
of the army
1948

1980s–1990s

Costa Rica takes
steps to protect
its tropical rain
forests and dry
forests

Rafael Angel
Calderón is
elected president

Strong economic
growth; José
María Figueres is
elected president

Other oft-given reasons for Costa Rica's stability are the high levels of toleration exhibited by its people and the absence of a military establishment. Costa Rica has had no military establishment since a brief civil war in 1948. Government officials have long boasted that they rule over a country that has more teachers than soldiers. There is also a strong public tradition that favors demilitarization. However, Costa Rica is not without auxiliary forces that could form the nucleus of an army in times of emergency.

The press is among the most unrestricted in Latin America; differing opinions are openly expressed. Human-rights abuses are virtually nonexistent, but there is a general suspicion of communists in this overwhelmingly middle-class, white society. And some citizens are concerned with the antidemocratic ideas expressed by ultra-conservatives.

The strain placed on the Costa Rican economy by the violence in the region and the press of refugees, at one time as high as 250,000, helped to create a climate of fear and uncertainty, especially with regard to the government's ability to deliver social services. (More than 80 percent of the population are covered by social-security programs, and approximately 60 percent are provided with pension and medical benefits.) But in 1993, with a measure of peace returning to the region and many refugees returning to their homes, the Costa Rican economy experienced a vibrant revival. Impressive economic growth, reductions in the levels of inflation and unemployment, and a hopeful decrease in the number of families below the poverty line all gave cause for optimism. Clearly, consensus-based reform-ist approaches to government-policy formulation stood up to the formidable challenges thrown up by regional chaos and economic recession.

THE ENVIRONMENT

At a time when tropical rain forests globally are under assault by developers, cattle barons, and land-hungry peasants, Costa Rica has taken concrete action to protect its environment. Minister of Natural Resources Álvaro Umana was one of those responsible for engineering an imaginative debt-for-nature swap. In his words: "We would like to see debt relief support conservation . . . a policy that everybody agrees is good." Since 1986 the Costa Rican government has authorized the conversion of $75 million in commercial debt into bonds. Interest generated by those bonds has supported a variety of projects, such as the enlargement and protection of La Amistad, a 1.7 million-acre reserve of tropical rain forest.

About 13 percent of Costa Rica's land is protected currently in a number of national parks. It is hoped that very soon about 25 percent of the country will be designated as national parkland in order to protect tropical rain forests as well as the even more endangered tropical dry forests.

Much of the assault on the forests typically has been dictated by economic necessity and/or greed. In one all-too-common scenario, a small- or middle-size cacao grower discovers that his crop has been decimated by a blight. Confronted by disaster, he will usually farm the forest surrounding his property for timber and then torch the remainder. Ultimately, he will likely sell his land to a cattle rancher, who will transform what had once been rain forest, or dry forest, into pasture.

In an effort to break this devastating pattern, at least one Costa Rican environmental organization has devised a workable plan to save the forests. Farmers are introduced to a variety of cash crops so that they will not be totally dependent on a single crop. Also, in the case of cacao, for example, the farmer will be provided with a disease- or blight-resistant strain to lessen further the chances of crop losses and subsequent conversion of land to cattle pasture.

Scientists in Costa Rica are concerned that tropical forests are being destroyed before their usefulness to humankind can be fully appreciated. Such forests contain a treasure-trove of medicinal herbs. In Costa Rica, for example, there is at least one plant common to the rain forests that might be beneficial in the struggle against AIDS.

DEVELOPMENT

In 1992 gross domestic product grew by an impressive 7.8%, among the strongest rates in Latin America and better than Japan or the United States. Inflation fell from 27% in 1991 to 12% in 1993. Exports rose 15%, and there was a 20% increase in tourist revenues.

FREEDOM

Despite a generally enviable human-rights record for the region, there is some de facto discrimination against blacks, Indians, and women (domestic violence against women is a serious problem). The press is free. A stringent libel law, however, makes the media cautious in reporting of personalities.

HEALTH/WELFARE

Costa Ricans enjoy the highest standard of living in Central America. There is little malnutrition, school attendance is high, and sanitation services are adequate. But Costa Rica's indigenous peoples, in part because of their remote location, have inadequate schools, health care, and access to potable water. Because many lack citizenship papers, they cannot vote or hold office.

ACHIEVEMENTS

In a region torn by civil war and political chaos, Costa Rica's years of free and democratic elections stand as a remarkable achievement in political stability and civil rights. President Óscar Arias was awarded the Nobel Peace Prize in 1987; he is an internationally recognized and respected world leader.

El Salvador (Republic of El Salvador)

GEOGRAPHY

Area in Square Kilometers (Miles):
21,476 (8,292) (about the size of Massachusetts)
Capital (Population): San Salvador (1,400,000)
Climate: semitropical; distinct wet and dry seasons

PEOPLE

Population
Total: 5,574,000
Annual Growth Rate: 2.2%
Rural/Urban Population Ratio: 56/44
Ethnic Makeup of Population: 89% Mestizo; 10% Indian; 1% white

Health
Life Expectancy at Birth: 68 years (male); 73 years (female)
Infant Mortality Rate (Ratio): 26/1,000
Average Caloric Intake: 94% of FAO minimum
Physicians Available (Ratio): 1/2,830

Religion(s)
93% Roman Catholic; Protestant groups throughout the country

Education
Adult Literacy Rate: 73%

COMMUNICATION

Telephones: 116,000
Newspapers: 6 dailies

THE NEED TO FLEE

During its history El Salvador has often been in a state of turmoil. Because revolution and counterrevolution have been a large element in their lives, the people of El Salvador have had to decide which military or political factions to back. Often the people of the villages have had to hide in the bush to avoid soldiers—so often, in fact, that this occurrence has been called *aquinda*, a word not found in any dictionary, which means "to flee in the middle of the night with everything you've got." It is hoped that the lexicon of El Salvador will become more life-affirming with the formal 1992 cease-fire to the Civil War.

TRANSPORTATION

Highways—Kilometers (Miles):
12,164 (7,541)
Railroads—Kilometers (Miles): 602 (374)
Usable Airfields: 77

GOVERNMENT

Type: republic
Independence Date: September 21, 1821
Head of State: President Armando Calderón Sol
Political Parties: Democratic Party; National Republican Alliance Party; Salvadoran Authentic Institutional Party; Party of National Conciliation; Christian Democratic Party; Salvadoran Popular Party; others
Suffrage: universal at 18

MILITARY

Number of Armed Forces: 31,500
Military Expenditures (% of Central Government Expenditures): 24.5%
Current Hostilities: none: cease-fire declared for Civil War in February 1992

ECONOMY

Currency ($ U.S. Equivalent): 8.1 colones = $1
Per Capita Income/GDP: $1,010/$5.5 billion
Inflation Rate: 19.0%
Total Foreign Debt: $2.0 billion
Natural Resources: hydroelectric and geothermal power
Agriculture: coffee; cotton; sugar; livestock; corn; poultry; sorghum
Industry: food and beverages; textiles; footwear and clothing; chemical products; petroleum products

FOREIGN TRADE

Exports: $580 million
Imports: $1.2 billion

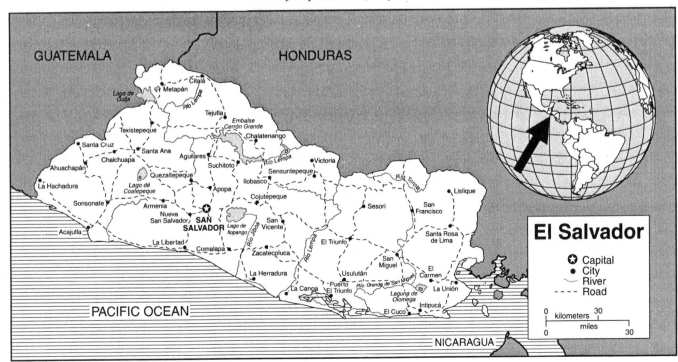

EL SALVADOR:
A TROUBLED LAND

El Salvador, a small country, until 1992 was engaged in a civil war that cut through class lines, divided the military and the Roman Catholic Church, and damaged the social and economic fabric of the nation. It was the latest in a long series of violent sociopolitical eruptions that have plagued the country since its independence in 1821.

In the last quarter of the nineteenth century, large plantation owners—spurred by the sharp increase in the world demand for coffee and other products of tropical agriculture—expanded their lands and estates. Most of the new land was purchased or taken from Indians and Mestizos (those of mixed white and Indian blood) who, on five occasions between 1872 and 1898, took up arms in futile attempts to preserve their land. The once-independent Indians and Mestizos were reduced to becoming tenant farmers, sharecroppers, day laborers, or peons on the large estates. Indians, when deprived of their lands, also lost their cultural and ethnic distinctiveness. Today El Salvador is an overwhelmingly Mestizo society.

The uprooted peasantry was controlled in a variety of ways. Some landowners played the role of *patrón* and assured workers the basic necessities of life in return for their labor. Laws against "vagabonds" (those who, when stopped by rural police, did not have a certain amount of money in their pockets) assured plantation owners a work force and discouraged peasant mobility.

To enforce order further, a series of security organizations—the National Guard, the National Police, and the Treasury Police—were created by the central government. Many of these security personnel actually lived on the plantations and estates and followed the orders of the owner. Although protection of the economic system was their primary function, over time elements of these organizations became private armies.

This phenomenon lay at the heart of much of the "unofficial" violence in El Salvador in recent years. In Salvadoran society, personal loyalties to relatives or local strongmen competed with and often superseded loyalty to government officials. Because of this the government was unable to control some elements within its security forces.

In an analysis of the Salvadoran Civil War, it is tempting to place the rich, right-wing landowners and their military allies on one side; and the poor, the peasantry, and the guerrillas on the other. Such a division is artificial, however, and fails to reflect the complexities of the conflict. Granted, since 1945 the military and landowners had enjoyed a mutually beneficial partnership. But there were liberal and conservative factions within the armed forces, and since the 1940s there had been some movement toward needed social and economic reforms. It was a military regime in 1949 that put into effect the country's first social-security legislation. In 1950 a Constitution was established that provided for public-health programs, women's suffrage, and extended social-security coverage. The reformist impulse continued in the 1960s, when it became legal to organize opposition political parties.

A TIME FOR CHANGE

Food production increased in the 1970s by 44 percent, a growth that was second in Latin America only to Brazil's. Although much of the food grown was exported to world markets, some of the revenue generated was used for social programs in El Salvador. Life expectancy increased; the death rate fell; illiteracy declined; and the percentage of government expenditures on public health, housing, and education was among the highest in Latin America.

The programs and reforms, in classic Hispanic form, were generated by the upper classes. The elite believed that state-sponsored changes could be controlled in such a way that traditional balances in society would remain intact and elite domination of the government would be assured.

El Salvador's Civil War may be traced to 1972, when the Christian Democratic candidate for president, José Napoleón Duarte, is believed to have won the popular vote but was deprived of his victory when the army declared the results false and handed the victory to its own candidate. Impatient and frustrated, middle-class politicians and student leaders from the opposition began to consider more forceful ways to oust the ruling class.

By 1979 guerrilla groups had become well established in rural El Salvador, and some younger army officers grew concerned that a successful left-wing popular revolt was a distinct possibility. Rather than wait for revolution from below, which might result in the destruction of the military as an institution, the officers chose to seize power in a coup and manipulate change from above. Once in power this *junta,* or ruling body, moved quickly to transform the structure of Salvadoran society. A land-reform program, originally developed by civilian reformers and Roman Catholic clergy, was adopted by the military. It would give the *campesinos* ("peasants") not only land but also status, dignity, and respect.

In its first year, 1980, the land-reform program had a tremendous impact on the landowning elite: 37 percent of the lands producing cotton and 34 percent of the coffee-growing lands were confiscated by the government and redistributed. The junta also nationalized the banks and assumed control of the sale of coffee and sugar. Within months, however, several peasant members of the new cooperatives and the government agricultural advisers sent to help them were gunned down. The violence spread. Some of the killings were attributed to government security men in the pay of dispossessed landowners, but most of the killings may have been committed by the army.

In the opinion of a land-reform program official, the army was corrupt and had returned to the cooperatives it had helped to establish to demand money for protection and bribes. When the peasants refused, elements within the army initiated a reign of terror against them.

In 1989 further deterioration of the land-reform program was brought about by Supreme Court decisions and by policies adopted by the newly elected right-wing government of President Alfredo Cristiani. Former landowners who had had property taken for redistribution to peasants successfully argued that seizures under the land reform were illegal; five successive land-reform cases have been decided by the Supreme Court in favor of former property owners.

Cristiani, whose right-wing National Republican Alliance Party (ARENA) fought hard against land reform, would not directly attack the land-reform program—only because such a move would further alienate rural peasants and drive them into the arms of left-wing guerrillas. Instead Cristiani favored the reconstitution of collective farms as private plots. Such a move, according to the government, would improve productivity and put an end to what authorities perceived as a form of U.S.-imposed "socialism." Critics of the government's policy charged that the privatization plan would ultimately result in the demise of land reform altogether.

Yet another problem was that many of the collectives established under the reform were (and remain) badly in debt. A 1986 study by the U.S. Agency for International Development reported that 95 percent of the cooperatives could not pay interest on the debt they were forced to acquire to compensate the landlords. *New York Times* reporter Lindsey Gruson noted that the world surplus of agricultural products as well as mismanagement by peasants who suddenly found themselves in the unfamiliar role of owners were a large part of the reason for the failures. But the government did not help. Technical assistance was not provided, and the tremendous debt gave the cooperatives a poor credit rating, which made it difficult for them to secure needed fertilizer and pesticides.

Declining yields and, for many families, lives of increasing desperation have been the result. Some peasants will leave the land and sell their plots to the highest bidder. This will ultimately bring about a reconcentration of land in the hands of former landlords.

Other prime farmland lay untended because of the Civil War. Violence drove many peasants from the land to the slums of the larger cities. And free-fire zones established by the military (in an effort to destroy the guerrillas' popular base) and guerrilla attacks against cooperatives (in an effort to sabotage the economy and further destabilize the country) had a common victim: the peasantry.

Some cooperatives and individual families failed to bring the land to flower because of the poor quality of the soil they inherited. Reporter Gruson told the story

of one family, which was, unfortunately, all too common:

José . . . received 1.7 acres on a rock-pocked slope an hour's walk from his small shack. José . . . used to sell some of his beans and rice to raise a little cash. But year after year his yields have declined. Since he cannot afford fertilizers or insecticides, the corn that survives the torrential rainy season produces pest-infested ears the size of a baby's foot. Now, he has trouble feeding his wife and seven children.

"The land is no good," he said. "I've been working it for 12 years and my life has gotten worse every year. I don't have anywhere to go, but I'll have to leave soon."

After the coup, several governments came and went. The original reformers retired, went into exile, or went over to the guerrillas. The Civil War continued into 1992, when a UN-mediated cease-fire took effect, and the extreme right and left regularly utilized assassination to eliminate or terrorize both each other and the voices of moderation who still dared to speak out. The death squads and guerrillas claimed their victims from all social

classes. Some leaders, such as former President Duarte, described a culture of violence in El Salvador that had become part of the national character.

HUMAN-RIGHTS ISSUES

Through 1992 human-rights abuses still occurred on a wide scale in El Salvador. Public order was constantly disrupted by military operations, guerrilla raids, factional hatreds, acts of revenge, personal grudges, pervasive fear, and a sense of uncertainty · about the future. State-of-siege decrees suspended all constitutional rights to freedom of speech and press. However, self-censorship, both in the media and by individuals, out of fear of violent reprisals, was the leading constraint on free expression in El Salvador.

Release of the report in 1993 by the United Nations's "Truth Commission," a special body entrusted with the investigation of human-rights violations in El Salvador, prompted the right-wing–dominated Congress to approve an amnesty for those named. But progress has been made in other areas. The National Police have been separated from the Defense Ministry; and the National Guard, Civil Defense forces, and the notorious Treasury Police have been abolished. A new National Ci-

(United Nations photo)

Unloading the fish catch in El Salvador.

Present-day El Salvador is occupied by Spanish settlers from Mexico
1524

Independence of Spain is declared
1821

El Salvador is part of the United Provinces of Central America
1822

Independence as a separate state
1838

A brief war between El Salvador and Honduras
1969

Guerrilla warfare in El Salvador
1970

Army officers seize power in a coup; Civil War
1979

1980s–1990s

Right-wing President Alfredo Cristiani is elected

The cease-fire takes effect on February 1, 1992, officially ending the Civil War

Armando Calderón Sol of the ARENA party wins the Presidential run-off election

vilian Police, comprised of 20 percent of National Police, 20 percent former Farabundo Martí National Liberation Front (FMLN) guerrillas, and 60 percent with no involvement on either side in the Civil War, will be instituted in mid-1994.

In El Salvador, as elsewhere in Latin America, the Roman Catholic Church was divided. The majority of church officials backed government policy and supported the United States's contention that the violence in El Salvador was due to Cuban-backed subversion. Other clergy strongly disagreed and argued convincingly that the violence was deeply rooted in historical social injustice.

GOVERNANCE

The election to the presidency of José Napoleón Duarte in 1984 was an important first step in establishing the legitimacy of government in El Salvador, as were municipal elections in 1985. The United States supported Duarte as a representative of the "democratic" middle ground between the guerrillas of the FMLN and the right-wing ARENA party. Ironically, U.S. policy in fact undermined Duarte's claims to legitimacy and created a widespread impression that he was little more than a tool for U.S. interests.

Yet while the transfer of power to President Cristiani via the electoral process in 1989 reflected the will of those who voted, it did not augur well for the lessening of human-rights abuses. With respect to the guerrillas of the FMLN, Cristiani made it clear that the government would set the terms for any talks about ending the Civil

War. For its part the FMLN warned that it would make the country "ungovernable." In effect, then, the 1989 election results polarized the country's political life even more.

After several unsuccessful efforts to bring the government and the guerrillas to the negotiating table, the two sides in April 1991 reached a tentative agreement on constitutional reforms at a UN-sponsored meeting in Mexico City. The military, judicial system, and electoral process were all singled out for sweeping changes. By October the FMLN had promised to lay down its arms, and near midnight on December 31 the final points of a peace accord were agreed upon. Final refinements of the agreement were drawn up in New York, and a formal signing ceremony was staged in Mexico City on January 16, 1992. The official cease-fire took effect February 1, thus ending the 12-year Civil War that had claimed more than 70,000 lives and given El Salvador the reputation of a bloody and abusive country.

Implementation of the agreement reached between the government and the FMLN has proven contentious. "But," according to *Boston Globe* correspondent Pamela Constable, "a combination of war-weariness and growing pragmatism among leaders of all persuasions suggests that once-bitter adversaries have begun to develop a modus vivendi." President Cristiani reduced the strength of the army from 63,000 to 31,500 by February 1993, earlier than provided for by the agreement; and the class of officers known as the *tondona,* who have long dominated the mili-

tary and are likely responsible for human-rights abuses, were forcibly retired by the president on June 30, 1993. Land, judicial, and electoral reforms will follow. Despite perhaps inevitable setbacks because of the legacy of violence and bitterness, editor Juan Comas wrote that "most analysts are inclined to believe that El Salvador's hour of madness has passed and the country is now on the road to hope."

ECONOMIC PROSPECTS

El Salvador has always been an inherently rich country in terms of its resources. The Civil War wreaked havoc on the economy, with damage to the infrastructure in excess of $300 million, and displaced hundreds of thousands of people. Recovery has been impressive. Inflation is relatively low, the level of foreign indebtedness modest, and the gross domestic product has grown steadily since 1990. Of primary importance was the role played by the 10 percent of the population living in the United States. In 1989 alone their remittances to El Salvador totaled an estimated $760 million, 53 percent more than export earnings. Money in these amounts will serve to prime the pump of economic recovery.

DEVELOPMENT

Since 1991 the government has been able to attract substantial investment in a new industry of low-wage, duty-free assembly plants patterned after the *maquiladora* industries along Mexico's border with the United States. Advantageous tax laws and a free-market climate favorable to business are central to the government's development policy.

FREEDOM

The end of the Civil War brought an overall improvement in human rights in El Salvador. The number of extrajudicial killings fell significantly, and politically motivated killings seem to be on the wane. News from across the political spectrum, often critical of the government, is reported in El Salvador, although foreign journalists seem to be the target of an unusually high level of muggings, robberies, and burglaries.

HEALTH/WELFARE

Many Salvadorans suffer from parasites and malnutrition. El Salvador has one of the highest infant mortality rates in the Western Hemisphere, largely because of polluted water. Potable water is available to only 10% of the population. Violence against women is widespread. Judges often dismiss rape cases on the pretext that the victim provoked the crime.

ACHIEVEMENTS

Despite the violence of war, political power has been transferred via elections at both the municipal and national levels. Elections help to establish the legitimacy of civilian leaders in a region usually dominated by military regimes.

Guatemala (Republic of Guatemala)

GEOGRAPHY

Area in Square Kilometers (Miles): 108,780 (42,000) (about the size of Tennessee)
Capital (Population): Guatemala City (1,800,000)
Climate: temperate in highlands; semitropical on coasts

PEOPLE

Population
Total: 9,784,000
Annual Growth Rate: 2.4%
Rural/Urban Population Ratio: 61/39
Ethnic Makeup of Population: 56% Ladino (Mestizo and Westernized Indian); 44% Indian

Health
Life Expectancy at Birth: 61 years (male); 66 years (female); 44 years (Indian population)
Infant Mortality Rate (Ratio): 56/1,000
Average Caloric Intake: 93% of FAO minimum
Physicians Available (Ratio): 1/289

Religion(s)
predominantly Roman Catholic; also Protestant and traditional Mayan

Education
Adult Literacy Rate: 55%

COMMUNICATION

Telephones: 180,000
Newspapers: 4 dailies

MIGUEL ÁNGEL ASTURIAS

For years the infamous United Fruit Company, based in Boston, Massachusetts, played an important role in the economy and political life of Guatemala. Nobel Prize-winning author Miguel Ángel Asturias bitterly criticized the excesses of this company in a famous trilogy of novels: *Strong Wind, The Green Pope,* and *The Eyes of the Interred.* For these and other novels—notably, *El Señor Presidente,* which is the story of one of Guatemala's most ruthless dictators—Asturias has been called "the conscience of his country."

TRANSPORTATION

Highways—Kilometers (Miles): 18,000 (11,160)
Railroads—Kilometers (Miles): 953 (590)
Usable Airfields: 400

GOVERNMENT

Type: republic
Independence Date: September 15, 1821
Head of State: President Ramiro de León Carpio
Political Parties: Christian Democratic Party; National Liberation Movement; National Authentic Center; Anticommunist Unification Party; Democratic Institutional Party; National Centerist Union; Solidarity Action Movement; National Advancement Party; Social Democratic Party; others
Suffrage: universal at 18

MILITARY

Number of Armed Forces: 43,500
Military Expenditures (% of Central Government Expenditures): 13.3%
Current Hostilities: civil war

ECONOMY

Currency ($ U.S. Equivalent): 5.28 quetzals = $1
Per Capita Income/GDP: $1,260/$11.7 billion
Inflation Rate: 14.0%
Total Foreign Debt: $2.6 billion
Natural Resources: oil; nickel; timber
Agriculture: corn; beans; coffee; cotton; cattle; sugarcane; bananas; timber; rice; cardamon
Industry: food processing; textiles; construction materials; pharmaceuticals; furniture; tires

FOREIGN TRADE

Exports: $1.2 billion
Imports: $1.7 billion

GUATEMALA: PEOPLES IN CONFLICT

Ethnic relations between the descendants of Mayan Indians, who comprise 44 percent of Guatemala's population, and whites and Ladinos (Hispanicized Indians) have always been unfriendly and have contributed significantly to the nation's turbulent history. During the colonial period and since independence, Spaniards, Creoles (whites born in the New World—as opposed to in Nicaragua, where Creoles are native-born blacks), and Ladinos have repeatedly sought to dominate the Guatemalan Indian population, largely contained in the highlands, by controlling the Indians' land and their labor.

The process of domination was accelerated between 1870 and 1920, as Guatemala's entry into world markets hungry for tropical produce such as coffee resulted in the purchase or extensive seizures of land from Indians. Denied sufficient lands of their own, Indians were forced onto the expanding plantations as debt peons. Others were forced to labor as seasonal workers on coastal plantations, and there many died because of the sharp climatic differences.

THE INDIAN AND INTEGRATION

Assaulted by the Ladino world, highland Indians withdrew into their own culture and built social barriers between themselves and the changing world outside their villages. Those barriers have persisted until the present.

For the Guatemalan governments that have thought in terms of economic progress and national unity, the Indians have always presented a problem. (In 1964 the Guatemalan national census separated the population into two social categories: whites and Ladinos, and Indians.) Traditionally the white world has perceived them as a burden. "Backward," "custom-bound," "superstitious," "uneducated," and "unassimilable" is how the Indians were described in the late nineteenth century. Those same descriptions are used today. According to anthropologist Leslie Dow, Jr., Guatemalan governments too easily explain the Indian's lack of material prosperity in terms of the "deficiencies" of Indian culture. Indian "backwardness" is better explained by elite policies calculated to keep Indians subordinate. Social, political, and economic deprivations have consistently and consciously been utilized by governments anxious to maintain the Indian in an inferior status.

Between 1945 and 1954, however, there was a period of remarkable social reform in Guatemala. Before the reforms were cut short by the resistance of landowners, factions within the military, and a CIA-sponsored invasion, Guatemalan governments made a concerted drive to integrate the Indian into national life. Some Indians who lived in close proximity to large urban centers such as the capital, Guatemala City, learned that their vote had the power to effect changes to their benefit. They also realized that they were unequal not because of their illiteracy, "backwardness," poverty, or inability to converse in Spanish, but because of governments that refused to reform their political, social, and economic structures.

In theory, indigenous peoples in Guatemala enjoy equal legal rights under the Constitution. In fact, they remain largely outside the national culture, do not speak Spanish, and are not integrated into the national economy. Indian males are far more likely to be impressed into the army or guerrilla units. Indigenous peoples in Guatemala have suffered most of the combat-related casualties and repeated abuses of basic human rights. There is a pervasive discrimination against Indians in white society. Indians have on occasion challenged state policies that they have considered inequitable and repressive. But if they become too insistent on change, threaten violence or societal upheaval, or support and/or join guerrilla groups, government repression is usually swift and merciless.

GUERRILLA WARFARE

For much of the 1980s, Guatemala was plagued by violence, attributed both to left-wing insurgencies in rural areas and to armed forces' counterinsurgency operations. Led by youthful middle-class rebels, guerrillas gained strength because of several factors: the radical beliefs of some Roman Catholic priests in rural areas; the ability of the guerrillas to mobilize Indians for the first time; and the "demonstration effect" of events elsewhere in Central America. Some of the success is explained by the guerrilla leaders' ability to converse in Indian languages. Radical clergy increased the recruitment of Indians into the guerrilla forces by suggesting that revolution was an acceptable path to social justice. The excesses of the armed forces in their search for subversives drove other Indians into the arms of the guerrillas. And in some parts of the highlands, the loss of ancestral lands to speculators or army officers was sufficient to inspire the Indians to join the radical cause.

According to the *Latin American Regional Report* for Mexico and Central America, government massacres of guerrillas and their actual or suspected supporters were frequent and "characterized by clinical savagery." At times the killing was selective, with community leaders and their families singled out. In other instances entire villages were destroyed and all the inhabitants slaughtered. "Everything depends on the army's perception of the local level of support for the guerrillas," according to the report.

To counterbalance the violence, once guerrillas were cleared from an area, the government implemented an Aid Program to Areas in Conflict. Credit was offered to small farmers to boost food production in order to meet local demand, and displaced and jobless people were enrolled in food-for-work units to build roads or other public projects.

By the mid-1980s, most of the guerrillas' military organizations had been destroyed. This was the result not only of successful counterinsurgency tactics by the Guatemalan military but also of serious errors of judgment by guerrilla leaders. Impatient and anxious for change, the guerrillas overestimated the willingness of the Guatemalan people to rebel and underestimated the power of the military establishment. Surviving guerrilla units maintained an essentially defensive posture for the remainder of the decade. In 1989, however, the guerrillas regrouped. The intensification of human-rights abuses from 1990 until the present and the climate of violence are indicative of the military's response.

There was some hope for improvement in 1993 in the wake of the ouster of President Jorge Serrano, whose attempt to emulate the "self-coup" of Peru's Alberto Fujimori failed. Guatemala's new president, Ramiro de León Carpio, is a human-rights activist who has been sharply critical of security forces in their war against the guerrillas of the Guatemalan National Revolutionary Unity (URNG). Peace talks between the government and guerrillas had been pursued with the Roman Catholic Church as intermediary for several years, with sparks of promise but no real change. De León, in July 1993, announced a new set of proposals to bring to an end 30 years of bloodshed. The creation of a "forum" with the participation of all sectors, including the guerrillas, would discuss the means to remove the causes of the conflict. Other changes envisaged the reduction of the size of the military establishment, as has been the case in El Salvador, and the reestablishment of a "truth commission" to investigate human-rights abuses. De León planned to work with the Organization of American States and the United Nations as mediators.

Other signs of change included the appointment of a "moderate" to the office of defense minister and the selection of Celestino Tay Coyoy as minister of education. Tay is active in the National Assembly of the Maya People and reflects the willingness of the government to respond to the needs of 60 percent of the population who are indigenous. But the willingness of the guerrillas to negotiate and the genuine efforts on de León's part to begin the process of healing ultimately depend on the intentions of Guatemala's military, which remains the most powerful force in the country. If past history provides a lesson, the prospects for change supported by the military are not auspicious.

URBAN VIOLENCE

Although most of the violence has occurred in rural areas, urban Guatemala has not escaped the horrors of the conflict. The following characterization of Guatemalan politics, written by an English traveler in 1839, is still relevant today: "There is but one side to the politics in Guatemala. Both parties have a beautiful way of producing unanimity of opinion, by driving out of the country all who do not agree with them."

Since 1978 right-wing killers have murdered dozens of leaders of the moderate political left to prevent them from organizing viable political parties that might challenge the ruling elite. These killers have also assassinated labor leaders if their unions were considered leftist or antigovernment. University student leaders

(United Nations photo/152/271/Antoinette Jongen)

This elderly Indian woman of San Mateo looks back on a life of economic and social prejudice. In recent years Indians in Guatemala have pursued their rights by exercising their voting power. On occasion they have resorted to violence, which has been repressed swiftly and mercilessly by the government. But the power of the ballot box has begun to reap gains.

| Guatemala is conquered by Spanish forces from Mexico **1523** | Independence **1821** | Guatemala is part of the United Provinces of Central America **1822–1838** | Independence as a separate state **1838** | Revolution; many reforms **1944** | A CIA-sponsored coup deposes the reformist government **1954** | Miguel Ángel Asturias wins the Nobel Prize **1967** | An earthquake leaves 22,000 dead **1976** | Human-rights abuses lead to the termination of U.S. aid **1977** |

1980s–1990s

President Jorge Serrano is removed after a failed "self-coup"

Human-rights activist Ramiro de León Carpio is named to the presidency

Talks between the government and guerrillas commence to end 30 years of violence

and professors have "disappeared" because the national university has a reputation as a center of leftist subversion. Media people have been gunned down if they were critical of the government or the right wing. Left-wing extremists also have assassinated political leaders associated with "repressive" policies; civil servants whose only "crime" was government employment; military personnel and police; foreign diplomats; peasant informers; and businesspeople and industrialists associated with the government.

Common crime has risen to epidemic proportions in Guatemala City (as well as in the capitals of other Central American republics). Many of the weapons that once armed the Nicaraguan militias and El Salvador's civil-defense patrols found their way onto the black market, where, according to the Managua newspaper *Pensamiento Propio,* they were purchased by the Guatemalan Army, the guerrillas of the URNG, and criminals. In 1992 the Ministry of the Interior created the *Hunahpu* task-force patrols. Composed of elements of the National Police, the Treasury Police, and the Mobile Military Police, the Hunahpu has tended to adopt the policy of "catch in the act, shoot on the spot" in an effort to control common crime.

The fear of official or unofficial violence has always inhibited freedom of the press. Early in the 1980s, the Conference on Hemispheric Affairs noted that restrictions on the print media and the indiscriminate brutality of the death squads "turned Guatemala into a virtual no-man's land for journalists." Lingering fears and memories of past violence tend to limit

the exercise of press freedoms guaranteed by the Constitution. The U.S. State Department's *Country Reports* notes that "the media continues to exercise a degree of self-censorship on certain topics. . . . The lack of aggressive investigative reporting dealing with the military and human rights violations apparently is due to self-censorship."

One Guatemalan journalist who dared to begin publication of an antigovernment daily in 1988 was repeatedly threatened with bodily harm. His newspaper office was firebombed, his home was ransacked and burglarized, and the police let it be known that they were not especially interested in investigating the charges. He writes in a climate of intimidation, leading him to comment: "To invest in Guatemala as a journalist is to invest in a desert."

HEALTH CARE AND NUTRITION

In rural Guatemala half the population has a diet that is well below the minimum daily caloric intake established by the Food and Agricultural Organization. Growth in the staple food crops (corn, rice, beans, wheat) has failed to keep pace with population growth. Marginal malnutrition is endemic.

Health services vary, depending on location, but are uniformly poor in rural Guatemala. The government has begun pilot programs in three departments to provide basic primary health care on a wide scale. But some of these well-intentioned policies have failed because of a lack of sensitivity to cultural differences. Anthropologist Linda Greenberg observed that the Ministry of Health, as part of its cam-

paign to bring basic health care services to the hinterlands, introduced midwives ignorant of Indian traditions. For Guatemalan Indians, pregnancy is considered an illness and demands specific care, calling for certain foods, herbs, body positions, and interpersonal relations between expectant mother and Indian midwife. In the Mayan culture, traditional medicine has spiritual, psychological, physical, social, and symbolic dimensions. Ministry of Health workers too often dismiss traditional practices as superstitious and unscientific. This insensitivity and ignorance creates ineffectual health care programs.

THE FUTURE

Guatemala's turmoil will persist as long as elite-dominated governments treat Indians as second-class citizens and rob them of their land and their dignity. Political war will also continue because of the polarization that has taken place between a murderous right wing that refuses to acknowledge the need for meaningful societal changes and a left wing that considers armed confrontation its only resort. Meaningful dialogue has begun, but violence and an intransigent military persist.

DEVELOPMENT

The Guatemalan economy grew 4.6% in 1992, which produced an increase in per capita income of about 1.4%. Inflation continued to decline, from 22% in January 1990 to 14% at the end of 1992. In all respects the economy showed marked improvement over the levels attained in the late 1980s.

FREEDOM

President de León Carpio has warned those who would violate human rights and said that the law would punish those guilty of abuses, "whether or not they are civilians or members of the armed forces." The moment has come, he continued, "to change things and improve the image of the army and of Guatemala."

HEALTH/WELFARE

While constitutional bars on child labor in the industrial sector are not difficult to enforce, in the informal and agricultural sectors, such labor is common. It is estimated that 5,000 children live on the streets and survive as best they can. They are often targeted for elimination by police and death squads.

ACHIEVEMENTS

The novelist Miguel Ángel Asturias gained an international reputation for his works about political oppression. In 1967 he was awarded the Nobel Prize for Literature.

Honduras (Republic of Honduras)

GEOGRAPHY

Area in Square Kilometers (Miles):
109,560 (42,300) (slightly larger than Tennessee)
Capital (Population): Tegucigalpa (550,000)
Climate: subtropical, but varies with elevation (temperate highlands)

PEOPLE

Population

Total: 5,093,000
Annual Growth Rate: 2.8%
Rural/Urban Population Ratio: 56/44
Ethnic Makeup of Population: 90% Mestizo (European and Indian mix); 7% Indian; 2% African; 1% European, Arab, and Oriental

Health

Life Expectancy at Birth: 65 years (male); 68 years (female)
Infant Mortality Rate (Ratio): 54/1,000
Average Caloric Intake: 96% of FAO minimum
Physicians Available (Ratio): 1/1,724

Religion(s)

about 97% Roman Catholic; a small Protestant minority

Education

Adult Literacy Rate: 73%

ANTONIO VELÁZQUEZ

Honduras's most important twentieth-century artist, Antonio Velázquez, was self-taught. He won international acclaim and fame for his renditions of his hometown of San Antonio de Oriente, a sixteenth-century mining town. Detailed without being photographic, his style has been classified as an example of the primitive school. Velázquez was also able to serve simultaneously as mayor and town barber.

COMMUNICATION

Telephones: 35,100
Newspapers: 4 dailies

TRANSPORTATION

Highways—Kilometers (Miles): 18,494 (11,466)
Railroads—Kilometers (Miles): 955 (592)
Usable Airfields: 133

GOVERNMENT

Type: republic
Independence Date: September 15, 1831
Head of State: President Carlos Roberto Reina
Political Parties: Liberal Party; National Innovation and Unity Party; Christian Democratic Party; others
Suffrage: universal and compulsory at 18

MILITARY

Number of Armed Forces: 18,900
Military Expenditures (% of Central Government Expenditures): 7%
Current Hostilities: none

ECONOMY

Currency ($ U.S. Equivalent): 5.4 lempira = $1 (fixed rate)
Per Capita Income/GDP: $1,050/$5.2 billion
Inflation Rate: 26.0%
Total Foreign Debt: $2.8 billion
Natural Resources: forest products; minerals; fish
Agriculture: coffee; bananas; corn; beans; livestock; cotton; sugarcane; tobacco
Industry: textiles; wood products; cement; cigars

FOREIGN TRADE

Exports: $1.0 billion
Imports: $1.3 billion

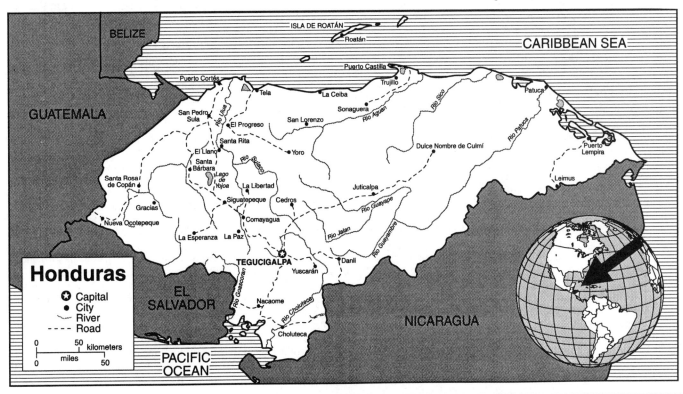

HONDURAS: PEACEABLE KINGDOM?

In political terms, Honduras resembles much of the rest of Central America. Frequent changes of government, numerous constitutions, authoritarian presidents, widespread corruption, and an inability to solve basic problems are common to Honduras and to the region. A historian of Honduras once wrote that his country's history could be "written in a tear." In terms of social policy, however, Honduras stands somewhat apart from its neighbors. It was slower to modernize, there were no great extremes of wealth between landowners and the rest of the population, and society appeared more paternalistic and less exploitive than was the case in other Central American states.

Honduras is a poor country. It has serious social problems—widespread illiteracy, malnutrition, and inadequate health care. "Ironically," journalist Loren Jenkins wrote, "the land's precarious existence as a poor and unstable backwater has proven almost as much a blessing as a curse." Honduras lacks the sharp social divisions that helped to plunge Nicaragua, El Salvador, and Guatemala into rebellion and civil war. And Honduran governments have seemed somewhat more responsive to demands for change.

A WILLINGNESS TO CHANGE

In 1962 and 1975, agrarian-reform laws were passed and put into effect with relative success. The Honduran government, with the aid of peasant organizations and organized labor, was able to resettle 30,000 families on their own land. Today two-thirds of the people who use the land either own it or have the legal right to its use. Labor legislation and social-security laws were enacted in the early 1960s. Even the Honduran military, usually corrupt, has at times brought about reform. An alliance of the military and organized labor in the early 1970s produced a series of reforms in response to pressure from the less advantaged sectors of the population; in 1974 the military government developed a 5-year plan to integrate the rural poor into the national economy and to increase social services in the area. The state has often shown a paternalistic face rather than a brutal, repressive one. The capacity for reform led one candidate in the 1981 presidential campaign to note: "We Hondurans are different. There is no room for violence here."

There are now many signs of change. Agrarian reform slowed after 1976, prompting a peasant-association leader to remark: "In order to maintain social peace in the countryside, the peasants' needs will have to be satisfied to avoid revolt." In 1984 the Honduran government initiated a land-titling program and issued about 1,000 titles per month to landless peasants. The government's agrarian-reform program, which is under the control of the National Agrarian Institute, has always been characterized by the carrot and the stick. While some *campesinos* ("peasants") have been granted titles to land, others have been jailed or killed.

Honduran campesinos, according to *Central America Report*, "have had a long and combative history of struggling for land rights." In 1987 hundreds of peasants were jailed as "terrorists" as a result of land invasions. Occupation of privately owned lands has become increasingly common in Honduras and reflects both population pressure on and land hunger of the peasantry. Sometimes the land seizures by squatters are recognized by the National Agrarian Institute. In other cases, the government has promoted the relocation of people to sparsely populated regions of the country. On the negative side, the chosen regions are tropical rain forests which are already endangered throughout the region. The government wishes to transform the forests into rubber and citrus plantations or into farms to raise rice, corn, and other crops.

Peasants who fail to gain access to land usually migrate to urban centers in search of a better life. What they find in cities such as Tegucigalpa are inadequate social services, a miserable standard of living, and a municipal government without the resources to help. Tegucigalpa in 1989 was deeply in debt, mortgaged to the limit, months behind in wage payments to city workers, and plagued by garbage piling up in the streets.

In the late 1980s, the nation's economy fared badly. But by 1992 the economy, following painful adjustments occasioned by the reforms of the government of President Rafael Callejas, again showed signs of growth. Real gross domestic product reached 3.5 percent, and inflation was held in check. Unemployment is a persistent problem; some agencies have calculated that two-thirds of the work force lack steady employment. A union leader warned: "Unemployment leads to desperation and becomes a time bomb that could explode at any moment."

In addition to internal problems, pressure has been put on Honduras by the International Monetary Fund. Before the IMF will approve further loans, the Honduran government must introduce stiff austerity measures, including higher taxes on consumer goods, the elimination of price controls on basic commodities, and a reduction in state spending on social welfare and public projects. The demands provoked a bitter response from a conservative Honduran newspaper: "This level of sacrifice will inevitably serve as a provocation: the country will explode socially, and those who now deny us money for production will only have to provide exorbitant sums for arms, violence, repression, and death."

HUMAN AND CIVIL RIGHTS

Not surprisingly, President Callejas met with strong opposition to his plans for economic adjustment. Throughout early 1990 his currency devaluation, price increases on basic commodities, and the mass dismissal of public employees provoked social unrest and the strong condemnation of trade-union and church leaders. On the positive side, Callejas's willingness to make unpopular decisions deemed necessary for economic recovery resulted in loans of $1 billion from international institutions and from the Japanese government.

In theory, despite the continuing violence in the region, basic freedoms in Honduras are still intact. The press is privately owned and free of government censorship. There is, however, a quietly expressed concern about offending the government, and self-censorship is considered prudent. Moreover, it is an accepted practice in Honduras for government ministries and other agencies to have journalists on their payrolls.

Honduran labor unions are free to organize and have a tradition of providing their rank and file certain benefits. They are allowed to bargain, but labor laws guard against "excessive" activity. A complex procedure of negotiation and arbitration must be followed before a legal strike can be called. If a government proves unyielding, labor will likely pass into the ranks of the opposition.

In 1992 Honduras's three major workers' confederations convinced the private sector to raise the minimum wage by 13.7 percent, the third consecutive year of increases. Nevertheless, the minimum wage, which varies by occupation and location, is not adequate to provide a decent standard of living, especially in view of inflation. According to one labor leader, the minimum wage will "not even buy tortillas." To compound the problems of workers, the labor minister admitted that about 30 percent of the enterprises under the supervision of his office paid wages *below* the minimum. To survive, families must pool the resources of all its working members. Predictably, health and safety laws are usually ignored. As is the case in the rural sector, the government has listened to the complaints of workers—but union leaders have also on occasion been jailed.

The government is also confronted by the problem of an increasing flow of rural poor into the cities. Employment opportunities in rural areas have declined as landowners convert cropland into pasture for beef cattle. Because livestock-raising requires less labor than growing crops, the surplus rural workers seek to better their opportunities in the cities. But the new migrants have discovered that Honduras's commercial and industrial sectors are deep in recession and cannot provide jobs.

Fortunately, many of the 300,000 refugees from Nicaragua and El Salvador have returned home. With the election of President Violeta Chamorro in Nicaragua, most of the 20,000 rebel Contras lay down their arms and returned home, thus eliminating—from the perspective of the Honduran government—a source of much violence in its border regions.

To the credit of the Honduran government, which is under strong pressure from conservative politicians and businesspeople as well as elements within the armed forces for tough policies against dissent, allegations vis-à-vis human-rights abuses are taken seriously. (In one celebrated case, the Inter-American Court of Human Rights, established in 1979, found the government culpable in at least one person's "disappearance" and ordered the payment of an indemnification to the man's family. While not accepting any premise of guilt, the government agreed to pay. More importantly, according to the COHA *Washington Report*, the decision sharply criticized

"prolonged isolation" and "incommunicado detention" of prisoners and equated such abuses with "cruel and inhuman punishment.") While Honduras may no longer be characterized as "the peaceable kingdom," the government has not lost touch with its people and still acts out a traditional role of patron.

Perhaps the most serious threat to civilian government comes from the military. The recent Central American policy of the United States boosted the prestige, status, and power of the Honduran military, which is increasingly confident in its ability to forge the nation's destiny. It is ironic that U.S. policy, which is committed to the spread of democracy, may again produce military rule in Honduras. The appearance of small bands of guerrillas, assaults on human rights, and the call for discipline and order—so common in much of Central America—are increasingly obvious in Honduras.

In 1993 the administration of President Callejas announced the creation of a commission to study proposals for reform of the security services. At the top of the Callejas's list was a constitutional change that would allow the president, and not the Superior Council of the Armed Forces, to nominate the commander-in-chief of the armed forces, as had been the case. Other reforms would force the military to divest themselves of state agencies such as the telecommunications company (Hondutel), the directorates of civil aviation and migration, and the merchant marine.

Callejas introduced Honduras to winds of free-market economics which continue to blow strongly throughout Latin America. He took the first steps toward reduc-

ing the role of the government in the economy, a difficult task since the military holds many lucrative concessions. Indeed, the military proved resistant to any cuts in its budget or privileges. In the words of armed forces commander General Luis Alonso Discua: "We are not prepared to dismantle our structures to please those who think that we are not necessary...." Callejas's austerity programs, in part induced by the insistence of the International Monetary Fund, caused widespread misery, but by 1992 the economy showed signs of strengthening.

A pragmatist who was willing to strike out in fresh directions, Callejas also moved to improve relations with his neighbors. The pace of refugee repatriation was accelerated, and Honduras joined the new Central American Free Trade Zone.

On November 28, 1993, the presidential elections resulted in Carlos Roberto Reina, of the Liberal Party, easily defeating Oswaldo Ramos Soto, the incumbent National Party's candidate. The Honduran people thereby expressed their dissatisfaction with the sacrifices that Callejas had asked them to make to slow inflation and curb the budget deficit. The new administration faces formidable challenges in economic, political, and social arenas; however, the Honduran democratic institution has again allowed for an orderly transfer of power.

DEVELOPMENT

The Central American Free Trade Zone, of which Honduras is a member, will reduce tariffs by 5% to 20% on more than 5,000 products traded within the region. Over the coming years, more products will be included and tariffs will be progressively lowered.

FREEDOM

The military remains a strong force in Honduras but continues to support civilian government. The turmoil in neighboring countries has had an adverse effect on human rights as security has been tightened. In 1992 there were numerous cases of extrajudicial killing committed by members of the police and military.

HEALTH/WELFARE

Although minimum wages, working hours, vacations, and occupational safety are regulated by law, in practice they are frequently ignored. Minimum wages are established by occupation, with the lowest set at the equivalent of under $3.00 *per day*.

ACHIEVEMENTS

The small size of Honduras, in terms of territory and population, has produced a distinctive literary style that is a combination of folklore and legend.

Nicaragua (Republic of Nicaragua)

GEOGRAPHY

Area in Square Kilometers (Miles):
148,000 (57,143) (about the size of Iowa)
Capital (Population): Managua (1,000,000)
Climate: subtropical, but varies with elevation (temperate highlands)

PEOPLE

Population

Total: 3,878,000
Annual Growth Rate: 2.0%
Rural/Urban Population Ratio: 40/60
Ethnic Makeup of Population: 69% Mestizo; 17% white; 9% black; 5% Indian

Health

Life Expectancy at Birth: 60 years (male); 66 years (female)
Infant Mortality Rate (Ratio): 57/1,000
Average Caloric Intake: 99% of FAO minimum
Physicians Available (Ratio): 1/1,678

Religion(s)

primarily Roman Catholic; Protestant

Education

Adult Literacy Rate: 57%

COMMUNICATION

Telephones: 60,000
Newspapers: 3 dailies; 105,000 circulation

TRANSPORTATION

Highways—Kilometers (Miles): 25,930 (16,102)

Railroads—Kilometers (Miles): 373 (233)
Usable Airfields: 155

GOVERNMENT

Type: republic
Independence Date: September 15, 1821
Head of State: President Violeta Barrios de Chamorro
Political Parties: Political Alliance in Opposition; Sandinista National Liberation Front; Social Democratic Party; Social Christian Party; Democratic Conservative Party; Constitutionalist Liberal Party; many others
Suffrage: universal at 16

MILITARY

Number of Armed Forces: 60,600
Military Expenditures (% of Central Government Expenditures): 13.3%
Current Hostilities: border skirmishes with Honduras

ECONOMY

Currency ($ U.S. Equivalent): 25,000,000 córdobas = $1
Per Capita Income/GDP: $425/$1.6 billion
Inflation Rate: 9.9%
Total Foreign Debt: $10.0 billion
Natural Resources: arable land; livestock; timber; fisheries
Agriculture: cotton; coffee; sugarcane; cattle
Industry: food processing; chemicals; metals; textiles; petroleum; beverages

FOREIGN TRADE

Exports: $342 million
Imports: $738 million

FILIBUSTERS

A U.S. adventurer named William Walker, known to his admirers as the "grey-eyed man of destiny," led 58 armed men called filibusters (from the Spanish word *filibustero*, or "freebooter") in a coup against the government of Nicaragua in 1855. After capturing the city of Granada, he arranged for Patricio Rivas to become provisional president. Effective power was held by Walker, however, as he was commander-in-chief of the army. The government was recognized by the United States in 1856. Walker was forced to flee Nicaragua in 1857 after he confiscated interests belonging to Cornelius Vanderbilt, who supported and financed a Central American force that drove Walker from power. William Walker was executed in Honduras in 1860, following an abortive coup against the Honduran government.

NICARAGUA:
A NATION IN REVOLUTION

Nicaraguan society, culture, and history have been molded to a great extent by its geography. A land of volcanoes and earthquakes, the frequency of natural disasters in Nicaragua has profoundly influenced its peoples' perceptions of life, death, and fate. What historian Ralph Woodward has written about Central America is particularly apt for Nicaraguans. Fatalism may be said to be a "part of their national mentality, tempering their attitudes toward the future. Death and tragedy always seem close in Central America. The primitive states of communication, transportation, and production, and the insecurity of human life, have been the major determinants in the region's history. . . ."

Nicaragua is a divided land, with distinct geographic, cultural, racial, ethnic, and religious zones. The west-coast region, which contains about 90 percent of the total population, is overwhelmingly white or Mestizo (mixed blood), Catholic, and Hispanic. The east coast is a sharp contrast, with its scattered population and multiplicity of Indian, Creole (in Nicaragua, native-born blacks), and Hispanic ethnic groups.

The east coast's geography, economy, and isolation from Managua (the nation's capital city) have created a distinct identity among its people. Many east-coast citizens think of themselves as *costeños* ("coast dwellers") rather than Nicaraguans. Religion reinforces this common identity. About 70 percent of the east-coast population, regardless of ethnic group, are members of the Protestant Moravian Church. After more than 135 years of missionary work, the Moravian Church has become "native," with locally recruited clergy. Among the Miskito Indians, Moravian pastors commonly replace tribal elders as community leaders. The black Creoles speak English and originally arrived either as shipwrecked or escaped slaves or as slave labor introduced by the British to work in the lumber camps and plantations in the seventeenth century. Many Creoles and Miskitos feel a greater sense of allegiance to the British than to Nicaraguans from the west coast, who are regarded as foreigners.

SANDINISTA POLICIES

Until the successful 1979 Revolution that drove the dictator Anastasio Somoza from power, Nicaraguan governments generally ignored the east coast. Revolutionary Sandinistas—who took their name from a guerrilla, Augusto César Sandino, who fought against occupying U.S. forces in the late 1920s and early 1930s—adopted a new policy toward the neglected region. The Sandinistas were concerned with the east coast's history of rebelliousness and separatism, and they were attracted by the economic potential of the region (palm oil and rubber). Accordingly, they hastily devised a bold campaign to unify the region with the rest of the nation. Roads, communications, health clinics, economic development, and a literacy campaign for local inhabitants were planned. The Sandinistas, in defiance of local customs, also tried to organize the local population into mass formations—that is, organizations for youth, peasants, women, wage earners, and the like. It was believed in Managua that such groups would unite the people behind the government and the Revolution and facilitate the economic, political, and social unification of the region.

In general, the attempt failed, and regional tensions within Nicaragua persist. Historically, costeños were unimpressed with the exploits of the guerrilla Sandino, who raided U.S. companies along the east coast in the 1930s. When the companies left or cut back on operations, workers who lost their jobs blamed Sandino rather than the worldwide economic crisis of the 1930s. Consequently, there was a reluctance to accept Sandino as the national hero of the new Nicaragua. Race and class differences increased due to an influx of Sandinistas from the west. Many of the new arrivals exhibited old attitudes and looked down on the east-coast peoples as "uncivilized" or "second class."

The Miskito Question

In 1982 the government forced 10,000 Indians from their ancestral homes along the Río Coco because of concern with border security. As a result, many Indians joined the Contras, U.S.-supported guerrillas who fought against the Sandinista regime.

In an attempt to win back the Miskito and associated Indian groups, the government decided on a plan of regional autonomy. In 1985 Interior Minister Tomás Borge finished a draft plan. Its main proposals included the following features: a regional assembly for the east coast, with each of the six ethnic groups (Miskito, Sumo, Rama, Garifuna, Creole, Mestizo) having the same number of representatives; regional control over Sandinista federal officials working in the region; natural resources under the control of regional governments; and bilingual-education programs. Defense of the east-coast region remained in the hands of Managua, in coordination with the autonomous governments. The Sandinista government initiated a "repatriation" scheme in 1984, allowing 1,000 Miskitos to return to their homes.

The significance of the Sandinista policy was that the government finally appreciated how crucial regional differences are in Nicaragua. Cultural and ethnic differences must be respected if Managua expects to rule its peoples effectively. The lesson learned by the Sandinistas was taken to heart by the Chamorro government, which was the first in history to appoint a Nicaraguan of Indian background to a ministerial-level position. The limited self-government granted to the east-coast region by the Sandinistas in 1987 has been maintained; local leaders were elected to office in 1990.

A Mixed Record

In general terms, the record of the Sandinista government was mixed. When the rebels seized power in 1979, they were confronted by an economy in shambles. Nineteen years of civil war had taken an estimated 50,000 lives and destroyed half a billion dollars' worth of factories, businesses, medical facilities, and dwellings. Living standards had tumbled to 1962 levels, and unemployment was estimated at 25 percent.

Despite economic difficulties, the government made great strides in the areas of health and nutrition. A central goal of official policy was to provide equal access to health services. The plan had more success in urban areas than in rural ones. The government emphasized preventive, rather than curative, medicine. Preventive medicine included the provision of clean water, sanitation, immunization, nutrition, and maternal and child care. People were also taught basic preventive medical techniques. National campaigns to wipe out malaria, measles, and polio had reasonable success. But because of restricted budgets, the health system was overloaded, and there was a shortage of medical supplies. In the area of nutrition, basic foodstuffs such as grains, oil, eggs, and milk were paid for in part by the government in an effort to improve the general nutritional level of Nicaraguans.

By 1987 the Sandinista government was experiencing severe economic problems that badly affected all social programs, and in 1989 the economy for all intents and purposes collapsed. Hyperinflation ran well over 100 percent a month; and in June 1989, following a series of mini-devaluations, the nation's currency was devalued by an incredible 100 percent. Commerce was virtually paralyzed.

The revolutionary Sandinista government, in an attempt to explain the economic debacle, with some justice argued that the Nicaragua it inherited in 1979 had been savaged and looted by former dictator Somoza. The long-term costs of economic reconstruction; the restructuring of the economy to remove the vast concentrations of wealth in a few hands that existed before 1979; the trade embargo erected by the United States and North American diplomatic pressure designed to discourage lending or aid from international institutions such as the International Monetary Fund; and the high cost of fighting a war against U.S.-supported Contra rebels formed the backdrop to the crisis. Opposition leaders added to the list Sandinista economic policies that discouraged private business.

The impact of the economic crisis on average Nicaraguans was devastating. Overnight, prices of basic consumer goods such as meat, rice, beans, milk, sugar, and cooking oil experienced increases of between 40 and 80 percent. Gasoline prices doubled. Primary and secondary school teachers engaged in work stoppages in an effort to increase their monthly wages of about $15, equal to the pay of a domestic servant. (To put the teachers' plight into perspective, note that the cost of a liter of milk absorbed fully 36 percent of a day's pay.) As a hedge against inflation, other Nicaraguans purchased dollars on the black market. *Regionews,* published in

Managua, noted that conversion of córdobas into dollars was "seen as a better proposition than depositing them in savings accounts."

Economic travail inevitably produces dissatisfaction; opinion polls taken in July 1989 signaled political trouble for the Sandinistas. According to *Latin American Weekly Report,* the surveys reflected an electorate with mixed feelings. While nearly 30 percent favored the Sandinistas, 57 percent indicated that they would not vote for President Daniel Ortega.

The results of the election of 1990 were not surprising, for the Sandinistas had lost control of the economy. They failed to survive a strong challenge from the opposition, led by the popular Violeta Chamorro.

Sandinista land reform, for the most part, consisted of the government's confiscation of the huge estates of the ousted Somoza family. These lands amounted to more than 2 million acres, about 40 percent of the nation's best farmland. Some peasants were given land, but the government preferred to create cooperatives. This policy prompted the criticism that the state simply had become an old-fashioned landowner. Sandinistas replied that "the state is not the same state as before; it is a state of producers; we organized production and placed it at the disposal of the people." In 1990 there were several reports of violence between Sandinista security forces and peasants and ex-Contras who petitioned for private ownership of state land.

The Role of the Church

The Revolution caused a sharp division within the Roman Catholic Church in Nicaragua. Radical priests, who believed that Christianity and Marxism share similar goals and that the church should play a leading role in social change and revolution, were at odds with traditional priests fearful of "godless communism." Since 1979 many radical Catholics had become involved in social and political projects; several held high posts in the Sandinista government.

One priest of the theology of liberation was interviewed by *Regionews.* The interviewer stated that an "atheist could say, 'These Catholics found a just revolution opposed by the Church hierarchy. They can't renounce their religion and are searching for a more convenient theology. But it's their sense of natural justice that motivates them.' " The priest replied: "I think that's evident and that Jesus was also an 'atheist,' an atheist of the religion as practiced in his time. He didn't believe in the God of the priests in the temples who were allied with Caesar. Jesus told of a new life. And the 'atheist' that exists in our people doesn't believe in the God that the hierarchy often offers us. He believes in life, in man, in development. God manifests Himself there. A person who believes in life and justice in favor of the poor is not an atheist." The movement, he noted, would continue "with or without approval from the hierarchy."

(United Nations photo/Jerry Frank)

A lakeside section of Managua, Nicaragua, was destroyed by an earthquake. Central America is often shaken by both large and small earthquakes.

| Nicaragua is explored by Gil González **1522** | Independence of Spain **1821** | Nicaragua joins the United Provinces of Central America **1823** | Independence as a separate state **1838** | William Walker and filibusters (U.S. insurgents) invade Nicaragua **1855** | Augusto César Sandino leads guerrillas against occupying U.S. forces **1928–1934** | Domination of Nicaragua by the Somoza family **1934–1979** | Sandinista guerrillas oust the Somoza family **1979** | Sharp deterioration of relations with the United States |

1980s–1990s

| A cease-fire allows an opening for political dialogue | Violeta Chamorro and UNO defeat Sandinistas in the 1990 elections | Political instability and rural violence plague reconstruction |

The Drift to the Left

As has historically been the case in revolutions, after a brief period of unity and excitement, the victors begin to disagree over policies and power. For a while in Nicaragua, there was a perceptible drift to the left, and the Revolution lost its image of moderation. While radicalization was a dynamic inherent in the Revolution, it was also pushed in a leftward direction by a hostile U.S. foreign policy that attempted to bring down the Sandinista regime through its support of the Contras. In 1987, however, following the peace initiatives of Latin American governments, the Sandinista government made significant efforts to project a more moderate image in the region. *La Prensa*, the main opposition newspaper, which the Sandinistas shut down in 1986, was again allowed to publish. Radio Católica, another source of opposition to the government, was given permission to broadcast after its closure the year before. And antigovernment demonstrations were permitted in the streets of Managua.

Significantly, President Ortega proposed reforms in the country's election laws in April 1989, to take effect before the national elections in 1990. Although the Bush administration was not convinced that the changes would ensure free elections, a report prepared by the Hispanic Division of the Library of Congress was generally favorable. The new Nicaraguan legislation was based on Costa Rican and Venezuelan models and in some instances was even more forward-looking.

An important result of the laws was the enhancement of political pluralism, which allowed the National Opposition Union (UNO) victory in 1990. Rules for organizing political parties, once stringent, were loosened; opposition parties were granted access to the media; foreign funding of political parties was allowed; the system of proportional representation permitted minority parties to maintain a presence; and the opposition was allowed to monitor closely the elections.

The Sandinistas realized that to survive, they had to make compromises. In need of breathing space, the government embraced the Central American Peace Plan designed by Costa Rican president Óscar Arias and designed moderate policies to isolate the United States.

On the battlefield, the cease-fire unilaterally declared by the Sandinistas was eventually embraced by the Contras as well, and both sides moved toward a political solution of their differences. Armed conflict formally ended on June 27, 1990, although sporadic violence continued in rural areas.

CHAMORRO AND UNO

It was the critical condition of the Nicaraguan economy that in large measure brought the Sandinistas down in the elections of 1990. Even though the Chamorro government made great progress in the demilitarization of the country and national reconciliation, the economy remains a time bomb.

The United States has continued to withhold aid because congressional critics feel that President Chamorro allows too much Sandinista influence in her government and failed to compensate U.S. citizens for land expropriated by the Sandinistas. Of particular concern is the continued presence of a Sandinista, General Humberto Ortega, as army chief. It is alleged that the army, through him, remains the real power behind the Nicaraguan political system. Inflation has been brought down, from 674 percent in 1991 to 9.9 percent; but currency devaluation is routine, and a tough economic austerity program was put in place in 1993. More than 800,000 people are now out of work.

The continuing economic crisis and disagreements over policy directions have destroyed the original base of Chamorro's political support. At the end of 1992, the battle between the executive and legislative branches of government came to a head when President Chamorro closed the Assembly building and called for new elections. UNO legislators criticized what they called Chamorro's "self-coup," moved definitively into opposition, and renamed the party the Political Alliance in Opposition. Further complicating the reconstruction of the country was renewed violence in the countryside by re-armed Contras ("Recontras") and demobilized Sandinista fighters ("Recompas"). The Recontras allege that the government has given them land of poor quality, failed to provide titles, and denied them access to bank loans and housing.

Thus, Nicaragua again stands on the edge of a precipice. Political stability is precarious, the economy continues its depressed state, and violence again stalks the countryside.

DEVELOPMENT

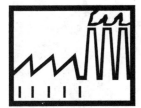

Nicaragua began the transition from a state-run economy to a mixed economy in 1990. Enterprises confiscated by the Sandinistas were returned to former owners.

FREEDOM

Diverse points of view have been freely and openly discussed in the media. Radio, the most important medium for news distribution in Nicaragua, has conveyed a broad range of opinion.

HEALTH/WELFARE

Almost 60% of the households in Nicaragua are headed by women. Of these, 72% live in poverty. Of the unemployed, 57% are women; and 75% of these are single mothers.

ACHIEVEMENTS

The Nicaraguan poet Rubén Darío was the most influential representative of the Modernist Movement, which swept Latin America in the late nineteenth century. Darío was strongly critical of injustice and oppression.

Panama (Republic of Panama)

GEOGRAPHY

Area in Square Kilometers (Miles):
75,650 (29,208) (slightly larger than West Virginia)
Capital (Population): Panama City (1,064,000)
Climate: tropical

PEOPLE

Population
Total: 2,530,000
Annual Growth Rate: 2.0%
Rural/Urban Population Ratio: 47/53
Ethnic Makeup of Population: 70% Mestizo; 14% West Indian; 10% white; 6% Indian and others

Health
Life Expectancy at Birth: 73 years (male); 77 years (female)
Infant Mortality Rate (Ratio): 17/1,000
Average Caloric Intake: 103% of FAO minimum
Physicians Available (Ratio): 1/841

Religion(s)
93% Roman Catholic; 7% Protestant and others

Education
Adult Literacy Rate: 88%

COMMUNICATION

Telephones: 241,900
Newspapers: 5 Spanish dailies; 1 English

THE GREAT "SOUTH SEA"

In 1502, on his fourth voyage to the New World, Christopher Columbus visited the north coast of what today is Panama. As a result the first colonies of this area were settled along the Caribbean coast. The first head of the European colony, Vasco Nuñez de Balboa, ruled the natives through friendship rather than by force. After listening to an Indian chief's son talk about the "South Sea," Balboa set out on an expedition in 1513 and became the first white man to view the Pacific Ocean.

TRANSPORTATION

Highways—Kilometers (Miles): 8,530 (5,297)
Railroads—Kilometers (Miles): 737 (457)
Usable Airfields: 133

GOVERNMENT

Type: centralized republic
Independence Date: November 3, 1903
Head of State: President Guillermo Endara
Political Parties: Nationalist Republican Liberal Movement; Authentic Liberal Party; Arnulfista Party; Christian Democratic Party; Democratic Revolutionary Party; Agrarian Labor Party; Liberal Party; Popular Action Party; others
Suffrage: universal and compulsory at 18

MILITARY

Number of Armed Forces: all armed forces were disbanded in 1990
Military Expenditures (% of Central Government Expenditures): —
Current Hostilities: none

ECONOMY

Currency ($ U.S. Equivalent): 1 balboa = $1 (fixed rate)
Per Capita Income/GDP: $2,040/$5.0 billion
Inflation Rate: 2.0%
Total Foreign Debt: $5.4 billion
Natural Resources: geographic location; copper ore; timber
Agriculture: bananas; rice; sugarcane; corn; coffee
Industry: food processing; beverages; petroleum products; construction materials; clothing

FOREIGN TRADE

Exports: $380 million
Imports: $1.5 billion

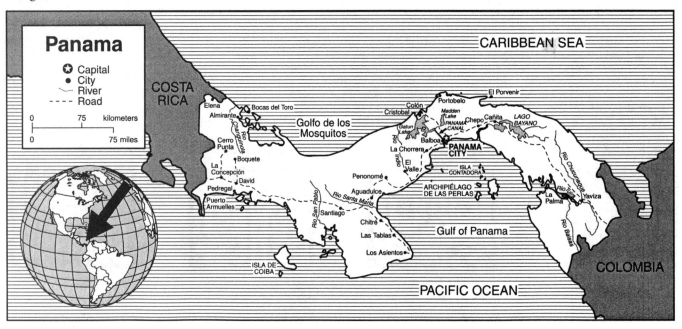

PANAMA:
A NATION AND A CANAL

The Panama Canal, opened to shipping in 1914, has had a sharp impact on Panamanian political life, foreign policy, economy, and society. Panama is a country of minorities and includes blacks, Mestizos (mixed Indian and white), Indians, and Chinese. Many of the blacks and Chinese are the children or grandchildren of the thousands of workers who were brought to Panama to build the canal. Unable to return home, they remained behind, an impoverished people, ignored for decades by a succession of Panamanian governments. The government has usually been dominated by whites, although all the country's minorities are politically active. In areas where Indians comprise a majority of the population, they play significant roles in provincial political life. Some, such as the San Blas islanders—famous for the art form known as Mola, which consists of different colored fabrics that are cut away to make designs—live in self-governing districts. Although Indians are not restricted to tribal areas, most remain by choice, reflecting a long tradition of resistance to assimilation and defense of their cultural integrity.

Panama's economy has both profited and suffered from the presence of the canal. Because governments traditionally placed too much reliance on the direct and indirect revenues generated by the canal tolls, they tended to ignore other types of national development. Much of Panama's economic success in the 1980s, however, was the result of a strong service sector associated with the presence of a large number of banks, the Panama Canal, and the Colón Free Zone. Agriculture and industry, on the other hand, usually experienced slow growth rates.

Because of U.S. control of the canal and the Canal Zone, this path between the seas continuously stoked the fires of Panamanian nationalism. The high standard of living and the privileges enjoyed by U.S. citizens residing in the zone contrasted sharply with the poverty of Panamanians. The late President Omar Torrijos became a national hero in 1977 when he signed the Panama Canal Treaties with U.S. President Jimmy Carter. The treaties ultimately provide for full Panamanian control over the canal and its revenues by the end of this century.

Panamanian officials speak optimistically of their plans for the bases they will soon inherit and mention universities, modern container ports, luxury resorts, and retirement communities. But, according to *New York Times* correspondent Howard W. French, there is much concern over the loss of an estimated $500 million that tens of thousands of U.S. troops, civilians, and their dependents pump into the Panamanian economy. Moreover, while all agree that the canal itself will be well run because Panamanians have been phased into its operation, there is pessimism about the lack of planning for ancillary facilities. Already several properties have been overrun by squatters and one tank farm is in danger of rusting from lack of use.

A RETURN TO CIVILIAN GOVERNMENT

President Torrijos, who died in a suspicious plane crash in 1981, left behind a legacy that included much more than the treaties. He elevated the National Guard to a position of supreme power in the state and ruled through a National Assembly of community representatives.

The 1984 elections appeared to bring to fruition the process of political liberalization initiated in 1978. But even though civilian rule was officially restored, the armed forces remained the real power behind the throne. Indeed, spectacular revelations in 1987 strongly suggested that Defense Forces Chief General Manuel Antonio Noriega rigged the 1984 elections. He was also accused of drug trafficking, gun running, and money laundering.

Indeed, in February 1988 Noriega was indicted by two U.S. grand juries and charged with using his position to turn Panama into a center for the money-laundering activities of the Medellín, Colombia, drug cartel and protection of cartel members living temporarily in Panama.

Attempts by Panamanian President Eric Arturo Delvalle to oust the military strongman failed, and Delvalle himself was forced into hiding. Concerted efforts by the United States to remove Noriega from power—which included an economic boycott, plans to kidnap the general and have the CIA engineer a coup, and saber-rattling by the dispatch of thousands of U.S. troops to the Canal Zone—proved fruitless.

The fraud and violence that accompanied an election called by Noriega in 1989 to legitimize his government and the failure of a coup attempt in October ultimately resulted in the invasion of Panama by U.S. troops in December. Noriega was arrested, brought to the United States for trial, and convicted on drug-trafficking charges.

(United Nations photo)

The Panama Canal has been of continuing importance to the country since it opened in 1914. Full control of the canal will be turned over to Panama in 1999, marking the end of U.S. involvement and representing a source of Panamanian nationalism.

Panama City is
established
1518

Panama is a
department of
Colombia
1821–1903

Independence
of Colombia
1903

The signing of
the Panama
Canal treaties
1977

The death of
President Omar
Torrijos creates a
political vacuum

1980s–1990s

Deterioration in
U.S.-Panama
relations

American troops
invade Panama;
Noriega surren-
ders to face drug
charges in the
United States

Guillermo
Endara is
appointed
president;
economic
recovery is
accompanied by
political disarray

The U.S. economic sanctions succeeded in harming the wrong people. Noriega and his cronies were shielded from the economic crisis by their profits from money-laundering. But some other Panamanians were devastated by the U.S. policy.

Members of Panama's electoral commission declared Guillermo Endara president (although his victory in the election of May 1989 was annulled on Noriega's orders). Among the major problems faced by the new Endara government were rebuilding the economy and restoring law and order.

Ominously, the Endara government has continued to lose support among Panamanians. Parties have argued over the proper share of government jobs, factions within the ruling party have paralyzed government, and there is constant feuding within the bureaucracy. "Equally troublesome," according to political scientist Steve C. Ropp, writing in *Current History,* "is the fact that these quarrels and divisions among civilian politicians are mirrored in the existing distribution of control over the instruments of force." Seven government-sanctioned organizations have the legal right to bear arms, while there are an additional 100 private-security agencies that may have as many as 12,000 armed personnel. The danger is that the government organizations will become politicized and that the other forces will in essence become private armies.

Ropp notes further that one of the "most important consequences of [Endara's] . . . coalition and the attendant feuding among civilian politicians has been a dramatic decline in the civilian political leadership's legitimacy." Endara could not avoid the

albatross of his installation by a foreign power; and now the combination of a leadership crisis, corruption, and crime have eroded most of his support. It is "clear that Panamanians are increasingly becoming dissatisfied not only with their leaders but with democracy itself," Ropp states. An opposition close to the military leadership that controlled Panama between 1968 and 1989 has rapidly rebounded.

The Panamanian economy, on the other hand, has recovered from the crisis induced by the anti-Noriega policies of the Reagan and Bush administrations. In 1992 real gross domestic product growth reached an impressive 8 percent; and most sectors of the economy, led by the canal, banking, and the Colón Free Zone, moved forward. At the same time, Endara's privatization of state enterprises and tariff reduction, while necessary to diversify an economy overly dependent on canal revenues and traditional agricultural exports, have resulted in the loss of jobs. Unemployment hovers around the 15 percent mark, which further fuels the fires of discontent.

SOCIAL POLICIES

As in most Latin American nations, Panama's Constitution authorizes the state to direct, regulate, replace, or create economic activities designed to increase the nation's wealth and to distribute the benefits of the economy to the greatest number of people. In reality, the income of 35 to 40 percent of Panama's population frequently fails to provide a family's basic needs. One-fifth of the population are classified as extremely poor and cannot

provide for basic necessities. On the positive side, the government has made moderately successful attempts to improve health care in both urban and rural areas.

Women, who won the right to vote in the 1940s, are accorded equal political rights under the law and hold a number of important government positions. But, as is the case in all of Latin America, women do not enjoy the same opportunities for advancement as do men. There are also domestic constraints to their freedom. Panamanian law, for example, does not recognize community property; divorced or deserted women have no protection and can be left destitute, if that is the will of their former spouses. Many female heads of household from poor areas are obliged to work for the government, often as street cleaners, in order to receive support funds from the authorities.

With respect to human rights, Panama's record is mixed. The press and electronic media, while theoretically free, have experienced some harassment. In 1983 the Supreme Court ruled that journalists need not be licensed by the government. Nevertheless, both reporters and editors exercise a calculated self-censorship, and press conduct in general is regulated by an official Morality and Ethics Commission, whose powers are broad and vague.

DEVELOPMENT

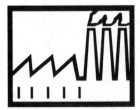

Real growth in gross domestic product, which stood at –0.4% in 1989 as a result of U.S. economic sanctions, rebounded to 9.3% in 1991 and more than 8% in 1992. Privatization of the economy was accelerated.

FREEDOM

Panama's indigenous population of 194,000 have the same political rights as other citizens. In 1992 Kuna Indians asked for the creation of an additional reserve to prohibit incursions by squatters into areas traditionally considered their own.

HEALTH/WELFARE

Even though a Tripartite Commission composed of business, labor, and government decreed a 20.5% increase in the minimum wage in 1993, such income is insufficient to meet a family's basic nutritional and housing needs.

ACHIEVEMENTS

The Panama Canal, which will pass wholly to Panamanian control in 1999, is one of the greatest engineering achievements of the twentieth century. A maze of locks and gates, it cuts through 50 miles of the most difficult terrain on Earth.

South America

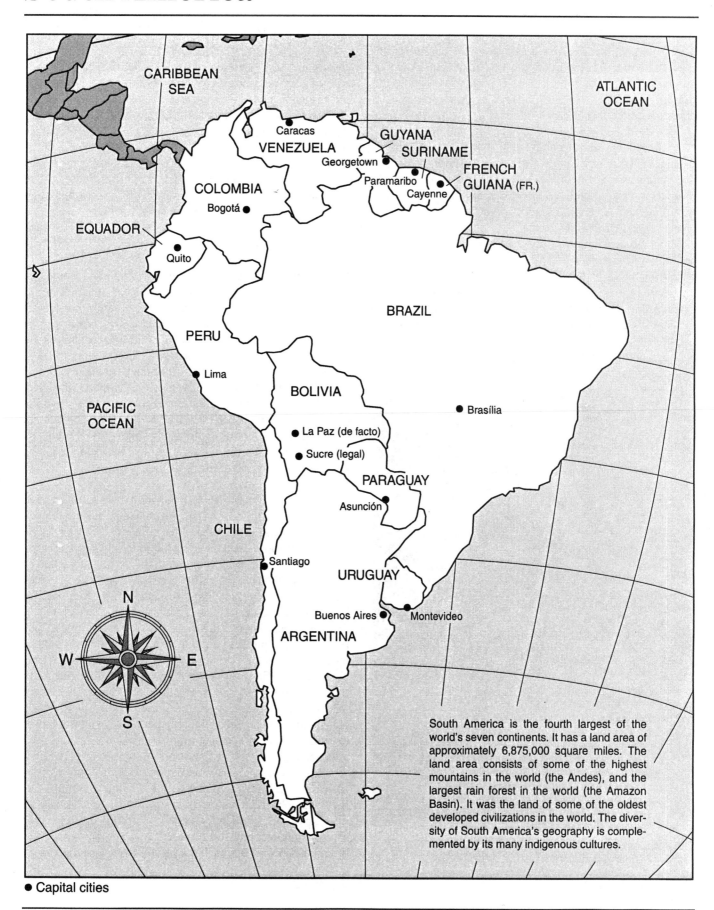

CARIBBEAN SEA

ATLANTIC OCEAN

Caracas

VENEZUELA

GUYANA

SURINAME

Georgetown

FRENCH GUIANA (FR.)

Paramaribo

Cayenne

COLOMBIA

Bogotá ●

EQUADOR

Quito ●

PERU

BRAZIL

● Lima

BOLIVIA

PACIFIC OCEAN

● Brasília

● La Paz (de facto)

● Sucre (legal)

PARAGUAY

Asunción ●

CHILE

Santiago ●

URUGUAY

Buenos Aires ● ● Montevideo

ARGENTINA

N
W · E
S

South America is the fourth largest of the world's seven continents. It has a land area of approximately 6,875,000 square miles. The land area consists of some of the highest mountains in the world (the Andes), and the largest rain forest in the world (the Amazon Basin). It was the land of some of the oldest developed civilizations in the world. The diversity of South America's geography is complemented by its many indigenous cultures.

● Capital cities

South America: An Imperfect Prism

Any overview of South America must first confront the incredible geographic and climatic diversity of the region. Equatorial rain forests are found in Brazil, Ecuador, Colombia, and Venezuela, and other countries; while the coastal deserts in Peru and northern Chile are among the driest and most forbidding in the world. Naturalist Charles Darwin described the area as "a complete and utter desert." More hospitable are the undulating pampas and plains of Argentina, Uruguay, central Venezuela, eastern Colombia, and southeastern Brazil. The spine of the continent is formed by the Andes Mountains, majestic and snow-capped. South America, because of its topography and the many degrees of latitude in which it lies, also has extremes of temperatures, ranging from desert heat to the steaming humidity of the tropics to the cold gales of Tierra del Fuego, which lies close to the Antarctic Circle. To add further to the perils of generalization, wide-ranging differences often occur within each country. Geography has played a critical role in the evolution of each of the nations of South America; it has been one of several major influences in their histories and their cultures.

(United Nations photo)

In many parts of South America, producing enough food to feed the people has been a constant problem. The natural diversity of land, extremes of weather, and unpredictable natural disasters have made food production difficult.

NATURE'S CHALLENGE

Nature has always presented the inhabitants of South America with an unrelenting challenge. On the west coast, most of the major cities are located in geologically active zones. All too frequently, earthquakes, tidal waves, volcanic activity, and landslides have taken a staggering toll of human life. For all the region, floods and droughts make agriculture a risky business. In 1982–1983, for example, the worst drought in living memory struck Peru and Bolivia. With food supplies dwindling, thousands of farmers and their families were forced to migrate to the cities.

REGIONALISM

South America's diverse topography has also helped to foster a deep-seated regionalism that has spawned innumerable civil wars and made national integration an extremely difficult task. In Colombia, for instance, the Andes fan out into three distinct ranges, separated by deep valleys. Each of the nation's three major cities—Bogotá, Medellín, and Cali—dominates a valley and is effectively isolated from the others by the mountains. The broad plains to the east have remained largely undeveloped because of the difficulty of access from the centers of population. Troubling to Colombian governments is the fact that, in terms of topography, the eastern plains are tied to Venezuela and not to the Colombian cities to the west.

Similarly, mountains divide Ecuador, Peru, Bolivia, and Venezuela. In all these nations, there is a permanent tension between the capital cities and the hinterlands. Often, as is the case in those republics that have large Indian populations, the tension is as much cultural as it is a matter of geography. But in the entire region, geography interacts with culture, society, politics, and economics. Regionalism has been a persistent theme in the history of Ecuador, where there has been, and continues to be, an often bitter rivalry between the capital city of Quito, located high in the central mountains, and the port city of Guayaquil. Commonly, port cities, with their window on the world outside, tend to be more cosmopolitan, liberal, and dynamic than cities that are more isolated. Such is the case with freewheeling Guayaquil, which stands in marked contrast to conservative, traditional, deeply Catholic Quito.

Venezuela boasts six distinct geographical regions, which include mountains and valleys, plains and deserts, rivers and jungles, and a coastline. Historian John Lombardi has observed that each of these regions has had an important role in identifying and defining the character of Venezuela's past and present: "Over the centuries the geographical focus has shifted from one region to another in response to internal arrangements and external demands."

(United Nations photo)

The countries of the Southern Cone—Argentina, Uruguay, Paraguay, and Chile—have had their cultures shaped by the geography of their vast, fertile plains. These latter-day gauchos herd their animals to the auction pens.

THE SOUTHERN CONE

The cultures of the countries of the so-called Southern Cone—Argentina, Uruguay, Paraguay, and Chile—have also been shaped by the geographical environment. Argentina, Uruguay, and Brazil's southern state of Rio Grande do Sul developed subcultures that reflected life on the vast, fertile plains, where cattle grazed by the millions. The *gaucho* ("cowboy") became symbolic of the "civilization of leather." Fierce, independent, a law unto himself, the gaucho was mythologized by the end of the nineteenth century. At a time when millions of European immigrants were flooding into the region, the gaucho emerged as a nationalist symbol of Argentina and Uruguay, standing firm in the face of whatever natives viewed as "foreign."

Landlocked Paraguay, surrounded by powerful neighbors, has for most of its history been an introspective nation, little known to the outside world. Because of its geography, most of Paraguay's population is concentrated near the capital city of Asunción. A third of the nation is tropical and swampy—not suitable for settlement. To the west, the desolate Chaco region, with its lack of adequate sources of drinkable water, is virtually uninhabitable.

Chile, with a coastline 2,600 miles long, is a country of topographic and climatic extremes. If superimposed on a map of North America, Chile would stretch from Baja California to the Yukon in Alaska. It is on Chile's border with Argentina that the Andes soar to their greatest heights. Several peaks, including Aconcagua, reach to nearly 23,000 feet in elevation. That mountain barrier has historically isolated Chile from eastern South America and from Europe. The central valley of Chile is the political, industrial, social, and cultural heart of the nation. With the capital city of Santiago and the large port of Valparaíso, the valley holds about 70 percent of Chile's population. The valley's Mediterranean climate and fertile soil have long acted as a magnet for Chileans from other, less hospitable, parts of the country.

BRAZIL

Historian Rollie Poppino has noted that the "major miracle of Brazil is its existence as a single nation." What he implies is that Brazil embraces regions that are so distinct that they could well be separate countries. "There are actually many Brazils within the broad expanse of the national territory, and the implication of uniformity conveyed by their common flag and language is often deceptive." In Brazil, there exists a tremendous range of geographical, racial, cultural, and economic contrasts. But part of the Brazilian "miracle" lies in the ability of its people to accept the diversity as normal. For years many Brazilians were unaware of the great differences within their country, until the improvement of transportation and communications as well as the impact of the mass media informed them not only of their common heritage but also of their profound regional differences.

DIVERSE PEOPLES

In many respects the peoples of South America are as diverse as its geography. While the populations of Argentina and Uruguay are essentially European, with virtually no Indian intermixture, Chilean society is descended from Spanish conquerors and the Indians they dominated. The Indian presence is strongest in the Andean republics of Bolivia, Peru, and Ecuador—the heart of the ancient Inca civilization. Bolivia is the most Indian, with well over half its population classified as such. *Mestizos* (mixed white and Indian) constitute about a quarter of the population, and whites make up only about 10 percent.

Three ethnic groups are found among the populations of Colombia and Venezuela: Spanish and Indian predominate, and there are small black minorities. About 60 percent of the populations of both countries are of Mestizo or *pardo* (mixed blood) origin. One of Brazil's distinctive features is the rich racial mixture of its population. Indians, Europeans,

Africans, and Japanese live in an atmosphere largely free of racial enmity.

Taken as a whole, the predominant culture is Iberian (that is, Spanish or Portuguese), although many mountain areas are overwhelmingly Indian in terms of ethnic makeup. With the conquest and colonization of South America in the sixteenth century, Spain and Portugal attempted to fasten their cultures, languages, and institutions on the land and its peoples. Spanish cities—laid out in the familiar grid pattern consisting of a large central plaza bordered by a Catholic church, government buildings, and the dwellings of the ruling elite—represented the conscious intention of the conquerors to impose their will not only on the defeated Indian civilizations but also on nature itself. By way of contrast, the Brazilian cities that were laid out by early Portuguese settlers tended to be less formally structured, suggesting that their planners and builders were more flexible and adaptable to the new world around them. Roman Catholicism was imposed on all citizens by the central authority. Government, conforming with Hispanic political culture, was authoritarian in the colonial period and continues to be so today. The conquerors created a stratified society of essentially two sectors: a ruling white elite and a ruled majority. But Spain and Portugal also introduced institutions that knit society together. Paternalistic patron–client relationships that bound the weak to the strong were common; they continue to be so today.

INDIAN CULTURE

Among the isolated Indian groups of Ecuador, Peru, and Bolivia, Spanish cultural forms were strongly and, for the most part, successfully resisted. Suspicious and occasionally hostile, the Indians refused integration into the white world outside their highland villages. By avoiding integration, in the words of historian Frederick Pike, "they maintain the freedom to live almost exclusively in the domain of their own language, social habits, dress and eating styles, beliefs, prejudices, and myths."

Only the Catholic religion was able to make some inroads, and that was, and still is, imperfect. The Catholicism practiced by Quechua- and Aymara-speaking Indians is a blend of Catholic teachings and ancient folk religion. For example, in an isolated region in Peru where eight journalists were massacred by Indians, a writer who investigated the incident reported in the *New York Times* that while Catholicism was "deeply rooted" among the Indians, "it has not displaced old beliefs like the worship of the *Apus*, or god mountains." When threatened, the Indians are "zealous defenders of their customs and mores." The societies' two cultures have had a profound impact on the literature of Ecuador, Peru, and Bolivia. The plight of the Indian, social injustice, and economic exploitation are favorite themes of these nations' authors.

(United Nations photo/Bruno J. Zehnder)

The region's Indian cultures and the development of the twentieth century have never really mixed. The native cultures persist in many areas, as exemplified by this Indian woman at a market in Ecuador.

Other Indian groups more vulnerable to the steady encroachment of "progress" did not survive. In the late nineteenth century, pampas Indians were virtually destroyed by Argentine cavalry armed with repeating rifles. Across the Andes, in Chile, the Araucanian Indians met a similar fate in the 1880s. Unfortunately, relations between the "civilized" world and the "primitive" peoples clinging to existence in the rain forests of Brazil, Peru, Bolivia, and Venezuela have generally improved little, although events in Brazil, Ecuador, and Venezuela in the early 1990s may signal a significant shift to greater Indian rights. Indigenous peoples throughout the Amazon Basin, however, are still under almost daily assault from settlers hungry for land, road builders, developers, and speculators—most of whom care little about the cultures they are annihilating.

AFRICAN-AMERICAN CULTURE

In those South American countries where slavery was widespread, the presence of a large black population has contributed yet another dimension to Hispanic culture (or, in the case of Guyana and Suriname, English and Dutch culture). Slaves, brutally uprooted from their cultures in Africa, developed new cultural forms that were often a combination of Christian and pagan. To insulate themselves against the rigors of forced labor and to forge some kind of common identity, slaves embraced folk religions that were heavily oriented toward magic. Magic helped blacks to face an uncertain destiny, and folk religions built bridges between peoples facing a similar, horrible fate. Folk religions not only survived the emancipation of slaves but have remained a common point of focus for millions of Brazilian blacks.

This phenomenon had become so widespread that the Roman Catholic Church in the 1970s made a concerted effort to win Afro-Brazilians to a religion that was more Christian and less pagan. This effort was partly negated by the development of close relations between Brazil and Africa, which occurred at the same time as the church's campaign. Brazilian blacks became more acutely aware of their African origins and began a movement of "re-Africanization." So pervasive had the folk religions become that one authority stated that Umbada (one of the folk religions) was now the religion of Brazil. The festival of *Carnaval* in Rio de Janeiro, Brazil, is perhaps the best-known example of the blending of Christianity with spiritism. Even the samba, a sensuous dance form that is central to the Carnaval celebration, had its origins in black folk religions.

IMMIGRATION AND CULTURE

Italians, Eastern and Northern Europeans, Chinese, and Japanese have also contributed to the cultural, social, and economic development of several South American nations. The great outpouring of Europe's peoples that brought millions of immigrants to the shores of the United States also brought millions to South America. From the mid-nineteenth century to the outbreak of World War I in 1914, great numbers of Italians and Spaniards and much smaller numbers of Germans, Russians, Welsh, Scots, Irish, and English boarded ships that would carry them to South America. Many were successful in the New World. Indeed, immigrants were largely responsible for the social restructuring of Argentina, Uruguay, and southern Brazil, as they created a large and dynamic middle class where none had existed before.

Italians and Spaniards
Many of the new arrivals came from urban areas, were literate, and possessed a broad range of skills. Argentina received the greatest proportion of immigrants. So great was the influx that an Argentine political scientist labeled the years 1890–1914 "the alluvial era" (the flood). His analogy was apt, for by 1914 half the population of the capital city of Buenos Aires were foreign-born. Indeed, 30 percent of the total Argentine population were of foreign extraction. Hundreds of thousands of immigrants also flocked into Uruguay.

In both countries they were able to move quickly into middle-class occupations in business and commerce. Others found work on the docks or on the railroads that carried the produce of the countryside to the ports for export to foreign markets. Some settled in the interior of Argentina, where they usually became sharecroppers or tenant farmers, although a sizable number were able to purchase land in the northern province of Santa Fe or became truck farmers in the immediate vicinity of Buenos Aires. Argentina's wine industry underwent a rapid transformation and expansion with the arrival of Italians in the western provinces of Mendoza and San Juan. In the major cities of Argentina, Uruguay, Chile, Peru, and Brazil, Italians built hospitals and established newspapers; they formed mutual aid societies and helped to found the first labor unions. Today their presence is still strong, and Italian words have entered into everyday discourse in Argentina and Uruguay.

Other Groups
Other immigrant groups also made their contributions to the formation of South America's societies and cultures. Germans colonized much of southern Chile and were instrumental in creating the nation's dairy industry. In the wilds of Patagonia, Welsh settlers established sheep ranches and planted apple, pear, and cherry trees in the Río Negro valley.

In Buenos Aires, despite the 1982 conflict over the Falkland Islands, there remains a distinct British imprint. Harrod's is the largest department store in the city, and one can board a train on a railroad built with English capital and journey to suburbs with names such as Hurlingham, Temperley, and Thames. In both Brazil and Argentina, soccer was introduced by the English, and two Argentine teams still bear the names "Newell's Old Boys" and "River Plate." Collectively, the immigrants who flooded into South America in the late nineteenth and early twentieth centuries introduced a host of new ideas, methods, and skills. They were especially important in stimulating and shaping the modernization of Argentina, Uruguay, Chile, and southern Brazil.

PROBLEM IMMIGRATION: VENEZUELA

In other countries that were bypassed earlier in the century, immigration has become a new phenomenon. Venezuela—torn by political warfare, its best lands long appropriated by the elite, and its economy only slowly developing—was far less attractive than the lands of opportunity to the north (the United States) and south (Argentina, Uruguay, and Brazil). In the early 1950s, however, Venezuela embarked on a broad-scale development program that included an attempt to attract European immigrants. Thousands of Spaniards, Portuguese, and Italians responded to the economic opportunity. Most of the immigrants remained in the capital city of Caracas, where they eventually became important in the construction business, retail trade, and the transportation industry.

Venezuela is currently experiencing a new wave of immigration that many citizens perceive as more of an invasion. Since the 1970s Colombians, attracted by tales of high salaries and golden employment opportunities, have crossed illegally into Venezuela by the tens of thousands. As is the case with Mexicans who cross into the United States, the Colombians experience discrimination and fail to win the better jobs. Most find employment that is low-paying and unskilled. Some move to the countryside and sign on as agricultural workers on coffee plantations or as hired hands on the cattle ranches that dot the plains. Those Colombians who do manage to find employment in Venezuelan industry are a source of anger and frustration to labor-union members, who resent workers who accept low rates of pay.

On the positive side, the presence of hundreds of thousands of immigrants in Venezuela has begun to soften the nation's deep racism. Venezuela today is a more equitable multiracial society than it was just a few decades ago.

INTERNAL MIGRATION

Paralleling the movement of peoples from across the oceans to parts of South America has been the movement of populations from rural areas to urban centers. In every nation, cities have been gaining in population for years. What prompts people to leave their homes and strike out for the unknown? In the cases of Bolivia and Peru, the very real prospect of famine has driven people out of the highlands and into the larger cities. Frequently, families will plan the move carefully. Vacant lands around the larger cities will be scouted in advance and suddenly, in the middle of the night, the new "settlers" will move in and erect a shantytown. With time, the seizure of the land is usually recognized by city officials and the new neighborhood is provided with urban services. Where the land seizure is resisted, however, violence and loss of life are common.

Factors other than famine also force people to leave their ancestral homes. Population pressure and division of the land into parcels too small to sustain families compel people to migrate. Others move to the cities in search of economic opportunities or chances for social advancement that do not exist in rural regions. In sum, a combination of push and pull factors are involved in a family's decision to begin a new life.

Since World War II, indigenous migration in South America has rapidly increased urban populations and has forced cities to reorganize. Rural people have been exposed to a broad range of push–pull pressures to move to the cities. Land hunger, extreme poverty, and rural violence might be included among the push factors; while the hope of a better job, upward social mobility, and a more satisfying life help to explain the attraction of a city. The phenomenon can be infinitely complex.

In Lima, Peru, there has been a twofold movement of people. While the unskilled and illiterate, the desperately poor and unemployed, the newly arrived migrant, and the delinquent have moved to or remained in inner-city slums, former slum dwellers have in turn moved to the city's perimeter. Although less centrally located, they have settled in more spacious and socially desirable shantytowns. In this way some 16,000 families created a squatter settlement practically overnight in the south of Lima. Author Hernando DeSoto, in his groundbreaking and controversial book *The Other Path,* captures the essence of the shantytowns. "Modest homes cramped together on city perimeters, a myriad of workshops in their midst, armies of vendors hawking their wares on the street, and countless minibus lines crisscrossing them—all seem to have sprung from nowhere, pushing the city's boundaries ever outward."

Significantly, DeSoto notes, collective effort has increasingly been replaced by individual effort, upward mobility exists even for the inner-city slum dwellers, and urban culture and patterns of consumption have been transformed. Opera, theater, and *zarzuela,* or comic opera, have gradually been replaced by movies, soccer, folk festivals, and television. Beer, rice, and table salt are now within the reach of much of the population; consumption of more expensive items, such as wine and meat, has declined.

On the outskirts of Buenos Aires there exists a *villa miseria* (a slum) built on the bottom and sides of an old clay pit. Appropriately, the *barrio,* or neighborhood, is called La Cava (literally "The Digging"). The people of La Cava are poor; most have moved there from rural Argentina or from Paraguay. Shacks seem to be thrown together from whatever was available—scraps of wood, packing crates, sheets of tin, and cardboard. There is no source of potable water, garbage litters the narrow alleyways, and there are no sewers. In the summer, because of the concave character of the barrio, the heat is unbearable. Rats and flies are legion. At times the smells are extraordinarily disagreeable. The first-time visitor to La Cava experiences an assault on the senses; this is Latin America at its worst.

But there is another side to the slums of Buenos Aires, and Lima, and Santiago. A closer look at La Cava reveals a community in transition. Some of the housing is more substantial, with adobe replacing the scraps of wood and tin; other homes double as places of business and sell general merchandise, food, and bottled drinks. One advertises itself as a food store, bar, and butcher shop. Another sells watches and repairs radios. Several promote their merchandise or services in a weekly newspaper that circulates in La Cava and two other *barrios de emergencia* ("emergency"—that is, temporary—neighborhoods). The newspaper addresses items of concern to the inhabitants. There are articles on hygiene and infant diarrhea; letters and editorials plead with people not to throw their garbage in the streets; births and deaths are recorded. The paper is a chronicle of progress as well as frustration: people are working together to create a viable neighborhood; drainage ditches are constructed with donated time and equipment; collections and raffles are held to provide materials to build sewers and, in some cases, to provide minimal street lighting; and men and women who have contributed their labor are singled out for special praise.

The newspaper also reproduces municipal decrees that affect the lives of the residents. The land on which the barrio sits was illegally occupied, the stores that service the neighborhood were opened without the necessary authorization, and the housing was built without regard to municipal codes, so city ordinances aimed at the barrios de emergencia are usually restrictive. "The sale, renting or transfer of *casillas* [homes] within the boundaries of the barrio de emergencia is prohibited; casillas can not be inhabited by single men, women or children; the opening of businesses within the barrio is strictly prohibited, unless authorized by the Municipality; dances and festivals may not be held without the express authorization of the Municipality." But there are also signs of accommodation: "The Municipality is studying the problem of refuse removal." For migrants, authority and the legal system are not helpful but are hindrances.

Hernando DeSoto found this situation to be true also of Peru, where "the greatest hostility the migrants encountered was from the legal system." Until the end of World War II, the system had either absorbed or ignored the migrants "because the small groups who came were hardly likely to upset the status quo." But when the rural to urban flow became a flood, the system could no longer remain disinterested. Housing and education were barred to them, businesses would not hire them. Over time the migrants discovered that they would have to fight for every right and every service from an unwilling establishment. To survive, they became part of the informal sector, otherwise known as the underground or parallel economy.

This is true not only in the squatter settlements on the fringes of South America's great cities but also of the inner-city slums. Slum dwellers *have* been able to improve their market opportunities and *have* been able to acquire better housing and some urban services, because they organized on their own, outside formal political channels. In the words of sociologist Susan Eckstein, "They refused to allow dominant class and state interests to determine and restrict their fate. Defiance and resistance won them concessions which quiescence would not."

DeSoto found this to be the case with Lima: Migrants, "if they were to live, trade, manufacture, or even consume . . . had to do so illegally. Such illegality was not antisocial in intent, like trafficking in drugs, theft, or abduction, but was designed to achieve such essentially legal objectives as building a house, providing a service, or developing a business."

This is also the story of Buenos Aires's La Cava. To open a shop in the barrio with municipal approval, an aspiring businessperson must be a paragon of patience. Various levels of bureaucracy, with their plethora of paperwork and fees, insensitive municipal officials, inefficiency, and interminable waiting drive people outside a system where the laws do not seem to conform to social need.

AN ECCLESIASTICAL REVOLUTION

During the past 20 years, there have been important changes in the religious habits of many South Americans. Virtually everywhere Roman Catholicism, long identified with the traditional order, has been challenged by newer movements such as Evangelical Protestantism and the Charismatics. Within the Catholic Church, the theology of liberation has gained ground. The creation of Christian communities in the barrios, people who bond together to discuss their beliefs and act as agents of change, has become a common phenomenon throughout the region. Base communities from the Catholic perspective instill Christian values in the lives of ordinary people. But it is an active form of religion that pushes for change and social justice. Hundreds of these communities exist in Peru, thousands in Brazil.

NATIONAL MYTHOLOGIES

In the midst of geographical and cultural diversity, the nations of South America have created national mythologies designed to unite people behind their rulers. Part of that mythology is rooted in the wars of independence that tore through much of the region between 1810 and 1830. Liberation from European colonialism imparted to South Americans a sense of their own national histories, replete with military heroes such as José de San Martín, Simón Bolívar, Bernardo O'Higgins, and Antonio José de Sucre, as well as a host of revolutionary myths. This coming to nationhood paralleled what the United States experienced when it won its independence from Britain. South Americans, at least those with a stake in the new society, began to think of themselves as Venezuelans, Chileans, Peruvians, or Brazilians. The architects of Chilean national mythology proclaimed the emergence of a new and superior being who was the result of the symbolic and physical union of Spaniards and the tough, heroic Araucanian Indians. The legacy of Simón Bolívar lives on in Venezuela, and even today the nation's foreign policymakers speak in Bolivarian terms about Venezuela's rightful role as a leader in Latin American affairs. In some instances the mythology generated by the wars for independence became a shield against foreign ideas and customs and was used to force immigrants to become "Argentines" or "Chileans." It was an attempt to bring national unity out of diversity.

Argentines have never solved the question of their identity. Many consider themselves European and hold much of the rest of Latin America in contempt. Following the unsuccessful conclusion of the Falklands War with Britain, one scholar suggested that perhaps Argentines should no longer consider themselves as "a forlorn corner of Europe" but should wake up to the reality that they are Latin Americans. Much of Argentine literature reflects this uncertain identity and may help to explain author Jorge Luis Borges's affinity for English gardens and Icelandic sagas. It was also an Argentine military government that invoked Western Catholic civilization in its fight against a "foreign" and "godless" communism in the 1970s.

THE ARTIST AND SOCIETY

There is a strongly cultured and humane side of South America. Jeane Franco, an authority on Latin American cultural movements, has observed that to "declare oneself an artist in Latin America has frequently involved conflict with society." The art and literature of South America, in particular, and Latin America, in general, represent a distinct tradition within the panorama of Western civilization. It is an art that has as its focus social questions and ideals. It expresses love for one's fellow human beings and "has kept alive the vision of a more just and humane form of society." It rises above purely personal relationships and addresses humanity.

Much change is also evident at the level of popular culture. Andean folk music, for example, is being replaced by the more urban and upbeat *chicha* music in Peru; and in Argentina, the traditional *tango* has lost much of its early appeal. Radio and television programs are more and more in the form of soap operas, adventure programs, or popular entertainment, once considered vulgar by cosmopolitan city dwellers.

South America is rather like a prism. It can be treated as a single object or region. Yet when exposed to a shaft of sunlight of understanding, it throws off a brilliant spectrum of colors that exposes the diversity of its lands and peoples.

Argentina (Republic of Argentina)

GEOGRAPHY

Area in Square Kilometers (Miles):
2,771,300 (1,100,000) (about 4 times
the size of Texas)
Capital (Population): Buenos Aires
(metropolitan area, 10,500,000)
Climate: varied; predominantly
temperate

PEOPLE

Population
Total: 32,901,000
Annual Growth Rate: 1.1%
Rural/Urban Population Ratio: 14/86
Ethnic Makeup of Population: 85%
white; 15% Mestizo, Indian, and
others

Health
Life Expectancy at Birth: 67 years
(male); 74 years (female)
Infant Mortality Rate (Ratio):
34/1,000
Average Caloric Intake: 125% of
FAO minimum
Physicians Available (Ratio): 1/370

Religion(s)
90% Roman Catholic (fewer than
20% practicing); 2% Protestant; 2%
Jewish; 6% others

Education
Adult Literacy Rate: 95%

COMMUNICATION

Telephones: 3,250,000
Newspapers: 227

THE TANGO

The dance known as the tango had its origins in the outskirts of
Argentina's capital city of Buenos Aires in the closing decades of the
nineteenth century. It initially lacked respectability and social accep-
tance, but around the turn of the century the tango became popular in
Paris, where it gained respectability. By 1910 the tango had returned to
Buenos Aires and eventually became a national symbol of Argentina.
That which had been shunned by "proper society" was now warmly
embraced by all.

TRANSPORTATION

Highways—Kilometers (Miles):
208,350 (129,385)
Railroads—Kilometers (Miles):
34,172 (21,221)
Usable Airfields: 1,473

GOVERNMENT

Type: republic
Independence Date: July 9, 1816
Head of State: President Carlos
Menem
Political Parties: Radical Civic
Union Party; Justicialist Party
(Peronist); Intransigent Party; Union
of the Democratic Center; others
Suffrage: compulsory at 18

MILITARY

Number of Armed Forces: 80,000
*Military Expenditures (% of Central
Government Expenditures):* 8.6%
Current Hostilities: none

ECONOMY

Currency ($ U.S. Equivalent): 0.99
new austral = $1
Per Capita Income/GDP:
$2,134/$90.1 billion
Inflation Rate: 10%
Total Foreign Debt: $62.0 billion
Natural Resources: fertile plains
(pampas); minerals
Agriculture: grains; oilseeds;
livestock products
Industry: food processing; motor
vehicles; consumer durables; textiles;
metallurgy; chemicals

FOREIGN TRADE

Exports: $12.0 billion
Imports: $8.0 billion

Argentina
- ✪ Capital
- ● City
- ⌇ River
- - - - Road

0 ___ 300 kilometers
0 ___ 300 miles

ARGENTINA:
THE DIVIDED LAND

"Incomprehensible," "arrogant," and "brutal" are terms that have been used by writers to describe contemporary Argentina. Others, as far back as the mid-nineteenth century, have perceived two Argentinas; Domingo F. Sarmiento, the president of Argentina in the 1860s, entitled his classic work *Civilization and Barbarism.* More contemporary writers speak of Argentina as a divided land or as a city and a nation. All address the relationship of the capital city, Buenos Aires, to the rest of the country. Buenos Aires is cultured, cosmopolitan, modern, and dynamic. The rural interior is in striking contrast in terms of living standards, the pace of life, and, perhaps, expectations as well. For years Buenos Aires and other urban centers have drawn population away from the countryside. Today Argentina is 86 percent urban.

There are other contrasts. The land is extremely rich and produces a large share of the world's grains and beef. Few Argentines are malnourished, and the annual per capita consumption of beef is comparable to that of the United States. Yet this land of promise, which seemed in the 1890s to have a limitless future, has slowly decayed. Its greatness is now more myth than real. Since the Great Depression of the 1930s, the Argentine economy has, save for brief spurts, never been able to return to the sustained growth of the late nineteenth and early twentieth centuries.

Today the Argentine economy is more stable than it has been for years. Inflation

has dropped from 200 percent per annum to about 10 percent; inefficient and costly state enterprises have been privatized, including petroleum, traditionally a strategic sector reserved to the state; the foreign debt is under control; and the pace of business activity, employment, and foreign investment has quickened. Whether the economic turnaround can be sustained is problematical, however, for Argentine economic history has been full of dramatic phases full of promise but ultimately empty of results. Much depends on the continued confidence of the Argentine people in the leadership and policies of President Carlos Menem.

AUTHORITARIAN
GOVERNMENT

In political terms Argentina has revealed a curious inability to bring about the kind of stable democratic institutions that seemed assured in the 1920s. Since 1930 the military has seized power at least half a dozen times. It must be noted, however, that it has been civilians who have encouraged the generals to play an active role in politics. Historian Robert Potash writes: "The notion that Argentine political parties or other important civilian groups have consistently opposed military takeovers bears little relation to reality."

Argentina has enjoyed civilian rule since 1983, but the military is still a presence. Indeed, one right-wing faction, the *carapintadas* ("painted faces") responsible for mutinies against President Raúl Alfonsín in 1987 and 1988, have organized a nationwide party and have attracted enough

votes to rank as Argentina's third-largest political party. An authoritarian tradition is very much alive in Argentina, as is the bitter legacy of the so-called Dirty War.

THE DIRTY WAR

What made the most recent period of military rule different is the climate of political violence that gripped Argentina starting in the late 1960s and early 1970s. The most recent period of violence began with the murder of former President Pedro Aramburu by left-wing guerrillas (Montoneros) who claimed to be fighting on behalf of the exiled popular leader Juan Perón (who was president from 1946 to 1955 and from 1973 to 1974). The military responded to what it saw as an armed challenge from the left with tough antisubversion laws and official violence against suspects. Guerrillas increased their activities and intensified their campaign to win popular support. Worried by the possibility of a major popular uprising and divided over policy, the military called for national elections in 1973, hoping that a civilian government would calm passions. The generals could then concentrate their efforts on destroying the armed left. The violence continued, however, and even the brief restoration of Juan Perón to power failed to bring peace.

In March 1976, with the nation on the verge of economic collapse and guerrilla warfare spreading, the military seized power once again and declared a state of internal war, popularly called the Dirty War. Between 1976 and 1982, approximately 6,000 Argentine citizens "disappeared." Torture, the denial of basic human rights, harsh press censorship, officially directed death squads, and widespread fear came to characterize Argentina.

The labor movement—the largest, most effective, and most politically active on the continent—was, in effect, crippled by the military. Identified as a source of leftist subversion, the union movement was destroyed as an independent entity. Collective-bargaining agreements were dismantled, pension plans cut back, and social-security and public-health programs eliminated. The military's intent was to destroy a labor movement capable of operating on a national level.

The press was one of the immediate victims of the 1976 coup. A law was decreed warning that anyone spreading information derived from organizations "dedicated to subversive activities or terrorism" would be subject to an indefinite sentence. To speak out against the military was punishable by a 10-year jail term. The state also directed its terrorism tactics

(United Nations photo/P. Teuscher)

Few people are malnourished in Argentina. Well known for its abundant grains and beef, Argentina also has a large fishing industry, as shown by these fishing boats in the bay of the Plata River in Buenos Aires.

against the media, and approximately 100 journalists disappeared. Hundreds more received death threats, were tortured and jailed, or fled into exile. Numerous newspapers and magazines were shut down, and one, *La Opinión,* passed to government control.

The ruling junta justified these excesses by portraying the conflict as the opening battle of "World War III," in which Argentina was valiantly defending Western Christian values and cultures against hordes of communist, "godless" subversives. It was a "holy war," with all of the unavoidable horrors of such strife.

By 1981 leftist guerrilla groups had been annihilated. Argentines slowly began to recover from the shock of internal war and talked of a return to civilian government. The military had completed its task; the nation needed to rebuild. Labor attempted to re-create its structure and threw the first tentative challenges at the regime's handling of the economy. The press carefully criticized both the economic policies of the government and the official silence over the fate of the *desaparecidos* (the "disappeared ones"). Human-rights groups pressured the generals with redoubled efforts.

THE WAR IN THE FALKLANDS

Against this backdrop of growing popular dissatisfaction with the regime's record, together with the approaching 150th anniversary of Britain's occupation of Las Islas Malvinas (Falkland Islands), then-President Leopoldo Galtieri decided in 1982 to regain Argentine sovereignty and attack the Falklands. A successful assault, the military reasoned, would capture the popular imagination with its appeal to Argentine nationalism. The military's tarnished image would regain its luster. Forgiven would be the excesses of the Dirty War. But the attack ultimately failed.

OPPOSITION TO THE MILITARY

In the wake of the fiasco, which cost thousands of Argentine and British lives, the military lost its grip on labor, the press, and the general population. Military and national humiliation, the continuing economic crisis made even worse by war costs, and the swelling chorus of discontent lessened the military's control over the flow of information and ideas. Previously forbidden subjects—such as the responsibility for the disappearances during the Dirty War—were raised in the newspapers.

The labor movement made a rapid and striking recovery and is now in the forefront of renewed political activity. Even though the movement is bitterly divided into moderate and militant wings, it is a force that cannot be ignored by political parties on the rebound.

The Falklands War may well prove to be a watershed in recent Argentine history. A respected Argentine observer, Torcuato DiTella, argues that the Falklands crisis was a "godsend," for it allowed Argentines to break with "foreign" economic models that had failed in Argentina. Disappointed with the United States and Europe over their support of Britain, he concluded: "We belong in Latin America and it is better to be a part of this strife-torn continent than a forlorn province of Europe."

Popularly elected in 1983, President Raúl Alfonsín's economic policies initially struck in bold new directions. He forced the International Monetary Fund to renegotiate Argentina's huge multibillion-dollar debt in a context more favorable to Argentina, and he was determined to bring order out of chaos.

One of his most difficult problems centered on the trials for human-rights abuses against the nation's former military rulers. According to *Latin American Regional Reports,* Alfonsín chose to "distinguish degrees of responsibility" in taking court action against those who conducted the Dirty War. Impressively, Alfonsín put on trial the highest authorities, to be followed by action against those identified as responsible for major excesses.

Almost immediately, however, extreme right-wing nationalist officers in the armed forces opposed the trials and engineered a series of mutinies that undermined the stability of the administration. In 1987, during the Easter holiday, a rebellion of dissident soldiers made its point, and the Argentine Congress passed legislation that limited the prosecution of officers who killed civilians during the Dirty War to only those at the highest levels. Further mini-mutinies in 1988 resulted in further concessions by the Alfonsín government to the mutineers, including reorganization of the army high command and higher wages.

Political scientist Gary Wynia aptly observed: "The army's leadership is divided between right-wing officers willing to challenge civilian authorities with force and more romantic officers who derive gratification from doing so. Many of the latter refuse to accept the contention that they are 'equal' to civilians, claiming that they have a special role that prevents their subordination to civilian authorities." To this day the Argentine military has come to terms neither with itself nor with democratic government.

Argentina's current president, Carlos Menem, was supported by the military in the elections of May 1989, with perhaps 80 percent of the officer corps casting their votes for the Peronist Party. Menem adopted a policy of rapprochement with the military, which included the 1990 pardon of former junta members convicted of human-rights abuses. Historian Peter Calvert argues that Menem chose the path of amnesty because elements in the armed forces "would not be content until they got it." Rebellious middle-rank officers were well disposed toward Peronists, and Menem's pardon was "a positive gain in terms of the acceptance of the Peronists among the military themselves." In essence, then, Menem's military policy is consistent with other policies in terms of its pragmatic core.

On the other hand, significant progress was made in 1992 with regard to "disappeared" people. President Menem agreed to create a commission to deal with the problem of children of the disappeared who were adopted by other families. Many have had their true identities established as a result of the patient work of "The Grandmothers of the Plaza de Mayo" and by the technique of cross-generational genetic analysis.

ECONOMIC TRAVAIL AND RECOVERY

Former President Alfonsín was fond of telling the following story of the frustrations of high office. George Bush, praying in the White House, asked God, "Will the hostages in the Middle East ever be released?" The reply came from above: "Yes, but not during your term in office." Similarly, Mikhail Gorbachev, alone in his library in the Kremlin, looked heavenward and asked: "Will perestroika succeed?" Once again the reply was heard: "Yes, but not during your time in office." And then, Alfonsín continued, "I myself looked up to God and asked, 'Will Argentina's economic, military and political crises ever be solved?' " Once more comes God's answer: "Yes, but not in *my* time in office." The humor is bitter and suggests the intractable character of crisis in Argentina. Indeed, Argentina's runaway inflation forced President Alfonsín to hand over power to Carlos Menem 6 months early.

Menem's government has worked a bit of an economic miracle, despite an administration nagged by corruption and early policy indecision, which witnessed the appointment of 21 ministers to 9 cabinet positions during his first 18 months in office. In Menem's favor, he is not an ideologue but, rather, an adept politician

Pedro de Mendoza establishes the first settlement at Buenos Aires 1536	Independence from Spain 1816	War with Paraguay 1865–1870	Electoral reform— compulsory male suffrage 1912	Juan Perón is in power 1946–1955 and 1973–1974	The Dirty War 1976–1982

1980s–1990s

War with Britain over the Falkland Islands; military mutinies and economic chaos

Carlos Menem is elected president; Argentina introduces a new unit of currency, the austral

Privatization of the economy accelerates; presidential elections are scheduled for 1995

whose acceptance by the average voter is equaled by his ability to do business with almost anyone. He quickly identified the source of much of Argentina's chronic inflation: the state-owned enterprises. From the time of Perón, these industries were regarded as wellsprings of employment and cronyism rather than as instruments for the production of goods or the delivery of the services such as electric power and telephone service. "Ironically," in the words of Luigi Manzetti, writing in *North-South FOCUS,* "it took a Peronist like Menem to dismantle Perón's legacy." While Menem's presidential campaign stressed "traditional Peronist themes like social justice and government investments" to revive the depressed economy, once in power, "having inherited a bankrupt state and under pressure from foreign banks and domestic business circles to enact a stiff adjustment program, Menem reversed his stand." He embraced the market-oriented policies of his political adversaries, "only in a much harsher fashion." State-owned enterprises were sold off in rapid-fire fashion. Argentina underwent a rapid transformation, from one of the world's most closed economies to one of the most open.

Economic growth began again in 1991, but the social costs were high. Thousands of public-sector workers lost their jobs; a third of Argentina's population of 32 million lived below the poverty line, and the gap between the rich and poor tended to increase. But both inflation and the debt were contained, foreign investment in-

creased, and confidence began to return to Argentina.

Menem has turned his economic success into political promise. Early in 1993 he announced a $1.5 billion antipoverty initiative, which set the stage for machinations aimed at securing a second term despite a constitutional prohibition against consecutive terms in office.

Continuismo, or the continuation of a president in office, has long plagued Latin American politics. President Menem's bid for a second term has raised warning flags. Former President Alfonsín, as reported in *Latin American Regional Reports,* noted that Menem's reelection could result in an "Argentine version" of former Paraguyan dictator Alfredo Stroessner or, "worse still," of Peru's President Alberto Fujimori.

The Peronist Party, as of this writing, plans a plebiscite on Menem's possible reelection. The will of the people, in this scenario, would result in a constitutional reform allowing his reelection when his current term ends in 1995. Obviously, the Peronists feel that Menem's popularity, undergirded by Argentina's economic success, will triumph over any constitutional constraints.

FOREIGN POLICY IN THE NATIONAL INTEREST

The Argentine government's foreign policy has usually been determined by realistic appraisals of the nation's best interests. Since 1946 the country has moved be-

tween the two poles of pro-West and non-aligned. President Menem has firmly supported the foreign-policy initiatives of the United States and the United Nations. Argentine participation in the Persian Gulf War and the presence of Argentine troops under UN command in Croatia, Somalia, and other trouble spots have paid dividends. Washington has agreed to supply Argentina with military supplies for the first time since the Falklands War in 1982. Such a policy obviously wins points for Menem with the Argentine military.

ARGENTINA'S FUTURE

The Argentine economy, despite recent successes, still remains volatile, and there is always the possibility of a return to high inflation. Politically, Argentina will witness an interesting experiment in attempts to reform the Constitution to allow for Menem's continuation in office. And the military remains a constant source of uncertainty.

DEVELOPMENT

The sale of the state-owned oil company, YPF to local and international investors for more than $3 billion was, in Latin American terms, extraordinary. By converting stock into government bonds, Argentina will likely be able to retire about $2 billion of its $62 billion debt and to settle a large portion of its debt with pensioners. Argentina is the first Latin American country to sell its state energy company and could trigger similar moves elsewhere in the hemisphere.

FREEDOM

The U.S. State Department reported significant and steady improvement in Argentina's human-rights record. There have been some credible reports of torture, extrajudicial killing at the hands of the police, and several incidents of discrimination against the Jewish community, but nothing like the excesses of the 1970s. The International Press Society gave the country good marks for freedom of expression; Argentine newspapers since 1992 have been unfettered and often critical of corruption in government.

HEALTH/WELFARE

Argentina's inflation rate of about 10%, although appreciably lower than past years, still has an adverse impact on the amount of state spending on social services. Moreover, the official minimum wage falls significantly lower than the $12,000 per year necessary to support a family of four. Consequently, many workers are forced to labor overtime to compensate for inadequate wages. On the other hand, vacation, maternity, and sick-leave regulations are among the best in Western industrialized countries.

ACHIEVEMENTS

Argentine citizens have won four Nobel Prizes—two for peace and one each for chemistry and medicine. The nation's authors— Jorge Luis Borges, Julio Cortazar, Manuel Puig, and Ricardo Guiraldes, to name only a few—are world famous. In sports, Emilio Firpo and Gabriela Sabatini have excelled in, respectively, boxing and tennis.

Bolivia (Republic of Bolivia)

GEOGRAPHY

Area in Square Kilometers (Miles):
1,098,160 (424,162) (about the size
of California and Texas combined)
Capital (Population): La Paz (de
facto) (669,000); Sucre (legal)
(105,800)
Climate: varies from humid and
tropical to semiarid and cold

PEOPLE

Population
Total: 7,323,000
Annual Growth Rate: 2.3%
Rural/Urban Population Ratio: 49/51
Ethnic Makeup of Population: 30%
Quechua; 25% Aymara; 30%
Mestizo; 15% white

Health
Life Expectancy at Birth: 59 years
(male); 64 years (female)
Infant Mortality Rate (Ratio):
82/1,000
Average Caloric Intake: 91% of FAO
minimum
Physicians Available (Ratio): 1/1,595

Religion(s)
95% Roman Catholic; also Methodist
and other Protestants

Education
Adult Literacy Rate: 78%

COMMUNICATION

Telephones: 144,300
Newspapers: 14 dailies

TRANSPORTATION

Highways—Kilometers (Miles):
38,836 (24,117)

Railroads—Kilometers (Miles): 3,684
(2,288)
Usable Airfields: 934

GOVERNMENT

Type: republic
Independence Date: August 6, 1825
Head of State: President Gonzalo
Sánchez de Lozada
Political Parties: Movement of the
Revolutionary Left; Nationalist
Democratic Action; Nationalist
Revolutionary Movement; Civic
Solidarity Union; Conscience of the
Fatherland; Christian Democratic
Party; others
Suffrage: universal and compulsory
at 18 if married, 21 if single

MILITARY

Number of Armed Forces: 29,800
*Military Expenditures (% of Central
Government Expenditures):* 14.1%
Current Hostilities: dispute with
Chile regarding a sovereign access to
the sea for Bolivia

ECONOMY

Currency ($ U.S. Equivalent): 3.75
bolivianos = $1
Per Capita Income/GDP: $630/$3.3
billion
Inflation Rate: 15%
Total Foreign Debt: $3.3 billion
Natural Resources: tin; natural gas;
petroleum; zinc; tungsten; antimony;
silver; iron ore
Agriculture: potatoes; corn;
sugarcane; rice; wheat; coffee; coca;
bananas
Industry: textiles; mining; food
processing; chemicals; plastics

FOREIGN TRADE

Exports: $970 million
Imports: $760 million

LA DIABLADA

Each year in the Indian city of Oruro, there occurs a remarkable
ceremony known as *La Diablada*. Dating from colonial times, La
Diablada combines Catholic and indigenous religious themes in pro-
cessions and short plays that depict the ageless conflict between good
and evil. In one play the Spanish conquest is re-created; the Inca, sad
but noble, are defeated. There is little doubt left in the minds of the
native audience as to which side is "good" and which side "evil."

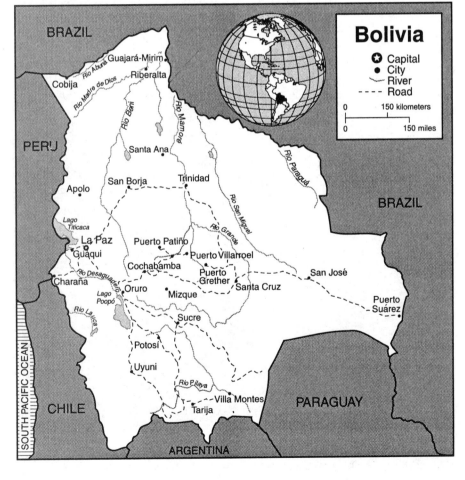

BOLIVIA: AN INDIAN NATION

Until recently the images of Bolivia captured by the world's press were uniformly negative. Human-rights abuses were rampant, a corrupt and brutal military government was deeply involved in cocaine trafficking, and the nation was approaching bankruptcy.

Other images might include Bolivia's complex society. So intermixed has this multiethnic culture become that one's race is defined by one's social status. So-called whites, who look very much like the Indians with whom their ancestors intermarried, form the upper classes only because of their economic, social, and cultural positions—that is, the degree to which they have embraced European culture.

Another enduring image is Bolivia's extreme instability. Granted, there were 200 changes of government in less than 200 years, with an average regime lasting 9 months. Actually, what outsiders perceive as typical Latin American political behavior clouds what is unusual and positive about Bolivia.

One nineteenth-century leader, Manuel Belzu, played an extremely complex role that combined the forces of populism, nationalism, and revolution. Belzu encouraged the organization of the first trade unions, abolished slavery, promoted land reform, and praised Bolivia's Indian past.

In 1952 a middle-class–led and popularly supported revolution swept the country. The ensuing social, economic, and political reforms, while not erasing an essentially dual society of "whites" and Indians, did significantly ease the level of exploitation. Most of the export industries, including those involved with natural resources, were nationalized. Bolivia's evolution—at times progressive, at times regressive—continues to reflect the impulse for change.

SOCIETY: POSITIVE AND NEGATIVE ASPECTS

Bolivia, despite the rapid and startling changes that have occurred in the recent past, remains a poor society. In terms of poverty, life expectancy, death rates, and per capita income, it ranks among the worst in the Western Hemisphere.

Rights for women have made slow progress, even in urban areas. In 1975 a woman was appointed to the Bolivian Supreme Court, and in 1979 Congress elected Lidia Gueiler Tejada, leader of the lower house, as president. Long a supporter of women's rights, Tejada earlier had drafted and pushed through Congress a bill that created a ministry to provide social bene-

fits for women and children. That remarkably advanced legislation has not guaranteed that women enjoy a social status equal to that of men, however. Many women are likely unaware of their rights under the law.

Bolivia's press is reasonably free, although many journalists are reportedly paid by politicians, drug traffickers, and officials to increase their exposure or suppress negative stories. A few journalists who experienced repression under previous governments still practice self-censorship.

URBANIZATION

Santa Cruz, commonly known as "the other capital" of Bolivia, in the last 40 years has been transformed from an isolated backwater into a modern city with links to the other parts of the country and to the rest of South America. From a population of 42,000 in 1950, the number of inhabitants quickly rose to half a million in the mid-1980s and is now growing at the rate of about 8 percent a year. Bolivia's second

largest city, in the 1990s its population is expected to surpass that of the capital of La Paz.

The city's political and economic strength has kept pace with the population growth. Politically, Santa Cruz represents the interests of lowland regionalism against the traditional hegemony of the highlands. Santa Cruz is also a growing commercial center; much of its wealth derives from the production and export of cocaine.

Most of the city's population growth has been the result of rural-to-urban migration, a phenomenon closely studied by geographer Gil Green. On paper Santa Cruz is a planned city, but since the 1950s there has been a running battle between city planners and new settlers wanting land. "Due to the very high demand for cheap land and the large amount of flat, empty, nonvaluable land surrounding it, the city has tended to expand by a process of land invasion and squatting. Such invasions are generally overtly or covertly organized by political parties seeking electoral support of the low-income population." In the wake of a successful "invasion," the land is divided into plots

(United Nations photo)

Bolivia has a complex society, tremendously affected by the continued interplay of multiethnic cultures. This woman illustrates the persistent influence of indigenous peoples on Bolivia.

Timeline:

Spanish settle the altiplano (high plain) **1538**	Bolivian declaration of independence from Spain **1825**	The War of the Pacific with Chile; Bolivia loses access to the sea **1879–1880**	The Chaco War with Paraguay **1932–1935**	Reforms: nationalization of mines, land reform, universal suffrage, creation of labor federation **1952–1964**	**1980s–1990s**

Privatization of the economy accelerates; labor unrest grips the mining sector

"Goni" Sánchez de Lozada is elected president

Bolivia's indigenous people achieve a new political voice

that are allocated to the squatters, who then build houses from whatever materials are at hand. Then begins the lengthy process of settlement consolidation and regularization of land tenure. Once again the new land is subdivided and sold cheaply to the low-income population.

Mass migration to Santa Cruz has drawn people from different geographical regions in Bolivia who are also different from one another in terms of their ethnicity. Once they arrive in Santa Cruz, they are labeled either as Cambas or Kollas. Cambas, from the tropical lowlands, are of European stock and speak Spanish, are the politically dominant ethnic group in Santa Cruz, and discriminate against the Kollas. Kollas are Aymara- or Quechua-speaking Indians from the Andean highlands.

The labels are used by the city dwellers to determine how one should behave in social interactions and reflect profound differences in language, dress, food, and music. Racial differences reinforce the tensions between the two groups. Kollas are particularly unwilling to adopt the lowland culture of the city, for the Indians' cultural heritage is an important part of their identity. The constant infusion of highland culture into Santa Cruz is resisted by Cambas, who use racial and cultural differences to retain their own "elite" status in the city. In Green's words: "What may in fact be happening, is that whilst some cultural divisions are becoming less marked, the ideology of difference is maintained in order that city residents born in certain areas of the country are excluded from local positions of power."

One's migrant status usually determines housing status in Santa Cruz. Kollas, who are long-distance migrants and the most recent arrivals in the city, lack information about Santa Cruz and have the fewest contacts to offer them help with accommodations. Thus, they are forced to rent. Cambas, who are city natives or long-term residents, for the most part have well-developed support networks of interdependence with other Camba residents. They know the city and can best take advantage of land invasions and sales of cheap property. Kin and acquaintances are a critical part of the process.

FOREIGN POLICY AND DRUGS

Nonalignment has characterized Bolivian foreign policy since the 1952 Revolution. Relations with the United States have until recently been strained because of official involvement in drug trafficking. Bolivian politicians have repeatedly promised to put an end to the trade and substitute other crops, a policy that most Bolivians view with suspicion.

Recent estimates published by GATT suggest that illegal exports of coca paste and cocaine contributed the equivalent of 13 to 15 percent of gross domestic product in 1991 and that coca by-products accounted for about 40 percent of total exports, legal and illegal, in 1990. About 400,000 Bolivians are estimated to live off coca and cocaine production. U.S. wishes run afoul of the multifaceted heritage of coca, the sacred plant of the Incas. There is virtually no activity in domestic, social,

or religious life in which coca does not play a role; thus, attempts to limit its cultivation would have profound repercussions among the peasantry.

CHALLENGES

Bolivia's problems are formidable. Although the economic horizon is less threatening and the country is blessed with substantial natural resources, Bolivia's people remain the poorest, most malnourished, and least educated in the Andean region; and extensive drug trafficking and the widespread corruption associated with it may prove resistant to any action the Bolivian government may choose to take.

Bolivian politics has enjoyed an unusual period of stability. Elections in 1993 resulted in victory for Gonzalo ("Goni") Sánchez de Lozada, who won in large part because his running mate, the indigenous politician Victor Hugo Cárdenas, was leader of the Movimiento Revolucionario Túpaj Katari de Liberación and attracted the votes of Bolivia's Aymara-speaking majority. For the future "Goni" announced his "Plan of Everyone," which has as its object privatization of the economy. Bolivians, however, will be able to participate in shareholding and profits.

DEVELOPMENT

Bolivia's economy, after years of contraction, began to expand again in the late 1980s; in 1991 the growth rate was 4.1% and in 1992 about 3.3%. President-elect Sánchez de Lozada promised to continue the economic policies of President Paz Zamora, which emphasized privatization, debt reduction, and export development.

FREEDOM

A corrupt judicial system, overcrowded prisons, and violence and discrimination against women and indigenous peoples are perennial problems in Bolivia, despite protective legislation. A government campaign against narcotics traffickers has resulted not only in abuses by the police but also the further corruption of law enforcement.

HEALTH/WELFARE

Provisions against child labor in Bolivia are frequently ignored; children may be found shining shoes, selling lottery tickets, and as street vendors. Although urban children generally attend school through the elementary level, more than half of rural children do not. Taken together, fewer than 30% of Bolivian children are educated beyond elementary school.

ACHIEVEMENTS

The Bolivian author Armando Chirveches, in his political novel La Candidatura de Rojas (1909), produced one of the best examples of this genre in all of Latin America. It captures the politics of the late nineteenth century extraordinarily well.

Brazil (Federal Republic of Brazil)

GEOGRAPHY

Area in Square Kilometers (Miles):
8,512,100 (3,285,670) (larger than the 48 contiguous U.S. states)
Capital (Population): Brasília (1,400,000)
Climate: mostly tropical or semitropical; temperate zone in the south

PEOPLE

Population
Total: 158,200,000
Annual Growth Rate: 1.8%
Rural/Urban Population Ratio: 25/75
Ethnic Makeup of Population: 55% white; 38% mixed; 6% black; 1% others

Health
Life Expectancy at Birth: 62 years (male); 69 years (female)
Infant Mortality Rate (Ratio): 67/1,000
Average Caloric Intake: 107% of FAO minimum
Physicians Available (Ratio): 1/684

Religion(s)
90% Roman Catholic; others

CARNAVAL: A FORM OF SOCIAL CONTROL?

Every year, just before the Lenten season, the wild 3-day celebrations of Carnaval take place in Brazil. It is a time to release pent-up frustrations and to immerse oneself in song and dance. Brazilian social critics have long accused the government of using Carnaval as an emotional safety valve for the disadvantaged, that the celebrations are little more than psychological therapy. But Carnaval is also a popular mass art form that allows Brazil's subcultures to express themselves through music and dance. In this sense it has become central to the complex culture of Brazil.

Education
Adult Literacy Rate: 81%

COMMUNICATION

Telephones: 13,905,290
Newspapers: 322 dailies

TRANSPORTATION

Highways—Kilometers (Miles):
1,673,735 (1,037,715)
Railroads—Kilometers (Miles):
28,828 (17,902)
Usable Airfields: 2,911

GOVERNMENT

Type: federal republic; democratically elected president since 1985
Independence Date: September 7, 1822
Head of State: President Itamar Franco
Political Parties: National Reconstruction Party; Brazilian Democratic Movement Party; Liberal Front Party; Workers' Party; Brazilian Labor Party; Democratic Labor Party; Brazilian Social Democratic Party; Popular Socialist Party; Communist Party of Brazil; Christian Democratic Party
Suffrage: voluntary at 16; compulsory between 18 and 70; voluntary at 70

MILITARY

Number of Armed Forces: 324,200
Military Expenditures (% of Central Government Expenditures): 4.2%
Current Hostilities: none

ECONOMY

Currency ($ U.S. Equivalent): 73.5 cruzeiros = $1 (changes frequently)
Per Capita Income/GDP: $2,300/$358 billion
Inflation Rate: 478%
Total Foreign Debt: $118.0 billion
Natural Resources: iron ore; manganese; bauxite; nickel; uranium; gemstones; petroleum
Agriculture: coffee; rice; corn; sugarcane; soybeans; cotton; manioc; oranges
Industry: textiles; chemicals; cement; lumber; steel; motor vehicles; metalwork; capital goods

FOREIGN TRADE

Exports: $31.6 billion
Imports: $21.0 billion

Brazil
- ✪ Capital
- ● City
- River
- --- Road

0   500   kilometers
0   500   miles

BRAZIL: A TROUBLED GIANT

Former Brazilian President Ernesto Geisel stated in 1977 that progress was based on "an integrated process of political, social, and economic development." Democracy, he argued, was the first necessity in the political arena. But democracy could only be achieved "if we also further social development . . . , if we raise the standard of living of Brazilians." The standard of living, he continued, "can only be raised through economic development."

It was clear from his remarks that the three broad objectives of becoming a democracy, social progress, and economic development were interconnected. He could not conceive of democracy in a poor country or in a country where there were "gaps, defects, and inadequacies in the social realm."

CONCEPTS OF PROGRESS

Geisel's comments offer a framework within which to consider not only the current situation in Brazil but also historical trends that reach back to the late nineteenth century—and, in some instances, to Portugal. Historically, most Brazilians have believed that progress would take place within the context of a strong, authoritarian state. In the nineteenth century, for example, a reform-minded elite adapted European theories of modernization that called for government-sponsored changes. The masses would receive benefits from the state; in this way, the elite reasoned, pressure for change from the poorer sectors of society would be eliminated. There would be progress with order. *Ordem e Progresso* ("Order and Progress") is the motto that graces the Brazilian flag; the motto is as appro-

priate today as it was in 1889, when the flag first flew over the new republic.

The tension among modernization, social equity, and order and liberty was first obvious in the early 1920s, when politically isolated middle-class groups united with junior military officers (*tenentes*) to challenge an entrenched ruling class of coffee-plantation owners. By the mid-1920s the tenentes, bent on far-reaching reforms, conceived a new role for themselves. With a faith that bordered at times on the mystical and a philosophy that embraced change in the vaguest of terms, they felt that only the military could shake Brazil from its lethargy and force it to modernize. Their program demanded the ouster of conservative, tradition-minded politicians, an economic transformation of the nation, and, eventually, a return to strong, centralized constitutional rule. The tenentes also proposed labor reforms that included official recognition of trade unions; a minimum wage and maximum work week; restraints on child labor; land reform; nationalization of natural resources; and a radical expansion of educational facilities. Although the tenentes were frustrated in their attempts to mold policy, many of their reforms were taken up by Getulio Vargas, who seized power in 1930 and imposed a strong, authoritarian state on Brazil.

THE 1964 REVOLUTION

In some respects the goals of the tenentes were echoed in 1964 when a broad coalition of civilians—frustrated by an economy that seemed to be disintegrating, concerned with the "leftist" slant of the government of João Goulart, and worried about social revolution that might well challenge the status and prestige of the wealthy and the middle classes—called on the military to impose order on the country.

The military leaders did not see their intervention as just another coup but, rather, as a revolution. They foresaw change but believed it would be dictated from above. Government was highly centralized, the traditional parties were virtually frozen out of the political process, and the military and police ruthlessly purged Brazil of elements considered "leftist" or "subversive." (The terms were used interchangeably.) Order and authority triumphed over liberty and freedom. The press was muzzled and human-rights abuses were rampant.

Brazil's economic recovery eventually began to receive attention. The military gave economic growth and national security priority over social programs and political liberalization. Until the effects of

(United Nations photo/J. Frank)

Diversification of its agricultural production is regarded as necessary for the economic development of Brazil. This view of the central vegetable market in São Paulo shows the grass-roots movement toward agricultural diversity.

the OPEC-generated oil crisis in 1973 began to be felt, the recovery of the Brazilian economy was dubbed a "miracle," with growth rates averaging 10 percent a year.

The benefits of that growth went primarily to the upper and middle classes, who enjoyed the development of industries based largely on consumer goods. Moreover, Brazil's industrialization was flawed. It was heavily dependent on foreign investment, foreign technology, and foreign markets. It required large investments in machinery and equipment but needed little labor, and it damaged the environment through pollution of the rivers and air around industrial centers. Agriculture was neglected to the point that basic foodstuffs had to be imported.

THE IMPACT OF RURAL-URBAN MIGRATION

The stress on industrialization tremendously increased rural-to-urban migration and complicated the government's ability to keep up with the expanded need for public health and social services. In 1970 nearly 56 percent of the population were concentrated in urban areas; by the early 1990s, 75 percent of the population were so classified. These figures also illustrate the inadequacies of an agrarian program based essentially on a "moving frontier." Peasants evicted from their plots have run out of new lands to exploit, unless they move to the inhospitable Amazon region. As a result many have been attracted by the cities.

The pressure of the poor on the cities, severe shortages of staple foods, and growing tension in rural areas over access to the land forced the government to act. In 1985 the civilian government of José Sarney announced an agrarian-reform plan to distribute millions of acres of unused private land to peasants. Implementation of the reform was not easy, and confrontations between peasants and landowners occurred.

MILITARY RULE IS CHALLENGED

Nineteen seventy-four was a crucial year for the military government of Brazil. The virtual elimination of the urban-guerrilla threat challenged the argument that democratic institutions could not be restored because of national-security concerns.

Pressure grew from other quarters as well. Many middle- and upper-class Brazilians were frightened by the huge state-controlled sector in the economy that had been carved out by the generals. The military's determination to promote the rapid development of the nation's resources, to control all industries deemed vital to the nation's security, and to compete with multinational corporations concerned Brazilian businesspeople who saw their role in the economy decreasing.

Challenges to the military regime also came from the Roman Catholic Church, which attacked the government for its brutal violations of human rights and constantly called for economic and social justice. One Brazilian bishop publicly called the government "sinful" and in "opposition to the plans of God" and noted that it was the church's moral and religious obligation to fight it. After 1974, as Brazil's economic difficulties mounted, the chorus of complaints grew insistent.

THE RETURN OF DEMOCRACY

The relaxation of political repression was heralded by two laws passed in 1979. The Amnesty Bill allowed for the return of hundreds of political exiles; the Party Reform Bill in essence reconstructed Brazilian politics. Under the provisions of the Party Reform Bill, new political parties could be established—provided they were represented in 9 states and in 20 percent of the counties of those states. The new parties were granted the freedom to formulate political platforms, as long as they were not ideological and did not favor any one economic class. The Communist Party was outlawed, and the creation of a workers' party was expressly forbidden. (Communist parties were legalized again in 1985.)

The law against the establishment of a workers' party reflected the regime's concern that labor, increasingly anxious about the state of the economy, might withdraw its traditional support for the state. Organized labor had willingly cooperated with the state since the populist regime of Getulio Vargas (1937–1945). For Brazilian workers in the 1930s, the state was their patron, the source of benefits. This dependence on the government, deeply rooted in Portuguese political culture, replaced the formation of a more independent labor movement and minimized industrial conflict. The state played the role of mediator between workers and management. President Vargas led the workers to believe that the state was the best protector of their interests. Polls have indicated that workers still cling to that belief.

If workers expect benefits from the state, however, the state must then honor those expectations and allocate sufficient resources to assure labor's loyalty. A deep economic crisis, such as the one that occurred in the early 1960s and the one that grips Brazil today, endangers the state's control of labor. In 1964 organized labor supported the coup because workers felt that the civilian regime had failed to perform its protective function. This phenomenon also reveals the extremely shallow soil in which Brazilian democracy has taken root.

Organized labor tends not to measure Brazilian governments in political terms but within the context of the state's ability to address labor's needs. For the rank-and-file worker, it is not a question of democracy or military authoritarianism but of bread and butter. Former President Sarney, in an effort to keep labor loyal to the government, sought the support of union leaders for a proposal to create a national pact with businesspeople, workers, and his government. But pervasive corruption, inefficient government, and a continuing economic crisis eventually, in the words of political scientist Margaret Keck, "eroded the legitimacy of these elites" and favored nontraditional parties in the 1989 election. The candidacy of Luís Inácio da Silva, popularly known as "Lula" and leader of the Workers' Party, "was stunning evidence of the Brazilian electorate's dissatisfaction with the conduct of the country's transition to democracy and with the political class in general." He lost the election by a very narrow margin.

Yet workers continue to regard the state as the source of benefits, as do other Brazilians. Many social reformers, upset with the generals for their neglect of social welfare, believe that social reform should be dispensed from above by a strong and paternalistic state. Change is possible, even welcome—but it must be the result of compromise and conciliation, not confrontation or non-negotiable demands.

THE NEW CONSTITUTION

The *abertura* (political liberalization) climaxed in January 1985 with the election of civilian President Sarney following 21 years of military rule. Importantly, the military promised to respect the Constitution and promised a policy of nonintervention in the political process. In 1987, however, with the draft of a new constitution under discussion, the military strongly protested language that removed its responsibility for internal law and order and restricted its role to that of defense of the nation against external threats. According to *Latin American Regional Reports: Brazil,* the military characterized the draft constitution as "confused, inappropriate, at best a parody of a constitution, just as Frankenstein was a gross and deformed imitation of a human being."

Military posturing aside, the new Constitution went into effect in October 1988. It reflects the input of a wide range of interests: The Constituent Assembly—which also served as Brazil's Congress—heard testimony and suggestions from Amazonian Indians, peasants, and urban poor, as well as from rich landowners and the military. The Constitution is a document that captures the byzantine character of Brazilian power politics and influence peddling and reveals compromises made by conservative and liberal vested interests.

The military's fears about its role in internal security were removed when the Constituent Assembly voted constitutional provisions to grant the right of the military independently to ensure law and order, a responsibility it has historically claimed. But Congress also arrogated to itself the responsibility for appropriating federal monies. This is important because it gives Congress a powerful check on both the military and the executive office.

Nationalists won several key victories. The Constituent Assembly created the concept of "a Brazilian company of national capital" that can prevent foreigners from engaging in mining, oil-exploration risk contracts, and biotechnology. Brazilian-controlled companies were also given preference in the supply of goods and services to local, state, and national governments. Legislation re-affirmed and strengthened the principle of government intervention in the economy should national security or the collective interest be at issue.

Conservative congressional representatives were able to prevail in matters of land reform and defeated a proposal that would have allowed the compulsory appropriation of property for land reform. Although a clause that addressed the "social function" of land was included in the Constitution, it was clear that powerful landowners and agricultural interests had triumphed over Brazil's landless peasantry.

In other areas, however, the Constitution is remarkably progressive on social and economic issues. The work week was reduced to a maximum of 44 hours, profit sharing was established for all employees, time-and-a-half is promised for overtime work, and paid vacations include a bonus of 30 percent of one's monthly salary. Day-care facilities are to be established for all children under age 6, maternity leave of 4 months and paternity leave of 5 days are envisaged, and workers are protected against "arbitrary dismissal." The Constitution also introduced a series of innovations that would increase significantly the ability of Brazilians to claim their guaranteed rights before the nation's courts and ensure the protection of human rights, particularly the rights of Indians and peasants involved in land disputes.

Despite the ratification of the new Constitution, a functioning Congress, and an independent judiciary, the focus of power in Brazil is still the president. A legislative majority in the hands of the opposition in no way erodes the executive's ability to govern as he chooses. Any measure introduced by the president automatically becomes law after 40 days, even without congressional action. Foreign observers perceive "weaknesses" in the new parties, which in actuality are but further examples of well-established political practices. The parties are based on personalities rather than issues, platforms are vague, goals are so broad that they are almost illusions, and party organization conforms to traditional

(United Nations photo)

By the late 1980s, agrarian reforms that were designed to establish the peasants in plots of workable land had caused the depletion of Brazilian jungle and, as space ran out, a large movement of these people to the cities. This urban crowding is illustrated in this photo of the Vavella section of Rio de Janeiro.

alliances and the "rules" of patronage. Democratic *forms* are in place in Brazil; the *substance* remains to be realized.

The election of President Fernando Collor de Mello, who assumed office in March 1990, proves the point. As Margaret Keck explains, Collor fit well into a "traditional conception of elite politics, characterized by fluid party identifications, the predominance of personal relations, a distrust of political institutions, and reliance on charismatic and populist appeals to *o povo*, the people." Unfortunately, such a system is open to abuse; revelations of widespread corruption that reached all the way to the presidency brought down Collor's government in 1992 and gave Brazilian democracy its most difficult challenge to date. The scandal brought to light a range of strengths and weaknesses that present a number of insights.

THE PRESS AND THE PRESIDENCY

Brazil's press was severely censored and harassed from the time of the military coup of 1964 until 1982. Not until passage of the Constitution of 1988 was the right to free speech and a free press guaranteed. It was the press, and in particular the news magazine *Veja*, that opened the door to President Color's impeachment. In the words of *World Press Review*, "Despite government pressure to ease off, the magazine continued to uncover the president's malfeasance, tugging hard at the threads of Color's unraveling administration. As others in the media followed suit, Congress was forced to begin an investigation and, in the end, indict Collor." The importance of the event to Brazil's press, according to *Veja* editor Mario Sergio Conti, is that "It will emerge with fewer illusions about power and be more rigorous. Reporting has been elevated to a higher plane. . . ."

While the failure of Brazil's first directly elected president in 29 years was tragic, it should not be interpreted as the demise of Brazilian democracy. Importantly, according to Brazilian journalist Carlos Eduardo Lins da Silva, writing in *Current History*, many "Brazilians and outside observers saw the workings of the impeachment process as a sign of the renewed strength of democratic values in Brazilian society. They were also seen as a healthy indicator of growing intolerance to corruption in public officials." The military, despite persistent rumors of a possible coup, has to date allowed the constitutional process to dictate events. For the first time, most civilians do not see the generals as part of the solution to

political shortcomings. And Congress, to its credit, chose to act responsibly and not be "bought off" by the executive office.

THE RIGHTS OF WOMEN AND CHILDREN

Major changes in Brazilian households have occurred over the last decade as the number of women in the work force has dramatically increased. In 1990 just over 35 percent of women were in the work force, and the number was expected to grow. As a result women are limiting the size of their families. More than 20 percent use birth-control pills, and Brazil is second only to China in the percentage of women who have been sterilized (16 percent as opposed to 17 percent). The tradi-

tional family of 5 or more children has shrunk to an average of 3.4. With two wage earners, the standard of living has risen slightly for some families. Many homes now have electricity and running water, and television sales increased by more than 1,000 percent in the last decade.

In relatively affluent, economically and politically dynamic urban areas, women are more obvious in the professions, education, industry, the arts, media, and political life. In rural areas, especially in the northeast, traditional cultural attitudes, which call upon women to be submissive, are still well entrenched.

Women are routinely subjected to physical abuse in Brazil. Americas Watch, an international human-rights group, re-

(United Nations photo/Shelley Rotner)

The status of blacks in Brazil is considered better than in most other multiracial societies. The class structure is determined by a number of factors: income, family history, education, social behavior, cultural tastes, and talent. Still, the upper class remains mainly white, and the lower class principally of color.

ports that more than 70 percent of assault, rape, and murder cases take place in the home and that many incidents are unreported. Even though Brazil's Supreme Court struck down the outmoded concept of a man's "defense of honor," local courts acquit men who kill unfaithful wives. Brazil, for all intents and purposes, is still a patriarchy.

Children are also in many cases denied basic rights. According to official statistics, almost 18 percent of children between the ages of 10 and 14 are in the work force and oftentimes labor in unhealthy or dangerous environments. Violence against urban street children has reached frightening proportions. Between January and June 1992, 167 minors were killed in Rio de Janeiro; 306 were murdered in São Paulo over the first 7 months of the year. In July 1993 the massacre in a single night of 7 street children in Rio resulted, for a time, in cries for an investigation of the matter.

THE STATUS OF BLACKS

Scholars continue to debate the actual status of blacks in Brazil. Not long ago an elected black member of Brazil's federal Congress blasted Brazilians for their racism. In fairness, however, writes historian Bradford Burns, Brazil probably has less racial tension and prejudice than other multiracial societies.

A more formidable barrier, Burns says, may well be class. "Class membership depends on a wide variety of factors and their combination: income, family history and/or connections, education, social behavior, tastes in housing, food and dress, as well as appearance, personality and talent." But, he notes, "The upper class traditionally has been and still remains mainly white, the lower class principally colored." Upward mobility exists and barriers can be breached. But if such advancement depends upon a symbolic "whitening out," does not racism still exist?

This point is underscored by the 1988 celebration of the centennial of the abolition of slavery in Brazil. In sharp contrast to government and church emphasis on racial harmony and equality were public protests by militant black groups claiming that Brazil's much-heralded "racial democracy" was a myth. In 1990 blacks earned 40 percent less than whites in the same professions.

THE INDIAN QUESTION

Brazil's estimated 200,000 Indians have suffered greatly in recent decades from the gradual encroachment of migrants from the heavily populated coastal regions and from government efforts to open the Amazon region to economic development. Highways have penetrated Indian lands, diseases for which the Indians have little or no immunity have killed thousands, and additional thousands have experienced a profound culture shock. Government efforts to protect the Indians have been largely ineffectual.

The two poles in the debate over the Indians are captured in the following excerpts from *Latin American Regional Reports: Brazil:* A Brazilian Army officer observed that the "United States solved the problem with its army. They killed a lot of Indians. Today everything is quiet there, and the country is respected throughout the world." And in the words of a Kaingang Indian woman: "Today my people see their lands invaded, their forests destroyed, their animals exterminated and their hearts lacerated by this brutal weapon that is civilization."

Sadly, the assault against Brazil's Indian peoples has accelerated and disputes over land have become more violent. One case speaks for itself. In the aftermath of a shooting incident in which several Yanomamö Indians were killed by prospectors, the Brazilian federal government declared that all outsiders would be removed from Yanomamö lands, ostensibly to protect the Indians. Those expelled by the government included anthropologists, missionaries, doctors, and nurses. A large number of prospectors remained behind. By the end of 1988, while medical personnel had not been allowed back in, the number of prospectors had swelled to 50,000 in an area peopled by 9,000 Yanomamö. Evidence suggests that the Indians have been devastated by diseases, particularly malaria, and by mercury poisoning as a result of prospecting activities upriver from Yanomamö settlements. In 1991 cholera began to spread among indigenous Amazon peoples, due to medical waste dumped into rivers in plague-ridden Peru and Ecuador.

The new Constitution devotes an entire chapter to the rights of Indians. For the first time in the country's history Indians are granted the authority to bring suits in court to defend their rights and interests. In all such cases, they will be assisted by a public prosecutor. In 1991, even though the government established a large protected zone for Brazil's Yanomamö Indians, reports of confrontations between Indians and prospectors have persisted. There are also Brazilian nationalists who insist that a 150-mile-wide strip along the border with Venezuela be excluded from the reserve as a matter of national security. The Yanomamö cultural area extends well into Venezuela; such a security zone would bisect Yanomamö lands.

THE BURNING OF BRAZIL

Closely related to the destruction of Brazil's Indians is the destruction of the tropical rain forests. The burning of the forests by peasants clearing land in the traditional slash and burn method, or by developers and landowners constructing dams or converting forest to pasture, has become a source of worldwide concern and controversy.

Ecologists are horrified by the mass extinction of species of plants, animals, and insects, most of which have not even been catalogued. The massive annual burning, equivalent in 1987 to the size of Kansas, also fuels the debate on the greenhouse effect and global warming. The problem of the burning of Brazil is indeed global, because we are all linked to the tropics by climate and the migratory patterns of birds and animals.

World condemnation of the destruction of the Amazon basin has produced a strong xenophobic reaction in Brazil. Foreign Ministry Secretary-General Paulo Tarso Flecha de Lima informed a 24-nation conference on the protection of the environment that the "international community cannot try to strangle the development of Brazil in the name of false ecological theories." He further noted that foreign criticism of his government in this regard was "arrogant, presumptuous and aggressive." The Brazilian military, according to *Latin American Regional Reports: Brazil,* has adopted a high-profile posture on the issue. The military sees the Amazon as "a kind of strategic reserve vital to national security interests." Any talk of transforming the rain forests into an international nature reserve is rejected out of hand.

Over the next decade, however, Brazilian and foreign investors will create a 2.5 million-acre "green belt" in an area of the Amazon rain forest already devastated. Fifty million seedlings have been planted in a combination of natural and commercial zones. It is hoped that responsible forestry will generate jobs to maintain and study the native forest and to log the commercial zones. Steady employment would help to stem the flow of migrants to cities and to untouched portions of the rain forest.

FOREIGN POLICY

If Brazil's Indian and environmental policies leave much to be desired, its foreign

				The Brazilian Expeditionary Force participates in the Italian campaign		
Pedro Alvares Cabral discovers and claims Brazil for Portugal **1500**	Declaration of Brazil's independence **1822**	The Golden Law abolishes slavery **1888**	The republic is proclaimed **1889**	**1944**	The military seizes power **1964**	Economic, social, and ecological crises

1980s–1990s

President Collor is convicted on impeachment charges; he is replaced by Vice President Itamar Franco

High inflation threatens social violence

Continued violence is reported against Brazil's native peoples

policy has won it respect throughout much of Latin America and the Third World. Cuba, Central America, Angola, and Mozambique seem far less threatening to the Brazilian government than they do to Washington. Brazil is more concerned about its energy needs, capital requirements, and trade opportunities. Its foreign policy, in short, is one of pragmatism. Former Foreign Minister Olavo Setúbal has repeatedly stated that he is a great believer in the "diplomacy of results" and not the diplomacy of ideology.

ECONOMIC POLICY AND THE DEBT

Many experts believe that Brazil's political liberalization is linked to its economy—which is in difficult straits. Inflation and the foreign debt preoccupy the government. The economy is in shambles, hyperinflation looms, and concerns have been expressed about the social and political impact of failed policies.

Economic reform has been significantly delayed by the fall of the Collor government. Collor's successor, President Itamar Franco, has given mixed signals in terms of his economic policy. Even though he served as Collor's vice president, Franco was critical of rapid privatization of state-owned companies, opposed opening Brazil's market to foreign competition, and favored growth over the battle against inflation. But in mid-1993 Finance Minister Fernando Henrique Cardoso announced a new plan calculated to slash government spending and accelerate privatization. In the meantime inflation has surged ahead, with monthly averages of 40 percent not uncommon.

A fundamental problem is the state of Brazilian industry. According to reports in *World Press Review,* Brazil is 15 to 20 years behind the economies of the Northern Hemisphere in the modernization of machinery and products. In the 1980s the nation's industries "went into hibernation" and stopped investing in themselves. As a result there was no increase in productive capacity. The steel industry is characterized as "lazy and rusty," and the automotive industry is described as the "least productive in the world and among the worst for quality." Electricity generation is stagnant. However, the scope of Brazilian industry is impressive and "produces virtually everything."

Inflation remains a problem because its solution, in large measure, demands unpopular political measures. Tax increases for the middle class and the wealthy, cuts in state spending, and the elimination of some of the inefficient and costly state-owned enterprises will be difficult to accomplish. As it is, a general lack of resources forced by austerity measures has left the promises of politicians unfulfilled. Without resources, education will not be expanded and basic services will not be extended to poor urban districts.

Austerity may have a high political cost for Brazil. Increasing rates of unemployment, upwardly spiraling prices for basic commodities for the poor, and a sharp re-duction in the purchasing power of the middle classes are an explosive mix. Despite strong pressure from international lending agencies to cut further state spending, Brazil will most likely impose only those austerity measures that fall within the political tolerance of Brazilians. This state of affairs led journalist Lins da Silva to lament: "Brazilian elites have once again shown how capable they are of solving political crises in a creative and peaceful manner but also how unwilling to promote change in inequitable social structures." There has been a lack of "commitment to reforms to promote prosperity for most of the population or to shake the well-established interests of small groups." Ominously, while the military has remained aloof to Brazil's political agonies, it has spoken out about the dangers posed by poverty, unemployment, and inflation. Brazilian political analyst Villasvoas Correa warned that "if the crisis starts to explode, I cannot see the military staying in their barracks watching." In April 1993 the commanders of the armed forces announced that their priority was the "struggle against misery."

DEVELOPMENT

Brazil's diverse economy, with a strong agricultural base, ample natural resources, and a large industrial sector, lags behind other Latin American countries in terms of privatization. This reflects the failure of economic and administrative reforms to move the country toward a market economy. In the meantime, the nation's informal economic sector continues to grow and may comprise as much as 60% of the total.

FREEDOM

Violence against street children, indigenous peoples, homosexual people, and common criminals at the hands of the police, landowners, vigilante groups, gangs, and hired thugs is commonplace. Homicide committed by police is the third leading cause of death among children and adolescents. Indigenous peoples continue to clash with miners and landowners. Investigation of such crimes is lax and prosecution of the perpetrators is sporadic.

HEALTH/WELFARE

Official statistics showed that in 1993, 32 million Brazilians, or one-fifth of the entire population, lived below the poverty line. Millions were virtually indigent. The area hardest hit was the drought-stricken northeast, which held some 60% of the worst cases of poverty. The government planned to combat the poverty by public-works projects to repair roads and construct dams, wells, and housing. Improved public health was also a priority.

ACHIEVEMENTS

Brazil's cultural contributions to the world are many. Authors such as Joaquim Maria Machado de Assis, Jorge Amado, and Graciliano Ramos are evidence of Brazil's high rank in terms of important literary works. Brazilian music has won devotees throughout the world, and Brazil's *Cinema Novo* (New Cinema) has won many awards.

Chile (Republic of Chile)

GEOGRAPHY

Area in Square Kilometers (Miles):
756,945 (292,180) (nearly 2 times
the size of California)
Capital (Population): Santiago
(5,100,000)
Climate: mild; desert in north;
Mediterranean in center; cool and
damp in south

PEOPLE

Population
Total: 13,529,000
Annual Growth Rate: 1.6%
Rural/Urban Population Ratio: 14/86

"A SYNTHESIS OF THE PLANET"

Gabriela Mistrál, the Nobel Prize–winning Chilean poet and writer, described her nation in the following terms:

> Something like a synthesis of the planet is fulfilled in the geography of Chile. It starts in the desert, which is like beginning with sterility that loves no man. It is humanized in the valleys. It creates a home for living beings in the ample fertile agricultural zone, it takes on a grandiose sylvan beauty at the end of the continent as if to finish with dignity, and finally crumbles, offering half life, half death, in the sea.
> "My Country," *United Nations World* (May 1950), p. 51.

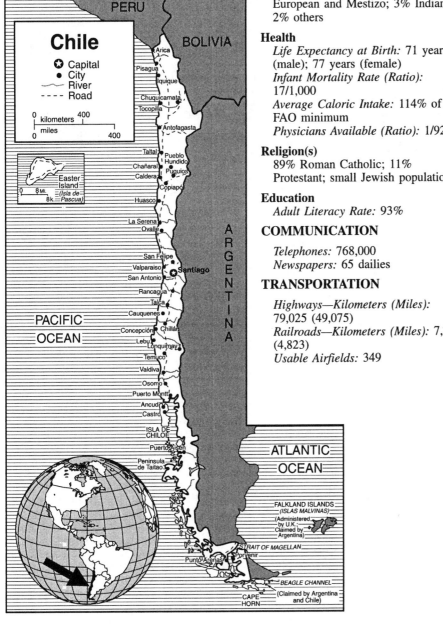

Ethnic Makeup of Population: 95%
European and Mestizo; 3% Indian;
2% others

Health
Life Expectancy at Birth: 71 years
(male); 77 years (female)
Infant Mortality Rate (Ratio):
17/1,000
Average Caloric Intake: 114% of
FAO minimum
Physicians Available (Ratio): 1/922

Religion(s)
89% Roman Catholic; 11%
Protestant; small Jewish population

Education
Adult Literacy Rate: 93%

COMMUNICATION

Telephones: 768,000
Newspapers: 65 dailies

TRANSPORTATION

Highways—Kilometers (Miles):
79,025 (49,075)
Railroads—Kilometers (Miles): 7,766
(4,823)
Usable Airfields: 349

GOVERNMENT

Type: republic
Independence Date: September 18,
1818
Head of State: President Eduardo
Frei Ruiz-Tagle
Political Parties: Christian
Democratic Party; Party for
Democracy; Radical Party; Social
Democratic Party; Socialist Party;
National Revolution; Independent
Democratic Union; others
Suffrage: universal and compulsory
at 18

MILITARY

Number of Armed Forces: 95,800
*Military Expenditures (% of Central
Government Expenditures):* 8.4%
Current Hostilities: none

ECONOMY

Currency ($ U.S. Equivalent): 395.1
pesos = $1
Per Capita Income/GDP:
$2,300/$30.5 billion
Inflation Rate: 18.7%
Total Foreign Debt: $17.0 billion
Natural Resources: copper; timber;
iron ore; nitrates; precious metals;
molybdenum
Agriculture: wheat; potatoes; sugar
beets; onions; beans; fruits; livestock
Industry: mineral refining; metal
manufacturing; food processing; fish
processing; wood products

FOREIGN TRADE

Exports: $8.9 billion
Imports: $7.4 billion

CHILE: A NATION ON THE REBOUND

In September 1973 the Chilean military, with the secret support of the U.S. Central Intelligence Agency (CIA), seized power from the constitutionally elected government of President Salvador Allende. Chile, with its long-standing traditions of free and honest elections, respect for human rights, and freedom of the press, was quickly transformed into a brutal dictatorship that arrested, tortured, and killed thousands of its own citizens. In the larger sweep of Chilean history, however, the coup seemed to be the most recent and severe manifestation of a lengthy conflict between social justice, on the one hand, and the requirements of order dictated by the nation's ruling elite, on the other. This was true in the colonial period when there was conflict between the Roman Catholic Church and landowners over Indian rights. It has also been apparent in recent confrontations among Marxists, reformers, and conservatives.

FORM AND SUBSTANCE

Form, as opposed to substance, characterized the rule of the Christian Democrats in the 1960s, when they created many separate rural unions, supposedly to address the needs of *campensinos* ("peasants"). A divided union movement in effect became a form of government control that prevented the emergence of a single powerful rural organization.

In the early 1970s, President Allende—despite his talk of socialism and his genuine attempt to destroy the institutions and values of an old social order—used a centralized bureaucracy that would have been recognized by sixteenth-century viceroys and nineteenth-century presidents as his weapon of transformation. Allende's attempts to institute far-reaching social change led to a strong reaction from powerful sectors of Chilean society who felt threatened.

THE 1973 COUP D'ETAT

When the military ousted Allende, it had the support of many Chileans, including the majority of the middle classes, who had been hurt by the government's economic policies, troubled by continuous political turmoil, and infuriated by official mismanagement. The military, led by General Augusto Pinochet, began a new experiment with another form of centrist rule: military authoritarianism. The generals made it clear that they had not restored order merely to return it to the "discred-

(Reuters/Bettmann)

On October 5, 1988, the voters of Chile denied General Augusto Pinochet an additional 8-year term as president. To his credit, his military regime accepted defeat peacefully.

ited" constitutional practices of the past. They spoke of regeneration, of a new Chile, and of an end to the immorality, corruption, and incompetence of all civilian politics. The military announced in 1974 that "guided by the inspiration of [Diego] Portales," who was one of nineteenth-century Chile's greatest civilian leaders, "the government of Chile will energetically apply the principle of authority and drastically punish any outburst of disorder and anarchy."

The political, economic, and social reforms proposed by the military aimed at restructuring Chile to such an extent that there would no longer be a need for traditional political parties. Economic policy favored free and open competition as the main regulator of economic and social life. The Chilean state rid itself of hundreds of state-owned corporations, struck down tariffs designed to protect Chilean industry from foreign competition, and opened the economy to widespread foreign investment. The changes struck deeply at the structure of the Chilean economy and produced a temporary but sharp recession, high unemployment, and hundreds of bankruptcies. A steep decline in the standard of

living for most Chileans was the result of the government's anti-inflation policy.

Social-welfare programs were reduced to a minimum. The private sector was encouraged to assume many functions and services once provided by the state. Pensions were moved entirely to the private sector as all state programs were phased out. In this instance the state calculated that workers tied through pensions and other benefits to the success of private enterprise would be less likely to be attracted to "non-Chilean" ideologies such as Marxism, socialism, and even Christian democracy. State-sponsored health programs were also cut to the bone, and many poor now pay for services once provided by the government.

THE DEFEAT OF A DICTATOR

To attain a measure of legitimacy, Chileans expected the military government to produce economic achievement. By 1987, and continuing into 1989, the regime's economic policies seemed successful. The growth rate for 1988 was an impressive 7.4 percent, but it also masked critical weaknesses in the Chilean economy. For example, much of the growth was overdependent on exports of raw materials—notably copper, pulp, timber, and fishmeal.

Modest economic success and an inflation rate of less than 20 percent convinced General Pinochet that he could take his political scenario for Chile's future to the voters for their ratification. But in the October 5, 1988, plebiscite, Chile's voters upset the general's plans and decisively denied him an additional 8-year term. (He did, however, continue in office until the next presidential election determined his successor.) Importantly, the military regime (albeit reluctantly) accepted defeat at the polls, which signifies the reemergence of a deep-rooted civic culture and long democratic tradition.

Where had Pinochet miscalculated? Public-opinion surveys on the eve of the election showed a sharply divided electorate. Some political scientists even spoke of the existence of "two Chiles." In the words of government professor Arturo Valenzuela and *Boston Globe* correspondent Pamela Constable, one Chile "embraced those who had benefited from the competitive economic policies and welfare subsidies instituted by the regime and who had been persuaded that power was best entrusted to the armed forces." The second Chile "consisted of those who had been victimized by the regime, who did not identify with Pinochet's anti-Communist cause, and who had quietly nurtured a belief in democracy." Polling data from the respected Center for Public Studies showed that 72 percent of those who voted against the regime were motivated by economic factors. These were people who had lost skilled jobs or who had suffered a decrease in real wages. While Pinochet's economic reforms had helped some, it had also created a disgruntled mass of downwardly mobile wage earners.

Valenzuela and Constable explain how a dictator allowed himself to be voted out of power. "To a large extent Pinochet had been trapped by his own mythology. He was convinced that he would be able to win and was anxious to prove that his regime was not a pariah but a legitimate government. He and other officials came to believe their own propaganda about the dynamic new Chile they had created." The closed character of the regime, with all lines of authority flowing to the hands of one man, made it "impossible for them to accept the possibility that they could lose." And when the impossible occurred and the dictator lost an election played by his own rules, neither civilians on the right nor the military were willing to override the constitutional contract they had forged with the Chilean people.

In March 1990 Chile returned to civilian rule for the first time in almost 17 years, with the assumption of the presidency by Patricio Aylwin. His years in power revealed that tensions still exist between civilian politicians and the military. In 1993, for example, General Pinochet mobilized elements of the army in Santiago, a move that, in the words of the independent newspaper *La Época,* "marked the crystallization of long-standing hostility" between the Aylwin government and the army. The military had reacted both to investigations into human-rights abuses during the Pinochet dictatorship and proposed legislation that would have subordinated the military to civilian control. On the other hand, the commanders of the navy and air force as well as the two right-wing political parties refused to sanction the actions of the army. President Aylwin regained the initiative when he publicly chastised General Pinochet. Congress, in a separate action, affirmed its supremacy over the judiciary in 1993, when it successfully impeached a Supreme Court justice for "notable dereliction of duty." The court system had been notorious for transferring human-rights cases from civil to military courts, where they were quickly dismissed. The impeachment augured well for further reform of the judicial branch.

Further resistance to the legacy of General Pinochet was expressed by the people when, on December 11, 1993, the center-left coalition candidate Eduardo Frei Ruiz-Tagle won the Chilean presidential election with 58 percent of the vote. As part of his platform, Frei had promised to bring the military under civilian rule. The parliamentary vote, however, did not give him the two-thirds majority needed to push through such a reform, but the trend toward civilian government seems to be continuing.

The rural areas of Chile have presented challenges to agrarian reformists. The pressure to produce higher levels of fresh produce has gradually poisoned the land and the people with pesticides.

The founding of
Santiago de Chile
1541

Independence of
Spain is
proclaimed
1818

The
administration of
Eduardo Frei;
revolution in
Liberty
dramatically
alters Chilean
society
1964–1970

A military coup
ousts President
Salvador Allende;
General Augusto
Pinochet
becomes
president
1973

1980s–1990s

Chile returns to
civilian rule with
the election of
Patricio Aylwin

Economic growth
in Chile
surpasses all
modern records

Eduardo Frei is
elected president

In 1993, the Chilean economy grew for the ninth consecutive year, a diversified range of exports reached record levels, and unemployment was at an official level of 5 percent. Even if this figure seems improbably low and fails to consider underemployment, Chile still enjoys the lowest unemployment rate in South America. The foreign debt has been reduced to $17 billion from a high of $30 billion at the beginning of economic restructuring, during the dictatorship of Pinochet.

Novelist and politician Mario Vargas Llosa observed that, while Chile "is not paradise," it does have a "stability and economic dynamism unparalled in Latin America." Indeed, "Chile is moving closer to Spain and Australia and farther from Peru or Haiti." He suggests that there has been a shift in Chile's political culture. "The ideas of economic liberty, a free market open to the world, and private initiative as the motor of progress have become embedded in the people of Chile."

In part, the change was the product of the harsh policies of the Pinochet regime. To quote Vargas Llosa, "For many people it is difficult to admit that Chile's extraordinarily successful economic programs were carried out under a brutally repressive dictatorship." The results do not justify the regime's crimes; neither do they invalidate the crimes.

LAND AND ENVIRONMENT

In 1955 Chile was a country where fewer than 5 percent of the population owned more than 80 percent of the farmland.

Thousands of landless day laborers and owners of *minifundia*, tiny subsistence plots, lived on the margins of the great estates or around small towns. Others lived as a permanent work force on the estates, called *fundos*. Together they constituted a pool of cheap agricultural labor.

According to Patrick Breslin, an analyst working with the Inter-American Foundation, the arrangement was exploitive and inefficient. At any given time, about 40 percent of prime farmland was left uncultivated. "And the system didn't meet the country's needs." Agricultural output in the 1950s was constantly outstripped by demand; Chile had to import increasing amounts of foodstuffs. "But so long as the traditional fundo system existed, it insured social and political control to a small ruling class. As in much of Latin America, agrarian reform was debated, and resisted, for decades."

In the Cachapoal Valley in Central Chile, it was the Roman Catholic Church that implemented the first experiments with agrarian reform. In 1962 church estates were divided among 76 families, most of them former workers, who were given 20 years at low interest to pay for the land. Breslin notes that three successive governments of the right, center, and left followed the example of the church and implemented increasingly sweeping land-reform policies. This was a major issue during the 1960s, and Socialist President Salvador Allende stepped up the pace. With the military coup of 1973, the cause of land reform fell on bad times; Many *campesino* ("peasant") leaders were ar-

rested or killed, and workers who had gained control of the land under the various reform programs now lost it—through debt or fraud—to the former owners. The cooperatives in the Cachapoal Valley survived, although they had to compete with the competitive market system forced through by the military. During a 30-year timespan, the agricultural workers of Cachapoal experienced a wide range of systems, ranging from semifeudalism, through cooperativism and collectivism, to capitalism.

Now the land is imperiled by a new danger common to Third World countries: the gradual poisoning of the land and the people by pesticides. The birds are disappearing from Cachapoal. Farmers, according to Breslin, fear that this may be the harbinger of catastrophe. The farmers are integrally connected to an expanding and highly competitive world market in fresh produce; they thus are pressured to use ever-increasing amounts of pesticides as well as fertilizers. Pesticide poisoning is just as important as the destruction of rain forests in other parts of Latin America. Solutions are difficult, and farmers living on the economic edge are reluctant to change, even though the birds no longer fly over the valley. Another threat to portions of Chile is the depletion of the ozone layer.

DEVELOPMENT

Economic growth for 1992, predicted at 6%, was actually closer to 10%; and the government produced a budgetary surplus for the second year in a row. Foreign investment in 1992 was 21% higher than in 1991. Bilateral trade agreements were made with Mexico, Venezuela, and Bolivia; and were preferred to membership in subregional trade organizations such as Mercosur.

FREEDOM

According to the U.S. State Department's *Country Reports on Human Rights Practices,* Chile's human-rights record has improved significantly in recent years. There is still the need to adress hundreds of abuses committed during the years of military rule. The military pursues obstructionist tactics in this regard.

HEALTH/WELFARE

It has been estimated that 25% of Chile's women have been subjected to physical violence at the hands of husbands or partners. The level of violence is highest in society's lowest strata; 34% of women interviewed in Santiago reported abuse. Society, the police, and courts continue to tolerate or ignore instances of wife-beating.

ACHIEVEMENTS

Chile's great literary figures, such as Gabriela Mistrál and Pablo Neruda, have a great sympathy for the poor and oppressed. This places Chilean authors in the mainstream of Latin American literature. Another major Chilean writer, Isabel Allende, has won worldwide acclaim.

Colombia (Republic of Colombia)

GEOGRAPHY

Area in Square Kilometers (Miles):
1,139,600 (440,000) (about the size
of Texas and New Mexico combined)
Capital (Population): Bogotá
(4,819,000)
Climate: tropical on coast and
eastern plains; cooler in highlands

PEOPLE

Population
Total: 34,297,000
Annual Growth Rate: 1.9%
Rural/Urban Population Ratio: 30/70
Ethnic Makeup of Population: 58%
Mestizo; 20% white; 14% mulatto;
4% African; 3% African-Indian; 1%
Indian

Health
Life Expectancy at Birth: 69 years
(male); 74 years (female)
Infant Mortality Rate (Ratio):
31/1,000; Indians 233/1,000
Average Caloric Intake: 108% of
FAO minimum
Physicians Available (Ratio): 1/1,240

Religion(s)
95% Roman Catholic

Education
Adult Literacy Rate: 87% (Indians
40%)

COMMUNICATION

Telephones: 2,547,222
Newspapers: 31 dailies

THE STONE MONUMENTS OF SAN AGUSTÍN

The archaeological site of San Agustín is an important testimony to the
artistic and cultural achievements of the Indians who inhabited the
southwestern region of Colombia more than 2,000 years ago. Impressive contributions of this culture include the imposing, larger-than-life
stone monuments with part-human, part-jaguar features. The jaguar
played an important role in the people's religious system and persisted
as a popular symbol for centuries. The jaguar theme also links the
inhabitants of San Agustín with other cultures in the Americas.

TRANSPORTATION

Highways—Kilometers (Miles):
75,450 (46,885)
Railroads—Kilometers (Miles): 3,386
(2,103)
Usable Airfields: 1,023

GOVERNMENT

Type: republic
Independence Date: July 20, 1810
Head of State: President César
Gaviria Trujillo
Political Parties: Liberal Party;
Social Conservative Party; National
Salvation Movement; Democratic
Alliance M-19; Patriotic Union;
Communist Party
Suffrage: universal at 18

MILITARY

Number of Armed Forces: 130,400
plus 50,000 national police
*Military Expenditures (% of Central
Government Expenditures):* 7.0%
Current Hostilities: territorial dispute
with Venezuela

ECONOMY

Currency ($ U.S. Equivalent): 681.5
pesos = $1
Per Capita Income/GDP:
$1,300/$45.0 billion
Inflation Rate: 26.8%
Total Foreign Debt: $17.0 billion
Natural Resources: petroleum; natural
gas; coal; iron ore; nickel; gold;
copper; emeralds
Agriculture: coffee; bananas; rice;
corn; sugarcane; marijuana; coca;
plantains; cotton; tobacco
Industry: textiles; food processing;
clothing and footwear; beverages;
chemicals; metal products; cement

FOREIGN TRADE

Exports: $7.5 billion
Imports: $6.1 billion

Colombia

⊛ Capital
● City
〰 River
- - - - Road

COLOMBIA: THE VIOLENT LAND

Colombia has long been noted for its violent political history. The division of political beliefs in the mid-nineteenth century into conservative and liberal factions produced not only debate but also civil war. To the winner went the presidency and the spoils of office. That competition for office came to a head during the savage War of the Thousand Days (1899–1902). Nearly half a century later, Colombia was again plagued by political violence which took perhaps 200,000 lives. Although on the surface it is distinct from the nineteenth-century civil wars, *La Violencia* ("The Violence," 1946–1958) offers striking parallels to the violence of the last century. Competing factions were again led by conservatives and liberals, and the presidency was the prize. Explanations for this phenomenon have tended to be at once simple and powerful. Colombian writers blame a Spanish heritage and its legacy of lust for political power.

Gabriel García Márquez, in his classic novel *One Hundred Years of Solitude*, spoofed the differences between liberals and conservatives. "The Liberals," said Aureliano Buendia's father-in-law, "were Freemasons, bad people, wanting to hang priests, to institute civil marriage and divorce, to recognize the rights of illegitimate children as equal to those of legitimate ones, and to cut the country up into a federal system that would take power away from the supreme authority." On the other hand, "the Conservatives, who had received their power directly from God, proposed the establishment of public order and family morality. They were the defenders of the faith of Christ, of the principle of authority, and were not prepared to permit the country to be broken down into autonomous entities." Aureliano, when later asked if he was a Liberal or a Conservative, quickly replied: "If I have to be something I'll be a Liberal, because the Conservatives are tricky."

THE ROOTS OF VIOLENCE

The roots of the violence are far more complex than a simple quest for spoils caused by a flaw in national character. Historian Charles Bergquist has shown that "divisions within the upper class and the systematic philosophical and programmatic positions that define them are not merely political manifestations of cultural traits; they reflect diverging economic interests within the upper class." These opposing interests developed both in the nineteenth and twentieth centuries. Moreover, to see Colombian politics solely as a violent quest for office ignores long periods of relative peace (1902–1935). Whatever the underlying causes of violence, it has profoundly influenced contemporary Colombians.

La Violencia was the largest armed conflict in the Western Hemisphere since the Mexican Revolution (1910–1917). It was a civil war of ferocious intensity that cut through class lines and mobilized people from all levels of society behind the banners of either liberalism or conservatism. That elite-led parties were able to win popular support was evidence of their strong organization rather than their opponents' political weakness.

(United Nations photo/M. Grant)

Colombia, as is the case of other Andean nations, has experienced rapid urbanization. Large numbers of migrants, drawn to urban areas, spread into slums on the outskirts of cities, as exemplified by this picture of a section of Colombia's capital, Bogotá. Most of the migrants are poorly paid, and the struggle to meet daily basic needs precludes political activism.

These multiclass parties still dominate Colombian political life, although the fierce interparty rivalry that characterized the civil wars of the nineteenth century as well as La Violencia has been stilled. In 1957 Colombia's social elite decided to bury partisan differences and devised a plan to end the widespread strife. Under the National Front agreement, the two parties agreed to divide legislative and bureaucratic positions equally and to alternate the presidency every 4 years from 1958 to 1974. This form of coalition government proved a highly successful means of elite compromise.

THE IMPACT OF LA VIOLENCIA

The violence has left its imprint on Colombia in other ways. Some scholars have suggested that peasants now shun political action because of fears of renewed violence. Refugees from La Violencia generally experienced confusion and a loss of values. Usually, rising literacy rates, improved transportation and communications, and integration into the nation's life produce an upsurge of activism as people clamor for more rapid change. This has not been the case in rural Colombia. Despite guerrilla activity in the countryside—some of which is a spin-off from La Violencia, some of which until recently had a Marxist orientation, and some of which is banditry—the guerrillas have not been able to win significant rural support.

La Violencia also led to the professionalization and enlargement of the Colombian armed forces in the late 1950s and early 1960s. Never a serious participant in the nation's civil wars, the military has acquired a new prestige and status unusual for Colombia. It must be considered an important factor in any discussion of Colombian politics today.

A standoff between guerrillas and the military prompted the government of Virgilio Barco to engage reluctantly in a dialogue with the insurgents, with the ultimate goal of peace. In 1988 he announced a three-phase peace plan to end the violence, to talk about needed reforms, and ultimately to re-incorporate guerrillas into society. This effort came to fruition in 1991, when the guerrilla movement M-19 laid down its arms after 16 years of fighting and engaged in political dialogue. Indeed, former guerrilla Antonio Navarro Wolf won 24 percent of the popular vote in an election and was named minister of health. Other guerrilla groups, notably the long-lived (since 1961) Colombian Revolutionary Armed Forces (FARC) and the National Liberation Army (ELN), led by a Spanish priest, have chosen to remain in the field. In November 1992 President César Gaviria and his advisers concluded that, in historian Christopher Abel's words, "the leaders of the main guerrilla organisations were insincere in their professions of determination to reach a peaceful settlement . . . and were cynically exploiting the 'peace process' . . . to purchase new weapons and regroup their forces for a renewed offensive." Accordingly, the ad-

(United Nations photo/J. Frank)

Coffee is a very important element in the economy of Colombia. The country is the world's second-largest exporter of the crop. This warehouse in Bogotá can store up to a half million bags of coffee.

ministration decided to take a hard line toward not only the guerrillas but also the drug cartels and organized crime. Violence would be escalated to bring peace to the most violent country on earth.

Hundreds of politicians, judges, and police officers have been murdered in Colombia. In the last presidential election alone, three candidates were assassinated. It has been estimated that 10 percent of the nation's homicides are politically motivated. Murder is the major cause of death for men between ages 15 and 45. While paramilitary violence accounts for many deaths, drug-trafficking and the unraveling of Colombia's fabric of law are responsible for most. As political scientist John D. Martz has written: "Whatever the responsibility of the military or the rhetoric of government, the penetration of Colombia's social and economic life by the drug industry [is] proving progressively destructive of law, security and the integrity of the political system."

DRUGS AND DEATH

Drug traffickers, according to *Latin American Update,* "represent a new economic class in Colombia; since 1981 'narcodollars' have been invested in real estate and large cattle ranches." The Colombian weekly newsmagazine *Semana* noted that drug cartels had purchased 2.5 million acres of land since 1984 and now own one-twelfth of the nation's productive farmland in the Magdalena River Basin. More than 100,000 acres of forest have been cut down to grow marijuana, coca, and opium poppies. Of particular concern to environmentalists is the fact that opium poppies are usually planted in the forests of the Andes at elevations above 6,000 feet. "These forests," according to *Semana,* "do not have great commercial value, but their tree cover is vital to the conservation of the sources of the water supply." The cartels have also bought up factories, newspapers, radio stations, shopping centers, soccer teams, and bullfighters. The emergence of Medellín as a modern city of gleaming skyscrapers and expensive cars also reflects the enormous profits of the drug business. In rural Colombia, drug traffickers have utilized paramilitary groups to clear areas of guerrillas who had themselves forced traditional landowners to leave. The drug traffickers have taken possession of the land and defend it with private "armies."

Drug warfare among rival drug cartels contributes to the climate of violence. The high level of drug-related killings in Medellín and Cali and attempts by the Cali cartel to purchase 550-pound bombs

from the Salvadoran military testify to the horrific character of the competition.

Political scientist Francisco Leal Buitrago argues that while trafficking in narcotics in the 1970s was economically motivated, by the 1980s it had evolved into a social phenomenon. "The traffickers represent a new social force that wants to participate like other groups—new urban groups, guerrillas and peasant movements. Like the guerrillas, they have not been able to participate politically. . . ." Constitutional reforms that prevent the extradition of drug traffickers to the United States convinced several of the more notorious drug barons to surrender in return for lenient sentences. That policy shifted abruptly when the head of the Medellín cartel, Pablo Escobar, escaped from jail and when it was shown that the levels of violence between the cartels had not diminished despite a softer government line.

Domestic consumption has also emerged as a serious problem in Colombia's cities. *Latin American Regional Reports* notes that the increase in consumption of the Colombian form of crack, known as *bazuko,* "has prompted the growth of gangs of youths in slum areas running the bazuko business for small distributors." In Bogotá, police reported that more than 1,500 gangs operated from the city's slums.

URBANIZATION

As is the case in other Andean nations, urbanization has been rapid. But the constantly spreading slums on the outskirts of the larger cities have not produced significant urban unrest or activism. Most of the migrants to the cities are first generation and are less frustrated and demanding than the general urban population. The new migrants perceive an improvement in their status and opportunities simply because they have moved into a more hopeful urban environment. Also, since most of the migrants are poorly paid, their focus tends to be on daily survival, not political activism.

Migrants make a significant contribution to the parallel Colombian economy. As is the case in Peru and other South American countries, the informal sector amounts to approximately 30 percent of gross domestic product.

The Roman Catholic Church in Colombia has also tended to take advantage of rapid urbanization. Depending on the individual beliefs of local bishops, the church has to a greater or lesser extent embraced the migrants, brought them into the church, and created or instilled a sense of community where none existed before. The church has generally identified with

the expansion and change taking place and has played an active social role.

Marginalized city dwellers are often the targets of violence. Hired killers, called *sicarios,* have murdered hundreds of petty thieves, beggars, prostitutes, indigents, and street children. Such "clean-up" campaigns are reminiscent of the activities of the Brazilian death squads since the 1960s. An overloaded judicial system and interminable delays have contributed to Colombia's high homicide rate. Increasingly, violence and murder have replaced the law as a way to settle disputes. Private justice is now commonly resorted to for a variety of disputes. Debts, for example, are more easily and quickly resolved through murder than by lengthy court proceedings.

SOCIAL CHANGE

The government has responded to calls for social change and reform. Former President Virgilio Barco sincerely believed that the eradication of poverty would help to eliminate guerrilla warfare and reduce the escalating scale of violence in the countryside. Unfortunately, his policies lacked substance, and he was widely criticized for his indecisiveness. President Gaviria feels that political reform must precede social and economic change and is confident that Colombia's new Constitution will set the process of national reconciliation in motion.

The constitutional debate generated some optimism about the future of liberal democracy in Colombia. As Christopher Abel wrote, it afforded a forum for groups ordinarily denied a voice in policy formulation—"to civic and community movements in the 40 and more intermediate cities angry at the poor quality of basic public services; to indigenous movements. . . ; and to cooperatives, blacks, women, pensioners, small businesses, consumer and sports groups." Unfortunately, the debates have not been transformed into a viable social policy. The distribution of income in Colombia has been deteriorating since 1983, and the significant improvement in the incomes of the poor in the 1970s has not been sustained. Successful social policy springs from committed politicians. But Colombia's political parties are in disarray, which in turn weakens the confidence of people in the ability of the state to govern.

ECONOMIC POLICIES

Colombia has a mixed economy. While state enterprises control domestic participation in the coal and oil industries and play a commanding role in the provision

| The first Spanish settlement at Santa Marta **1525** | Independence of Spain **1810** | The creation of Gran Colombia (including Venezuela, Panama, and Ecuador) **1822** | Independence as a separate country **1830** | War of the Thousand Days **1899–1902** | La Violencia; nearly 200,000 lose their lives **1946–1958** | Women's suffrage **1957** | |

1930s–1990s

César Gaviria is elected president; Congress undertakes constitutional reforms

Government offensive against guerrillas, narcotraffickers, and organized crime

Drug king Pablo Escobar is killed

of electricity and communications, most of the economy is dominated by private business. Colombia is a moderate oil producer, although recent attacks on pipelines and storage facilities by guerrillas have cut seriously into export earnings from this sector. A third of the nation's legal exports comes from the coffee industry, while exports of coal, cut flowers, seafood, and other nontraditional exports have experienced significant growth. In that Colombia is not saddled with an onerous foreign debt, its economy is relatively prosperous.

Contributing to economic success is the large informal sector. Also of tremendous importance are the profits from the illegal drug industry. *The Economist* estimated that Colombia grossed perhaps $1.5 billion in drug sales in 1987, as compared to official export earnings of $5.5 billion. Drugs contributed an estimated 4 percent of gross domestic product in 1989. Perhaps half the profits are repatriated—that is, converted from dollars into local currency. An unfortunate side effect of the inflow of cash is an increase in the inflation rate (which, at 26.8%, is still low by Latin American standards).

FOREIGN POLICY

In the foreign-policy arena, former President Barco's policies were attacked as low-profile, shallow, and too closely aligned to the policies of the United States. President Gaviria has taken a more independent line, especially in terms of the drug trade.

With an uneasy peace reigning in Central America, Colombia's focus has turned increasingly toward its neighbors and a festering territorial dispute with Venezuela over waters adjacent to the Guajira Peninsula. Colombia has proposed a multilateral solution to the problem, perhaps under the auspices of the International Court of Justice. Venezuela continues to reject a multilateral approach and seeks to limit any talks to the two countries concerned. It is likely that a continued deterioration of internal conditions in either Venezuela or Colombia will keep the territorial dispute in the forefront. A further detriment to better relations with Venezuela is justified Venezuelan fears that Colombian violence as a result of guerrilla activity, military sweeps, and drugs, will cross the border. As it is, thousands of Colombians have fled to Venezuela to escape their violent homeland.

More positively, Gaviria's support of free-trade initiatives has stimulated a bilateral trade with Venezuela. Mexico and Chile have also been targeted by the Colombian government for similar bilateral agreements to liberalize import policies, stimulate exports, and attract foreign capital.

THE CLOUDED FUTURE

Francisco Leal Buitrago, a respected Colombian academic, argues forcefully that his nation's crisis is above all "political." "It is the lack of public confidence in the political regime. It is not a crisis of the state itself. . . , but in the way in which the state sets the norms—the rules for participation—for the representation of public opinion. . . ." Constitutional reforms are considered a step in the right direction and, once completed, will be tested in new congressional elections. Significant changes include, in addition to no extradition to the United States, a ban on those currently holding public office to seek election unless they resigned before the middle of June 1991; a reduction in the number of senators; and the granting to the president of extraordinary special powers to be overseen by a commission chosen proportionally from parties represented in the next Congress. The Supreme Court's Office of the Constitution will be replaced by a Constitutional Court to guard the integrity of the Constitution.

Endemic violence and lawlessness, the continued operation of some guerrilla groups, the emergence of mini-cartels in the wake of the eclipse of drug kingpins such as Escobar, and the attitude of the military toward conditions in Colombia all threaten the new constitutional accord.

DEVELOPMENT

Colombia prepared to join the oil-producing nations of the world with the declaration that the rich Cusiana field, to the east of Bogotá, was commercial. Proven reserves might be as much as 2 billion barrels and could double Colombia's foreign exchange earnings in the near future.

FREEDOM

Colombia continues to have the highest rate of violent deaths in Latin America. Guerrillas, the armed forces, and right-wing vigilante groups are responsible for many deaths. Criminals, especially those connected to drug trafficking, are also the cause of much violence.

HEALTH/WELFARE

Rapid urbanization has led to a dramatic rise in the number of women in the work force. Women comprise about 41% of the active labor force; as a rule they earn 33% less pay than men for the same job. In the universities 40% of the student body are female, which augurs well for the future professional employment of women.

ACHIEVEMENTS

Colombia has a long tradition in the arts and humanities and has produced international figures such as the Nobel Prize–winning author Gabriel García Márquez; the painters and sculptors Alejandro Obregón, Fernando Botero, and Edgar Negret; the poet León de Greiff; and many others well known in music, art, and literature.

Ecuador (Republic of Ecuador)

GEOGRAPHY

Area in Square Kilometers (Miles):
276,840 (106,860) (about the size of Colorado)
Capital (Population): Quito
(1,200,000)
Climate: varied; tropical on coast and inland jungle; springlike year-round on Andean plateau

PEOPLE

Population
Total: 10,933,000
Annual Growth Rate: 2.2%
Rural/Urban Population Ratio: 44/56
Ethnic Makeup of Population: 55% Mestizo; 25% Indian; 10% Spanish; 10% black

Health
Life Expectancy at Birth: 67 years (male); 72 years (female)
Infant Mortality Rate (Ratio): 42/1,000
Average Caloric Intake: 97% of FAO minimum
Physicians Available (Ratio): 1/933

Religion(s)
95% Roman Catholic

Education
Adult Literacy Rate: 86%

COMMUNICATION

Telephones: 318,000
Newspapers: 22 dailies

TRANSPORTATION

Highways—Kilometers (Miles):
36,187 (22,435)

Railroads—Kilometers (Miles): 1,067 (661)
Usable Airfields: 142

GOVERNMENT

Type: republic
Independence Date: May 24, 1822
Head of State: President Sixto Durán-Ballén
Political Parties: Democratic Left Party; Social Christian Party; Concentration of Popular Forces; Broad Leftist Party; others
Suffrage: universal at 18; compulsory for literates

MILITARY

Number of Armed Forces: 57,800
Military Expenditures (% of Central Government Expenditures): 12.9%
Current Hostilities: unresolved long-smoldering dispute with Peru over a 49-mile stretch of border

ECONOMY

Currency ($ U.S. Equivalent): 1,890 sucres = $1
Per Capita Income/GDP: $1,070/$11.5 billion
Inflation Rate: 49.0%
Total Foreign Debt: $12.4 billion
Natural Resources: petroleum; fish; timber
Agriculture: bananas; coffee; cocoa; seafood; sugarcane; rice; corn; livestock
Industry: food processing; wood products; textiles; chemicals; fishing; petroleum

FOREIGN TRADE

Exports: $2.9 billion
Imports: $1.9 billion

THE NECESSARY INDIAN

Galo Plaza Lasso, the president of Ecuador from 1948 to 1952, once said:

Indians raise most of the food we eat in Ecuador. What nonsense it is to say that Indians are a drag on the economies of our Andean countries. Forty percent of Ecuadorians are Indians. Most of the rest are Mestizos. With love and understanding, the Indians are ready to forget four centuries of abuse and increase their stature in our society. We need their common sense—and their colorful dress.

Ecuador
- ✪ Capital
- • City
- River
- - - - Road

ECUADOR:
A LAND OF CONTRASTS

Several of Ecuador's great novelists have had as the focus of their works the exploitation of the Indians. Jorge Icaza's classic *Huasipungo* (1934) describes the actions of a brutal landowner who first forces Indians to work on a road so that the region might be "developed" and then forces them, violently, from their plots of land so that a foreign company's operations will not be impeded by a troublesome Indian population. That scenario, while possible in some isolated regions, is for the most part unlikely in today's Ecuador.

In recent years Ecuador has apparently made great strides forward in health care, literacy, human rights, press freedom, and representative government. Since 1990 Conaie, an organization of Ecuadorean Indians, has become increasingly assertive in national politics and reflects developments in other Latin American countries with significant indigenous populations. Nobel Peace Prize-winner Rigoberta Menchú, a Quiché-Mayan from Guatemala, has used her new-found position to intervene in favor of indigenous peoples in countries like Ecuador. Conaie, which has from time to time aligned itself with urban unions, has pressed for an agrarian-reform law from the center-right government of President Sixto Durán-Ballén.

Although Ecuador is still a conservative, traditional society, it has recently shown an increasing concern for the plight of its rural inhabitants, including the various endangered Indian groups inhabiting the Amazonian region. The new attention showered on rural Ecuador—traditionally neglected by policymakers in Quito, the capital city—reflects in part the government's concern with patterns of internal migration. Even though rural regions have won more attention from the state, social programs continue to be implemented only sporadically.

Two types of migration are currently taking place: the move from the highlands to the coastal lowlands and the move from the countryside to the cities. In the early 1960s, most of Ecuador's population was concentrated in the mountainous central highlands. Today the population is about equally divided between that area and the coast, with more than half the nation's people crowded into the cities. So striking and rapid has the population shift been that the director of the National Institute of Statistics commented that it had assumed "alarming proportions" and that the government had to develop appropriate policies if spreading urban slums were not to develop into "potential focal points for insurgency."

Despite the large-scale movement of people in Ecuador, it still remains a nation of regions. Political rivalry has always characterized relations between Quito, in the sierras, and cosmopolitan Guayaquíl, on the coast. The presidential elections of 1988 illustrated the distinctive styles of the country. Rodrigo Borja's victory was regionally based, in that he won wide support in Ecuador's interior provinces. Usually conservative in its politics, the interior voted for the candidate of the Democratic Left, in part because of the extreme populist campaign waged by a former mayor of Guayaquíl, Abdalá Bucaram. Bucaram claimed to be a man of the people who was persecuted by the oligarchy. He spoke of his lower-class followers as the "humble ones," or, borrowing a phrase from former Argentine President Juan Perón, *los descamisados* ("the shirtless ones"). Bucaram, in the words of political scientist Catherine M. Conaghan, "honed a political style in the classic tradition of coastal populism. He combined promises of concrete benefits to the urban poor with a colorful anti-oligarchic style."

EDUCATION AND HEALTH

Central to the government's policy of development is education. Twenty-nine percent of the national budget was set aside for education in the early 1980s, with increases proposed for the following years. Adult literacy improved from 74 percent in 1974 to 86 percent in 1993. In the central highlands, however, illiteracy rates of more than 35 percent are still common, largely because Quechua is still the preferred language among the Indian peasants.

The government has approached this problem with an unusual sensitivity to indigenous culture. Local Quechua speakers have been enlisted to teach reading and writing both in Quechua and Spanish. This approach has won the support of Indian leaders who are closely involved in planning local literacy programs built around indigenous values.

Health care has also shown steady improvement, but the total statistics hide sharp regional variations. Infant mortality and malnutrition are still severe problems in rural areas. In this sense Ecuador suffers from a duality found in other Latin American nations with large Indian populations—social and racial differences persist between the elite-dominated capitals and the Indian hinterlands. Income, services, and resources tend to be concentrated in the capital cities. Ecuador, at least, is attempting to correct the imbalance.

The profound differences between Ecuador's highland Indian and European cultures is illustrated by the story of an Indian peasant who, when brought to a

(United Nations photo)

The migration of the poor to the urban areas of Ecuador has been very rapid and of great concern to the government. The increase in inner-city population can easily lead to political unrest.

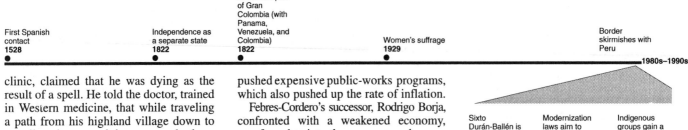

First Spanish
contact
1528

Independence as
a separate state
1822

Ecuador is part
of Gran
Colombia (with
Panama,
Venezuela, and
Colombia)
1822

Women's suffrage
1929

Border
skirmishes with
Peru
1980s–1990s

Sixto
Durán-Ballén is
elected president

Modernization
laws aim to
speed the
privatization of
the economy

Indigenous
groups gain a
national political
voice

clinic, claimed that he was dying as the result of a spell. He told the doctor, trained in Western medicine, that while traveling a path from his highland village down to a valley, he passed by a sacred place, where a witch cast a spell on him. The man began to deteriorate, convinced that this had happened. The doctor, upon examination of the patient, could find no physical reason for the man's condition. Medicine produced no changes. The doctor finally managed to save his patient, but only after a good deal of compromise with Indian culture. "Yes," he told the peasant, "a witch has apparently cast a spell on you and you are indeed dying." And then the doctor announced: "Here is a potion which will remove the spell." The patient's recovery was rapid and complete. Modern medicine can work miracles, but health care workers must also be sensitive to cultural differences that can spell the difference between life and death.

THE ECONOMY

The high expectations of the León Febres-Cordero administration, which was voted out of power in 1988, were dashed by poor and self-serving economic policies, compounded by the deterioration of Ecuador's export performance and a growing debt. Revenue fall-off from declining oil prices hurt the economy badly; to offset the lost revenues, the government was forced to contract more debt. Other export sectors, notably coffee, cocoa, and shrimp, could not compensate for the lost income. Rather than pursue a policy of fiscal restraint, Febres-Cordero, anxious to win a place in his nation's history as a man of accomplishment,

pushed expensive public-works programs, which also pushed up the rate of inflation.

Febres-Cordero's successor, Rodrigo Borja, confronted with a weakened economy, was forced to introduce an unpopular austerity program, including currency devaluation in the range of 75 percent, tax increases, import restrictions, higher fuel and electricity prices, and controls on banks on hard-currency transactions. A modest increase in the minimum wage temporarily prevented the United Workers' Front (FUT), the country's most powerful union confederation, from organizing serious opposition to the measures. By mid-1989, however, the FUT threatened a national strike if improvements in wages were not forthcoming. The confederation demanded an increase of more than 100 percent in the minimum wage (to raise it to the equivalent of $109 a month).

The government attempted to balance its unpopular economic measures with a show of nationalism, in terms both of Ecuador's economy and its foreign policy. President Borja announced that the state would assume control of four petroleum operations, two involving Texaco. The Trans-Ecuadorean pipeline became state-operated as of October 1989; oil fields managed by Texaco passed to full state control in July 1990.

On the other hand, Borja made some changes in the nation's policy that reflected the new impetus toward free-market economics. The government announced that foreign investors would enjoy the same rights and treatment as national investors. The current president, Sixto Durán-Ballén, has accelerated the pace of economic change and pushed a modern-

ization law that would result in the privatization of 160 state-owned enterprises and a reduction in the number of public employees from 400,000 to 280,000. Ecuador's unions have strongly resisted such policies, and Congress has tied the president's hands by repeatedly summoning his ministers to defend themselves against votes of censure by the Legislature.

HUMAN RIGHTS

Ecuador's human-rights record is among the best in the Western Hemisphere. Trade unions operate freely, and newspapers representing a broad spectrum of views are privately owned and are free from government intervention. Women are still considered second-class citizens, however—not because they are discriminated against by law, but rather because of a male-oriented cultural tradition.

With respect to the law, as is the case in most civil law (as opposed to English common law) systems, there is no trial by jury in Ecuador. Judges play a central role in investigations as well as in deciding guilt or innocence. Defendants have the right to counsel, to call witnesses on their own behalf, to cross-examine all witnesses, to refuse to testify against themselves, and to appeal sentences to higher courts. Inefficiency and corruption, however, often delay trials for 2 or more years.

DEVELOPMENT

Ecuador's development problems have been exacerbated by problems with debt negotiations with and interest payments to foreign creditors. Further complicating the picture is the uncertain future of petroleum revenues, which have fallen below expectations.

FREEDOM

Ecuador's media, with the exception of two government-owned radio stations, are in private hands and represent a broad range of opinion. They are often critical of government policies although they practice a degree of self-censorship in coverage involving high-level military personnel in corruption.

HEALTH/WELFARE

Educational and economic opportunities in Ecuador are often not made available to women, blacks, and indigenous peoples. Most of the nation's peasantry, overwhelmingly Indian or Mestizo, are poor. Infant mortality, malnutrition, and epidemic disease are common among these people.

ACHIEVEMENTS

Ecuadorian poets have often made their poetry an expression of social criticism. The so-called Tzántzicos group has combined avant-garde techniques with social commitment and has won a measure of attention from literary circles.

Guyana (Cooperative Republic of Guyana)

GEOGRAPHY

Area in Square Kilometers (Miles):
215,000 (82,990) (about the size of Idaho)
Capital (Population): Georgetown (170,000)
Climate: tropical; two rainy seasons (May to mid-August and mid-November to mid-January)

PEOPLE

Population
Total: 739,000
Annual Growth Rate: -0.6%
Rural/Urban Population Ratio: 61/39
Ethnic Makeup of Population: 51% East Indian; 43% African and mixed African; 4% Amerindian; 2% European and Chinese

Health
Life Expectancy at Birth: 61 years (male); 68 years (female)
Infant Mortality Rate (Ratio): 50/1,000
Average Caloric Intake: 110% of

FAO minimum
Physicians Available (Ratio): 1/5,307

Religion(s)
57% Christian; 33% Hindu; 9% Muslim; 1% others

Education
Adult Literacy Rate: 95%

COMMUNICATION

Telephones: 27,000
Newspapers: 1 daily

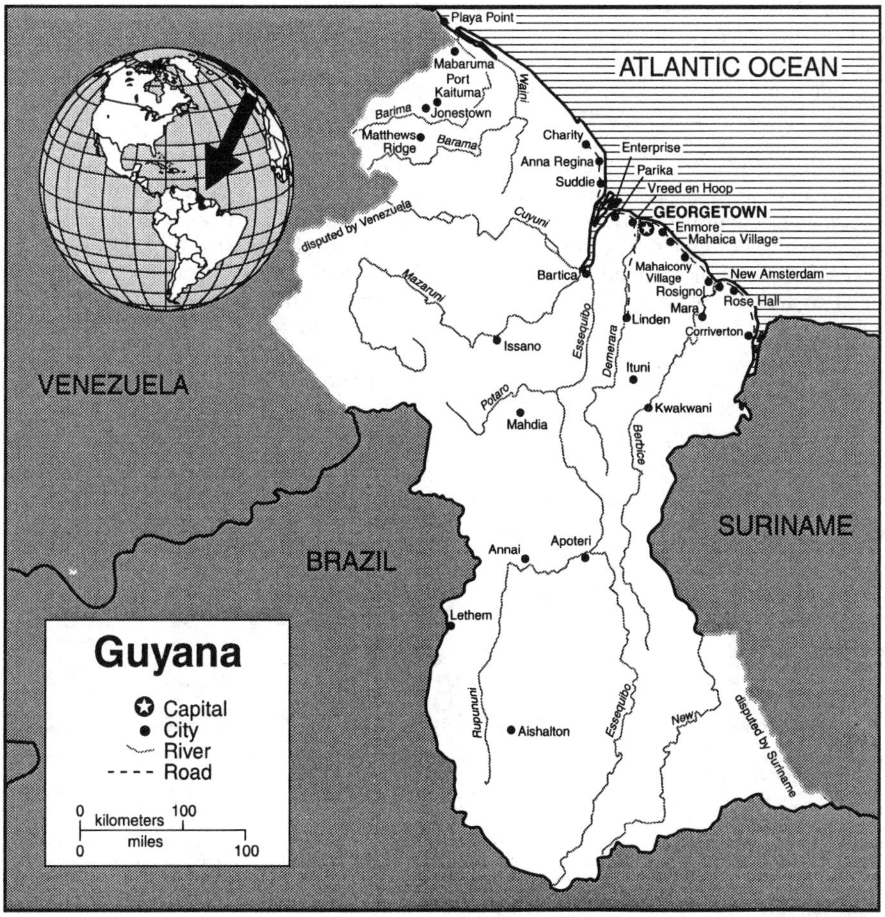

THE JUNGLE FALLS

Deep in the jungles of Guyana, the Potaro River cascades over the Kaieteur Falls. After a sheer drop of 741 feet over the edge of a sandstone plateau, the rushing water has gouged out a chasm 5 miles long. The falls are the central attraction of the Kaieteur National Park, which was established in 1930. Getting to the falls can be accomplished by car or boat, but the trip is easier by using a chartered aircraft out of the capital city of Georgetown.

TRANSPORTATION

Highways—Kilometers (Miles): 7,665 (4,760)
Railroads—Kilometers (Miles): 187 (116)
Usable Airfields: 49

GOVERNMENT

Type: republic within Commonwealth
Independence Date: May 26, 1966
Head of State: President Cheddi Jagan
Political Parties: People's National Congress; Working People's Alliance; People's Progressive Party; United Force; Democratic Labor Movement; People's Democratic Movement; National Democratic Front
Suffrage: universal at 18

MILITARY

Number of Armed Forces: 5,550
Military Expenditures (% of Central Government Expenditures): 6%
Current Hostilities: none

ECONOMY

Currency ($ U.S. Equivalent): 124.1 Guyana dollars = $1
Per Capita Income/GDP: $300/$250 million
Inflation Rate: 75%
Total Foreign Debt: $2.0 billion
Natural Resources: bauxite; gold; diamonds; hardwood timber; shrimp; fish
Agriculture: sugarcane; rice
Industry: bauxite mining; alumina production; sugar and rice milling

FOREIGN TRADE

Exports: $189 million
Imports: $246 million

Guyana
⊛ Capital
● City
River
---- Road

0 kilometers 100
0 miles 100

The first permanent Dutch settlements on Essequibo River
1616

The Netherlands cedes the territory to the United Kingdom
1814

Independence
1966

Territorial disputes with Suriname and Venezuela
1980s–1990s

President Forbes Burnham dies

President Cheddi Jagan backs away from wholesale privatization

The government promises to end racial and ethnic discrimination

GUYANA: ETHNIC TENSIONS

Christopher Columbus, who cruised along what are now Guyana's shores in 1498, named the region Guiana. The first European settlers were the Dutch, who settled in Guyana late in the sixteenth century, after they had been ousted from Brazil by a resurgent Portuguese Crown. Dutch control ended in 1796, when the British gained control of the area. In 1815, as part of the treaty arrangements that brought the Napoleonic wars to a close, the Dutch colonies of Essequibo, Demerera, and Berbice were officially ceded to the British. In 1831 the former Dutch colonies were consolidated as the Crown Colony of British Guiana.

Guyana is a society deeply divided along racial lines. East Indians make up the majority of the population. They predominate in rural areas, constituting the bulk of the labor force on the sugar plantations, and they comprise nearly all of the rice-growing peasantry. They also dominate local businesses and are prominent in the professions. Blacks are concentrated in urban areas, where they are employed in clerical and secretarial positions in the public bureaucracy, in teaching, and in semiprofessional jobs. A black elite dominates the state bureaucratic structure.

Before Guyana's independence in 1966, plantation owners, large merchants, and British colonial administrators consciously favored some ethnic groups over others, providing them with a variety of economic and political advantages. The regime of President Forbes Burnham revived old patterns of discrimination for political gain.

Burnham, after ousting the old elite when he nationalized the sugar plantations and the bauxite mines, built a new regime that simultaneously catered to lower-class blacks and discriminated against East Indians. In an attempt to address the blacks' basic human needs, the Burnham government greatly expanded the number of blacks holding positions in public administration. To demonstrate his largely contrived black-power ideology, Burnham spoke out strongly in support of African liberation movements. The government played to the fear of communal strife in order to justify its increasingly authoritarian rule.

In the mid-1970s, a faltering economy and political mismanagement generated an increasing opposition to Burnham that cut across ethnic lines. The government increased the size of the military, packed Parliament through rigged elections, and amended the Constitution so that the president held virtually imperial power.

There has been some improvement since Burnham's death in 1985. The appearance of newspapers other than the government-controlled *Guyana Chronicle* and the public's dramatically increased access to television has served to curtail official control of the media. In politics, the election of Indo-Guyanese leader Cheddi Jagan to the presidency reflects the deep-seated disfavor of the behavior and economic policies of the previous government of Desmond Hoyte. Indeed, Guyana's economic crisis has become endemic and has resulted in continued poor health care and shortages of essential foodstuffs. President Jagan has identified the nation's foreign debt of $2 billion as a "colossally big problem, because the debt overhang impedes human development."

Former President Hoyte at one time pledged to continue the socialist policies of the late Forbes Burnham but in the same breath talked about the need for privatization of the crucial sugar and bauxite industries. Jagan's economic policies, according to *Latin American Regional Reports,* have outlined an uncertain course. During his campaign Jagan stated that government should not be involved in sectors of the economy where private or co-operative ownership would be more efficient. But in 1993 he backed away from the sale of the Guyana Electric Company and had some doubts about selling off the sugar industry. In Jagan's words: "Privatisation and divestment must be approached with due care. I was not elected president to preside over the liquidation of Guyana. I was mandated by the Guyanese people to rebuild the national economy and to restore a decent standard of living."

DEVELOPMENT

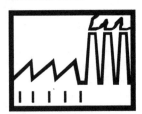

According to *Caribbean Contact,* President Jagan has decided to review the development record of the Hoyte government. Contracts with transnational gold, diamond, and oil companies that have allowed intensified exploitation of Guyana's Amazon rain forest will be renegotiated if they are perceived as a threat to the country's natural and social environments.

FREEDOM

One of the priorities of the Jagan government is the elimination of all forms of ethnic and racial discrimination, a difficult task in a country where political parties are organized along racial lines. Not to be ignored are Guyana's indigenous peoples, who will be offered accelerated development programs to enhance their health and welfare.

HEALTH/WELFARE

The government has initiated policies designed to lower the cost of living for Guyanese. Prices for essentials have been cut. Money has been allocated for school lunch programs and for a "food-for-work" plan. Pensions have been raised for the first time in years. The minimum wage, however, will not sustain an average Guyanese family.

ACHIEVEMENTS

The American Historical Association selected Walter Rodney for the 1982 Beveridge Award for his study of the Guyanese working people. The award is for the best book in English on the history of the United States, Canada, or Latin America. Rodney, the leader of the Working People's Alliance, was assassinated in 1980.

Paraguay

GEOGRAPHY

Area in Square Kilometers (Miles):
406,752 (157,048) (about the size of
California)
Capital (Population): Asunción
(607,000)
Climate: temperate east of the
Paraguay River; semiarid to the west

PEOPLE

Population
Total: 4,930,000
Annual Growth Rate: 2.9%
Rural/Urban Population Ratio: 52/48
Ethnic Makeup of Population: 95%
Mestizo; 5% white and Indian

Health
Life Expectancy at Birth: 71 years
(male); 74 years (female)
Infant Mortality Rate (Ratio):
28/1,000
Average Caloric Intake: 126% of
FAO minimum
Physicians Available (Ratio): 1/1,458

Religion(s)
90% Roman Catholic; 10%
Mennonite and other Protestant
denominations

Education
Adult Literacy Rate: 90%

COMMUNICATION

Telephones: 78,300
Newspapers: 5 dailies

SELLING POWER

The government of Paraguay is authoritarian but welcomes development by outsiders. This atmosphere may well allow Paraguay to realize
its great potential as an exporter of electric power. In fact, by the year
2000 it could be the world's largest producer of electric power. The first
hydro turbine is at the Itaipú Dam project on the Paraná River. This dam
was jointly constructed by Paraguay and Brazil, and there has been
international interest in the project.

TRANSPORTATION

Highways—Kilometers (Miles):
21,960 (13,637)
Railroads—Kilometers (Miles): 970
(602)
Usable Airfields: 716

GOVERNMENT

Type: constitutional republic with a
powerful executive branch
Independence Date: May 14, 1811
Head of State: President Juan Carlos
Wasmosy
Political Parties: Colorado Party;
Liberal Party; Radical Liberal Party;
Christian Democratic Party; Febrerist
Revolutionary Party; Popular
Democratic Party
Suffrage: universal and compulsory
from 18 to 60

MILITARY

Number of Armed Forces: 16,000
*Military Expenditures (% of Central
Government Expenditures):* 13.3%
Current Hostilities: none

ECONOMY

Currency ($ U.S. Equivalent): 1,447
guaranis = $1 (fixed rate)
Per Capita Income/GDP: $1,460/$7.0
billion
Inflation Rate: 15%
Total Foreign Debt: $1.7 billion
Natural Resources: hydroelectric
sites; forests
Agriculture: meat; corn; sugarcane;
soybeans; lumber; cotton
Industry: sugar; cement; textiles;
beverages; wood products

FOREIGN TRADE

Exports: $642 million
Imports: $1.8 billion

| The Spanish found Asunción 1537 | Independence is declared 1811 | War against the "Triple Alliance": Argentina, Brazil, and Uruguay 1865–1870 | General Alfredo Stroessner begins his rule 1954 | Women win the right to vote 1961 | 1980s–1990s |

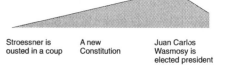

A COUNTRY OF PARADOX

Paraguay is a country of paradox. Although there is little threat of foreign invasion and guerrilla activity is insignificant, a state of siege was in effect for 35 years, ending only in 1989 with the ouster of President (General) Alfredo Stroessner, who had held the reins of power since 1954. Government expenditures on health care are among the lowest in the Western Hemisphere; yet life expectancy is impressive, and infant mortality reportedly has fallen to levels comparable to more advanced developing countries. On the other hand, nearly a third of all reported deaths are of children under 5 years of age. Educational achievement, especially in rural areas, is low.

Paraguayan politics, economic development, society, and even its statistical base are comprehensible only within the context of its geography and Indo-Hispanic culture. Geographic isolation in the midst of powerful neighbors has encouraged Paraguay's tradition of militarism and self-reliance—of strongmen who tolerate little opposition. There is no tradition of constitutional government or liberal democratic procedures upon which to draw. Social values influence politics to the extent that politics becomes an all-or-nothing struggle for power and its accompanying prestige and access to wealth. These political values, in combination with a population that is poor and politically ignorant, contribute to the type of paternalistic, personal rule characteristic of a dictator such as Stroessner.

The paradoxical behavior of the Acuerdo Nacional, a block of opposition parties under Stroessner, was understandable within the context of a quest for power or at least a share of power. Stroessner, always eager to divide and conquer, identified the Acuerdo Nacional as a fruitful field for new alliances. Leaping at the chance for patronage positions but anxious to demonstrate to Stroessner that they were a credible political force worthy of becoming allies, Acuerdo members tried to win the support of unions and the peasantry. At the same time, the party purged its youth wing of leftist influences.

Just when it seemed that Stroessner would rule until death, Paraguayans were surprised in February 1989 when General Andrés Rodríguez—second-in-command of the armed forces, a member of the Traditionalist faction of the Colorado Party, which was in disfavor with the president, and a relative of Stroessner—seized power. Rodríguez's postcoup statements promised the democratization of Paraguay, respect for human rights, repudiation of drug trafficking, and the scheduling of presidential elections. Not surprisingly, General Rodríguez emerged as President Rodríguez. When asked about voting irregularities, Rodríguez indicated that "real" democracy would begin with elections in 1993 and that his rule was a necessary "transition."

"Real" democracy, following the 1993 victory of President Juan Carlos Wasmosy, had a distinct Paraguayan flavor. Wasmosy won the election with 40 percent of the vote; and the Colorado Party, which won most of the seats in Congress, was badly divided.

Stroessner is ousted in a coup   A new Constitution   Juan Carlos Wasmosy is elected president

When an opposition victory seemed possible, the military persuaded the outgoing government to push through legislation to reorganize the armed forces. In effect, they were made autonomous. Unsettling were remarks made just days before the election when army strongman General Lino Oviedo said, according to *Latin American Regional Reports,* that "the military would not stomach an opposition victory [and] . . . that the military would 'co-govern' with the Colorado Party forever, 'whether anyone likes it or not, no matter who dislikes it, and no matter who squeals.' " What was clear was that the military is still the arbiter of Paraguayan politics.

It is difficult to acquire accurate statistics about the Paraguayan economy, in part because of the large informal sector and in part because of large-scale smuggling and drug trafficking. From the government's perspective, the economic problems are manageable. Wasmosy has promised to push ahead with plans to privatize the Paraguayan economy, but the military may stand in his way: The generals control the most important state-owned enterprises. There is also concern about the "Brazilianization" of the eastern part of Paraguay, which has developed to the point at which Portuguese is heard as frequently as Spanish or Guaraní, the most common Indian language.

DEVELOPMENT

Monies earned from the sale of state-owned companies, according to President Wasmosy, will be used, together with profits from the Itaipú hydroelectric facility, to create a national development fund. But, he emphasized, economic development should be led by the private sector.

FREEDOM

The continued domination of Paraguay's politics by the Colorado Party stems from its ability to dispense party patronage and to co-opt the opposition. Access to government positions, high ranks in the military and police, and lucrative contracts are usually offered to party members.

HEALTH/WELFARE

The Paraguayan government spends very little on human services and welfare. As a result, its population is plagued with health problems—including poor levels of nutrition, lack of drinkable water, absence of sanitation, and a prevalence of fatal childhood diseases.

ACHIEVEMENTS

Paraguay has produced several notable authors, including Gabriel Casaccia and Augusto Roa Bastos. Roa Bastos makes extensive use of religious symbolism in his novels as a means of establishing true humanity and justice.

Peru (Peruvian Republic)

GEOGRAPHY

Area in Square Kilometers (Miles): 1,280,000 (496,222) (about ⅚ the size of Alaska
Capital (Population): Lima (5,659,000)
Climate: coast area, arid and mild; Andes, temperate to frigid; eastern lowlands, tropically warm and humid

PEOPLE

Population
Total: 22,768,000
Annual Growth Rate: 2.0%
Rural/Urban Population Ratio: 30/70
Ethnic Makeup of Population: 45% Indian; 37% Mestizo; 15% white; 3% black, Asian, and others

Health
Life Expectancy at Birth: 63 years (male); 67 years (female)
Infant Mortality Rate (Ratio): 59/1,000
Average Caloric Intake: 98% of FAO minimum
Physicians Available (Ratio): 1/1,016

Religion(s)
more than 90% Roman Catholic

Education
Adult Literacy Rate: 85% (estimate)

COMMUNICATION

Telephones: 702,037
Newspapers: 12 dailies

TRANSPORTATION

Highways—Kilometers (Miles): 69,942 (43,364)

Railroads—Kilometers (Miles): 1,801 (1,118)
Usable Airfields: 201

GOVERNMENT

Type: constitutional republic
Independence Date: July 28, 1821
Head of State: President Alberto Fujimori
Political Parties: Change 90; Popular Action Party; American Popular Revolutionary Alliance; Popular Christian Party; United Left; Liberty Movement; Front of Workers and Peasants; Independent Mora Lizing Front; Socialist Left; Democratic Front
Suffrage: universal at 18

MILITARY

Number of Armed Forces: 120,000
Military Expenditures (% of Central Government Expenditures): 11.2%
Current Hostilities: none

ECONOMY

Currency ($ U.S. Equivalent): 2.02 soles = $1
Per Capita Income/GDP: $1,920/$20.6 billion
Inflation Rate: 56%
Total Foreign Debt: $19.4 billion
Natural Resources: minerals; metals; petroleum; forests; fish
Agriculture: coffee; cotton; cocoa; sugar; wool; corn
Industry: mineral processing; oil refining; textiles; food processing; light manufacturing; automobile assembly

FOREIGN TRADE

Exports: $3.3 billion
Imports: $3.5 billion

A LOST KINGDOM

Peru has an exciting and rich cultural history, as evidenced most dramatically by Machu Picchu and other influences and tangible remains of the Incas. In 1985 explorer Gene Savoy discovered another "lost kingdom," Gran Vilaya, in the rain forest of Peru north of Lima. Because of the inaccessibility of the region, archaeologists are just beginning to learn about this ancient culture. It has an exciting start: Savoy's expedition found stone complexes and terracing, indications of a well-organized and complex society.

Peru
- ✪ Capital
- ● City
- ⌇ River
- --- Road

PERU: HEIR TO THE INCAS

The culture of Peru, from pre-Hispanic days to the present, has in many ways reflected the nation's variegated geography and climate. While 55 percent of the nation is covered with jungle, coastal Peru boasts one of the world's driest deserts. Despite its forbidding character, irrigation of the desert is made possible by run-offs from the Andes. This allows for the growing of a variety of crops in fertile oases that comprise about 5.5 percent of the land area.

Similarly, in the highlands, or sierra, there is little land available for cultivation. Because of the difficulty of the terrain, only 6.8 percent of the land is able to produce crops. Indeed, Peru contains the lowest per capita amount of arable land in South America. The lack of good land has had—and continues to have—profound social and political repercussions, especially in the southern highlands near the city of Ayacucho.

THE SUPREMACY OF LIMA

Historically, coastal Peru and its capital city of Lima have attempted to dominate the sierra politically, economically, and, at times, culturally. Long a bureaucratic and political center, Lima in the twentieth century has presided over the economic expansion of the coast. Economic opportunity in combination with severe population pressure in the sierra have caused Lima and its port of Callao to grow tremendously in population, if not in services. Ironically, the capital city has one of the worst climates for dense human settlement. Thermal inversions are common and, between May and September, produce a cloud ceiling and a pervasive cool fog.

Middle- and upper-class city dwellers have always been ignorant of the people of the highlands. Very few are knowledgeable of either Quechua or Aymara, the Indian languages spoken daily by millions of Peruvians. Yet this ignorance of the languages—and by extension, of the cultures—has not prevented government planners or well-meaning intellectuals from trying to impose a variety of developmental models on the inhabitants of the sierra. In the late nineteenth century, for example, modernizers known collectively in Latin America as Positivists sought in vain to transform native culture by Europeanizing it. Other reformers sought to identify with the natives. In the 1920s a young intellectual named Victor Raúl Haya de la Torre fashioned a political ideology called APRISMO, which embraced the idea of an alliance of Indoamerica to recover the American

states for their original inhabitants. While his broader vision proved to be too idealistic, the specific reforms he recommended for Peru were put into effect by reform-minded governments in the 1960s and 1970s. Sadly, reform continued to be developed and imposed from Lima without an understanding of the rationale behind existing agrarian systems or an appreciation of a peasant logic that was based not on production of a surplus but on attaining a satisfying level of well-being. Much of the turmoil in rural Peru today stems from the agrarian reform of 1968–1979.

AGRARIAN REFORM

From the mid-1950s rural laborers in the central and southern highlands and on the coastal plantations demonstrated an increasingly insistent desire for agrarian reform. Peasant communities in the sierra staged a series of land invasions and challenged the domination of the large estate, or *hacienda,* from outside. Simultaneously, tenants living on the estates pressured the hacienda system from within. In both cases, peasants wanted land.

The Peruvian government responded with both the carrot and the stick. A military regime, on the one hand, tried to crush peasant insurgency in 1962 and, on the other, passed agrarian-reform legislation. The laws had no practical effect, but they did give legal recognition to the problem of land reform. In the face of continued peasant unrest in the south, the military enacted more substantial land laws in 1963, confiscating some property and redistributing it to peasants. The trend toward reform continued with the election of Francisco Belaunde Terry as president of a civilian government.

In the face of continued peasant militancy, Belaunde promised far-ranging reforms, but a hostile Congress refused to provide sufficient funds to implement the proposed reforms. Peasant unrest increased, and the government feared the development of widespread rural guerrilla warfare.

Against this backdrop of rural violence, the Peruvian military again seized power in 1968. To the astonishment of most observers, the military chose not to crush popular unrest but, rather, to embrace reforms. Clearly, the military had become sensitive to the political, social, and economic inequalities in Peru that had bred unrest. The military was intent on revolutionizing Peru from the top down rather than waiting for revolution from below.

In addition to land reform, the military placed new emphasis on Peru's Indian past. Tupac Amaru, an Incan who had rebelled against Spanish rule in 1780–1781, became a national symbol. In 1975 Quechua, the ancient language of the Inca, became Peru's second official language, along with Spanish. School curricula were revised and approached Peru's Indian heritage in a new and positive light.

NATIONALIZATION AND INTEGRATION

Behind the reforms, which were extended to industry and commerce and included the nationalization of foreign enterprises, lay the military's desire to provide for Peru a stable social and political order. The military leaders felt they could provide better leadership in the quest for national integration and economic development than could "inefficient" civilians. Their ultimate goal was to construct a new society based on citizen participation at all levels.

As is so often the case, however, the reform model was not based on the realities of the society. It was naively assumed by planners that the Indians of the sierra were primitive socialists and wanted collectivized ownership of the land. In reality, each family's interests tended to make it competitive, rather than cooperative, with every other peasant family. Collectivization in the highlands failed because peasant communities outside the old hacienda structure clamored for the return of traditional lands that had been taken from them over the years. The Peruvian government found itself, awkwardly, attempting to defend the integrity of the newly reformed units from peasants who wanted their own land.

THE PATRON

Further difficulties were caused by the disruption of the patron–client relationship in the more traditional parts of the sierra. Hacienda owners, although members of the ruling elite, often enjoyed a tight bond with their tenants. Rather than a boss–worker relationship, the patron–client tie came close to kinship. Hacienda owners, for example, were often godparents to the children of their workers. A certain reciprocity was expected and given. But with the departure of the hacienda owners, a host of government bureaucrats arrived on the scene, most of whom had been trained on the coast and were ignorant of the customs and languages of the sierra. The peasants who benefited from the agrarian reform looked upon the administrators with a good deal of suspicion. The agrarian laws and decrees, which were all written in Spanish, proved impossible for the

Machu Picchu, a famous Inca ruin, stands atop a 6,750-foot mountain in the Peruvian Andes.

peasants to understand. Not surprisingly, fewer than half of the sierra peasants chose to join the collectives; and in a few places, peasants actually asked for the return of the hacienda owner, someone with whom they could relate. On the coast the cooperatives did not benefit all agricultural workers equally, since permanent workers won the largest share of the benefits. In sum, the reforms had little impact on existing trends in agricultural production, failed to reverse income inequalities within the peasant population, and did not ease poverty.

The shortcomings of the reforms—in combination with drought, subsequent crop failures, rising food prices, and population pressure—created very difficult and tense situations in the sierra. The infant mortality rate rose 35 percent between 1978 and 1980, and caloric intake dropped well below the recommended minimum. More than one-half of the children under age 6 suffered some form of malnutrition. Rural unrest continued.

RETURN TO CIVILIAN RULE

Unable to solve Peru's problems and torn by divisions within the ranks, the military stepped aside in 1980, and Belaunde was again elected as Peru's constitutional president. Despite the transition to civilian government, unrest continues in the highlands, and the appearance of a left-wing guerrilla organization known as Sendero Luminoso (Shining Path) led the government to declare repeated states of emergency and to lift civil guarantees.

In an attempt to control the situation, the Ministry of Agriculture won the power to restructure and, in some cases, to liquidate the cooperatives and collectives established by the agrarian reform. Land was divided into small individual plots and given to the peasants. Because the plots can be bought, sold, and mortgaged, some critics argue that the undoing of the reform may hasten the return of most of the land into the hands of a new landed elite.

Civilian rule, however, has not necessarily meant democratic rule for Peru's citizens. This helps to explain the spread of Sendero Luminoso despite its radical strategy and tactics of violence. By 1992, according to Diego García-Sayán, the executive director of the Andean Commission of Jurists, the Sendero Luminoso controlled "many parts of Peruvian territory. Through its sabotage, political assassinations, and terrorist actions, Sendero Luminoso has helped to make political violence, which used to be rather infrequent, one of the main characteristics of Peruvian society."

Violence was not confined to the guerrillas of Sendero Luminoso or of the Tupac Amaru Revolutionary Movement (MRTA). Economist Javier Iguíñiz of the Catholic University of Lima told another WOLA forum that a solution to violence requires an understanding that it flows from disparate, autonomous, and competing sources, including guerrillas, right-wing paramilitary groups, the Peruvian military and po-

lice forces, and cocaine traffickers, "particularly the well-armed Colombians active in the Huallaga Valley." Sendero Luminoso is also active in the Huallaga Valley and profits from taxing drug traffickers. Raúl González of Lima's Center for Development Studies observed that as both the drug traffickers and the guerrillas "operate outside the law, there has evolved a relationship of mutual convenience in certain parts of Huallaga to combat their common enemy, the state."

Ex-President Alan García vacillated on a policy towards the Sendero Luminoso insurgency but ultimately authorized the launching of a major military offensive against Sendero Luminoso bases thought to be linked to drug trafficking. Later, determined to confront an insurgency that has claimed 22,200 victims over the past decade, President Alberto Fujimori armed rural farmers, known as *rondas campesinas,* to fight off guerrilla incursions. The arming of peasants is not new to Peru; it is a practice that dates to the colonial period. Critics correctly feared that the accelerated war against insurgents and drug traffickers would only strengthen the Peruvian military's political power.

A BUREAUCRATIC REVOLUTION?

Peruvian author Hernando DeSoto's best-selling and controversial book, *The Other Path* (as opposed to Sendero Luminoso, or Shining Path), argues convincingly that both left- and right-wing governments in Latin America in general and in Peru in particular are neomercantile—that is, both intervene in the economy and promote the expansion of state activities. "Both strengthened the role of the government's bureaucracy until they made it the main obstacle, rather than the main incentive, to progress, and together they produced, without consulting the electorate, almost 99 percent of the laws governing us." There are differences between left- and right-wing approaches: The left governs with an eye to redistributing wealth and well-being to the neediest groups, and the right tends to govern to serve foreign investors or national business interests. "Both, however, will do so with bad laws which explicitly benefit some and harm others. Although their aims may seem to differ, the result is that in Peru one wins or loses by political decisions. Of course, there is a big difference between a fox and a wolf but, for the rabbit, it is the similarity that counts."

DeSoto attacked the bureaucracy head-on when his private research center, the Institute for Liberty and Democracy,

The Inca Empire is at its height 1500	The Spanish found Lima 1535	Independence is proclaimed 1821	Women gain the right to vote 1955	Military coup: far-reaching reforms 1968	The Pope visits Peru: attacks adherents of liberation theology 1980s–1990s

President Alberto Fujimori executes a "self-coup"   Guerrilla activity declines with the arrest of key leaders   Elections are scheduled for 1995

drafted legislation to abolish a collection of requirements built on the assumption that citizens are liars until proven otherwise. The law, which took effect in April 1989, reflects a growing rebellion against bureaucracy in Peru. Another law, which took effect in October 1989, radically simplifies the process of gaining title to land. DeSoto discovered that to purchase a parcel of state-owned land in Peru, one had to invest 56 months of effort and 207 visits to 48 different offices. The legislation will have an important impact on the slum dwellers of Lima, for it will take much less time to regularize land titles as the result of invasions and seizures. Slum dwellers with land titles, according to DeSoto, invest in home improvements at a rate 9 times greater than that of slum dwellers without titles. Slum dwellers who own property will be less inclined to turn to violent solutions to their problems.

The debureaucratization campaign has been paralleled by grass-roots social movements that grew in response to a state that no longer could or would respond to the needs of its citizenry. Cataline Romero, director of the Bartolome de Las Cases Institute of Lima, told a WOLA forum that "grass-roots social movements have blossomed into political participants that allow historically marginalized people to feel a sense of their own dignity and rights as citizens."

Poor people have developed different strategies for survival as the government has failed to meet even their most basic needs. Most have entered the informal sector and have learned to cooperate through the formation of unions, mothers'

clubs, or cooperatives. Concluded Romero: "As crisis tears institutions down, these communities are preparing the ground for building new institutions that are more responsive to the needs of the majority." DeSoto concurs and adds: "No one has ever considered that most poor Peruvians are a step ahead of the revolutionaries and are already changing the country's structures, and what politicians should be doing is guiding the change and giving it an appropriate institutional framework so that it can be properly used and governed."

DEMOCRACY AND THE "SELF-COUP"

President Fujimori, increasingly isolated and unable to effect economic and political reforms, in April 1992 suspended the Constitution, arrested a number of opposition leaders, shut down Congress, and openly challenged the power of the judiciary. The military, Fujimori's staunch ally, openly supported the *autogolpe,* or "self-coup," as did business leaders and about 80 percent of the Peruvian people. In the words of political scientist Cynthia McClintock, writing in *Current History,* "Fujimori emerged a new caudillo, destroying the conventional wisdom that institutions, whether civilian or military, had become more important than individual leaders in Peru and elsewhere in Latin America." The president's popularity eroded somewhat in 1993 but was still relatively high. In November 1992 elections were held for a Constituent Assembly to effect constitutional reform. In 1993 it amended

the 1979 Constitution to allow Fujimori to run for a second consecutive term.

Much of the president's popularity stems from the fact that Peru's two major guerrilla groups, Sendero Luminoso and the MRTA, were badly mauled by security forces. The internal strife had cost 29,000 lives since 1980. The leaders of both groups had been captured and given life sentences, and most of MRTA's leadership surrendered. And the economy, even though still in difficult straits, has seen some improvement. Inflation fell off from a daunting 7,649 percent in 1990 to 56 percent in 1992; and the international community, with a leading role played by Japan, returned Peru to the good graces of the international financial community. Reportedly, Fujimori wants to devote greater state expenditure to social programs to create jobs and help the poor. With the defeat of terrorism, poverty and misery are the new enemies.

Whether Fujimori will survive depends not only on his continued popularity but also on the mood of the military. While he enjoys the support of the high command, Fujimori has also politicized the armed forces. Such a threat to the institutional integrity of the military could trigger a coup, especially if the economy fails to turn around dramatically.

DEVELOPMENT

Proposed amendments to the 1979 Constitution would give the primary role in the economy to the private sector. It would support the continued privatization of state-owned companies as well as Peru's pension system.

FREEDOM

President Fujimori's increasing centralization of power poses a threat to the civil and political rights of Peruvians. Proposed amendments to the Constitution would allow the president to dissolve Congress without cause, veto legislation, rule by emergency decree, and be eligible for immediate reelection.

HEALTH/WELFARE

The news magazine *Caretas* of Lima notes that violence against women in Peru has reached unprecedented levels. Much of the violence assumes the form of rape and murder perpetrated by security forces as well as the guerrillas of Sendero Luminoso. Offenders have not been punished.

ACHIEVEMENTS

Peru has produced a number of literary giants, including José Maria Mariategui, who believed that the "socialism" of the Indians should be a model for the rest of Peru; and Mario Vargas Llosa, always concerned with the complexity of human relationships.

Suriname

GEOGRAPHY

Area in Square Kilometers (Miles):
163,265 (63,037) (about the size of
Georgia)
Capital (Population): Paramaribo
(192,000)
Climate: tropical

PEOPLE

Population
Total: 410,000
Annual Growth Rate: 1.5%
Rural/Urban Population Ratio: 30/70
Ethnic Makeup of Population: 37%
Hindustani (East Indian); 31%
Creole; 15.3% Javanese; 10.3% Bush
Negro; 2.7% Amerindian; 1.7%
Chinese

Health
Life Expectancy at Birth: 66 years
(male); 71 years (female)
Infant Mortality Rate (Ratio):
34/1,000
Average Caloric Intake: 108% of
FAO minimum
Physicians Available (Ratio): 1/1,903

THE FIRST SYNAGOGUE

Suriname (once known as Guiana) was pretty much left alone by the
early Spanish and Portuguese explorers because of its lack of gold. The
first successful settlement was established by Britain's Lord Willoughby in 1651. Willoughby welcomed people from unsuccessful West
Indian and other South American colonies, who brought capital and
skills to the new settlement. Because of his policy, the first synagogue
in the Western Hemisphere was erected in Suriname in 1665 by Jewish
immigrants from Brazil.

Religion(s)
27% Hindu; 25% Protestants; 23%
Roman Catholic; 20% Muslim; 5%
others

Education
Adult Literacy Rate: 95%

COMMUNICATION

Telephones: 27,500
Newspapers: 2 dailies

TRANSPORTATION

Highways—Kilometers (Miles): 8,300
(5,154)
Railroads—Kilometers (Miles): 166
(103)
Usable Airfields: 40

GOVERNMENT

Type: military-civilian executive
Independence Date: November 25,
1975
Head of State: President Ronald
Venetiaan
Political Parties: New Front;
Progressive Reform Party; National
Democratic Party; National Party;
others
Suffrage: universal at 18

MILITARY

Number of Armed Forces: 2,950
*Military Expenditures (% of Central
Government Expenditures):* 9%
Current Hostilities: none

ECONOMY

Currency ($ U.S. Equivalent): 1.78
Suriname guilders = $1
Per Capita Income/GDP: $3,400/$1.4
billion
Inflation Rate: 50.0%
Total Foreign Debt: $138 million
Natural Resources: bauxite; iron ore;
minerals; forests; hydroelectric
potential; fish; shrimp
Agriculture: rice; sugarcane; bananas;
timber
Industry: aluminum; alumina; food
processing; lumber; bricks; cigarettes

FOREIGN TRADE

Exports: $594 million
Imports: $331 million

British
colonization
efforts
1650

The Dutch
receive Suriname
from the British in
exchange for
New Amsterdam
1667

Independence of
the Netherlands
1975

A military coup

1980s–1990s

The rural Maroon
insurgency ends

The election of
President Ronald
Venetiaan
restores civilian
government

Civilian/military
tensions continue

A SMALL-TOWN STATE

Settled by the British in 1651, Suriname, a small colony on the coast of Guiana, prospered with a plantation economy based on cocoa, sugar, coffee, and cotton. The colony came under Dutch control in 1667. In exchange, the British were given New Amsterdam (Manhattan, New York). The colony was often in turmoil because of Indian and slave uprisings, which took advantage of a weak Dutch power. When slavery was finally abolished, in 1863, plantation owners brought contract workers from China, India, and Java.

Suriname, on the eve of independence of the Dutch in 1975, was a complex multiracial society. Although existing ethnic tensions were heightened as communal groups jockeyed for power in the new state, other factors cut across racial lines. Even though Creoles (native-born whites) were dominant in the bureaucracy as well as in the mining and industrial sectors, there was sufficient economic opportunity for all ethnic groups, so acute socioeconomic conflict was avoided.

THE POLITICAL FABRIC

Until 1980 Suriname enjoyed a parliamentary democracy that, because of the size of the nation, more closely resembled a small town or extended family in terms of its organization and operation. The various ethnic, political, and economic groups that comprised Surinamese society were united in what sociologist Rob Kroes described as an "oligarchic web of patron-client relations" that found its expression in government. Through the interplay of the various groups, integration in the political

process and accommodation of their needs were achieved. Despite the fact that most interests had access to the center of power, and despite the spirit of accommodation and cooperation, the military seized power early in 1980.

THE ROOTS OF MILITARY RULE

In Kroes's opinion, the coup originated in the army among noncommissioned officers, because they were essentially outside the established social and political system—they were denied their "rightful" place in the patronage network. The officers had a high opinion of themselves and resented what they perceived as discrimination by a wasteful and corrupt government. Their demands for reforms, including recognition of an officers' union, were ignored. In January 1980 one government official talked of disbanding the army altogether.

The coup, masterminded and led by Sergeant Desire Bouterse, had a vague, undefined ideology. It claimed to be nationalist; and it revealed itself to be puritanical, in that it lashed out at corruption and demanded that citizens embrace civic duty and a work ethic. Ideological purity was maintained by government control or censorship of a once-free media. Wavering between left-wing radicalism and middle-of-the-road moderation, the rapid shifts in Bouterse's ideological declarations suggest that this was a policy designed to keep the opposition off guard and to appease factions within the military.

The military rule of Bouterse seemed to come to an end early in 1988, when President Ramsewak Shankar was inaugurated. However, in December 1990 Bouterse

masterminded another military coup. The military and Bouterse remained above the rule of law, and the judiciary was not able to investigate or prosecute serious cases involving military personnel.

With regard to Suriname's economic policy, most politicians see integration into Latin American and Caribbean markets as critical. The Dutch, who suspended economic aid after the 1990 coup, restored their assistance with the election of President Ronald Venetiaan in 1991. But civilian authorities are well aware of the roots of military rule and pragmatically allow officers a role in government befitting their self-perceived status.

In 1993 Venetiaan confronted the military when they refused to accept his choice of officers to command the army. Despite open attempts by military elements to intimidate the National People's Assembly, that body supported the president. Only the National Democratic Party, led by Bouterse, demurred. The beleaguered government welcomed a show of support from the Organization of American States, Venezuela, Brazil, and the United States. Most important, the Dutch government hinted that assistance could, when coordinated with the OAS, take a military form. In the words of one Dutch observer, "Bouterse will think twice before attempting to mount another coup."

DEVELOPMENT

Suriname's economy did not grow in 1992; and, to complicate matters, shortages of foreign exchange, inflation, and a vibrant parallel market were apparent. Economic assistance from the Dutch was expected to produce an improvement in 1993 and 1994.

FREEDOM

The Venetiaan government successfully brought to an end the Maroon insurgency of 8 years' duration. Under the auspices of the OAS, the rebels turned in their weapons, and an amnesty for both sides in the conflict was declared.

HEALTH/WELFARE

Amerindians and Maroons (the descendants of escaped African slaves) who live in the interior have suffered from the lack of educational and social services, partly from their isolation and partly from insurgency. With peace, however, it is hoped that the health, education, and general welfare of these people will improve.

ACHIEVEMENTS

Suriname, unlike most developing countries, has a small foreign debt and a relatively strong repayment capacity based on its export industry.

Uruguay (Oriental Republic of Uruguay)

GEOGRAPHY

Area in Square Kilometers (Miles):
176,215 (68,037) (about the size of
Washington State)
Capital (Population): Montevideo
(1,310,000)
Climate: temperate

PEOPLE

Population

Total: 3,142,000
Annual Growth Rate: 0.6%
Rural/Urban Population Ratio: 14/86
Ethnic Makeup of Population: 88%
white; 8% Mestizo; 4% black

Health

Life Expectancy at Birth: 69 years
(male); 76 years (female)
Infant Mortality Rate (Ratio):
23/1,000
Average Caloric Intake: 110% of
FAO minimum
Physicians Available (Ratio): 1/447

Religion(s)

66% Roman Catholic; 2% Protestant;
2% Jewish; 30% nonprofessing or
other

Education

Adult Literacy Rate: 96%

COMMUNICATION

Telephones: 337,000
Newspapers: 5 dailies; 210,000
circulation

CULTURAL LIFE

Uruguayan literary figures and artists have won worldwide acclaim.
The essayist José Enrique Rodo (1872–1917) has been called "the
greatest modernist prose writer." Another luminary was the short-story
writer Horacio Quiroga (1878–1937), whose jungle stories from the
Argentine province of Misiones made the outdoors a popular subject
for story material. The artist Joaquín Torres García (1874–1949) went
to Spain as an art student and studied under Joan Miró and Pablo
Picasso. It was Torres who introduced Picasso's style to South America.

TRANSPORTATION

Highways—Kilometers (Miles):
49,900 (30,988)
Railroads—Kilometers (Miles): 2,991
(1,854)
Usable Airfields: 83

GOVERNMENT

Type: republic
Independence Date: August 25, 1828
Head of State: President Luis Alberto
Lacalle
Political Parties: National (Blanco)
Party; Colorado Party; Broad Front
Coalition; Civic Union Party; New
Space Coalition
Suffrage: universal and compulsory
at 18

MILITARY

Number of Armed Forces: 25,200
*Military Expenditures (% of Central
Government Expenditures):* 9.2%
Current Hostilities: none

ECONOMY

Currency ($ U.S. Equivalent): 4.21
pesos = $1
Per Capita Income/GDP: $2,935/$9.1
billion
Inflation Rate: 60%
Total Foreign Debt: $4.2 billion
Natural Resources: soil; hydroelectric
potential; minerals (minor)
Agriculture: beef; wool; wheat; rice;
corn; sorghum; fish
Industry: meat processing; wool and
hides; textiles; footwear; leather
apparel; tires; cement; fishing;
petroleum refining

FOREIGN TRADE

Exports: $1.6 billion
Imports: $1.3 billion

Uruguay

⊗ Capital
● City
∿ River
- - - - Road

0 — 40 kilometers
0 — 40 miles

Jesuits and Franciscans establish missions in the region
1624

Uruguay is established as a buffer state between Argentina and Brazil
1828

The era of President José Batlle y Ordoñez; social reform
1903–1929

Women win the right to vote
1932

Tupamaro guerrillas wage war against the government
1963–1973

1980s–1990s

Luis Alberto Lacalle of the Blanco Party is elected president

Voters reject a government privatization plan

Constitutional reform becomes an issue

URUGUAY: ONCE A PARADISE

The modern history of Uruguay begins with the administration of President José Batlle y Ordoñez. Between 1903 and his death in 1929, Batlle's Uruguay became one of the world's foremost testing grounds for social change, and it eventually became known as "the Switzerland of Latin America." Batlle's Colorado Party supported a progressive role for organized labor and formed coalitions with the workers to challenge the traditional elite and win benefits. Other reforms included the formal separation of church and state, nationalization of key sectors of the economy, and the emergence of mass-based political parties.

Batlle's masterful leadership was aided by a nation that was compact in size; had a small, educated, and homogeneous population; and had rich soil and a geography that facilitated easy communication and national integration. Although the spirit of Batllismo eventually faded, Batlle's legacy is still reflected in many ways. Reports on income distribution reveal an evenness that is uncommon in developing countries. Extreme poverty is unusual in Uruguay, and most of the population enjoy an adequate diet and minimal standards of living. Health care is within the reach of all citizens. And women in Uruguay are granted equality before the law, are present in large numbers at the national university, and have access to professional careers.

Unfortunately, this model state fell on bad times beginning in the 1960s. Runaway inflation, declining agricultural production, a swollen bureaucracy, corruption,

and bleak prospects for the future led to the appearance of youthful middle-class urban guerrillas. Known as Tupamaros, they first attempted to jar the nation to its senses with a Robin Hood-style approach to reform. When that failed, they turned increasingly to violence and terrorism in an effort to destroy a state that resisted reform. The Uruguayan government was unable to quell the rising violence. Eventually it called on the military, which crushed the Tupamaros and then drove the civilians from power in 1973.

RETURN TO CIVILIAN RULE

In 1980 the military held a referendum on a new constitution. Despite extensive propaganda, 60 percent of Uruguay's population rejected the military's proposals and forced the armed forces to move toward a return to civilian government. Elections in 1984 returned the Colorado Party to power and José María Sanguinetti as president.

By 1989 Uruguay was again a country of laws, and its citizens were anxious to heal the wounds of the 1970s. A test of the nation's democratic will involved the highly controversial 1986 Law of Expiration, which effectively exempted military and police personnel from prosecution for alleged human-rights abuses committed under orders during the military regime. Many Uruguayans objected and created a pro-referendum commission. They invoked a provision in the Constitution that is unique to Latin America: Article 79 states that if 25 percent of eligible voters sign a petition, it will initiate a referendum, which, if passed, will implicitly annul the

Law of Expiration. Despite official pressure, the signatures were gathered. The referendum was held on April 16, 1989. It was defeated by a margin of 57 to 43 percent.

With respect to the Uruguayan economy, which is generally depressed, President Luis Alberto Lacalle has urged change on his country. But attempts to implement a privatization law were defeated in a referendum at the end of 1992. With more than 10 percent of the nation on the state payroll, a Congress dominated by the opposition, and elections scheduled for 1995, any attempts to privatize will experience political rough waters. Most of Uruguay's population are more comfortable with a shabby status quo. According to *The Wall Street Journal,* this widespread sentiment against change is a paradox: "The smallest and one of the richest countries per capita in South America is the one most vocal in its opposition to the free-market winds blowing throughout the continent." Uruguayans rely on the state and enjoy a cradle-to-grave welfare system. As Lacalle phrased it, "We were brought up in a country where the ethics of security overrode the ethics of change." The inability of the president to effect his policies has led him to suggest constitutional reform in order to give the executive office more power.

DEVELOPMENT

Although the Uruguayan people rejected the government's privatization plan, a previously announced sale of the state airline, PLUNA, went ahead. Four airlines, Vasp (Brazil), Iberia (Spain), Aerolíneas Argentinas, and American Airlines have all qualified to bid for PLUNA.

FREEDOM

Uruguay's military is constitutionally prohibited from involvement in issues of domestic security unless ordered to do so by civilian authorities. The press is free and unrestricted, as is speech. The political process is open, and academic freedom is the norm in the national university.

HEALTH/WELFARE

Uruguay compares favorably with all of Latin America in terms of health and welfare. Medical care is outstanding, and the quality of public sanitation equals or exceeds that of other developing countries. Women, however, still experience some discrimination in the workplace.

ACHIEVEMENTS

Uruguay, of all the small countries in Latin America, has been the most successful in creating a distinct culture. High levels of literacy and a large middle class have allowed Uruguay an intellectual climate that is superior to many much-larger nations.

Venezuela (Republic of Venezuela)

GEOGRAPHY

Area in Square Kilometers (Miles):
912,050 (352,143) (about the size of Texas and Oklahoma combined)
Capital (Population): Caracas (4,000,000)
Climate: varies from tropical to temperate

PEOPLE

Population
Total: 20,676,000
Annual Growth Rate: 2.4%
Rural/Urban Population Ratio: 16/84
Ethnic Makeup of Population: 67% Mestizo; 21% white; 10% black; 2% Indian

Health
Life Expectancy at Birth: 71 years (male); 78 years (female)
Infant Mortality Rate (Ratio): 23/1,000
Average Caloric Intake: 107% of FAO minimum
Physicians Available (Ratio): 1/643

Religion(s)
96% Roman Catholic; 4% Protestant and others

Education
Adult Literacy Rate: 88%

COMMUNICATION

Telephones: 1,440,000
Newspapers: 25 dailies

TRANSPORTATION

Highways—Kilometers (Miles):
77,785 (48,304)
Railroads—Kilometers (Miles): 542 (336)
Usable Airfields: 278

GOVERNMENT

Type: federal republic
Independence Date: July 5, 1821
Head of State: President Rafael Caldera
Political Parties: Social Christian Party; Democratic Action; Movement Toward Socialism; others
Suffrage: universal at 18

MILITARY

Number of Armed Forces: 51,000
Military Expenditures (% of Central Government Expenditures): n/a
Current Hostilities: none

ECONOMY

Currency ($ U.S. Equivalent): 118 bolívars = $1
Per Capita Income/GDP: $2,590/$53.2 billion
Inflation Rate: 30.7%
Total Foreign Debt: $30.9 billion
Natural Resources: petroleum; natural gas; iron ore; gold; hydroelectric power; bauxite
Agriculture: rice; coffee; corn; sugar; bananas; dairy; meat; poultry products
Industry: oil refining; iron-ore mining; petrochemicals; textiles; transport equipment; food processing

FOREIGN TRADE

Exports: $15.1 billion
Imports: $10.2 billion

VENEZUELA: CHANGING TIMES

Venezuela is a country in transition. After decades of rule by a succession of *caudillos* (strong, authoritarian rulers), national leaders can now point to more than 3 decades of unbroken civilian rule and peaceful transfers of presidential power. Economic growth—stimulated by mining, industry, and petroleum—has until re-cently been steady and, at times, stunning. With the availability of better transportation; access to radio, television, newspapers, and material goods; and the presence of the national government in once-isolated towns, regional diversity is less striking now than a decade ago. Fresh life styles and perspectives, dress and music, and literacy and health care are changing the face of rural Venezuela.

(United Nations photo/H. Null)

When oil was discovered in Venezuela, rapid economic growth caused many problems in national development. By depending on petroleum as the major source of wealth, Venezuela was at the mercy of the often fickle world energy market.

THE PROBLEMS OF CHANGE

Such changes have not been without problems. Venezuela, despite its petroleum-generated wealth, remains a nation plagued by imbalances, inequalities, contradictions, and often-bitter debate over the meaning and direction of national development. Some critics note the danger of the massive rural-to-urban population shift and the influx of illegal immigrants (from Colombia and other countries), both the result of Venezuela's rapid economic development. Others warn of the excessive dependence on petroleum as the means of development and are concerned about the agricultural output at levels insufficient to satisfy domestic requirements. Venezuela, once a food exporter, periodically has had to import large amounts of basic commodities—such as milk, eggs, and meat—to feed the expanding urban populations. Years of easy, abundant money also promoted undisciplined borrowing abroad to promote industrial expansion and has saddled the nation with a serious foreign-debt problem. Government corruption is rampant and, in fact, led to the impeachment of President Carlos Andrés Pérez in 1993.

THE CHARACTER OF MODERNIZATION

The rapid changes in Venezuelan society have produced a host of generalizations as to the nature of modernization in this Andean republic. Commentators who speak of a revolutionary break with the past—of a "new" Venezuela completely severed from its historic roots reaching back to the sixteenth century—ignore what is enduring about Venezuela's Hispanic culture.

Venezuela, before it began producing petroleum, was not a sleepy backwater. Venezuela's Andean region had always been the most prosperous area in the South American continent and was a refuge from the civil wars that swept other parts of the country. There were both opportunity and wealth in the coffee-growing trade. With the oil boom and the collapse of coffee prices in 1929, the Andean region experienced depopulation as migrants left the farms for other regions or for the growing Andean cities. In short, Venezuela's rural economy should not be seen as a static point from which change began but as a part of a dynamic process of continuing change, which now has the production of petroleum as its focus.

CULTURAL IDENTITY

Historian John Lombardi has identified language, culture, and an urban network centered on the capital city of Caracas as primary forces in the consolidation of the nation. "Across the discontinuities of civil war and political transformation, agricultural and industrial economies, rural life styles and urban agglomerations, Venezuela has functioned through the stable network of towns and cities whose interconnections defined the patterns of control, the directions of resource distribution, and the country's identity."

One example of the country's cultural continuity can be seen by looking into one dimension of Venezuelan politics. Political parties are not organized on class lines but tend to cut across class divisions. This is not to deny the existence of class consciousness—which is certainly ubiquitous in Venezuela—but it is not a major *political* force. Surprisingly, popular support for elections and strong party affiliations are more characteristic of rural areas than of cities. The phenomenon cannot be explained as a by-product of modernization. Party membership and electoral participation are closely linked to party organization, personal ties and loyalties, and charismatic leadership. The party, in a sense, becomes a surrogate *patrón* that has power and is able to deliver benefits to the party faithful.

AN IMPACT OF URBANIZATION

Another insight into Hispanic political culture can be found in the rural-to-urban shift in population that has often resulted in large-scale seizures of land in urban areas by peasants. Despite the illegality of the seizures, such actions are frequently encouraged by officials because, they argue, it provides the poor with enough land to maintain political stability and to prevent peasants from encroaching on richer neighborhoods. Pressure by the new urban dwellers at election time usually results in their receiving essential services from government officials. In other words, municipal governments channel resources in return for expected electoral support from the migrants. Here is a classic Hispanic response to challenge from below—to bend, to cooperate.

Cultural values also underlie both the phenomenon of internal migration and the difficulty of providing adequate skilled labor for Venezuela's increasingly technological economy. While the attraction of the city and its many opportunities is one reason for the movement of population out of rural areas, so too is the Venezuelan culture, which belittles the peasant and rural life in general. Similarly, the shortage

(United Nations photo)

From the rain forest to the Caribbean, from the Andes to vast inland plains, from peasant villages to large cities, Venezuela is an interesting and diversified country. This photo shows the modern capital city of Caracas, nestled in the northern coastal mountain range.

of skilled labor is not only the result of inadequate training but also of social values that neither reward nor dignify skilled labor.

THE SOCIETY

The rapid pace of change has contributed to a reexamination of the roles and rights of women in Venezuela. In recent years women have occupied positions in the cabinet and in the Chamber of Deputies; several women deputies have held important party posts.

Yet while educated women are becoming more prominent in the professions, there is a reluctance to employ women in traditionally "men's" jobs, and blatant inequality still blemishes the workplace. Women, for example, are paid less than men for similar work. Although modern feminist goals have become somewhat of a social and economic force, at least in urban centers, the traditional roles of wife and mother continue to hold the most prestige, and physical beauty is still often viewed as a woman's most precious asset. In addition, many men seek deference from women rather than embracing social equality. Nevertheless, the younger generations of Venezuelans are experiencing the social and cultural changes that have tended to follow women's liberation in Western industrialized nations: higher levels of education and career skills; broadened intellectualism; increasing freedom and equality for both men and women; relaxed social mores; and the accompanying personal turmoil, such as rising divorce and single-parenthood rates.

Venezuelans generally enjoy a high degree of individual liberty. Civil, personal, and political rights are protected by a strong and independent judiciary. Citizens enjoy a free press. There exists the potential for governmental abuse of press freedom, however. Several laws leave journalists vulnerable to criminal charges, especially in the area of libel. Journalists must be certified to work, and certification may be withdrawn by the government if journalists stray from the "truth," misquote sources, or refuse to correct "errors." But as a rule, radio, television, and newspapers are free and are often highly critical of the government.

The civil and human rights enjoyed by most Venezuelans have not necessarily extended to the nation's Indian population in the Orinoco Basin. For years extra-regional forces—in the form of rubber-gatherers, missionaries, and developers—have, in varying degrees, undermined the economic self-sufficiency, demographic viability, and tribal integrity of indigenous peoples. A government policy that stresses the existence of only one Venezuelan culture poses additional problems for Indians.

In 1991, however, then-President Pérez signed a decree granting a permanent homeland, encompassing some 32,000 square miles in the Venezuelan Amazon forest, to the country's 14,000 Yanomamö Indians. As James Brooke reported in *The New York Times,* "Venezuela's move has left anthropologists euphoric." Venezuela will permit no mining or farming in the territory and will impose controls on existing religious missions. President Pérez stated that "the primary use will be to preserve and to learn the traditional ways of the Indians."

Race relations are outwardly tranquil in Venezuela, but there exists an underlying racism in nearly all arenas. People are commonly categorized by the color of their skin, with white being the most prized. Indeed, race, not economic level, is still the major social-level determinant. This unfortunate reality imparts a sense of frustration and a measure of hopelessness to many of Venezuela's people, in that even those who acquire a good education and career training may be discriminated against in the workplace because they are "of color." Considering that only one-fifth of the population are of white extraction, with 67 percent Mestizos and 10 percent blacks, this is indeed a widespread and debilitating problem.

A VIGOROUS FOREIGN POLICY

Venezuela has always pursued a vigorous foreign policy. In the words of former President Luis Herrera Campins: "Effective action by Venezuela in the area of international affairs must take certain key facts into account: economics—we are a producer-exporter of oil; politics—we have a stable, consolidated democracy; and geopolitics—we are at one and the same time a Caribbean, Andean, Atlantic, and Amazonian country." Venezuela has long assumed that it should be the guardian of Simón Bolívar's ideal of creating an independent and united Latin America. The nation's memory of continental leadership, which developed during the Wars for Independence (1810–1826), has been rekindled in Venezuela's desire to promote the political and economic integration of both the continent and the Caribbean. Venezuela's foreign policy remains true to the Bolivarian ideal of an independent Latin America. It also suggests a prominent role for Venezuela in Central America. In the Caribbean, Venezuela has emerged as a source of revenue for the many microstates in the region; the United States is not without competitors for its Caribbean Basin Initiative.

PROMISING PROSPECTS TURN TO DISILLUSIONMENT

The 1980s brought severe turmoil to Venezuela's economy. The boom times of the 1970s turned to hard times as world oil prices dropped. Venezuela became unable to service its massive foreign debt (currently $30.9 billion) and to subsidize the "common good," in the form of low gas and transportation prices and other amenities. In 1983 the currency, the bolívar, which had remained stable and strong for many years at 4.30 to the U.S. dollar, was devalued to an official rate of 14.5 bolívars to the dollar. By early 1993 the exchange rate was approaching 110 bolivars to the dollar on the free market. This was a boon to foreign visitors to the country, which became known as one of the world's greatest travel bargains, but a catastrophe for Venezuelans.

President Jaime Lusinchi of the Democratic Action Party, who took office early in 1984, had the unenviable job of trying to cope with the results of the preceding years of free spending, high expectations, dependence on oil, and spiraling foreign debt. Although the country's gross national product grew during his tenure (agriculture growth contributed significantly, rising from 0.4 percent of GNP in 1983 to 6.8 percent in 1986), austerity measures were in order. The Lusinchi government was not up to the challenge. Indeed, his major legacy was a corruption scandal at the government agency Recadi, which was responsible for allocating foreign currency to importers at the official rate of 14.5 bolívars to the dollar. It was alleged that billions of dollars were skimmed, with a number of high-level government officials, including three Finance ministers, implicated. Meanwhile the distraught and economically pinched Venezuelans watched inflation and the devalued bolívar eat up their savings; the once-blooming middle class started getting squeezed out.

In the December 1988 national elections, another Democratic Action president, Carlos Andrés Pérez, was elected. Pérez, who had served as president from 1974 to 1979 (presidents may not serve consecutive terms), had been widely rumored to have stolen liberally from Venezuela's coffers during that tenure. Venezuelans joked at first that "Carlos Andrés is coming back to get what he left behind," but as the campaign wore on, some political observers were surprised to hear the preponderance of the perhaps naive sentiment that "now he has enough

President Carlos Andrés Pérez is suspended for alleged embezzlement of state funds

Some 200 die in a prison uprising, fanning tourists' fears; Venezuelan involvement in cocaine trafficking intensifies

Rafael Caldera is elected president in 1993

and will really work for Venezuela this time." It now appears that the early skepticism should have been heeded.

One of Pérez's first acts upon reentering office was to raise the prices of government-subsidized gasoline and public transportation. Although he had warned that tough austerity measures would be implemented, in February 1989 the much-beleaguered and disgruntled urban populace took to the streets in the most serious rioting to have occurred in Venezuela since it became a democracy. Army tanks rolled down the major thoroughfares of Caracas, the capital; skirmishes between the residents and police and military forces were common; looting was widespread. The government announced that 287 people had been killed. Unofficial hospital sources charge that the death toll was closer to 2,000. A stunned Venezuela quickly settled down in the face of the violence, mortified that such a debacle, widely reported in the international press, should take place in this advanced and peaceable country. But tourism, a newly vigorous and promising industry as a result of favorable currency-exchange rates, subsided immediately; it has yet to recover.

On February 4, 1992, an even more ominous event highlighted Venezuela's continuing political and economic weaknesses. Rebel military paratroopers attacked the presidential palace in Caracas and government sites in several other major cities. The coup attempt, the first in Venezuela since 1962, was rapidly put down by forces loyal to President Pérez, who escaped what he described as an as-

sassination attempt. Reaction within Venezuela was mixed, reflecting widespread discontent with Pérez's tough economic policies, government corruption, and declining living standards. A second unsuccessful coup attempt, on November 27, 1992, followed months of public demonstrations against Pérez's government. Perhaps the low point was reached in May 1993, when President Pérez was suspended from office and impeachment proceedings initiated. Allegedly, the president had embezzled more than $17 million and had facilitated other irregularities. Against a backdrop of military unrest, Ramón José Velásquez was named interim president. In December 1993 Venezuelans elected as president Rafael Caldera, who had been president in a more prosperous and promising era (1969–1974). How Caldera will go about lifting Venezuela out of recession and reestablishing public faith in social and political structures and institutions is not yet clear. Judith Ewell, writing in *Current History,* among other journalists, makes it clear that creative and positive steps must be taken soon to solve the country's deep problems. Seemingly relentless government scandals, the continuing devaluation of the bolívar, increased drug trafficking and related violence, military dissatisfaction, the collapse of one of Venezuela's major banks, and an appallingly high murder rate in the capital are among the most ominous signs that this once peaceable and progressive country is in dire need of decisive leadership.

The Venezuelan people have good reason to be anxious about how they will fare

in the future. The country is blessed with an extraordinary amount and diversity of geographic beauty and natural resources—including the versatile Venezuelans themselves. Whether or not Venezuela can retain its reputation as a model of democracy in Latin America will depend on the restraint of the military, a future-directed improvement in the economy, politicians willing to enact meaningful change that includes the elimination of corruption, and dedicated efforts to address widespread social problems, including worrisome inequities in the justice system. Because of its exceptional political, social, and economic history, the decisions that Venezuela makes in the next few years will be of acute interest not only to Latin America but to the entire world.

DEVELOPMENT

Even though the free-market policies of suspended president Pérez were unpopular, the interim government of President Velásquez made no radical changes; the strategy of the Caldera administration remains to be seen. The foreign debt, an inflation rate topping 30%, and capital flight continue to plague the Venezuelan economy.

FREEDOM

Venezuela has a free and vigorous daily press, numerous weekly news magazines, 3 nationwide television networks, and nearly 200 radio stations. Censorship or interference with the media on political grounds is rare. Venezuela has traditionally been a haven for refugees and displaced persons. "Justice" in the justice system remains elusive for the poor.

HEALTH/WELFARE

Rising unemployment and harsh economic austerity measures have taken a devastating toll on the poorest strata of the population, whose existence is marginal at best. The government is trying to maintain a commitment to improve education, housing, and public-health services for the disadvantaged but seems to be fighting a losing battle. Critics blame government corruption.

ACHIEVEMENTS

Venezuela's great novelists, such as Rómulo Gallegos and Artúro Uslar Pietri, have been attracted by the barbarism of the backlands and the lawlessness native to rural regions. Gallegos's classic *Doña Barbara,* the story of a female regional chieftain, has become world-famous.

The Caribbean

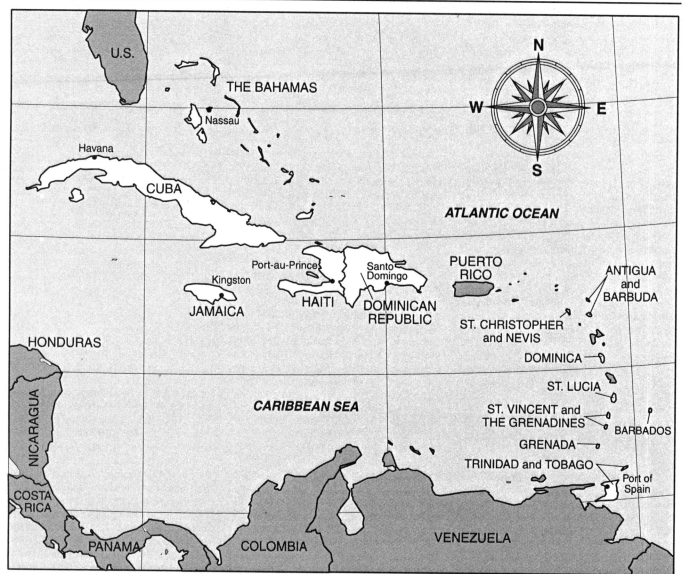

● Capital cities

The Caribbean region consists of hundreds of islands stretching from northern South America to the southern part of Florida. Many of the islands cover just a few square miles and are dominated by a central range of mountains; only Cuba has any extensive lowlands. Almost every island has a ring of coral, making approaches very dangerous for ships. The land that can be used for agriculture is extremely fertile; but many islands only grow a single crop, making them susceptible to fluctuations in the world market in that particular commodity.

The Caribbean: Sea of Diversity

To construct a coherent overview of the Caribbean is an extremely difficult task because of the region's geographical and cultural diversity. "The history of the Caribbean is the examination of fragments, which, like looking at a broken vase, still provides clues to the form, beauty, and value of the past." So writes historian Franklin W. Knight in his study of the Caribbean. Other authors have drawn different analogies: geographer David Lowenthal and anthropologist Lambros Comitas note that the West Indies "is a set of mirrors in which the lives of black, brown, and white, of American Indian and East Indian, and a score of other minorities continually interact."

For the geographer the pieces fall into a different pattern, consisting of four distinct geographical regions. The first contains the Bahamas as well as the Turks and Caicos Islands. The Greater Antilles—consisting of Cuba, Hispaniola (Haiti and the Dominican Republic), Jamaica, the Cayman Islands, Puerto Rico, and the Virgin Islands—make up the second region. Comprising the third region are the Lesser Antilles—Antigua and Barbuda, Dominica, St. Lucia, St. Vincent and the Grenadines, Grenada, and St. Kitts–Nevis as well as various French departments and British and Dutch territories. The fourth group consists of islands that are part of the South American continental shelf: Trinidad and Tobago, Barbados, and the Dutch islands of Aruba, Curaçao, and Bonaire.

No comparable area of Latin America has such a diversity of physical and human geography. Within the broad geographical regions, each nation is different. On each island there often is a firmly rooted parochialism—a devotion to a parish or a village, a mountain valley or a coastal lowland.

CULTURAL DIVERSITY

To break down the region into culture groups presents its own set of problems. The term "West Indian" inadequately describes the culturally Hispanic nations of Cuba and the Dominican Republic. On the other hand, "West Indian" does capture the essence of the cultures of Belize, the Caribbean coast of Central America, and Guyana, Suriname, and Cayenne (French Guiana). In Lowenthal's view: "Alike in not being Iberian [Hispanic], the West Indies are not North American either, nor indeed do they fit any ordinary

(United Nations photo/King)

These Jamaican agricultural workers, who reflect the strong African heritage of the Caribbean, contribute to the ethnic and cultural diversity of the region.

regional pattern. Not so much undeveloped as overdeveloped, exotic without being traditional, they are part of the Third World yet ardent emulators of the West."

FAILURE OF THE FEDERATION

To complicate matters further, few West Indians would identify themselves as such. They are Jamaicans, or Bajans, or Grenadans. Their economic, political, and social worlds are usually confined to the islands on which they live and work. In the eyes of its inhabitants, each island, no matter how small, is—or should be—sovereign. Communications by air, sea, and telephone are ordinarily better with the rest of the world than communications within the Caribbean. Trade, even between neighboring islands, has always been minimal. Economic ties with the United States or Europe, and in some cases Venezuela, are more important.

A British attempt to create a West Indies Federation in 1958 was reduced to a shambles by 1962. Member states had the same historical background; spoke the same languages, had similar economies; and were interested in the same kinds of food, music, and sports. But their spirit of independence triumphed over any kind of regional federation that "threatened" their individuality. In the words of a former Barbados prime minister: "We live together very well, but we don't like to live together *together*." A Trinidadian explanation for the failure of the federation is found in a popular calypso verse from the early 1960s:

Plans was moving fine
When Jamaica stab we from behind
Federation bust wide open
But they want Trinidad to bear the burden.

Recently, however, the Windward Islands (Dominica, Grenada, St. Lucia, and St. Vincent and the Grenadines) have discussed political union. While each jealously guards its sovereignty, leaders are nevertheless aware that integration is necessary if they are to survive in a changing world. The division of the world into giant economic blocs points to political union and the creation of a Caribbean state with a combined population of nearly half a million. Antigua and Barbuda resist because, in the words of Prime Minister Vere Bird, "political union would be a new form of colonialism and undermine sovereignty."

Similar problems plague the Dutch Caribbean. Caribbean specialist Aaron Segal notes that the six-island Netherlands Antilles Federation has encountered severe internal difficulties. Aruba has never had a good relationship with the larger island of Curaçao and has announced that it will declare its independence in 1995. "The other Netherlands Antillean states have few complaints about their largely autonomous relations with the Netherlands but find it hard to get along with one another."

Interestingly, islands that are still colonial possessions generally have a better relationship with their "mother" countries than with one another. Over the past few decades, smaller islands, with populations of less than 50,000, have learned that there are advantages to a continued colonial connection. Extensive subsidies paid by the United Kingdom, France, or the Netherlands have turned dependency into an asset. Tax-free offshore sites for banks and companies as well as tourism and hotel investments have led to modest economic growth.

CULTURAL IDENTIFICATION

Despite the local focus of the islanders, there are broad cultural similarities. To the horror of nationalists, who are in search of a Caribbean identity that is distinct from Western civilization, most West Indians identify themselves as English or French in terms of culture. Bajans—people from Barbados—take a special pride in identifying their country as "The Little England of the Caribbean." English or French dialects are the languages spoken in common.

Nationalists argue that the islands will not be wholly free until they shatter the European connection. In the nationalists' eyes, that connection is a reminder of slavery. After World War II, several West Indian intellectuals attacked the strong European orientation of the islands and urged the islanders to be proud of their black African heritage. The shift in focus was most noticeable in the French Caribbean, although this new ethnic consciousness was echoed in the English-speaking islands as well as in the form of a black-power movement during the 1960s and 1970s. It was during those years, when the islands were in transition from colonies to associated states to independent nations, that the Caribbean's black majority seized political power by utilizing the power of their votes.

It is interesting to note that, at the height of the black-power and black-awareness movements, sugar production was actually halted on the islands of St. Vincent, Antigua, and Barbuda—not because world market prices were low but because sugar cultivation was associated with the memory of the slavery of the past.

African Influences

The peoples of the West Indies are predominantly black, with lesser numbers of mixed bloods and small numbers of whites. Culturally, the blacks fall into a number of groups. In Haiti, blacks, throughout the nineteenth century, strove to realize an African-Caribbean identity. African influences have remained strong on the island, although they have been blended with European Christianity and French civilization. Mulattos, traditionally the elite in Haiti, have strongly identified with French culture in an obvious attempt to distance themselves from the black majority, who comprise about 95 percent of the population. African-Creoles, as blacks of the English-speaking islands prefer to be called, are manifestly less "African" than the mass of Haitians. An exception to this generalization is the Rastafarians, common in Jamaica and found in lesser numbers on some of the other islands. Convinced that they are Ethiopians, the Rastafarians hope to return to Africa.

Racial Tension

The West Indies have for years presented an image of racial harmony to the outside world. Actually, racial tensions are not only present but also have tended to become sharper during the past few decades. Racial unrest broke to the surface in Jamaica in 1960 with riots in the capital city of Kingston. Tensions heightened again in 1980–1981 and in 1984, to the point that the nation's tourist industry drastically declined. The recent slogan of the Jamaican tourist industry, "Make It Jamaica Again," was a conscious attempt to downplay racial antagonism. The black-power movement in the 1960s on most of the islands also put to the test notions of racial harmony.

Most West Indians, however, believe in the myth of racial harmony. It is essential to the development of nationalism, which must embrace all citizens. Much racial tension is officially explained as class difference rather than racial prejudice. There is some merit to the class argument. A black politician on Barbuda, for example, enjoys much more status and prestige than a poor white "Redleg" from the island's interior. Yet if a black and a Redleg competed for the job of plantation manager, the white would likely win out over the black. In sum, race does make a difference, but so too does one's economic or political status.

The East Indians

The race issue is more complex in Trinidad and Tobago, where there is a large East Indian (*i.e., originally from India*) minority. The East Indians, for the most part, are agricultural workers. They were originally introduced by the British between 1845 and 1916 to replace slave labor on the plantations. While numbers of East Indians have moved to the cities, they still feel that they have little in common with urban blacks. Because of their large numbers, East Indians are able to preserve a distinctive, healthy culture and community and to compete with other groups for political office and status.

East Indian culture has also adapted, but not yielded, to the West Indian world. In the words of the prize-winning contemporary Trinidadian author V. S. Naipaul: "We were steadily adopting the food styles of others: The Portuguese stew of tomato and onions . . . the Negro way with yams, plantains, breadfruit, and bananas," but "everything we adopted became our own; the outside was still to be dreaded. . . ." The East Indians in Jamaica, who make up about 3 percent of the population, have made even more accommodations to the cultures around them. Most Jamai-

(United Nations photo/Milton Grant)

The African influence on the population of the Caribbean is substantial; a large majority of African descendants are represented on just about every island. This woman is from Haiti.

can East Indians have become Protestant (the East Indians of Trinidad have maintained their Hindu or Islamic faith).

East Indian conformity and internalization and their strong cultural identification have often made them the targets of the black majority. Black stereotypes of the East Indians describe them in the following terms: "secretive," "greedy," and "stingy." East Indian stereotypes describing blacks as "childish," "vain," "pompous," and "promiscuous" certainly do not help to ease ethnic tensions.

REVOLUTIONARY CUBA

In terms of culture, the Commonwealth Caribbean (former British possessions) has little in common with Cuba or the Dominican Republic. But Cuba has made its presence felt in other ways. The Cuban Revolution, with the social progress that it entailed for many of its people and the strong sense of nationalism that it stimulated, impressed many West Indians. For new nation-states still in search of an identity, Cuba offered some clues as to how to proceed. For a time Jamaica experimented with Cuban models of mass mobilization and programs designed to bring social services to the majority of the population. Between 1979 and 1983, Grenada saw merit in the Cuban approach to problems. The message that Cuba seemed to represent was that a small Caribbean state could shape its own destiny and make life better for its people.

The Cuba of Fidel Castro, while revolutionary, is also traditional. Hispanic culture is largely intact. The politics are authoritarian and personalist, and Castro himself easily fits into the mold of the Latin American leader, or *caudillo,* whose charisma and benevolent paternalism win him the widespread support of his people. Castro's relationship with the Roman Catholic Church is also traditional and corresponds to notions of a dualistic culture that has its roots in the Middle Ages. In Castro's words: "The same respect that the Revolution ought to have for religious beliefs, ought also to be had by those who talk in the name of religion for the political beliefs of others. And, above all, to have present that which Christ said: 'My kingdom is not of this world.' What are those who are said to be the interpreters of Christian thought doing meddling in the problems of this world?" Castro's comments should not be interpreted as a communist assault on religion. Rather, they express a time-honored Hispanic belief that religious life and everyday life exist in two separate spheres.

The social reforms that have been implemented in Cuba are well within the powers of all Latin American governments to enact. Those governments, in theory, are duty-bound to provide for the welfare of their peoples. Constitutionally, the state is infallible and all-powerful. Castro has chosen to identify with the needs of the majority of Cubans, to be a "father" to his people. Again, his actions are not so much communistic as Hispanic.

Where Castro has run against the grain is in his assault on Cuba's middle class. In a sense, he has reversed a trend that is evident in much of the rest of Latin America—the slow, steady progress of a middle class that is intent on acquiring a share of the power and prestige traditionally accorded to elites. Cuba's middle class was effectively shattered—deprived of much of their property; their livelihood; and, for those who fled into exile, their citizenship. Expatriate Cubans remain bitter toward what they see as Castro's betrayal of the Revolution and the middle class.

(United Nations photo/M. Hopp)

Certain crops in Caribbean countries generate a disproportionate amount of the nations' foreign incomes—so much so that their entire economies are susceptible to world demand. This harvest of bananas in Dominica is ready for shipment to a fickle world market.

EMIGRATION AND MIGRATION

Throughout the Caribbean emigration and migration are a fact of life for hundreds of thousands of people. These are not new phenomena; their roots extend to the earliest days of European settlement. The flow of people looking for work is deeply rooted in history, in contemporary political economy, and even in Caribbean island culture. The Garifuna (black-Indian mixture) who settled in Belize and coastal parts of Mexico, Guatemala, Honduras, and Nicaragua originally came from St. Vincent. There, as escaped slaves, they intermixed with remnants of Indian tribes who had once peopled the islands, and adopted many of their cultural traits. Most of the Garifuna (or Black Caribs, as they are also known) were deported from St. Vincent to the Caribbean coast of Central America at the end of the eighteenth century.

From the 1880s onward, *patois*-speaking (French dialect) Dominicans and St. Lucians migrated to Cayenne (French Guiana) to work in the gold fields. The strong identification with Europe has drawn thousands more to what many consider their cultural homes. High birth rates and lack of economic opportunity have forced others to seek their fortunes elsewhere. Many citizens of the Dominican Republic have moved to New York, and Haitian "boat people" have thrown themselves on the coast of Florida by the thousands. Other Haitians seek seasonal employment in the Dominican Republic or the Bahamas.

On the smaller islands, stable populations are the exception rather than the rule. The people are constantly out-migrating to larger places in search of higher pay and a better life. Such emigrants moved to Panama when the canal was being cut in the early days of this century or sought work on the Dutch islands of Curaçao and Aruba when oil refineries were built there in the 1920s. They provided much of the labor for the banana plantations in Central America. There are sizable Jamaican communities in the Dominican Republic, Haiti, the Bahamas, and Belize.

The greatest number by far have left the region altogether and emigrated to the United States, Canada, and Europe. Added to those who have left because of economic or population pressures are political refugees. The majority of these are Cubans, most of whom have resettled in southern Florida.

Some have argued that the prime mover of migration from the Caribbean lies in the ideology of migration—that is, the expectation that all nonelite males will migrate abroad. Sugarcane slave plantations left a legacy that included little possibility of island subsistence; and so there grew the need to migrate to survive, a fact that was absorbed into the culture of lower-class blacks. But for these blacks there has also existed the expectation to return. (In contrast, middle- and upper-class migrants have historically departed permanently.) Historian Bonham Richardson has written: "By traveling away and returning the people have been able to cope more successfully with the vagaries of man and nature than they would have by staying at home. The small islands of the region are the most vulnerable to environmental and economic uncertainty. Time and again in the Lesser Antilles, droughts, hurricanes, and economic

(United Nations photo/J. Viesti)

Poverty in the Caribbean region is exemplified by this settlement in Port-au-Prince, Haiti. Such grinding poverty causes large numbers of people to migrate in search of a better life.

depressions have diminished wages, desiccated provision grounds, and destroyed livestock, and there has been no local recourse to disease or starvation." Hence men and women of the small West Indian islands have been obliged to migrate. "And like migrants everywhere, they have usually considered their travels temporary, partly because they have never been greeted cordially in host communities."

On the smaller islands, such as St. Kitts and Nevis, family and community ceremonies traditionally reinforce and sustain the importance of immigration and return. Funerals reunite families separated by vast distances; Christmas parties and carnival celebrations are also occasions to welcome returning family and friends. Monetary remittances from relatives in the United States, or Canada, or the larger islands are a constant reminder of the importance of migration. According to Richardson: "Old men who have earned local prestige by migrating and returning exhort younger men to follow in their footsteps . . . Learned cultural responses thereby maintain a migration ethos . . . that is not only valuable in coping with contemporary problems, but also provides continuity with the past."

The Haitian diaspora offers some significant differences. While Haitian migration is also a part of the nation's history, a return flow is noticeably absent. One of every six Haitians now lives abroad—primarily in Cuba, the Dominican Republic, Venezuela, Colombia, Mexico, and the Bahamas. In French Guiana, Haitians now comprise more than 25 percent of the population. They are also found in large numbers in urban areas of the United States, Canada, and France. The typical Haitian emigrant is poor, has little education, and has few skills or job qualifications.

Scholar Christian A. Girault remarked that, although "ordinary Haitian migrants are clearly less educated than the Cubans, Dominicans, Puerto Ricans and even Jamaicans, they are not Haiti's most miserable; the latter could never hope to buy an air ticket or boat passage, or to pay an agent." Those who establish new roots in host countries tend to remain, even though they experience severe discrimination and are stereotyped as "undesirable" because they bring with them "misery, magic and disease," particularly AIDS.

There is also some seasonal movement of population on the island. Agricultural workers by the tens of thousands are found in neighboring Dominican Republic. *Madames sara,* or peddlars, buy and sell consumer goods abroad and provide "an essential provisioning function for the national market." And students studying abroad are expected to return to Haiti upon completion of their educations.

AN ENVIRONMENT IN DANGER

When one speaks of soil erosion and deforestation in a Caribbean context, Haiti is the example that usually springs to mind. While that image is accurate, it is also too limiting,

for much of the Caribbean is threatened with ecological disaster. Part of the problem is historical, for deforestation began with the development of sugarcane cultivation in the seventeenth century. But now soil erosion and depletion as well as the exploitation of marginal lands by growing populations perpetuate a vicious cycle between inhabitants and the land on which they live. Cultivation of sloping hillsides creates a situation in which erosion is constant.

A 1959 report on soil conditions in Jamaica noted that in one district of the Blue Mountains, on the eastern end of that island, the topsoil had vanished, a victim of rapid erosion. The problem is not unique to the large islands, however. Bonham Richardson observes that ecological degradation on the smallest islands is acute. Thorn scrub and grasses have replaced native forest. "A regional drought in 1977, leading to starvation in Haiti and producing crop and livestock loss south to Trinidad, was severe only partly because of the lack of rain. Grasses and shrubs afford little protection against the sun and thus cannot help the soil to retain moisture in the face of periodic drought. Neither do they inhibit soil loss."

Migration of the islands' inhabitants has at times exacerbated the situation. In times of peak migration, a depleted labor force on some of the islands has resulted in landowners resorting to the raising of livestock, which is not labor intensive. But livestock contribute to further ecological destruction. "Emigration itself has thus indirectly fed the ongoing devastation of island environments, and some of the changes seem irreversible. Parts of the smaller islands already resemble moonscapes. They seem simply unable to sustain their local resident populations, not to mention future generations or those working abroad who may someday be forced to return for good."

MUSIC, DANCE, FOLKLORE, AND FOOD

Travel accounts of the Caribbean tend to focus on local music, dances, and foods. Calypso, the limbo, steel bands, reggae, and African–Cuban rhythms are well known. Much of the music derives from Amerindian and African roots. Calypso music apparently originated in Trinidad and spread to the other islands. Singers improvise on any theme and are particularly adept at poking fun at politicians and their shortcomings. Indeed, governments are as attentive to the lyrics of a politically inspired calypso tune as they are to the opposition press. On a broader scale, calypso is a mirror of West Indian society.

Some traditional folkways, such as storytelling and other forms of oral history, are in danger of being replaced by electronic media, particularly radio, tape recorders, and jukeboxes. The new entertainment is both popular and readily available.

Scholar Laura Tanna has gathered much of Kingston, Jamaica's, oral history. Her quest for storyteller Adina

Henry took her to one of the city's worst slums, the Dungle, and was reprinted in *Caribbean Review:* "We walked down the tracks to a Jewish cemetery, with gravestones dating back to the 1600s. It, too, was covered in litter, decaying amid the rubble of broken stones. Four of the tombs bear the emblem of the skull and crossbones. Popular belief has it that Spanish gold is buried in the tombs, and several of them have been desecrated by treasure seekers. We passed the East Indian shacks, and completed our tour of Majesty Pen amidst greetings of 'Love' and 'Peace' and with the fragrance of ganja wafting across the way. Everywhere, people were warm and friendly, shaking hands, chatting, drinking beer, or playing dominos. One of the shacks had a small bar and jukebox inside. There, in the midst of pigs grunting at one's feet in the mud and slime, in the dirt and dust, people had their own jukeboxes, tape recorders, and radios, all blaring out reggae, the voice of the ghetto." Tanna found Miss Adina, whose stories revealed the significant African contribution to West Indian folk culture.

In recent years Caribbean foods have become more accepted than ever before. Part of the search for an identity involves a new attention to traditional recipes. French, Spanish, and English recipes have been adapted to local foods—iguana, frogs, seafood, fruits, and vegetables. Cassava, guava, and mangoes figure prominently in the islanders' diets.

The diversity of the Caribbean is awesome, with its potpourri of peoples and cultures. Its roots lie in Spain, Portugal, England, France, the Netherlands, Africa, India, China, and Japan. There has emerged no distinct West Indian culture, and the Caribbean peoples' identities are determined by the island—no matter how small—on which they live. For the Commonwealth Caribbean, nationalist stirrings are still weak and lacking in focus; while Cuba and the Dominican Republic have a much surer grasp on who they are. Nationalism is a strong integrating force in both of these nations. The Caribbean is a fascinating corner of the world that is far more complex than the travel posters imply.

Antigua and Barbuda

GEOGRAPHY

Area in Square Kilometers (Miles):
442 (171) (about 2½ times the size
of Washington, D.C.)
Capital (Population): Saint John's
(27,000)
Climate: tropical

PEOPLE

Population
Total: 64,000
Annual Growth Rate: 0.4%
Rural/Urban Population Ratio: 66/34
Ethnic Makeup of Population: almost
entirely black African origin; some of
British, Portuguese, Lebanese, or
Syrian origin

Health
Life Expectancy at Birth: 71 years
(male); 75 years (female)
Infant Mortality Rate (Ratio):
20/1,000
Average Caloric Intake: 90% of FAO
minimum
Physicians Available (Ratio): 1/2,187

Religion(s)
predominantly Anglican; other
Protestant sects; some Roman Catholic

Education
Adult Literacy Rate: 89%

COMMUNICATION

Telephones: 6,700
Newspapers: n/a

ENGLISH HARBOUR

English Harbour in Antigua was the key to British naval power in the
Caribbean—it was the stop-off where warships were refitted in order
to avoid having to go to England. By the end of the eighteenth century,
English Harbour was at its zenith and its dockyard could handle almost
any need of the British warships. There were more than 1,000 troops in
the shore guard; and the harbor was a crowded and lively place, with
constant parties and pageants. The importance of the English Harbour
gave the small, arid island of Antigua a lasting role in the history of the
Caribbean.

TRANSPORTATION

Highways—Kilometers (Miles): 240
(150)
Railroads—Kilometers (Miles): 64
(40)
Usable Airfields: 3

GOVERNMENT

Type: parliamentary democracy;
independent state; recognizes Queen
Elizabeth II as chief of state
Independence Date: November 1,
1981
Head of State: Prime Minister Vere
C. Bird
Political Parties: Antigua Labour
Party; United Progressive Party
Suffrage: universal at 18

MILITARY

Number of Armed Forces: 700 in
defense force
*Military Expenditures (% of Central
Government Expenditures):* n/a
Current Hostilities: none

ECONOMY

Currency ($ U.S. Equivalent): 2.7
East Caribbean dollars = $1
Per Capita Income/GDP:
$6,500/$418 million
Inflation Rate: 7.0%
Total Foreign Debt: $250 million
Natural Resources: seafood
Agriculture: cotton
Industry: tourism; cotton production

FOREIGN TRADE

Exports: $33.2 million
Imports: $326 million

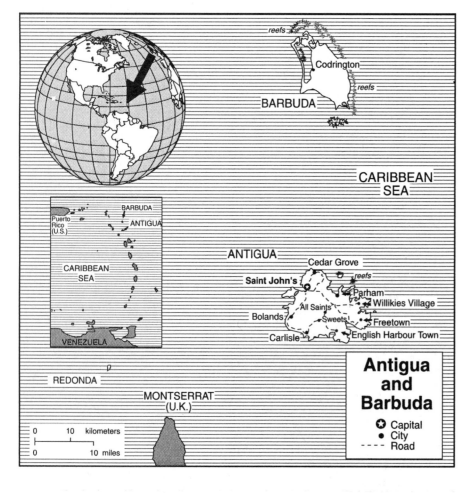

The English
settle Antigua
1632

Antigua
abolishes slavery
1834

Antigua becomes
part of the West
Indies Federation
1958–1962

Independence of
the United
Kingdom

1980s–1990s

The Organization
of Eastern
Caribbean States
proposes political
unity

Barbuda talks of
secession

The Bird
administration is
accused of
widespread
corruption

ANTIGUA AND BARBUDA: A STRAINED RELATIONSHIP

The nation of Antigua and Barbuda gained its independence of the United Kingdom on November 1, 1981. Both islands, tenuously linked since 1967, illustrate perfectly the degree of localism characteristic of the West Indies. Barbudans—who number approximately 1,200—culturally and politically believe that they are not Antiguans; indeed, since independence of Britain they have been intent on secession. Barbudans view Antiguans as little more than colonial masters.

MEMORIES OF SLAVERY

Antigua was a sugar island for most of its history. This image changed radically in the 1960s, when the black-power movement then sweeping the West Indies convinced Antiguans that work on the sugar plantations was "submissive" and carried the psychological and social stigma of historic slave labor. In response to the clamor, the government gradually phased out sugar production, which ended entirely in 1972. The decline of agriculture resulted in a strong rural-to-urban flow of people. To replace lost revenue from the earnings of sugar, the government promoted tourism.

Tourism, however, also created tension. Most of the hotel industry was owned by foreigners, and some of the exclusive clubs were all but racist. One, the prestigious Mill Reef Club, was for whites only and was physically separated from the rest of the island by a high barbed-wire fence.

RE-CREATION OF THE SUGAR INDUSTRY

Convinced that sugar imports were a foolish waste of badly needed revenue, the Antiguan government reactivated the production of sugar in 1981, but on a scale sufficient only to meet local needs. As a result, in 1984 agriculture accounted for less than 15 percent of the gross domestic product. This figure dropped to 7 percent in 1986. Rebuilding the agricultural sector, including the sugar industry, is a priority for the government, which has initiated a "back to the land" movement and has provided financial incentives for young men and women willing to work in the agricultural sector.

CULTURAL PATTERNS

Antiguans and Barbudans are culturally similar. Many islanders still have a strong affinity for England and English culture, while others identify more with what they hold to be their African-Creole roots. On Antigua, for example, Creole, which is spoken by virtually the entire population, is believed to reflect what is genuine and natural about the island and its culture. Standard English, even though it is the official language, carries an aura of falseness in the popular mind.

FOREIGN RELATIONS

Despite the small size of the country, Antigua and Barbuda are actively courted by regional powers. The United States maintains a satellite-tracking station on Antigua, and Brazil has provided loans and other assistance. A small oil refinery, jointly supported by Venezuela and Mexico, began operations in 1982 and is expected eventually to meet the petroleum needs of the island nations in the Eastern Caribbean.

Prime Minister Vere Bird has also actively courted the world's powers. In 1983 he undertook a month-long tour of Asia, where he met with representatives of the governments of South Korea and China. In Bird's words: "We can show the world the benefits of cooperation by transferring the experience gained in China to the development problems of Antigua and Barbuda."

THE FUTURE

For years allegations of corruption had dogged the administration of Vere Bird. But because his party, the Antigua Labour Party, has held power with only one interruption since 1951, he controls patronage and access to government jobs. Consequently, it is unlikely that the opposition, an unusual coalition of religious, private-sector, and opposition parties, will be able to oust the Bird dynasty.

DEVELOPMENT

For the first time since 1988, the government expected economic growth, anticipated to be in the range of 2.5% for 1993. Hurricane Hugo, the Gulf War, recession, and the concomitant loss of tourist dollars have been blamed for the decline. The political opposition would add corruption to the list.

FREEDOM

Pervasive government control of the electronic media has resulted in virtually no access for opposition parties or persons representing opinions divergent from or critical of those held by the government. The government has used the media in a deliberate campaign of disinformation on a number of occasions.

HEALTH/WELFARE

The government has initiated programs to enhance educational opportunities for men and women and to assist in family planning. The new Directorate of Women's Affairs helps women to advance in government and in the professions. It has also sponsored educational programs for women in health, crafts, and business skills.

ACHIEVEMENTS

Antigua has preserved its rich historical heritage, from the dockyard named for Admiral Lord Nelson to the Ebenezer Methodist Church. Built in 1839, the latter was the "mother church" for Methodism in the West Indies.

The Bahamas (Commonwealth of the Bahamas)

GEOGRAPHY

Area in Square Kilometers (Miles):
13,934 (5,380) (about the size of
Connecticut)
Capital (Population): Nassau
(135,400)
Climate: tropical

PEOPLE

Population
Total: 256,000
Annual Growth Rate: 1.4%
Rural/Urban Population Ratio: 40/60
Ethnic Makeup of Population: 85%
black; 15% white

Health
Life Expectancy at Birth: 69 years
(male); 76 years (female)
Infant Mortality Rate (Ratio):
19/1,000
Average Caloric Intake: 98% of FAO
minimum
Physicians Available (Ratio): 1/1,218

Religion(s)
32% Baptist; 20% Anglican; 19%
Roman Catholic; 18% Protestant;
11% unaffiliated or unknown

Education
Adult Literacy Rate: 90%

COMMUNICATION

Telephones: 99,000
Newspapers: 2 dailies

THE BAHAMAS: A STRATEGIC LOCATION

The name "Bahamas" comes from the Spanish *bajamar* (shallow
water). This island group, independent since 1973, consists of nearly
700 islands and cays (small islands) as well as almost 2,400 low, barren
rock formations. Only about 22 of the islands are occupied on this
archipelago. The Bahamas are strategically located in the Atlantic just
off the coast of Florida and southward along the Cuban coast. Because
they bridge the entrance to the Caribbean, the Bahamas have had a
tumultuous history. Explorers (Christopher Columbus is believed to
have landed on one island on October 12, 1492), pirates, and slavers
have all had an impact on the islands' cultures.

TRANSPORTATION

Highways—Kilometers (Miles): 2,400
(1,480)
Railroads—Kilometers (Miles): none
Usable Airfields: 54

GOVERNMENT

Type: independent state; recognizes
Queen Elizabeth II as chief of state
Independence Date: July 10, 1973
Head of State: Prime Minister Hubert
A. Ingraham
Political Parties: Progressive Liberal
Party; Free National Movement
Suffrage: universal at 18

MILITARY

Number of Armed Forces: no defense
force as such; Royal Bahamas Police
Force organized along paramilitary
lines; the United Kingdom is
responsible for external defense
*Military Expenditures (% of Central
Government Expenditures):* 3%
Current Hostilities: none

ECONOMY

Currency ($ U.S. Equivalent): 1
Bahamian dollar = $1 (fixed rate)
Per Capita Income/GDP: $9,900/$2.5
billion
Inflation Rate: 7.3%
Total Foreign Debt: $1.2 billion
Natural Resources: salt; aragonite;
timber
Agriculture: vegetables; lobster, fish
Industry: tourism; fishing; petroleum;
pharmaceuticals; banking; rum

FOREIGN TRADE

Exports: $306 million
Imports: $1.1 billion

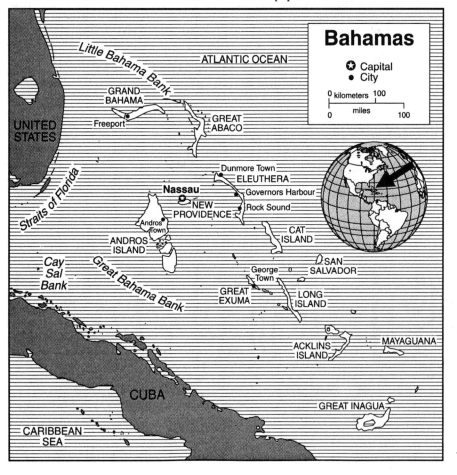

Christopher Columbus first sights the New World at San Salvador Island
1492

The first English settlement in the Bahamas
1647

Black-power controversy
1967

Independence of the United Kingdom
1973

1980s–1990s

Violent crime, drug trafficking, and narcotics addiction become serious social problems

The Progressive Labour Party, in power since 1967, is defeated

Hubert A. Ingraham, leader of the Free National Movement, is sworn in as prime minister

BAHAMAS: A NATION OF ISLANDS

Christopher Columbus made his first landfall in the Bahamas in 1492, when he touched ashore on the island of San Salvador. Permanent settlements on the islands were not established by the British until 1647, when the Eleutheran Adventurers, a group of English and Bermudan religious dissidents, landed. The island was privately governed until 1717, when it became a British Crown colony. During the U.S. Civil War, Confederate blockade runners used the Bahamas as a base. The tradition continued in the years after World War I, when Prohibition rum runners used the islands as a base. Today drug traffickers utilize the isolation of the out-islands for their illicit operations.

Although the Bahamas are made up of almost 700 islands, only 10 have populations of any significant size. Of these, New Providence and Grand Bahama contain more than 75 percent of the Bahamian population. Because most economic and cultural activities take place on the larger islands, other islands—particularly those in the southern region—have suffered depopulation over the years as young men and women have moved to the two major centers of activity.

Migrants from Haiti and Jamaica have also caused problems for the Bahamian government. There are an estimated 50,000 illegal Haitians now resident in the Bahamas—equivalent to approximately 20 percent of the total Bahamian population of 256,000—and more arrive daily. The Bahamian response to date has been humane, but the government insists on its right to repatriate the illegals to their country of origin. One official noted in 1991 that "the problem . . . is so vast and potent in relation to the size of this country that it will in a relatively short time . . . result in a very fundamental economic and social transformation that even the very naïve would understand to be undesirable." Bahamian problems with Jamaicans are rooted differently. The jealous isolation of each of the new nations is reflected in the West Indians' fears and suspicions of the activities of their neighbors. As a result, interisland freedom of movement is subject to strict scrutiny.

A SHIFT IN POLITICAL POWER

The Bahamas were granted their independence of the United Kingdom in 1973 and established a constitutional parliamentary democracy governed by a freely elected prime minister and Parliament. Upon independence there was a transfer of political power from a small white elite to the black majority, who comprise 85 percent of the population. Whites continue to play a role in the political process, however, and several hold high-level civil-service and political posts.

HEALTH AND EDUCATION

According to Bahamian statistics, the country enjoyed a marked improvement in health conditions over the past few decades. Life expectancy rose and infant mortality declined. Virtually all people living in urban areas have access to good drinking water, although the age and dilapidated condition of the capital's (Nassau) water system could present problems in the near future.

The government has begun a broad program to restructure education on the islands. The authorities have placed a new emphasis on technical and vocational training so that skilled jobs in the economy that are now held by foreigners will be performed by Bahamians. While the literacy rate has remained high, there remains a shortage of teachers, equipment, and supplies.

CURRENT PROBLEMS

High unemployment, estimated at nearly 25 percent in the 16-to-24 age group, has produced frustration, outmigration, and a rising crime rate. Illegal immigration of Haitians has severely taxed education and health facilities and has convinced many Bahamians that their own sense of identity may be threatened. Not surprisingly, this has led to some abuse of Haitians.

Tourism, the mainstay of the economy, accounting for about half of the gross national product, experienced a sharp downturn in 1990–1992. Offshore banking and finance is the second most important sector. Government efforts to diversify the economy have proven fruitless, and drug trafficking remains a problem.

DEVELOPMENT

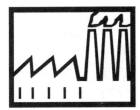

Because the Bahamian economy is service-oriented, especially in tourism and offshore banking, there are no significant industrial and occupational health hazards. Tourism accounts for nearly half the gross national product.

FREEDOM

Women generally enjoy equal rights in the Bahamas, in law and in practice. They participate actively in all levels of government and business and are well represented in the professional and private sectors. The Constitution does, however, make some distinctions between males and females with regard to citizenship and permanent-resident status.

HEALTH/WELFARE

The number of cases of child abuse and neglect rose in 1992. The Government and Women's Crisis Centre focused on the need to fight child abuse through a public-awareness program that had as its theme: "It shouldn't hurt to be a child."

ACHIEVEMENTS

The natural beauty of the islands has had a lasting effect on those who have visited them. As a result of his experiences in the waters off Bimini, Ernest Hemingway wrote his classic *The Old Man and the Sea.*

Barbados

GEOGRAPHY

Area in Square Kilometers (Miles):
431 (166) (about 2½ times the size
of Washington, D.C.)
Capital (Population): Bridgetown
(7,400)
Climate: tropical

PEOPLE

Population
Total: 255,000
Annual Growth Rate: 0.1%
Rural/Urban Population Ratio: 58/42
Ethnic Makeup of Population: 80%
black; 16% mixed; 4% white

Health
Life Expectancy at Birth: 70 years
(male); 76 years (female)
Infant Mortality Rate (Ratio):
22/1,000
Average Caloric Intake: 129% of
FAO minimum
Physicians Available (Ratio): 1/1,042

Religion(s)
67% Protestant (Anglican,
Pentecostal, Methodist, others); 4%
Roman Catholic; 17% none; 3%
unknown; 9% others

Education
Adult Literacy Rate: 99%

COMMUNICATION

Telephones: 89,000
Newspapers: 2 dailies

BARBADOS: AN OLD DEMOCRACY

In February 1627 the first permanent settlers arrived aboard the *William and John* to start the British colony of Barbados. So began a democracy that is one of the oldest in the Western Hemisphere; in fact, the writers of the U.S. Constitution borrowed wording from the Charter of Barbados of 1635. Independent of the United Kingdom since 1966, the government of Barbados contends that its election process is no more chaotic than that between the Republicans and Democrats in the United States.

TRANSPORTATION

Highways—Kilometers (Miles): 1,669
(1,035)
Railroads—Kilometers (Miles): none
Usable Airfields: 1

GOVERNMENT

Type: parliamentary democracy;
independent sovereign state within
Commonwealth
Independence Date: November 30,
1966
Head of State: Prime Minister Lloyd
Erskine Sandiford
Political Parties: Democratic Labour
Party; Barbados Labour Party;
National Democratic Party
Suffrage: universal at 18

MILITARY

Number of Armed Forces: small
Barbados regiment
*Military Expenditures (% of Central
Government Expenditures):* 3.0%
Current Hostilities: none

ECONOMY

Currency ($ U.S. Equivalent): about
2 Barbadian dollars = $1 (fixed rate)
Per Capita Income/GDP: $6,500/$1.7
billion
Inflation Rate: 3.4%
Total Foreign Debt: $540 million
Natural Resources: negligible
Agriculture: sugarcane; subsistence
foods
Industry: tourism; sugar milling; light
manufacturing; component assembly
for export

FOREIGN TRADE

Exports: $211 million
Imports: $704 million

Barbados
⊛ Capital
● City
〜 River
--- Road

| 0 | 3 kilometers |
| 0 | 3 miles |

Barbados is occupied by the English **1625**	The first sugar from Barbados is sent to England **1647**	Full citizenship is granted to nonwhites **1832**	Independence of the United Kingdom **1966**	**1980s–1990s**
			Prime Minister Lloyd Erskine Sandiford's Democratic Labour Party is returned to power	Economic contraction begins; fiscal deficit grows	The economic austerity program pushes unemployment above 23%

THE LITTLE ENGLAND OF THE CARIBBEAN

A parliamentary democracy that won its independence of Britain in 1966, Barbados boasts a House of Assembly that is the third oldest in the Western Hemisphere, after Bermuda's and Virginia's. A statement of the rights and privileges of Bajans (as Barbadians are called), known as the Charter of Barbados, was proclaimed in 1652 and has been upheld by those governing the island. The press is free, labor is strong and well organized, and human rights are respected. While the majority of the populations of the English-speaking West Indies still admire the British, this admiration is carried to extremes in Barbados. In 1969, for example, Bajan soccer teams chose English names and colors— Arsenal, Tottenham Hotspurs, Liverpool, and Coventry City. Among the primary religions are Anglican and Methodist Protestantism.

Unlike most of the other islands of the Caribbean, European sailors initially found Barbados uninhabited. It has since been determined that the island's original inhabitants, the Arawak Indians, were destroyed by Carib Indians who overran the region and then abandoned the islands. Barbados, settled by the English, was always under British control until its independence.

A SUGAR ECONOMY

As compared to other West Indian nations, Barbados, in terms of wealth, is well off. One important factor is that Barbados has been able to diversify its economy; thus, the country no longer is dependent solely on sugar and its by-products, rum and molasses. Manufacturing, financed by foreign investment, now contributes to the country's exports. Tourism is also an important source of revenue.

The Constitution of 1966 authorized the government to promote the general welfare of the citizens of the island through equitable distribution of wealth. While governments have made a sincere effort to wipe out pockets of poverty, a great disparity in wealth still exists. Most of the nation's landed estates and businesses are owned by whites, even though they comprise a small percentage of the population (4 percent).

RACE AND CLASS

Barbados is a class- and race-conscious society. One authority noted that there are three classes (elite, middle class, and masses) and two colors (white/light and black). Land is highly concentrated; 10 percent of the population own 95 percent of the land.

While discrimination based on one's color is legally prohibited, color distinctions continue to correlate with class differences and dominate most personal associations. Although whites have been displaced politically, they still comprise more than half of the group considered "influential" in the country.

QUALITY-OF-LIFE FACTORS

Even though Barbados's class structure is more rigid than other West Indian states, there is upward social mobility for all people, and the middle class has been growing steadily in size. Poor whites, known as "Redlegs," have frequently moved into managerial positions on the estates. The middle class also includes a fairly large percentage of blacks and mulattos. Bajans have long enjoyed access to public and private educational systems, which have been the object of a good deal of national pride. Adequate medical care is available to all residents through local clinics and hospitals under a government health program. All Bajans are covered under government health-insurance programs.

Given the nation's relative wealth and its dynamism, Bajans have been inclined to seek a strong role in the region. In terms of Caribbean politics, economic development, and defense, Bajans feel that they have a right and a duty to lead.

Some of that optimism has been tempered in the 1990s by economic recession. Recovery in 1993 saw a growth of 1 to 2 percent, a result of an International Monetary Fund-induced austerity program. Yet this turnaround was not without cost, as contraction in the labor force pushed unemployment to a 15-year high of 23.1 percent. Prime Minister Lloyd Erskine Sandiford has also pressed for privatization of state enterprises and a 2-year wage freeze.

DEVELOPMENT

The government's privatization program was, in the words of Finance Minister David Thompson, "based on a pragmatic assessment of the state of the economy and of the policies that must be implemented to achieve economic dynamism."

FREEDOM

Barbados has maintained an excellent human-rights record. The government officially advocates strengthening the human-rights machinery of the United Nations and the Organization of American States. Women are active participants in the country's economic, political, and social life.

HEALTH/WELFARE

Women's-rights groups in 1992 identified violence against women and children as a significant problem in Barbados. Domestic violence, incest, and rape among family members are increasing. Legislation has been passed in an attempt to address the problem.

ACHIEVEMENTS

The Bajan novelist George Lamming has won attention from the world's literary community for his novels, each of which explores a stage in or an aspect of the colonial experience. He explains, through his works, what it is to be simultaneously a citizen of one's island and a West Indian.

Cuba (Republic of Cuba)

GEOGRAPHY

Area in Square Kilometers (Miles):
114,471 (44,200) (about the size of
Pennsylvania)
Capital (Population): Havana
(2,077,000)
Climate: tropical

PEOPLE

Population
Total: 10,847,000
Annual Growth Rate: 1.0%
Rural/Urban Population Ratio: 28/72
Ethnic Makeup of Population: 51%
mulatto; 37% white; 11% black; 1%
Chinese

Health
Life Expectancy at Birth: 74 years
(male); 79 years (female)
Infant Mortality Rate (Ratio):
11/1,000
Average Caloric Intake: 121% of
FAO minimum
Physicians Available (Ratio): 1/333

Religion(s)
85% Roman Catholic before Castro
assumed power

Education
Adult Literacy Rate: 94%

COMMUNICATION

Telephones: 311,100
Newspapers: 1 daily

THE LANGUAGE OF REVOLUTION

Cuban males still make passes at virtually every passing female on the
streets of Havana. But *señorita* (miss) is no longer viewed as a proper
form of address. Gone from Cuban speech are *señorita*, *señora*, and
señor. They have been replaced by the revolutionary words *compañera*
and *compañero*, meaning "comrade" or "companion." The accepted
farewell is *hasta luego* ("until later"), taking the place of *adios*, with its
religious connotation of "go with God."

TRANSPORTATION

Highways—Kilometers (Miles):
26,477 (16,442)
Railroads—Kilometers (Miles):
12,947 (8,040)
Usable Airfields: 167

GOVERNMENT

Type: communist state
Independence Date: May 20, 1902
Head of State: President Fidel Castro
Ruz
Political Parties: Cuban Communist
Party
Suffrage: universal at 16

MILITARY

Number of Armed Forces: 180,500
*Military Expenditures (% of Central
Government Expenditures):* 8.0%
Current Hostilities: none

ECONOMY

Currency ($ U.S. Equivalent): 1.0
peso = $1 (linked to U.S. dollar)
Per Capita Income/GDP:
$1,580/$17.0 billion
Inflation Rate: n/a
Total Foreign Debt: $6.8 billion
Natural Resources: metals; primarily
nickel
Agriculture: sugar; tobacco; coffee;
citrus and tropical fruits; rice; beans;
meat; vegetables
Industry: sugar refining; metals; oil
refining; food processing; wood
products; cement; chemicals; textiles

FOREIGN TRADE

Exports: $3.6 billion
Imports: $3.7 billion

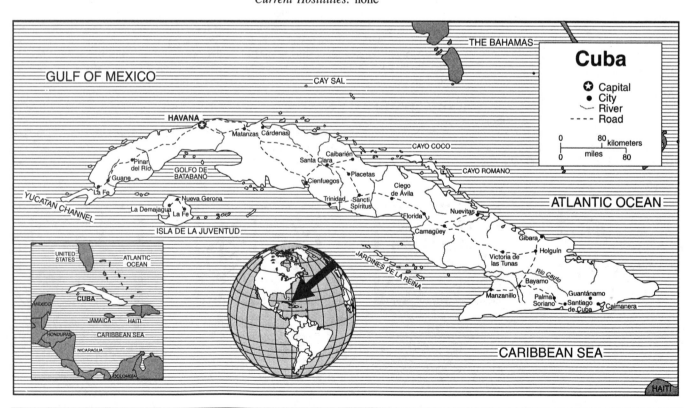

REFLECTIONS ON A REVOLUTION

Cuba, which contains about half the land area of the West Indies, has captured the attention of the world since 1959. In that year Fidel Castro led his victorious rebels into the capital city of Havana and began a revolution that has profoundly affected Cuban society. The Cuban Revolution had its roots in the struggle for independence of Spain in the late nineteenth century, in the aborted Nationalist Revolution of 1933, and in the Constitution of 1940. It grew from Cuba's history and must be understood as a Cuban phenomenon.

The Revolution in some respects represents the fulfillment of the goals of the Constitution of 1940, a radically nationalist document that was never fully implemented. It banned *latifundia* (the ownership of vast landed estates) and discouraged foreign ownership of the land. It permitted the confiscation of property in the public or social interest. The state was authorized to provide full employment for its people and to direct the course of the national economy. Finally, the Constitution of 1940 gave the Cuban state control of the sugar industry, which at the time was controlled by U.S. companies.

The current Constitution, written in 1976, incorporates 36 percent of the articles of the 1940 Constitution. In other words, many of Castro's policies and programs are founded in Cuban history and the aspirations of its people. Revolutionary Cuba has been very successful in solving the nation's most pressing problems of poverty. But those successes must be balanced against the loss of basic freedoms imposed by a strong authoritarian state.

REVOLUTIONARY ACHIEVEMENTS

One of the Revolution's most impressive successes was in the area of education. In 1960 the Castro regime decided to place emphasis on raising the minimum level of education for the whole population. To accomplish this some 200,000 Cubans were mobilized in 1961 under the slogan "Let those who know more teach those who know less." In a single year, the literacy rate rose from 76 to 96 percent. Free education was made available to all Cubans. The literacy campaign involved many Cubans in an attempt to recognize and attack the problems of rural impoverishment. For many women who were students or teachers, it was their first taste of active public life, and because of their involvement they began to redefine sex roles and attitudes.

While the literacy campaign was a resounding triumph, long-term educational policy was less satisfactory. Officials blamed the high dropout rate in elementary and junior high schools on poor school facilities and inadequate teacher training. Students also apparently lacked enthusiasm, and Castro himself acknowledged that students needed systematic, constant, daily work and discipline. "Scholarship students and students in general," in Castro's words, "are willing to do anything, except to study hard."

Health Care

The Cuban Revolution also took great strides forward in improving the health of the Cuban population, especially in rural regions. Success in this area is all the more impressive when one considers that between one-third and one-half of all doctors left the country between 1959 and 1962. Health care declined sharply, and the infant mortality rate rose rapidly. But with the training of new health care professionals, the gaps were filled. The infant mortality rate is now at a level comparable to that in developed countries.

From the outset the government decided to concentrate on rural areas, where the need was the greatest. Medical treatment is free, and newly graduated doctors must serve for at least 2 years in the countryside. The Cuban health service was founded on the principle that good health for all, without discrimination, is a birthright of Cubans. All Cubans are also included under a national health plan.

The first national health standards were developed between 1961 and 1965, and eight priority areas were identified: infant and maternal care, adult health care, care for the elderly, environmental health, nutrition, dentistry, school health programs, and occupational health. A program of spraying and immunization eradicated malaria and poliomyelitis. Cuban life expectancy is now one of the highest in the world, and Cuba's leading causes of death are the same as in the United States—heart disease, cancer, and stroke. With an increasingly greater number of the population over 60 years of age, Cuba's social benefits will have to be markedly expanded.

Before the Revolution of 1959 there was very little health and safety regulation for workers. Since 1959, however, important advances have been made in the training of specialized inspectors and occupational physicians. In 1978 a Work Safety and Health Law was enacted, which defined the rights and responsibilities of government agencies, workplace administrators, unions, and workers.

Cuba has also exported its health care expertise. One health authority has called Cuba a "health power." It has had medical teams in countries from Nicaragua to Yemen and more doctors overseas than the World Health Organization. Cuba's heavily ideological literacy programs and public-health training in Africa prompted Cuban vice president Carlos Rafael Rodríguez to say that, in Africa, "the United States looks to win, and we look to the future."

Redistribution of Wealth

The third great area of change presided over by the Revolution was income redistribution. The Revolution changed the lives of rural poor and agricultural workers. They gained the most with respect to other groups in Cuban society—especially in terms of urban groups. From 1962 to 1973, for example, agricultural workers saw their wages rise from less than 60 percent to 93 percent of the national average.

Still, Cuba's minimum wage of approximately $130 a month is inadequate for most families. The figure is badly overvalued; a family's real buying power is about $18 per month, which means that many families must have two wage earners to make ends meet. All wages are enhanced by the so-called social wage, which consists of free medical care and education, subsidized housing, and low food prices. Yet persistent shortages and tight rationing of food undermine a good portion of the social wage. Newly married couples find it necessary to live with relatives, sometimes for years, before they are able to obtain their own housing, which is in short supply. Food supplies, especially those provided by the informal sector, have been adversely affected by a 1986 decision to eliminate independent producers because an informal private sector was deemed antithetical to "socialist morality" and promoted materialism.

Women in Cuba

From the outset of the 1959 Revolution, Fidel Castro appealed to women as active participants in the movement and redefined their political roles. Women's interests are protected by the Federation of Cuban Women, an integral part of the ruling party. The Family Code of 1975 equalized pay scales, reversed sexual discrimination against promotions, provided generous maternity leave, and gave employed women preferential access to goods and services. Although women comprise approximately 30 percent of the Cuban work force, most are employed in traditional female occupations; the Third Congress of the Cuban

Communist Party admitted in 1988 that both racial minorities and women were underrepresented in responsible government and party positions at all levels. This continues to be a problem.

SHORTCOMINGS

The new Cuba does have some shortcomings. Wayne Smith, a former chief of the U.S. Interest Section in Havana who is sympathetic to the Revolution, has written: "There is little freedom of expression and no freedom of the press at all. It is a command society, which still holds political prisoners, some of them under deplorable conditions. Further, while the Revolution has provided the basic needs of all, it has not fulfilled its promise of a higher standard of living for the society as a whole. Cuba was, after all, an urban middle-class society with a relatively high standard of living even before the Revolution. . . . The majority of Cubans are less well off materially."

Castro, to win support for his programs, has not hesitated to take his revolutionary message to the people. Indeed, the key reason why Castro has enjoyed such widespread support in Cuba is because the people have the sense of being involved in a great historical process.

Alienation

Not all Cubans identified with the Revolution, and many felt a deep sense of betrayal and alienation. The elite and most of the middle class strongly resisted the changes that robbed them of influence, prestige, and property. Some were particularly bitter; for at its outset, the Revolution was largely a middle-class movement. Castro, for them, was a traitor to his class. Thousands fled Cuba, and some formed the core of an anti-Castro guerrilla movement based in South Florida.

There are signs that Castro's government, while still popular, has lost the widespread acceptance it enjoyed in the 1960s and 1970s. While Castro still has the support of the older generation and those in rural areas who benefited from the social transformation of the island, limited economic growth has led to dissatisfaction among urban workers and youth, who are less interested in Castro as a revolutionary hero and more interested in economic gains.

More serious disaffection may exist in the army. Journalist Georgie Anne Geyer, writing in *World Monitor,* suggests that the 1989 execution of General Arnaldo Ochoa, ostensibly for drug-trafficking, was actually motivated by Castro's fears of an emerging competitor for power.

"The 1930s-style show trial effectively revealed the presence of an 'Angola generation' in the Cuban military. . . . That generation, which fought in Angola between 1974 and 1989, is the competitor generation to Castro's own Sierra Maestra generation." The condemned officers argued that their dealings with drug traffickers were not for personal enrichment but were designed to earn desperately needed hard currency for the state. Some analysts are convinced that Castro knew about drug-trafficking and condoned it; others claim that it took place without his knowledge. But the bottom line is that the regime had been shaken at the highest levels, and the purge was the most far-reaching since the 1959 Revolution.

The Economy

The state of the Cuban economy and the future of the Cuban Revolution are inextricably linked. Writing in *World Today,* James J. Guy predicted that, given the economic collapse of the former Soviet Union and its satellites, "Cuba is destined to face serious structural unemployment: its agrarian economy cannot generate the white-collar, technical jobs demanded by a swelling army of graduates. . . . The entire system is deteriorating—the simplest services take months to deliver, water and electricity are constantly interrupted. . . ," and there is widespread corruption and black-marketeering.

Oil is particularly nettlesome. Just as Soviet oil imports fell off and Cuba was forced to make petroleum purchases on the world market, Kuwait was invaded by Iraq. Oil prices skyrocketed. Active development of the tourism industry offers some hope, but Western banks and governments since the mid-1980s have been reluctant to invest in Cuba.

Although Castro prides Cuba on being one of the last bulwarks of untainted Marxism-Leninism, in April 1991 he said: "We are not dogmatic . . . we are realistic. . . . Under the special conditions of this extraordinary period we are also aware that different forms of international cooperation may be useful." He noted that Cuba had contacted foreign capitalists about the possibility of establishing joint enterprises and remarked that more than 49 percent foreign participation in state businesses was a possibility.

In 1993 Castro called for economic realism. Using the rhetoric of the Revolution, he urged the Legislative Assembly to think seriously about the poor condition of the Cuban economy: "It is painful, but we must be sensible. . . . It is not only with decisiveness, courage and heroism that one saves the Revolution, but also with intelligence. And we have the right to invent ways to survive in these conditions without ever ceasing to be revolutionaries." What Castro appeared to suggest was the "dollarization" of the economy and the

(United Nations photo)

Fidel Castro has been the prime minister of Cuba since he seized power in 1959. Pictured above is Castro at the United Nations, as he looked in 1960.

The island is
discovered by
Christopher
Columbus
1492

The founding of
Havana
1511

The Ten Years'
War in Cuba
1868–1878

The Cuban War
of Independence
1895–1898

The Republic of
Cuba is
established
1902

Cuba writes a
new, progressive
Constitution
1940

Fidel Castro
seizes power
1959

An abortive
U.S.–sponsored
invasion at the
Bay of Pigs
1961

The OAS votes
to allow
member states
to normalize
relations with
Cuba
1975

1980s–1990s

Mass exodus
from Cuba; trial
and execution of
top military
officials for
alleged dealing in
drugs

The last Soviet
troops leave Cuba

Radical
economic
restructuring is
announced

legalization of the huge parallel market. Taken in combination with the participation of foreign investors in Cuban enterprises and the greater autonomy given to managers of state-owned companies, "this," according to *Latin American Regional Reports,* "spells a peculiarly Cuban version of the roll-back of the state." Castro has always been pragmatic; his adherence to doctrinaire communism may grow increasingly flexible despite rhetorical flourishes to the contrary.

Freedom Issues

Soon after the Revolution, the government assumed total control of the media. No independent news organization is allowed, and all printed publications are censored by the government or the Communist Party. The arts are subject to strict censorship, and even sports must serve the purposes of the Revolution. As Castro noted: "Within the Revolution everything is possible. Outside it, nothing."

In many respects, there is less freedom now in Cuba than there was before the Revolution. Cuba's human-rights record is not good. There are thousands of political prisoners, and rough treatment and torture—physical and psychological—occur. The Constitution of 1976 allows the repression of all freedoms for all those who oppose the Revolution. U.S. political scientist William LeGrande, who is sympathetic to the Revolution, nevertheless notes that "Cuba is a closed society. The Cuban Communist Party does not allow dissenting views on fundamental policy. It does not allow people to challenge the basic leadership of the regime."

FOREIGN POLICY

Cuban foreign policy has been the subject of much debate, especially with respect to the degree of Soviet involvement in its formulation. Until recently there was undoubtably a Soviet influence, but Cuban policy has always reflected the internal dynamics of the Cuban, not the Russian, Revolution.

For years Cuba has asserted that small nations have a right to pursue their own foreign policies; they need not be passive observers. Moreover, Castro's aggressive foreign policy has helped to bolster his image in Cuba. Cubans, who in the 1920s and 1930s were searching for a national identity, revel in Cuba's assertion of national strength and in the projection of that strength in other parts of the world. One of the real successes of the Revolution is that Cuba is the only Latin American state whose foreign policy is truly global in perspective.

THE FUTURE

It will be difficult for Castro to maintain the support of the Cuban population. There must be positive accomplishments in the economy. Health and education programs are successful and will continue to be so. "Cubans get free health care, free education and free admission to sports and cultural events [and] 80% of all Cubans live in rent-free apartments, and those who do pay rent pay only between 6 and 10% of their salaries," according to James J. Guy. But there must be a recovery of basic political and human freedoms. Criticism must not be the occasion for jail terms or exile. The Revolution must be more inclusive and less exclusive.

Although Castro has never been effectively challenged, there are signs of unrest on the island. The military, as noted, is a case in point. Castro has also lost a good deal of luster internationally, as most countries have moved away from statism and toward free-market economies and more open forms of government.

The question is increasingly asked, What will happen once Fidel, through death or retirement, is gone from power? Castro's assumption is that the new Constitution, which institutionalizes the Revolution, will provide a mechanism for succession. Over the past few years he has made some effort to depersonalize the Revolution; his public appearances are fewer and he does less traveling around the countryside. Change must come to Cuba. More than half of all Cubans alive today were born after the Revolution. They are not particularly attuned to the rhetoric of revolution and seem more interested in the attainment of basic freedoms and consumer goods. Castro is resistant to those demands and appears more as a tired revolutionary. Perhaps he realizes that his time has past, for he announced that he will not run for another term as president when elections are held in 1998.

DEVELOPMENT

Cuba's economic crisis has forced President Castro to consider legalizing both the holding of foreign currencies and the huge black market. At the present time, the state benefits from neither.

FREEDOM

Amnesty International has voiced concern over Cuba's prisoners of conscience and continued imprisonment of political prisoners after the expiration of their sentences.

HEALTH/WELFARE

Health delivery systems in Cuba are still impressive for the region, although the poor state of the Cuban economy has forced the introduction of severe austerity. There is less disparity in basic social services between rural and urban areas than in any other Latin American nation.

ACHIEVEMENTS

A unique cultural contribution of Cuba to the world was the Afro-Cuban movement, with its celebration of black song and dance rhythms. Prize-winning contemporary Cuban authors such as Alejo Carpentier and Edmundo Desnoes have been translated into many languages.

Dominica (Commonwealth of Dominica)

GEOGRAPHY

Area in Square Kilometers (Miles):
752 (289) (about ¼ the size of
Rhode Island)
Capital (Population): Roseau (22,000)
Climate: tropical

PEOPLE

Population
Total: 87,000
Annual Growth Rate: 1.6%
Rural/Urban Population Ratio: entire
island considered urban
Ethnic Makeup of Population: mostly
black; some Carib Indians

Health
Life Expectancy at Birth: 74 years
(male); 79 years (female)
Infant Mortality Rate (Ratio):
11/1,000
Average Caloric Intake: 90% of FAO
minimum
Physicians Available (Ratio): 1/2,619

Religion(s)
77% Roman Catholic; 15%
Protestant; 8% others

Education
Adult Literacy Rate: 94%

COMMUNICATION

Telephones: 4,600
Newspapers: n/a

THE SWITZERLAND OF THE CARIBBEAN

The tiny island of Dominica was discovered by Christopher Columbus
on his second voyage to the New World in 1493. The island was sighted
on the Christian Sabbath (*Domingo* in Spanish), hence the name
Dominica. Today, as in 1493, Dominica's very mountainous terrain is
densely covered with heavy tropical growth. Described as the most
ruggedly beautiful island in the Caribbean, Dominica has been called
"the Switzerland of the Caribbean."

TRANSPORTATION

Highways—Kilometers (Miles): 750
(466)
Railroads—Kilometers (Miles): none
Usable Airfields: 2

GOVERNMENT

Type: independent state within the
Commonwealth; recognizes Queen
Elizabeth II as chief of state
Independence Date: November 3,
1978
Head of State: Prime Minister Mary
Eugenia Charles
Political Parties: Dominica Labor
Party; Dominica Freedom Party;
United Workers Party
Suffrage: universal at 18

MILITARY

Number of Armed Forces: n/a
*Military Expenditures (% of Central
Government Expenditures):* 4.6%
Current Hostilities: none

ECONOMY

Currency ($ U.S. Equivalent): 2.7
East Caribbean dollars = $1
Per Capita Income/GDP:
$2,000/$170 million
Inflation Rate: 4.7%
Total Foreign Debt: $73 million
Natural Resources: timber
Agriculture: bananas; citrus;
coconuts; coca; essential oils
Industry: agricultural processing;
tourism; soap and other
coconut-based products; cigars

FOREIGN TRADE

Exports: $60 million
Imports: $104 million

DOMINICA PASSAGE

Vieille Case
Calibishie
Portsmouth
Glanvillia
Wesley
Toulaman
Marigot
Colihaut
Salibia
Morne
Raquette
Castle
Bruce
Layou
Salisbury
Saint Joseph
CARIBBEAN SEA
Pont
Cassé
Rosalie
Massacre
Laudat
Roseau
La Plaine
Roseau
Pointe
Michel
Berekua
Soufrière
DOMINICA CHANNEL

DOMINICA
CARIBBEAN
SEA
VENEZUELA
ATLANTIC
OCEAN

Dominica
⊛ Capital
● City
〜 River
--- Road
0 kilometers 6
0 miles 6

Dominica is
sighted on
Christopher
Columbus's
second voyage
1493

Dominica is
deeded to the
British by France
1783

Independence of
the United
Kingdom
1978

Hurricanes
devastate
Dominica's
economy
1979–1980

1980s–1990s

Hurricane Hugo
devastates the
island

Prime Minister
Eugenia Charles
is the
Caribbean's first
woman head
of state

Elections are
scheduled for
1995

A FRAGMENTED NATION

Dominica is a small and poor country that was granted its independence of the United Kingdom in 1978. Culturally, the island reflects a number of patterns. Ninety percent of the population speak French *patois* (dialect) and most are Roman Catholic, while a small minority speak English and are Protestant. Yet English is the official language. There are also small groups of Indians who may have descended from the original Carib inhabitants; they are alternately revered and criticized. While many Dominicans perceive the Carib Indians as drunken, lazy, and dishonest, others see them as symbolically important because they represent an ancient culture and fit into the larger West Indian search for cultural and national identity. There is also a small Rastafarian sector (those who identify with their black African roots).

Christopher Columbus discovered the island of Dominica on his second voyage to the New World in 1493. Because of the presence of Carib Indians, who were known for their ferocity, Spanish efforts to settle the island were rebuffed. It was not until 1635 that France took advantage of Spanish weakness and claimed Dominica as its own. French missionaries became the island's first European settlers. Because of continued Carib resistance, the French and English agreed in 1660 that both Dominica and St. Vincent should be declared neutral and left to the Indians. Definitive English settlement did not occur until the eighteenth century, and the island again became a bone of contention between the French and English. It became British by treaty in 1783.

REGIONALISM

Dominica's population is broken up into sharply differentiated regions. The early collapse of the plantation economy left pockets of settlements which still are virtually isolated from one another. A difficult topography and poor communications exaggerate the differences between these small communities. This contrasts with nations such as Jamaica and Trinidad and Tobago, which have a greater sense of national awareness because there are good communications and mass media that reach most citizens and foster the development of a national perception.

EMIGRATION

Although Dominica has a high birth rate and life expectancy has measurably increased over the past few years, the growth rate has been dropping due to significant outmigration. Outmigration is not a new phenomenon. From the 1880s until well into this century, many Dominicans sought economic opportunity in the gold fields of French Guiana. Today most move to the neighboring French departments of Guadeloupe and Martinique.

THE ECONOMY

Dominica's economy had just recovered from the shattering hurricanes of 1979 and 1980 that destroyed banana crops and the trees that produced them when Hurricane Hugo devastated the island again in 1989.

Foreign investment has been encouraged and foreign donors sought to reha-bilitate the basic economic infrastructure. Prime Minister Mary Eugenia Charles has identified good roads as essential for the development of agriculture and industry and for attracting tourists. With aid from the United States, roads are being widened and, for the first time, adequate drainage is being provided to cope with the island's seasonal torrential downpours. Recovery of the agricultural sector and an expansion of the tourist industry are critical if Dominica is to prevent further erosion of the quality of life of its people.

POLITICAL FREEDOM

Despite economic difficulties and several attempted coups, Dominica still enjoys a parliamentary democracy patterned along British lines. The press is free and has not been subject to control—save for a brief state of emergency in 1981, which corresponded to a coup attempt by former Prime Minister Patrick John and unemployed members of the disbanded Defense Force. Political parties and trade unions are free to organize. Labor unions are small but enjoy the right to strike. Women have full rights under the law and are active in the political system; Prime Minister Charles is the Caribbean's first woman head of state.

DEVELOPMENT

Dominica's agrarian economy is heavily dependent on earnings from banana exports to Great Britain. Attempts are being made to diversify agricultural production, to develop a tourist industry, and to promote light manufacturing.

FREEDOM

Freedom House, an international human-rights organization, listed Dominica as "free." It also noted that "the rights of the native Caribs may not be fully respected." The example set by Prime Minister Charles has led to greater participation by women in the island's political life.

HEALTH/WELFARE

With the assistance of external donors, Dominica has rebuilt many primary schools destroyed in Hurricane Hugo. A major restructuring of the public-health administration has improved the quality of health care, even in the previously neglected rural areas.

ACHIEVEMENTS

Traditional handcrafts—especially intricately woven baskets, mats, and hats—have been preserved in Dominica. Schoolchildren are taught the techniques to preserve this dimension of Dominican culture.

Dominican Republic

GEOGRAPHY

Area in Square Kilometers (Miles): 48,464 (18,712) (about the size of Vermont and New Hampshire combined)
Capital (Population): Santo Domingo (1,700,000)
Climate: maritime tropical

PEOPLE

Population

Total: 7,516,000
Annual Growth Rate: 1.9%
Rural/Urban Population Ratio: 40/60
Ethnic Makeup of Population: 73% mixed; 16% white; 11% black

Health

Life Expectancy at Birth: 66 years (male); 70 years (female)
Infant Mortality Rate (Ratio): 56/1,000
Average Caloric Intake: 106% of FAO minimum
Physicians Available (Ratio): 1/2,147

Religion(s)

95% Roman Catholic; 5% others

Education

Adult Literacy Rate: 83%

COMMUNICATION

Telephones: 190,000
Newspapers: 9 dailies

COLUMBUS AND THE FIRST CATHEDRAL IN AMERICA

Christopher Columbus discovered Hispaniola (part of which today is the Dominican Republic, the rest Haiti) on his initial voyage to the New World in 1492. After the first northern colony was destroyed by Indians, Columbus established a second colony, only to abandon it when gold was reported in the south. This colony eventually became the city of Santo Domingo, on the Caribbean coast. The Catedrál de Santo Domingo was built soon after the founding of the city. Completed in 1540, it is the oldest cathedral in the Americas. In 1542 the remains of Christopher Columbus and his son Diego were moved from Sevilla, Spain, to this cathedral, allowing the discoverer of the Americas a final resting place in the "new world" that made him famous.

TRANSPORTATION

Highways—Kilometers (Miles): 17,120 (10,614)
Railroads—Kilometers (Miles): 1,655 (1,026)
Usable Airfields: 30

GOVERNMENT

Type: republic
Independence Date: February 27, 1844
Head of State: President Joaquín Balaguer Ricardo
Political Parties: Dominican Revolutionary Party; Social Christian Reformist Party; Dominican Liberation Party; Independent Revolutionary Party; others
Suffrage: universal and compulsory at 18 or if married, except members of the armed forces or the police, who cannot vote

MILITARY

Number of Armed Forces: 22,800
Military Expenditures (% of Central Government Expenditures): 4.6%
Current Hostilities: none

ECONOMY

Currency ($ U.S. Equivalent): 12.7 pesos = $1
Per Capita Income/GDP: $950/$7.0 billion
Inflation Rate: 4.7%
Total Foreign Debt: $4.7 billion
Natural Resources: nickel; bauxite; gold; silver
Agriculture: sugarcane; coffee; cocoa; cacao; tobacco; rice; corn; beef
Industry: tourism; sugar refining; textiles; cement; mining

FOREIGN TRADE

Exports: $775 million
Imports: $1.8 billion

The founding of Santo Domingo, the oldest European city in the Americas 1496	Independence of Spain is declared 1821	Haitian control 1822–1844	Independence as a separate state 1844	The era of General Rafael Trujillo 1930–1961	Civil war and U.S. intervention 1965	The IMF approves $78 million in a stand-by loan

1980s–1990s

Joaquín Balaguer is elected president; promises reforms	Workers press for a higher minimum wage; labor-related violence spreads	Elections are scheduled for 1994

DOMINICAN REPUBLIC: RACIAL STRIFE

Occupying the eastern two-thirds of the island of Hispaniola (Haiti comprises the western third), the Dominican Republic historically has feared its neighbor to the west. Much of the fear has its origins in race. From 1822 until 1844, the Dominican Republic—currently 73 percent mixed, or mulatto—was ruled by a brutal black Haitian regime. One authority noted that the Dominican Republic's freedom from Haiti has always been precarious: "Fear of reconquest by the smaller but more heavily populated (and, one might add, black) neighbor has affected Dominican psychology more than any other factor."

In the 1930s, for example, President Rafael Trujillo posed as the defender of Catholic values and European culture against the "barbarous" hordes of Haiti. Trujillo ordered the massacre of from 12,000 to 20,000 Haitians who had settled in the Dominican Republic in search of work. For years the Dominican government had encouraged Haitian sugar cane cutters to cross the border to work on the U.S.-owned sugar plantations. But with the world depression in the 1930s and a fall in sugar prices and production, many Haitians did not return to their part of the island; in fact, additional thousands continued to stream across the border. The response of the Dominican government was wholesale slaughter.

HAITIAN WORKERS

Since 1952 a series of 5-year agreements have been reached between the two gov-ernments to regularize the supply of Haitian cane cutters. An estimated 20,000 cross each year into the Dominican Republic legally, and an additional 60,000 enter illegally. Living and working conditions are very poor for these Haitians, and the migrants have no legal status and no rights. Planters prefer the Haitian workers because they are "cheaper and more docile" than Dominican laborers, who expect reasonable food, adequate housing, electrical lights, and transportation to the fields. Today, as in the 1930s, economic troubles have gripped the Dominican Republic; the president has promised across-the-board sacrifices.

There is a subtle social discrimination against darker-skinned Dominicans, although this has not proved to be an insurmountable obstacle, as many hold elected political office. Discrimination is in part historical, in part cultural, and must be set against a backdrop of sharp prejudice against Haitians. This prejudice is also directed against the minority in the Dominican population who are of Haitian descent.

If one ignores the plight of the Haitians in the Dominican Republic, the society would appear to be free and open. Freedom of the press has generally been respected since 1978, although some censorship was exercised in 1981, when there were rumblings of peasant unrest. Dominicans enjoy the broad range of human rights guaranteed them under the 1966 Constitution.

WOMEN'S RIGHTS

Women in the Dominican Republic have enjoyed political rights since 1941. President Joaquín Balaguer Ricardo, in an unprecedented move, named women governors for 8 of the country's 29 provinces. Sexual discrimination is prohibited by law, but women have not shared equal social or economic status or opportunity with men. Divorce, however, is easily obtainable, and women can hold property in their own names.

THE ECONOMY

The Dominican Republic has a mixed economy based largely on agriculture and services. Key industries, such as sugar, the national airline, and public utilities, are controlled by the state. The winds of privatization that are sweeping over most of Latin America have not as yet touched the Dominican Republic. The sugar industry has been the traditional earner of foreign exchange, although in recent years tourism, free-trade zones, and remittances from Dominicans living abroad now generate more foreign exchange. The nation is threatened by a large foreign debt—$4.7 billion—although inflation has been brought under control. But a rapidly rising population, high unemployment and underemployment, and wages that never recovered from the losses to inflation in 1990 and 1991 have produced unrest and uncertainty.

DEVELOPMENT

An inefficient state sector and rising levels of inflation imperil the Dominican economy. Budget austerity in response to the foreign-debt crisis has resulted in layoffs and dismissals, in a country where unemployment and underemployment are already serious problems.

FREEDOM

The Dominican Republic has established a representative democratic system despite a violence-torn history, the poverty of most of its people, and an increasingly difficult economic situation.

HEALTH/WELFARE

Poverty is widespread in the Dominican Republic, and health conditions, especially in the countryside, are extremely poor. Living standards have once again begun to deteriorate and have seriously affected the poor and lower middle class.

ACHIEVEMENTS

Dedicated in 1973, the National Theater of the Dominican Republic is a professional showcase of Caribbean arts. It is located on the Plaza de la Cultura along with the Museum of the Dominican Man, the Gallery of Modern Art, and the National Library. The theater has become the cultural heart of the city of Santo Domingo.

Grenada

GEOGRAPHY

Area in Square Kilometers (Miles):
344 (133) (about 2 times the size of
Washington, D.C.)
Capital (Population): St. George's
(35,700)
Climate: tropical

PEOPLE

Population
Total: 83,500
Annual Growth Rate: −0.3%
Rural/Urban Population Ratio: 70/30
Ethnic Makeup of Population: mainly
black

Health
Life Expectancy at Birth: 69 years
(male); 74 years (female)
Infant Mortality Rate (Ratio):
28/1,000
Average Caloric Intake: 87% of FAO
minimum
Physicians Available (Ratio): 1/4,400

Religion(s)
largely Roman Catholic; Church of
England; other Protestant sects

Education
Adult Literacy Rate: 85%

COMMUNICATION

Telephones: 5,650
Newspapers: n/a

GRENADA: STABILIZATION

Grenada is less than 100 miles off the coast of Venezuela, in a channel
through which half of the United States's imported oil enters the
Caribbean. In 1983 there was considerable interest in this tiny island
when Prime Minister Maurice Bishop and most of his cabinet were
killed by the military. The United States responded to this seemingly
Cuban-inspired coup by sending in U.S. Marines to protect the 700 to
1,000 Americans living on the island. This American "invasion" defused the hostilities in a week. On December 3, 1984, the Grenadans
elected a new prime minister, Herbert Blaize, along with his New
National Party. Blaize's election was favored by the United States.

TRANSPORTATION

Highways—Kilometers (Miles): 930
(577)
Railroads—Kilometers (Miles): none
Usable Airfields: 3

GOVERNMENT

Type: independent state; recognizes
Queen Elizabeth II as chief of state
Independence Date: February 7, 1974
Head of State: Prime Minister
Nicholas Braithwaite
Political Parties: New National
Party; Grenada United Labor Party;
National Party; National Democratic
Congress; Maurice Bishop Patriotic
Movement; JEWEL Movement
Suffrage: universal at 18

MILITARY

Number of Armed Forces: 6,500
police; Royal Grenada Police Force
*Military Expenditures (% of Central
Government Expenditures):* n/a
Current Hostilities: none

ECONOMY

Currency ($ U.S. Equivalent): 2.7
East Caribbean dollars = $1 (fixed
rate)
Per Capita Income/GDP:
$2,800/$238 million
Inflation Rate: 7.0%
Total Foreign Debt: $90 million
Natural Resources: spices
Agriculture: nutmeg; cocoa; bananas;
mace
Industry: food processing; garments

FOREIGN TRADE

Exports: $26 million
Imports: $105 million

GRENADA: A FRESH BEGINNING

On his third voyage to the New World in 1496, Christopher Columbus discovered Grenada, which he named Concepción. The origin of the name "Grenada" cannot be clearly established, although it is believed that the Spanish renamed the island for the Spanish city of Granada. Because of a fierce aboriginal population of Carib Indians, the island remained uncolonized for 100 years.

Grenada, like most of the West Indies, is ethnically mixed. Its culture draws on several traditions. The island's French past is preserved among some people who still speak *patois* (a French dialect). There are few whites on the island, save for a small group of Portuguese who immigrated earlier in the century. The primary cultural identification is with Britain, from which Grenada won its independence in 1974.

Grenada's political history has been tumultuous. The corruption and violent tactics of Grenada's first prime minister, Sir Eric Gairy, resulted in his removal during a bloodless coup in 1979. Even though this action marked the first extraconstitutional change of government in the Commonwealth Caribbean (former British colonies), most Grenadans supported the coup, led by Maurice Bishop and his New Joint Endeavor for Welfare, Education, and Liberation (JEWEL) Movement. Prime Minister Bishop, like Jamaica's Michael Manley before him, attempted to break out of European cultural and institutional molds and mobilize Grenadans behind him.

Bishop's social policies laid the foundation for basic health care for all Grenadans. With the departure of Cuban medical doctors in 1983, however, the lack of trained personnel created a significant health-care problem. Moreover, although medical-care facilities exist, these are not always in good repair, and equipment is aging and not reliable. Methods of recording births, deaths, and diseases lack systemization, so it is risky to rely on local statistics to estimate the health needs of the population.

There has also been some erosion from Bishop's campaign to accord women equal pay, status, and treatment. Skilled employment for women tends to be concentrated in the lowest-paid sector. Two women, however, were elected to Parliament.

On October 19, 1983, Bishop and several of his senior ministers were killed during the course of a military coup led by the hard-line Marxists Bernard Coard and General Hudson Austin. Six days later the United States, with the token assistance of soldiers and police from the states of the Eastern Caribbean, invaded Grenada, arrested Coard and Austin, restored the 1974 Constitution, and prepared the way for new elections (which were held in December 1984). Most Grenadans welcomed the U.S. action. But they also remember with much fondness the regime of Maurice Bishop and his social policies.

Grenada's international airport, once the focus of so much controversy, is now open and has pumped new blood into the tourist industry. Moves have also been made by the Grenadan government to promote private-sector business and to diminish the role of the government in the economy. Large amounts of foreign aid, especially from the United States, have helped to repair the infrastructure. Significant problems remain, however. Unemployment has not decreased; it remains at nearly 30 percent of the work force. Not surprisingly, the island is plagued by a rising crime rate, which is a reflection of the feeble state of the economy. Prime Minister Nicholas Braithwaite's tough-minded economic policy and leadership style have created infighting within his party, which has spread to government. The Trades Union Council has been particularly critical of the government's privatization policy because it will likely translate into a loss of jobs. Nevertheless, Grenadans enjoy full political freedom, a free press, the right to organize unions, and freedom of assembly and association.

DEVELOPMENT

The privatization policy of the National Democratic Congress has generated much opposition from Grenadans. The opposition claim that two state-owned enterprises, the Grenada Bank of Commerce and the Grenada Electricity Company, are profitable.

FREEDOM

Grenadans are guaranteed full freedom of the press and speech. Newspapers, most of which are published by political parties, freely criticize the government without penalty.

HEALTH/WELFARE

Grenada still lacks effective legislation for regulation of working conditions, wages, and occupational safety and health standards. Although discrimination is prohibited by law, women often are paid less than men for the same work. There tends to be less wage discrimination in higher-paying jobs, but few women hold such positions.

ACHIEVEMENTS

The government is attempting to continue the "participatory democracy" style of late Prime Minister Bishop. A series of public consultations have been held with respect to the reestablishment of local government in the villages. Some 52 village councils work with the government in an effort to set policies that are both responsive and equitable.

Haiti (Republic of Haiti)

GEOGRAPHY

Area in Square Kilometers (Miles):
27,750 (10,714) (about the size of
Maryland)
Capital (Population): Port-au-Prince
(514,000)
Climate: warm; semiarid

PEOPLE

Population
Total: 6,432,000
Annual Growth Rate: 2.3%
Rural/Urban Population Ratio: 72/28
Ethnic Makeup of Population: 95%
black; 5% mulatto and European

Health
Life Expectancy at Birth: 53 years
(male); 55 years (female)
Infant Mortality Rate (Ratio):
104/1,000
Average Caloric Intake: 96% of FAO
minimum
Physicians Available (Ratio): 1/6,039

HAITI: A LAND OF GINGERBREAD HOUSES

The origins of the architecture of Haiti's gingerbread houses are a
mystery. Did they spring from the Paris Exposition of 1900 or did they
evolve from the styles popular in the United States in the late 1800s?
Whatever the reason, Haiti abounds with these elegant, intricate, and
multicolored homes. No two are identical. Today these houses need
constant and expensive maintenance; as a result the Haitian gingerbread
house is an endangered species. It is hoped that public awareness will
keep them from becoming extinct.

Religion(s)
80% Roman Catholic (of which the
overwhelming majority also practice
voodoo); 6% Protestant; 4% others

Education
Adult Literacy Rate: 53%

COMMUNICATION

Telephones: 36,000
Newspapers: 6 dailies

TRANSPORTATION

Highways—Kilometers (Miles): 4,000
(2,480)
Railroads—Kilometers (Miles): 40
(25)
Usable Airfields: 10

GOVERNMENT

Type: provisional; still in a state of
turmoil
Independence Date: January 1, 1804
Head of State: President Jean
Bertrand Aristide (overthrown by a
military coup in October 1991; fled
the country and remains in exile as
of this writing); de facto Prime
Minister Marc Bazin
Political Parties: National Front for
Change and Democracy; National
Konbite Movement; National
Alliance for Democracy and Progress
(coalition)
Suffrage: universal over 18

MILITARY

Number of Armed Forces: 7,600
*Military Expenditures (% of Central
Government Expenditures):* 11.0%
Current Hostilities: none

ECONOMY

Currency ($ U.S. Equivalent): 5
gourdes = $1 (fixed rate)
Per Capita Income/GDP: $440/$2.7
billion
Inflation Rate: 20%
Total Foreign Debt: $838 million
Natural Resources: bauxite
Agriculture: coffee; sugarcane; rice;
corn; sorghum
Industry: sugar refining; textiles;
flour milling; cement; tourism;
light-assembly industries

FOREIGN TRADE

Exports: $169 million
Imports: $348 million

| The island is discovered by Christopher Columbus; named Hispaniola **1492** | The western portion of Hispaniola is ceded to France **1697** | Independence of France **1804** | The era of President François Duvalier **1957–1971** | Jean-Claude Duvalier is named president-for-life **1971** | Thirty-three Haitians drown in an attempt to reach Florida by boat **1980s–1990s** |

| Duvalier flees into exile; a 1991 military coup against President Jean-Bertrand Aristide | A UN/OAS agreement with the Haitian military in 1993 to return Aristide to power | Attempts to implement the UN/OAS plan are rebuffed |

HAITI

Haiti, which occupies the western third of the island of Hispaniola (the Dominican Republic comprises the other two-thirds), was the first nation in Latin America to win independence of its mother country—in this instance, France. It is the poorest country in the Western Hemisphere and one of the least developed in the world. Agriculture, which employs about 70 percent of the population, is pressed beyond the limits of the available land; the result has been catastrophic deforestation and erosion. While only roughly 30 percent of the land is suitable for planting, 50 percent is actually under cultivation. Haitians are woefully poor, suffer from poor health and lack of education, and seldom find work. Haiti's urban unemployment is estimated at 40 to 50 percent. Even when employment is found, wages are miserable, and there is no significant labor movement to intercede on behalf of the workers.

For most of its history Haiti has experienced a series of harsh authoritarian regimes. The ouster in 1986 of President-for-Life Jean-Claude Duvalier promised, for the moment, a more democratic opening as the new ruling National Governing Council announced as its primary goal the transition to a freely elected government. Political prisoners were freed; the dreaded Duvalier secret police, the Tontons Macoute, were disbanded; and the press was unmuzzled.

The vacuum left by Duvalier's departure was filled by a succession of governments that were either controlled or heavily influenced by the military. Significant change was heralded in December 1990 with the election to power of an outspoken Roman Catholic priest, Jean-Bertrand Aristide, with 66.7 percent of the vote. By the end of 1991 he had moved against the military and had formulated a foreign policy that sought to move Haiti away from the United States and closer to the nations of Latin America and the Caribbean. Aristide's promotion of the "church of the poor," which combines local beliefs with standard Catholic instruction, earned him the enmity of both conservative church leaders and voodoo priests. The radical language of his Lavalas (Floodtide) movement, which promised sweeping economic and social changes, made business leaders and rural landowners uneasy.

Perhaps not surprisingly in this coup-ridden nation, the army, always dangerous and unpredictable, ousted President Aristide in October 1991. The Organization of American States, the United Nations, and the United States condemned the coup, moved to isolate the new military government, and imposed economic sanctions. In July 1993 Aristide and General Raoul Cédras, the leader of the coup, agreed to accept a UN/OAS plan to return Haiti to democracy and Aristide to power. But effecting this plan has proved difficult, and Aristide still remained in exile and the military in power in mid-1994.

A persistent theme in Haiti's history has been a bitter rivalry between a small mulatto elite, consisting of 3 to 4 percent of the population, and the black majority. When François Duvalier, a black country doctor, was president (1957–1971), his avowed aim was to create a "new equilibrium" in the country—by which he meant a major shift in power from the established, predominantly mulatto, elite to a new, black middle class. Much of Haitian culture explicitly rejects Western civilization, which is identified with the mulattos. The Creole language of the masses and their practice of voodoo, a combination of African spiritualism and Christianity, has not only insulated the population from the "culturally alien" regimes in power but has also given Haitians a common point of identity.

Haitian intellectuals have raised sharp questions about the nation's culture. Modernizers would like to see the triumph of the French language over Creole and Roman Catholicism over voodoo. Others argue that significant change in Haiti can come only from within, from what is authentically Haitian. The refusal of Haitian governments to recognize Creole as the official language has only added to the determination of the mulatto elite and the black middle class to exclude the rest of the population from effective participation in political life.

DEVELOPMENT

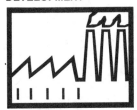

Haiti's economic decline accelerated in 1992 because of political instability, poor management, and a trade embargo imposed as a result of the coup of 1991.

FREEDOM

Despite the government's initiative to introduce human-rights legislation in 1992, nothing was done, and widespread abuses continued. Extrajudicial killings, disappearances, beatings, torture, arbitrary arrest and detention, and violence and intimidation of the press are common.

HEALTH/WELFARE

Deep-seated conflicts among Haiti's complex social groups have left little tradition of national service. Mass education has seldom been encouraged and at times has been actively discouraged. The same attitudes apply to health care. A consequence of this social disorganization has been a lack of respect for political and civil rights by those in authority.

ACHIEVEMENTS

In the late 1940s Haitian "primitive" art created a sensation in Paris and other art centers. Although the force of the movement has now been spent, it still represents a unique, colorful, and imaginative art form.

Jamaica

GEOGRAPHY

Area in Square Kilometers (Miles):
10,991 (4,244) (slightly smaller than
Connecticut)
Capital (Population): Kingston
(104,000)
Climate: tropical

PEOPLE

Population

Total: 2,507,000
Annual Growth Rate: 0.9%
Rural/Urban Population Ratio: 48/52
Ethnic Makeup of Population: 76%
black; 15% Afro-European; 3% East
Indian and Afro-East Indian; 3%
white; 1% Chinese and Afro-Chinese;
2% others

Health

Life Expectancy at Birth: 72 years
(male); 76 years (female)
Infant Mortality Rate (Ratio):
18/1,000
Average Caloric Intake: 119% of
FAO minimum
Physicians Available (Ratio): 1/5,723

Religion(s)

56% Protestant; 5% Roman Catholic;
39% others, including some
spiritualistic cults

Education

Adult Literacy Rate: 82%

REGGAE

Reggae is the only Caribbean music and beat to have had a significant
impact outside the region in recent years. The music derives from the
traditional rhythms of the Rastafarian cult. Originally called "ska,"
reggae was introduced to the United States at the World's Fair in 1964.
This combination of folk, rock, soul, blues, and revival has become
popular in the United States and Europe. The lyrics usually follow a
protest theme and are sharply critical of the injustices of society.

COMMUNICATION

Telephones: 127,000
Newspapers: n/a

TRANSPORTATION

Highways—Kilometers (Miles):
18,200 (11,310)
Railroads—Kilometers (Miles): 294
(183)
Usable Airfields: 23

GOVERNMENT

Type: constitutional monarchy;
recognizes Queen Elizabeth II as
chief of state
Independence Date: August 6, 1962
Head of State: Prime Minister
Percival J. Patterson
Political Parties: People's National
Party; Jamaica Labour Party
Suffrage: universal at 18

MILITARY

Number of Armed Forces: 3,500
*Military Expenditures (% of Central
Government Expenditures):* 1.1%
Current Hostilities: none

ECONOMY

Currency ($ U.S. Equivalent): 21.9
Jamaican dollars = $1
Per Capita Income/GDP: $1,400/$3.6
billion
Inflation Rate: 80.0%
Total Foreign Debt: $3.8 billion
Natural Resources: bauxite; gypsum;
limestone
Agriculture: sugar; bananas; citrus
fruits; coffee; allspice; coconuts
Industry: tourism; bauxite; textiles;
processed foods; sugar; rum; molasses;
cement; metal; chemical products

FOREIGN TRADE

Exports: $1.2 billion
Imports: $1.8 billion

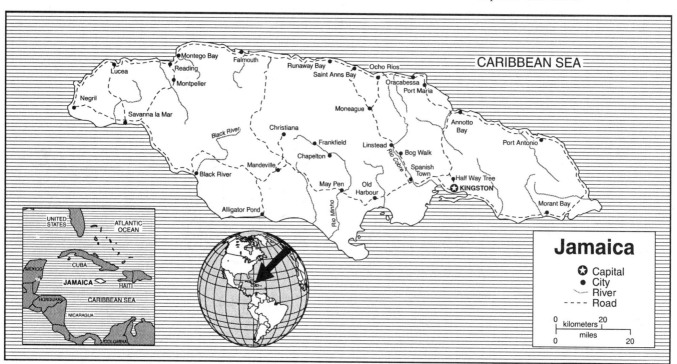

The first Spanish settlement **1509**	Jamaica is seized by the English **1655**	An earthquake destroys Port Royal **1692**	Universal suffrage is proclaimed **1944**	Independence of the United Kingdom **1962**	**1980s–1990s**

Violent crime and strong-armed police responses plague the island

Percival J. Patterson is elected prime minister

Electoral reforms are promised following political violence

JAMAICA: "OUT OF MANY, ONE PEOPLE"

In 1962 Jamaica and Trinidad and Tobago were the first of the English-speaking West Indies to gain their independence. A central problem since that time has been the limited ability of Jamaicans to forge a sense of nation. "Out of many, one people" is a popular slogan, but it belies an essential division of the population along lines of both race and class. The elite, consisting of a small white population and Creoles (Afro-Europeans), still think of themselves as English. Local loyalties notwithstanding, Englishness permeates much of Jamaican life, from the language to sports. According to former Prime Minister Michael Manley: "The problem in Jamaica is how do you get the Jamaican to divorce his mind from the paralysis of his history, which was all bitter colonial frustration, so that he sees his society in terms of this is what crippled me?"

SOCIAL CHANGE

Manley's first government (1975–1980) was one of the few in the West Indies to incorporate the mass of the people into a political process. He was aware that in a country such as Jamaica—where the majority of the population were poor, ill educated, and lacked essential services—the promise to provide basic needs would win him widespread support. Programs to provide Jamaicans with basic health care and education were expanded, as were services. Many products were subject to price controls or were subsidized to make them

available to the majority of the people. Cuban medical teams and teachers were brought to Jamaica to fill the manpower gaps until local people could be trained. However, Jamaica's fragile economy could not support Manley's policies, and he was eventually opposed by the entenched elite and voted out of office. In 1989, however, Manley was returned to office with a new image as a moderate, willing to compromise and aware of the need for foreign-capital investment. Manley retired in 1992 and was replaced by Prime Minister Percival J. Patterson, who promised to accelerate Jamaica's transition to a free-market economy.

SOCIAL PROBLEMS

The problems remain. An increase in racial tensions over the past few decades reflects not only a new black awareness but the fact that color is still an important factor in Jamaican society. Blacks and whites are far from equal. The Rastafarian movement symbolizes the kinds of tensions that are growing: Rastafarians believe that they are not Jamaicans at all, but Ethiopians. The Rastafarian movement is a genuine rejection on the part of poor Jamaicans of Western white man's civilization.

Increasing crime and violence have been a major social problem in Jamaica in recent years. A stagnant economy, rising unemployment, problems associated with urbanization, and a lessened respect for authority have contributed to the rising crime rate.

As is the case in many Third World countries where unemployment and disaf-

fection are common, drug use is high in Jamaica. The government is reluctant to enforce drug control, however, for approximately 8,000 rural families depend on the cultivation of *ganga* (marijuana) to supplement their already marginal incomes.

HUMAN RIGHTS

Jamaica suffers from a high level of violent crime, some of which is politically motivated and tends to be associated with election campaigns. Both major parties have supporters who employ violence for political purposes. The legal system has been unable to contain the violence or bring the guilty to justice because of a pervasive code of silence enforced at the local level.

On the positive side, Jamaica's press is basically free and human rights are generally respected. Press freedom is observed in practice within the broad limits of libel laws and the State Secrets Act. Opposition parties publish newspapers and magazines that are highly critical of government policies, and foreign publications are widely available.

Jamaica's labor-union movement is strong and well organized and has contributed many leaders to the political process. Unions are among the strongest and best organizations in the country and are closely tied to political parties.

DEVELOPMENT

Jamaica's 1993–1994 budget is designed to lower inflation, which at one point in the 1992–1993 fiscal year reached 105%. Tax increases in combination with aggressive pursuit of tax evaders highlight the new budget. The government hopes to encourage investment and stresses production, with an eye to increasing employment opportunities.

FREEDOM

General elections in March 1993 were marked by violence and irregularities. Prime Minister Patterson has resolved "to complete the process of electoral reform . . . to ensure that elections are not marred by acts of violence and malpractices." He hoped for cooperation from the opposition Jamaica Labour Party.

HEALTH/WELFARE

Reports of violence against women increased dramatically in 1992 and 1993 and for the first time forced the Jamaica Council on Human Rights, founded in 1968, to focus on women's issues. In domestic cases women are reluctant to bring charges against their partners, for conviction would result in jail and a loss of "security" and income.

ACHIEVEMENTS

Marcus Garvey was posthumously declared Jamaica's first National Hero in 1964 because of his leading role in the international movement against racism. He called passionately for the recognition of the equal dignity of human beings regardless of race, religion, or national origin. Garvey died in London in 1940.

St. Kitts–Nevis

GEOGRAPHY

Area in Square Kilometers (Miles):
261 (101) (about 2 times the size of
Washington, D.C.)
Capital (Population): Basseterre
(15,000)
Climate: subtropical

PEOPLE

Population
Total: 40,100
Annual Growth Rate: 0.3%
Rural/Urban Population Ratio: n/a
Ethnic Makeup of Population: mainly
of black African descent

Health
Life Expectancy at Birth: 63 years
(male); 69 years (female)
Infant Mortality Rate (Ratio):
22/1,000
Average Caloric Intake: n/a
Physicians Available (Ratio): 1/3,125

Religion(s)
Anglican; other Protestant sects;
Roman Catholic

Education
Adult Literacy Rate: 90%

COMMUNICATION

Telephones: 9,367
Newspapers: n/a

TRANSPORTATION

Highways—Kilometers (Miles): 305
(189)

Railroads—Kilometers (Miles): 58
(36)
Usable Airfields: 2

GOVERNMENT

Type: independent state within
Commonwealth; recognizes Queen
Elizabeth II as chief of state
Independence Date: September 19,
1983
Head of State: Prime Minister
Kennedy Alphonse Simmonds
Political Parties: St.
Christopher–Nevis Labor Party;
People's Action Movement; Nevis
Reformation Party
Suffrage: universal adult

MILITARY

Number of Armed Forces: n/a
*Military Expenditures (% of Central
Government Expenditures):* n/a
Current Hostilities: none

ECONOMY

Currency ($ U.S. Equivalent): 2.7
East Caribbean dollars = $1 (fixed
rate)
Per Capita Income/GDP:
$3,650/$147 million
Inflation Rate: 4.2%
Total Foreign Debt: $26.4 million
Natural Resources: n/a
Agriculture: sugarcane on St. Kitts;
cotton on Nevis
Industry: sugar processing; tourism;
cotton; salt; copra

FOREIGN TRADE

Exports: $24.6 million
Imports: $103.2 million

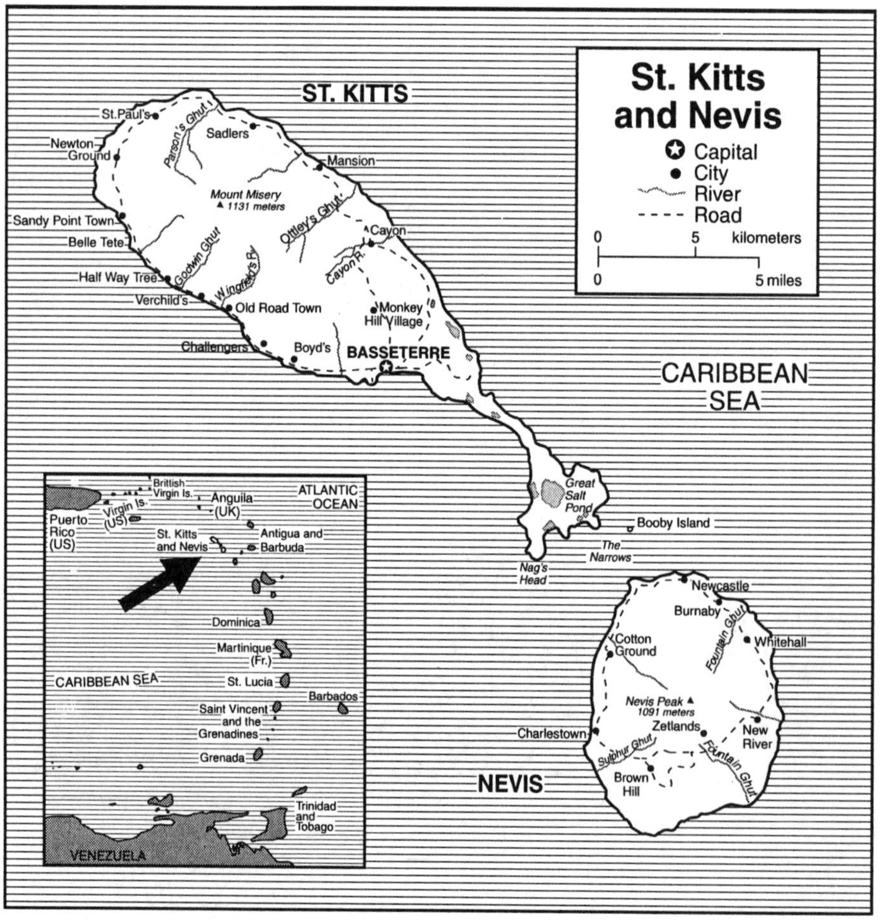

FIFTY-FIFTY GOVERNMENT?

St. Kitts–Nevis declared its independence on September 19, 1983,
making it the third two-island country in the Caribbean (the others are
Trinidad/Tobago and Antigua/Barbuda). The desire on the part of the
citizens of the smaller island of Nevis for an equal say in the government
is potentially a source of considerable friction. Allowing people on
Nevis—who comprise less than 20 percent of the nation's total population—to have a 50 percent vote in governmental decisions is bitterly
opposed by the citizens in St. Kitts. This conflict may prove to be a
more serious problem now that independence has been gained.

The islands are discovered and named by Christopher Columbus
1493

The British colony is settled by Captain Thomas Warner
1623

A land battle at Frigate Bay disrupts a peaceful accord between France and England
1689

The English are expelled by French at the siege of Brimstone Hill
1782

The French are beaten at the sea battle of Frigate Bay, the beginning of continuous British rule
1792

Self-government as an Associate State of the United Kingdom
1967

1980s–1990s

Independence of the United Kingdom

Kennedy Simmonds becomes prime minister

The promotion of tourism stimulates economic growth

ST. KITTS–NEVIS: THE NEWEST NATION

As of September 19, 1983, the twin-island state of St. Kitts–Nevis became an independent nation. The country had been a British colony since 1623, when Captain Thomas Warner landed with his wife and eldest son, along with 13 other settlers. The colony fared well, and soon other Caribbean islands were being settled by colonists sent out from St. Kitts (also commonly known as St. Christopher). As a result St. Kitts has been referred to as "the Mother Isle of the British West Indies."

The history of this small island nation is the story of the classic duel between the big sea powers of the period—Great Britain, France, and Spain—and the natives—in this case, the Carib Indians. (Although much of the nation's history has centered around St. Kitts, the larger of the two islands, Nevis, only 2 miles away, has always been considered a part of the main island, and its history is tied into that of St. Kitts.) The British were the first settlers on the island of St. Kitts but were followed that same year by the French. In a unique compromise, considering the era, the British and French divided the territory in 1627 and lived in peace for a number of decades. A significant reason for this British/French cooperation was the constant pressure from their common enemies: the aggressive Spanish and the fierce Carib Indians.

This peaceful alliance lasted until 1689, when a raging land battle at Frigate Bay, St. Kitts, put an end to the peaceful coex-

istence and opened hostilities between the two factions that would last for 100 years. Finally, in 1782, the siege of Brimstone Hill, "the Gibraltar of the West Indies," settled the affair in the French's favor. When several thousand French troops rousted some 700 Britons from the fort, everyone felt the battle had been so well fought that the French allowed the defenders to march out in full formation to honor their bravery. The expression "peace with honor" has its roots in this historic encounter. The next year the tide turned in favor of the British at the sea battle of Frigate Bay. British Admiral Hood, through a series of brilliant maneuvers, soundly defeated French Admiral Count de Grasse. This time the British allowed the French to have "peace with honor." Thereafter the islands remained under British rule until independence in 1983.

AGRICULTURE

Before the British colonized the island, St. Kitts was called *Liamiuga* ("Fertile Isle") by the Carib Indians. The name was, and is, apt, because agriculture plays a big role in the economy of the islands. Almost 90 percent of the nation's economy is based on the export of sugar; the rest derives from the tourist trade. Because the sugar market is so unstable, the islands' economy fluctuates considerably. Nearly one-third of St. Kitts's land (some 16,000 acres) is under cultivation. In a good year, sugar production can exceed 50,000 tons. Although over the years growers have experimented with a number of other crops, they always have come back to sugarcane.

TOURISM

Unlike such islands as Barbados and Antigua, St. Kitts–Nevis for years chose not to use tourism as a buffer to offset any disastrous fluctuations in sugar prices. On St. Kitts there is an antitourism attitude that can be traced back to the repressive administration of Robert Bradshaw, the first prime minister of St. Kitts–Nevis after it achieved self-government as an Associate State of the United Kingdom on February 27, 1967. A black nationalist, Bradshaw worked to discourage tourism and threatened to nationalize all land holdings. Under the moderate leadership of Prime Minister Kennedy Simmonds, the opening of a major resort on St. Nevis and plans for the construction of a deepwater port have attracted investment and contributed to significant economic growth.

FUTURE CHALLENGES

The future of St. Kitts–Nevis will depend on its ability to broaden its economic base. A potential problem of some magnitude looms. The island of Nevis, long in the shadow of the more populous and prosperous St. Kitts, has raised the possibility of secession. Under the Constitution, the Nevis Assembly can initiate secession proceedings by a two-thirds vote.

DEVELOPMENT

The nation has a mixed economy based on sugarcane, tourism, and light industry. While most commercial enterprises are privately owned, the sugar industry and 85% of all arable land are owned by a state corporation. Economic growth improved to 6% in 1992.

FREEDOM

The election in 1984 of Constance Mitcham to Parliament signaled a new role for women. She was subsequently appointed minister of women's affairs, a position she still holds. Despite her success, women still occupy a very small percentage of senior civil-service positions.

HEALTH/WELFARE

Since the economy of St. Kitts–Nevis is so dependent on the sugarcane crop, the overall welfare of the country is at the mercy of the world sugar market. Although a minimum wage is established in law, the amount is generally recognized as less than what a person can reasonably be expected to live on.

ACHIEVEMENTS

St. Kitts–Nevis was the first successful British settlement in the Caribbean. St. Kitts–Nevis was the birthplace of Alexander Hamilton, the first U.S. secretary of the Treasury Department and an American statesman.

St. Lucia

GEOGRAPHY

Area in Square Kilometers (Miles):
619 (238) (about ⅕ the size of
Rhode Island)
Capital (Population): Castries
(55,000)
Climate: maritime tropical

PEOPLE

Population
Total: 151,800
Annual Growth Rate: 1.7%
Rural/Urban Population Ratio: 50/50
Ethnic Makeup of Population: 90%
black; 6% mixed; 3% East Indian;
1% white

Health
Life Expectancy at Birth: 70 years
(male); 75 years (female)
Infant Mortality Rate (Ratio):
18/1,000
Average Caloric Intake: 99% of FAO
minimum
Physicians Available (Ratio): 1/2,636

Religion(s)
90% Roman Catholic; 3% Church of
England; 7% other Protestant sects

Education
Adult Literacy Rate: 78%

COMMUNICATION

Telephones: 9,500
Newspapers: none

TRANSPORTATION

Highways—Kilometers (Miles): 806
(500)

Railroads—Kilometers (Miles): none
Usable Airfields: 2

GOVERNMENT

Type: independent state within
Commonwealth, recognizes Queen
Elizabeth II as chief of state
Independence Date: February 22,
1979
Head of State: Prime Minister John
George Compton
Political Parties: United Workers
Party; St. Lucia Labor Party;
Progressive Labor Party
Suffrage: universal at 18

MILITARY

Number of Armed Forces: no army;
special unit for defense within police
force
*Military Expenditures (% of Central
Government Expenditures):* n/a
Current Hostilities: none

ECONOMY

Currency ($ U.S. Equivalent): 2.7
East Caribbean dollars = $1 (fixed
rate)
Per Capita Income/GDP:
$1,930/$295 million
Inflation Rate: 4.2%
Total Foreign Debt: $54.5 million
Natural Resources: forests; minerals
(pumice); mineral springs
Agriculture: bananas; coconuts;
cocoa; citrus fruits; spices, livestock
Industry: garments; electronic
components; beverages; corrugated
boxes; tourism

FOREIGN TRADE

Exports: $127 million
Imports: $270 million

DRIVE-IN VOLCANO

St. Lucia is a small, mountainous island. Amid the deep valleys and
beautiful tropical flowers lies the smoldering volcano Soufrière. It is
possible to drive a car right to the lip of the fuming crater and boil an
egg in one of the many surrounding streams. The area around the crater
has a number of hot springs, some of which have been in use as sulphur
baths since 1785, when King Louis XVI had the water channeled for
the benefit of his troops.

St. Lucia

- ✪ Capital
- ● City
- ⌇ River
- - - - Road

The English take
possession of St.
Lucia
1638

The English
regain
possession
from
France
1794

Riots in St. Lucia
1908

Universal adult
suffrage
1951

Independence of
the United
Kingdom
1979

1980s–1990s

John Compton
wins the election
in 1992

Economic growth
remains strong;
unemployment
remains high

Poet Derek
Walcott wins the
Nobel Prize for
Literature

ST. LUCIA: ENGLISH POLITICS, FRENCH CULTURE

The history of St. Lucia gives striking testimony to the fact that the sugar economy together with the contrasting cultures of various colonial masters were crucial in shaping the land, social structures, and life-styles of its people. The island changed hands between the French and the English at least seven times, and the influences of both cultures are still evident today. Ninety percent of the population speak French *patois* (dialect), while the educated and the elite prefer English. Indeed, the educated perceive patois as suitable only for proverbs and curses. On St. Lucia and the other patois-speaking islands (Dominica, Grenada), some view the common language as the true reflection of their uniqueness. English, however, is the language of status and opportunity. In terms of religion, most St. Lucians are Roman Catholic.

HISTORY

The original inhabitants of St. Lucia were Arawak Indians who had been forced off the South American mainland by the cannibalistic Carib Indians. Gradually, the Carib also moved onto the Caribbean islands and destroyed most of the Arawak culture. Evidence of that early civilization has been found in rich archaeological sites on St. Lucia. The date of the European discovery of the island is uncertain; it may have occurred in 1499 or 1504 by the navigator and map maker Juan de la Cosa, who explored the Windward Islands dur-

ing the early years of the sixteenth century. The Dutch, French, and English all established small settlements or trading posts on the island in the seventeenth century but were resisted by the Caribs. The first successful settlement dates from 1651, when the French were able to maintain a foothold.

POLITICAL CULTURE

The island's political culture is English. Upon independence of the United Kingdom in 1979, St. Lucians adopted the British parliamentary system, which includes specific safeguards for the preservation of human rights. Despite several years of political disruption caused by the jockeying for power of several political parties and affiliated interests, St. Lucian politics is essentially stable.

THE ECONOMY

St. Lucia has an economy that is as diverse as any in the Caribbean. Essentially agricultural, the country has also developed a tourism industry, manufacturing, and related construction activity. A recent "mineral inventory" has located possible gold deposits, but exploitation must first await the creation of appropriate mining legislation.

The Caribbean Basin Initiative of the United States has produced mixed reviews in St. Lucia. While textile, clothing, and nontraditional categories exported to the United States increased by 476 percent between 1983 and 1990, Prime Minister John Compton complained that the CBI

largely had failed to deliver, primarily because of nontariff trade barriers. He also expressed concern about the potential impact on the Caribbean of the U.S.–Mexican free-trade agreement. Mexico enjoyed key advantages over Caribbean nations in trade with the United States, Compton said, including a common border, lower labor costs, a tradition of cooperation, and a huge Mexican market that cannot be ignored by the United States.

EDUCATION AND EMIGRATION

Education in St. Lucia has traditionally been brief and perfunctory. Few students attend secondary school, and very few (3 percent) ever attend a university. Although the government reports that 95 percent of those eligible attend elementary school, farm and related chores severely reduce attendance figures. In recent years St. Lucia has channeled more than 20 percent of its expenditures into education and health care. In 1980 patient care in the general hospital was made free of charge. Population growth is relatively low, but emigration off the island is a significant factor. For years St. Lucians, together with Dominicans, traveled to French Guiana to work in the gold fields. More recently they have crossed to neighboring Martinique, a French department, in search of work.

DEVELOPMENT

St. Lucia has enjoyed several years of sustained economic growth. The agricultural, tourist, and, more recently, the manufacturing and construction sectors were strong through 1992. Unemployment remains a problem, however, and stands at about 18%.

FREEDOM

The political system is healthy, with opposition parties playing an active role in and out of Parliament. Women participate fully and hold prominent positions in the civil service.

HEALTH/WELFARE

The minister of agriculture has linked marginal nutrition and malnutrition with economic adjustment programs in the Caribbean. He noted that the success achieved earlier in raising standards of living was being eroded by "onerous debt burdens."

ACHIEVEMENTS

St. Lucians have won two Nobel prizes. Sir W. Arthur Lewis won the prize in 1979 for economics, and in 1993 Derek Walcott won the prize for literature. Wolcott, when asked how the island had produced two Nobel laureates, replied: "It's the food."

St. Vincent and the Grenadines

GEOGRAPHY

Area in Square Kilometers (Miles): 340 (131) (about 2 times the size of Washington, D.C.)
Capital (Population): Kingstown (18,400)
Climate: tropical

PEOPLE

Population
Total: 115,400
Annual Growth Rate: 1.1%
Rural/Urban Population Ratio: n/a
Ethnic Makeup of Population: mainly black African descent; remainder mixed, with some white and East Indian and Carib Indian

Health
Life Expectancy at Birth: 71 years (male); 74 years (female)
Infant Mortality Rate (Ratio): 19/1,000
Average Caloric Intake: 91% of FAO minimum
Physicians Available (Ratio): 1/4,737

Religion(s)
Anglican; Methodist; Roman Catholic; Seventh-Day Adventist

Education
Adult Literacy Rate: 85%

COMMUNICATION

Telephones: 6,500
Newspapers: n/a

GREEN GOLD

Historically, St. Vincent grew and exported huge amounts of arrowroot (a tuberous plant used to make certain kinds of starch). In fact, its economy was quite dependent on this single crop. Then, in 1954, the price of bananas skyrocketed and United States manufacturers replaced arrowroot with cornstarch. Bananas became St. Vincent's new major crop and its major export. St. Vincent's soil is so fertile that just about any plant will grow and flourish. This, coupled with the rise of the banana market, make St. Vincent a land of "green gold."

TRANSPORTATION

Highways—Kilometers (Miles): 861 (534)
Railroads—Kilometers (Miles): none
Usable Airfields: 6

GOVERNMENT

Type: independent state within Commonwealth; recognizes Queen Elizabeth II as chief of state
Independence Date: October 27, 1979
Head of State: Prime Minister James F. Mitchell
Political Parties: St. Vincent Labor Party; New Democratic Party; United People's Movement; others
Suffrage: universal at 18

MILITARY

Number of Armed Forces: none
Military Expenditures (% of Central Government Expenditures): n/a
Current Hostilities: none

ECONOMY

Currency ($ U.S. Equivalent): 2.7 East Caribbean dollars = $1 (fixed rate)
Per Capita Income/GDP: $1,300/$146 million
Inflation Rate: 3.0%
Total Foreign Debt: $50.9 million
Natural Resources: n/a
Agriculture: bananas; arrowroot
Industry: food processing

FOREIGN TRADE

Exports: $75 million
Imports: $130 million

St. Vincent and the Grenadines

CARIBBEAN SEA

St. Vincent Passage
PORTER POINT — Owia Bay
Orange Hill
Wallibu
Georgetown
DARK HEAD
Chateaubelair
Cumberland Bay
ST. VINCENT
COLONARIE POINT
Colonarie
Barrouallie
ATLANTIC OCEAN
Layou
Camden Park
KINGSTOWN
YAMBOU HEAD
Kingstown Bay
Greathead Bay
Calliaqua

St. Vincent and the Grenadines
⊗ Capital
● City
River
--- Road
kilometers
miles

Puerto Rico (U.S.)
CARIBBEAN SEA
ST. VINCENT
GRENADINES
VENEZUELA

NORTHEAST POINT
Bequia
ISLE QUATRE
BALICEAUX ISLAND
THE GRENADINES

Christopher Columbus discovers and names St. Vincent
1498

Ceded to the British by France
1763

The Carib War
1795

St. Vincent's La Soufrière erupts and kills 2,000 people
1902

Independence of the United Kingdom
1979

Political fragmentation creates 8 political parties
1980s–1990s

Parliamentary elections are scheduled for 1994

Banana earnings fall off

A new minimum wage law takes effect

ST. VINCENT AND THE GRENADINES: POOR BUT FREE

Vincentians, like many other West Indians, either identify with or, from a different perspective, suffer from a deep-seated European orientation. Critics argue that it is an identification that is historical in origin and that it is negative. For many the European connection is nothing more than the continuing memory of a master–slave relationship.

St. Vincent is unique in that it was one of the few Caribbean islands where runaway black slaves intermarried with Carib Indians and produced a distinct racial type known as the Garifuna, or black Caribs. Toward the end of the eighteenth century, the Garifuna and other native peoples mounted an assault on the island's white British planters. They were assisted by the French from Martinique but were defeated in 1796. As punishment the Garifuna were deported to what is today Belize, where they formed one of the bases of that nation's population.

In 1834 the black slaves were emancipated, which resulted in disrupting the island's economy by decreasing the labor supply. In order to fill this vacuum, Portuguese and East Indian laborers were imported to maintain the agrarian economy. This, however, was not done until later in the nineteenth century—not quickly enough to prevent a lasting blow to the island's economic base.

St. Vincent, along with Dominica, is one of the poorest islands in the West Indies. The current unemployment rate is estimated at between 20 and 40 percent.

With more than half the population under age 15, unemployment will continue to be a major problem.

Formerly one of the West Indian sugar islands, St. Vincent's main crops are now bananas and arrowroot. The sugar industry was a casualty of low world-market prices and a black power movement in the 1960s that associated sugar production with memories of slavery. Limited sugar production has been renewed to meet local needs.

THE POLITICS OF POVERTY

Poverty affects everyone, except a very few who live in comfort. In the words of one Vincentian, for most people, "life is a study in poverty." In 1969 a report identified malnutrition and gastroenteritis as being responsible for 57 percent of the deaths of children under age 5. Those problems persist.

Deep-seated poverty also has an impact on the island's political life. Living on the verge of starvation, Vincentians cannot appreciate an intellectual approach to politics. They find it difficult to wait for the effects of long-term trends or coordinated development. Bread-and-butter issues are what concern them. Accordingly, parties speak little of basic economic and social change, structural shifts in the economy, or the latest economic theories. Politics are reduced to personality contests and rabble-rousing.

Despite its economic problems, St. Vincent is a free society. Newspapers are uncensored. Some reports, however, have noted that the government has on occasion granted or withheld advertising on the basis of a paper's editorial position.

Unions enjoy the right of collective bargaining. They represent about 11 percent of the labor force. St. Vincent, which won its independence in 1979, is a parliamentary, constitutional democracy. Parties have the right to organize.

NATURAL DISASTERS

Contributing to the island's economic problems was the eruption of the volcano La Soufrière on St. Vincent in 1979, which caused considerable agricultural damage. Hurricane Allen followed the next year; it utterly destroyed the banana crop and severely damaged the island's infrastructure. No sooner had the banana industry recovered than Tropical Storm Danielle destroyed much of the 1986 crop and severely cut into export earnings.

In an attempt to diversify the economy, the government has explored the possibilities of tourism and manufacturing. Development schemes for the Grenadines are in the planning stages. Tourism may well hold one of the keys to solving the nation's economic difficulties.

DEVELOPMENT

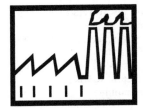

St. Vincent has a very young population, a relatively high rate of illiteracy, and serious unemployment problems. The banana industry has recovered from weather-related disasters, but the manufacturing sector has suffered from the closure of three factories with a concomitant loss of jobs.

FREEDOM

In 1989 the government took a great step forward in terms of wage scales for women by adopting a new minimum wage law, which provided for equal pay for equal work by men and women. The law took effect in 1990. Violence against women remains a significant problem.

HEALTH/WELFARE

Minimum wages have been established and range from $3.85 per day in agriculture to $7.40 in industry. Clearly the minimum is inadequate, although most workers earn significantly more than the minimum.

ACHIEVEMENTS

A regional cultural organization was launched in 1982 in St. Vincent. Called the East Caribbean Popular Theatre Organisation, it reaches out to Dominica, Grenada, and St. Lucia.

Trinidad and Tobago

GEOGRAPHY

Area in Square Kilometers (Miles):
5,128 (1,980) (about the size of
Delaware)
Capital (Population): Port-of-Spain
(300,000)
Climate: tropical

PEOPLE

Population

Total: 1,299,000
Annual Growth Rate: 1.1%
Rural/Urban Population Ratio: 31/69
Ethnic Makeup of Population: 43%
black; 40% East Indian; 14% mixed;
1% white; 1% Chinese; 1% others

Health

Life Expectancy at Birth: 68 years
(male); 73 years (female)
Infant Mortality Rate (Ratio):
17/1,000
Average Caloric Intake: 121% of
FAO minimum
Physicians Available (Ratio): 1/2,198

Religion(s)

32% Roman Catholic; 24% Hindu;
14% Anglican; 14% other Protestant;
6% Muslim; 10% others

Education

Adult Literacy Rate: 95%

COMMUNICATION

Telephones: 182,325
Newspapers: 4 dailies

THE STEEL BAND

Trinidadians, with an inventive skill that has astounded musicologists,
created a whole range of instruments, from oil drums, gas tanks, pots,
and pans, to empty metal containers of all descriptions. Collectively,
these are known as the steel band. The music from these homemade
instruments became popular after World War II and quickly spread to
other islands. The rhythms have their origin in the islands' black culture,
which reaches back to Africa. The sound is unique and compelling.

TRANSPORTATION

Highways—Kilometers (Miles): 8,000
(4,960)
Railroads—Kilometers (Miles): none
Usable Airfields: 5

GOVERNMENT

Type: parliamentary democracy
Independence Date: August 31, 1962
Head of State: Prime Minister Patrick
Augustus Mervyn Manning
Political Parties: People's National
Movement; National Alliance for
Reconstruction; United National
Congress; Movement for Social
Transformation; National Joint Action
Committee
Suffrage: universal at 18

MILITARY

Number of Armed Forces: about 2,650
*Military Expenditures (% of Central
Government Expenditures):* 4.6%
Current Hostilities: none

ECONOMY

Currency ($ U.S. Equivalent): 4.25
Trinidad & Tobago dollars = $1
Per Capita Income/GDP: $3,600/$4.9
billion
Inflation Rate: 11.1%
Total Foreign Debt: $2.5 billion
Natural Resources: oil and gas;
petroleum
Agriculture: sugarcane; cocoa; coffee;
rice; citrus; bananas
Industry: food processing; fertilizers;
cement; petroleum; tourism;
automobile assembly

FOREIGN TRADE

Exports: $2.0 billion
Imports: $1.2 billion

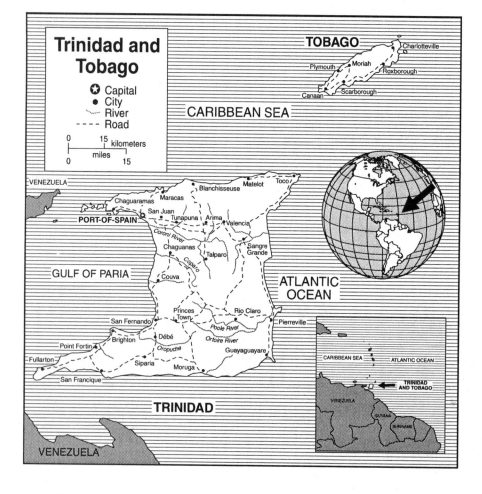

The island now
called Trinidad is
discovered by
Columbus and
later colonized by
Spain
1498

Trinidad is
captured by the
British
1797

Tobago is added
to Trinidad as a
colonial unit
1889

Independence of
the United
Kingdom
1962

Oil-export
earnings slump

1980s–1990s

An attempted
coup by Muslim
army officers

Patrick Manning
is elected prime
minister

The state
announces a
privatization
policy for the
economy;
organized-labor
protests

TRINIDAD AND TOBAGO: A MIDDLE-CLASS SOCIETY

The nation of Trinidad and Tobago, which became independent of Britain in 1962, differs sharply from other West Indian countries, in terms of both its wealth and its societal structure. More than one-third of its revenues derive from the production of crude oil. Much of the oil wealth has been redistributed and has created a society that is essentially middle class. Health conditions are generally good, education is widely available, and the literacy rate is a very high 95 percent.

The country also enjoys an excellent human-rights record, although there is a good deal of tension between the ruling urban black majority and East Indians, who are rural. The divisions run deep and parallel the situation in Guyana. East Indians feel that they are forced to submerge their culture and conform to the majority. In the words of one East Indian, "Where do Indians fit in when the culture of 40 percent of our people is denied its rightful place and recognition; when most of our people exist on the fringes of society and are considered as possessing nothing more than nuisance value?" Resented are the lyrics of a black calypso artist that state:

If you are an East Indian
And you want to be an African
Just shave your head just like me
And nobody would guess your
nationality.

The prosperity of the nation, however, tends to mute these tensions.

Freedom of expression and freedom of the press are constitutionally guaranteed as well as respected in practice. Opposition viewpoints are freely expressed in the nation's Parliament, which is modeled on British lines. There is no political censorship. Opposition parties are usually supported by rural Hindu East Indians. While they have freely participated in elections, some East Indians feel that the government has gerrymandered electoral districts to favor the ruling party.

A small group of black fundamentalist Muslim army officers, known as the Jamaat al Muslimeen, attempted a coup in 1990. Their leader in 1993 threatened another round of violence "because we will no longer take oppression." What is worrisome is that some groups seem willing to act outside of the parliamentary process.

Trade-union organization is the most extensive among the Commonwealth Caribbean nations and includes about 30 percent of the work force. In contrast to other West Indian states, unions in Trinidad and Tobago are not government controlled, nor are they generally affiliated with a political party.

Women are well represented in Parliament, serve as ministers, and hold other high civil-service positions. Several groups are vocal advocates of women's rights.

In an attempt to redress imbalances in the nation's agricultural structure, which is characterized by small landholdings—half of which are less than 5 acres each—the government has initiated a land-redistribution program using state-owned properties and estates sold to the government. The program is designed to establish more efficient medium-size family farms of 5 to 20 acres, devoted to cash crops.

TOBAGO

Residents of Tobago have come to believe that their small island is nothing more than a dependency of Trinidad. It has been described as a "weekend resort," a "desert island," and a "tree house"—in contrast to "thriving," "vibrant" Trinidad. Tobagans feel that they receive less than their share of the benefits generated by economic prosperity.

In 1989 the Constitution was reviewed with an eye to introducing language that would grant Tobago the right to secede. The chair of the Tobago House of Assembly argued that "in any union, both partners should have the right to opt out if they so desire." Others warn that such a provision would ultimately snap the ties that bind two peoples into one.

Trinidadian opposition leaders have also observed that the areas that have historically supported the ruling party have more and better roads, telephones, and schools than those backing opposition parties. An admission by a government minister during a local election campaign that the government would deliberately follow such a policy in the future did nothing to allay the charges.

DEVELOPMENT

Prime Minister Patrick Manning has targeted more than 20 state companies for total or partial privatization. The state will limit its activity to areas of strategic importance, such as oil and gas and enterprises that provide social services. In mid-1993 the state held an interest in 83 companies.

FREEDOM

Freedom of expression is guaranteed by the Constitution. The independent judiciary, pluralistic political system, and independent and privately owned print media assure that free expression exists in practice as well as in theory.

HEALTH/WELFARE

Legislation passed in 1991 greatly expanded the categories of workers covered by the minimum wage. The same legislation provided for 3 months' maternity leave for household and shop assistants as well as other benefits.

ACHIEVEMENTS

Eric Williams, historian, pamphleteer, and politician, left his mark on Caribbean culture with his scholarly books and his bitterly satirical *Massa Day Done*. V. S. Naipaul is another influential and well-known Trinidadian author.

Articles from the World Press

Regional Articles

Mexico

Central America

Topic Guide to Articles

TOPIC AREA	TREATED IN	TOPIC AREA	TREATED IN
The Caribbean	22. The Caribbean: Small Is Scary 24. A Place Called Fear	**Politics**	
		Regional Overview	1. Latin America Survey 2. Latin America: Post-Adjustment Blues 3. Latin America Transformed 4. Privatization Is Not Democratization
Human Rights			
Regional Overview	4. Privatization Is Not Democratization		
Central America	11. Central America's Latest War	*Mexico*	5. Can NAFTA Change Mexico? 7. A New Chapter in Mexican Politics?
South America	17. "I Fight for Our Future"		
Indians		*Central America*	11. Central America's Latest War 12. Even in Peace 14. Nicaragua: Sandinistas Still in the Driver's Seat
Mexico	6. The Revolution Continues		
South America	17. "I Fight for Our Future" 20. Indian Leader's Goal Is Land		
		South America	18. The Sick Man of Latin America 20. Indian Leader's Goal Is Land
The Caribbean	22. The Caribbean: Small Is Scary		
Industrial Development		*The Caribbean*	22. The Caribbean: Small Is Scary 23. Cuba Alone 24. A Place Called Fear
Regional Overview	1. Latin America Survey 2. Latin America: Post-Adjustment Blues 3. Latin America Transformed		
		Population	
		Central America	10. Can Central America Cope?
Mexico	5. Can NAFTA Change Mexico?	*South America*	16. Pollution Is Growing Threat in Argentina
Central America	9. The Lost Decade	**Privatization**	
South America	16. Pollution Is Growing Threat in Argentina	*Regional Overview*	4. Privatization Is Not Democratization
Labor		**Roots**	
Mexico	5. Can NAFTA Change Mexico?	*Central America*	15. The Star System
Medicine		*South America*	17. "I Fight for Our Future"
South America	19. Healing Secrets in a Shaman's Forest	*The Caribbean*	22. The Caribbean: Small Is Scary
Migration		**Social Reform**	
Central America	10. Can Central America Cope?	*Regional Overview*	1. Latin America Survey 4. Privatization Is Not Democratization
Military			
Central America	12. Even in Peace	*Central America*	10. Can Central America Cope?
NAFTA		*South America*	21. Kicking the Habit
Mexico	5. Can NAFTA Change Mexico? 6. The Revolution Continues 7. A New Chapter in Mexican Politics? 8. Mexico's Environmental Future	*The Caribbean*	24. A Place Called Fear
		Turmoil	
		Regional Overview	2. Latin America: Post-Adjustment Blues
Natives		*Mexico*	6. The Revolution Continues
Mexico	6. The Revolution Continues	*Central America*	9. The Lost Decade 10. Can Central America Cope? 11. Central America's Latest War 12. Even in Peace
Central America	10. Can Central America Cope? 15. The Star System		
South America	17. "I Fight for Our Future" 19. Healing Secrets in a Shaman's Forest 20. Indian Leader's Goal Is Land	*The Caribbean*	24. A Place Called Fear
		Urban Life	
Natural Resources		*Central America*	11. Central America's Latest War
South America	17. "I Fight for Our Future" 19. Healing Secrets in a Shaman's Forest	*South America*	16. Pollution Is Growing Threat in Argentina
		Violence	
Peasantry		*Mexico*	6. The Revolution Continues
Central America	10. Can Central America Cope? 12. Even in Peace	*Central America*	11. Central America's Latest War 12. Even in Peace
South America	16. Pollution Is Growing Threat in Argentina		

Article 1   *The Economist*, November 13, 1993

LATIN AMERICA

Yes, we have no mañanas

Latin Americans have been through a painful decade of economic and political reform. Will they now entrench it, or destroy it, asks John Grimond?

Once in a while, something big hits Latin America. About 65m years ago it was an object from outer space that released roughly as much energy as 2 billion atomic bombs the size of the one that blitzed Hiroshima. The heat and dust generated by that impact put paid to the world's dinosaurs. In recent years Latin America has been struck by something similar: not so big, not so destructive and not a meteorite from outer space, but something that has already released enormous quantities of energy and wiped out many of the region's latter-day dinosaurs. That something is the creed of democracy and market economics. It promises to have an effect almost as dramatic as that gigantic boulder from the sky.

The landscape has already been changed. For decades, the most prominent political features of Latin America were militarism, Marxism and populism, and the dominating economic one was the closed economy, whose engine of growth was import substitution. Today reform is under way almost everywhere, even—hesitantly—in Cuba, though Fidel Castro's joyless island still exemplifies the old more than the new.

Elsewhere, however, the transformation is remarkable. At the beginning of the 1980s it was difficult to find a country in Latin America that was not ruled by an authoritarian government, often a military one. There were some democracies (Venezuela and Costa Rica, for example), but several places that superficially looked democratic (such as Mexico) were in fact autocracies, and most countries were straightforwardly under military rule.

Today, on the mainland at least, the soldiers are back in their barracks. From time to time General Augusto Pinochet, no longer Chile's head of government but still its commander-in-chief, dons his fatigues, clears his throat in stentorian fashion and makes Chile's civilian politicians jump nervously to attention. Rumours of coups arise intermittently in countries such as Venezuela (despite its democratic traditions) and even Bolivia (now stable, but not always so: it had 189 putsches in its first 168 years of independence). Though already in power, President Alberto Fujimori even managed to carry out a sort of coup in Peru last year, suspending both Congress and the constitution, with the army's backing. But international opposition was such that Mr Fujimori was obliged to let the people elect a new Congress seven months later. And Guatemala's president, Jorge Serrano, who was tempted to emulate Mr Fujimori in June this year, found that he could not muster the army's support; indeed, it played an influential part in his downfall.

Soldiers, it seems, have lost their taste for running things, maybe because they made such a hash of it when they had the chance. For the most part they were as incompetent as civilians. Not all of them: General Alfredo Stroessner, who bossed Paraguay from 1945 to 1989 as a caricature of a 19th-century *caudillo*, briefly managed to give it one of the highest growth rates in the world in 1976–81. But in most countries, the soldiers found that they could not make a success of economics. In Argentina they could not even make a success of war.

Marxism, too, is in eclipse. Latin America, the stamping-ground of Fidel Castro and Che Guevara, was where revolutionary communism, according to some, was going to take off in the 1960s. Chile was the only country in the world where a freely-elected Marxist government—under Salvador Allende, in 1970—came to power. To this day Maoists can still be found among the peasants of Peru (as they cannot be among the peasants of China) and Marxists lurk within the ranks of opposition parties (such as Mexico's PRD) and teach on many a Latin American campus.

But the puff has gone out of Latin America's left-wing revolutionaries. Chile has turned its back on Marxism and militarism alike; the consensus that is its strongest political characteristic is held in place by the general recognition that it would be folly to return to either. Cuba's Mr Castro is cheered to the ideological echo when he travels in South America, but for his pig-headed defiance of the United States, not for his impoverishing communism. In Nicaragua, his sympathisers, the *comandantes* under Daniel Ortega, were firmly rejected by the voters in February 1990. The people of Colombia and El Salvador have declined to rise up in support of the left-wing guerrillas who have urged them on.

Just as striking, populism is also out of vogue, at least for the moment. Carlos Andres Perez, who presented himself as the populist darling of Venezuela in the 1970s, returned in 1989 as a purveyor of ultra-unpopular orthodoxy. In Peru, Alan Garcia, who ran his country's economy into the ground with his frenetic dynamism in the late 1980s, saw his party repudiated at the polls in 1990. Carlos Menem, elected as a Peronist in Argentina in 1989, spun round to market economics with all the abruptness and skill of a tango dancer. He now presides over one of Latin America's biggest privatisation programmes, and urges Argentines to abandon their dependence on the state. In Mexico, where not so long ago presidents such as Luis Echeverria and Jose Lopez Portillo splashed out on patronage, prestige and political projects, President Carlos Salinas keeps a frugal house and hopes to end his term of office with a free-trade agreement with the United States—the Latin American populist's traditional enemy number one.

Accompanying these three political changes is the transformation of the economic landscape. For the 40 years after the second world war, most Latin American economies were kept as tightly sealed as biscuit boxes. The prevailing economic theory was handed down from the United Nations Economic Commission on Latin America and the Caribbean (as it is now called), ECLAC, founded by Raul Prebisch in 1947.

It is a little unfair to characterise the policies that this theory spawned as promoting import substitution rather than export-led growth, the protection of domestic industry, artificially high exchange rates, help for the public sector at the expense of the private and a tendency to create huge budget deficits—but only a little. It is also a little unfair to describe these policies as disastrous: between 1950 and 1980 the GDP of the region as a whole grew at an average annual rate of 5.5% and in the 1970s Brazil, whose economy is easily the biggest in Latin America, had one of the world's highest growth rates. But they certainly proved unsustainable.

The first signs of their inadequacy emerged in the 1970s, when countries such as Brazil found themselves facing higher oil prices, lower savings rates, bigger budget deficits, growing national debts and rising inflation. The collective response was to borrow and spend, a policy in which lenders readily acquiesced until August 12th 1982, when Mexico announced it could no longer pay its debts. So began the long Latin American debt saga, in which almost every country in the region, with

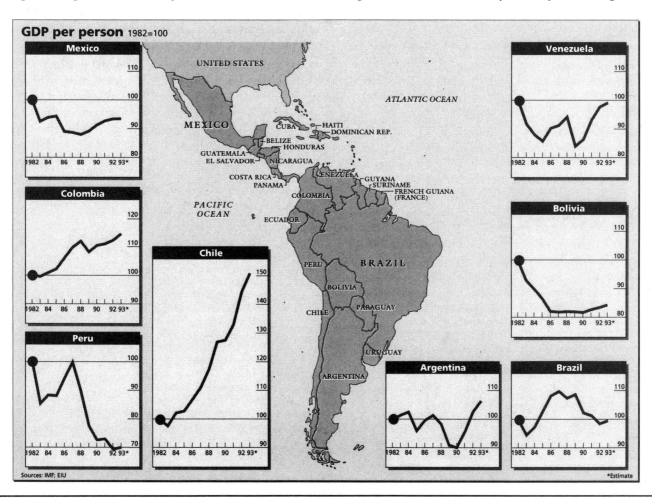

GDP per person 1982=100

Sources: IMF; EIU

*Estimate

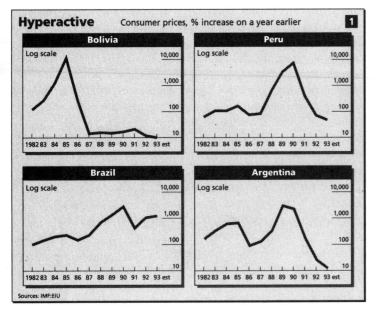

Hyperactive Consumer prices, % increase on a year earlier **1**

Bolivia

Peru

Brazil

Argentina

Sources: IMF:EIU

11,800% (some estimates even put the figure at 23,000%), in Nicaragua 14,300%.

Debt and inflation brought other woes: recession, unemployment, falling real wages. At the end of the 1980s, the region had transferred more than $223 billion abroad in servicing its debts and paying dividends to foreigners on their investments, and Latin Americans' income per head was lower than it had been ten years earlier. The 1980s became known as the lost decade.

Young liberals

Yet something was also gained: a realisation that the old ways could not be continued. Accordingly from Argentina to Mexico, reformers started work under the watchful eyes of the International Monetary Fund, the World Bank and other creditors, to put matters right. For several years many Latin American countries have been going through the equivalent of a wrenching health cure, complete with purgatives, exercise and the economic equivalent of a grapefruit diet. Structural adjustment, a phrase that strikes terror in politicians' hearts all over the world, has followed stabilisation. Budgets have been balanced, workers sacked, markets liberalised; regulations have been scrapped and state companies sold off. Tariffs and quotas are passé; free trade all round is the order of the day.

Not surprisingly, the people in charge are a new breed. Whether long-haired and wild in appearance, like Hernan Büchi in Chile, or sober and respectable, like Pedro Aspe in Mexico, the reforming finance ministers have tended to be young, American-trained and highly capable. The half-dozen men running Mexico are nearly all American-educated, usually in economics, intellectually sharp and in their 40s. Their Colombian counterparts, known as the *Kinder* cabinet, are even younger. An equally impressive team can be found in Bolivia, the poorest country in South America.

The results are already apparent. Last year Chile grew by 10.4%, Argentina by 9%, Venezuela by 7%. Inflation will be below 10% in Bolivia and Mexico this year and heading that way in Costa Rica. Argentina sold 45% of its oil company YPF in June for $3 billion. In 1989–92 Mexico attracted more than $35 billion in foreign investment—enough to make poor Boris Yeltsin viridian with envy.

In short, Latin America seems destined at last to become a serious place, where responsible politicians, not beribboned generals, run functioning democracies and prosperous economies. It is almost as though the entire region is going through a change analogous to one it went through in the 19th century, when church and state were painfully separated; only this time the separation is between economy and state. Some countries, such as

the notable exception of Colombia, had to reschedule its debts.

For many countries, the handmaiden of uncontrolled debt was uncontrolled inflation (see charts 1 and 2). Until the 1980s the world had known few hyperinflations and all had been generated by either the first world war (Germany, Austria, Hungary, Russia) or the second (China, Greece, Hungary again). Latin America's contribution to economic history—alas, since emulated in Russia and Eastern Europe—has been to bring about hyperinflation by sheer mismanagement. Dizzying figures for consumer-price rises were recorded all over the region between 1980 and 1990; annual inflation in Brazil hit 2,750%, in Argentina 3,080%, in Peru 7,500%, in Bolivia

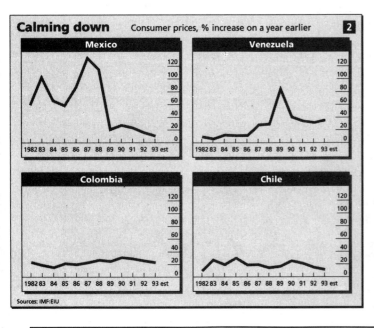

Calming down Consumer prices, % increase on a year earlier **2**

Mexico

Venezuela

Colombia

Chile

Sources: IMF:EIU

Chile, which has been leading the pack since the mid-1970s, have been reforming for several years; others, such as Ecuador, have only just started. Yet everywhere the intention seems to be to continue with reform, not to turn back.

Or is it? Outsiders have entertained high hopes of Latin America before, and lived to see them dashed. Argentines must weary of being reminded that at the beginning of this century they were among the world's richest people; indeed between 1870 and 1930 they had Latin America's most successful economy. In the following 60 years they sank as inexorably as they had risen. Mexico too, another showcase of reform, has gone through great economic changes at the end of each of the past two centuries; on each occasion turbulence, indeed war, has ensued.

You do not have to be a pessimist to see that all is not rosy in Latin America. In general the race to make money is only just outdoing the race to make babies: income per head for the region grew at about 0.5% last year. That figure would have been higher but for Brazil, where economic growth was negative in 1992 and where inflation is still running at about 30% a month. Reform has yet to take root in Brazil. Until it does, it will be impossible to be optimistic for the region as a whole.

Even elsewhere the picture is patchy. Peru's economy shrank in 1992, for the fourth year out of five. In better-run Colombia, the annual rate of inflation is about 20%. Many countries' exchange rates, borne up by high interest rates and sound fiscal policies, are appreciating—to the alarm of exporters. The region's stockmarkets, whose buoyancy is often touted as a measure of Latin America's new vigour, may well be just as vulnerable to collapse as they were in the early 1980s, when those of Argentina

and Chile, puffed up by capital inflows, rose beguilingly, only to deflate like failed soufflés. On several stockmarkets, including those of Argentina, Chile, Colombia and Venezuela, fewer companies were listed in 1990 than ten years earlier.

Moreover, reform is losing its appeal as a slogan. The voters have lived with it for several years; they have tightened their belts, and tightened them again, and now they want to let them out a bit. If reform is so good, they ask, why do a third of Latin Americans live in poverty? Though average incomes per head are well above $2,000, millions of people—in the Altiplano of Bolivia, central Guatemala, Guyana, Haiti, Nicaragua, Peru and northeast Brazil—are no better off than sub-Saharan Africans. Even in model Mexico, a little under a quarter of the population (or 17m people) lives in absolute poverty. All told 70m Latin Americans survive on an income of less than $1 a day.

The pressure for social spending, on health, education, housing and so on, is already building. It will intensify. Elections, either presidential or congressional or both, will be held next month in Chile and Venezuela, next year in Brazil, Colombia, Costa Rica, the Dominican Republic, Ecuador, El Salvador, Panama, Mexico and Uruguay. Voters will not automatically accept another round of structural adjustment.

In the end, the success or failure of this bout of reform depends on Latin Americans. Are they really determined this time to become mature and responsible countries? Or have they done no more than what they had to do to survive, under the tutelage of the IMF and World Bank, before reverting to type? Are they, in other words, still just a bunch of *mañana* republics? The rest of this survey will assess the prospects for enduring reform....

The other obstacles to change

Inequalities, injustice, violence and drugs

Eventually. The word has an ominous ring to it in Latin America, because in many places eventually may be too late. Mexico, after nearly six years under Mr Salinas, has seen some dramatic changes. Yet it is not clear that the proportion of people living in poverty has fallen, despite the efforts of Solidarity: ECLAC says it has, but the World Bank is completing its figures only for 1989. At any rate about half of all Mexicans live below the poverty line (1.13 times the minimum wage) and at least a fifth live on less than $1 a day. If this is the situation in one of Latin America's best run economies, imagine what it must be like in the others.

That thought worries many Latin Americans—social development was the theme of their leaders when they

met last July in Brazil for their annual get-together—as well as international organisations such as ECLAC and the World Bank. A few weeks ago the World Bank issued a gloomy warning that "failures to act aggressively on poverty will likely encourage distributive conflicts, prompting discontent and perhaps even a return to populism dirigisme and chaos." Certainly, stabilisation and structural adjustment have brought magnificent returns to the rich—in a continent with the world's most unequal distribution of income. Mexico has 13 dollar billionaires today, compared with one in 1988, according to *Forbes*. Though in many countries the extent of inequality has recently fallen, on average the poorest fifth of the population receives little more than 4% of the income.

Slow progress ◼3

Latin America, social indicators

	1970	1980	1990
Illiterate population as % of population aged 15 and over	29	23	15
Enrolment ratios ages 6-11	71	82	87
Gross enrolment ratios, secondary level	32	47	55
Population per doctor	2,053	1,315	1,083
% of population with access to safe water	54	70	80*
Infant mortality rate (per 1,000 live births)	85	63	48
Life expectancy at birth	60	64	68

Source: World Bank   *1988

Worse still, Latin Americans are indifferent savers and reluctant investors. In 1990 Latin America's domestic savings and investment rates were less than half those of the high-performing Asian countries. Unless there are incentives to save (as in Chile), Latin Americans are natural spenders: look at the fur coats in Buenos Aires, the plastic surgeons in Rio de Janeiro, the pets' grooming parlours in Bogota. And when it comes to finding a place for their money, many prefer Miami to their own uncertain economies.

As a result, the current burst of growth has been financed to a large extent by foreign capital, at rates which may well not persist. Foreigners have seen sure returns from privatised telecoms and energy companies: Mexicans must pay their telephone bills, just as Argentines must fill up their cars with petrol. But once the plums have gone, the next companies—the steelworks and decrepit railways—are more problematic. Moreover, popular opinion is turning against conventional privatisation in many places. In recognition of this, the new government in Bolivia talks of "capitalisation", a scheme to win foreign capital by offering voting rights and management to investors without relinquishing complete ownership.

One difficulty is that most Latin American countries have yet to establish unambiguously independent judicial systems. It is not just that corruption is common almost everywhere. It is that judges tend to take their orders from the executive. Probably only in Chile and Costa Rica, two countries largely ignored by the Spanish crown, is there a tradition of the rule of law; elsewhere everything is ignorable or negotiable. In Santiago during the 1973 coup, it is said that the tanks stopped at red lights; in Sao Paulo or Bogota, red lights are for shooting, especially at night: stop and you risk being pulled from your car.

In most countries judges have tended to be underpaid. In Colombia, where in the past they could easily be suborned by drug traffickers, their salaries have now been tripled—and the judicial system has been completely reformed, changed from an inquisitorial one to an adversarial one. In Bolivia, the United States is helping to reform and strengthen a sclerotic judicial system. But

generally judges are held, at best, in only moderate esteem. In Mexico, for instance, a Supreme Court judge retired recently to become a deputy state governor. For foreign investors everywhere, the honest settlement of disputes is a persistent worry.

But not perhaps their biggest. Though democracy has swept Latin America and revolution is in decline, violence lives on. In Brazil rich businessmen dress unostentatiously and drive beaten-up jalopies in order to avoid kidnapping or attack; the alternative is bodyguards, fortified houses and armour-plated cars. When the boss of the local subsidiary of a foreign firm is shot in a traffic jam on his way home from work, word soon spreads among foreigners. Foreigners, too, take note when Rio's slum-dwellers rise up to invade the tourist beaches of Copacabana and Ipamena, as happened last month. But most of the victims of violence are Brazilians, in remote Amazonia, in the *favelas* (shanty towns), or on the streets—where many of them are probably shot by the police. According to Human Rights Watch, a group based in New York, 1,470 of the 2,774 deaths last year in Sao Paulo alone were attributable to the police.

Colombia, however, has the doubtful distinction of being rated the most violent country in Latin America. Last year it had 28,237 murders, 83 for every 100,000 inhabitants (nine times the rate for the United States); it also had 1,320 kidnappings. In Bogota even exuberance can bring violence: the day after Colombia beat Argentina five-nil in a World Cup soccer qualifier in September, 98 people were reported killed—a figure that Bogota's police chief later said was "exaggerated".

About a sixth of Colombia's murders, however, are associated with guerrillas. The government has made efforts, some of them successful, to make peace with the guerrillas and bring them into conventional political life; the M-19 guerrilla group, for instance, has become a recognised political party. But three other groups remain active, though hardly ideologically fired; their main motive appears to be plunder and brigandry, and some at least of the guerrillas are in cahoots with drug traffickers. If the government were able to persuade the guerrillas that it could guarantee them against reprisals from their former comrades, it might be able to secure the surrender of at least one group. No general surrender, however, is likely until a new government takes over next year, and it may not happen even then.

Terrorism can be found in other countries—an outbreak of bombing took place in Venezuela in July—but the two other places that have suffered conspicuously from guerrillas are Central America and Peru. In El Salvador, long one of the region's most violent countries, peace seems to be holding between the government and the rebel Farabundo Marti National Liberation Front. In Nicaragua, armed bands are still active in the north, some made up of bandits, some of ex-Sandinists, some of ex-contras. In July a gang of ex-Sandinists took over a provincial capital, and outbreaks of violence continue. Kidnapping is commonplace.

Peru is even more violent, thanks to the Shining Path guerrillas, Latin America's answer to the Khmers Rouges. Although Abimael Guzman, the Shining Path leader, has been in captivity for more than a year and is now talking peace, it is far from certain that the war he started in 1980 is over. Part of the potency of the Shining Path lies in its indiscriminate use of violence. It will kill officials, leftists, rightists, trade unionists, tourists, anyone; on August 19th, for instance, it slaughtered 60 Indians in Peru's Amazon jungle. Not only does its butchery deter tourism and investment, and otherwise inhibit economic activity; it has also led to the emergence in Peru of that Latin American speciality, death squads.

Peru is paying the price of a divided society. Unlike its neighbour, Bolivia, another country with a large Indian population, Peru has never succeeded in giving its peasantry, the *campesinos*, a stake in society. Whereas the revolution in Bolivia in 1952 brought land reform that gave small landholdings to the hitherto landless, the poor in Peru have always felt excluded. Thus the Shining Path, with its grim Maoist message, has established a foothold in Peru that Mr Fujimori has yet to destroy.

Today Bolivia is one of the most peaceful, albeit poorest, countries in Latin America. Its social cohesion is one of its greatest assets—and is being sensibly strengthened by the current government (Vice-President Victor Hugo Cardenas is an Indian). Neither Bolivia nor Peru is, however, free of Latin America's most pernicious affliction, drugs.

The scourge of drugs

A huge war is being waged on drugs in Latin America. It involves billions of dollars from the United States and a vast effort on the part of several much poorer governments. It is being lost.

The war has had three elements—interdiction (cutting off supplies), eradication (destroying plants) and substitution (encouraging drug growers to produce other crops). It has been concentrated in the Andean countries of Bolivia, Peru and Colombia, and the main drug against which it has been directed is cocaine. The bulk of the effort, and of the money, has gone into police and soldiers; much less has gone into economic aid to get peasants to grow other crops or to improve the judicial systems of the countries concerned.

There have been successes. Shipments of cocaine are habitually intercepted; swathes of land are cleansed of their crops; thousands of migrants who had rushed to Bolivia's Chapare valley to grow coca have been resettled. But for every success there is at least one failure. Some of these could, conceivably, be put right: the outside world could, in theory, choose to pay enough for pineapples to make a Bolivian *campesino* reckon it was worth his while growing them instead of coca. But that is just in theory. And other solutions do not even have a theoretical basis. The central difficulty of concentrating on the supply rather than the demand for drugs is that the greater the success in reducing supply, the higher the market price of whatever is produced and thus the greater the incentive to produce more.

Furthermore, as long as demand for drugs persists, success in cutting supplies in one place merely means that production moves elsewhere. It may also mean that production shifts from one drug to another. Since Colombia became viewed as the main cocaine producer, its manufacturers have moved to Peru, Bolivia and other countries. Similarly, as the war against Colombia's Medellin cartel has brought results, the rival Cali cartel has merely increased its share of the market. And as the war on cocaine has intensified, production has shifted to poppies (for heroin), which are now being grown in Guatemala and Colombia, as well as in Mexico and, in smaller quantities, in Belize and Peru. The cultivation of epadu, a variety of coca, is expanding in Brazil, where the more highly valued coca plant does not grow. And cocaine labs, now largely driven out of Colombia, are increasingly to be found in countries to the south.

The zealous Americans fighting drugs in the field know all this; they call it the balloon effect—squeeze in one place and you get a swelling somewhere else. But they reckon, some of them at least, that if they can save Bolivia that will be a worthwhile achievement. In itself it would be. As Bolivia's President Sanchez himself recognises, his country's institutions—army, police, judges, political parties—are weak and could easily be overwhelmed by the drugs business. But it is far from clear that it will ever be possible to put a *cordon sanitaire* round even one country.

In one form or another, the consequences of the drugs business can be seen not just in the Andean countries but all over the region. Profits are laundered from Argentina to Mexico. Pass a new hotel in this capital or that, and you will be told it was built with drugs money. Venture into the *favelas* of Rio de Janeiro and you discover that drug traffickers are providing rudimentary social services that the state disdains. Drive through Santa Cruz in Bolivia and see the spanking new buildings, partly financed by the cocaine that is now consumed by the smart set in their four-wheel-drives.

In the Andes, chewing coca leaves is an age-old habit. But nowadays drug production means hard-core drug consumption on a wider scale, and among many more people in many more countries. So long as it is illicit, it also means corrupt police, politicians, judges; and it means violence. The one certainty about illegal drugs is that in due course they bring bloodshed.

The spring in the step of the llama

But not all will bound forward

Will Latin America pull it off despite the difficulties? Will the changes endure? Will development prove sustainable, to use the jargon?

The chances are best in those countries that can achieve fast economic growth and ensure that the benefits are reasonably spread throughout the population. Chile is perhaps the only country where the prospects of this happening are strong. It still has plenty of poverty. Ricardo Lagos, a Chilean Socialist, likes to describe the vineyards on the edge of the Atacama desert where computers control irrigation drop by drop to ensure that the grapes ripen exactly on December 6th to catch the European market in time for Christmas; just next door, says Mr Lagos, goatherds tend their beasts as their forefathers have done for hundreds of years. Yet Chile has managed partly to reduce its dependence on commodities like copper that can be dug out of the ground by becoming an efficient producer of wine, grapes, computer software and other exports.

Mexico also has a good chance of success, given that so many of its changes have already been institutionalised. The system is still a corporatist one, in which a huge pyramid of authority is controlled by the president at its apex. And questions remain about whether such a system can be democratised. But questions also remain about whether Mexicans really want democracy, or merely some of the things—like freedom from corruption—associated with it. Mexicans are deferential, almost Confucian in their outlook. One benefit they enjoy is their relative social homogeneity. Society is hierarchical, but it is not divided by lines of colour in the way many Latin American societies are: the great liberal hero of Mexican history, Benito Juarez, was a Zapotec Indian. Such a figure would be unimaginable in countries such as Peru or Argentina.

With luck, Argentina will enjoy some dramatic economic growth. But now that the economy has been tackled, the task of rebuilding the state must begin. Here the signs are much harder to read. President Menem is trying to change the constitution to allow himself a second term. Recent attacks on critical journalists are just one of

the indications that the commitment to democracy may not run very deep. It is not even certain that Mr Menem would continue to back his finance minister, Mr Cavallo, if it seemed expedient to change tack.

Almost everywhere, in Uruguay, Bolivia, Peru, Venezuela and throughout Central America, the prospects for democratisation depend on economic success. Any country that has gone through hyperinflation seems to have some extra time, but not an indefinite amount. Reform must start making people feel richer, which means creating jobs in paid employment, not just in the informal sector—the world of gathering cardboard for recycling and selling biscuits to motorists in traffic jams. Growth must benefit poor as well as rich.

The legacy of the cold war seems destined to hold back many countries in Central America. Costa Rica has remained an island of civilisation, but too many others have inherited the familiar problems of Latin America— oligarchical rule, an overweening army and a bloated government bureaucracy—with death squads, guerrilla warfare and cold war rivalry thrown in. They will take time to evolve into modern countries.

Brazil holds out the greatest uncertainty, along with its perpetual promise. Things have a tendency to fall apart in Brazil under civilian governments; the states prove recalcitrant and go their own way. It seems likely that before Brazil becomes a serious country, ready to embark on a course of genuine reform, it will have to find a Garibaldi to unify it. Brazil has politicians who might conceivably do the job (Tasso Jereisatti, a former governor of Ceara state? Jaime Lerner, a former mayor of Curitiba?), but they are outsiders in the race to succeed President Franco. At some stage an *autogolpe*, like Mr Fujimori's in Peru, may be on the cards.

Even if that does not happen, it is likely that many Latin American countries will evolve into authoritarian democracies. Not everywhere: the democratic tradition in Latin America, though broken with appalling frequency in some places, is long and strong in others. Yet many countries are too violent to allow true respect for human rights, even if voting is reasonably free and power changes hands regularly. And anyway many Latin Americans welcome order and maybe even a dose of sternness. That is part of the appeal of the Protestant evangelicals who are making so many converts throughout the region.

The shadow of the generals hangs over virtually every cabinet; few countries—Bolivia, Chile, Colombia and Argentina are exceptions—dare to appoint civilian defence ministers. The soldiers have little to do, but as long as drugs and violence abound it will be hard to cut them back. It is not even clear that the people want to. Although there is unmet demand for justice almost everywhere, in many countries where atrocities took place under military rule, most people simply want to forget; they have little appetite for trials.

Drugs, already corrosive, threaten to become more so. Their biggest victim is Colombia, which might well have a more cheerful economic future than Argentina but for the narcotics business. But plenty of other countries, maybe with Peru leading the way, could fall victim to the same poison.

Of llamas and jaguars

The solution to the drugs problem, if there is one, lies outside Latin America, in the consuming countries. The outside world can help Latin America in other ways, too. The main one is by opening its markets to Latin America's exports. The countries of the region are doing their bit: they have formed a network of free-trade agreements, some of which have led to a remarkable expansion of trade (for instance, between Venezuela and Colombia). NAFTA, if it comes to pass, will open up the markets of the United States and Canada to Mexico, and maybe in time to other countries. If it does not pass, its failure will be seen as a rebuff not just to Mexico's President Salinas but to all Latin American reformers.

The good news is that in few countries are politicians openly calling for an end to the policies of economic reform. Suspicions may be harboured about the statist tendencies of Luis Ignacio da Silva in Brazil, who could win the presidency next year, or of Mr Cardenas in Mexico, or indeed of several others elsewhere; but most politicians recognise that the old model is no longer an option. Where "heterodox" solutions were applied, as in Peru in the late 1980s, the results were disastrous; in Lima, for instance, the poorest suffered disproportionately, their average consumption falling by more than 60% between 1985 and 1990.

The outlook therefore is reasonably bright. With pauses here and backsliding there, economic change will continue, bringing a slow evolution of democratic civil society. The landscape may not be filled with bounding jaguars; but llamas can be sturdy beasts, and their temperament is stolid. For all its uncertainties, Latin America looks more hopeful today than for half a century.

Article 2   *Foreign Policy*, Fall 1993

LATIN AMERICA: POST-ADJUSTMENT BLUES

Moises Naim

Moises Naim, a senior associate at the Carnegie Endowment, is a former minister of industry in Venezuela and World Bank executive director. His book Paper Tigers and Minotaurs: The Politics of Venezuela's Economic Reforms *was just published by the Carnegie Endowment.*

One of the policy achievements of the 1980s was a new hemispheric consensus about the role of the state in the economy. In one country after another, reform movements tore down government-imposed obstacles to growth and trade, and it seemed that North and South America could end their bitter ideological disagreements about the roles of markets and government in economic development. But now, as Latin America moves toward the end of the 1990s, Washington may encounter some surprises to the south. Latin America, which has spent the last 10 years demolishing the state, will spend the next 10 rebuilding it.

The market-oriented reforms that almost all Latin American countries have adopted in recent years are showing strains: a fragile macroeconomic situation, lagging export growth, regulatory failures, and the epidemic of poverty. Those and other issues are pushing Latin governments into more activist roles. That does not mean that the pendulum will swing back: No regime in the area can afford, financially or politically, to resurrect the ways of the past. But the need for a new inter-American synthesis of the roles of market and state is rapidly becoming evident. While the practical difficulties of reversing many market reforms are obvious, the problems resulting from the absence or the incompetence of the state are also increasingly visible. Countries that have just discovered the market are now rediscovering the state and rehabilitating public agencies devastated by years of abuse and, lately, neglect. The danger, of course, is that many of the conditions that in the past made the state a powerful source of poverty and inequality will persist. Voracious business sectors, labor unions, military establishments, and other such groups continue to exert inordinate influence on government bureaucracies, where lack of resources, corruption, and institutional devastation remain the norm in most countries.

The outcomes of the rediscovery of the state will differ in each country. But the broadly similar factors that led to the adoption of market reforms throughout Latin America will remain important, limiting the scope and shape of state intervention. All countries are experiencing the same set of post-reform problems that erode enthusiasm for the market and increase demands for more vigorous state action.

In economics as in politics, events in Latin America have often caught observers by surprise. The region has gone from being the fuse of the debt bomb that threatened the international financial system to being a powerful magnet for global capital. Once plagued by dictators and authoritarian regimes, the continent is now almost entirely governed by elected presidents. Sweeping economic reforms have calmed the region's past macroeconomic shakiness. Episodes of hyperinflation are now rarer and the economy is slowly starting to grow after more than a decade of economic decay. Once the cradle of the import-substitution doctrine, Latin America has embraced export-led growth with the fervor of the East Asian dragons. Almost overnight, one of the most protectionist regions in the world has become one of the most open to trade.

All that happened quickly. In 1979, 12 out of 19 Latin American governments were authoritarian. By 1990, every country but Cuba had elected its president. Import tariffs that, on average, had reached more than 50 per cent in the mid-1980s were lowered to the teens in the early 1990s, while the extensive system of non-tariff restrictions to trade was also for the most part dismantled.

By the early 1990s, all of the region's countries—save Cuba—were liberalizing trade, privatizing state-owned enterprises, deregulating entire sectors of the economy, and fighting fiscal deficits. The pace and scope of reforms varied; the direction of change was the same everywhere: more markets, less state.

It was easy to interpret Latin America's break with its past as nothing short of an ideological revolution. Many articles and speeches extolled the new vision of markets and democracy that replaced the state-centered and authoritarian beliefs dominant in Latin America since the 1940s. Certainly, governments embellished their policies by launching them as new, all-encompassing programs for development. Undoubtedly, a major reconsideration of the region's economic ills and probable cures did occur among influential elites. But an ideological revolution it was not.

Not one of the democratic governments that launched market-oriented reforms ran on a platform of free trade, price liberalization, and privatization. The drastic reforms of elected governments almost uniformly surprised Latin American voters. The victories of Carlos Andrés Perez in Venezuela and Carlos Menem in Argentina were influenced more by expectations nurtured by their past nationalistic and state-centered rhetoric and action than by the promise of free markets. Peru's Alberto Fujimori won by stridently denouncing such reforms, which constituted the platform of his main opponent, writer Mario Vargas Llosa. Once elected, however, Fujimori immediately adopted the same approach. In Brazil, Fernando Collor de Mello won on an anticorruption, antigovernment platform, and his successor, Itamar Franco, built much of his popular support by opposing Collor's attempts at economic liberalization. The Uruguayan government's privatization plans were stalled by a national referendum in 1992. A cursory reading of opinion polls and newspapers in the region shows that doubts about the market and hopes for a more activist state are still very much a part of public debate.

Despair, lack of alternatives, international circumstances, and political realism motivated Latin America's economic reforms—not fresh ideological commitments to capitalism and free trade. Newly elected governments had to respond with new strategies to pressing problems that left them little room to maneuver. An emerging view among economists about how to avoid earlier failed experiments to tame inflation and restore growth helped shape the new policies, which were dubbed the "Washington consensus."

The situation had deteriorated to the point that governments could no longer afford to postpone unpopular economic corrections. High and persistent inflation, for example, paved the way for the unprecedented commitment of most governments to sound fiscal and monetary policies. Latin American countries learned from bitter experience that large fiscal deficits and a lax monetary policy were a recipe for inflationary levels that ravaged the poor, inhibited growth, and threatened the survival of any regime incapable of controlling spiraling prices. Privatization, in turn, was fueled by the realization that public funds desperately needed for other goals were being soaked up by the constant losses of state-owned enterprises. Moreover, the simple promise of working telephones and reliable garbage collection could build popular support for the sale of public utilities far more easily than ideological sermons about the private sector.

To restore consumer products to the shops and eliminate rationing, hoarding, and black-market profiteering, price controls had to be minimized or eliminated. But free prices in closed, cartel-dominated economies did not work: Therefore, import barriers had to be eased to inject a dose of competitive pricing in the system. Freer trade with an overvalued local currency is untenable. The aim was an exchange rate that did not facilitate imports but, instead, encouraged exports. Capital flight financed by borrowing locally at artificially cheap interest rates also had to be stopped. Therefore, interest rates had to be high enough to discourage borrowing for speculation, to reward deposits in local currency, and to stimulate capital repatriation. The disappearance of the abundant international credit that was available in the 1970s forced a change in attitudes toward export promotion and foreign investment. Hence, policies that relied on exports for growth and foreign investment for capital, technology, and access to world markets were embraced across the region.

International experience also legitimized many of the changes. The success of East Asian economies showed that Latin American pessimism about the capacity of newcomers to compete in world markets was exaggerated. Spain's economic turnaround under Felipe González, Peru's debacle under Alan Garcia, Chile's success, and Mexico's progress generated strong—and culturally closer—demonstration effects. The collapse of the communist regimes in Eastern Europe and the Soviet Union also put Latin proponents of state intervention on the defensive. Finally, the only remaining suppliers of external credit to the region—the International Monetary Fund, the World Bank, and the Inter-American Development Bank—used their leverage bluntly, making loans contingent on comprehensive market-oriented economic reforms.

Restructuring Latin America

The failure of prior stabilization efforts in Latin America showed that trying to correct macroeconomic imbalances through slashing budget deficits, eliminating price distortions, and adopting tight money policies does not suffice. Those measures must be accompanied by more permanent changes in the structure of the economy. The core sources of fiscal imbalances—a bloated state, money-losing public enterprises, and low tax collections—must be addressed. Outward-oriented economic growth cannot be sustained without eliminating the export-impairing conditions and institutions left by decades of import-substitution policies. From ports and financial regulation to the trade regime and vocational training, fundamental aspects of a country's economic organization need to be reformed and integrated with the new export-led strategy.

Governments that adopted such a reform agenda have made rapid progress in correcting some of the worst problems. In most countries, after an initial and traumatic surge, prices, exchange rates, and the balance of payments began to stabilize. The cost of that gain was a dramatic drop in economic activity and an increase in unemployment. Usually, however, the resulting stability, combined with deregulation, led to the return of foreign investment, mostly in the form of portfolio flows. Privatization stimulated direct, non-portfolio investment by foreigners. In many countries, economic growth eventually resumed, and employment and real salaries, which had been falling for a decade, halted their decline and in some cases began to grow again.

But the rapid pace of reforms proved impossible to maintain. With the exception of Chile and, to a lesser extent, Mexico, most governments encountered growing difficulties in attaining the deeper structural reforms. Many factors accounted for the slowdown. Stabilization programs are difficult and politically costly to launch, but their technical and administrative requirements are much simpler than those of structural reforms. In most countries, the executive branch of government has the power to

cut public budgets unilaterally, liberalize prices, devalue the local currency, and tighten the money supply. In contrast to those "decree driven" measures, structural changes like privatization, the restructuring of social security systems, tax reform, and the institutional transformation of industry, agriculture, and higher education require more than the stroke of a pen and are immensely more complex. The public bureaucracy, Congress, the courts, state and local governments, political parties, labor unions, private sector organizations, and other interest groups all get involved in the process. The technical nature of structural changes makes for even more complexity. While foreign exchange controls can only be eliminated in a few ways, the debate about revamping the tax system or labor legislation can seem endless.

> *Not one of the democratic governments that launched market-oriented reforms ran on a platform of free trade, price liberalization, and privatization.*

Structural changes also tend to take place at a very different political stage of the reform process. Stabilization measures typically are started within the first months of a new administration, when the opposition is disorganized and discredited and the government still enjoys a honeymoon with the electorate. The consequences of stabilization policies quickly eat up that political capital, however. When the time comes to proceed with structural reforms, the opposition has usually regrouped and regained popularity and has more political power and institutional opportunities to block, delay, or water down the government's initiatives. Also, while macroeconomic stabilization tends to hurt everyone more or less equally, structural changes normally inflict the most harm on particular groups benefit-

ing from the old policies. Farmers threatened with losing their subsidies or managers of public companies slated for privatization are more likely to organize effective opposition to reform than are consumers or workers surprised by countrywide stabilization measures. Moreover, the impact of such measures is, by definition, temporary. In contrast, structural changes are permanent.

The international context in which most Latin American countries are implementing their structural reforms is very different from the one in which they launched their stabilization policies. Euphoria about the collapse of communism and market-oriented reforms in the East has itself collapsed. Today, China's gradualism in economic reforms is widely praised, while Russia's attempts at shock therapy are constantly criticized. In the United States, the chief economist of the Clinton administration, Laura D'Andrea Tyson, has written that "free trade is not necessarily . . . the best policy." Ideas about "managed trade," "strategic industries," and "activist industrial policies" that Latin American governments had abandoned have begun to emerge as part of official U.S. economic doctrine, itself a reaction to similar policies practiced by the Japanese and Europeans.

Meanwhile, in Latin America itself, Haiti's coup, Venezuela's new political instability, the Fujimori administration's suspension of constitutional rule in Peru, its failed imitation by President Jorge Serrano Elías in Guatemala, and the political obstacles to ratification of the North American Free Trade Agreement (NAFTA) have led to a more cautious mood about economic reforms and democracy. The 14 Latin American presidential elections scheduled between 1993 and 1995 are also bound to affect the pace of economic liberalization. As elections approach, unpopular decisions are postponed and calls from electoral contenders to "revise" or "rectify" the economic policies and "give them a human face" will become common. It remains to be seen whether the pattern of newly elected presidents pursuing economic policies they had disavowed as candidates will persist.

Governments in Latin America face a set of similar and important challenges. Some of the post-adjustment problems may undermine the benefits of successful efforts at stabilizing the economy. Others are creating political conditions that may impair the consolidation of democracy. The list of the burning issues for Latin American governments in the 1990s and beyond is long and varies in each country, but several areas of great concern have surfaced in almost all of them.

First, on the macroeconomic front, most countries continue to face enormous destabilizing pressures. Second, countries are experiencing growing difficulties in the management of their international trade policies. International protectionism and domestic obstacles to increased competitiveness inhibit export growth, while a unilateral liberalization of trade and a propensity for overvalued exchange rates lead to import surges. Together, those two factors create trade deficits and political pressures against freer trade. Third, states must meet the intense demand for sophisticated, and unprecedented, regulatory policies and institutions. Privatization, deregulation, and trade and financial liberalization impose new requirements for which governments throughout the region have little or no experience. Fourth, policymakers urgently need to upgrade the delivery of public services in general, and of health care and education in particular. None of those challenges can be met unless Latin America finds a way to rehabilitate and strengthen the state without repeating the errors of the past.

Life After Adjustment

With the exception of Brazil, a country suffering from 1,500 per cent inflation in 1993, all Latin American countries have made impressive strides in putting their macroeconomic houses in order. Enormous fiscal deficits, once common, are now rare. Finance ministers in Argentina, Chile, and Mexico can even boast to their colleagues in the industrialized countries about their budget *surpluses*. Deep budget cuts, income from privatization, tax reform, and other such measures created a much sounder fiscal stance. As a result, inflation throughout Latin America has abated. But it has not yet been exorcised.

The single-digit inflation that was supposed to be a reward for the region's painful efforts has eluded all reforming countries. Even in Chile, which began its reforms more than a decade ago and has enjoyed immense macroeconomic success, yearly inflation runs at 12 per cent. For most countries, such persistent inflation can be traced to the legacy of indexation, which automatically adjusts salaries and other prices to inflation. Indexation is now deeply rooted in expectations, economic structures, and institutional and even individual habits. It takes time to eliminate this stubborn

source of inertial inflation. The main threat, however, is that the newfound fiscal discipline, which in all countries has been a valuable ally in fighting inflation, will come under rapidly growing strains. Since the late 1970s, the region has accumulated a massive backlog of indispensable public investments that will be almost impossible to postpone for much longer. Thirty per cent of the population lacks electricity, almost a third have no access to public sanitation, more than a quarter cannot get safe drinking water, and about half of all the roads badly need rehabilitation or even reconstruction. The World Bank has estimated that it will take more than $7 billion per year over the next eight years to satisfy just the *current* unmet demand for electricity.

The regional decentralization that has accompanied democratization in Latin America adds further demands on public budgets as newly elected state and local officials stake their regional claims on national resources. Also, while the losses of once publicly owned companies no longer burden the state, the proceeds from privatization, which have contributed immensely to balanced budgets, will dry up as fewer companies are left for sale. Perhaps most important, public budgets will have to respond to the urgent need to expand social programs. Without measures to cushion the social impact of the structural reforms, people's fatigue from constantly adjusting to higher prices and lower budgets can easily develop into dangerous adjustment exhaustion. Under such circumstances, fiscal austerity becomes political suicide and governments lose their capacity or will to keep public budgets from bloating again.

Extremely high real interest rates throughout Latin America are also becoming a major source of macroeconomic stress. In countries with fiscal deficits, public borrowing is constantly pushing interest rates up. But paradoxically, in both Mexico and Argentina, which run fiscal surpluses and have crushed hyperinflation, misaligned exchange rates and other conditions have greatly stimulated imports, thus nurturing large, growing, and potentially destabilizing trade deficits. In Mexico, the current account deficit went from $6 billion in 1989 (3 per cent of GDP) to almost $23 billion in 1992 (nearly 7 per cent of GDP), and it will stay in that range in 1993. In Argentina, the current account deficit grew from $2.8 billion to $8 billion between 1991 and 1992. To make up for that imbalance, governments have

pushed interest rates high enough to attract sufficient foreign flows of capital to partially offset their trade deficits. Mexico's $23 billion current account deficit in 1992 was largely compensated by the inflow of $18.9 billion of foreign funds, $13.6 billion of which was short-term portfolio investment—the kind least suitable for stable development. Similarly, in 1992 Argentina attracted $8 billion of foreign investment.

The precariousness of the situation is evident. Sooner or later, Argentina and Mexico will be forced to make complex adjustments. Their inflation continues to exceed the U.S. rate, thus eroding their current exchange rate policies. Without broader reforms, high interest rates cannot maintain stability forever. The flow of foreign capital into Latin America is also likely to dwindle—at least temporarily—as investors see heightened devaluation risks and find fewer public companies to buy.

But the financial vulnerability brought about by the surge of foreign investment is not isolated to those two large countries. The combination of regionwide high interest rates, privatization, and deregulation pulled into Latin America substantial amounts of international capital, which was also pushed there by the industrialized countries' simultaneous slow growth and low interest rates. Flows of foreign direct investment to Latin America doubled in the last three years; since 1989 the region has drawn more foreign portfolio investment than any other developing region of the world. Latin stock markets have, since 1988, outperformed the Standard and Poor's index by 26 per cent in dollar terms. As a result of the inflows of capital, as well as of lower debt service payments, Latin America in 1992 amassed the highest accumulation of international reserves in history: $72 billion.

Nonetheless, the region's monetary authorities will in coming years confront new challenges associated with large inflows of capital—in particular, the vulnerabilities posed by short-term international money attracted by high interest rates. An immediate problem is that capital inflows are boosting the value of local currencies, thus damping exports. The major devaluations that accompanied the wave of reforms in the late 1980s created great incentives for exporters. But the competitiveness of exchange rates is constantly eroded by both capital inflows and the increasing attractiveness to governments of using a pegged, relatively fixed exchange rate to hold down inflation. For that approach to last, a country needs high international reserves and a tightly controlled fiscal situation. But as elections near—or impatience over resilient inflation sets in—governments will become more vulnerable to the seduction of exchange-based stabilization, regardless of their capacity to meet its prerequisites. New ministers will soon discover that politics makes for slippery fiscal control but sticky fixed exchange rates; the former is hard to maintain while the latter are difficult to adjust quickly enough. Maintaining the new, painfully learned fiscal discipline will be a central preoccupation of Latin American policy-makers as they strive to restore growth and manage the effects of political pressures on public finances. They will also face difficult choices in trying to balance the need to limit the inflationary impact of a constantly depreciating currency with the need to maintain the exchange rate at a level low enough to give new export sectors a chance in international markets. Without creating conditions for more exports, growth rates will probably sag, and with them the enthusiasm for market reforms and the governments that promote them.

Coping with Trade Frustration

Export growth will likely emerge as the issue where the expectations and promises of reforming governments are most unrealistic. The new policies have undoubtedly endowed most Latin countries with a greater potential to compete successfully in world markets than ever before. One surprise of trade liberalization is that the dream of regional integration that for centuries inspired more speeches than action is finally becoming a fact. As neighboring countries that historically kept each other at bay with high import controls eliminate them, cross-border trade and investment are soaring. Trade between Argentina and Chile went from less than $400 million in 1987 to more than $1 billion in 1992, while that between Colombia and Venezuela has been growing at double-digit rates. Total intraregional trade is climbing at unprecedented rates.

But trading with neighbors with a roughly similar mixture of exports has limits. The hope, therefore, is to move into world markets. Governments are quickly realizing that it takes much more than a major devaluation for their industries to become world-class players. Eliminating the anti-export bias embedded in the economic structure and in public and private institutions will take

much longer and be more traumatic than was generally anticipated. Years of underinvestment, protectionism, and technological backwardness have made Latin America's manufacturing firms utterly inadequate to meet the exacting requirements of international markets. Most local financial institutions have yet to learn how to handle export risks effectively, courts cannot be relied on to resolve commercial conflicts fairly and promptly, and the decaying physical infrastructure of the region sorely needs to be upgraded, as do health and education policies and the institutions that deliver them. In addition, labor legislation throughout the region still reflects the old schemes of protectionism and heavy subsidies. As a result, labor taxes are too high, dismissal costs are enormous, incentives for training are inadequate, labor mobility is restricted, and public employees tend to get automatic tenure. Meanwhile, the backward-looking indexation of wages is a source of inflationary inertia: In sum, the link between productivity and wages is absent.

Most of those obstacles are slowly being removed. But the lag in the reforms crimps the international competitiveness of Latin American exporters. As a result, the total export of goods from 1985 to 1992 increased only from $92 billion to $126 billion, while imports grew from $58 billion to $132 billion, thus creating in 1992 the first trade deficit for the entire region in many years. Notwithstanding some stellar performances like Chile's, since the 1950s Latin America has seen a steady decline in its export performance that the reforms have yet to reverse. The region's share of world exports sank from more than 12 per cent in 1950 to 3.6 per cent in 1992, the lowest in the century. Part of the reason is that the prices of the commodities like oil, sugar, coffee, and tin that still constitute the bulk of exports plummeted in the 1980s and have not recovered. But Latin exporters have also had to cope with extraregional trading partners that are lowering trade barriers much more slowly. The Japanese markets continue to be largely impenetrable to manufactures, and the European Community's Common Agriculture Policy and other obstacles severely hinder the expansion of Latin American exports. NAFTA's dimming prospects* are also being taken in Latin America as evidence that if free trade with Mexico is politically difficult in the United States, enacting a free trade

*NAFTA passed in the Congress November 1993.

agreement between the United States and any other Latin country would be close to a miracle.

Those domestic and international obstacles to export growth are already prompting industrialists to pressure governments to more actively support their foreign expansion. The region's press is full of businesses' complaints about how hard it is to compete when phones do not work, interest rates are so high, workers are not well trained, new technology is inaccessible, and foreign competitors enjoy support from their governments. Moreover, unilateral trade opening makes the region vulnerable to dumping by overseas exporters, common in certain industries such as clothing. Under these circumstances, trade liberalization and industrial policies that do not target specific sectors for governmental support become increasingly unpopular.

Latin America's experience with targeted industrial policies was disastrous. They mostly enriched the few shareholders of companies in "priority" industries and a few public bureaucrats. The policies also neutered any competitive instincts that might have existed in those industries. Nonetheless, given the widely publicized success of Japan and other East Asian countries with that approach, the attempts of the Clinton administration to resurrect it, and the difficulties of Latin governments in achieving the export success crucial to much of their political platforms, the political tide toward a more activist state role and targeted industrial policies is rising. But the conditions that earlier made such policies fail in Latin America remain. The private sector has not lost its enormous influence to steer public action to its benefit, while the public sector still lacks the capacity to resist. Without a more autonomous state, capable of interacting with the private sector more effectively, state support for industries will only bring back the corruption and the disincentives to compete that have prevailed for decades.

Rediscovering the State

The need to increase the autonomy of Latin governments' economic decision making goes well beyond export-promotion policies. Market reforms have created an overwhelming, mostly unprecedented demand for public regulation. When telephone or electric power companies were in the public sector, governments felt little pressure to develop an effective regulatory framework and a competent cadre of public regulators to oversee their operations. Privatization, however, creates an immediate need for such public services. The stock market can be liberalized with the stroke of a pen. Building the equivalent of the Securities and Exchange Commission takes much longer—especially since an effective competition policy and reliable antitrust agencies and courts were never a top priority under the state-centered, import substitution industrialization policies.

Governments will have to develop these new capacities as fast as possible, though the effort is bound to lag behind needs and expectations. Institution building is inherently a cumbersome process whose complexity, in this case, is amplified by the lack of experience, trained personnel, and financial resources as well as by the general weakness of the state in Latin America. It should come as no surprise that market failures and scandals resulting from poor regulatory frameworks and agencies will periodically rock all reforming countries. In some cases, such problems may accelerate remedial action and strengthen regulatory agencies. In other cases, however, regulatory failures will create a political backlash against reforms. A privatized utility's disappointing performance may increase the government's direct interference in its operation and erode public support for privatization; insider trading scandals in stock markets could spark a public reaction against their deregulation; the concentration of corporate ownership in a few economic groups might induce the state to intervene; and bankruptcies in the financial sector can lead to backtracking in reform there. Any government would have to react to such mishaps. But inexperience and political expediency are likely to lead to improvised reactions influenced by old habits in society, the bureaucracy, and the political system. Economic reforms will not be reversed because of localized regulatory failures. But they will add to the heavy political burden that reformers in the region have to carry.

Latin America's extreme poverty and social inequities have been a fixture for centuries, as have government attempts to alleviate them. In most cases, such actions backfired, increasing poverty and further skewing income distribution. Too often, extensive price controls and generalized subsidies ended up subsidizing the rich, discouraging investment in the basic goods used by the poor, and encouraging the smuggling of under-priced "social products" (milk, bread, corn, sardines, beans, and basic medicines) to countries where they could fetch higher prices. Shortages of those goods often became chronic, burdening the public budget and fueling inflation.

In 1992 Latin America suffered the first trade deficit for the entire region in many years.

Another preferred way to deal with the social situation was through labor legislation. But those laws only covered the small portion of the urban labor force formally employed. By offering generous conditions and benefits often superior to those in industrialized countries, the laws made employment so costly that employers had strong incentives to evade them. The supply of jobs in the formal sector was sharply limited. And even the most generous labor laws failed to protect workers from the harsh declines in real wages the region experienced in the 1980s. That sort of legislation uniformly reduced competitiveness in the private sector.

But labor legislation hurt the poor perhaps most by devastating the capacity of governments to deliver the services they need most. State agencies in charge of health, education, housing, public transportation, and social security typically are the largest employers in the country. Therefore, they must deal with the most powerful unions. By capturing ever larger shares of government social spending in the form of wages, and by creating formidable obstacles to institutional reform, organized labor greatly contributed to the inefficiency of social agencies. The administrative expenses of social security in Latin America are the highest in the world and normally make up the largest component of total social security outlays. Thus, contrary to common misconceptions, governments in Latin America have paid plenty of attention to social programs; overall budgetary limitations alone cannot explain the region's dire social conditions.

Recent economic reforms have had mixed consequences for the poor in Latin America. The recessions usually triggered by the launching of adjustment policies obviously hurt the poor. But at the same time, lower inflation and, subsequently, increased economic activity help. Also, governments have largely scrapped indirect subsidies, replacing them with compensatory social programs directly aiding the most vulnerable groups of society. In most countries, new public institutions and programs channel sizable resources straight to mothers, children, the elderly, and those living in "critical poverty." Until now, such innovations have avoided the deep operational problems that plague most other social initiatives. Maintaining the efficiency of the new "social emergency funds" and expanding their coverage will be a crucial task, and a daunting one. The direct delivery of goods and services to people in a specific group requires a sophisticated distribution and logistical network along with effective coordination and control systems. When the target population is hard to pinpoint and then reach systematically, that task is particularly hard. Expanding the population covered by direct subsidies will stretch to the limit the managerial capacities of new, inexperienced agencies.

But Latin America's social situation cannot improve through compensatory programs alone. Without major improvements in governments capacity to deliver education and health care, progress in poverty alleviation and income distribution will be stunted. While in the late 1980s Latin countries could deal with their macroeconomic disarray through "shock therapies," without "institutional shocks" aimed at transforming policies and institutions in charge of helping the poor, the social situation will stagnate and continue to breed instability.

In all countries, a principal aim of economic reforms is "to get prices right," from exchange rates to eggs. But the price that is seldom corrected in time, if at all, is that of the pay scale of managers in charge of getting all the other prices right. The always wide salary gap between public and private sector managers, which robs the state of skilled personnel needed to run it, has been wrenched open further by economic reforms. Fiscal austerity depresses government salaries, while economic liberalization boosts the demand—and the salaries—of managers in private business.

That is happening as states tackle the difficult post-adjustment challenges, which all generate political pressure for a greater role for governments. The regulation of business activities, trade and investment promotion, the direct distribution of goods and services to the poor, and macroeconomic management—all pull the state into new policy arenas.

The expansion of the state will not take the same forms or go as far as it did in the past. Financial realities, the painful lessons of macroeconomic instability, international trends, and the evident success of the new policies in certain areas will mitigate against that. But the problems of reform will begin to unleash political forces in Latin America that will slow the pace of reform and force midcourse corrections. Economic performance and political circumstances will determine how those contrary forces will balance out in different countries.

It is a paradox that after a decade of shrinking the role of the state economically, the future of Latin American market reforms will rest on the speed with which the state is rehabilitated and strengthened. Throughout the hemisphere reforms will stand a much better chance where governments can improve their performance and give institutional reforms the same priority macroeconomic stabilization has received in the recent past.

Article 3

New Perspectives Quarterly, Fall 1993

Latin America Transformed: An Accounting

Albert Fishlow

Dean of International and Area Studies and Professor of Economics at the University of California-Berkeley, Albert Fishlow was Deputy Assistant Secretary of State from 1975–1976. This article is excerpted from the book, Latin America in a New World, *edited by Abraham Lowenthal and Gregory Treverton (Westview Press, 1993).*

BERKELEY—This is a new world, not merely in the vast restructuring of political relationships that have occurred in the past five years, but also in the dramatic economic change that has taken place. Put directly and simply, capitalism has triumphed. What remains are important differences in direction and style, between European, Japanese and American variants. Socialism is dead: Even the increasingly successful Chinese model concedes that.

For Latin America, this has reinforced the need for substantial reduction in the size and functions of the state. Indeed, this requirement was already defined as early as 1982, when the debt crisis first presented itself. The last decade has been one of dramatic change in the region. Incomes have declined more than in any comparable period—including the Depression of the 1930s—and for the first time in the post-war era, aggregate per capita income actually fell in the 1980s.

The key issue now is whether global economic changes in the 1990s will incorporate and reinvigorate Latin America as a whole, or whether new regional divisions will dominate. Will the next decade belong to Chile and Mexico, as the period from 1950–1980 belonged to Brazil? The next few years will prove decisive. In a world in which Asian per-capita incomes have been increasing at rates of five percent a year, there is clear evidence for the possibility of accelerating growth especially through exports within the region.

Brazil is the only country in the region with a continuing triple-digit level of price increase, and its separateness has begun to have repercussions.

FROM THERE TO HERE

Latin America emerges from the debt crisis a much different continent than it was a decade ago. When Mexico defaulted in 1982, the countries of the hemisphere were plunged into searing difficulties that persisted until the present. Growth ceased and, what was proclaimed by some to be a temporary balance-of-payments adjustment, turned into the region's longest period of negative development in the 20th century. At the end of 1992, national per capita income, including the negative effects of a decline in terms of trade, stood at less than 90 percent of its 1980 value.

The key issue now is whether global economic changes in the 1990s will incorporate and reinvigorate Latin America as a whole, or whether new regional divisions will dominate.

The process of adjustment passed through four stages. First, there was a phase of drastic balance-of-payments correction between 1982 and 1984. The second phase, associated with worsening international prices and declining export earnings, exposed a fundamental reality: Banks were not inclined to lend more, but rather were committed to reducing their exposure abroad, and especially in the region. Latin America was forced to deal with the crisis through much more fundamental realignment than had been imagined.

Phase three of the readjustment began with the Baker Plan in 1985, which was a tripartite strategy of reliance on banks, international institutions and country adjustment. But, having failed to secure much-needed bank support, it eventually gave way to the Brady Plan, which enabled a substantial reduction of country indebtedness to banks for the first time, as in 1988 when Citibank independently wrote down its balance sheet of loans to Latin American countries. The Brady policy was confirmed by the settlement the following year of the outstanding Mexican debt at a price of about 65 cents to the dollar. Other countries soon settled at parallel discounts. The only major outstanding case at the beginning of 1993 is that of Brazil, on which agreement had been reached in 1992, before President Collor's impeachment. Discussions have recently begun anew to complete negotiations.

A fourth phase has followed, where in the last half of 1991 and during 1992, a rather large and unexpected amount of capital has flowed into the region. The change has been substantial. Early estimates for 1992 show a net movement of capital of well over $50 billion into the region in 1991–1992. This was equivalent to more than the total for all years from 1983–1989.

Latin America is again a place for foreign funds to go, but not entirely for long-term investment prospects.

Rather, the dominant motivation has been a combination of high Latin American internal interest rates and very low United States rates, along with the prospect of new Mexican opportunities made available by the conclusion of NAFTA negotiations.

The realignment of the domestic economy of the region has also been critical to escaping the shadows of the past. This has shown itself in three important changes. First, there has been a structural shift in government fiscal capability, and, with it a decline in the domestic rate of inflation. Brazil is the only country in the region with a continuing triple-digit level of price increase, and its separateness has begun to have repercussions. Second, there has been a realignment of ownership from public to private hands. And third, there has been a significant reduction of external tariffs and quotas protecting domestic industry, and a much greater reliance on internal productive capability.

The change in fiscal capability and rates of inflation is a major shift in regional patterns. What has happened in most countries is a continuous process, especially over the last three years, of increasing government control over revenues and expenditures. Another beneficial consequence has come from lower international interest costs: The decline in rates coupled with favorable results of debt reduction has added up to important benefits. The net impact has been dramatic. The fiscal balance shifted from 7.8 percent of GDP in 1987–89 to seven percent in 1992 for countries undertaking formal stabilization programs in the region. Even for others, it went from 5.1 percent to 2.8 percent.

Such improvement was mainly due to increased public sector revenues. Still, we cannot yet say that fiscal accounts are in "structural" balance in most of Latin America. For this to be the case, current income must be solidly backed by a stable tax base, which in turn is consistent with a level of current spending that can support the normal functioning of government administration and the provision of basic social services. The tax base must also be able to support the public investment required to revamp and develop infrastructure necessary for economic growth and enhanced social equity.

If continued, however, the major efforts at stabilization bode well overall. It is no accident that price inflation has been dramatically reduced. Indeed, excluding Brazil, overall inflation in Latin America fell to only 22 percent in the last year, less than half its 1991 value, and extraordinarily lower than the 900 percent registered in 1990.

Latin America has thus begun to emerge from the 1980s with much greater fiscal and monetary discipline. Contributing to the former has been a willingness to entrust the private sector with greater responsibility and control. Sales of formerly nationalized enterprises have accounted for sizable revenues, amounting from one to four percent of total government receipts in recent years. Airlines, telephone and telegraph operations, steel facilities, and countless other enterprises have been turned over to private hands again. It is essential, however, that private investment be sustained and rationalized in its new areas of responsibility. Not least, there must be regular increases of capital formation. If the shift to private hands is simply a one-time transaction, the projected benefits will not be realized.

Privatization should not be viewed simply as part of the process of fiscal reform. It encompasses a broader conception of the role of the state. Enterprises which should be sold are not merely those which are able to yield an immediate return to public authorities. Rather, the objective must be greater and continuing economic efficiency through productivity gains. The immediate financial gain is small compared to the potential longer term benefits.

Excluding Brazil, overall inflation in Latin America fell to only 22 percent in the last year, less than half its 1991 value, and extraordinarily lower than the 900 percent registered in 1990.

The third important policy modification has occurred in the government's strategy for protecting domestic production. Latin America began the post-1950 period committed to import substitution industrialization. Barriers to free exchange were erected to allow domestic sectors to rise up and to develop their efficiency. By 1960, it was apparent that protection was not working well; Only Brazil and Mexico, with their large size and natural limits to trade, had succeeded in growth. But it was not until the balance-of-payments crisis of the 1980s that all countries in the region had become converted to freer trade. Tariff reductions in recent years have been spectacular. Virtually everywhere, the value of domestic production subject to restriction has been substantially reduced and the average tariff significantly lowered. It now stands at little more than 20 percent, compared to almost 50 percent before tariff reduction began.

This change has contributed to the sharp rise of imports in the last two years. Between 1990 and 1992, the region's imports grew from $94.4 billion to some $132 billion, an annual rate of increase of more than 18 percent. Rising prices cancel out only little more than one percent of each year's expansion. The only large country whose behavior is at variance with this pattern is Brazil; excluding its slight decline, the region as a whole secured real gains of well over 20 percent for the last two years.

Latin America is thus a different continent economically than it was a decade ago. Its fiscal situation has much improved, and, with it inflation is now under control for virtually the first time since the 1950s. Its bloated public sector has been compressed, yielding in the process revenues to public authorities much in need of them. Its external barriers to trade have been substantially removed in recent years, and commitment to greater competitiveness has emerged. As elsewhere around the globe, a new reliance on markets has become the rule.

The question for leaders in the region is what strategy of international integration is likely to be the most effective source of growth in future years. Substantially, but not unanimously, the answer has been to seek greater association with the U.S. For the first time since World War II, closer economic links in the Americas are a distinct possibility.

On June 27, 1990, President Bush announced his Enterprise for the Americas Initiative, formally opening the possibility of a free-trade agreement ranging from the Yukon to the straits of Patagonia. This opportunity, like its much earlier 1982 predecessor, the Caribbean Basin Initiative, rested on three bases: investment promotion, aid accompanied by debt reduction, and the elimination of trade barriers. The centerpiece of the new initiative, and its greater departure from past policy, were its trade provisions.

First, Bush offered closer cooperation with the Latin American countries in the Uruguay Round, including the promise to seek deeper tariff cuts in products of special relevance. Second, Bush announced that the U.S. stands ready to enter into free-trade agreements with other markets in Latin America and the Caribbean, particularly with groups of countries that have associated for purposes of trade liberalization. Finally, given that such a step was likely to be too dramatic for some countries to consider, Bush also offered the negotiation of bilateral "framework" agreements that would permit more incremental negotiations covering particular issues of relevance.

By the end of 1990, seven countries had negotiated bilateral framework agreements with the U.S.—Bolivia, Chile, Colombia, Costa Rica, Ecuador, Honduras and Mexico. Subsequently, an agreement was concluded in 1991 that added a first regional grouping, the "Mercosur," involving four countries as a unit—Argentina, Brazil, Paraguay and Uruguay. By 1993 there are a total of 15 framework agreements covering 30 countries, including one with the 13 members of CARICOM (Caribbean Economic Community). But real attention was focused in the first instance on free trade with Mexico. Agreement to move ahead was signaled in September 1990 when Bush notified Congress of his intention to negotiate a free trade agreement with Mexico.

Two years of negotiation were required, involving not only the U.S. and Mexico, but also Canada, with which the U.S. had concluded an earlier pact that went into effect at the beginning of 1989. A final agreement was reached in August 1992. It is still subject to approval by the U.S. Congress this year.

Exactly because Latin America offers the prospect of lower costs, and because of its substantially lower income, it stands to gain the most from continually growing trade.

Mexico's decision to press for closer association with the U.S. was motivated by three factors. First, despite the fact that trade between the two countries was relatively free—especially after Mexico began to liberalize trade in 1985—an accumulation of adverse U.S. decisions affecting bilateral exchange began in the 1980s. Second, an agreement would serve to lock in a variety of wide-ranging economic reforms that Salinas wanted to continue and consolidate. Integration meant permanence for a more liberal Mexican economic model. But there was also a third motive: to influence positively the perceptions and expectations of the private sector, both foreign and domestic.

Though foreign investment increased after 1987, it did not respond as positively to the Mexican debt agreement and other policy changes as the government had hoped. The prospect for free trade, by encouraging new flows of capital, primarily but not exclusively from the U.S., could become the means for stimulating a needed increase in domestic investment. How right such an as-

sessment would be, at least for foreign flows, is offered by the simple comparison of subsequent capital intake: In 1991 and 1992 these grew to more than $20 billion, permitting an increase of some 50 percent in imports.

The rest of Latin America now has to decide on its response to the prospects of new trade linkage. Chile has already indicated its desire for free trade with the U.S. and has been accepted as a second potential partner. Talks will await decision on NAFTA. Despite the apparent interest of other countries, adherence is still very much a debatable issue. There are costs as well as potential benefits.

The gains are associated with the possibility of assured access to the U.S. market, and to the prospect for increased investment seeking to exploit this new boost to comparative advantage. I emphasize this dynamic effect. For given the already substantial reduction in tariffs and trade limitations throughout the hemisphere noted above, the static advantages are a trivial percentage of national income. They derive from one-time increased trade created by lower barriers. But it is to the future, and continuing expansion, that one must look.

Exactly because Latin America offers the prospect of lower costs, and because of its substantially lower income, it has the most to gain from continually growing trade.

On the other side, three principal costs confront the countries of the region. First, engagement in close alliance automatically sets limits to national macroeconomic policy. Renunciation of the use of trade and exchange rate instruments limits the ability to operate independently. It is no accident that Mexico and Chile are moving rapidly to lower inflation rates more comparable to U.S. values, or that Argentina has adopted a gold standard to fix exchange rates. These adaptations become a necessary component of policy. Such limitations are seen by adherents as advantages rather than costs.

Second, benefits from a closer association may not be distributed evenly: It is the likely attraction to future investments that will be decisive for individual members. Indeed, it is precisely such a reality that serves as a disciplinary device limiting national economic autonomy. There is no assurance that all countries will derive significant benefits. Indeed, unlike the previous emphasis upon domestic markets, it is now the possibility of effective export that counts.

Third, protection levels in Latin America will have to change more radically in order to conform to lower U.S. levels. But the much larger share of U.S. trade in Latin American imports than the reverse simply emphasizes the much greater adjustment that will be necessary in these countries. And it raises the issue of whether there will be additional sources of finance to help meet the burden. In the absence of new investment, freer trade agreements will simply mean mass entry of exports from the U.S.

THE LIMITS OF FREE TRADE

Preliminary calculations support this emphasis on dynamics and adaptability as the crucial factors determining future success. One recent study shows a one-time increase of Latin American imports to the U.S. of less than 10 percent if all trade restrictions were removed. The implicit maximum gain in Latin American income would then be less than two percent. Further, the only two large gainers would be Mexico and Brazil. Note as well that the positive effect gained by the U.S. is of an order of magnitude smaller: in the range of 0.1 percent.

Indeed, one reaction to such calculations is the conclusion that, in view of the limited potential of the free trade association approach, Latin American countries might do better by assigning relatively greater importance to multilateral liberalization efforts within the GATT.

This assessment correctly places a much larger part of the decision on the ability of Latin American countries to derive gains through time by attracting investment and increasing their trade. The choice depends on whether a new association to the U.S. market can set in motion a more rigorous commitment to effective policy than a GATT reduction. Recall that Latin American participation in world exports has declined by two-thirds since 1950. The appeal of a regional trade option is its hope of defining and disciplining a new economic strategy that can reverse that unfortunate history.

A central part in framing the Latin American response will be played by the countries of the Mercosur and, in particular, Brazil. These countries stand apart from the others in the region. They are precisely differentiated by the limited extent to which they are integrated into the U.S. market, and by the high inflation rates to which both Argentina and Brazil have been subject in recent years. It is not entirely accidental that these two countries have been the last to have agreed to a debt renegotiation, in contrast to Mexico's initial acceptance in 1988 and Chile's willingness to assume its obligations in full. Brazil has been quite active in the GATT round, moreover opposing U.S. positions in pursuit of a more independent stance.

Calculations of the static gains from export expansion, as already mentioned, show that Brazil is able to increase its exports by a greater percentage than any other country, precisely because it is trading manufactured products subject to higher duties. But the absolute value of such benefits is still a full 50 percent greater for Mexico. Note as well that these two countries alone capture some 90 percent of the aggregate advantages to the region. But these refer to immediate gain. The dynamic effects deriving from continuing investment and greater growth count much more.

Capital mobility promises to assure consistency between regional integration and the goals of global liberalization.

If the effects of an operational NAFTA and Chile's speedy accession mushroom well beyond the immediate gains of more efficient trade, there is little doubt that both Argentina and Brazil would reevaluate their initial positions and seek early inclusion. In turn, that would require macroeconomic stability, becoming a new and significant pressure on the internal policies of both. Argentina would have to confront its exchange rate overvaluation and Brazil its high rate of inflation.

What we see within the region, then, is uncertainty but a strengthening commitment to the possibility of freer trade. What we see in the U.S. is less clear, the more so after the election of President Clinton. No broad strategy is evident, other than the apparent commitment to support NAFTA.

The turn to regionalism in U.S. trade policy was somewhat accidental, the result of two independent circumstances. First, it was part of a U.S. effort to push the Uruguay Round of GATT negotiations to a satisfactory conclusion. There is little reason to believe that a major new advance focusing exclusively on the hemisphere was an expected result of Bush's Enterprise of the Americas initiative. Second, Mexico's early willingness to move ahead was more a product of fear that new freedom in Eastern Europe would deter needed American investment than belief in the virtues of integration. Thereafter, other potential hemispheric partners soon joined.

So much has changed in the intervening years that one is obliged to ask what basis for this regional thrust still remains in the 1990s. Is there hope any longer for the Uruguay Round? And, even if concluded, can it serve as the principal focus for new U.S. trade initiatives? Increasingly, these two questions lead to negative conclusions. There is increasing pressure within the U.S. for greater protectionism and more vigorous pursuit of specifically national objectives. That the U.S. balance-of-trade deficit with Japan is rising again does not help. And trade tensions are proliferating with Europe. All this seems to signal the end of a model for global free trade.

But that analysis misses two realities. First, a third Asian bloc is unlikely. ASEAN (Association of South East Asian Nations) and others in the region well appreciate that their economic future is better served by maintaining both the U.S. and Japan as active sources and active market possibilities. On its side, the patterns of recent trade confirm strong U.S. interest and commitment in this part of the world. Second, the increasing role of foreign investment is crucial. Capital mobility promises to assure consistency between regional integration and the goals of global liberalization. What is sometimes forgotten is that fully half of U.S. investment abroad is in Western Europe; and during the 1980s, East Asia rose to become parallel with Latin America's receipts of U.S. capital. Regionalism is not equivalent to rejection of important outside interests.

Quickly rising trade surpluses on the Pacific Rim, especially in Japan, threaten to extinguish any recovery elsewhere in the world.

A U.S. global concern remains, but it may now be advanced through more attention to a regional focus rather than through the traditional GATT route. Independently of whether or not there is a successful conclusion to the current global negotiations, trade interests are now likely to have a more self-conscious regional dimension. NAFTA opens a new path. But then the question immediately emerges, what kind of regional approach? Will it be Mexico alone, Mexico in conjunction with Central America and the Caribbean, or the Western Hemisphere as a whole?

Here the answer seems to be clear. The U.S. has agreed to negotiate with Chile next, not with the range of smaller countries in Central America and the Caribbean. They remain on the list of applicants, but without substantial appeal for early action. They already have the advantages of the Caribbean Basin Initiative, concluded back in 1982. This was initially motivated primarily by security rather than economic motives. It was consequently handicapped by the exclusion of key merchandise from free trade and the elimination of investment incentives. But the absence of continuing strong political pressures having to do with Nicaragua that were its initial motivation, and the lack of powerful economic interests requiring accommodation, suggest that this modified route is unlikely to evolve. If it were to, it would more suggest diminished U.S. interest in pursuing a hemispheric route, rather than a means to that end. Trade and investment are much too small to count, not for the countries in the region to be sure, but for the U.S. Now that Central America is no longer seen as the next breeding ground for Communist expansion, economics is likely to dominate in defining policy.

PLURILATERAL TRADE

This then makes a hemispheric free trade area the likely central policy focus, assuming congressional approval of NAFTA. Here a core issue is the form that such a widened structure might embody. Will it be "hub-spoke" in structure, centered around the U.S. and extending out to later acquisitions individually, or will it be a "plurilateral regionalism"?

Economists are virtually unanimous in their preferences for the latter, or more exactly, their opposition to the former. A hub-and-spoke model, where the U.S. would negotiate separate treaties with each successive member, would grant the U.S. tariff-free access to all the others; each of the partners, however, would face continuing limitations in their relation with other members, hence creating possibilities for trade diversion. In addition, investment in the U.S. is given a relative advantage, free access to all other countries, while access among members remains limited. Third, in the hub-and-spoke model the U.S. is placed in a superior bargaining position. It negotiates separate agreements with each of its smaller partners so that each has no chance to make common cause against the U.S. in areas of mutual, small-country interest.

These limitations, however accurate they may be, incorrectly exaggerate potential economic losses and neglect important political gains. Countries joining a hemispheric group would typically have a much larger bloc of trade with the U.S. than with other countries. The only exceptions to such a rule are Bolivia, Paraguay, Uruguay and Argentina; the last has a much larger trade and is much closer to conforming to the general rule. In the second instance, all of the countries already have preferential arrangements with a neighboring group, so that virtually all privilege would automatically extend to others in the group.

Here it is noteworthy that Chile, about to negotiate with the U.S., already has concluded a free trade treaty with Mexico. Others would do the same. Consequently, even without an identical free trade treaty, the degree of discrimination is likely to be minuscule.

TAIWAN AFTER CHILE?

Thus far, most discussions of multilateral trade associations have been limited to a Western Hemisphere group. But that is not inevitable. One could well imagine, after Mexican and Chilean adherence, that the next petitioner could be Taiwan or Korea. "To preserve the outward-looking image and reality of the WHFTA (Western Hemisphere Free Trade Association)," the political economist Richard Lipsey has written, "countries outside the Western Hemisphere that meet the preconditions should be welcomed." Such a trade thrust would be inherently consistent with general trade liberalization. But extension of the agreement in this direction would imply something very different for the future of the hemisphere. Instead of setting forth preferential market access as a potential and rational reward for taking hard domestic decisions, it would alter the picture. Being part of the hemisphere would be no advantage and yield no special privilege.

> *There is agreement on the need for competitiveness and productivity advances. Higher protection and more attention to exclusively domestic interests will not produce these outcomes.*

Once again the politics and the economics diverge. If the Clinton Administration intends to proceed with a Western Hemisphere model, it must clearly give precedence to its members. Otherwise, the model becomes one of selective negotiation—like that with Israel—and loses any regional significance. The real question is the extent to which a WHFTA can become a mechanism for assuring better domestic policy throughout the region by demonstrating the close relationship between that initial step and greater trade access. Mexico and Chile are two obvious cases. Brazil is another, where the gains from better fiscal policy can bring international, and not merely domestic rewards.

For the U.S., the free trade model holds the prospect of offering to countries of Latin America a genuine chance to renew their growth more productively. In the initial years, the U.S. economy would continue to expand, driven by the repressed demand for our exports in the region. Ironically, calculations indicating advantages for poorer neighbors ignore their desperate and long-postponed need for new investment. Eventually, a return flow of imports would mount, but hardly so soon as to cause great concern. Such a policy, aggressively pursued, holds the promise of broad hemispheric allegiance. Certainly, the large number of countries interested in adherence to such a model provides a basis for greater regional solidarity than at any time since the initial proposal of the Alliance for Progress during the Kennedy era. It would be tragic were it not actively promoted. The U.S. has no international reason not to assume aggressive leadership. The real issue is consistency with domestic politics.

LIGHT IN THE LATIN TUNNEL

Latin America has passed through a difficult decade. The light at the end of the tunnel finally seems visible. In the changing world economy now taking form, the region must soon choose its options. Clearly, future success requires a much greater outward orientation than was characteristic earlier. On this, there is virtual unanimity. And in turn, there is equal recognition that much greater macroeconomic stability is required. The real question is whether to pursue much looser association with the U.S. or, as in the past, to seek to diversify ever more the economic ties of the region.

For the U.S., there is an equal moment of decision. The Reagan reliance upon government deficits as the basis for economic expansion has now fully run its course and the Clinton Administration proposals for approaching closer budget balance are the central items for policy discussion. What remains to be decided is trade policy, both at the global and regional level. There is agreement on the need for competitiveness and productivity advances. Higher protection and more attention to exclusively domestic interests will not produce these outcomes.

> *Regionalism must become a route to globalism, not an alternative.*

A Western Hemisphere Free Trade Association offers a common direction to both parts of the region in search of new directions. It is a way to integrate Latin America more effectively and to revive necessary capital formation both North and South. It is equally a way to check protectionist tendencies in the U.S., while boosting current exports of capital goods. Nor does it imply that the rest of the world is a loser. The tripartite division of world markets that is so much feared is unlikely to occur. Rather, such a new regional emphasis may now be required to assure a continuing expansion of global trade.

The 1990s are likely to see a continuing effort to reconcile globalism and regionalism rather than an exclusive commitment to the latter. This is all to the good. Insistence upon a regional route as a single alternative is a potentially dangerous course without firm economic basis.

Isolated regionalism is desirable neither for the U.S. nor Latin America because it would deprive both of important and positive roles in the world economy in the next decade. Regionalism must become a route to globalism, not an alternative.

Article 4 *New Perspectives Quarterly*, Fall 1993

Privatization Is Not Democratization

The Browning of Latin America

Privatization, which has not disseminated property ownership, and the "disappearing of the state" in Latin America which has led to the neglect of infrastructure, education and social spending, may be inhibiting the emergence of lasting democracy. In this section one of Latin America's best known writers and a prominent political scientist worry about whether the reform path now being followed will lead to modern democracy.

Guillermo O'Donnell

An Argentine, Guillermo O'Donnell is one of Latin America's most prominent political scientists. He is presently Academic Director of the Helen Kellogg Institute for International Studies at Notre Dame and author of the forthcoming book, Sustainable Democracy.

In the following comments adapted from an interview with NPQ, *O'Donnell offers a theoretical perspective on how the free-market policies that have led to rapid growth in countries like Argentina and Mexico may also be preventing the emergence of effective democracy.*

NOTRE DAME—There is a tendency when discussing democracy in Latin America to talk in terms of nation-states as if they were cogent, unified entities. In fact, social relations within the political boundaries of nations are highly differentiated and the presence of the state is very uneven. The kind of democracy emerging in Argentina, Brazil, Peru and other Latin American countries can only be properly understood if we look closely at this reality. If effective democracy presumes an effective presence of the state, most of Latin America has a long way to go.

To grasp this reality I have found it useful to imagine a map of Latin America in which the areas covered by *blue* would designate a high degree of presence of the state both functionally and territorially, that is, a zone in which the rule of law is efficiently and equally applied across class and ethnic groups, and the bureaucracy is efficacious in administering policies across the entire territory.

A *green* zone would indicate a high degree of the presence of the state across the territory of a given nation, but a significantly lower presence in terms of the efficient and equal application of the rule of law. For example, a bureaucracy may have a presence in the entire country, but may be subverted to the use of private goals instead of public purpose—corruption. Food distribution programs in the poorest areas of Latin America are notorious instances of this.

Brown would signify a zone in which the presence of the state is very low, or even non-existent.

Following this color coding scheme, Norway, say, would be dominated by blue and post-Communist Russia by brown; the United States would show a combination of blue and green—indeed with flares of brown as when Rodney King was beaten by the Los Angeles police and when looting and riots later erupted, spotlighting a large strata of people in the cities living at the very edge of the nominal legal order and the social mainstream.

In Latin America, Brazil and Peru would be dominated by brown. Peru cannot even rightly be called a nation-state. Think not only of the *Sendero Luminoso* and the drug cartels that control entire areas of the provinces in Peru, but also of the child gangs that roam the streets of Rio and the police who arbitrarily murder them on behalf of exasperated merchants. The bureaucratic presence of the state in Mexico is pervasive across its territory due to the long history of centralization—and, sadly, it is pervasively corrupt. In Sinaloa and other places it is common knowledge that the police are working with the drug traffickers. In fact, the areas that have become drug centers were able to do so because they were already brown and beyond the rule of law. Such a scale of corruption has led to the delegitimation of state authority. In Mexico, including large sections of the major cities, the brown zones are growing even as the economy grows.

The brown zones in Argentina, a greenish country with patches of blue the closer one gets to the center of Buenos Aires, are less extensive, but have grown at an accelerating pace over the past 20 years. Effective tax collection, for example, is a notorious problem there. As the economy under President Menem is rapidly privatized and as the state contracts, even more people are being pushed from the formal, legal economy into the informal one.

Chile, a smaller country with a long history of democratic traditions before the authoritarian interlude of General Pinochet, shares the bluest hue in Latin America along with Uruguay and Costa Rica.

SPREADING BROWN ZONES

Why are the brown zones spreading? A country like Argentina, of course, has been in perpetual political and economic crisis for the past 40 years, so the depth and sustained nature of the crisis has caused the spread of brownish areas. Yet, there is no question that the drastic manner in which neoliberal policies—balanced budgets, tight money, privatization—have been implemented across Latin America has significantly worsened the browning of the region.

A serious consequence of slashing public budgets is that while public investment has been cut, private investment in most of Latin America has lagged in filling the gap which might absorb growing unemployment.

The result of "disappearing the state," as some have called it in Argentina, can also be seen in the deteriorating infrastructure. In Buenos Aires, it has been aptly noted, you can eat dinner in a glitzy restaurant crowded with affluent couples, only to stumble into the gaping holes on the crumbled public sidewalks when you step outside. This is a perfect metaphor not only for Argentina but for much of the neoliberal project in Latin America today: The private sphere flourishes as the public sphere crumbles.

If effective democracy means an effective presence of the state, Latin America has a long way to go.

Perhaps the most devastating impact has been the result of policies that aim to reduce the fiscal deficit at all costs. Since the state sector was the largest employer in Latin American, this policy has consigned great numbers of former state, provincial and municipal employees to the ranks of misery without a social safety net of any consequence to cushion their fall. The labor laws established over the decades to protect workers from summary firings due to restructuring are being dismantled in the name of "flexibility," in adjusting to the demands of technological change and the imperatives of competition in the global marketplace.

Public education in particular has been practically destroyed in Argentina and many other Latin American states as funds have been cut in order to balance public budgets. That is undermining the long-term capacity of these privatizing nations to sustain economic growth with a skilled and literate workforce. The consequence of cutting back the state in this way is that many who were formerly taxpaying members of the formal economy have had to join the informal, semi-clandestine economic underground in order to make a go of it, further eroding the reach and effectiveness of the state and its ability to attract the cooperation and legitimate consent of its subjects, whether in the implementation of policies or in respecting the rule of law.

The "structurally poor," who have always been with us in Argentina, have constituted about 10 percent of the population. The "new poor" who have come into existence in recent years have grown to 16 percent, with their ranks swelling at an accelerating rate in the 1980s, leaving, altogether, nearly 30 percent of the country below the poverty line. While further contributing to the ranks of the new poor, neoliberal policies have done nothing to reverse this trend.

BROWN VS. BLUE

The danger for democracy of brown zones becoming so pervasive, of course, is that growing numbers of people have no stake in the system and thus no allegiance to it. Under such circumstances, people become atomized and a kind of "de-solidarization" takes place that further accentuates the disintegration of the political community. As Carlos Monsivais says of Mexico: "A god will be made of opportunism. If people lose their stake in the future, the only way to make it is by crass opportunism, not only as a way of life, but as a religion, as the only thing people believe and trust in."

If the simultaneous opening of politics and the economy in Latin America means to most people a demotion in their standard of living or even impoverishment, who needs it? That is the kind of attitude which will put Latin America's democratic hopes in serious danger.

Since the state sector was the largest employer in Latin America, balanced budgets have consigned great numbers of former public employees to misery.

Mario Vargas Llosa talks about the "intellectual revolution" in favor of privatization that has taken place in Latin

America over the past few years after centuries of state centralization since pre-Columbian times. I would argue that yet another turn of that revolution now must take place among Latin American intellectuals: The recognition that without an effective state to accompany the open economy—albeit a state that is lean and efficient not bloated, corrupt and overly centralized—democracy cannot endure in Latin America.

The disintegration of the state apparatus and the decreasing efficiency of the "state-as-law" makes it incapable of implementing minimally complex policies. How should the commercial and financial opening of the economy be sequenced? How will salaries and employment policies be agreed? What industrial policy will be chosen and how will it be implemented?

If effective democracy is to take hold in Latin America, the new role of the state must involve reclaiming the brown areas by attaining greater equality of justice and the fair implementation of social policies across its administrative terrain. Modern social nets will have to be built to accommodate the more rapid shifts in economies integrated into the world system through open trade; social spending will have to be increased and better targeted for the poor; educational systems will have to be revamped; infrastructure will have to be replenished, not neglected.

All this will require a public administrator class that can make a decent living so they do not resort to corruption. And it will require a far less manic pace in reducing budget deficits. Why do the leaders of Latin American states, with their heavy burden of the poor and a middle class devastated by years of hyperinflation, feel they must slash spending faster than even the United States or privatize more rapidly and thoroughly than Great Britain? Why not seek a social accord that more gradually introduces reform while minimizing the pain of transition?

To succeed at democracy, both private and public sectors must have at least a medium term time frame (5–10 years) in which they know conditions will be stable; privatization policies must become more than the crude transfer of state assets to private monopolies, requiring competent and honest state agencies to manage the restructuring; and the state must be able to broker complex social negotiations, which requires legitimate access to the process by labor, educators and other social groups as well as the business elites.

FUJIMORI AND PURGATORY

In the absence of reclaiming the brown zones through this rediscovery of an efficient state, there seems little prospect of institutionalizing stability and democracy across the region.

Rather, there will be a propensity toward what I call "delegative democracy," or the handing over of authoritarian powers to a strong man, a Caesar, "to get the job done." That is the Fujimori phenomenon in Peru.

Already one hears exasperated cries for "the Fujimorization of Brazil." And what will be the fate of Mexico's reforms in 1994 as the presidential transition takes place? Will Mexico turn further toward a proto-authoritarian presidency, or open toward institutionalized democracy with a freer election?

The new democracies of Latin America today dwell in a kind of purgatory. Some will save themselves by following the felicitous course of institutionalizing stability and democracy; some will revert to all-out authoritarianism.

The only certainty for the foreseeable future is that we will see schizophrenic states across Latin America, countries with brown zones and strongmen—and blue areas striving mightily to emerge.

Torture Without Inflation

Mario Vargas Llosa

One of Latin America's most popular writers, Mario Vargas Llosa ran for president of Peru against Alberto Fujimori in 1989 and has since become one of the most severe critics of that regime. Included among his works are Aunt Julia and the Script Writer *and* In Praise of the Stepmother *(1990). Vargas Llosa's autobiography will be published in the spring by Farrar, Straus, Giroux.*

NPQ You were one of the first and most energetic proponents of privatization in Latin America. How do you assess the changes that have taken place in recent years on this vast Spanish-speaking continent?

MARIO VARGAS LLOSA An intellectual revolution has taken place in Latin America. For the first time in our history there is a broad consensus in favor of a predominant role for civil society and private enterprise; a consensus in favor of privatization not only in the economic sphere, but in the institutional life of society as well.

An intellectual revolution has taken place in Latin America. For the first time in our history there is a broad consensus for a predominant role for civil society and private enterprise.

This is new. Our tradition—and it is a very old one—has been that all aspects of life must fall under the responsibility of the state. The state was seen as the solution for everything; it was thought to be the only guarantor of efficiency and justice despite the opposite experience of the state being the source of inefficiency and corruption.

Of course, this transformation of mentality has not yet decisively won out. Populism still lurks about and there is a lot of confusion about the nature of the privatization that is necessary. But if we compare where we are today with where Latin America was a mere 10 years ago, the change is more than remarkable.

On the other hand, I think we Latin Americans are missing an extraordinary opportunity to use privatization not only as a technical measure to transfer the responsibility of creating wealth from the state to private hands, but as a means to disseminate private property as broadly as possible among the population.

When I have spoken of privatization, my idea has always been that the workers, the poor and the dispossessed of

Latin America who were outside the system of property ownership should be brought in. Without widespread dissemination of property ownership, it has long been clear, modernization cannot take hold in any society.

What has mostly happened with privatization efforts in Peru, Mexico and Argentina is little more than the transfer of monopolies from the state to the largest private owners. This contradicts the moral reason for privatization, which is the opening of markets and the creation of competition that will drive the process of wealth creation.

Too often privatization has just been used to replenish bankrupt states with fresh resources through the corrupt sell-off of assets to cronies of the political leaders.

Privatization ought instead to be the key tool of modernization for social as well as economic reform. It ought to be the means of giving people both a stake in the system and autonomy within the society. If formal political participation is not accompanied by direct participation in the market economy through ownership, democratization will not lead too far.

During the recent privatization in England, for example, people at least were enabled to buy shares in former state companies such as Telecom, or buy their state-owned apartments at a good price.

Privatization ought to mean dissemination of private property as broadly as possible among the population.

In Latin America where the economic differences are so enormous, social stability will be little improved unless the poor obtain some property of their own. Only in Chile has this begun to happen.

With the kind of privatization now being generally pursued, the chief benefits of growth accrue exclusively to a very tiny elite. This is a big mistake because 10 years from now there will be a reaction against the market and privatization. Populism will then again find propitious ground in Latin America.

NPQ In Brazil, populism is already making significant headway against the market orientation of the rest of the region. . . .

VARGAS LLOSA Brazil is way behind. It still has too much old populist politics and mercantilistic economics.

But even in Mexico, where the advances of reform have been far reaching, social inequality remains so enormous that it threatens to frustrate the process of modernization.

The only way to avert this outcome is to make sure that the market becomes rooted in the practical life of most people. Only grass-roots modernization will do the trick. Otherwise everything is reversible because economically disenfranchised people just will not believe in the market as the instrument of progress.

NPQ Chile, as you suggest, is one place where things are different. The gap between rich and poor is closing, not widening. Unemployment has fallen below five percent and the government has made special efforts to stimulate the formation of "microbusiness," where only a few people join together to make a small business that can provide a decent living.

VARGAS LLOSA And what is the result? In Chile you have the extraordinary case of a government that is more popular now than when it was elected four years ago! For this reason the Christian Democratic candidate in December's election, Eduardo Frei Jr., is certain to win.

There is no question that Chile is in the avant-garde of Latin America. It has improved not only statistically, but socially. And politically it has advanced much further than Mexico or Argentina. I mean, Chile is a modern democracy. Leaders in the region should take notice.

NPQ Has Chile discovered a "middle way" for Latin America, a development model that combines orthodox economic and fiscal policies with aggressive social spending aimed at alleviating poverty?

VARGAS LLOSA I don't think this is a middle way; it is the classic liberal way. The social programs in Chile are not populist at all. They have, for instance, been promoting private participation in educational reform so that the state does not monopolize the teaching of the young.

NPQ Would Chile's "economic coup"—the switch from an import-substitution to an export economy, privatization, balanced budgets, tight money—have been possible under democracy? Could it have been so efficiently executed if General Pinochet

didn't have the society under his armed thumb?

Maybe Fujimori can do the same thing for Peru?

VARGAS LLOSA I certainly don't accept that. This is wrong. Freedom is not divisible. That is why I have been criticizing Fujimori since his *autogolpe* on April 5, 1992.

In Chile it is true that the economic reforms took place during a dictatorship. But this is not a model. The building up of a market economy in England or the United States did not require a dictatorship. Why, then, do we need dictators for this purpose in Latin America?

It is true that the market reforms are taking place much more rapidly in Latin America than even in England under Thatcher. But that is because our state sector was much bigger and more had to be done. In order to get the benefits, we know we need to move fast. Gradualism has been tried too often in Latin America, and it doesn't work. So, you need radical reforms.

But radical reforms are not incompatible with democratic practice if politicians are honest and ask for a mandate. Costa Rica, to take one example, modernized without destroying its democratic practices.

We can also not accept the idea that we need a dictatorship to have a market economy because dictatorships in Latin America have traditionally been deeply corrupt. You can't have modernization of a country if government is nothing but a system of corruption.

Democracy is the best way to fight corruption because corruption can only be eliminated if the institutions of governance are opened to scrutiny and public criticism.

What happened in Chile was an exception not only because they gave civilians a free hand to shape the economy, but unlike other Latin American dictatorships, the Chilean military was not populist. Traditionally, Latin American dictators have favored a strong, authoritarian intervention by the state in every aspect of social and economic life.

NPQ Of course, Argentina is attempting a more radical economic opening than Chile or Mexico in a relatively open, competitive, democratic environment.

VARGAS LLOSA But I am very nervous about Argentina because the level of corruption is too high. Oh, there have [been] so many scandals with the way privatization has been handled. Argentina is the case *par excellence* of the transfer of monopolies from the state to the private sector, as in the case of the denationalized telephone company.

NPQ Fujimori, of course, is highly popular in Peru today because of his strongman approach. The public has delegated their trust to him to save Peru because they think that democracy was just too messy and because it did not eliminate corruption or end Shining Path terrorism.

VARGAS LLOSA Fujimori is not cleaning up corruption; he is giving it a new lease on life. And Peru has returned to the worst of times in Latin America in terms of human rights abuses. The army has a free hand to kill and torture whomever they summarily and arbitrarily choose.

What is happening now in Peru is a classic case where practically everything—the judiciary, the media, the Congress—is controlled by the state.

So the official image of the country is the one modelled by the regime. This image is positive, but it hasn't much to do with the reality.

> *Privatization in Latin America has mostly meant the transfer of monopolies from the state to the largest private owners.*

Although I don't totally believe the polls, I do admit that the regime is popular, but mainly out of rejection of the memory of the hyperinflation, demagoguery and chaos of the Alan Garcia period. At least there is some order now with Fujimori and inflation is down.

But this kind of nostalgic order is destined to collapse and will, I fear, bring

down with it the modern idea of the free-market economy.

This is why we must be very strong critics of the Fujimori approach. If it catches on—some are calling for "the Fujimorization of Brazil"—all the progress of the past decade can be reversed. All across Latin America there are generals watching Peru with great enthusiasm.

Peru, for them, is the new model of dictatorship for the 21st century: the military using a civilian leader who instead of sloganeering about socialism talks about private enterprise. This is not democracy. This is not modernization. This is torture without inflation.

In the end this new model of authoritarianism will have the same result as the old one: It will only bring about more corruption, more social inequality and destabilizing public disaffection. If the Fujimori model spreads, it will stoke the flames of extremism and ruin the new hope born in Latin America during the past decade.

Mexico: Articles Section

Article 5   *Foreign Affairs*, September/October 1993

Can NAFTA Change Mexico?

Jorge G. Castañeda

Jorge G. Castañeda is Professor of International Relations at the National Autonomous University of Mexico. His new book is Utopia Unarmed: The Latin American Left After the Cold War.

THE RISKS OF FREE TRADE

Many Mexicans have welcomed NAFTA as an undisguised blessing, whatever its effects on the United States. In the government and among the general population the agreement is seen as a ready course to modernization. President Carlos Salinas de Gortari's policies have consciously supported this impression. His administration has determinedly pursued NAFTA as part of a dual strategy. Economically, the trade agreement was to provide Mexico's ailing economy with the foreign capital injections it has long required for sustainable growth. Politically, an expanding Mexican economy—one linked to

the United States—would help lay the foundations for an eventual and controlled democratic transition.

Overlooked, however, has been the fact that NAFTA itself entails great risks. No country has ever attempted to develop an export manufacturing base by opening its borders so quickly and indiscriminately to more efficient and lower-cost producers. No nation today, not even the United States, has so willingly sacrificed an industrial policy or an equivalent form of managed trade. By unilaterally renouncing these advantages, Mexico will lose far more jobs in the next few years than it will create. Old industries and agricultural producers will die, be swallowed up or join with foreign ventures, long before the new jobs arrive.

Mexico is not a modern country. True, over the past half-century it has witnessed dramatic change. An inward-looking, illiterate and agrarian land has become an urban, partly industrialized nation with a growing middle class and a nascent civil society. But Mexico's underlying problems persist. It retains a largely corrupt and unchallenged state that possesses only the merest trappings of the rule of law. The enduring obstacles to Mexico's modernization—its repeated failure to transfer power democratically or to remedy the ancestral injustice of its society—remain and will require Mexico to continue to change itself, with or without a trade accord.

Any Mexican government's performance, as well as the virtues of a new relationship with the United States, must be measured against this background. Under certain conditions, NAFTA provides an opportunity to build a more prosperous, democratic and equitable nation. But NAFTA alone will not modernize Mexico. In the short term especially, the accord as it stands may only exacerbate the country's already stark disparities and dislocations. Rather than speeding and facilitating Mexico's long-awaited and much-hoped-for democratic transition, the near-term effect may be to slow the momentum for political reform. This must not happen.

WAITING FOR DEMOCRACY

Whatever political advances may have occurred under President Salinas, Mexico has yet to devise a system to transfer power democratically. The 1994 presidential succession promises to be as traditional a ritual as ever. The outgoing president will choose his successor, and then do everything necessary at the polls to secure his election. This system worked adequately for more than a half-century. But it dealt only with half the problem of modern government—order—leaving the other half—democratic representation—unresolved.

This quasi-magical procedure functioned properly only so long as everyone accepted its rules. But by the mid-1980s parts of the political establishment began to wonder whether they might not do better outside the system. In the 1988 election former Governor Cuauhtémoc Cárdenas, son of Mexico's most revered president this century, and former Institutional Revolutionary Party Chairman Porfiro Muñoz Ledo broke with the PRI and ran for office on their own, faring much better than they would have otherwise. Muñoz Ledo was elected senator for Mexico City, and Cárdenas, in the opinion of many Mexicans, won the presidency.

The opposition and Mexicans generally believe that the 1994 elections will again be a sham.

Since then, despite two electoral reform laws under Salinas, Mexico's democratic transition has not come to pass. The opposition and Mexicans generally, according to polls, believe that the 1994 elections will again be a sham. The umbilical cord between party and government has not been severed. This was demonstrated by the "shake-down dinner" at which the PRI, in the presence of President Salinas, attempted to extract campaign contributions of $25 million each from 30 of Mexico's richest business leaders. But this time, the PRI's central problem of appointing a candidate and securing the election and accession of a new president will be further aggravated by Mexico's economic doldrums and social deterioration. Salinas seems unable to satisfy either of the two desires of his middle class constituency: a democratic and orderly transfer of power and a growing economy with low inflation and a stable exchange rate. The only solution, as Carlos Ramírez, the most widely read columnist in Mexico, has put it, lies in the de facto exclusion of the presidency from the electoral arena, ensuring that, come what may, the next president will be the PRI candidate.

Part of the problem is that Mexico's opposition has yet to become a viable alternative to the status quo. The National Action Party (PAN) lacks strong national leadership and a nationwide presence; Cárdenas and his Party of the Democratic Revolution are still perceived as too radical, divided and inexperienced to take office. Yet both probably maintain sufficient strength to prevent the PRI from tampering with next year's election without incurring exorbitant costs. Thus, in addition to winning the election more or less cleanly, the PRI candidate will also have to convince his rivals of their defeat and his victory. Mexican politicians and pundits across the spectrum believe that the 1988 crisis must not be repeated. It would be terribly costly to carry into office another PRI candidate whose victory at the polls was disputed by adversaries representing half the electorate.

The need to manage a difficult succession makes a political solution more likely. Instead of emphasizing continuity in economic policy, Salinas will more likely choose a successor who can both win and persuade the opposition he won. Manuel Camacho, the mayor of Mexico City, and Luis Donaldo Colosio, the Minister of Social Development, look best placed to accomplish this task, although Finance Minister Pedro Aspe and Education Minister Ernesto Zedillo cannot be overlooked. The appointment of either Camacho or Colosio would enhance the possibility of what many are calling for privately: a pact among the PRI, PAN and Cárdenas to set ground rules for the campaign, the election itself and some sort of post-election national reconciliation. Camacho best understands the need for such an arrangement, but has aroused suspicions among the business community that he is a closet populist who places negotiation above a firm hand. Colosio, meanwhile, is experiencing difficulties in gaining national support.

While the PAN seems to pose no serious challenge in the presidential race, Cárdenas' situation is more complex. Conventional wisdom holds that he has squandered the popular support garnered in 1988 but that he will still fare better than the nine percent his party obtained in the 1991 midterm elections. Polls give him strong recognition ratings—over 60 percent—higher than any other contender. But he also has high negatives. A poll for the daily *Excelsior* showed 35 percent of those questioned felt Cárdenas should run again, while 44 percent said he should not.

Cárdenas' fate will ultimately be determined by the state of the economy, the extent of social inequities and the eventual divisions within the PRI. Also critical will be his ability to focus the campaign on his strong suits—democratization, social justice and the fight against corruption—and at least to neutralize his weaknesses—the lack of a detailed economic alternative and the fear that he represents instability.

MEXICO'S FLAGGING ECONOMY

Mexico's lacerating social and economic inequality stems partly from the antidemocratic nature of its politics. High levels of postwar economic growth, progress in education and health, and the emergence of a significant middle class have not remedied Mexico's atrociously lopsided income distribution. If 40 years of growth did not help, then a decade of economic stagnation in the 1980s only made matters worse. A recently published survey found that the richest ten percent of Mexicans, those who earned 32.8 percent of national income in 1984, saw their share jump to 37.9 percent by 1989. Conversely, the share of the poorest 40 percent shrank from 14.3 percent to 12.9 percent. The 1990 census, moreover, revealed that 63.2 percent of the nation's inhabitants made no more than twice the minimum wage—$200 per month—while price levels approached those in the United States. The long absence of free elections, of an emancipated labor movement and of the rule of law has helped keep the fruits of any economic expansion in the hands of a minority.

Much of the problem has been Mexico's inability to hurdle an apparently immovable obstacle to its economic growth: the need for substantial foreign capital injections. Since 1972 Mexico has been unable to overcome this external constraint on growth, except during the ephemeral convergence of exceptional circumstances—high oil prices, cheap and abundant lending, wholesale privatization or high yields in the stock market. The costs of attracting foreign capital—higher interest rates and re-

duced domestic spending—have become a severe burden and have engendered boom-bust cycles in the economy. Either the economy does not grow or, if it does, immense current account deficits spring up, requiring equivalent magnitudes of capital to finance them. The outcome of each cycle has been a currency devaluation, like those in 1976, 1982 and 1987, or an economic downturn with equally devastating consequences.

The Salinas administration sought to break these frustrating cycles and to achieve high growth—five to six percent a year—with a moderate external imbalance. Trade liberalization, privatizations and reduced restrictions on foreign investment were means to this end. After an initial, prudent economic expansion, however, the trade balance began to deteriorate drastically, rising from $4.3 billion in 1990 to more than $20 billion in 1992. Imports have risen by approximately 25 percent annually since 1988. At the same time, exports have stagnated, growing less than one percent in 1991 and 1.5 percent in 1992. This imbalance was made largely inevitable by the rapid opening to foreign trade, an appreciating real exchange rate and the remarkable propensity of the Mexican middle class to consume imported goods. By 1992 the overall current account deficit had reached $23 billion, or seven percent of GDP—Mexico's highest level ever.

Consequently, the Salinas administration was forced to throw the economy into a virtual recession, as the foreign capital imbalance prevented faster growth. After expanding in 1990 at 4.5 percent, economic growth slowed to 3.5 percent in 1991 and 2.6 percent in 1992. Government figures forecast slightly lower levels for both 1993 and 1994. Mexico's per-capita growth has thus once again fallen dangerously close to zero.

Moreover, Salinas was forced to make a series of bold moves to attract enough foreign capital to finance even these reduced and more realistic growth rates. He thus pursued a free trade agreement with the United States, the privatization of the Mexican banking system and a policy of encouraging powerful local investors to transform the Mexico City stock exchange, or Bolsa, into a magnet for money from abroad. These steps paid off. There has not been, and probably will not be, a major devaluation of the currency, and Mexico has built up an unprecedented $20 billion of reserves.

But there were costs. Yields on the Bolsa had to stay astronomically high (over 60 percent in dollars in 1991), and when they declined or stagnated, as they have since mid-1992, interest rate differentials between the United States and Mexico had to rise to stabilize portfolio or speculative investment (estimated at approximately 70 percent of the total). Direct foreign investment remains dismally low, as in the 1980s, ranging from 1.5 percent to 1.8 percent of GDP. And overall investment, despite the unprecedented inflow of funds, has not budged, remaining at a disappointing 19 percent of GDP. The dire need for foreign capital drove domestic real interest rates to nearly 15 percent in dollars by mid-1993; lending rates reached 30 percent. Besides, the capital these moves attracted was not ideal. Two-thirds was speculative, and the rest was concentrated not in the creation of new wealth but in services, largely tourism, and in foreign purchases of existing Mexican assets.

In the end, the course Salinas set is more responsible than that of his predecessors, but it still has not achieved the long-sought goal of high growth combined with manageable external accounts. The economic downturn, together with the effects of the previous decade of stagnation, has contributed to rising unemployment and social decay. Manufacturing employment, flat even while the economy was growing, has now fallen: in an index in which the year 1980 equaled 100, it never rose above 87 under Salinas, and by early 1993 it was down to nearly 80. By 1993 tens of thousands of factory workers, bank employees and retail store clerks had lost their jobs. Although a number of new jobs have been created, many more have been lost as a result of the economic downturn and the growing, and so far irresistible, competition from abroad.

Salinas' strategy in the face of myriad economic and political difficulties was simple: free trade with the United States.

Many in the United States nonetheless believe that economic integration and NAFTA have moved jobs on a "fast track" to a modernizing Mexico. In fact, the country's disparities are deepening. Ever more dispossessed accompany the growing number of Mexican "yuppies." The loud "sucking noise" of American jobs going south that U.S. presidential candidate Ross Perot ominously announced last fall is, from the Mexican side of the border, singularly difficult to hear.

IS NAFTA THE ANSWER?

The Salinas regime's strategy in the face of these myriad economic and political difficulties was simple and singleminded: free trade with the United States. To hold a clean election and at the same time to secure the victory

of Salinas' hand-picked candidate, the economy had to deliver high growth and create near the million jobs per year necessary to absorb population increases and facilitate social spending.

The only way to attract the foreign capital necessary to stabilize the exchange rate and to fund the ensuing current account deficit was to provide hesitant potential investors with guarantees of continuity of economic policy and access to the U.S. market through an ironclad agreement with Washington. NAFTA, it was hoped, would satisfy both requirements. The sustained economic growth generated by NAFTA would narrow income differentials by creating jobs. President Salinas' antipoverty program, known as Solidaridad, would ease the transition from past stagnation to NAFTA-fueled high growth. As the fruits of growth trickled down and discontent no longer threatened economic policy, Mexico would gradually evolve into a democracy.

More than a complement to the modernization policies embarked upon since 1985, NAFTA was seen as a silver bullet to neutralize the obstacles those policies engendered. When more capital than expected was needed and greater reluctance to invest was encountered, NAFTA would make up the difference. It would also relieve pressure from abroad to accelerate political reform, as U.S. supporters of NAFTA toned down their criticisms of human rights violations and electoral fraud in Mexico to avoid imperiling free trade. Investment from abroad would enable the economy to grow while introducing new technology and greater efficiency and modernizing Mexican society. Most Mexicans' traditional identification of modernity with the United States would be reinforced; their traditional resentment of the United States over past injuries and present asymmetries would be softened.

While it was hoped that NAFTA would address many of these problems, it has not defused the end-of-term crisis that Mexico's succession process has traditionally generated. Granted, the government's expectations, however inaccurate or overblown, touched a receptive chord among large sectors of the population. Polls repeatedly indicate strong support for NAFTA, as well as unfounded reasons for it: a recent survey found that 45.8 percent of those interviewed believed NAFTA would make it easier for Mexicans to get jobs in the United States. Similarly, it has created illusions in the United States that it would help stem Mexican immigration. Most immigration scholars in both countries expect NAFTA and the economic policies it will encourage in Mexico to stimulate migratory flows in the short run, as displaced peasants and laid-off employees take advantage of large wage differentials and head north.

But the dichotomy between the short and long term runs through the debate on NAFTA'S advantages and drawbacks. Economic integration between the United States and Mexico, already under way for years, is surely better served by a legal framework to rationalize and administer it. And Mexican economic development and living standards—if not national autonomy or cultural identity—will benefit in the long run from more investment and trade with the United States. The problem lies in the interim: How will the adjustment costs of NAFTA be distributed among the three partners and among different regions and sectors of the population within each country? How should the agreement address these questions?

NAFTA either ignores these problems or leaves their solution to the market. The trade pact presupposes that the amount of money needed to bring together economies and societies as distinct as Mexico, the United States and Canada is not overwhelming and that market forces alone will provide it. In fact the United States will have to retrain tens of thousands of workers and cushion the shock to innumerable communities and factories. Canada is already losing jobs and markets, while Mexico confronts its balance-of-payments difficulties. The three countries will also have to tackle environmental problems and infrastructure deficiencies, along the border and inside Mexico, together with major regional disruptions and a costly process of harmonization.

NAFTA'S HIDDEN COSTS

As the Europeans have learned, bringing together advanced and backward economies is an expensive proposition. Since the disparities between Mexico and its neighbors are greater than any comparable differences in Western Europe, odds are that the North American experience will be more costly. The three governments hope whatever must be done will be accomplished by private investment: low wages and solid business opportunities will attract private capital to Mexico, paying for infrastructure, environmental cleanup, the trade gap and debt service. But private money is unlikely to prove sufficient; nor will it flow to Mexico as freely as expected. For now NAFTA incorporates no contingency provision— no special funds and no special taxes.

Moreover, Mexico's regulatory situation was largely excluded from NAFTA, with the exception of those areas where strong American interests are involved: foreign investment, intellectual property and the textile industry. But if Mexico profoundly differs from its neighbors in any way besides overall wealth, it is in the absence of the rule of law and the regulatory framework that characterize developed market economies. The Mexican judicial branch is totally subservient to the executive; regulatory agencies have no independence whatsoever; corruption is egregious. By omitting both supranational

mechanisms for enforcement of norms and rights—on the environment, labor, consumer protection, due process—and any demand for the overhaul of Mexico's political and legal system, NAFTA's signatories ignored a fundamental facet of the Mexican reality.

Finally, NAFTA does not address the issue of whether Mexico has—or should have—the same type of market economy as that espoused by United States. Is Mexico more like the United States, where nearly everything is left to the private sector and the relatively free workings of the market? Or are Mexican traditions closer to those of the European social market economy model, with greater emphasis on state involvement and more stringent regulations and constraints on the market? Will NAFTA be an association of like-minded partners, like Europe before Britain joined, or will Mexico always play the role of former British Prime Minister Margaret Thatcher, defending seemingly eccentric customs and preferences? In the initial euphoria of negotiations, these matters were all shunted aside, dismissed as irrelevant or to be taken up at a later time. That time may have suddenly arrived.

NAFTA NEEDS REFORM

In the same way that the Clinton administration decided that a series of so-called supplemental agreements would serve U.S. interests, a number of changes would render NAFTA far more beneficial to Mexico as well. Various proposals have been placed on the table to transfer resources from NAFTA-winners to NAFTA-losers: border transaction taxes, a windfall profit tax, a North American development bank, a European-style regional fund scheme and a deeper reduction in Mexico's debt, among others.

These proposals are viable because their proponents come from the two wealthier nations, who would have to foot most of the bill. Moving forward with NAFTA without provisions along these lines would mean missing an excellent opportunity to attack the key obstacle to Mexico's development. A long-term program, including social conditionality and accountability—whereby local authorities and non-governmental organizations receive and supervise part of the funding—would work wonders for Mexico's balance of payments, the reconstruction of infrastructure and the redistribution of resources.

NAFTA should also be designed to contribute to political change in Mexico. It should only go into effect with a preamble like that issued in 1978 by the European Community at the start of negotiations to include Spain, Portugal and Greece: "The heads of state and government solemnly declare that respect for and maintenance of representative democracy and human rights in each member state are essential elements of the European communities." The application of the European precedent would entail a crucial test: submitting Mexico's August 1994 presidential elections to international monitoring by the United Nations and the Organization of American States. U.S. or Canadian congressional certification of the elections should be explicitly excluded; the multilateral nature of the exercise should be firmly proclaimed.

Support exists in Mexico for the idea. PAN has often called for international observers, and grass-roots groups have invited contingents from abroad. Cárdenas met with former President Jimmy Carter in May to explore the possibility of Carter's participation in Mexican election monitoring. Ratification of NAFTA and its entry into law could be postponed until the elections, as may occur anyway. Or NAFTA could be ratified, but its entry into law conditioned on free, fair and internationally monitored elections in 1994.

Finally, there is a necessary social facet to the new U.S.-Mexican relationship. Money of the right sort will not flow to Mexico in adequate volumes, nor can it be put to good use, unless a series of deep changes are carried out in social policy and structure. These policy changes must extend to unions and the environment and include efforts to reduce income disparities through tax reform and higher social spending, as well as measures to strengthen civil society. These are the famously debated labor and environmental chapters of NAFTA—side agreements with teeth, that is, commissions independent from the three governments with the resources and power to impose sanctions.

Beyond the side agreements, though, the bilateral relationship must empower Mexican society to achieve its own aims and fight its own battles. Mexico's social inequities can only be redressed through major efforts in education, health, housing and combating poverty. This enterprise, in turn, can only be achieved through significant tax reform. Other than improvements in collection, little has been achieved on this score; the adjustment in Mexican public finances over the past decade occurred entirely on the spending side. According to the Organization for Economic Cooperation and Development, total tax revenues over GDP stagnated from 1980 (17 percent) through 1991 (16.8 percent), remaining at a level well below not only that of Europe and the United States but also that of most successful developing nations.

There are, of course, other additions to the trade pact that would be beneficial to Mexico, such as beginning immigration negotiations on temporary domestic service workers. And there are issues of concern to the United States—and to many Mexicans—that can be partially approached through democratization: the authentic establishment of the rule of law, improved drug enforcement and an end to corruption.

CHANGE WITH OR WITHOUT NAFTA

The question in the final analysis is whether a free trade agreement without these improvements is still in both countries' interests and, conversely, what consequences NAFTA's rejection or postponement would have for Mexico. As with the rest of the NAFTA debate, hyperbole has contaminated the discussion of what these options would imply: a collapse of the Mexican economy, a reversal of the structural reforms, a run on the currency, a dramatic drying up of investment, a deep-rooted nationalist backlash.

Except for short-term pressure on the peso—manageable in many ways, including the Federal Reserve's intervention in exchange markets—should the agreement not be approved by the U.S. Congress by January 1, 1994, these catastrophic scenarios are unlikely. They are mainly a scare tactic to expedite passage. The Mexican economy is already in recession. Adopting NAFTA on time might set off a rush of short-term financing, but raising the long-term volume of direct foreign investment is an arduous task, especially given the global economic slowdown. The economic reforms undertaken in Mexico over the past few years were largely inevitable; with logical, and necessary, rectifications and adjustments, they are here to stay.

NAFTA's rejection would lead to a nationalist backlash only if the Mexican people felt strongly enough about it. But while polls show they support NAFTA, Mexicans are increasingly skeptical and vastly uninformed about the accord. Undoubtedly, some would engage in "gringo-bashing," but outside the immediate circle surrounding Salinas and the largest Mexican conglomerates, NAFTA's postponement may be either regretted or hailed but would not mean the end of the world.

Indeed, the most severe consequences of postponement may well be political. President Salinas bet the store on NAFTA, and if passage is his triumph, rejection or delay is his defeat. There was no need to frame the issue in those terms, but now that Salinas has, damage to his prestige and power may be unavoidable. That this complicates the succession is beyond dispute, although it is already clear that Salinas will have to choose the PRI candidate without knowing the outcome of the NAFTA debate. It is equally evident that quick approval of NAFTA would strengthen Salinas' hand in the succession; its postponement or rejection would weaken him. But whether it would weaken Mexico is highly dubious.

The broader issue is which process for transferring power will help to address Mexico's deep-rooted dilemmas. The case has been made that the most desirable outcome can, under present conditions, only be secured through the traditional authoritarian process; a NAFTA-induced crisis would favor supposed "nationalist-populist" options, either within the PRI itself or in the Cárdenas camp. But others argue, more persuasively, that if postponement of NAFTA forced an opening of the political system and a clean election in 1994, the process itself would guarantee the outcome: whoever was elected—even a closet populist from the PRI, Cárdenas or an inexperienced PAN candidate—would have to govern in the center, because that is where the votes are. Instead of the perfect outcome resulting from an increasingly unstable process, a reformed democratic process would ensure an acceptable outcome for everyone.

In the end, this is the central issue Mexicans and their neighbors to the north must face. The country has enjoyed unparalleled stability for more than seventy years, but the levers and gears that maintained it are worn out.

There are two risks to choose from: sticking with the old system until it breaks down, seriously and irreparably; or taking the leap into a new system, knowing full well that both the transition period and the new order itself will not be free of dangers. Had everything neatly fallen into place—the economy buzzing along at six percent, jobs and social spending up, corruption and drugs under control, NAFTA approved on time and with minimal damage—a painless and risk-free, gradual and perfectly managed transition might have been feasible. But in the real world, everything does not always break the right way; many of the things that could have gone wrong did. In view of the options, the best choice for Mexico is evident: change at last. It is not without perils, but it offers the chance of finally making Mexico the country its people have always deserved, and never possessed.

Article 6   *The Economist, January 22, 1994*

The revolution continues

President Salinas's economic reforms and free-trade policies are fundamentally sound. But his successor, to be elected in August, should read the bloody Chiapas rebellion as a warning that political reforms are also needed urgently.

MEXICO CITY

As Carlos Fuentes, a novelist, has noted, just when Mexico was moving closer to North America, its rulers were forcibly reminded that parts of their country still belonged to Central America. On January 1st, the day the North American Free-Trade Agreement (NAFTA) sent trade barriers tumbling between Mexico, the United States and Canada, a previously unknown guerrilla group was seizing half a dozen towns in the southern state of Chiapas and bloodily rewriting the political agenda.

President Carlos Salinas and his team of free-market reformers have been nastily shaken. Basking in international applause for his liberal economic policies, Mr Salinas had been looking forward to ending his six-year term on a high note and handing over smoothly to his heir-apparent, Luis Donaldo Colosio, candidate of the ruling Institutional Revolutionary Party (PRI) in August's presidential election. Instead, thanks to the intervention of the Zapatist National Liberation Army, as the guerrillas call themselves, Mexico faces a turbulent year in which the social costs of eco-

nomic reform, and of the lack of a properly functioning democracy, have suddenly acquired new prominence.

The Zapatists take their name from Emiliano Zapata, a peasant leader who fought to defend village lands during Mexico's 1910–20 revolution; they claim to have been preparing their present campaign for years, drawing on social injustices which are particularly acute in Chiapas where a third of the population is Indian and many of the rural poor have lost their land to cattle barons with political clout. When the Zapatists launched their attack, officials tried at first to dismiss them as a small bunch of agitators. But it took the army four days to drive them back into the mountains; and even then, with more than a hundred dead, there was no sign that the rebels suffered a decisive defeat. In fact, they may have two thousand or more well-drilled fighters, their nucleus drawn from Mexicans who fought as volunteers with Nicaragua's Sandinists and El Salvador's left-wing guerrillas in the Central American wars of the 1980s.

Nobody expects the rest of Mexico to rise in armed rebellion. But already the

Zapatists have taken some of the gloss off Mexico's economic transformation by exposing the flawed political base on which it rests and by denouncing the unequal distribution of its rewards. They have also humbled a government accustomed to ignoring opposition. Mr Salinas himself began by calling for their surrender, then quickly changed tack. He sacked his hard-line interior minister, Patrocinio Gonzalez, a former governor of Chiapas; declared a unilateral cease-fire; and sent Manuel Camacho, his foreign minister and most experienced negotiator, to open talks.

The Salinas solution

Even before Chiapas, sceptics feared that Mexico was condemning itself to having to sprint in a competitive world when much of its economy was still learning to walk unaided. NAFTA, momentous as it is for Mexico, is merely a trade agreement which in itself can guarantee neither growth nor prosperity and which involves none of the social and regional funds that the European Union offers its poorer members. The pressures and

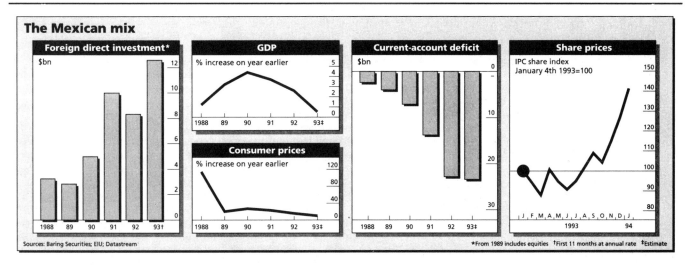

The Mexican mix

Foreign direct investment* ($bn): 1988, 89, 90, 91, 92, 93†

GDP (% increase on year earlier): 1988, 89, 90, 91, 92, 93‡

Consumer prices (% increase on year earlier): 1988, 89, 90, 91, 92, 93‡

Current-account deficit ($bn): 1988, 89, 90, 91, 92, 93‡

Share prices (IPC share index January 4th 1993=100): J F M A M J J A S O N D J, 1993, 94

Sources: Baring Securities; EIU; Datastream

*From 1989 includes equities †First 11 months at annual rate ‡Estimate

strains of forced economic adjustment must be borne by Mexico alone: and, with the Zapatists' leader, Comandante Marcos, denouncing NAFTA from a seized hotel balcony as a "death sentence" for Mexico's Indians, small wonder if some foreign investors, still counting their profits from the recently soaring stockmarket, began to have second thoughts about just how great those pressures and strains might be.

Mr Salinas's economic policies have widened already-huge disparities of wealth. Mexico now has seven dollar-billionaires, according to *Forbes* magazine—as many as Britain. Some have grown rich from a privatisation programme which brought large capital sums to the state but which also converted public monopolies into private ones. At the other extreme, despite sharply increased social spending by the government, 16% of Mexico's population—13.5m people—is officially classified as living in "extreme poverty" and another 23.6m as "poor". The government claims, improbably, that unemployment is only 3.7%; private-sector economists say that 25–30% of the labour force is out of work or scraping a living in the informal economy.

In the countryside, where most of the poor live, reform has so far done little to end chronic stagnation. Almost a quarter of the population works in agriculture, but it receives only 8% of national income. The government has begun to phase out its last significant crop subsidy, on maize. Instead, it will make cash payments to farmers, encouraging them to switch to more profitable crops. Though sensible in economic terms, this policy will pose political challenges by speeding the drift from the land—and provide more fuel for the Zapatists or their like.

Importantly, the Zapatists claim to be fighting not only for their land and culture, but also for free elections—a rare departure for Latin American guerrillas. If they fail, they should at least ensure an unusually complicated year for the PRI, which has ruled Mexico since the 1920s under various names and never lost a national election.

The PRI's designated candidate for the August presidential election, Mr Colosio,* who used to be Mr Salinas's social development minister, has been pushed into the background by the Chiapas revolt. Some even suggest that if Mr Camacho, who was Mr Colosio's closest rival for the nomination, succeeds in pacifying Chiapas, he could make his own bid for the presidency, perhaps as an independent. Mr Colosio has his work cut out to show that he can win the election convincingly (as Mr Salinas did not in 1988) and without recourse to his party's long tradition of ballot-box fraud.

Mr Colosio may be helped by a divided opposition. Mr Camacho aside, his main challenger is likely to be Cuauhtemoc Cardenas, a left-of-centre former PRI leader who some believe won more votes than Mr Salinas in 1988. The conservative National Action Party (PAN) is fielding a skilled parliamentarian, Diego Fernandez de Cevallos, as its candidate, and has strong pockets of regional support. Also working in Mr Colosio's favour will be the fact that, despite two electoral reforms under Mr Salinas, the system still favours the PRI. The government controls the electoral authority; the party enjoys privileged television coverage and—opponents claim—access to state resources.

*In March 1994, Luis Donaldo Colosio was assassinated in Tijuana.

Mr Colosio, or whoever else wins the August election, will find himself running an economy changed in some areas beyond recognition under Mr Salinas. The budget has been in surplus; foreign debts have been renegotiated; private investment has become the driving force of what was previously a state-led economy; import tariffs have been cut—the highest is now 20%, compared with more than 100% ten years ago; inflation, running at 159% annually in 1987, fell to 8% in 1993; more than 390 state-owned companies have been privatised, raising $23 billion; the constitution has been amended to allow communal farmers to own their land and do deals with private investors; regulations hindering private business have been systematically scrapped.

Mr Salinas's crowning achievement, Mexico's accession to NAFTA, surmounted a history of prickly nationalism and set his country on a course of economic integration with the United States which will be difficult and expensive for any future Mexican government to change. Now, 11 years after Mexico's moratorium triggered the Latin American debt crisis, the process of structural adjustment is almost complete. With NAFTA in place, optimists are hoping for economic growth strong enough to bring Mexico into the developed world some time early in the next century.

NAFTA and after

But for these high hopes to be realised, Mexico's businesses will first have to compete with America's, and survive. For the moment, that prospect appears at least as daunting as it does inspiring. Despite Mr Salinas's reforms and an inflow of about $25 billion in foreign capital, Mexico's GDP probably grew by only about 0.5% in 1993, down from 2.6% in 1992. In the third quarter of 1993, output shrank by 1.2%, the first drop since 1986. While bigger companies raise cheap funds on international capital markets and prepare to take on the world, smaller ones are struggling to cope with real interest rates of up to 15% and thousands have gone bust.

Officials attribute the present slowdown mainly to a sluggish world economy and to the prolonged uncertainty over NAFTA's fate in Congress which held up investment decisions: after growing by 20.4% in 1992, private investment rose by only 2.8% in the first three quarters of 1993. The government expects a rebound to 6.4% in 1994: so long as political violence does not spread, this may prove an underestimate. NAFTA should improve Mexico's credit rating (and so make its borrowing cheaper), though Chiapas has probably caused American rating agencies to hold off upgrading Mexican debt from speculative to investment quality.

Recovery will also get a boost from the government's decision, with one eye on the presidential election, to spend its budget surplus. Some of the extra money will go to the poor. Fulfilling a promise made to Bill Clinton to help smooth NAFTA's passage, workers on the minimum wage will receive an extra 14–17% this year, partly through a new negative income tax for low earners.

The challenge facing Mr Salinas's successor will be to sustain growth without yielding to inflationary pressures. Failure will be painful: Mexico's economy needs to grow by 5–6% in real terms each year merely to provide jobs for the 1m new workers entering the labour market. Growth provides the best hope of reducing income inequalities and increasing domestic savings, thus lessening Mexico's dependence on foreign capital. But the next government will also have to resist pressures to deal with social problems simply by opening its chequebook—a self-discipline which should be helped by a new law giving the central bank greater autonomy in credit policy.

In practice, Mexico's capacity to achieve sustainable growth will depend on three related variables: microeconomic reforms to raise productivity; the current account deficit; and post-NAFTA capital inflows.

First, productivity. Big companies have worked hard in the past three or four years to become more competitive. They have shed peripheral businesses, cut workers and found foreign partners

with new technologies and markets. Some have expanded into the United States or elsewhere through acquisition. Many are now highly efficient. Their efforts have contributed to a steady productivity rise in manufacturing industry, up 19% between 1990 and 1992. But many smaller companies have barely begun to work out what they need to do to compete, and are holding the economy back. Guillermo Ortiz, deputy finance minister, admits that the process has taken "longer than we thought it would—the inefficiencies and distortions in the productive apparatus were much greater than we realised."

Growth has also been slowed because Mexico's more open and competitive environment has obliged many firms to scrap plant and machinery installed in the protectionist era sooner than would normally have been the case; and to adjust to sharp changes in the relative prices of capital, labour, energy and imported goods. Energy prices, for example, are now 50% higher in real terms than they were in 1982. Capital was also cheaper then, and many imported goods were inaccessible. According to Jesus Reyes Heroles of GEA, an economic consultancy, companies in industries such as textiles, leather goods and petrochemicals were stuck with the wrong technology when relative prices changed. Despite a growth in investment from 17% of GNP in 1988 to 22% in 1992, the economy's capital stock is barely bigger than it was a decade ago.

Restructuring has been made harder during the past year by the tough combination of a faster-than-expected fall in inflation, high real interest rates and an appreciating real exchange rate. To the first of those, lower inflation, companies are now adjusting. Interest rates are set to fall: Baring Securities, a stockbroker, forecasts the peso interbank lending rate falling from 19% to 11% during 1994. That leaves the exchange rate. The peso was undervalued in the late 1980s when trade liberalisation began, so the initial impact on competitiveness was slight. Since then, the government has emphasised productivity as a means to raise competitiveness, while profiting from a firm currency to cut inflation and to break inflationary expectations. That policy is more controversial now that the biggest cloud over Mexico's growth prospects is a current-account deficit that reached $22.8 billion, or 6.8% of GDP, in 1992.

Miguel Mancera, president of the central bank, argues that the deficit is not inherently dangerous, because it is associated with the inflow of foreign funds, swelling the capital account, rather than expansionary fiscal or monetary policy. "It only becomes a problem because people think it's a problem," Mr Mancera says. Perhaps; but market perceptions do matter, and inflows could cease or reverse, making the deficit harder to finance. And, though import growth has slowed along with the economy, Mexican companies have shifted, probably permanently, to a greater dependence on imports. Officials point out that Mexico's non-oil exports have been growing faster than those of South Korea and Singapore since 1985, but there are also fears that the export-growth rate of 15% recorded in the first eight months of 1993 will fall sharply once the domestic market revives.

Rogelio Ramirez de la O, an economic consultant, says that each unit of investment in Mexico since 1988 has pulled in 1.8 units of imports, while the equivalent figure for Chile has been only 1.1. He argues that with NAFTA in place and the budget balanced, Mexico can afford to tackle the current-account deficit by letting the peso slide further against the dollar, without reviving inflation; a fall to the bottom of the band fixed by the central bank would mean a devaluation against the dollar of about 13% over the next 18 months. Without that, says Mr Ramirez, concern about the current account will dog growth again in 1995.

Finishing the job

Even if foreign investors do stay enthusiastic about Mexico, and growth is sustained without too much strain on the balance of payments, there are still many areas the next government needs to address to help Mexican companies compete. They include:

- **Deregulation.** Although the federal government has cut through swathes of red tape, state and municipal governments have been more grudging. A typical example: road haulage is now deregulated in federal law, allowing lorries to travel on any route, but some states still require goods to be re-loaded on to local transport for the final leg of their journey.
- **Monopolies.** Many still exist, public and private. A "competition commission", set up by the government last year, has been all but invisible—not least in December when the government decided to award 62 vacant television frequencies to Televisa, a private near-monopoly, without public tender.

- **Infrastructure.** Although labour costs in Mexico are low, poor infrastructure keeps transport and energy costs high. Private investors financed 4,000 kilometres of new motorway, but found that the high tolls deterred traffic. Ports, airports and railways all need big new investments.
- **Industrial policy.** The Salinas government dislikes it in principle, but officials have not always resisted it in practice. Mr Reyes Heroles argues for a disciplined blend of credits and information-sharing rather than crude subsidy.

But most of this relatively fine tuning will be academic if the government fails to maintain civil peace. The message of Chiapas is that bolder social and political reforms are needed. Mr Salinas's administration made a start on the former, but barely touched the latter. It increased social spending by almost 85% in real terms, much of that new money going via Solidarity, a high-profile anti-poverty agency. But to make any significant impact on poverty, Mr Salinas's successor will have to ensure that money is spent more wisely and impartially. Solidarity has too often allowed political criteria to dictate the direction of its disbursements.

Education is just as vital. Mr Salinas put more money into it, but quality and content still have a long way to go. Good universal education will be the precondition for a more productive workforce and for the redressing of what will otherwise be entrenched and perhaps worsening inequalities. Despite all its recent changes, much of Mexico remains locked in a feudal culture, accustomed to being told what to do—whether by an Aztec king, a Spanish viceroy or a PRI bureaucrat.

Feudal attitudes are at their most entrenched in far-flung places like Chiapas. Though more Solidarity money has gone there than anywhere else, its impact has often been neutered by the iron control of local PRI bosses whose main concern is with keeping the vote-machine well oiled: improbably, Mr Salinas was declared to have won 89.9% of the Chiapas vote in 1988.

By treating too much of Mexico too often as still its fief, the PRI may be storing up trouble. At the most recent municipal elections in Chiapas in 1991, for example, Mr Cardenas's opposition party believed it had won in the towns of Ocosingo and Las Margaritas. Mr Gonzalez, then the state governor, had other ideas. He jailed 153 Cardenas supporters in the two towns and awarded victory to the PRI. It may not be coincidence that both towns were among those occupied earlier this month by the Zapatists.

NAFTA and Chiapas should probably now be pulling Mexico in the same direction: towards a more responsive and efficient—and therefore open—political system which would place Mexico on a more equal footing with its other North American partners. A more inclusive political system might also be the best way for Mexico to lock in its gains from economic reform, by dissuading the poor and angry from venting their frustration by extra-political means.

Article 7   *World Press Review,* January 1994

A New Chapter in Mexican Politics?

Second thoughts about the NAFTA windfall

Mexican President Carlos Salinas de Gortari once appeared to stake the fortunes of his ruling party on the North American Free Trade Agreement (NAFTA). Despite U.S. ratification of the pact, however, victory in upcoming national elections is not guaranteed for Salinas's Institutional Revolutionary Party, which has dominated Mexican politics for more than 50 years. For one thing, there is a serious backlash in Mexico against the trade agreement. Two reports from the liberal news weekly "Proceso," by Carlos Puig and Carlos Acosta Córdova, indicate the depths of dissatisfaction with NAFTA and the relationship it establishes between Mexico and the United States. But the ruling party has another worry. Cynics will shrug, but political scientist and government critic Lorenzo Meyer writes in the centrist "Excélsior" of Mexico City that the 1994 presidential race could actually be won by Cuauhtémoc Cárdenas, who many believe would have beaten Salinas in the 1988 election if the ballots had been counted honestly.

Cuauhtémoc Cárdenas is running for the presidency of Mexico again, an act that departs from precedents and opens up possibilities. Mexico seems to be endowing itself with real political parties, breaking with tradition and the will of the government. First, there was the National Action Party (PAN), established in 1939. Now there is Cárdenas's Democratic Revolutionary Party (PRD), which formed in 1989. All that is lacking is for the ruling Institutional Revolutionary

Party (PRI) to cease to be the automatic party of government. Then and only then will elections be competitive and credible; then and only then will Mexico's politics enter the modern age.

The PRD was created in a hostile environment after the presidential election of nearly six years ago. Mexican society now has a center-left option. Without that, the political spectrum would remain tilted toward the right and lack any real pluralism.

An observer recently pointed out that, in Mexico, the only people who reach power are those who show an obsession for it, regardless of the compromises they make to get it. If one accepts that view, the fact that Cárdenas and his group have refused to make concessions and have remained staunchly in the opposition would mean that they lack a real will to power, that they want to remain eternal dissidents. Events are showing, however, that Cárdenas and his movement are serious contenders for public office. They are campaigning aggressively and uncompromisingly.

By announcing his candidacy, Cárdenas has brought down one of the great walls that define Mexico's authoritarian presidency. That wall was the unwritten, but never before broken, rule that no dissident within the political elite could survive after having challenged the right of the ruling president or party leader to choose presidential candidates. Until Cárdenas, the price of laying hands on the supposed right of the leader of the "revolutionary family" to name the next president was, at minimum, political death—and, in some cases, literal death. Cárdenas is the first person since 1923 to throw down the gauntlet and survive to try again.

If either the PRD or PAN candidate manages to win a majority of the vote in August, and—this is the hard part—if that candidate manages to convince the government that the best way out is to acknowledge its defeat, then a completely new chapter will open in the country's political history. The possibility of changing the incumbent party would completely change the nature of Mexican political and civil society.

It must have been difficult for Cárdenas and his followers not to feel powerless and discouraged in the aftermath of the 1988 elections, deflated by events such as the breakdown of the [vote-tallying] system in the presidential election and its sequels in murky state elections. Add to that an ongoing smear campaign, violence against followers that has already taken more than 200 lives, a

THE AMERICAN ERA BEGINS

There is no more room for doubt: Beginning this year, Mexicans are American citizens. Through the provisions of NAFTA, Mexico ties itself to the most powerful nation on the planet in order to continue the economic policies of the last six years. Beyond elections or national decisions, the treaty will force the abandonment of the mixed economy and our national development policy. There will be fewer subsidies, more privatization, and greater restrictions on nationalizations.

But the new relationship with the United States also means political costs for the Mexican system, and these have already begun. At the U.S. State Department, members of non-governmental organizations and academic centers in both Mexico and the United States are meeting to discuss how to observe the forthcoming Mexican elections in August. At the same time, members of Congress who voted on NAFTA have plans to send an observer delegation.

This new scrutiny is the result of a declaration, open and unanimous: "Mexico is not a democracy." This was the only thing upon which both sides of the debate in the United States, from Vice President Al Gore to Representative David Bonior, not to mention former President Jimmy Carter, could agree.

The new relationship also implies new collaborations. The government of Carlos Salinas de Gortari has promised new programs and actions to solve U.S. problems—although the treaty that was ratified on November 17 was a "trade agreement."

Mexico will start to take care of Mexicans arrested in the United States—with America footing half the bill. This eases the burden caused by illegal aliens in the American penal system.

The urgent need to secure votes in the U.S. Congress has meant that various Mexican "victories" in the negotiating of the agreement had to be "revised" at the last moment, granting U.S. industries greater protection. Added to the NAFTA package were letters of understanding, parallel accords, and other agreements designed to protect American business and create barriers that the treaty was supposed to eliminate. All this is, among other things, what it means to be Americans.

—Carlos Puig, "Proceso."

clampdown on the media, desertions, the support of big money for the PRI, the endless problems of creating an opposition party in a system governed by a state party, the double standards of foreign governments and opinion, the general crisis of the left, etc. Despite all of this and more, Cárdenas has emerged as a credible candidate with a constructive platform and a great many followers. There is no doubt that he has won the right to be considered a central actor.

That 1988 did not spell his end is due not only to the staunchness of Cárdenas, the PRD, and their followers but also to the slow but steady maturing of the civic culture of Mexico. With the passage of

time, urbanization, the spread of education, growth of communications, and modernization of the economy, today's Mexico has fewer subjects and more citizens. The system that has given the PRI more than a half century of uninterrupted monopoly—with the obvious and inevitable train of corruption, abuse of power, and inefficiency—is an affront and a daily humiliation. The opposition now offers the dissatisfied Mexican an opportunity to move away from the frustration, resignation, and passivity that authoritarianism breeds.

The international environment is also beginning to work in favor of Mexican pluralism and efforts toward democracy.

In 1988, there was still a Soviet Union. Therefore, the inertia of anti-communism was still operative, affecting the Cárdenas coalition and allowing foreign governments and the foreign press to look the other way when fraud was committed. Today, without the anti-communist veil, Mexican authoritarianism is being seen increasingly for what it is: a solitary dinosaur.

In short, as the candidacy of Cárdenas has gained strength, very much despite itself, one of the bulwarks of Mexican authoritarianism has fallen away. The voter has democratic choices. Now comes the more difficult part: forcing an honest count. But that fight is not the responsibility solely, or even mainly, of the opposition leaders and parties but of a larger group—all Mexicans who want to be worthy of calling themselves citizens.

—*Lorenzo Meyer, "Excélsior."*

Article 8   *Current History*, February 1993

Mexico's Environmental Future

Mexico confronts the interrelated and profound economic and environmental possibilities opened up by the North American Free Trade Agreement and increasing global integration. "Just as the United States will benefit from relocating some difficult environmental problems to its south," Steven Sanderson argues, "so Mexico should be able to count on a willing partner to the north."

Steven E. Sanderson

Steven E. Sanderson is a professor of political science and the director of the Tropical Conservation and Development Program at the University of Florida. Among his publications on Mexico are Agrarian Populism and the Mexican State *(Berkeley: University of California Press, 1981) and* The Transformation of Mexican Agriculture *(Princeton: Princeton University Press, 1986). His most recent book is* The Politics of Trade in Latin American Development *(Stanford: Stanford University Press, 1992).*

After conducting the region's most profound economic reform and abandoning its historical antipathy to its northern neighbor, Mexico has become the darling of the United States these days. It is apparently now ready to face together with the United States what many call "the inevitable future" of North American integration. The government of President Carlos Salinas de Gortari has made headlines by committing itself to free trade, by abandoning land reforms instituted after the revolution, and by subscribing to international environmental agreements that break with the country's sorry record of past abuse. For many, especially conservative internationalists, Mexico has become a model citizen, a regional leader in international affairs.

But behind the headlines, environmental concerns were treated at separate tables from general economic concerns at the North American Free Trade Agreement (NAFTA) negotiations, even though there is no doubt that the economy and the environment are inextricably linked. Although the course of economic growth will determine Mexico's environmental future, virtually no one in a position to make policy is discussing the impact North American free trade will have, on Mexico's environment, let alone Mexican economic reforms or land tenure changes. The architects of Mexico's impending wholesale integration into the world economy rarely speak about environmental protection. The ideology of the day has led free traders and fiscal reformers to condemn such concerns as belonging to an unaffordable nationalism of the past, and shrug off possible future costs.

Politicians have repeatedly stated that changes in economic policy actually strengthen environmental protection. From the United States trade representative to World Bank officials, talk of "sustainable," or ecologically sound, development is the order of the day. William Reilly, director of the Environmental Protection Agency under the Bush administration, hailed the agreement on free trade between the United States, Mexico, and Canada as "a watershed in the history of environmental protection, because it integrates economic and environmental concerns to an unprecedented degree."[1] But the evidence strongly suggests that environmental concerns are being ignored.

FREE TRADE, REGARDLESS

One of the most important indicators of Mexico's environmental trajectory is NAFTA, which would establish a trilateral free trade zone. Surprisingly, there is no substantive treatment of the environment in the most recent draft text of the agreement.[2] For example, the chapter on agriculture contains only a blanket expression of concern for "relevant ecological and other environmental conditions." The annex on the automotive industry refers neither to the environment nor to fuel efficiency, despite the alleged importance of environmental standards for automobile emissions and global concern over the release of greenhouse gases, which are believed to raise the temperature of the atmosphere. Perhaps most devastating, the word "environment" does not appear at all in the chapter on energy, nor any language professing concern for or recommending environmentally friendly energy policies for the free trade area.

Why the omission? First, the United States trade representative and other actors on the American side have always argued that crafting a treaty that addressed the environmental implications of free trade would create a "legislative Christmas tree" weighed down by ornaments inappropriate to the occasion. Such a document would not pass muster on Capitol Hill, or be welcomed in Mexico either.

Second, champions of economic integration—and of development in general—in both the United States and Mexico have neither the time, the intellectual disposition, nor the institutional mandate to deal with the environment. The environment is viewed as a "cost" billed against economic growth, while the opportunity to avoid unwanted future effects on the environment is missed. An otherwise valuable new assessment of NAFTA's impact published by the Brookings Institution barely touches on the environment, except in references to border pollution and in a more general essay by Robert Pastor, a member of President Jimmy Carter's administration.[3] The leading policy volume on NAFTA, published by the Institute for International Economics, says the big environmental issue in NAFTA is who will put up money to spend on the environment—a question the trade negotiators largely shirked, according to the authors.[4]

The third explanation for the omissions from NAFTA is even more troubling: that many policymakers worldwide believe good environmental outcomes naturally flow from sound economic practices. The global community has agreed since the 1987 report of the Brundtland Commission on the need to consider economic growth and development in light of environmental concerns, especially as the integration of the international economic system proceeds.[5] And in the United Nations Conference on Environment and Development (UNCED) documents emerging from the "Earth Summit" in Rio de Janeiro last June, the world signed on to a concept of sustainable development that would link economics and environment from the outset, and that identified free trade and economic policy reforms as the most important vehicles for ensuring sustainable development. (This allows environmentalists advocating sustainable development to paint a positive portrait of the trade-development-environment connection without examining more disturbing possibilities.)

But the dissonant tones of international integration are much more difficult than the fair music of rhetorical agreement. Today nations around the world face an environmental dilemma. The global community has recognized that the environmental condition of one country is a complex product of the environmental policies and economic dynamics of the global system at large. But the selfsame community also treats each nation as a separate, closed environment, in which uses and abuses of natural resources stem from domestic "policy choices." For Mexico, international economic integration means that its environmental future is no longer its exclusive purview—if indeed it ever was. Mexican policymakers must include the United States (and to a much lesser extent, Canada) in their calculations, and it is hard to imagine that the relatively tiny Mexican economy could exert any control over the domestic policy of its giant neighbors. But though outcomes are mainly determined at the trilateral and at the global level, still it is Mexico that is held responsible.

For Mexico, the global economic system is, in large measure, the United States. And the United States, by ignoring environmental problems or separating them from general trade and growth issues, permits itself the luxury of displacing a great deal of its own environmental policy failure to Mexico—perhaps to be later re-exported back over the border in other forms. Arid lands agriculture is moving to Mexico from the western United States as land, water, and labor become harder to find and more expensive, and questions about the use of agricultural chemicals become more pressing. Mexico in turn responds to the exigencies of United States–Mexican relations and internal political pressures and creates economic institutions and processes without regard for their likely environmental impact. For all the protests to the contrary, the environmental agenda is still marginal to the driving forces behind Mexican development and the United States–Mexican relations that frame it.

During the two years of negotiations over NAFTA, Mexico has often pushed its two northern neighbors toward agreement, so that NAFTA is very much a product of Mexican policy rather than a simple imposition of United States hegemony. Even so, given the widespread suspicion raised by the NAFTA talks and the general unhappiness of the developing countries with the Rio summit and the political jockeying surrounding it, some blame the United States for the environmental weakness of NAFTA. Others look to Mexico for new ways of tying economic recovery to environmental protection. It is impossible to leave NAFTA out when considering the Mexican environment (even though that is exactly what has been done up to now); for that reason alone, thinking about Mexico's environment requires an international focus. A look at agriculture and energy, only two out of a wide range of possible choices, will show how deeply Mexico's environmental futures are tied to international integration.

FOOD FACTS

Many of the reasons for Mexico's newfound internationalism are structural. Mexico cannot produce enough food for its burgeoning population or import the balance efficiently without recourse to free trade. Although Mexican agricultural production has increased substantially over the past two decades (the oft-repeated claim that Mexico's agriculture is stagnating is wrong), per capita agricultural production has not grown for a decade, hovering around levels that typified the early 1970s. In the past Mexico relied on heavy state intervention and costly public subsidies, as well as a restrictive import policy, to correct the food production problem. But none of these is politically or fiscally possible in the wake of the debt crisis and the subsequent economic reforms.[6] The virtue of free trade and privatization of agriculture is that they allow the public sector to retire from the subsidy business and allow cheap border prices of foodstuffs to lower the cost for consumers of grain products, cooking oil, and other basic consumer items.

The environmental future of trade-based food policy is unclear. Everyone seems to agree that the reorganization of food production on the basis of free trade will inevitably mean marginal agricultural land will no longer be competitive; some, but not all, argue that it will go out of cultivation. In this scenario, the environmental cost of rain-fed agricultural production in Mexico will be displaced to the grain belt in the United States, which is much better suited ecologically to the purpose. Marginal land in Mexico—arid lands and steep hillsides—will return to a more natural state, reducing soil erosion and exhaustion.

Some argue that agricultural adjustment will be devastating for poor farmers. Most estimates suggest that the impact will be broad and deep, and that it will be especially serious for maize and bean producers. Under most models, a substantial portion of the estimated 12 million to 15 million poor farmers in Mexico are expected to move to urban areas. The net environmental impact of such a demographic shift is unknown. It would depend on how, when, and why the farmers moved to the city, and on the ability of the cities to absorb them productively. Certainly, hundreds of thousands of rural poor moving to squalid shantytowns on the fringes of Mexican cities is not a positive social or environmental outcome, even if their land were to lie fallow. Others suggest that the deteriorating living conditions of poor farmers under free trade will lead to more, not less, poverty-induced soil degradation and deforestation. And to the extent—often underestimated—that poor farmers generate employment for poor landless people, who also would be displaced, the risk of the poor "mining" marginal lands and remnants of forest is heightened. In a country that has lost 11 million hectares of forest in the past two decades, this last prospect is a grim one.

The United States is a probable hedge against such possibilities. Some large percentage of the displaced rural poor would likely find their way to the border, reflecting the "pull" of chronic labor shortages in agriculture and services in the United States and the hard "push" of agricultural adjustment. Thus a more relaxed immigration policy on the part of the United States would be a most welcome environmental outcome for Mexico, while a restrictive policy would have the opposite effect. In neither case is Mexico in control of this element of its environmental future.

Mexico appears to recognize the inevitability of its integration into the international agricultural system, dominated by its relationship with the United States. So that it faces that future as much as possible on its own terms, it is taking a leadership role in defining those terms. Mexico's export agriculture has thus been cited as one of the most important winners under free trade. Most analysts predict that a significant portion of fruit and winter vegetable production will shift southward (as has been occurring over the last two decades) from the United States to northern Mexican irrigation districts as California, Texas, and Florida become less hospitable sites. Beyond that shift, free trade will create additional demand in the United States, and Mexico will even replace other regional competitors to some extent (for example, Brazil, for frozen orange juice concentrate).

Despite the positive effect on the volume and balance of Mexico's trade, this has a number of disturbing environmental implications. The debate over water supply and distribution in the western United States may very well be displaced in some measure to Mexico. And as the urbanization of northern Mexico continues, the competition between urban centers and agriculturalists for scarce water is likely to escalate. This is not a new debate in Mexico. Since World War II, the north has fought over groundwater use, and in the process conservation has lost out. The prospect of intensifying agriculture in northern Mexico does not bode well for problems of aquifer depletion and salinization, fertilizer runoff and contamination, and the like.

Moreover, much of the cost advantage of Mexican export agriculture revolves around heavily subsidized agricultural inputs, especially water and energy. Agricultural exports are overwhelmingly energy-intensive, because of mechanized cultivation practices and heavy fertilizer use. Yet Mexico intends to reduce many subsidies to agriculture. Will water prices actually seek market levels, or will some subsidization continue? And will Mexican fuel prices rise to reflect market realities? If so, the economic outcome for agricultural exports will be much less rosy; if not, Mexico will continue to subsidize energy and water consumption in the United States through a wasteful resource policy, with potentially disastrous environmental consequences. The essential question, though, is whether concern about the environment will take precedence over what are among the most promising exports in Mexico's agricultural sector. It certainly never has before.

THE OIL QUESTION

Mexico has a long history of oil production. Even before the revolution began in 1910 it was the world's largest oil exporter. After the Organization of Petroleum Exporting Countries (OPEC) enacted large price increases in 1973 and 1974, Mexico discovered huge new reserves and accelerated exploration and production to meet the needs of the 1970s oil boom. (Although Mexico was not a member of OPEC, it benefited from the high prevailing prices.) Now, after a decade of oil bust, the energy sector has reemerged as a determinant of domestic economic performance and environmental health.

Despite a decade of slow growth or no growth, energy consumption in Mexico grew 25 percent from 1980 to 1989, and average demand grew 3.4 percent annually. During that same period, the collapse of the oil boom and subsequent scandals within the state oil monopoly, Petróleos Mexicanos (PEMEX), caused investments in the sector to shrink drastically: from 1983 to 1991 PEMEX capital investments fell over 40 billion real pesos. Since then, Mexico has struggled to keep domestic production high enough to satisfy export and domestic demand.

The industrial growth projected as a result of economic recovery and integration through NAFTA will put tremendous new strains on domestic oil and gas production. If Mexico were to return to consumption rates of the good economic growth years of the 1970s, energy demand would grow at twice the rate it did during the 1980s. Problems with natural gas self-sufficiency cropped up some years ago, and the United States and Canada are both currently exporting natural gas to Mexico.

Demand for natural gas is expected to rise significantly over the next decade, as Mexico tries to change over its electrical energy production to natural gas-fired plants. The country is sure to take better advantage of its domestic gas, but much of its reserves are associated with southern oil fields, too remote for them to be competitive near the northern border. As a result, imports are likely to rise, with some expecting them to reach 1 billion cubic feet per day by the end of the century (current levels are about 350 million cubic feet per day). This would result in the production of cleaner technologies for energy production in Mexico.

The import solution does not follow for oil. As PEMEX is recapitalized and reorganized along more efficient lines, the main problem is to satisfy projected demand. Searching for more oil offshore and extracting more from known onshore reserves are the two main methods being employed. But numerous known environmental risks are associated with increased onshore drilling near the Lacandon Forest, the largest patch of tropical moist forest in Mexico and PEMEX's prime site for new exploration. Similar risks accompany offshore drilling in the Bay of Campeche, with potential consequences for tourism, coastal aquaculture, and offshore fisheries from the states of Tabasco to Texas. Here let us isolate two additional problems accompanying this strategy: the implications of industrial growth for domestic fossil fuel use, and increased energy use for the global environment.

The growth of Mexican society has of course resulted in more fossil fuel use, and the rate has accelerated in recent years. Automobiles alone now account for about 80 percent of the severe air pollution in Mexico City; the number of cars has grown six times faster than the population between 1940 and 1982. The economic reforms since 1985 have already meant new industrialization and exports. With NAFTA, industrialization is projected to increase, and the border industries (maquiladoras)—which have operated under special tax regulations and always been prohibited from selling in Mexico—will likely be folded into the general development plan. Certainly Mexico's hope is that industrial growth will speed up under NAFTA and provide more jobs. (The Mexican economy requires about a million new jobs annually just to cover new entrants into the labor market.)

What is disquieting is the virtual certainty that recent growth rates in fossil fuel consumption and carbon dioxide emissions are bound to increase with free trade and economic reform. Mexico is already the largest commercial consumer of energy in Latin America, far surpassing Brazil, which has nearly twice the population and economic output. Mexico's industrial carbon dioxide emissions exceed Brazil's by more than 50 percent, making Mexico the leading source in Latin America; even so, per capita emissions in Mexico are a small fraction of the United States figures, and would have to roughly triple for Mexico to break into the top 10 countries in the category.

But unless major changes take place in the way Mexico produces goods and services—reforms nowhere apparent in the country's current economic model—the steady upward trajectory of agricultural mechanization, industrial and commercial fuel-intensity, and carbon dioxide emissions is a part of the national environmental future. Critics in the United States have argued that Mexico should emulate American environmental standards, but as many have pointed out, Mexico's laws are as rigorous as any when it comes to industrial pollution. The real trouble lies in the fact that Mexico stands at the threshold of full integration into the community of developed nations—which has a miserable environmental record of its own, but has somehow been transformed into the standard for Mexico. The most positive possibilities for more open trade and freer competition lie in the more rapid transfer of clean technologies for new industrial production. And some customs receipts might be used for environmental cleanup and the implementation of safer standards.

REASSESSING THE FUTURE

The many economic reforms the Mexican government has undertaken are welcome to the extent that they eliminate gross distortions that allowed and even encouraged past environmental and economic abuses. But Mexico faces enormous environmental challenges for the future. If it displaces poor farmers from marginal lands, it must ensure that they have an alternative that is better socially and less harmful environmentally. It must also see to it that they do not make way for more intensive agriculture, with its energy waste and overuse of chemicals. If Mexico grows industrially, it must either devise new pathways to energy efficiency and lower levels of waste or risk becoming part of a Dickensian landscape of factories serving consumers in cleaner environments elsewhere. And if Mexico is to "mine" itself for oil, natural gas, water, and topsoil and export the products north, it should be confident that in the long run the proceeds will redound to the benefit of Mexicans.

Unfortunately, Mexico does not control the terms of its international integration. And its largest economic partner, the United States, is adopting a disingenuous position; it insists that Mexico emulate American environmental policies and trust that the benefits of free trade will be worth the environmental trouble. Free traders in the United States advocate doubling Mexican oil production in order to lower export prices, a policy that is environmentally unworthy on its face, and would contribute to more hydrocarbon consumption, not less. The United States has categorically refused to treat immigration in the free trade negotiations, and popular sentiment is certainly not pro-immigration. But "surplus population" is one of the consequences of economic efficiency in a country with a rapidly expanding population and a 3 percent growth rate in the labor force each year; it is well-nigh impossible for Mexico's teeming cities and worn-out, rain-fed lands to accept a million new hands a year without further environmental degradation. Just as the United States will benefit from relocating some difficult environmental problems to its south, so Mexico should be able to count on a willing partner to the north.

Whatever the bilateral, trilateral, or global framework, as Mexico looks into its environmental future, it must rely on something beyond the benevolence of the United States and Canada—or the global system, for that matter. To really make environmental progress, Mexico must reassess the use of energy in its economy, the cost of water and inorganic fertilizer in arid lands agriculture, and the virtues of industrializing on an American model. Otherwise, Mexico will not escape from the industrial and agricultural abuses that have beset societies of the developed world. Employing a model from the developed world's past is hardly a forward-looking strategy for a country with Mexico's potential.

NOTES

1. Quoted in "NAFTA Due to End Most Barriers to Trade between U.S., Mexico, Canada," *Oil and Gas Journal*, August 24, 1992, p. 30.
2. The draft referred to is dated September 8, 1992. It is not the only draft, and none of the drafts is official, in the sense of having been agreed on or submitted formally to the United States Congress. The final version is unlikely to differ in substance from this draft.
3. Nora Lustig, Barry P. Bosworth, and Robert Z. Lawrence, eds., *North American Free Trade: Assessing the Impact* (Washington, D.C.: Brookings Institution, 1992). See also Nora Lustig, Mexico: *The Remaking of an Economy* (Washington, D.C.: Brookings Institution, 1992).
4. Gary Clyde Hufbauer and Jeffrey J. Schott, *North American Free Trade: Issues and Recommendations* (Washington, D.C.: Institute for International Economics, 1992), p. 144.
5. World Commission on Environment and Development, *Our Common Future* (New York: Oxford University Press, 1987). The commission was chaired by Norwegian Prime Minister G. Harlem Brundtland.
6. For more details, see Steven E. Sanderson, "Mexican Public Sector Food Policy under Agricultural Trade Liberalization," *Policy Studies Journal*, vol. 20, no. 3 (1992), pp. 431–446.

Central America: Articles Section

Article 9   *The Washington Post*, June 14–20, 1993

The Lost Decade

Central America is staggering under its '80s legacy.

Douglas Farah

Washington Post Foreign Service

DANLI, Honduras
Santiago Montoya is the mayor of this
town, which for a decade was a cross-
roads in the Cold War conflicts that
wracked Central America. But he is
stumped by the question of what remained of the millions of dollars that
flowed through here to help U.S.-backed
contra rebels battle the leftist Sandinistas
in neighboring Nicaragua. "Well, some
Nicaraguans took over the cigar business," Montoya says after pondering a
moment. "I once heard of a reforesta-
tion project, but I don't know if it still
exists. Other than that, I can think of
nothing."

He is not the only Central American
who sadly records a blank when he
thinks of the 1980s. Across the region,
politicians, military leaders and policymakers are wrestling with the legacy of
the wars and revolutions that grabbed
world headlines and brought unprecedented overt and covert U.S. aid to this
usually neglected isthmus.

They are finding that the 1980s left behind few tangible improvements in the
lives of average citizens or solutions to
many of the socioeconomic issues that
underlay the conflicts. And they are
finding that the region lost a crucial decade in its development, making it difficult to compete now in a world market
where Central American products have
no guaranteed access.

Despite the large sums of U.S. aid—
about $5 billion to El Salvador, $2 billion
to Honduras, hundreds of millions to the
contras and $674 million in postwar re-
construction in Nicaragua—living standards in the three countries are lower
today than they were at the end of the
1970s.

The poverty rate, which stands at
about 70 percent in the three nations, is
higher. Illiteracy is also greater, at about

50 percent, and the national infrastruc-
tures are in worse condition. Nicaragua
is now ranked by some international
agencies as the second-poorest country
in the hemisphere, after Haiti.

"It was, for our countries, a lost decade in every sense, economically and socially," says Honduran President Rafael
Callejas. "It was an era of tremendous
dependence, because we were the place
where East and West met. And what that
brought us was death and violence."

President Alfredo Cristiani of El Salvador agrees that the 1980s were lost because "far from advancing as a country,
we have gone backwards . . . in the indicators that measure the advance and development of a country."

The Reagan and Bush administrations
saw U.S. Central American policy as
two-tracked: fighting Communist expansion that represented a threat to the
United States, and building democracies
that would address the fundamental
structural flaws that allowed the revolutions to flourish.

The Marxist-led Sandinistas in Nicaragua eventually were forced to hold
broad-based elections, and they lost. In
El Salvador, the Farabundo Marti National Liberation Front (FMLN) negotiated a peace pact under the mediation
of the United Nations and pressure from
the United States on the government,
and is now a legal political party.

El Salvador, Nicaragua and Honduras
also now have functioning electoral systems whose results have been respected.
Since the end of the conflicts, human
rights violations that made the region
notorious are down sharply in El Salvador and Nicaragua.

However, during interviews with dozens of political leaders, former guerrillas,
academics, and current and former U.S.
policy-makers in the three nations, a
consensus emerged that U.S. policy, although fostering elections, gave a
much lower priority to building the
kinds of democratic institutions that

could help transform society and guarantee stability and sustained economic
growth.

In fact, these sources say, U.S. policy
was driven primarily by military concerns. Washington often was willing to
settle for the appearance of democracy—
to satisfy U.S. congressional skeptics
holding purse strings—while allowing
its military clients to bypass the fragile
democratic institutions with impunity
when deemed necessary.

"Clearly, the two fundamental challenges left to consolidating democracy
are building strong, functioning systems
of law and order and clear, unequivocal
civilian authority over the armed
forces," says Bernard Aronson, assistant
secretary of State for inter-American affairs.

Aronson says criticizing U.S. policy in
the 1980s misses the most important
point: that the United States made "the
classic mistake" in earlier decades,
which "is to wait and ignore the region
while problems fester, then explode into
a crisis where all the choices are bad."

Many fear that mistake is already being repeated.

The U.S. aid that flowed freely into
Central America in the 1980s is
dropping rapidly. The Clinton administration is just beginning to fill the
top regional policy posts. Nicaragua and
El Salvador, the focal points of the 1980s,
have lacked U.S. ambassadors for more
than a year.

The Honduran town of Danli offers a
portrait of what happens in a region
where U.S. policy swings between ob-
sessive interest and utter neglect.
Throughout the 1980s, the town was an
important headquarters for the contra
rebels and their U.S. sponsors. Here,
they ran a small hospital, bought supplies, stored weapons and gathered intelligence.

Today, the rutted streets off the main
plaza remain, but the constant stream of

well-paid foreigners is gone, forcing hard times on the restaurants and other businesses that opened to accommodate them.

"Look at us now—we are worse off than ever," says a store owner on the main square. "They came, they did what they wanted, and then we had to live with the consequences."

As U.S. interest and aid dwindle, Honduras, Nicaragua, El Salvador and Guatemala have formed a common market they view as critical to sustaining economic growth.

They hope they will grow into a free-trade bloc that will unite with that proposed among the United States, Canada and Mexico under the planned North American Free Trade Agreement (NAFTA).

"What we are asking for from the United States is more commerce, strengthening of multilateral lending institutions, support for regional commercial blocs and treatment similar to that given its most privileged friends, meaning NAFTA," says Honduran President Callejas. "In Central America, we all have a similar mentality. We want to be treated the same as or better than NAFTA in terms of our competitive necessities."

But that is unlikely to happen under current conditions. Even if the United States were ready to extend free trade to Central America, the region's economies are years away from being prepared to join such an agreement.

"Attempting to resurrect economies on a base of poverty, after war, with minimal external resources is no easy task under any circumstances," wrote Marc Lindenberg in a 1993 World Peace Foundation report. "Modernizing the state and making it an efficient promoter of economic and social development will take decades."

With world prices of its main commodities—coffee and bananas—hovering at near record lows, and with few other natural resources, Central America's largest economic asset is cheap and abundant labor. But economists say that is simply not enough to make its industries competitive with those in rapidly growing countries in Asia or South America.

"Investors look for state-of-the-art telecommunications systems, infrastructure, a work force with some degree of training and . . . a functioning judicial system," says Mark Rosenberg, director of the Latin American and Caribbean Center at Florida International University. Clearly, he adds, cheap labor alone does not make a country competitive.

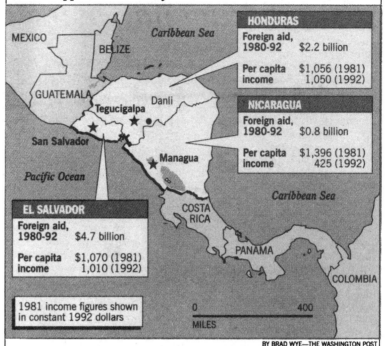

AID AND INCOME

Despite nearly $8 billion in U.S. aid from 1980 to the present, Honduras, El Salvador and Nicaragua have slipped economically ...

HONDURAS
Foreign aid, 1980-92	$2.2 billion
Per capita income	$1,056 (1981) 1,050 (1992)

NICARAGUA
Foreign aid, 1980-92	$0.8 billion
Per capita income	$1,396 (1981) 425 (1992)

EL SALVADOR
Foreign aid, 1980-92	$4.7 billion
Per capita income	$1,070 (1981) 1,010 (1992)

1981 income figures shown in constant 1992 dollars

0   400   MILES

BY BRAD WYE—THE WASHINGTON POST

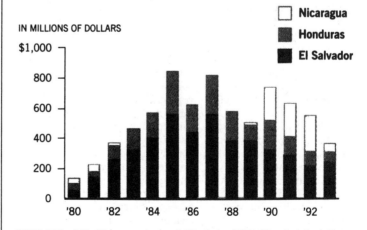

... while U.S. aid for the three countries, which peaked in 1985, shows a cumulative decline since 1990.

IN MILLIONS OF DOLLARS

Nicaragua
Honduras
El Salvador

NOTE: U.S. aid to Nicaragua was negligible during 1979-90, when the leftist Sandinistas were in power.

SOURCES: U.S. Agency for International Development, the World Factbook

THE WASHINGTON POST

One part of the problem is the legacy of disinvestment left by the war years. According to a study done in El Salvador by the Center for Scientific and Technological Investigations, linked to the opposition Christian Democratic Party, spending for education was two-thirds lower in 1992 than in

1977. Health-care spending was reduced by the same amount, and spending on public works was reduced by three-quarters. Only the defense budget was up, by 14 percent.

Victor Meza, director of the Honduran Center for Documentation, an independent think tank, says his country's standard of living has dropped to what it was "in the early 1970s, and we have higher unemployment than we had then."

Governments hard-pressed to wage war in many cases had no choice but to slash budgets for social and infrastructural investments. Yet U.S. officials and their regional allies argued at the time that they were working to address the roots of the region's economic problems—through special programs aimed at ending grossly unequal and inefficient distribution of land and encouraging financial reforms and privatization.

Today, it is clear that few of those non-military programs were aggressively pursued. Central American countries are struggling with the same structural economic handicaps that originally fueled their instability.

In El Salvador, land reform launched in 1980 and financed in large part by the United States is only now being fully implemented as part of the peace process. President Cristiani's conservative government is months behind schedule in dividing up land because there are not enough qualified people to carry out the necessary surveys.

Salvadoran banks, which were nationalized in the 1980s to ensure greater access to credit, proved so inefficient and corrupt under state control that they are being reprivatized by Cristiani's government. In all, they made more than $300 million in bad loans.

But the reprivatization also has come under fire. The opposition, led by the Christian Democrats, charges that banks are being bought by the same wealthy families and investors that owned them before 1980 and that credit would again be available only to wealthy businessmen and large farmers.

In Honduras, officials concede that U.S. aid programs actually inhibited stable economic development by fostering a corrupt climate of easy money.

"Our driving principle was that Honduras was a rental property for the contras and intelligence gathering," says a senior U.S. official involved in policy making. "The U.S. poured money in with little regard to where it went and fed all of the worst tendencies to corruption."

"If the level of corruption is not attacked now, in the future the democratic process will be affected," says Honduran national treasurer Israel Gonzalez, who has investigated, at the request of President Callejas, illicit enrichment of government officials. "We found [corruption] at every level."

Manuel Gamero, editor of El Tiempo newspaper, says the United States was only "interested in having their 'USS Honduras' battleship, and the rest did not matter."

"The result is that our future is bleak after the 1980s," Gamero says. "Our productive system is obsolete, our businesses are accustomed to subsidies, we have generalized corruption, and our human resources are precarious at best. ... At the end of the day, it would definitely have been better if the U.S. money had never come."

Shaky judicial systems are especially damaging to the region's economic prospects because foreign businesses generally are reluctant to invest in countries that lack due process to address grievances.

Despite U.S. support for judicial and institutional reform, these areas received only a fraction of the resources and attention that war efforts did.

"If there was a significant flaw in our assistance, it was that we did not sufficiently condition aid to macroeconomic reforms and the strengthening of democratic institutions such as the administration of justice," says U.S. Ambassador Cresencio S. Arcos Jr., who has worked on Honduran matters for 13 years.

During the regional wars, the focus was on human rights cases and the general inability to prosecute military officers for abuses. But courts have proved similarly incapable of dealing with such issues as property rights.

In Nicaragua, 13,000 cases involving properties confiscated by the Sandinistas during the 1980s are in dispute.

"The guiding principle in justice across Central America remains unchanged," says a veteran diplomat. "It is to protect those who can get protection and punish those who cannot."

In its 1992 human rights report on Honduras, the State Department says the country had "an endemically corrupt and inefficient criminal justice system" that was "in most cases incapable of rendering a verdict and passing a sentence in a timely manner."

Judges routinely earn less than $100 a month. Although largely untrained and often having only high school educa-

tions, they investigate crimes as well as judge them.

The low pay and backlog of cases have made the judiciaries easy targets of intimidation and corruption. Judicial appointments remain political: In El Salvador, for example, Cristiani's right-wing party controls the courts, but in Nicaragua, the opposition leftist Sandinistas still do.

Those arrested can spend years in prison without a hearing. A Salvadoran lawyer says his clients spent an average of three years in prisons before getting to trial. But those who can buy protection or intimidate their accusers never have to stand trial.

In San Salvador, three men were arrested recently for commandeering at gunpoint the car of a woman who had been a rebel commander in the war.

Relatives of the assailants turned up at the home of the woman's parents.

"They warned me and my parents not to pursue the case or something would happen to us," says the woman, who fought throughout the war. "Who was going to protect my family in this case? And we knew the judge had already been pressured. So we dropped all charges."

In Nicaragua, aside from property disputes, the government has been unable to investigate and prosecute several high-profile murders, or the killings of more than 200 members of the former contra movement.

In addition, the Sandinistas say more than 100 of their party members have been killed.

The most devastating indictment of the judicial system, however, may be in El Salvador, where the U.N.-mandated Truth Commission, formed to investigate war crimes, recommended that the entire supreme court be forced to resign for obstructing investigations.

As in economic affairs, U.S. attempts to reform the Salvadoran judicial system during the war years were unavailing.

From 1984 to 1990, the United States provided El Salvador with $13.7 million for judicial reform, including $5.5 million for the Special Investigative Unit. It was to be the investigative body handling major crimes. But the Truth Commission found that the unit's leaders tampered with evidence and covered up the military's involvement in the 1989 killings of six Jesuit priests.

Another institution that has been slow to develop is the legislature, with few resources, little power and virtually no experience. Ruben Zamora, vice president of the Salvadoran National Assembly, has no staff to help make policy.

Legislators across the region agree that they essentially are trying to build their institutions on the fly, at a time when the region is in crisis.

The polarization in Nicaragua and El Salvador, and the years of dependence on Washington for money, mean that many of the region's battles are still fought in the halls of the U.S. Congress, not in San Salvador or Managua.

Recently, all segments of the Nicaraguan political scene, who refuse to meet together in Managua, gathered for a forum at the Wilson Center in Washington. Supporters of President Violeta Chamorro and her opponents used the opportunity to lobby Congress for or against continued U.S. aid to the nation.

Antonio Lacayo, minister of the presidency, told the conference, "The element that has been lacking . . . is U.S. respect for our internal decisions, and [there is] a tendency of the Nicaraguans to resolve their problems here."

Article 10   *USA Today*, September 1991

Can Central America Cope With Soaring Population?

The "population is not just doubling or tripling; it is rising by a factor of seven. . . ."

Robert W. Fox

Mr. Fox, a former staff member of the Organization of American States and the Inter-American Bank, is the coauthor of a series of reports that present world population growth in three-dimensional computer graphics and text.

I was walking through the streets of Cartago, Costa Rica, some 20 years ago when the bells rang and the elementary schools let out. A thousand scrubbed and uniformed children flooded the streets. That Lilliputian world was a dramatic reminder that Costa Rica, like the rest of Central America, is a nation of children. Nearly half the population is under 15.

Central America's population explosion was captured for me in that incident. Today, ever larger numbers of children are pressing hard on small and shrinking economies. The 8,000,000 Central American children 15 or younger in 1970 represented a large increase from 4,000,000 in 1950. There are 13,000,000 now and, if projections hold true, there will be 19,000,000 by 2025.

Central America's population is not just doubling or tripling; it is rising by a factor of seven—if the ecology can support it— and growth will not stop in 2025.

In the first half of that 75-year period, only one-third of the expected increase occurred. The much larger share, nearly two-thirds, is projected between now and 2025. Past that year, the projections call for still further increases of about 1,000,000 annually. It is yesterday's, today's, and tomorrow's issue in Central America.

These amounts may seem modest next to the population size and growth in the U.S., but, by comparison, they actually are massive. Applying Central America's pace of growth, it is as though the U.S.'s population would be passing 1,000,000,000 in 2025.

The population explosion that began in the 1950s and continues today is arguably Central America's most significant historical event, overriding in importance the Spanish Conquest and the Independence Movement 270 years later. Never has the region experienced anything of this magnitude and force. Not only is the *amount* of growth of serious concern, but also the *speed* with which it is occurring.

It is wreaking havoc on the region's cultures, economies, social systems, and the natural resource base. Forget the failure of political systems and civil wars as the leading issue or economic depression and unemployment, which affect as much as half the labor force. Forget old debates over land-holding systems where power is concentrated in the hands of a few export crop producers. Forget low levels of living and miserable urban slums that appear occasionally to be clusters of smoking cardboard and tin boxes strung along the arroyos. Forget the exodus of tens and hundreds of thousands headed north to cross the porous Mexican and U.S. borders in search of jobs.

Focus instead on the rise in population as the single basic issue. Redoubling every 20–25 years, it has put an incredible burden on attempts to resolve old problems and, meanwhile, created new ones. In Central America today, you truly must run faster and faster just to stay in the same place.

Foreign writers covering Central America seem genuinely unaware of the issue's strength and the intertwining of demographic trends as well as political and economic concerns. A glance through recently published books in English on the region turn up only a few references to the subject, and they simply recite the facts of population size. There are at least two reasons for the inattention. Writers have little exposure or training in the basic principles of demography. It is a matter considered technical and best left to the experts. Secondly, the topic has been subjected to a concerted effort to narrow it down and find it a niche. Accordingly, it invariably is classified and bottled up in the health and family planning arena.

Largely ignoring it, writers instead focus on the visible results: rapid urbanization and growing slum settlements, crowded labor markets and high unemployment, declining purchasing power and falling levels of living, and a rapidly deteriorating natural resource base. These major problems have been exacerbated during Central America's "lost decade" of the 1980s. Now, in the 1990s, the economies continue to lose ground while population growth relentlessly moves ahead.

Central America's recent demographic history is typical of most Third World regions. Prior centuries of high fertility and mortality and the resulting small gap between these levels allowed for very low growth—well under one percent annually. Population grew slowly during the 16th- to 19th-century colonial era and in the first century of independence as well. By 1920, numbers had increased to 5,000,000 and, as the pace of growth quickened, to 7,000,000 20 years later.

By the 1940s, major health improvements were under way. The ages-old era of pestilence and plague faded and the modern one emerged. Radical changes took place in the next quarter-century. Field reports of the Pan American Health Organization from the 1940s discuss matters that seem current—the positive results from the installation of sewage and potable water systems, for example, rather than reports of plague or cholera outbreaks in port cities.

Following World War II, massive resources were invested in the region to improve general health conditions, including medical treatment, food processing, sanitation, education, and the control of communicable and transmissible diseases. As a result, the death rate—then high—dropped sharply in a very brief period of time.

The decline in deaths depended on imported technology such as medicines, pesticides, and insecticides. Meanwhile, the birth rate, which depended on slowly changing cultural norms, remained high. A growing gap developed between the two rates. This gap is the rate of natural increase, the basis of the population explosion.

While mortality levels plummeted, the birth rate—exceptionally high in 1950—stayed high. Compared to 24 births annually per 1,000 population in the U.S. in 1950, the rate was 40 in Panama and in a higher range elsewhere from 47 to 54. By the mid 1970s, while dropping substantially in Costa Rica, it fell just modestly elsewhere. Today, the birth rate still is moderately high—ranging from two-thirds to three-quarters its 1950 level. Women in Central America in 1950 averaged six to seven children; the range today is from three to six. These time period differences narrow, however, in terms of *surviving* children when the sharp drop in child mortality is applied.

Population growth represents the excess of births over deaths (minus migration). There were, on average, 290,000 more births than deaths annually in Central America during 1950–55; the difference is about 800,000 and, by 2020–25, it is projected to increase to 1,000,000 annually.

The rise is tied to the vast increase in the number of women of reproductive age, associated in turn with Central America's very young age structure. In 1950 there were 2,100,000 females of reproductive age. By 1990, they numbered 6,700,000 by 2000, 9,200,000 are projected; by 2025, 16,400,000. In essence, and although they are having fewer children apiece, this vastly greater *number* of women will produce many more offspring than before.

The population of Central America will continue to increase until these forces are played out and the number of births is equal to that of deaths in any given interval (minus migration). The youthful age structure that has emerged, however, combined with its product—the rising numbers of females 15–49—as well as the fertility and mortality trends, constitute the inertia that ensures this will not be attained for decades in spite of a falling birth rate.

Dwindling natural resources

Out of this population wellspring flow enormous consequences for the deteriorating natural resource base, particularly the forests—for urbanization and labor force growth, and eventually for the pressures that lead to flight to the U.S.

To accommodate the region's growing numbers, the pressures on natural resources are severe. With few mineral or petroleum reserves and limited amounts of good agricultural land—mostly tied up in large estates—the region depends heavily on its few remaining resources. Among them, the forests are prominent.

The forest resource increasingly has been drawn on to generate income in the "productive" economic sectors by supplying raw materials for manufacturing and processing industries. Precious woods are marketed abroad for making furniture, doors, beams, and carved figures. Local demand for less desirable wood is high. Sawmills provide timber and finished lumber for house construction to shelter the burgeoning urban population. Charcoal sellers ply the streets of the cities. The forests are being harvested, but there is little new growth to assure regeneration.

Man's forest incursions have led to a process of continuous deterioration. To bring out prized timbers such as mahogany, primitive logging roads are built.

These become waterways fed by tropical downpours. The local population exacerbates the situation by harvesting the readily available wood on the slopes next to the road. Heavy erosion results, soils in a widening radius are lost, and gullies develop.

Meanwhile, the roads permit penetration into the jungle by "forest farmers," who apply slash-and-burn techniques to clear small plots. This has gone on for centuries, but earlier involved far fewer people who worked a plot for only a few years, moving on as erosion and mineral leaching depleted the land's fertility. Now, under conditions of rapid rural population growth, other farmers follow in their footsteps and try to coax one or two more crops out of the soil. Rather than resting the land for many years as required to rebuild its fertility, this increased population pressure has led to even further soil deterioration.

As patches of cleared jungle coalesce and the forest line retreats, it then is valued only as pasture. From the early 1960s to 1987, the United Nation's Food and Agricultural Organization reports that land in permanent pasture increased from 7,000,000 to 13,000,000 hectares, while land in forests and woodlands dropped from 27,000,000 to 17,000,000 hectares. The newly cleared land has supported a vastly expanded cattle industry. Much of the beef is exported, and thus the "hamburger connection" is forged between tropical forest destruction and the economic demands of industrialized nations.

The deforestation in particular areas threatens to produce devastating results. Panama Canal operations depend on the water in Lake Gatun. Ships are raised from the Atlantic Ocean to the higher lake level through one set of locks. After crossing the Isthmus, they are lowered to the Pacific Ocean through other locks. Enormous amounts of lake water flush out to sea with these operations. Replenishing of Lake Gatun's water supply is vital, and that depends on the heavy rainfalls that regularly sweep the area.

Canal authorities now worry about the amount of forest clearance taking place in the immediately surrounding watershed basin. With reduced tree cover, the hydrological cycle is disturbed. Evapotranspiration is reduced, which diminishes local water vapor recycling in the atmosphere. In the absence of tree cover, the increased reflectivity heats the atmosphere, and this, in turn, counteracts cloud formation and rainfall. With the forest cover intact, the ground soaks up rainfall, releasing it slowly to the lake. Without cover, water runoff increases, eroding the land, carrying soils with it that threaten to silt up the lake.

Central America faces a dilemma. The remaining forest must be preserved for its intrinsic value along with the vast genetic diversity it contains that undoubtedly will lead to future medical and scientific discoveries. The tropics harbor many more times the number of species than exist in temperate climates. Tropical forests have taken millions of years to evolve into their extremely diversified biological states. Many species—plant, animal, and insect—survive symbiotically, all living in mutual interdependence. Thus, the felling of one commercially desirable tree in the tropical rain-forest may assure the destruction of an entire habitat and many of the distinct life forms it supports.

The region's explosive population growth exerts enormous pressures on this natural resource. Given economic demands, short-term interests often prevail to the detriment of forest preservation. The Central American nations are caught up in cycles that require income for new investments and old debt repayment. Earnings are needed to maintain current investments and satisfy basic needs of very young populations. The difficulties of meeting daily national expenses are compounded by economic stagnation and instability. Coping with these issues presses hard on the region's limited natural resource base, particularly its forests.

Urbanization

The growth of Central America's major cities since 1950 was an early sign of the population explosion. Shunning near-feudal agricultural conditions, attracted by the city lights, and bussed on good road systems in these relatively small countries, tens of thousands migrated to urban areas. Voting with their feet, it continues today.

Burgeoning urban populations pressed for expanded services. Dusty streets, torn up for months and years at a time to place water and sewer pipes, vied with overhead power line installations for general disruptiveness. In a very new development in the 1960s, expansive squatter settlements emerged on the outskirts, particularly around the capitals of Guatemala, Nicaragua, and Honduras. Sharp conflicts with municipal authorities arose over two very basic issues—ownership of the ground and legal recognition of the settlements—whose resolution was prerequisite to

(UN Photo/Claire Taplin)

The escalating population of Central America is putting enormous pressure on the enviorment and society.

home improvements and the extension into the communities of water, sewage, and electrical lines. In San Salvador, El Salvador, squatters built makeshift dwellings in the ravines that radiated outward from the city core, threading their way through upper- and middle-class residential zones. Social class in San Salvador literally is tied to one's topographical position.

Yet, that massive urban growth was but a harbinger of the much greater increases to come. Practically all cities and towns continue to grow rapidly, with no letup in sight. From 1950 to 1990, the urban population of Central America increased from 2,800,000 to 13,700,000. This net gain of 11,000,000, however, is just over a one-quarter of the expected total increase during 1950–2025. The much larger proportion—73%, or some 30,000,000 additional urban dwellers—lies immediately ahead.

The major cities already seem to have reached saturation and face significant constraints to further growth. Guatemala City is crowded into a small plateau; in San Jose, Costa Rica, and San Salvador, further physical expansion threatens to take scarce and fertile adjacent lands out of agricultural production; Tegucigalpa, Honduras, is wedged into a small valley; Panama City is bordered on three sides by the Pacific Ocean, the Canal, and hills to the north. Managua, Nicaragua, its vacant downtown area converted to cow pasture after the 1972 earthquake and now reeling

from the effects of a destroyed economy, must determine how to reconstruct a city around a hollow core, should confidence in the economy be regained and funds become available.

Automobile and bus fumes, factory smoke, and nearby burning fields contribute to a steady decline in the quality of the urban environment. The once clear sky over Guatemala City, for example, often is grey with smog. Generally crowded conditions are apparent, affecting the public transportation system in particular as old and overloaded busses, belching black smoke, slowly thread their way through narrow city streets. Most shocking of all is the contrast between clear upstream river and reservoir water before it passes through the cities and the black untreated sludge that pours into the stream beds at the other end—and from there is used in the agricultural fields. Resources to remedy these and many other deteriorating urban conditions are nowhere in sight.

The urban share of the total population in all the countries was about one-third in 1950. (Honduras was less than 18% urban.) It now has risen to about one-half. By 2025, it is expected to range from two-thirds to three-fourths. It will continue to increase as rural areas approach saturation in the amount of population they will absorb and as the "redundant" rural numbers pour into the cities. In earlier times, rural saturation resulted from miserable rural socio-economic conditions, including inequitable land ownership and tenure systems, rigid social stratification and the absence of social mobility, inadequate schools and medical facilities, and the lack of credit and financing institutions. While these conditions have changed little, they have been compounded by rising rural population densities and a rapidly increasing labor force.

A generation later, those children of Cartago, Costa Rica, now are working or looking for employment. Yet, the region is in the second decade of a severe recession. The economies are in disarray as the value of the currencies and primary export commodities—coffee, bananas, timber, cattle, cotton, and sugar—have fallen. Investors, jittery over unsettled political and economic conditions, have transferred capital to safer havens abroad.

Disadvantaged by falling export commodity earnings, limited in natural resources, short on investment capital, and supported by outmoded technology, few of Central America's huge new labor force entrants are finding meaningful employment. Over all, this parallels the urbanization trend; that is, about three-quarters of the 1950–2025 labor force increase will occur between now and 2025. With the agricultural labor force expected to increase by relatively small amounts, this will throw the largest burden on the cities.

As these massive urban labor force increases occur, and should the poor economic growth climate persist, unprecedented international labor force flows could result. This is already the case with El Salvador, where it is estimated that up to 15–20% of the total population has fled to the U.S. Affecting this potential, however, are other key issues, including the as yet unmeasured capacity of the informal employment sector to absorb labor increases in the cities, and the ability or desire of the U.S. to absorb the flow.

Other realities

For decades, Central Americans have sought to find a proper place for the population issue in their social and economic institutions. This has been a tough, uphill battle, made more difficult by moral and ethical implications in predominantly Roman Catholic societies. It has been and continues to be a struggle.

Economic development has dominated Central America's view of its future since the 1960s. A fast pace of economic growth was expected to more

than offset the demographic reality. All this was to be fostered through export earnings; "soft" loans and grants from the multilateral banking community (World Bank and Inter-American Development Bank); and loans from Organization for Economic Cooperation and Development nations and commercial bank funds.

National policies focused on development in the context of an eventual fully integrated economic union—the Central American Common Market. This was to be supported by the Central American Bank for Economic Integration that was to attract the resources of the international lending community, then awash with petrodollars.

Policies and programs were aimed at clearing the forests, colonizing and "developing" the land, and increasing export crops and livestock production levels. As the region's cities mushroomed in size, multiple urban industrialization options were advanced, some to deal with regional opportunities offered by the fledgling Central American Common Market, others to take advantage of the export market and the cheap and growing local labor force supply.

Such conscious policies for economic growth were not matched on the demographic front. Population increase was still considered a given. The idea of slowing it down, of tampering with "natural" forces, offended many and grated deeply on personal convictions. Besides, the notion of any limitations went completely against the grain of economic development and growth, its corollary. Instead, commercial interests advanced the notion that expanding markets would need more consumers. Rural interests stated that agricultural land remained to be developed. The military argued that more people were necessary to settle the fringes of national territory to prevent encroachments from neighboring nations. Indigenous leaders railed at the thought that their groups would be targets of population "control" efforts.

Religious orders fought against the very notion of family planning and provision of contraceptives. Many politicians behaved likewise in the male-dominated societies. Uncomfortable with the subject, they often were painfully shy to discuss it. Outright hostility to family planning was not unknown.

It always was recognized that economic growth had to keep pace with population increases. If the economies faltered, the continuing population gains would slip right on by, producing lower

and lower levels of living and wiping out the forward momentum of the 1960s and 1970s. This is precisely what happened. Living conditions in Central America have fallen back to 1960s levels.

The struggle to convey this demographic message in overwhelmingly "growth and development" oriented societies has been difficult. The principal actors have very divergent views and interests in mind.

It initially was confined to the resolve of private family planning organizations. Later, its base broadened with acceptance as a maternal and child health care issue in the Ministries of Public Health. During the 1970s, several countries even created demographic evaluation units at the national planning level. Elevating the topic to this level was both an attempt to raise awareness and yank control of it from economists, who more often than not considered population size and growth as a given, an "externality" to their analyses.

Demographers have informed politicians that they have a very major problem emerging for which there is no short-term solution. Further, it is guaranteed to continue to intensify for at least the next half-century, perhaps longer. To ameliorate it over the long term by implementing and supporting family planning programs will touch on and alter the deepest of cultural sensitivities. All this, they argue, will contribute to unrest and eventually bring about profound alterations in individual and family value systems.

Slowly but surely, the old attitudes are changing. The technical soundness of the population projections is recognized, and, accompanied by common sense observations in the increasingly crowded streets outside, politicians realize that a serious and intractable problem has emerged. Their response has become, "I already know [about it]. Don't bring me problems, bring me solutions."

Central America's demographic future contains hard messages that are difficult to swallow and the subject still is viewed from many different perspectives. Generally speaking, this is where the matter rests today.

What is occurring in Central America is a typical case of the demographic forces working in the Third World. It also has been at the center of much foreign policy debate in the U.S. (including proposals in Congress to make it possible for various Central Americans, once here, to stay here). The demographic future of Central America is linked with the U.S.'s population future through immigration, and the demographic trends in Central America imperil the prosperity and political stability of a region of considerable importance to the U.S.

Much of what has been said about Central America also could be said of Mexico, which is three times as populous as all of Central America and shares a long border with the U.S. High birth and rapidly falling death rates, a young age structure, and vast increases in the number of women of reproductive age are similar themes there.

The strongest distinction between Mexico and Central America is the Mexican government's deliberate decision in the 1970s to bring down its very high rate of population growth and to act quickly on this decision. Programs were drawn up and implemented and have been reinforced by each successive national administration. While the initial target of reaching a 100,000,000 population size by year 2000 may be overshot by some 6–10,000,000, this nevertheless represents a major change from the 132,000,000 Mexicans earlier projected for year 2000.

With shared features, Mexico long has realized that the demographic "passages" in store for Central America also are inevitable there. Appreciating that they have some control over the time required to work through these passages, Mexican authorities have made deliberate and concerted efforts to take advantage of this and speed up the process. Accordingly, while the age structure has changed very little (the Mexican median age was slightly over 18 years both in 1950 and today), the total fertility rate has dropped precipitously, from 6.7 children during 1950–70 to approximately 3.7. This represents enormous change in a very short period on the demographic scale of things. In Central America, only Costa Rica and Panama have had comparable fertility declines.

Nevertheless, with population momentum still driving their demography, neither Central America nor Mexico is likely to stabilize at a level and in time to take the pressures off their social, ecological, and economic systems—or ours.

Article 11   *World Press Review*, May 1993

Cities as 'casinos of crime'

Central America's Latest War

Yazmín Ross

Pensamiento Propio

In Central America, violence has entered everyday life, stimulated by social disintegration, an abundance of military arms, and thousands of people demobilized by armies, paramilitary organizations, and irregular forces. "At night, Central America is a no man's land," says Roberto Cuéllar of the Interamerican Institute for Human Rights in Costa Rica. "Today, our lives are chips in the casino of common crime." After 10 at night, anyone who goes out is on his own, and the risk to life and limb is the same in Guatemala City, San Salvador, Managua, Tegucigalpa, or Panama City. The cities are under a tacit state of siege, with their populations staying inside during certain hours, avoiding certain areas—such as the old downtown centers and some poorer suburbs, places where "nice people" have not gone for some time now. "Governments are reacting passively in the face of a rising crime rate," says Cuéllar. As if on a carousel, the political struggles of yesterday have passed into memory, leaving their methods and habits to haunt us. The use of weapons, too, has been depoliticized and now feeds ordinary criminality.

From the opposition bimonthly "Pensamiento Propio" of Managua.

Authorities say that this is a predictable aftermath of war. In a study entitled, "Civilian-Military Relations Under Democratic Rule," prepared by the Latin American Faculty of Social Sciences, researcher Augusto Varas maintains that the armies of Central America have perverted society by introducing massive violence. As a result, gangs of organized criminals have proliferated. These gangs often escape official control, and they make use of the structures formerly used by the forces of political repression, according to evidence gathered by human-rights organizations.

Since the cease-fire was signed in El Salvador in 1992, there have been 10 murders per day, part of a crime wave that has set off protests by business people and community groups. Former soldiers, police officers, and former death-squad members rob banks, restaurants, and other businesses with their AK-47s and even steal cattle and armed vehicles. In Nicaragua, land takeovers and attacks on the street have become commonplace, committed by former Contras and demobilized Sandinista soldiers, both angry because they have not received the land and aid promised to them in return for laying down their arms. In Panama, crime has increased by 300 percent since the American invasion in 1989. With the dissolution of the army and its replacement by the police, the streets and highways have been abandoned to criminal gangs, often made up of former soldiers and members of other forces created during the Manuel Noriega regime, according to authorities.

The number of private security agencies in Panama has increased from 20 to 110, and they employ 10,000 trigger-happy guards, who are blamed for the majority of street homicides. Last April, a "Death to Criminals" squad of vigilantes went into action, justifying its formation on the pre text that the legal and police systems were incapable of acting. At the same time, several international companies based in the Colón Free Trade Zone, among them Canon Latin America, Inc., announced that they were moving to Miami because of crime in the harbor and the kidnapping of Japanese executives, some of whom have been ransomed for as much as $700,000.

In Guatemala last March, the army began joint patrols with the police to stem the increase in street crime and bank robberies. In June, the Honduran army took similar action in the face of a crime wave that took 500 lives in the first four months of 1992.

Last year, after the peace accords were signed in El Salvador, President Alfredo Cristiani and Guatemalan President Jorge Serrano Elías agreed to measures to stop the black market in weapons. Before United Nations observers could take control of the weapons held by the army and the guerrillas, large-caliber weapons, army vehicles, and arms captured from the guerrillas during the conflict were quickly sold by Salvadoran officers. The arms were offered to anyone paying cash, and the customers included the Guatemalan army, leftist guerrillas, and criminals, according to official sources in both nations.

Drug smugglers are the best customers for surplus military equipment, and they have dealt with everyone from the Nicaraguan Contras to the Salvadoran air force. Lieutenant-Colonel Roberto Leiva of the air force sold four 550-pound bombs to rivals of Colombian drug boss Pablo Escobar Gaviria. The deal was worth $450,000, which was returned when the sale was exposed last March.

Large quantities of small arms, machine guns, and munitions that once armed the Nicaraguan militias and El Salvador's civil-defense patrols were bought in 1989 by followers of Panama's current president, Guillermo Endara, to fight Noriega. These guns are now back on the market, increasing the power of anti-social gangs and adding to instability. Many demobilized soldiers and guerrillas have, according to Mario Carías, foreign minister of Honduras, become "hired guns without ideologies." Raúl Benítez of the National Autonomous University's Center for Interdisciplinary Studies and Humanities Research in Mexico says that "these forces, which originated in a war for power, are now a potentially very large destabilizing factor. Even though regular and irregular forces are being demobilized, we are left with structural violence by out-of-control military forces."

Panama's David Smith, of the Central American Human-Rights Commission, says that "the war hid other forms of violence that affect the community." The abrupt transition from military-political confrontations to those of a civilian character has caused an increase in the quantity and quality of crimes committed in Central America. This includes Costa Rica, where the minister of public security, Luis Fishman, was kidnapped last September by a former member of the Honduran army, Orlando Ordóñez, who had a record of robbery, extortion, and sex offenses.

In Honduras, Fernando Marichal Callejas, a cousin of President Rafael Callejas, was murdered by kidnappers at the beginning of last year, shortly after they received a large ransom. President Callejas was able to prove a short time later that the head of the National Directorate of Investigations, Lieutenant Debbe Ramos, whose responsibility it was to investigate the case, was in fact responsible for the killing. Ramos is now in prison.

"At night, Central America is a no man's land."

It also was revealed that high military commanders and aides to President Callejas were involved in smuggling weapons, cocaine, and even infants. One of the most notorious scandals in recent months was the dismantling of a network of "nursing homes" that kept newborn babies until they could be exported to the United States. The homes were allegedly run by former Attorney General Rubén Zepeda and other politicians.

The processes of social disintegration and the recasting of the doctrines of national security, observes Raúl Benítez, will force the armies of Central America to assume a larger role in the fight against drug-smuggling and crime, which will continue to rise as unemployment and poverty increase and as refugees and those displaced by fighting return home.

In addition, this will mean a redefinition of the idea of human rights. Human-rights organizations, accustomed to reporting illegal detentions, disappearances, torture, political assassinations, and extra-judicial executions, will have to adapt, because most violence now comes from other sources. The new violence is uncontrollable and is forcing the adoption of new policies. Human-rights organizations are finding that their traditional formulas no longer fit, and they need new priorities.

Article 12   *The Washington Post National Weekly Edition*, June 14–20, 1993

Even in Peace, the Armies Remain Entrenched

The Central American militaries have joined forces against the civilians

Douglas Farah

TEGUCIGALOA, Honduras
When Gen. Luis Alonso Discua's term as head of the Honduran military was up earlier this year, he bullied a compliant congress into changing the law to allow his election to another three-year term.

In neighboring El Salvador, Gen. Rene Emilio Ponce, the defense minister who was supposed to be purged for human rights abuses by the end of last year, refused to go. When he finally presented his resignation in March, sources say, he warned President Alfredo Cristiani not to accept it, and Ponce is to remain in command until at least June 30.

Meanwhile, the head of the Nicaraguan army, Gen. Humberto Ortega, refuses to say when he will step aside even though his Sandinista party lost national elections three years ago and his presence has cost president Violeta Chamorro aid and credibility.

Analysts across Central America say the three cases exemplify the most dangerous long-term legacy of the Cold War conflicts that swept across the region in the 1980s—the military's continued dominance, even in nations that have civilian governments.

Today, after a decade of war, El Salvador, Nicaragua and Honduras all have democratically elected presidents and congresses. Washington no longer sees Central America's armies as essential and has slashed aid. The new civilian leaders, for their part, have begun to demand cuts in defense spending.

But the militaries in the region still view themselves as having ultimate responsibility in defining and protecting national interests. The feeling is summed up in the slogan painted at all military barracks in El Salvador: "The nation will live as long as the armed forces live." The generals believe civilians should be allowed to exercise power only as long as they do not interfere with the military or its self-defined mission.

And so, the armies of the region have set aside long-standing international rivalries and begun consulting with each other on the changing situation. They have bluntly rejected attempts by civilian politicians to control their budgets and commanders.

Moreover, all three forces have moved to expand their economic leverage, buying up or investing in businesses to guarantee independent and autonomous sources of funding for years to come.

"We are seeing the formation of a Central American guild of the military," says one veteran diplomat who has studied the militaries in the region for the past decade. "They have more in common with each other than with any national civilian government, and they are looking for preservation of privilege and power."

The diplomat warns that the "unequal competition" between the military and private sector was the "biggest threat to free, open market policies" because the military would be unwilling to tolerate competition in the industries it controlled.

As Central Americans struggle to curtail the swollen budgets and political turf of the military establishments, many accuse the United States of tolerating human rights abuses and economic corruption in the region's armies throughout the wars of the 1980s.

Even U.S. officials say that their efforts to help armies fight insurgencies sometimes conflicted with their attempts to promote good government. "What we were trying to do was extremely difficult," says Elliott Abrams, who led the Reagan administration's Central America policy. "We were trying to strengthen the military as an institution and at the same time strengthen civilian control of the government. It was quite a neat trick, but I think we had some success."

Still, the distorted balance of power perpetuated by U.S. policy is clearly evident in Honduras, which during the long U.S.-backed war against Nicaragua's Sandinista government earned the ironic nickname "USS Honduras" among Latin politicians, journalists and diplomats. Honduras served as a logistical base for the contra rebels fighting the Sandinistas, and U.S. officials acknowledge that military aid was handed out in Tegucigalpa with few strings attached.

"Everything that was being done here was being done to defeat Marxist-Leninism," says Alfredo Landaverde, a

A TEMPORARILY PERMANENT PRESENCE FOR A U.S. AIR BASE

PALMEROLA, Honduras

When the United States was pouring billions of dollars into Central America to defeat communism, this base was the nerve center for intelligence gathering, communications and logistical support for countless overt and clandestine missions viewed as crucial to protecting U.S. interests.

Now, with the Cold War over and the Central American wars largely ended, Palmerola is one of the last vestiges of the massive U.S. military presence in the region.

Though always billing it as a temporary facility, the Pentagon spent hundreds of millions of dollars after 1983 turning the once-sleepy Soto Cano Air Base into the most advanced base in Central America. It extended the airstrip to 8,500 feet, and mounted sophisticated listening devices and radars to track the communications and movements of El Salvador's leftist guerrillas and to coordinate air strikes against them.

The base also handled communications with U.S.-backed contra rebels seeking to overthrow Nicaragua's Marxist-led Sandinista government and served as the center for training National Guard units from across the United States. The U.S. troops mounted joint maneuvers with the Hondurans aimed at intimidating the Sandinistas, and the base is called Joint Task Force Bravo because it was planned as a joint operation with the Honduran military.

Despite the move to close unneeded military bases in the United States, Palmerola, located in a broad valley about 60 miles north of Tegucigalpa, appears safe for the near future. It is still home to some 1,200 U.S. troops who rotate through on a temporary basis, including National Guard units and 250 troops who maintain and fly a helicopter unit and other aircraft.

Palmerola is now responsible for helping track aircraft suspected of drug trafficking across the region,

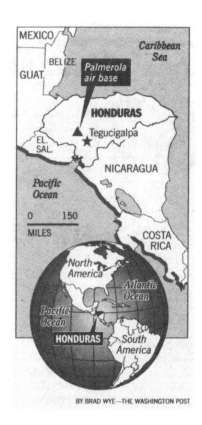

BY BRAD WYE—THE WASHINGTON POST

Christian Democratic congressman. "There was corruption in everything and the U.S. had to accept it because it was being done by their allies in the war."

With the help of the Reagan administration, the Honduran military used the threat of a Nicaraguan invasion to get millions of dollars of new equipment and buy a dozen F-5E fighter jets from the United States. The fleet, the most sophisticated in Central America, costs about $3 million a year to fly and maintain.

U.S. aid to the 24,000-man army peaked at $81 million in 1986 and totaled $509 million from 1981 to 1992. With the influx of money, analysts and diplomats say, the perks for officers were greatly increased and were viewed as rights rather than corruption.

Among them, according to diplomats who have dealt with the military, are padding brigade rolls with phantom soldiers and pocketing the extra salaries; siphoning off gasoline to sell; and selling extra rations. Directly or indirectly, these scams cost the United States millions of dollars.

"It is not like they stole directly from us," says a U.S. official who worked with the army. "They would steal

from themselves; then we would replace what they took."

During the 1980s, the army grew top-heavy with officers. The Honduran army is a third of the size of that in El Salvador, with which it fought a brief war in 1969, yet both have about 250 senior officers. A U.S. infantry division has 18,000 soldiers—only 6,000 fewer than the whole Honduran army—but normally only 20 to 25 senior officers.

The military is run by the Superior Council of the Armed Forces, a group of 63 officers from different graduating classes of the military academy that serves as a kind of congress where ideas are debated and discussed and institutional decisions made. Discua, the military chief who stayed in office, is its leader.

President Rafael Leonardo Callejas bristles at the suggestion that the council is the real ruler of Honduras. "I am the third elected president, and that shows civilian power is above military power," he says. "We civilians elect our governments, and each president has more pre-

and for providing intelligence. Year by year the base has taken on a more permanent appearance, with cement sidewalks and cement floors installed in many of the most important buildings.

"The role of [Palmerola] has changed over time," says Col. Robert Killebrew, the U.S. commander at the base. "Coincidentally with the end of the Cold War, we see a rise in concern over narcotics trafficking, and in many ways that is much more difficult to deal with than a good, old-fashioned insurgency."

Killebrew says the military favors staying in Palmerola until U.S. policy for Central America in the post–Cold War era is defined. U.S. officials say the base is also viewed as possible backup for some duties of the U.S. Southern Command, based in Panama and responsible for U.S. military activities in Latin America. It is not yet clear what will happen to Southcom facilities after the United States turns over the Panama Canal to Panama in 1994.

"Let's not just dash off somewhere when we don't know where we are going," Killebrew says as he gives a guided tour to journalists visiting the base. "Let's wait and see which way policy goes, and we probably won't get clear guidance for another year. . . . You can't deal with [Palmerola] in a vacuum—you have to deal with it as a part of the policy for the region."

U.S. officials say one reason for keeping Palmerola is that it is comparatively cheap. A senior U.S. official says Palmerola costs the United States $48 million to $52 million a year, including upkeep of the runway and buildings. Because it is officially a temporary facility on loan from the Honduran government, the United States pays no base rights, which could have cost Washington hundreds of millions of dollars more.

NOT EVERYONE THINKS THE new role justifies maintaining Palmerola or is happy that the United States does not pay more to use it.

"What the United States has is what it always wanted, a military stronghold in Central America," says Manuel Gamero, editor and influential columnist at El Tiempo, one of Honduras's largest newspapers. "It was supposed to be temporary, [but] we all know it is permanent. And they do not even pay rent."

But in a measure of how times have changed, President Rafael Leonardo Callejas talks openly about the U.S. presence in Palmerola and says he favors continuing it for an indefinite time. "Now there is little U.S. military presence compared to other eras," Callejas says. "I wish I could talk about them leaving in a short time, but I do not think that is feasible, because it contributes greatly to the anti-drug efforts."

—Douglas Farah

eminence and more authority over the military than his predecessor."

But when Discua's term was up in January, according to congressmen and diplomats, he bullied the congress into rewriting the law to allow his reelection. His brother Celin is a close friend of Callejas and is minister of justice. And when national congressmen and U.S. Ambassador Cresencio Arcos Jr. suggested the defense budget be cut, Discua went public.

He ridiculed what he called "irresponsible political apprentices" behind a "systematic campaign of slander" against the military and threatened to pull confidential files on those who challenged him—a credible threat because the U.S.-trained Discua was formerly the head of army intelligence.

Sociologist Leticia Salomon, who had studied civilian-military relations in Honduras, says one clear measure of the military's autonomy was that its budget is submitted as a single lump-sum amount to the congress for approval, usually without debate or dissent. It is not broken down at all, and civilians have no right to oversee how any of the money is spent.

The official military budget for 1993 is $50 million, up 20 percent in local currency but about the same in dollars as in 1992.

"That is what it looks like on paper, but in reality it is twice that or nearly $85 million," says a Jan. 4 editorial in El Tiempo, the only newspaper that seriously questions the military.

As U.S. aid began to fall at the end of the decade, the military, which already oversaw the police, immigration, ports, customs and the telephone company, started to branch out into businesses.

Now senior officers and the institution as a whole are involved in most aspects of Honduran economic life, scaring and angering their former allies—local businessmen, who now claim the military's entrance into their markets constitutes unfair competition.

Businessmen and diplomats say the military often does not pay the normal import duties on goods for its businesses, or business taxes on its profits, allowing its enterprises to operate at much lower cost than its civilian competitors do.

Most of the military investments are handled through the Military Pensions Institute (IPM), whose responsibility it is to provide retirement pensions to officers. Salomon and other analysts say officers essentially bought "shares" in IPM by becoming officers, and the value of those shares varied according to factors such as length of service, rank and how much one elected to pay into it. The goal, the sources say, was to be able to provide senior officers with incomes of more than $100,000 a year. The per capita income in Honduras is about $900.

A large problem, according to Salomon, Meza and legislators, is that no one knows how much the IMP makes, or all it is involved in.

"The military became much more active at the end of the 1980s and the beginning of the 1990s to try to make sure its retirement benefits were guaranteed," Salomon says. "They have gained much more economic power, and that is why the business class has protested. No one knows how much, but we are talking millions of dollars."

The head of the military, now Discua, is the president of the IPM. The profits from IPM's business interests go directly to the military and its retirement funds, not through the normal budgetary process or to the national treasury for accounting and appropriations.

According to diplomats who have studied the military, and businessmen, military-owned businesses now include the country's largest cement factory, Industria Cementera de Honduras; its most modern funeral home, Archangel Miguel; a bank that offers the public credit cards and loans; plus a real estate agency, cattle ranches, radio stations and scores of other concerns.

The sources say the military directly chooses the administrators of IMP businesses, although not all are military. For example, the head of the cement factory is Discua's brother-in-law.

In addition to the businesses owned openly by IMP, businessmen and diplomats say, individual officers, both on active duty and retired, are investing heavily but not always openly in the economy and further deterring free trade by using their military connections to undercut competition. Though a business registry exists, full disclosure is not enforced, the sources say. "In many cases an individual officer will own things, but another individual will appear again and again in the business registry," says the diplomat. "Those are the cutouts to hide the ownership."

The army now wants to buy the state telephone company, which is about to be privatized and is one of the government's most profitable businesses.

But President Callejas says the military is within its rights to do what it is doing. "In the decades of the 1970s and 1980s the military was authorized to participate in businesses . . . and have priority participation in buying enterprises that are privatized by the state," Callejas says. "That is the law. . . . If there are groups that are dissatisfied, their responsibility is to change the laws through congress, because what is happening is legal, and if it is legal it cannot be criticized."

But the process is coming under increasing fire because it creates uncertainty in the business community. "People tend to assume that because it is the military, the competition is unfair," says a senior banking official. "And I think that is probably true."

One of the more surprising developments since the end of Central America's wars has been the growing closeness between Discua and the Honduran army, and their former foes, the Nicaragua's Sandinistas, led by Ortega. Diplomats and military analysts in the region say there have been several meetings to share experiences and investment advice.

Lt. Col. Ricardo Wheelock, chief military spokesman in Nicaragua, says the Sandinista army is not involved in politics. Since President Chamorro was elected in 1990, he says, the army has been reduced from 87,000 to 15,250. During that same time, he says, military spending dropped from $177 million to $36.5 million.

But critics challenge both the assertion of civilian control of the army and its budget reduction figures. On the political side, the biggest bone of contention is the continued tenure of Ortega as head of the army. He has led the military since 1979, and his retention has caused anger among conservatives who supported Chamorro.

Just how sensitive the military is on the point was demonstrated again recently when published reports said Ortega had agreed to resign in late 1995, almost two years away. The military rushed out a statement saying the report was false. This followed an incident last year when Ortega said he would remain in office until at least 1997.

Critics charge that the Sandinistas are going into business much the same way the Honduran military is, to guarantee freedom from outside control.

In a document put out in April, the army said that "to initiate the capitalization process for retired officers, the government authorized the army to sell the surplus weapons it has as a result of the drastic reductions that have taken place from 1990 to 1992. In the future, the [retirement fund] will obtain additional funds for social security and professional development from different business activities the institution has begun in recent years within the laws of Nicaragua," the document said.

Wheelock says he cannot remember what these activities were except for a small well-drilling business and road repairs. "The money goes to a fund so that I do not have to turn into a criminal," Wheelock says, pulling out a monthly paycheck stub of about $200. "The government pays me enough to buy a good knife and some handkerchiefs to cover my face and go out and rob people. This money makes sure we have enough."

But opposition leader Alfredo Cesar, a former political leader of the contras, says the army controls agricultural products, cattle ranches, commercial warehouses, a business construction firm, and boot and clothing factories.

"That is only a partial list, because the ownership is often hidden," Cesar says. "They can give lower bids on things because they do not pay taxes. This is very serious because it allows the army to appear to be lowering its budget, but keep on spending. The money does not go to the national budget, and no one knows how much it is or where it goes."

Gilberto Cuadra, a business leader, says numerous businesses have gone into bankruptcy because the Sandinistas put in lower bids for construction projects. "This has to stop so the army does not remain a state within a state," he says.

Though earning a reputation as the most abusive and least submissive of the militaries in the 1980s, the Salvadoran military is seen as making the biggest strides in getting out of politics and successfully defining a role for itself. It is the only country that is developing a professional, civilian police force, and the only one where there has been a purge of officers accused of human rights abuses, corruption or incompetence.

Although, as in Honduras, the United States tolerated corruption and human rights abuses because the army was its ally, the military emerged from the war deeply changed. That was because the insurgent Farabundo Marti National Liberation Front (FMLN) was not de-

feated and made military reform a high priority at the negotiating table.

The peace agreement included a purge of suspected human rights abusers and a U.N.-sponsored "Truth Commission" that investigated the nation's worst crimes and then publicly fingered those responsible, mostly the military. It also guaranteed U.N.-verified reduction in troop strength from 55,000 to 25,000, now nearly complete.

Military analysts say the institution has not engaged in business activities like its counterparts in Honduras and Nicaragua, although individual officers have gone into lucrative businesses. But the bigger challenge in San Salvador remains political. Shortly before the Truth Commission issued its report March 15, Defense Minister Ponce presented his resignation, bitterly blaming the United States for trying to destroy the armed forces. But he did not leave. Sources say Ponce made it clear to Cristiani that the resignation should not be accepted, and Cristiani publicly says Ponce should stay until the end of his term in 1994.

U.N. sources now say Cristiani has agreed to remove Ponce and the other officers by June 30, and the United States is withholding $11 million in military aid until the purge is completed.

Ponce, however, appears to have prepared for that eventuality. "It would be inopportune and inappropriate," he warned recently, "to put in a civilian" as the next defense minister. "We do not think it would be convenient, and we have told the president so."

—*Douglas Farah*

Article 13   *The Economist*, July 17, 1993

Trade in Central America
To NAFTA and EMU, a child

MEXICO CITY
While much of Latin America was warming to free trade at the end of the 1980s, many Central Americans were fighting civil wars. Guerrillas, refugees and arms moved more easily than goods across the boundaries of their small and poor countries. Now that peace has come to most of the isthmus, its govern-

ments are making up for lost time. At a meeting in Guatemala next month, the presidents of six Central American countries will be asked to agree to a plan whose goal is economic union.

Already, trade within Central America has nearly doubled (to $1.8 billion last year) from its 1986 low-point. Four countries—Guatemala, El Salvador,

Honduras and, last month, Nicaragua—have begun to dismantle barriers to the movement of goods, labour and money across each other's borders. Unlike a previous common market in the 1960s, the new scheme also opens up the area to the rest of the world. The four countries have set a low common external tariff for most imports and are negotiat-

GROUNDS CONTROL

Another new mark of Latin co-operation is the pact signed on July 4th between the five Central American coffee-growing countries, and Brazil and Colombia, the world's two biggest coffee exporters. They agreed to put a fifth of this year's exports into storage, restricting supply and, they hope, raising prices. This is the first time since the old quota-system broke down in 1989 that producers' ambitions to control the market might actually amount to something.

Growers in Africa and Indonesia have said that they might join in. On the back of the pact and fears of a frost in Brazil, prices in New York have risen by 13% to 70 cents a pound (454 grams).

Colombia's delegate to the International Coffee Organisation (ICO) in London, Nestor Osorio, says the pact is in part a response to the breakdown in March of years of negotiations between producers and consumers. The latter were loth to launch a new price-stabilisation scheme when previous ones had proved unworkable. They wanted the ICO to count beans rather than control the trade in them.

But coffee prices sank below 60 cents a pound this year, little more than half of their level when quotas were in place. According to Mick Wheeler, a representative of Papua New Guinea, consuming countries took advantage, swelling their stocks to 20m bags of 60 kilograms each, twice their typical level—and persuading producers to establish a new mechanism to limit exports. The new pact will not have a rapid effect—its first year of operation would cut consumers' stocks only back to their historic levels. But the pact's modest aims are its greatest strength: as long as it is not too effective, signatories will be unlikely to cheat.

The area's pioneering multinational is TACA, El Salvador's private airline which has bought minority stakes in five other Central American airlines since 1989 in an effort to offer stiffer competition to American Airlines and United Airlines. But such companies are still rarities. Why then are governments so keen on greater economic union?

One prompt is the region's badly damaged balance of payments. With the cold war over, the United States is preparing to slash its economic aid to Central America. World prices for staple exports such as coffee, sugar, cotton and beef have plunged because of over-supply. And then there are the protectionist policies of its customers. This month the European Community began applying quotas on banana imports, hitting Honduras and Costa Rica—where the fruit accounts for more than 40% of total exports—particularly hard.

Meanwhile the North American Free Trade Agreement is threatening Central America's other recent export success, "non-traditional" products. These manufactured or processed goods (as opposed to "traditional" raw-materials or crops) include canned vegetables, clothing and the widgets assembled in Central America's *maquiladora* plants, many of which are exported to North America under the Caribbean Basin Initiative (CBI). NAFTA will give Mexican-based producers greater access to the North American market and better legal protection as investors in Mexico than the Caribbean initiative. Fearing that their *maquiladora* plants will move north to Mexico, Central American countries are all keen to make NAFTA-style pacts.

On their own, Central American countries cannot hope to carry any weight in the world. Taken together, the 30m people of the six countries offer a market of $32 billion—not much smaller than Chile's. For almost two decades after independence from Spain most of Central America hung shakily together as a single political entity. Visionaries—or maybe dreamers—are starting to talk of a new Central American Federation for early next century.

ing free-trade agreements with Mexico, Colombia and Venezuela.

The fifth Central American country, Costa Rica, the region's most stable and prosperous, has also been cutting tariffs, but is nervous about joining its neighbours' single-market scheme. Costa Rica's unemployment rate is 4% compared with at least 60% in Nicaragua, immediately to its north. It fears an invasion of job seekers if it drops border controls. However, Costa Rica has been seeking bilateral trade deals with Mexico and the United States.

The new "integration protocol" the presidents will be asked to sign sets out ambitious goals such as monetary union and a single currency, but sets no time-tables. Officials at the Secretariat for Central American Economic Integration in Guatemala say they are happy with the idea of a two-speed Central America. Costa Rica, for instance, will probably sign the protocol, but opt out of some provisions for the time being. The sixth country, Panama, which has never been quite sure if it is part of Central, rather than South, America, may opt out of the common external tariff.

Some businesses have been quick to exploit the newly expanded market. Banco Uno, a Guatemalan bank, has become binational, opening branches and raising equity in Honduras, for example.

Article 14   *USA Today,* January 1994

Nicaragua: Sandinistas Still in the Driver's Seat

Marvin Alisky

Dr. Alisky, Associate International Affairs Editor of USA Today, *is professor emeritus of political science, Arizona State University, Tempe.*

In 1990, Violeta Chamorro and her United Nicaraguan Opposition (UNO) Party enjoyed a stunning victory over the ruling Sandinista Party under Pres. Daniel Ortega. Marxist Sandinistas had taken power by force in 1979, ousting the corrupt dictatorship of Gen. Anastasio Somoza, then built their own version of an authoritarian state. The Ortega regime confiscated much of the private sector, expropriating farms, ranches, and industries.

Soviet and Cuban aid had bolstered the Sandinista government during the 1980s while the U.S. political establishment was fighting over whether it was right or wrong to support the Contras, opposition forces composed of Somoza supporters and others disenchanted with early Sandinista behavior. With the end of Soviet aid to Nicaragua in 1989, domestic pressures forced an election in February, 1990, and the UNO won in a landslide. As a compromise for a peaceful transition of presidential power, Sandinista police, army, and unions remained in place. The U.S. resumed economic aid to Managua to encourage a return to civil rights and a private sector economy, without success.

During 1990 and 1991, despite Sandinista unions calling strikes, the Chamorro government managed some monetary stabilization, marginal deregulation, and a degree of privatization. However, Ortega warned the Congress (National Assembly) not to repeal the giveaway the Sandinistas achieved just before they left power. He threatened a civil war if these expropriations were repealed, and the UNO Congressional majority and Chamorro's Cabinet backed down. The thousands of houses, land, and other property the Sandinistas gave to their leaders just before leaving office have remained in Sandinista hands.

The Chamorro government explained it was trying to avoid the winner-take-all politics of Nicaragua's past. By early 1992, though, the pro-Sandinista daily, *El Nuevo Diario*, reported that the UNO majority in Congress (National Assembly) could not keep Sandinista political groups from setting the government's agenda. Nicaragua continued to be without clear rules for property rights, whether they concerned financial instruments or fixed assets. This lack of clarity prompted the unwillingness of foreign investors to make significant investments. Chamorro managed to revive some private banks, but the government-owned ones continued to run as they had under Sandinista rule, having no capital requirements and monthly subsidies from the government's Central Bank. Economic recovery was blocked.

In September, 1992, the Senate Foreign Relations Committee issued a 140-page report stating that the $1,000,000,000 in U.S. aid sent to Nicaragua during the past two years had been misspent. It also noted that Sandinista military and policy apparatus and much of the old Marxist bureaucracy the Chamorro administration had attempted to dislodge had remained firmly in place.

Early in 1993, political analyst Emilio Alvarez observed: "Nicaragua today is run by two people, Antonio Lacayo [Chamorro's chief of staff and son-in-law] and Humberto Ortega [Daniel Ortega's brother, commander of the army and national security], who were never elected to any office. The Nicaraguan citizens should take back what they won at the polls." Yet, Washington continues to prop up a Chamorro government that has no large popular support.

If the $731,000,000 economic aid package for Nicaragua for 1994–95 could be suspended, it would encourage the Chamorro government to abandon its accommodationist policies towards the Sandinistas. The only hopeful sign is that the State Department has been discussing with the Organization of American States (OAS) the formation of a Multinational Verification Commission to monitor whether the Chamorro government is making any genuine efforts to restore human rights. This commission has been formed, but not yet activated, and also wants to probe the Sandinistas' continuing role in drug trafficking. Cardinal Miguel Obando y Bravo, a key intermediary between the UNO and Sandinistas, has indicated a stalemate, with divisions in politics and economics likely to continue and without relief from widespread poverty, unemployment, and lack of political freedom.

During August, 1993, Nicaragua suffered political violence that almost brought government operations to a standstill. Former Contras, now called Recontras, who fought the Sandinista regime in the 1980s, took officials as hostages to pressure the government to give 77,000 Recontras back their lands and the jobs they had been promised in 1990. Former Sandinista soldiers in turn grabbed Vice Pres. Virgilio Godoy and other conservatives hostage as counter-pressure. Neither set of kidnappings achieved success, and the hostages were freed. In September, 1993, Chamorro twice announced publicly that she would replace Humberto Ortega as commander of the army in 1994. In October, he stated that he expected a National Military Council to negotiate with the President on his replacement, indicating another Sandinista military leader could be chosen.

Nicaragua poses a symbolic, but critical, problem for Pres. Clinton's new foreign policy strategy. In an area where the U.S. has intervened regularly, the prospect of even financial arm-twisting would run counter to the image as well as the fact of multilateralist and cooperative strategies that are a cornerstone of the "Clinton Doctrine." An apparent "client" state now seems rife with abuses and potential reopening of revolutionary conflict. With a list of potential challenges to the coherence of his human rights plank already including Somalia, Bosnia, and Haiti, Clinton doesn't need another to provide the conclusion to his attempt to prove that he is more than a domestic president. In the absence of the Soviet threat that was used to justify most of Latin American (and especially Nicaraguan) policy over the last 15 years, perhaps it's time, at last, to let the Nicaraguans sink or swim on their own.

Article 15

The UNESCO COURIER, November 1993

The star system

In their quest to foretell the future, Mayan priests and astronomers entered the realm of pure mathematics.

Berthold Riese

Berthold Riese, of Germany, is a specialist in the field of Amerindian civilizations. His work Maya-Kalender und Astronomie *(The Mayan Calendar and Astronomy) appeared in* Altamerikanistik *(Early American Studies), edited by Ulrich Köhler and published by Dietrich Reimer Verlag, Berlin, 1988.*

Several million Indians living in Guatemala, southern Mexico and Belize today still speak one of the thirty or so Mayan languages, including Mam, Quiché, Cakchiquel, Kekchi and Myathan. A well-developed and broadly similar numerical system exists in all of these tongues.

Centuries of colonization and, more importantly, the introduction of the market economy have led to the gradual replacement of vernacular names for numerals by words borrowed from Spanish. Higher numerals have disappeared from general use and today even the primary numbers are being forgotten.

Numbers in everyday use

Archaeological excavations have yielded little information on how numerals were used in the economy of pre-Columbian America. We do know, however, that the Mayas' numerical system was initially based on counting on the fingers and toes. In Quiché, for example, the word for the number twenty, *buvinak*, literally means "a whole person". This method of counting is also reflected in the decimal divisions. The word for 11 is *hulahuh* or *hun* (one) plus *lahuh* (ten). These numbers were probably used in much the same way as we use numbers for counting today, with one difference. The Mayan languages use words known as "classifiers" to describe objects being counted, denoting whether they are round, elongated, stackable, solid or liquid food, etc. For example, a Yucatec would not say, "Here is a cigarette", but "Here is one (*hun*) long, cylindrical object (*dzit*) called a cigarette (*chamal*)".

Calendars

The conventional solar year
The Mayan calendar was based on the 365-day solar year, which the Mayas had inherited from the earlier civilizations of the Zapotecs (at Monte Alban) and the Olmecs (at La Venta and Tres Zapotes). The length of this calendar year never varied and was divided using the vigesimal system of numeration into eighteen months of twenty days each. The remaining five days were added at the end of the year. Each month had a name, which does not seem to have been related to the seasons or to

any particular festivals. Most of them were handed down by tradition and perhaps even borrowed from other languages and cultures. They do not seem to have had any meaning other than their calendar function, not unlike our own months whose original Roman meanings few people know today.

Each day was designated by a number from 0 to 19 which was placed in front of the name of the month, and from 0 to 4 in the case of the final, shorter month. It was therefore possible to identify each day of the year, as in our own calendar. The years followed each other without interruption and there were no leap years.

The diviner's calendar

Guatemala's Quiché, Ixil and Mam Indians still use a traditional 260-day calendar to predict the future. Why 260 days? In interviews with Guatemalan diviners in Chichicastenango and Momstenango, German ethnologist Leonhard Schultze Jena found that the number of days in the year matches the length of human pregnancy. Whatever its origin may be, the vigesimal system made it possible for early Mayan mathematicians to break this 260-day year down into thirteen months of twenty days each. Each calendar day was identified by attaching a number from one to thirteen to one of the twenty names of the vigesimal cycle, which referred to animals, natural forces and traditional or abstract concepts whose meanings are unknown today.

Like the solar calendar, the diviner's calendar is cyclical. The last day of one cycle is automatically followed by the first day of the next and so on.

The calendar round

Permutation of the 260-day calendar with the 365-day calendar gives a cycle of 52 years in which each day bears a different name derived from elements taken from the other two systems. This major cycle of 18,980 days—52 solar years of 365 days each or 73 divination years of 260 days each—is known as the "calendar round" and was the largest time-measuring unit for most of the Mesoamerican peoples during late pre-Columbian times. Unlike the Mixtecs and Aztecs, the Mayas were familiar with different systems and used other units for measuring longer periods of time, but they were an exception among the great pre-Columbian cultures.

Hieroglyphics

As we have seen, the calendar days were identified by names, some of which designated numbers. That is how Indian diviners still express them in their own languages. The pre-Hispanic Mayas could also write all the days of the year, of the divination calendar and the calendar round in hieroglyphic script. Four hieroglyphic books or codices

from that time have survived, and are today conserved in Paris, Dresden, Madrid and Mexico City.

Countless stone inscriptions, a few wall paintings and many painted clay pots and sherds are other sources of information about this highly original writing system.

The simplest way of writing numbers between 0 and 19 consisted of using dots for units and lines for fives in an additive system (**figure 1**). For higher numbers an additional symbol for 20 was used. A positional system was used to write numbers higher than 40, with an extra symbol equivalent to our zero identifying the unoccupied places. Each place represents a power of 20, until the third place in which a factor of 18 is used. Thus, the order of positional values was as follows: first place, 20^0 (=1), second place, 20^1 (=20), third place, 18×20^1 (=360), fourth place 18×20^2 (=7,200), fifth place $18 = 20^3$ (=144,000) and so on.

Counting the days

At an early stage, certainly no later than the beginning of the Christian era, the Central American Indians invented a new way of calculating time: the day number ("*cuenta larga*", or "long count"). This system, which is independent of the calendar cycles described above, consists of numbering the days continuously from a more or less mythical date far in the past. This extremely accurate dating system has proved to be of invaluable assistance to modern researchers, ever since scholars in the early twentieth century succeeded in correlating it with our own calendar. Its primary aim was to help the Mayas codify major historic dates concerning their rulers or deities.

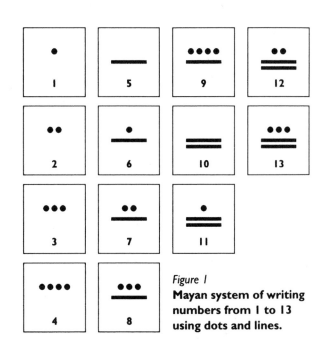

Figure 1
Mayan system of writing numbers from 1 to 13 using dots and lines.

Other calendar cycles

The Mayas of the classical period used other cycles for historical, divinatory and speculative purposes. For example, a cycle of days or nights devoted to nine deities is known from hieroglyphs G_1–G_9. Furthermore, the combination of short 7, 9 and 13-day cycles, each of which designated a category of gods, was used to come up with a complex divination cycle of 819 days.

Astronomy

The astronomy of the Mayas was not limited to observation of the stars and approximate predictions of the movements of the heavenly bodies. Using their sophisticated numerical systems and various tabular calculations in conjunction with the hieroglyphic script, Mayan astronomers were able to perform complex calculations with figures running into millions.

Their efforts were focused primarily on the sun and the moon. Different year lengths were used for different sorts of calculations. Normally they took the conventional 365-day year as a basis. However, years with a length of 364 days are also encountered, as are years of 365¼ days, similar to our own Julian calendar.

The moon played a prominent role in stone inscriptions, which often begin with a day number followed by the phase of the moon and the day's position in a calendar of six lunar months.

Mayan astronomers also calculated the synodic period of the planet Venus, and the figure of 584 days at which they arrived is astonishingly close to the modern astronomic value. But they went still further. A set of tables in the Dresden Maya codex cites correction factors to allow for the fractional deviations from this value, which can only be observed after decades and even centuries. Researchers also suspect that the Mayas were familiar with the synodic period of other planets, such as Mars and Jupiter, but this has not been proved conclusively.

A springboard into pure mathematics

For the Maya, all the calendar and astronomic cycles and systems were ultimately used for divination and religious or speculative purposes. Their calendar experts constantly strove to establish a relationship between the cycles by permutation, using the lowest common multiple and other methods, to predict the future and connect the present with historical dates. In this way they could also learn something about the destiny of their clients— the ruler and private individuals.

These practical goals often served as a springboard for complex calculations and research which transcended their original purpose. For example, some of their calculations were projected so far into the past or future that the primary purpose must have been to quench the calendar priests' own thirst for knowledge and desire to explore the limits of their mathematical system. It is therefore reasonable to assert that the Mayas, like the Babylonians, Greeks, Arabs and Indians before and after them, had entered the realm of pure mathematics.

South America: Articles Section

Article 16   *Latinamerica Press*, September 6, 1993

World Health Organization issues warning

Pollution Is Growing Threat in Argentina

Manuel Long

Argentine journalist

BUENOS AIRES (LP)—The Argentine capital has been criticized by the World Health Organization (WHO) for putting the health of its citizens at "serious risk" by failing to have contamination monitors and maintain statistics on pollution-related illnesses.

The critical picture, drawn in a WHO report on pollution in the world's 20 largest cities, only calls attention to one city in a country where water contamination causes 80 percent of all infant deaths, uncontrolled logging is causing the desertification of large tracts of land, hunting threatens 312 species of native animals with extinction, and excessively high levels of noise and lead are part of everyday life.

"The main environmental problem is poverty. It is only necessary to look at the dramas of cholera, floods or contaminated waters, which always affect the poor. That is why environmental conservation must always be accompanied by development, and vice versa," ecologist Inés Malvárez said.

"The suffering caused by slow death from contamination is as horrible as the pain the country went through under the military dictatorships," said Alberto Morán, environmental undersecretary for the city of Buenos Aires. "Eighty percent of the infant mortality is caused by waterborne illnesses. Children are slowly dying because of a sick environment."

The Plata River, whose banks are home to 6 million people, receives 300,000 metric tons of toxic residues a year, 250,000 of which are solvents and 50,000 are heavy metals. "In the last eight kilometers before emptying into the Plata River, the Matanza and Reconquista rivers have no oxygen in their waters. That means the only things flowing are liquid chemicals that do not even allow the growth of bacteria," Morán said.

Because it has no waste-recycling system, Buenos Aires cannot avoid the contamination caused by the 600,000 metric tons of dangerous household refuse dumped annually. "But the main source of contamination is the 7,300 industries, of which only 20 percent are inspected," he said.

In December 1991, after Argentines were outraged by the announcement that the country had agreed to receive 20,000 metric tons of human excrement from France *(LP, Nov. 7, 1991),* a law was passed that prohibited the importation of toxic materials and nuclear waste. But because the government has never ratified the law it cannot be enforced.

Last February, a business was fined for hydrocarbon contamination that was affecting animals such as penguins, walrus and seals on the Puerto Deseado Reserve in the province of Santa Cruz. But the US$1 symbolic fine was insulting to environmentalists.

In October of last year, a Buenos Aires judge sent 19 business people to jail who were responsible for the contamination of the Matanza-Reconquista basin. But after receiving strong government pressure, the judge released them on bail set at $550,000 each.

Secretary of the Environment María Julia Alsogaray and Economy Minister Domingo Cavallo accused the judge of putting the economic stability of the country at risk. Their concern was that the sanctions "could bring (potential) foreign investment in the country to a halt."

> *'The suffering caused by slow death from contamination is as horrible as the pain the country went through under the military dictatorships.'*

Water pollution has brought cholera to Argentina. Since February 1992 when the disease first appeared in the country, 2,000 cases have been registered and 23 people have died, while governmental propaganda continues to say it is just caused by dirty hands and is a problem that can be solved with a strong educational campaign.

But the WHO, like environmentalist Malvárez, maintains that cholera stems from lack of development.

"You can't just cynically say that it is a problem of poverty," Malvárez said.

Since the outbreak in Peru in 1990, the cholera epidemic has spread across local and national borders, affecting most of the countries in Latin America.

A January 1992 report from the United Nations World Conference On Water and the Environment in Dublin, Ireland, stated, "It is ironic that the amount lost in exports and tourism in the first three months of the epidemic would have been enough to provide sanitation services and potable running water for the entire population of Lima."

Another of the many problems that affect the environment is indiscriminate logging. According to statistics from the Forest Resources Directory, by the year 2025 Argentine forests will have disappeared, accelerating the desertification

process that has already been seen in various regions of the country.

Animal life also has been ravaged. There are 312 species of animals in danger of extinction, a problem that is made more acute by the contraband exportation of wild animals, which at the end of 1990 was estimated to be generating between $400 million and $500 million annually (*LP, June 27, 1991*).

More than 200 of the endangered species are fish. The causes that put them at risk of extinction range from indiscriminate and highly technical fishing methods to the toxicity of the rivers.

On another level, noise pollution in urban centers of Argentina is second to none. In residential areas of Buenos Aires and in three main population centers of the country, Córdoba, Rosario and Mendoza, sound levels often reach 85 decibels, almost triple the 30 suggested by WHO as "a tolerable limit."

Lead content in the air is another concern cited by environmentalists. In Buenos Aires lead levels in the air that are

four times greater than the WHO-suggested limits have been found in areas of highly concentrated vehicle traffic.

Lead content in food is another serious health issue. The daily lead content concentrated in the food of the rural population of the province of Córdoba is 8.54 micrograms, whereas that of Buenos Aires is three times higher, 26.15.

And on a larger scale, the possibility of contamination from leaks in one of the country's three nuclear power plants continues to haunt environmentalists.

John Schroeder, an expert in nuclear information with Greenpeace, Southern Cone, said a failure in the nuclear plant of Atucha I, 40 kilometers from Buenos Aires, "would have a similar effect here to the Chernobyl accident in the Soviet Union where, since 1986, more than 10,000 people have died." The Atucha I plant has been closed down three times so far this year due to heavy water leaks from its reactor.

Article 17   *Parade Magazine, April 12, 1992*

'I Fight for Our Future'

*It's a battle Chief Paiakan began for the survival of his people,
but what's at stake is the survival of us all.*

Hank Whittemore

Several years ago, a young Kayapo Indian named Paulo Paiakan left his village in the Amazon rain forest of Brazil in order to save it. He ventured to the outside world, warning that if the forest disappears, his people will die. Today he is still standing against the forces of destruction as time runs out. At stake is far more than the fate of a remote Kayapo village. The rain forest is one of the world's great biological treasures. If the Kayapo lose the forest that sustains their lives, so will we.

From the city of Belém at the mouth of the Amazon River in Brazil, the flight inland proceeds over vast devastation caused by cattle ranchers, gold miners and loggers. It's three hours to Rendenção, the farthest outpost on the tropical frontier. Then a tiny plane continues until, mercifully, the scene below is transformed into a canopy of lush green treetops shielding perhaps half the plant and animal species on earth.

Later the pilot dives and banks over a clearing of red dirt bordered by small thatch homes—a signal to the Kayapo

people of Aukre. When the plane drops amid tall trees to find a thin landing strip and rolls to a stop, scores of villagers emerge staring in silence. Their bodies and faces are painted with intricate designs; they wear colorful bracelets and necklaces of beads. Some of the men carry guns or knives or bows—they are warriors, with a heritage of fierce pride that is centuries old.

The visitor is led into the main yard of the village, where Chief Paiakan stands near the Men's Hut at the center. He is about 37, but the Kayapo do not

Paulo Paiakan, a chief of the Amazon-based Kayapo, addresses tribal leaders and rain-forest activists in Altamira, Brazil. "In the old days, my people were great warriors," he says. "Now, instead of war clubs, we are using words."

measure time that way, so his exact age is unknown. Shirtless, wearing shorts and sandals, he is a charismatic figure with flowing black hair and dark eyes that sparkle when he grins.

The first recorded contact with the Kayapo was just over a quarter century ago, in 1965, and since about 1977 their culture and way of life have been under siege. This year, during the 500th anniversary of Columbus' first contact with the Americas, Paiakan's village faces irrevocable change. Yet he greets the visitor warmly, speaking in Portuguese: "Your flight was safe. You are here. Everything is good."

After nightfall, as sounds of the forest fill the darkness, a Kayapo elder points to the stars and observes that they are distant campfires. Paiakan rests in a hammock under the roof outside his house, speaking softly: "Since the beginning of the world, we Indians began to love the forest and the land. Because of this, we have learned to preserve it. We

are trying to protect our lands, our traditions, our knowledge. We defend to not destroy. If there was no forest, there would be no Indians."

Rain forests are vital for the rest of us as well. Because they absorb carbon dioxide and emit oxygen into the atmosphere, rain-forest destruction affects weather patterns and contributes to global warming, the so-called Greenhouse Effect. Furthermore, half of the world's biogenetic diversity is within these tropical forests, yet 50 percent of those species are still unknown to the outside world. About one-third of the world's medicines currently are derived from tropical plants, but indigenous people like the Kayapo have even more knowledge of plants with curative powers—knowledge that is quickly vanishing along with the forests themselves.

Among the Kayapo, preparation for a new leader begins at birth. Such was the case for Paiakan, who is descended from

a long line of chiefs. His father, Chiciri, who lives in Aukre, is a highly regarded peacemaker; and when Paiakan was born, the tribe received a "vision" of his special destiny.

"When I was still a boy," Paiakan recalls, "I knew that one day I would go out into the world to learn what was coming to us."

As a teenager, Paiakan got his chance. He was sent to the Kayapo village of Gorotire for missionary school, where he met white men who were building the Trans-Amazonian Highway through the jungle. Paiakan was recruited to go out ahead of the road's progress, to approach the previously uncontacted tribes.

When he went back to see what was coming on the road, however, he saw an invasion of ranchers, miners and loggers using fires and chainsaws. As he watched them tearing down vast tracts of forest and polluting the rivers with mercury, he realized that his actual job

Kayapo children in Aukre, Brazil. Paiakan brought a small group of villagers here in 1983 to escape the approaching devastation. Soon, he realized they could not run forever, and he began his fight to preserve what was left of the forest and his tribe.

was to "pacify" other Indians into accepting it.

"I stopped working for the white man," he says, "and went back to my village. I told my people, 'They are cutting down the trees with big machines. They are killing the land and spoiling the river. They are great animals bringing great problems for us.' I told them we must leave, to get away from the threats."

Most of the Kayapo villagers did not believe him, arguing that the forest was indestructible. So Paiakan formed a splinter group of about 150 men, women and children who agreed to move farther away. For the next two years, advance parties went ahead to plant crops and build homes. In 1983, they traveled four days together, 180 miles downriver, and settled in Aukre.

"Our life is better here," Paiakan says, "because this place is very rich in fish and game, with good soil. Our real name is Mebengokre—'people of the water's source.' The river is life for the plants and animals, as well as for the Indian."

But the new security did not last. During the 1980s, most other Kayapo villages in the Amazon were severely affected by the relentless invasions. Along with polluted air and water came outbreaks of new diseases, requiring modern medicines for treatment. Aukre was still safe, but smoke from burning forests already could be seen and smelled. Paiakan, realizing that he could

The Amazon. Places of compelling beauty may soon be lost. With them will go the global atmospheric benefits of the rain forest, the "natural pharmacy" of Amazon plants and the homeland of a people.

not run forever, made a courageous decision. He would leave his people again—this time, to go fight for them.

He went to Belém, the state capital, where he learned to live, dress and act like a white man. He learned to speak Portuguese, in order to communicate with government officials. He even taught himself to use a video camera, to document the destruction of the forest—so his people could see it for themselves and so the Kayapo children would know about it.

Paiakan continued to travel between Aukre and the modern world, at one point becoming a government adviser on indigenous affairs for the Amazon. In 1988, when the rubber tapper Chico Mendes was shot dead by ranchers for

organizing grass-roots resistance to deforestation, it was feared that Paiakan himself might be a target.

"Many indigenous leaders have been killed," says Darrell Posey, an ethnobiologist from Kentucky who has worked with Indians of Brazil for 15 years, "but publicity surrounding the Mendes murder may have helped to protect Paiakan." The Brazilian Pastoral Commission for Land has counted more than 1200 murders of activist peasants, union leaders, priests and lawyers in the past decade.

In 1988, after speaking out against a proposed hydroelectric dam in the rain forest, both Paiakan and Posey were charged with breaking a Brazilian law against "foreigners" criticizing the government. Because Indians are not legally citizens, Paiakan faced three years in prison and expulsion from the country; but when other Kayapo learned of his plight, some 400 leaders emerged from the forest in warpaint. The charges were dropped.

"In the old days," Paiakan told the press, "my people were great warriors. We were afraid of nothing. We are still not afraid of anything. But now, instead of war clubs, we are using words. And I had to come out, to tell you that by destroying our environment, you're destroying your own. If I didn't come out, you wouldn't know what you're doing."

In 1989, Paiakan organized an historic gathering in Altamira, Brazil, that brought together Indians and members of the environmental movement. A major theme of the conference was that protecting natural resources involves using the traditional knowledge of indigenous peoples. "If you want to save the rain forest," he said, "you have to take into account the people who live there."

With increasing support, Paiakan acquired a small plane for flying to and from his village. He also made trips to the United States, Europe and Japan, even touring briefly with the rock star Sting, to make speeches about the growing urgency of his people's plight.

But the erosion of Indian culture in the Amazon forest was becoming pervasive. With the influx of goods ranging from medicines to flashlights to radios to refrigerators to hunting gear, village after village was succumbing to internal pressure for money to buy more. By 1990, only Aukre and one other Kayapo community had refused to sell their tree-cutting rights to the loggers, whose tactics included seductive offers of material goods to Indian leaders.

In June that year, racing against time, Paiakan completed negotiations for Aukre to make its own money while preserving the forest. Working with The Body Shop, an organic-cosmetics chain based in Britain, he arranged for villagers to harvest Brazil nuts and then create a natural oil to be used in hair conditioners. It would be their first product for export.

Paiakan returned with his triumphant news only to learn that other leaders of Aukre—during the previous month, in his absence—had sold the village's timber rights for two years. It was a crushing blow, causing him to exclaim that all his "talking to the world" had been in vain. He said that if he could not save his people, he would rather not live.

"He went through a period of intense, deep pain," says Saulo Petian, a Brazil-

Far from the rain forest: Paiakan in New York while on tour with the rock star Sting. He's trying to get his message to the world.

ian from São Paulo employed by The Body Shop to work with Kayapo. "He left the village and went far along the river, to be by himself. After about two months, when he got over his sadness and resentment, he came back and told me, 'Well, I traveled around the world and seemed to be successful, but the concrete results for the village were very little. These are my people. They have many needs. I can't go against them now.'"

So Paiakan made peace with the other leaders of his village and started over. "I was like a man running along but who got tired and stopped to rest," Paiakan recalls. "Then I came back, to continue my fight into the future."

What began was the simultaneous unfolding of two events, by opposing forces, in Paiakan's village. One was the beginning of construction by the Indians of a small "factory" with a palm-leaf roof for creation of the hair-conditioning oil. For Paiakan it was a way of showing his people how to earn money from the forest without allowing it to be destroyed. Meanwhile, loggers came through the forest constructing a road that skirted the edge of the village. By 1991, trucks were arriving from the frontier to carry back loads of freshly cut timber.

The white men left behind the first outbreak of malaria that Aukre had seen, mainly afflicting the elders and children. The only consolation for Paiakan was that the tree-cutters had just a couple of dry months each year when the road was passable.

"Through the Brazil-nut oil project," Petian says, "Paiakan is showing his people another possibility for satisfying their economic needs. He's giving them

a viable alternative that includes helping to save the forest and their way of life."

Throughout Brazil, there is similar effort by environmentalists and Indian groups to discourage deforestation by creating markets for nuts, roots, fruits, oils, pigments and essences that can be regularly harvested. Since 1990, about a dozen products using ingredients from the Brazilian Amazon have entered the American market. The nuts, for example, are being used to produce a brittle candy called Rainforest Crunch. The candy is also used by Ben & Jerry's Homemade Inc. for one of its ice cream flavors.

"Paiakan is one of the most important leaders looking at alternatives for sustainable development," says Stephan Schwartzman, a rain-forest expert at the Environmental Defense Fund in Washington, D.C. He cautions, however, that "nothing in the short term can compete economically" with cash from the sale of rights for logging and gold mining.

Up to 8 percent of the two million square mile Amazon rain forest in Brazil—an area about the size of California—already has been deforested. Once the trees are gone, the topsoil is quickly and irreversibly eroded, so that in just a few years hardly anything can grow, and both cattle-raising and agriculture become nearly impossible.

A hopeful sign is that Brazil's president, Fernando Collor de Mello, who took office in 1990, has taken some positive steps to protect both the forest and the Indians. (The population of indigenous people in Brazil, once at least 3 million, has fallen in this century to 225,000.) Last November, President Collor moved to reserve more than 36,000 square miles of Amazon rain forest as a homeland for an estimated 9000 Yanomami Indians in Brazil. He also approved 71 other reserves covering 42,471 square miles, some 19,000 of which will be set aside for the Kayapo—about 4000 people in a dozen villages.

It was a major victory for Paiakan, giving him more concrete evidence to show that his previous efforts outside the village had been worthwhile.

"Paiakan has a vision," Darrell Posey says. "He's trying in a lot of ways to maintain his traditions—setting up a village school for Kayapo culture, creating a scientific reserve. At the same time, he's making the transition to a modern world in which white men are not going to go away. He knows you either deal with them or you don't survive."

These days, Paiakan is working to organize an Earth Parliament of indigenous leaders in Rio de Janeiro in June.

The global parliament will run simultaneously with the UN Conference on Environment and Development, the so-called Earth Summit, which more than 70 percent of the world's heads of state are expected to attend to ponder the fate of the planet. . . .

"Paiakan has been at the center of incredible change, whether he has wanted to be or not," Posey says, "and now he's trying to straddle both the past and the future. I would hope that people in positions of power will see him as someone who can help the world turn back to its roots, to those whose lives depend on working with nature and not against it."

The Brazilian rain forest itself has taken on tremendous symbolic value worldwide, says Thomas Lovejoy, a leading Amazon researcher and assistant secretary for external affairs of the Smithsonian Institution. "It's a metaphor for the entire global crisis," Lovejoy

adds. "If we can't deal with that environment and with the people who live there properly, it's unlikely that we'll be able to deal with the rest."

At sunrise in the Kayapo village of Aukre, the red clay of the logging road is wet from rain. The trucks are gone, now, and there is serenity as the tropical heat moves in. A shaman, or medicine man, is treating Paiakan's wife for an illness, using plants from the "pharmacy" of the forest. Some of the men are going off on a hunting trip. Women and children bathe in the river as butterflies of brilliant colors swirl across a blue sky. Time seems to stand still, before it races on.

For a copy of the free "Rainforest Action Guide" with information about what you can do to help save the Amazon rain forest, write: Rainforest Action Network, Dept. J, 450 Sansome St., Suite 700, San Francisco, Calif. 94111.

Article 18   *Forbes*, September 13, 1993

The sick man of Latin America

Brazilians say: We are the country of the future— and always will be. But a lot of foreign investors are betting that the future is finally here. Will they lose their shirts?

Joel Millman

Hernan Büchi, the architect of Chile's spectacular 1980s reform, is addressing a gathering of brokers and investment bankers in New York. No, he assures his audience, he is not a candidate for Chile's presidency—a job he almost won three years ago. "My dream job is to be finance minister of Brazil," he says, breaking into a wide smile. "Fixing that country would be a miracle."

Having played a big role in Chile's emergence from stagnation to a model of economic growth, Büchi knows something about economic miracles. His skepticism

about Brazil's ability to stage one is shared by many others. A few weeks later Arminio Fraga, a former director of Brazil's central bank now working for George Soros, is addressing a similar gathering. All seriousness, Fraga calls himself a cautious optimist but warns: "I'm really afraid that time is running out for Brazil."

Brazil, the sick man of Latin America, seems to be getting sicker, not better.

With 7 million people, Rio de Janeiro is growing by 140,000 people a year. Yet Telerj, the local subsidiary of state-owned Telebrás, has suspended the installation of lines to serve new customers. It's too expensive. Since rates are kept artificially low by the government, Telerj

You think you got problems?

Hans Pryon, vice president of Cia. Hering, a 113-year-old Brazilian textile firm in the southern city of Blumenau, drives to work through lush emerald hills, past vineyards and Bavarian chalets. Mountain mists and tropic sunshine combine to throw up rainbows around each turn.

But when he gets to work he confronts problems that American executives rarely face. Selling cheap, light clothing in poor, hot Brazil should be easy. But cotton production has died with the brutal drought in Brazil's northeast, drying up raw materials; training workers is expensive and time-consuming. Brazil's long-protected economy means distribution is generally inefficient and wasteful. "It takes 30 days to get a shirt to the stores sometimes," he sighs. "By that time the product costs more here than it does in the States."

Then there's inflation, running at a rate of 32% a month. The continent's largest producer of knit garments, Cia. Hering has lost money the past three years. "Here," says Prayon, "retailers can't get credit like industries can. So we end up financing every one of our buyers."

That means 30-day financing at rates of up to 50% for thousands of buyers, each link in the distribution chain passing its finance costs on to the next. With state and federal taxes tacked on with each transaction, by the time one of Hering's $1 shirts reaches a major department store it may cost as much as $8 in cruzeiros, almost the price of the T shirts sold abroad.

Cia. Hering enjoyed sales of $300 million in both 1988 and 1989, the two years leading up to the recession, just 15% coming from exports. Sales have shrunk to under $250 million, and a doubling of the still

small export segment has been a lifesaver. If you're betting Brazil can shed its precapitalistic ways, Hering's stock is a bargain. It trades on the São Paulo and Rio stock exchanges at just 10% of book, for a market value of $100 million. "There's no liquidity," Prayon complains. "If you get 35% interest at the banks, who is going to buy our shares?"

What may save Hering is the outside world's new interest in investing in Brazil. In 1992 it became the first private Brazilian company to test the Eurobond market, issuing $50 million in notes. Meanwhile, it is exporting its own expertise, this year breaking ground on a $42 million factory in Spain, servicing customers such as Euro-Disney in Paris, major German department stores and mail-order outlets.

—J.M.

loses about $300 per installation. So millions of Cariocas go without telephone service.

A parallel free market tries to make up for the official market's failings. In Rio (and practically everywhere else) an established "Bolsa de Telefones" openly advertises the prices of line swaps throughout the city. (People with extra lines, or people moving from one part of the city to another, will call the Bolsa looking for a swap.) On Rio's Bolsa you can currently buy a line for cash; another informal exchange buys and sells blocks of shares in Telebrás, the telecommunications giant, which customarily issues a few shares with every line installed. Telerj tolerates these sales because it knows it can't service its customers. At least with this unofficial pricing system, the available phones are allocated according to their economic value.

Even where official policy is meant to encourage private enterprise, an unholy alliance of trade unions, bureaucrats and patronage-loving politicians often combines to frustrate the policy. In the resulting compromise—the Brazilians have a word for it, *jeitinho*, the quick fix—the cards get reshuffled, but the basic deck doesn't get changed.

Take the case of cellular telephones. The decision was made by the congress to open the business to private companies. The unholy alliance objected, pointing out

that the Brazilian constitution reserves telecommunications to the state. The resulting *jeitinho* permitted private licenses but also gave the state companies the right to compete. The jiggered compromise was challenged in court by telecommunications workers unions. As a result, after two years there are still no private cellular systems in Brazil—and a state system is only getting started.

Thus, despite attempts to free the economy, state corporations continue to dominate: Almost 40% of GNP is in the public sector.

So pervasive is state control of the economy that many of the shares that trade on the stock exchanges represent a minority interest in state-owned companies. Two-thirds of the Rio de Janeiro and São Paulo bolsas' daily volume is accounted for by shares of such companies. The state companies themselves are big investors, much of the trading volume coming from pension funds of state companies.

On the rare occasions a company is "privatized," the buyer is often a state company's pension fund; in Brazil both public and private pension funds are *required* to have a minimum 25% of their assets on the bolsa.

State banking—nearly 100 separate institutions—is another morass. State-controlled are the central bank, the national development banks, the regional banks and banks of each of Brazil's 26 states.

In order to service the state's debt, state-owned banks offer attractive rates of return on deposits, which are eagerly snapped up as hedges against Brazil's raging inflation. "We know the state will not let them go bankrupt, and they pay a premium," explains Daniel Dantas, an economist at Rio's Icatu Bank. "So one bank lends to the other. If Bradesco (Brazil's number one private bank) lends to Banespa (the state of São Paulo's bank), exposure is zero. The government couldn't afford to let either one of them go bankrupt. No risk, just money to be made."

During election years, local political machines issue high-yield certificates of deposit to finance their candidates' campaigns. Once in power, the winners "discover" their banks cannot honor the terms. But they can lobby Brasilia for a bailout. More *jeitinho*.

The system makes a banker's life incredibly easy. He can lend money to a state company at a good interest rate, secure in the knowledge that the state will bail the company out even if it is massively in the red. "According to the constitution, a state-owned company cannot go bankrupt," explains Eduardo Modiano, architect of Brazil's privatization program. "It gives confidence to investors, but it is a false idea. There is not going to be any individual bankruptcy, but Brazil altogether can go bankrupt."

An additional drawback of the system is that it tends to crowd out and make credit expensive for small business people *(see box on the previous page)*.

A system like this sharpens the wits in some ways. Not even Wall Street can beat the Brazilians when it comes to thinking about fancy financing schemes.

Take São Paulo's state power utility, the Companhia Energética de São Paulo, or CESP. CESP, has spent more than $2 billion erecting two new hydroelectric plants, but CESP can't pay for the foreign turbines it has ordered. Trouble is, CESP is strapped. Electric power rates in Brazil are set at artificially low levels—about half their 1973 level—as a subsidy to Brazilian industry.

So CESP hasn't any profits to use for payments, nor can it borrow: The constitution limits CESP's leverage. With its stock trading on the bolsa at 13% of book, an equity offering is also out of the question.

Jeitinho, the quick fix.

CESP is issuing something called Certificados a Têrmo de Energia, what São Paulo financiers are calling "megawatt futures." Sold by the megawatt-hour, they are being marketed as hedges against the next electricity rate hike, which is likely to be a whopper. For $50 per megawatt-hour, industrial consumers can buy CESP futures. After 12 months the paper becomes a voucher for energy use. Or the futures can be held another year and be redeemed at full value, plus 18% interest per year. Insurance companies and pension funds will be able to buy the futures and sell them on the secondary market.

Tomas Sá, the director of São Paulo's Banco Patente who helped design the scheme, says that if the electricity futures sell, then CESP's parent, Eletrobrás, may also issue futures, as will the National Water Works, the São Paulo Railroad and a dozen more state-owned industries.

With so many oddball financing schemes around, even the country's top economists are no longer sure how much internal debt the government is grappling with. The most widely used estimates run from $70 billion all the way up to $120 billion. Big chunks of that debt lie scattered like land mines on the balance sheets of billion-dollar companies like Petrobrás and CESP, ready to explode.

Privatization architect Modiano, now a private consultant, is hopeful that the era of *jeitinho* has run its course and the civil war between Brazil's public and private sectors may at last be drawing to an end. The same constitution that decrees profitability for the state is to be rewritten, starting in October with a national debate that many expect to pave the way for a comprehensive privatization. "Strategic" monopolies the state enjoys in telecommunications, banking and mining are to be reevaluated.

Investors are betting heavily that this will happen. Petrobrás, the state oil monopoly, has seen its share price rise 174% in the last 12 months, on speculation fueled by rumors of price hikes on things like gasoline and propane for cooking stoves, and some politicians' tepid comments from Brasilia that Petrobrá's may one day be privatized.

For years prices have been kept down, as a way to dampen Brazil's raging inflation, depriving Petrobrás of billions in revenues. The state requires—as a populist measure—Petrobrás to sell its products at prices well below world levels. Real privatization would not only permit Petrobrás to operate more efficiently but would also permit the company to raise prices. The result would be a huge surge in profitability. But it hasn't happened yet.

Thus constitutional reform, already the subject of bitter debate a year before Brazil's presidential elections, holds enormous potential for all of Latin America. A Brazilian boom would overshadow even Mexico's newfound prosperity. It would help spread prosperity throughout the continent, with Argentina, Chile, Venezuela, Peru and Colombia all cashing in.

Will it happen? Brazil could squander this opportunity, exercising *jeitinho* instead of discipline. Conditions could even get worse, postponing for perhaps another generation the true reform so many have been longing for.

Generations of corruption and compromise have made Brazilians cynical. Thus no one expects a neat, clean-cut solution. Icatu's Daniel Dantas sees the selloff of state enterprises as inevitable, but he expects a long, nasty struggle. "I don't think we can have anything but a government that is not good. The only choice now is to have a small one. I hope we are on our way."

Article 19   *AMÉRICAS*, July/August 1993

HEALING SECRETS IN A SHAMAN'S FOREST

DON PACHO'S BOTANICAL GARDEN IN THE COLOMBIAN AMAZONIA PRESERVES ANCIENT CURATIVE PLANTS, PROVIDING A POTENTIAL TREASURE FOR MODERN MEDICINE

Jimmy Weiskopf

Jimmy Weiskopf, a New York-born journalist who has lived in Colombia since 1977, has, during the past two years, made five visits to don Pacho's home in the Putumayo.

It is early Sunday morning on the banks of the Putumayo river in Colombia and Francisco (don Pacho) Piaguaje—*curandero* of the Siona Indian community of Buenavista—is sprawled out on the floor of the tin-roofed wooden house, raised up on pillars, that is his home, his consulting room and, just now, the center of the impromptu fiesta which follows his Saturday night healing sessions with the sacred hallucinogenic vine, yajé. On the front porch that looks out over the river-side clearing, a dozen Indians and creole colonists laugh and shout over a few bottles of *aguardiente*. In the back, a kitchen thatched with palm leaves, don Pacho's wife, *la abuela*, surrounded by three of her 37 grandchildren, prepares a breakfast of fish stew, plantains and *yuca* for the visitors. The daughter of a legendary Siona healer herself, she has been a *curandero*'s wife for over half a century and the boisterous crowd does not faze her.

Pacho has reached the final stage of his shamanistic cycle, where, talking loudly but paying little attention to anyone else, he vents his private obsessions. His moody introspection is in sharp contrast to his normal self: alert, kindly, patient, and calm. He has been up all night, curing some 30 patients by absorbing the negative energies, known as "bad airs" and attributed to maleficent energies, that are the cause of illness in the Siona shamanistic philosophy. He has entered into the *pinta* or mind-pictures which the vine often produces. He has stroked the focal points of evil in afflicted bodies and physically sucked the

sickness in and blown it away. He has sung, told stories and played the harmonica. So it is no wonder that he is emotionally drained.

The rest of us are as tired as he is, and I am the only one who listens to what is apparently a nonsensical flow of sermon and reminiscence broken by outbursts of anger and equally surprising gestures of tenderness and imbued with a heightened, poetic language that only emerges at such times. His broad Indian features, a map of contrasting planes shadowed by a peaked forage cap, reveal a multitude of expressions as he speaks in a deep, hoarse voice. "I have with the wisdom of my forefathers, worked with the powers of the healing plants and the benefits of my science have reached throughout Colombia. Doctors have come here to learn of them and they have, under my guidance, grown in wisdom. But I myself am nothing. All that I know has been given to me by God who illumined my forefathers and taught them the science of the plants which they passed on to me through their yajé chants. Now they are gone and I am the last of the knowers."

Pacho's is not an idle claim. One of the last authentic shamans of the Putumayo jungle region, he has a profound knowledge of a treasury of medicinal plants that is still largely unknown to modern science. But what makes him special is his willingness to share this knowledge with outsiders (not a common trait amongst the Indians of his generation) and his conviction that he has a mission to divulge and preserve it, one which he has honored by welcoming into his home during recent years scores of what he calls *universitarios*—doctors, anthropologists, botanists and the like—some of whom have come from as far away as France, Canada and Germany. Like them, he is aware that this heritage is threatened, not only by

the gradual erosion of his own cultural traditions but also by environmental threats to the native habitat of the Putumayo. The younger Sionas no longer speak their tribal language nor easily recognize or make use of the medicinal plants their grandfathers employed, and ironically, his current prestige in the community probably owes more to the respect shown him by eminent white visitors than traditional beliefs in herbalism. For, like ourselves, some of the Sionas have more faith in orthodox medicine.

The colonization of the region by small land-holders and coca growers, the influence of state schools and missionaries, the television and motorized transport, the ecological damage caused by extensive cattle-farming and oil exploitation, and other inroads of modern civilization are destroying both the material and cultural bases of a millenary science of healing that may be of great benefit to mankind and which, once it is gone, can never be replaced. Nevertheless, Pacho believes that this science can be saved through the creation, on land which he has donated, of a botanical garden where he will cultivate, classify and teach others to prepare the thousands of plants with which he works. It is a difficult enterprise because communications between his reservation and the outside world are slow; he is poor and the paperwork involved is nearly as baffling to his educated friends in the big cities as it is to the Sionas. Even so, after several years of fund-seeking, an initial grant for the project has been made by the Colombian semi-state electricity financing agency, the FEN, and Pacho has already cleared the terrain and gathered seeds and cuttings. Once the garden has been sown, with the help of contracted labor, the money will be used to construct lodgings and laboratories for the scientists who will eventually live and study there and for the publication of posters and books on the garden's plants that will be primarily directed at Colombian schoolchildren. Pacho hopes that by enlisting the younger members of the community in the work of planting and cataloguing his plants, he will awaken their pride and interest in the Siona medicinal heritage.

Don Pacho's role as an apostle of Indian folk medicine has evolved from his personal history and the idiosyncrasies of his character. In his lifetime, he has seen the indigenous culture of the lower Putumayo fall from its prime into an undeniable decadence. His childhood coincided with the first real thrust of Western civilization into the Putumayo which, up to the turn of the century, was largely untouched by outside influences. He grew up at a time when salt, machine-made fabrics, metal implements and other goods which the Sionas now take for granted were uncommon, and motorboats, electric lighting and airplanes were unheard of. Nevertheless, the founding, in 1912, of a Capuchin mission in what is now the nearby town of Puerto Asís led to dramatic changes. The region's entrance into the modern world was further accelerated by the war (along the lower Putumayo river frontier) between Colombia and Peru in the mid-1930s and the discovery of oil in the upper Putumayo in the 1950s.

Pacho belongs to the first generation of Putumayo Indians educated in the Capuchin's boarding school, and, although Siona is both his and his wife's original language, for all practical purposes Spanish is now his tongue. He spent most of his early manhood working alongside "whites" as a guide and a sailor along the Putumayo, both on commercial paddleboats and Colombian navy vessels and as a laborer and cook on road-building, construction and foundry gangs. This experience, curiously enough, not only broadened his cultural horizons but also made him realize that his true calling was to be a healer. During these voyages, he swapped botanical knowledge with herbalists from Ecuador, Peru and Brazil. Since the late forties, when he finally settled down in Buenavista, he has been the shaman of the community, a role which, amongst the Sionas, gives him the status of a chief.

During the last decade, in which he has treated an increasing number of non-Indian patients (not only neighboring colonists but city-dwellers as well) and shared his learning with anthropologists and other intellectuals, he has

established, without really seeking it, a nation-wide reputation as a healer, a gift which has been formally recognized by invitations to speak in academic assemblies in Ecuador and in the Colombian cities of Pasto and Bogota. During the 1992 Colombian Congress of Anthropology, he spoke before an international public about his plants and his dream of founding a botanical garden. He raised a mild scandal when, to the embarrassment of one of its organizers, he gave a practical demonstration of his healing powers by doing a shamanistic conjuration over a map of Colombia out of a sincere desire to bring peace to this troubled country. Recently, Pacho was invited to speak at a symposium on ethnobotany organized by the José Celestino Mutis botanical garden in Bogotá.

Beyond all this, however, he possesses a rare compassion, a universal human trait which makes a person seek fulfillment through healing no matter their origin. One evidence of it is his reluctance to charge for his curations and his general indifference to money. Another is his genuine love of mankind and his

Yajé, Banisteriopsis caapi

unfeigned interest in helping anyone who approaches him. Apart from the Saturday night yajé ceremonies, Pacho is available to treat, at any time, those who turn up to be cured. The *curanderos* of the Amazon are not specialists, like Western doctors, but ordinary *campesinos* whose daily life is an arduous, sweaty, mosquito-ridden and sometimes back-breaking routine of clearing land, weed-

ing crops, hunting, fishing and craftwork. These labors integrate quite naturally with their medical chores and despite the poverty and lack of modern creature comforts, such healers enjoy one great advantage over their counterparts in the city—they always have time for their patients, whom they often lodge and feed in their own homes without expecting any special payment.

This particular day, however, is quiet. I accompany Pacho to his *yuca* patch, where we spend a few hours clearing weeds with machetes. Despite his age, ("75 Aprils" as he says) he has the muscular body of an athlete and the strength of a youngster. I have seen him clear a half-hectare of dense tropical forest, under intense sun, in a matter of days, a job which left me gasping and axe-blistered after a few hours. Don Pacho then shows me the site which he has opened for the botanical garden. As ever, walking through the jungle with Pacho is a privilege. What for me is an unvariegated and repetitive succession of trunks and creepers, bushes and ferns, grasses and flowers is for Pacho a sharply-etched gallery of plant friends with familiar and instantly recognized faces. Before ten minutes have passed, he has stopped to point out at least a dozen that I am blind to: the spaded *mame-üko* leaf, used in the fan which "blows" away the evil airs; the red cedar, a prized hardwood used in construction, which has nearly been eradicated in the region; the *palo cruz*, whose carnation-like flower is one of the few spots of bright red in this sea of green and is used to treat hemorrhages and to regulate the menstrual cycle; the *curarina* vine, a traditional snake-bite remedy and another creeper, with a mossy texture and an orchid-like flower, used to treat diarrhea; and the sacristan, a cluster of those cable-formed, aerial roots with a scarlet color which is used to "seat" loose teeth in their canals or painlessly extract rotten ones.

An anthropologist friend of Pacho's who gathered samples of these plants in Buenavista told me that some of them turned out to be literally unclassifiable within the canons of modern botany when examined by the National University of Colombia's Institute of Sciences in Bogotá. The same is true of yajé, whose varieties and methods of preparation present no problems for native shamans but are still a great mystery for orthodox medicine.

The tunnel of vegetation which forms the path leading from the riverside clearing into the largely virgin jungle that occupies most of the 4,500 hectare reservation (established by the Colombian government's Bureau of Indian Affairs in 1969) opens up after about a quarter-mile into one of don Pacho's *chagras*. In these slash-and-burn clearings, today's Sionas follow the traditional practice of sowing a variety of crops—mostly *yuca*, maize, rice, sugar cane and plantains—in a seemingly haphazard manner amongst fallen tree trunks and uncleared weeds and bushes, a marvel of empirical conservation. Here again, there are many medicinal plants, some of which have been sown by Pacho, while others flourish in a semi-wild state. Some of them are familiar, like the tropical nettle, which is used, amongst other things, for calming through a stinging shock therapy, those who have a "bad trip" on yajé; and the *lombricera*, a parasite remedy. There are also a number of exotic fruits which, in addition to being delicious, have specific medicinal properties: the *caimito*, the *marañon* (a cough remedy): the *guanabana*, and *borojnó* (now being exported from Colombia as a cancer cure). It is also worth mentioning the hot chile pepper which, in addition to being a condiment and a remedy, is (in its Siona name) the denomination of Pacho's tribal lineage and was burnt in the traditional yajé rites to frighten off the evil spirits. Others, however, are rarer, like the tropical anís, native to Brazil, a natural analgesic and the *yajé-üco*, also known as the yajé of water or the companion of yajé, a vine whose leaves are boiled together with the yajé vines to prevent the resulting potion from "burning" internal organs.

Leaving the *chagra* behind, we trudge along a muddy footing, interrupted by streams bridged only by a slippery log. Pacho points out a plant which I have used many times (though I do not recognize it) and which, in addition to being one of the most important in Siona herbalism, perfectly exemplifies the need for his botanical garden. It is the vine *yoco*, which, like yajé, is a strong purgative, though without yajé's hallucinogenic effects. Nowadays, as Pacho uses it, it is taken at dawn on an empty stomach as a general preventative against tropical parasites. Traditionally, however, it was an important complementary plant in the yajé rites, whose practitioners would, after cleaning out their systems with yajé and staying up all night, use *yoco* to keep up their strength when they went out (without breakfast) to hunt the animals they had seen in their yajé visions. Jokingly called the "coffee of the Indians," it was also used on a daily basis, without yajé, to

sustain long treks through the jungle or to keep the Sionas awake during the long nights before the advent of petrol lamps and electric light when it was the custom to retire at sunset and then wake, around two in the morning, to do craftwork and other light domestic tasks.

Yoco is a much more remarkable plant than it is credited to be. It not only kills the appetite (a recognized property which leads one eminent Colombian botanist to suggest that it could be commercialized as a slimming remedy) but it does this without apparently weakening you. In fact, a light fast with *yoco* not only sharpens the senses and gives one the energy to work well at both manual and intellectual tasks, but it also brings a definite feeling of tranquility and well-being which has nothing to do with intoxication. If yajé is the plant of wisdom, then *yoco* is the vine of happiness. Unfortunately, *yoco* is becoming scarce and during my last visit to the community, despite Pacho's searches throughout the surrounding forests, sometimes a week or more went by before he finally encountered it. This is not only true of *yoco* but also applies to other food and/or medicinal plants that were formerly common in the region. The scarcity may have something to do with the increasing human intervention which has contaminated soils and waters and upset the delicate ecological equilibrium. One evidence of these threats is an oil installation which lies only a few hours walking distance from the community on the southern or Ecuadorian side of the Putumayo, whose banks are inhabited by the Sionas though it is not technically part of their reservation.

We continue walking and Pacho shows me other natural marvels, such as the wild coconut palm which has a diminutive nut and whose leaf-fibers are used for hammocks; the *matapalo*, an impressive parasitic root formation whose tentacles reach up to a height of ten meters and which is used for bone injuries; and the *chuchuhuasa*, a tree whose bark serves to clean the blood and cure arthritis and rheumatism and is one of the most celebrated Amazonian remedies. We also turn up another; more human surprise, a ceramic vessel, buried up to its neck alongside the trail in what seems to be a virgin stretch of forest. Pacho explains that some thirty years ago this was the site of the *chagra* and yajé house of Arsenio Yaiguaje, his deceased brother-in-law, the last great shaman of the Sionas in a direct father-to-son line that may go back a thousand or more

years. It was Arsenio who taught Pacho the secrets of yajé and left him the five yajé plants, cultivated with a graft of *datura*, which formed the basis of his present cultivations of the vine. In Arsenio's honor, Pacho's botanical garden will bear his name.

Finally, after an hour's walk, we reach the recently opened two hectares that will form the part of the botanical garden reserved for plants that grow in direct sunlight. As always in the region, the change of habitat from forest to clearing is abrupt and dramatic; the sunlight is hot and blinding after the relatively cool and perfectly shaded jungle. But what is more impressive is the way it brings into sharp relief the gigantic almost monstrous nature of the Putumayo wilderness. When you are in the depths of the forest, you cannot really appreciate the sheer majesty of it all, whereas in the open, the straightly cut borders reveal a bewilderingly intricate face of vegetation that forms a solid wall of green some 60 or more meters high. Within the rectangle itself, the fallen trunks, charred and still lightly smoldering after the firing of the undergrowth a week before, resemble the twisted pillars of a ruined titan's palace. Further burning and machete-work will prepare the ash-covered soil for sowing, which will be done, as in any other *chagra*, in between the enormous rubble of lumber. While these trunks will eventually decompose, they now serve as a convenient causeway that we walk across, some meters above-ground, to reach the clearing's far edge.

In the forest again, guided by markers that are indecipherable to me, Pacho walks the boundaries of the eight hectares that will make up the main, shaded part of the garden. Here, where vines like yajé, *yoco* and *curarina* will be sown, the idea is to leave the terrain in its natural state by clearing only the ground vegetation or selectively thinning trees. Pacho points out that both the shaded and sunny parts will have to be fenced-in because, despite being on a protected reserve, the paths through this part of the forest are used by colonists who live around the reservation and who may accidentally damage rare plants. All of the plants in the garden will, for the benefit both of visitors and the members of the community, bear placards with their scientific, Spanish and Siona names and in addition to the specialists working there, ordinary tourists will be invited to participate in the project through guided tours. While Pacho's idea is not unique, his reserve will be the first to preserve strictly lowland, jungle remedies. Another botanical garden—founded by the Indian healer don Pedro Juajibioy, who was guide to the world famous Harvard botanist Richard Schultes—is located in Sibundoy in the Andean foothills of the Department of Putumayo and is mostly demoted to "cold climate" plants.

Despite his occasional philosophizing, Pacho is a modest and down-to-earth man who is sarcastic about the kind of over-intellectual, citified visitors who only come to the community "to work with their mouths" and for this reason he is reluctant to talk about his ideals. Nevertheless, during the course of many conversations with him some of his underlying principles have emerged. Perhaps the most important is a genuine belief in the efficacy of natural medicine and shamanistic healing. "Many of these pharmacists," he once told me, "are only in it for money, and the pills and potions they sell you, which are mostly sugar and starch, only treat the symptoms not the real causes of the illness. They only give a temporary relief so that you have to go back to the same drugstore a few weeks later and buy something else. It is not only expensive, but also unnecessary, for the plants in the wilderness are very good, they cure everything. The trees have shown me, when I drink yajé, that they are like people, like ourselves; they don't like us to hurt them when we gather their leaves, they feel what one does to them. Yajé makes you see, in the drunkenness, a certain plant and the next day you go into the forest and there it is. The plants themselves tell you which one serves for the liver, for the kidneys, for the lungs, to make tumors disappear, everything."

Article 20   *The Christian Science Monitor,* June 23, 1993

Indian Leader's Goal Is Land

*Restlessly on the move in his effort to organize communities,
Miguel Angel is dedicated to improving life of his people*

David Holmstrom

Staff writer of The Christian Science Monitor

Photo by Melanie Stetson Freeman

Staff photographer of The Christian Science Monitor

OTAVALO, ECUADOR
The dark-haired boy rises from his desk in the schoolroom and comes to the doorway. His smile is shy, almost confused. Standing there is his father, Miguel Angel, a Quichua Indian with a long braid down his back.

Weeks have passed since son and father have seen each other. Miguel touches the boy on the shoulder. The boy looks up on awe, or shy strangeness, as if his father is just this—a man in a doorway. This awkward meeting outside a school room in Imbabura province, Ecuador, lasts two minutes. The father is quickly gone. The desperate needs of his people keep him from his family.

As the elected president of an Indian organization known as FICI (Indigenous and Compesino Federation of Imbabura), with a hand-lettered sign on a side-street office here, Mr. Angel's passion is to acquire more land for his people.

Partly for safety, he seldom spends the night in the same place twice as he moves through the villages of the Andean highlands in a province 100 miles north of Quito, Ecuador's capital. Although he is in his early 30s, Angel's tenacity and personal political beliefs echo an older, leftist Ecuador in which socialist and communist unions were the main opposition to government policies. In that Ecuador, before attention shifted to the new issues of oil exploration and colonization in the rain forests, 2 percent of landowners of highland haciendas controlled 66 percent of the arable land. Angel knows that the figures have not changed. Today, 90 percent of small farmers own less than 10 hectares each, often on the steepest slopes.

In his efforts to change the imbalance, Angel has been harassed, threatened, held captive, and spied upon by the military and the police. For the past 10 years, he has been a community organizer.

Once he was taken to a big hole in the earth by soldiers and told he was going to be buried alive. "But the whole community surrounded the [military] truck," he says. The hole stayed empty.

The Indians in the highlands have lived in poverty for centuries. Angel wears shoes borrowed from his brother and owns virtually nothing but his clothes. President of FICI is not a paid position. His strength, intelligence, and persistence command the respect and care of the people he serves. Support flows both ways.

Because of Ecuador's Agrarian Reform Law of 1973, indigenous communities can form associations and file a claim with the government to obtain land that could be used for farming.

But the Agricultural Development Law of 1979, which favors landowners, restricts agrarian reform and makes it difficult and expensive to file such claims.

For the past three years, the local military base has refused to relinquish any of several thousand acres for local native farmers to plant food.

"The Army uses some of the land for grazing horses," Angel says, pointing to a rolling hillside beyond a barbed-wire fence. "We've said that this land should be farmed for food to eat. People are fundamental here, not horses. We live in poverty while they feed their horses."

Angel and others have talked with military authorities in Quito several times. "The minister of defense said he would investigate the issue of land," Angel says, "but it has been three years. A legal challenge is very expensive."

Military intransigence stems from general hostility toward any challenge to its authority, Angel says, particularly from Indians. In political and ideological terms, he suggests, "the slaves are turning against the master."

FATHER AND SON: *Always on the move, Angel rarely sees his family. A surprise visit to Punguhuacu means a hand on the shoulder of his younger son.*

Angel is the son and grandson of Indians who worked all their lives as virtual slaves on a hacienda.

"If there is no land for indigenous people," he says in his subdued, direct manner, "then there is really nothing else, no other way to survive."

But Angel knows there are more punishing ways to survive; Indian men and women from the highlands increasingly migrate to the cities for jobs. With few skills to offer and multiple temptations to face, many are disillusioned and defeated.

"The power of the Indian movement," Angel says, "is the power of community. What happens in capitalism or the mestizo world is that when you are 15, suddenly you are independent. Family is lost. Community is lost. Individualism doesn't work here; community does."

Angel visits a small community close to the military base. Standing in front of a windowless community center with a dirt floor, Juan José Simbaua, the president of the community, explains the problem his village of 170 families faces.

"We live in critical poverty without work and water," he says. "We've asked that the military sell us the land, and they threaten us and say the blood will run if we try to buy the land. Some of us were caught on the land [trying to survey it] and brought to the Army barracks and kept overnight. They told us not to get

involved, because there will be blood. If they are going to kill us, it doesn't matter. We are not going to give up."

In front of the community center, village women have gathered to learn how to knit sweaters. Traditionally, men are the weavers and knitters in the highlands, and women embroider only for their families. "Our husbands can't get work," one of the women says, "so in this association, we organize to help them by starting to make sweaters to sell."

Another community leader explains that all the roads here were built by the community, not by the government. "We put up the electricity poles too," he says, "but if they fall, sometimes we don't have electricity for a week."

A few miles away, in the tiny village of Punguhuacu, inside a mud house with a dirt floor, another group of 20 women has started a bread-baking cooperative to raise money to buy land from a nearby hacienda.

With a gas-fired oven provided by a Dutch foundation, the women bake loaves of wheat bread to sell in Otavalo and other cities. Angel's wife, Maria Lola Criollo, is president of the cooperative. The mud house belongs to Angel's parents.

On the way to visit Mario Acosta Luna, the commander of the police in Imbabura province, Angel says that re-

spect for Indians is growing. "Marches and protests in Ecuador are having an effect," he says.

> *'The power of the Indian movement is the power of community. What happens in capitalism or the mestizo world is that when you are 15, suddenly you are independent. Family is lost. Community is lost. Individualism doesn't work here; community does.'*
> *—Miguel Angel*

Just a few years ago, entrance into the commander's office was impossible. Now Angel sits with Mr. Luna, sipping coffee, both men being much too polite in front of a reporter and photographer, discussing the importance of dialogue between Indians and the police.

"There must be a sharing of ideas so that everyone advances," the commander says. "I've always talked with all sides. The police are not repressive in Ecuador. We are a preventive element, but when things get out of hand, we use other methods, but only to prevent worse problems."

After the afternoon meeting, Angel concedes that Luna "has done some things for Indians. But the police, in conjunction with the military, are a repressive instrument," he adds.

As the sun goes down, Angel rejects the suggestion that the odds against him look overwhelming.

"Yes, I get tired," he says, "but this is my responsibility." Asked where he will spend the night, he replies with a smile, "I'm not telling you."

Article 21 *Harvard International Review,* Summer 1993

Kicking the Habit

Fujimori Strays from Peru's Beaten Path

Steve Xydas

Steve Xydas is a Staff Writer for the Harvard International Review.

The history of Latin America bears the imprint of tragedy. The nations of the region have been plagued by poverty and economic instability, their political fabric left tattered by a seemingly endless string of dictatorships and military coups. Peru has the unfortunate distinction of being one of the poorest countries in this already-beleaguered region.

For more than a decade, Peru has suffered from severe hyperinflation, a large foreign debt, a colossal and inefficient public sector, a lack of international reserves and a growing inequality of income. These conditions allowed the virtually unknown Alberto Fujimori, who had no affiliation with the distrusted traditional political parties, to win the presidency in 1990.

Since then, Fujimori's drastic economic stabilization and adjustment program has effectively curbed inflation, and his policy of trade liberalization and wide-scale privatization has eliminated many of the market distortions that had retarded Peru's economic growth.

With these economic reforms, however, has come political upheaval. In April 1992, Fujimori dissolved the National Congress, censored the press and, in effect, instituted martial law. Political disquiet has been accompanied by merciless economic contraction. GDP has fallen, unemployment has risen, net exports have decreased and the number of poor has grown.

If Peru is to turn its economy around, Fujimori will have to retain the support of the populace, his only protection against an "expected" coup this year, by ensuring that the poor experience a rise in their standard of living.

Military Intervention

Peru has a long and varied history. At the time of its discovery by the Spanish explorer Francisco Pizarro, Peru was the center of the highly developed Inca civilization. But the conquistadors pillaged the Inca's land of gold and silver and ravaged the indigenous culture. Peru remained the most important of Spain's holdings in the New World until its independence in 1879.

In the century since, a series of military takeovers have interrupted constitutional civilian governments, the most recent being a 1968 military junta led by Peru's army Chief of Staff, General Juan Velasco Alvarado, that deposed the democratically-elected President Fernando Belaúnde Terry. The Alvarado regime attempted to rapidly modernize the severely underdeveloped nation, mainly by nationalizing many private companies and instituting land reform, in what is now known as the "Peruvian experiment." This regime, however, gave way to the installation of General Morales Bermúdez in a bloodless military coup in 1975.

General Bermúdez inaugurated a second stage of economic reforms, but his government eventually fell in 1980, having failed to reach its goals of accelerating economic growth; equalizing the distribution of income, wealth and power; releasing Peru of its dependence on foreign aid and establishing the nation as a leader among less-developed countries In 1980, elections were held in Peru for the first time since 1963, with former president Belaúnde returning to power in a stunning public rejection of the dictatorial regimes.

President Belaúnde faced even worse economic problems than his military predecessors. The worldwide recession in the early 1980s exacerbated Peru's debt crisis. Belaúnde responded by implementing a program of fiscal austerity, leading to a waning of the economy. As a result, Alan García Peréz, a social democrat of the American Popular Revolutionary Alliance party, emerged as the winner of the 1985 presidential election. García, in turn, introduced his own radical economic policies, achieving great popularity with a successful reduction of inflation, a rise in the living standard of the poor and the fulfillment of high economic growth rates.

In 1987, however, García proposed to nationalize the Peruvian financial system, a move that the public strongly opposed. Living standards and demand for goods plunged and took with them García's popularity. In the subsequent election of 1990, Mario Vargas Llosa, the famous Peruvian novelist, ran against an obscure agronomist, Alberto Fujimori. The son of Japanese immigrants, Fujimori came to represent the face of change for the over 12 million poverty-stricken Peruvians. He failed to win the required majority, but became the surprise victor of the election in a runoff.

Stablilzation Under Fujimori

Once in power, Fujimori implemented what has been called the harshest economic stabilization program in the history of Latin America. Vigorous tax collection, large reductions in the real salaries of government employees and rises in the rates charged by inefficient state-owned utilities helped cut the large budget deficit and exorbitant inflation rate. A comprehensive austerity program has limited government spending to government revenues. With its budget balanced, the government has cleared the way for International Monetary Fund (IMF) financing. Fujimori also instituted a US$8 million credit line to help reconstruct and repair housing damaged by terrorism, set aside US$145 million for agricultural emergencies, increased infrastructure construction by US$25 million and established a fund of US$200 million to help the banking system and businesses. The latter act alone prompted a five percent drop in the interest rate last year.

Fujimori's tough economic reforms have attracted foreign investment and regained the confidence of foreign creditors. The IMF approved Peru's stabilization plan and accepted its fiscal and monetary targets, placing Peru in good standing with the organization and clearing the way for new loans, a necessity for investment and economic growth. The Inter-American Development Bank (IDB) recently approved a US$222 million loan to Peru to finance Fujimori's economic reforms. Peru also received a US$100 million loan from Japan tied to the IDB loan. In addition, Fujimori has requested an additional US$200 million loan from the IDB to help agricultural development and improve Peru's ailing health care system, paving the way for essential economic and social improvements.

Fujimori has succeeded in reducing the real exchange rate of the new Peruvian currency, the sol. The removal of price controls and fixed exchange rates allowed the overvalued sol to depreciate on the open market. Contributing to the fall in the value of the Peruvian currency, Fujimori's policy of monetary expansion has driven down interest rates and increased liquidity. The devaluation of the sol will make the country's exports more competitive on international markets and help curb the influx of imports that has resulted from the reduction of trade barriers.

Significant gains in the seemingly endless fight against inflation stand as one of Fujimori's most prized victories. The monthly rate of inflation in September 1992 was 2.6 percent, the lowest rate since 1980. The annual inflation rate has plunged from 7,650 percent in 1990 to 56 percent in 1992 with 39 percent projected in 1993.

Peru's Persistent Problems

Despite Fujimori's success in obtaining international economic aid, devaluing the sol and ending inflation, the economy has continued to contract, partly due to efforts to balance the fiscal budget. GDP decreased by three percent in 1992 after a promising increase of 2.6 percent the previous year. Rises in unemployment in almost all sectors indicate a general decline in economic conditions. Employment fell 10.4 percent from January 1990 to December 1992. It is evident that Peru's troubled economic state will not end anytime soon.

Throughout the political upheaval, Fujimori's popularity has never fallen below 50 percent, but unless his economic policies bring about rapid growth, he could fall prey to a military coup.

Living standards in Peru have also continued to drop. Between 1990 and 1992, the number of Peruvians whose incomes fell beneath the official poverty line increased by five million. Currently, 12 million Peruvians—more than half of the country's total population of 22 million—live in extreme poverty. About half of Peru's educational facilities are without electricity and drinking water. Education and health expenditure for young adults decreased from US$49 per student in 1981 to US$12.50 in 1990, in a country with an already low literacy rate and chronically inadequate medical care. Peru's infant mortality rate also remains one of the nation's most pressing problems; the death rate of 85 per thousand births is the second highest in Latin America. Peru's social sector must overcome these obstacles before the country can claim any sort of fundamental economic advancement.

Fujimori's economic reforms, such as his privatization efforts, have been only marginally effective, raising questions for his impatient supporters about the future economic state of Peru. Although the government has sold

Heirro Perú, a state owned iron monopoly, to a Chinese firm, attempts to sell Peru's national airline, several banks, chemical companies and oil refineries have been unsuccessful. This has been the case even though the government reduced its asking price for many state enterprises by as much as 15 percent, indicating that foreign investors are still wary of possible economic risks in Peru.

Production in almost all sectors is down. From June 1991 to June 1992, agricultural production dropped 7.7 percent, as the effects of a drought in the highlands were aggravated by the overvaluation of the sol. Farmers are reportedly continuing to switch from staple crops to coca, adding to Peru's prevalent drug problems. The mining sector has declined significantly, plagued by energy shortages, high financing costs, high taxes, labor strikes and acts of terrorism. In May 1992, manufacturing output was only 79.6 percent of the output in 1979, an unmistakable sign of Peru's ailing economy.

Fujimori's reforms have also incurred a large social cost. Since 1980, the Maoist guerrilla group *Sendero Luminoso* (Shining Path) has waged a war of terror that has so far claimed at least 22,500 lives. The Shining Path is based in the southern highlands of Peru, but has spread to the central Andes region and the coca growing jungle, as well as into the cities. Shining Path terrorists recently planted bombs at a number of targets in Lima, including bank branches and a research center where Fujimori's former Minister of Economy and Finance, Carlos Boloña Behr, once worked.

Numerous strikes have also left the country vulnerable. Strikes among hospital workers, for example, exacerbated Peru's cholera epidemic, which killed over 115 people and infected over 22,000 in February 1991.

Moreover, in order to deal with the terrorists, the drug war, corruption and conflicts in getting his reforms through Congress, Fujimori controversially dismissed the National Congress, suspended parts of the Peruvian constitution and censored the press with military support in April 1992. This loss of democratic principles was mitigated by Fujimori's invitation to an Organization of American States delegation to watch over constituent assembly elections held in November of that year, in which Fujimori again achieved a majority.

The restoration of constitutional legitimacy in Peru entitled the nation to receive international financial assistance, which had been suspended upon Fujimori's seizure of extra-constitutional power. Fujimori has also relentlessly battled the Shining Path, capturing the faction's leader, Abimael Guzmán Reynos, among hundreds of others.

These apparent triumphs, however, belie Peru's ongoing political instability, exemplified by a coup attempt in November that included a plan to take Fujimori's life.

Brighter Days Ahead?

The Peruvian economy has certainly benefited from Fujimori's reforms. The days of hyperinflation, terrorism and capital flight seem to be over. Though unemployment and production have declined, the groundwork for a healthy economy has been laid. Government revenues and expenditures are in balance for the first time in over a decade, while foreign investment, a critical factor in the turnaround of Peru's economy, has increased. With the unification of the exchange rate system, Peruvian banks are now accepting foreign currency deposits for the first time since the banking system was nationalized. The positive effects of Fujimori's reforms clearly outweigh the negative ones.

Fujimori, however, has taken it upon himself to implement martial law—a move that many of his political opponents view as a grab for power. The influential novelist Mario Vargas Llosa, who ran unsuccessfully against Fujimori in 1990, remains bitter over Peru's descent into dictatorship. Throughout the political upheaval, Fujimori's popularity has never fallen below 50 percent, but unless his economic policies bring about rapid growth, he could fall prey to a military coup. The failed attempt in November was stopped just hours before it was to take place.

The next and most crucial step that Fujimori must take is the restoration of economic growth coupled with a rise in the living standard of the poor. Public sector privatization is a good start, but needy Peruvians must benefit if Fujimori is to stay in power. Since the bulk of the poor are involved in export-oriented agriculture, a rise in income will accompany the recent devaluation of the sol. Tariffs must be removed, not merely lowered, in order to bring prices to market values and eliminate the distortions in imported agricultural goods. And agricultural subsidies must be completely eliminated if Fujimori's structural adjustment policies are to take full effect.

Unless changes reach the impoverished majority, on whose support Fujimori has been able to rely so far, his popularity will evaporate. Fujimori must protect the temporary mandate that has thus far enabled him to execute his economic reforms. If he does not, Peru's all too familiar history of military intervention will repeat itself once again.

The Caribbean: Articles Section

Aricle 22

Current History, March 1991

The Caribbean: Small Is Scary

Aaron Segal

Aaron Segal is the author of five books on the Caribbean, including Haiti: The Failure of Politics *(1992).*

The Caribbean competes with the Indian Ocean and South Pacific regions as the most fragmented and heterogeneous in the world. So deep is the fragmentation that several geographic definitions dispute what constitutes the region.[1] Rather than the broad Caribbean basin definition, which includes such mainland states as Mexico, Colombia and Venezuela, or the narrow Commonwealth Caribbean definition, which includes only the former British colonies, another regional definition is preferable. According to this definition, the Caribbean includes the entire Caribbean archipelago from the Bahamas in the north to Trinidad and Tobago next to northern South America. It also includes the culturally related societies of Belize on the Caribbean coast of Central America and the northern South American societies of Guyana, Suriname and French Guiana.

The diversity in this geographic region is impressive. Five million people live in nonindependent United States, British, French and Dutch territories—the last legacy of 450 years of colonialism. Since the failure of the West Indies Federation—a union of British possessions that was established in 1958 and dissolved in 1962—13 independent states have been created out of former British colonies. These 13 states maintain a Caribbean Community (CARICOM), the University of the West Indies, the Caribbean Development Bank and other forms of regional cooperation.

The Dominican Republic and Haiti share the island of Hispaniola, but their trade and political relations are limited and often hostile. Air, telephone and sea communications with Miami and New York are more efficient than cross-island communication. Cuba, with a population close to 11 million, is the largest society and island in the Caribbean and is the most isolated from its neighbors.

The region's political and economic diversity has led to four official language groupings: English, French, Spanish and Dutch. However, in most Caribbean societies the people also speak a Creole language or dialect. Creole languages have gained some degree of official recognition in Curaçao (Paliamiento), Suriname (Sranan) and Haiti (Kreyol).

In spite of this longstanding and continuing diversity, the Caribbean has a shared culture. Its Creole languages, dances, music and games are clearly related. Most Caribbean societies share histories of colonialism, African slavery, emancipation and Indian indentured labor; Afro-Caribbean religious, linguistic, familial and agricultural syncretisms range from Santería in Cuba to voodoo in Haiti and Shango in Trinidad and Tobago. The exploration of these cultural similarities and syncretisms has been a major accomplishment of Caribbean and foreign scholars.[2]

Caribbean states are small in size and population, although population densities are high (400 or more persons per square mile). Only Cuba, the Dominican Republic and Haiti have populations of more than 5 million. Twenty of the 26 societies in the Caribbean have populations under 1 million. The total population of the region is less than that of Colombia and only slightly greater than that of the five largest Central American states combined. The Caribbean consists essentially of micro- and mini-states dwarfed in size and resources by their continental neighbors. With one-third of the Caribbean's total population, Cuba could potentially exercise hegemony, but has instead chosen to project its influence in Angola and Nicaragua.

Since the coerced immigration of African slaves and Indian indentured laborers ended in the nineteenth century, the Caribbean has experienced massive net emigration; since the end of World War II, between 5 and 10 percent of nearly every Caribbean society has left the region.[3] An estimated 1 million people of Caribbean origin live in the United Kingdom, the Netherlands and France, and perhaps 5 million live in the United States and Canada. Except for Cuban refugees, most have left voluntarily. Many enjoy dual nationality and go back and forth between the home islands and the new societies.

Together with family planning, education and the changing status of women, emigration has sharply reduced population growth in all Caribbean societies except Haiti during the last two decades. Caribbean population growth rates are between 1 and 2 percent a year, down from 2 to 3 percent earlier. Cultural ties are maintained through frequent visits and the practice of sending Caribbean children born overseas home to be raised by grandparents and others. As anthropologist Raymond Smith has shown in his detailed studies, the Caribbean peoples have learned to stretch family ties from London, Toronto, New York and other foreign locales back to the islands.[4]

TOWARD COOPERATION

The emergence of Caribbean-wide problems is forcing once-isolated societies to learn to work together. There is pressure for limited forms of functional regional cooperation rather than political unity through an expanded CARICOM and associations of nongovernmental interests like the Caribbean Conservation Association and the Association of Caribbean Universities.

The fundamental problem the region shares is total dependence on imported energy. Only Trinidad and Tobago has oil reserves, but these offshore fields are being rapidly depleted. The August, 1990, Iraqi invasion of Kuwait and the ensuing crisis in the Persian Gulf have cost the Caribbean nations hundreds of millions of dollars in higher oil prices despite their ability to buy Mexican and Venezuelan oil at discount prices. Vulnerable to world energy price volatility, the Caribbean has been jolted by inflation and higher costs for its fuel-intensive exports; it has also had balance of payments difficulties. The Soviet Union's cutback on oil deliveries to Cuba has left the island unable to sell surplus oil on world markets for dollars.

The shared search for alternative energy has begun in the Caribbean.[5] Experiments with the conversion of sugarcane residue into energy, active and passive solar energy devices, windmills, biogas and other technologies have been undertaken. Much of this experimentation has been funded by foreign donors. Solar energy appears promising but will require sustained basic and applied research. No single Caribbean island can carry out an effective alternative energy program. Cuba learned this with the failure of its Soviet-designed nuclear reactor project.

The control of drug trafficking is also nudging the Caribbean toward cooperation. Belize and Jamaica are the only Caribbean countries where marijuana is grown and exported. However, the islands provide transit points for cocaine and other drugs from Colombia destined for either North America or Europe. Small planes and high-speed boats take advantage of secluded island airstrips or territorial waters to transfer drugs. Those islands that have offshore banks and minimal regulations are also used to launder drug money.

Drug trafficking in the Caribbean corrupts law officials, introduces violence, and even threatens national security on islands that are protected by only a handful of police and a tiny army. The United States Drug Enforcement Administration (DEA) claims that in 1989, drug trafficking to the United States through the Caribbean dropped by nearly half as dealers switched to Central American and Mexican routes. The DEA operates regional surveillance centers in the Dominican Republic, Haiti and Aruba. Meanwhile, the Caribbean is being used increasingly to ship Colombian cocaine to Europe. In 1990, French police intercepted the largest shipment ever on French territory on the tiny island of St. Martin. Dutch police claim that 60 percent of the cocaine entering the Netherlands comes by way of Suriname.

ECONOMIC CHANGES

Historically, most Caribbean states have been locked into preferential trade arrangements with former colonial powers. This is changing. In 1990, the Dominican Republic and Haiti signed the Lomé Convention with the European Community (EC), making all independent Caribbean states except Cuba parties to preferential trade agreements both with the EC and with the United States through the Caribbean Basin Initiative (CBI).[6] No other region of the world enjoys this nonreciprocal dual access to the most important markets in the world.

The Lomé Convention applies to 69 developing countries, including 16 in the Caribbean. It provides concessional aid on a five-year basis and price supports for major tropical exports like coffee, cacao and bananas. Designed primarily for extremely poor countries in sub-Saharan Africa, it is probably the most generous form of North-South cooperation in the world, although it does not extend to duty-free exports of manufactured products.

The 1988–1989 negotiations for the entry of the Dominican Republic and Haiti to the Lomé Convention were promoted by Spain and by Haiti's African friends. The new members will each receive an estimated $30 million to $40 million a year from the EC in aid and price supports. The EC also provides other Caribbean Lomé members with financial and technical aid. Additional flights and tourist promotion will increase European tourism to the Caribbean, which is currently about 10 percent of total tourism. The EC is also committed to increasing aid to the British, Dutch and French Caribbean, which are juridically parts of the EC.

The CBI has been in operation since 1983 and extends to Central America as well as to the Caribbean. It provides for nonreciprocal duty-free entry to the United States of certain products manufactured or assembled in the CBI states. Because of pressure from United States producers, sugar, rum, certain textiles and many other products are excluded. The CBI has generated new foreign investment, jobs and exports, especially in Jamaica, St. Lucia and the Dominican Republic. However the CBI has been curtailed in value by exemptions and has not lifted island economies out of deep economic slumps. The administration of United States President George Bush pressured Congress in 1990 to extend the CBI for another 15-year period, but many of the exemptions remain.[7]

The Caribbean has not been able to take full advantage of its unique trade access. Exports to the EC and the United States are limited by rules such as local value-added taxes, quotas and protection for sugar. The islands lack infrastructure and managerial personnel, and they are competing with Singapore, Mauritius and other better organized island exporters. Ports, shipping and air freight are costly and often inefficient. There is a critical shortage of island entrepreneurs capable of running subcontracting operations.

Meanwhile, the dual-market access may not last. Mexico and the United States are negotiating a free trade agreement that will undermine some CBI advantages. The EC is working out formulas to deal with 29 island dependencies from Corsica to the Madeiras, all of which are seeking preferences.

The Caribbean needs to move rapidly to take advantage of its dual-market access while it lasts. Its other options are in trouble. Passenger cruise ships are stopping at ports less frequently or only briefly. Peasant agriculture is in trouble everywhere after decades of official neglect, and food imports continue to grow. Traditional tropical export crops like bananas and sugar are curbed by foreign quotas and import schemes, and newer exports like cut flowers and exotic fruits require extensive investments and marketing.

MAINTAINING DEMOCRACY

Remarkably, a majority of Caribbean societies have remained democratic in spite of economic stagnation.[8] The exceptions are Cuba, with its personalist, Marxist regime; Haiti, which continues to try to shake the legacy of a 29-year family dictatorship that ended in 1986; multiethnic Suriname, where military rule has only partly given way to civilian rule; and multiethnic Guyana, where Afro-Guyanese use coercion to rule over an Indian majority. However, in Grenada, electoral democracy has been restored after breaking down in a 1979 coup and being revived in the wake of United States military intervention in 1983.

Throughout the Caribbean, opposition political parties win elections and take office. More significant, the courts retain their independence, the press is privately owned and relatively free, civil liberties are recognized and respected, and dissent is tolerated. The military and security forces are removed from politics and as a rule do not abuse citizens. Although there are exceptions, there is an active civil society that protests, dissents, takes its case to the courts, contests free elections and provides an effective opposition. It is hard to find similar regimes in such numbers anywhere else in the developing world.

Explanations abound for the persistence of political democracy in some parts of the Caribbean. One suggested explanation is the legacy of British colonialism and parliamentary rule. However, this legacy failed in Guyana and all of British Africa, and democracy is working in Puerto Rico and in the Dominican Republic in spite of a Spanish colonial legacy. Jamaican political scientist and pollster Carl Stone explains that among many West Indians, democracy—especially dissent and an independent judiciary—have acquired an absolute rather than instrumental value.[9] To them, democracy is a quality of life issue. Perhaps Grenada is the case study; its islanders have returned passionately to party politics and competitive elections since 1983, although the island economy (based on nutmeg and tourism) has shown little improvement.

What are the prospects for democracy in the rest of the Caribbean? Guyana and Suriname have failed in multiethnic power-sharing, yet there is no other way they can become democratic. Donor pressure has had some effect, but Guyana and Suriname have become police states, paying only lip service to democracy. They are examples of how steady economic decline and mismanagement can lead to dictatorship.

Haiti's chances for achieving democracy are poor. Its history and political culture are based on elite domination of an isolated peasantry. The pro-life ration of political parties and movements in Haiti since 1986 is an encouraging sign, but there is little consensus on the conduct of politics. The economy is deteriorating, reinforcing the pressure toward another dictatorship.

DECOLONIZING THE CARIBBEAN

The desire for independence is not a major force in the region. Only the island of Aruba, with a population of 95,000, has set an independence date (1995) to secede from the six-island Netherlands Antilles Federation. Aruba has contracted with a United States firm to refurbish an antiquated oil refinery for $100 million and is counting on Venezuela to provide a regular supply of crude oil. The remaining members of the federation are restructuring and further decentralizing under the benevolent gaze of the Netherlands, which has already granted them autonomy.

The perennial quarrel over the status of Puerto Rico took a new turn when the Commonwealth's pro-statehood government and the pro-independence parties asked the United States Congress to authorize a referendum on Puerto Rico's relationship with the United States.[10] House and Senate committees disagreed on whether Puerto Ricans living in the United States would be allowed to vote, whether the referendum would be binding or advisory, and whether Congress should spell out the terms of each form of status on the ballot. All three parties agreed, however, to keep the issue off the 1992 Puerto Rican gubernatorial and legislative ballot.

The French Caribbean islands of Guadeloupe and Martinique and the mainland territory of French Guiana sought not independence but affirmation of their ties to France. Many French Antilleans saw the EC as a threat to their preferential trade in bananas, rum, pineapples and other products to France.[11] There was also concern that EC investors and citizens would take advantage of French Antillean business opportunities. A series of visits by French President François Mitterrand and Prime Minister Michel Rocard took place in 1989 and 1990 to calm Antillean fears, and to accelerate French aid for the damage caused by Hurricane Hugo in 1988.

Currently, Cuba has only modest diplomatic relations with Barbados, Guyana, Suriname, Trinidad and Tobago, and Jamaica. Because of Cuba's isolation, Caribbean leaders were upset by the deterioration in Soviet-Cuban relations and the insistence of Cuban strongman Fidel Castro on maintaining one of the world's remaining austerity-based Marxist regimes.

A post-Castro Cuba would have several avenues of reentry to the region. The most acceptable would be Cuban prowess in sports, dance, music and the visual arts. Another would be renewed contacts with the Haitian and Jamaican communities that have lived in Cuba since the 1920's. Ironically, Cuba, with its massive joint-venture investment in international tourism, urgently needs help in promotion, flights, cruise ships and management from its Caribbean neighbors, especially the Dominican Republic and Puerto Rico.

Haiti's travail since the exile of President-for-Life Jean-Claude Duvalier in February, 1986, has included two coups, one general election aborted by violence and an interim government that gave way to the December, 1990, elections. Violence between Duvalierists and anti-Duvalierists, army factions, and landlords and peasants

has disrupted an already stricken economy.[12] The demise of tourism, the exit of many assembly plants and faltering yields of coffee imprisoned most Haitians in the deepest poverty in the region. Nearly a million Haitians living in the United States, Canada, the Bahamas and the Dominican Republic send between $100 million and $125 million a year to Haiti—enough to feed an estimated one out of every four Haitians.

Haiti has seemed ungovernable. Yet the Catholic Church and mainstream Protestant churches and several private radio stations broadcasting nationally in Creole have shown signs of providing a national conscience and curbing some of Haiti's worst human rights abuses. And the 1990 elections led to a victory for a 37-year-old populist priest, Father Jean-Bertrand Aristide, who lacked both a platform and a party, although he enjoyed wide popular support for his courageous opposition to the Duvalierists.

The Dominican Republic boasted an economy with buoyant tourism, an export duty-free zone, assembly plants, and mining sectors, but suffered from chaotic economic policies and political conflict. At the helm was 84-year-old President Joaquin Balaguer, reelected in 1990 in a hotly contested race with archrival and former President Juan Bosch. While these men swapped political charges, the economy deteriorated sharply. Balaguer's traditional practices of pump-priming patronage with public works were financed by printing money and acquiring an external debt of more than $4 billion. One result was an annual inflation rate close to 70 percent in 1990 and a series of crippling general strikes led by trade unions and the political opposition. Balaguer offered to move general elections up to 1992 and reluctantly agreed to some of the fiscal cuts and other austerity measures insisted on by international lending agencies.

The Dominican Republic is in trouble. It needs a restructuring of its political parties too long dominated by aging giants and a massive dose of economic structural adjustment. Remarkably, the military and the police have played a secondary role, and electoral democracy has survived a series of rude shocks. One stabilizer is a substantial middle class, although its numbers are being thinned by emigration to the United States.

THE COMMONWEALTH CARIBBEAN

The global process of regional economic integration brought new life into the semimoribund CARICOM. At its 1990 heads of state meeting, decisions were made to create a common market by 1992, provide further export credits for interisland trade and strengthen regional institutions like the University of the West Indies. CARICOM support was pledged to Belize in its negotiations with Guatemala in their boundary dispute, and a mission was sent to Haiti. Bogged down for years in protectionist disputes among its members, CARICOM has begun to show its potential as a regional political entity. There has even been discussion that the six small eastern Caribbean members might turn their cooperative effort into a renewed attempt at political union.[†]

While most CARICOM members experienced little or no economic growth in the late 1980's, the Bahamas was the exception; its booming economy was driven by tourism and offshore banking. Political democracy persisted, with the opposition returning to power in a narrow election victory in multiethnic Belize. In 1989 there were five hotly contested elections in the CARICOM states alone. That year, voters returned veteran Jamaican leader Michael Manley and his National Democratic party to power. Abandoning his socialist views of the 1970's, Manley opted for pragmatic economic policies and agreements with the International Monetary Fund (IMF) and the World Bank. Hurricane Hugo devastated Jamaica in 1988, but by 1990 there were signs of recovery based on tourism, new assembly plants and higher prices for bauxite, the country's main export.

With a population of only 300,000, Barbados found its bountiful but vulnerable economy declining. Exports from assembly plants were down, and sugar remained in a slump, partly because of EC and United States quotas and preferences for domestic products. Accustomed to sophisticated two-party politics in a highly literate society, Barbadians grumbled at belt-tightening imposed by younger politicians. Barbados placed its hopes on more tourism from Europe, especially from Great Britain, and on a further upswing in CARICOM trade. A 1987 visit from Queen Elizabeth II of England for the 350th anniversary of the Barbados Parliament was a source of pride for a society that takes democracy seriously as part of its heritage.

Trinidad and Tobago has run into massive problems. Its oil-based economy has been declining since the early 1980's because of low world prices, bankrupt state enterprises, fiscal deficits, inflation and a drop in the standard of living combined with high unemployment. Economic malaise brought the opposition Prime Minister Arthur N. R. Robinson to power in the 1986 elections. However, his governing coalition soon fell apart over economic policies.

This background helps to explain why a local Muslim group with ties to Libya took the Prime Minister and several members of his Cabinet hostage in late July, 1990. Led by an ex-policeman, Yasin Abu Bakr, this group was

finally dislodged by a combination of negotiations and limited force.

Trinidad and Tobago will have a long road back from these tragic events. Higher oil prices will help, but a breach has been opened between the largely Indian business community and the political leadership. The trial of Yasin Abu Bakr and 13 supporters on capital charges will do little to quiet racial and economic fears. Multiethnic Trinidad and Tobago has thus far avoided the violence of Guyana and Suriname. But it has been unable to put together an effective governing coalition that enjoys support from all ethnic communities.

The year 1992 is the quincentenary of the first voyage of Christopher Columbus to the New World. In some respects, the Caribbean that he encountered in 1492 was more united than the region is 500 years later.

Footnotes

1. Aaron Segal, "Caribbean Complexities," *Current History,* December, 1988, pp. 413–416, 434–437.
2. Sidney W. Mintz and Sally Price, eds., *Caribbean Contours* (Baltimore, Md.: Johns Hopkins University Press, 1985).
3. Barry Levine, ed., *Caribbean Exodus* (New York: Praeger, 1987).
4. Raymond T. Smith, *Kinship and Class in the West Indies: A Genealogical Study of Jamaica and Guyana* (New York: Cambridge University Press, 1988).
5. Wallace C. Koehler and Aaron Segal, "Caribbean Science and Technology: Do They Exist?" *Caribbean Review,* vol. 14, no. 3 (Summer, 1985), p. 11.
6. An international conference was held in Paris in June, 1990, with regard to the Caribbean and the European Community; see also Aaron Segal, "The Caribbean's Euro-American Links," *The Times of the Americas* (Washington, D.C.), March 21, 1990.
7. Ibid., December 13, 1989. This issue contains articles on the CBI.
8. Carl Stone, *Power in the Caribbean Basin: A Comparative Study of Political Economy* (Philadelphia: Institute for the Study of Human Issues, 1986).
9. Carl Stone, *Politics Versus Economics: The 1989 Elections in Jamaica* (Kingston, Jamaica: Heinemann, 1989).
10. Raymond Carr, *Puerto Rico: A Colonial Experience* (New York: New York University Press, 1985).
11. Alain-Philippe Blérald, *Histoire économique de la Guadeloupe et de la Martinique du XVII siècle à nos jours* (Paris: Karthala, 1986).
12. Recent books on Haiti since 1986 include Amy Wilentz, *The Rainy Season: Haiti since Duvalier* (New York: Simon and Schuster, 1989); Simon M. Fass, *Political Economy in Haiti* (New Brunswick, N.J.: Transaction Publishers, 1988); and Michel-Ralph Trouillot, *Haiti: State Against Nation* (New York: Monthly Review Press, 1990).

†St. Lucia, Grenada, St. Kitts and Nevis, St. Vincent and the Grenadines, Antigua, and Dominica.

Article 23   *Time,* December 6, 1993

Cuba Alone

Castro's socialist dream has turned into a nightmare. Isolated, hungry, and broke, the country hopes that a touch of capitalism will save it.

Johanna McGeary and Cathy Booth

HAVANA

We met Ana on the Avenue Galiano, a shopping street in downtown Havana, where she was gazing longingly into a store selling plastic shoes for 20 pesos (15¢). They are rationed, and it is not her year to buy new ones. Ana was eager to talk, but not in public, where the government's ever present watchers could see. Come to my home, she said, and you will see how terrible life is here.

Home is a rundown walk-up in Old Havana, where filth clings to peeling plaster and the reek of garbage sticks in the throat. Makeshift walls, festooned with frayed electric wires, subdivide the old apartments into tiny windowless warrens. When we arrive early one morning, she is locked behind massive doors. A woman with the face of a Madonna stares impassively over the half door to her dark flat. Down the hall another head pokes out: the Committee for the Defense of the Revolution has taken note of our arrival.

Ana is 24, separated from her husband, and does not trust her neighbors. Inside, she shows us her shabby living room, the dim bedroom she shares with her son, a rudimentary bathroom and a dank kitchen equipped with a leaky sink, hot plate and ancient refrigerator. Its contents: beans, rice and a frozen three-month-old piece of chicken that she is saving for two-year-old Rolando. "The state gives you six pounds of rice a month, but we eat that in three days," she says. When her rations ran out the week before, she sold her grandmother's 10-year-old boots to buy turnips.

Ana, a secretary in a food cooperative a long commute away—it takes her three hours to get there—knows she may well live and die in this apartment, like her grandmother before her. "People are disillusioned," she says. "We have education and health care, but we don't have food or freedom. What can I give my child?" She feels caged and angry. "They control everything," she says, making the gesture of a hand stroking a beard, which is how Cubans silently refer to their supreme leader, Fidel Castro. The woman down the hall reports regularly to the local block committee about her, says Ana, "because I am not a conformist." She finds peace in her Bible, though her faith has earned her a black mark on the dossier that follows all Cubans from childhood to death.

She pours out her dreams in poems. On old paper salvaged from her office wastebins, she writes *Días de Mis Sueños,* The Days of My Dreams: "I think of Mozart, Beethoven, Chopin and invite them to a party and give them a gift. Always the night ends with them drinking and playing music that makes me escape from this place."

If Cuba is a land of dreams, it is because reality is too cruel. Ana's house is a perfect metaphor for the country crumbling around her: the whole economy is in a state of advanced decay. After more than 30 years of Soviet-style socialism, life has turned much worse during what the Cubans call the "special period," the four years since the Berlin Wall crashed and carried away the Soviet lifelines. Cuba must now fend for itself.

Havana has turned into a decaying ghost of itself, its once vibrant life leached out by hard times.

It cannot. People are hungry: food is rationed, but there is almost none to buy. Factories are shut: there is no fuel to run machines, no raw materials to process. Harvests rot in the fields for want of distribution. We see no cars and few buses on the broad boulevards; people travel by bicycle, horse and buggy, or crammed aboard the occasional flatbed truck. There are swizzle sticks but no soap, no toilet paper, no plain paper either. By day a pall of smoke hangs over the city: the government, desperate to limit the daily 12-hour blackouts of summer, spent some of its precious cash on cheap, dirty oil to fire the electric plants. But nights are still dark and silent; only the light from the tourist hotels casts a faint glow over the ocean-front Malecón. Havana is a ghost of itself, its once vibrant life leached out by hard times.

Why aren't Cubans marching in the streets, demanding the downfall of Castro and communism?

So why aren't Cubans in the streets demanding the downfall of Castro and communism? Last week the State Department called Cuba's future grim, "a prolonged, slow decline waiting for a catastrophe." In a still-classified warning to President Clinton in August, the CIA predicted that "tensions and uncertainties are so acute that significant miscalculations by Castro, a deterioration of his health, or plotting in the military could provoke regime-threatening instability at virtually any time." The CIA report sketches out "serious instability" and "the risk of a bloodbath."

After a rare, two-week visit by American journalists to the island, it is apparent the issue is not so simple. Already Fidel Castro's Cuba is no more. Whether he is leading the way or merely acquiescing to it, the socialist Utopia he built is sliding inexorably toward capitalism. But Cubans still believe that Castro's revolution has given them something too precious to lose. People understand their economy is in ruins, but they see no one who could lead them out of their present misery but Fidel. The struggle under way is between Castro and the forces of history: Can he control Cuba's mutation to his liking, or will freeing the economy steal the country out from under him?

Circumstance, not a change of heart, is the driving force behind Cuba's grudging transformation. If the collapse of the Soviet empire had not cut Havana's imports from $8 billion to $1.7 billion today, change would not be coming at all. Beginning in July, Castro announced steps to open up the economy. He legalized the use of the dollar, granted more autonomy to farmers, and allowed people in more than 135 small-time occupations, from shoe repair to haircutting, to work for themselves. "For 30 years we did not do anything like this," Fidel told a group of 175 Americans visiting Cuba in violation of the 32-year U.S. embargo, "but the realities of today's life have forced us to do this. It is painful, but we have no other choice."

And more changes are coming: economics czar Carlos Lage has recently outlined plans to introduce a tax system, downsize the government work force, and restructure the agricultural sector. There is even talk of eliminating government control over who leaves the island.

But there seems to be no guiding strategy from the top. A diplomat tells this story about how the first changes came about. When the Communist Party realized the situation was desperate, it put out a call for advice. One plan proposed some 40 or 50 steps the government needed to take incrementally, beginning with putting food on the table. Then it moved on to reforms of various kinds and, finally, far down the list, to legalizing dollars. Fidel pointed to the dollar measure and said, We will start here.

The consensus says Castro is being forced to legitimize what the Cuban people are doing illicitly. "I think people push, and he eventually accedes," says a Western diplomat. "I don't see any fundamental decision by Fidel to change his ways of thinking." A foreign businessman exploring joint ventures is certain that Castro is simply showing the pragmatism of a smart politician: "He's not doing any of this because he likes it but because he will do whatever he has to do to survive."

However it is happening, optimists say the door to real reform is now open. Cynics look at the narrow nature of the changes and shake their heads. Each modest economic decree is hedged with restrictions. Social tension could erupt, since those with families in the U.S. or jobs in tourism have access to dollars while government bureaucrats, doctors, engineers and the military do not. Cubans seeking to work for themselves must pass a check by the feared Ministry of Interior before getting a license; professionals—anyone with a college degree—are barred from self-employment. Farmers who want to sell vegetables privately find that the local cooperative still sets the price.

Cubans look back on the time before 1989 as a Golden Age, when the system brought them a standard of living better than most Caribbean nations and roughly equal for every citizen. In four years all that has vanished, leaving Cubans confused, embittered—and open to change.

They want reform, but they don't know what kind. Bright young technocrats eagerly describe a world where capitalist energy will coexist with communist caretaking. An older woman involved in joint ventures insists that Fidel's system needs only modest tinkering. A grizzled mine worker warns against any changes that bring back inequality. Reporters are invited into the country, but top officials decline interviews: they no longer seem to know what the party line is. "There is a new incoherence," says a Western diplomat in Havana. "It's not pluralism, but different people have different ideas about where the country should go."

The results are schizophrenic. The government promotes Cubacel, a joint telephone venture with Mexican businessmen—and the government organizes a new category of medals called Combatants of the Revolution to keep old-think alive. While shops for Cubans stock a few rusted kitchen knives and cardboard toys, shiny Nissans carry tourists to refurbished hotels equipped with Sony TVs tuned to CNN.

If they have to change—and most accept that only reluctantly—Cubans are determined to change in their own way. No matter where you go on the island, what stratum of society you probe, you hear the same mantra: *the achievements of the revolution*. What they call the revolution is not communism, not socialist ideology, not even veneration for Fidel. "The achievements of the revolution" is code for cradle-to-grave health care, free and universal education, and generous social-security payments. Castro brought these benefits to millions who had almost nothing before the revolution, and after 34 years they are fiercely proud of the guarantees—so rare in Latin America—and are determined not to lose them. "There is no way you can take away the achievements of the revolution," says 35-year-old reformer Pedro Monreal. "They are installed on the hard disk of my generation." Cubans insist they will manage to keep these benefits and still revive their shattered economy.

We have to collect Julio Carranza, the young deputy director of the Communist Party's Center for American Studies, at his house. He has no gas for his car, and his neighborhood is blacked out. We enter another world when we sit down with him and Monreal in the gilded elegance of Havana's Ferminia Restaurant—dollars only. Wolfing down real meat, the two thirty-something economists paint glowing pictures of a wondrous second-generation Marxism where quasi-private enterprise pays for the nation's broad social safety net.

They are convinced that Cuba can have the best of both systems: the benefits of socialism and the wealth of the free market. Cuba can succeed where Russia and Eastern Europe have failed. But even these experts have only the vaguest notions of how. "I think we can do it if there is more income for the state," says Monreal. The two envision less central planning but government control over the shape of the economy: a system encompassing private, cooperative and state ownership, all working to the common good. They talk of taxes, salary scales, redundant employment, monetary reform, but have no idea how they would really work. "One day Cuba will not use any ism to describe our system," boasts Carranza.

Concepción Portela could not agree less. Maybe it is generational: she is 61. "I am a Marxist," she says. After years in a government ministry, she runs a private business advising foreign investors on joint ventures in tourism, biotechnology, construction. Her job—which she considers temporary, until "we work our way out of this situation"—is not to change the system but to preserve it by bringing capital into the country. Cuba, she insists, will never denationalize, never privatize: "I distribute what I produce to others."

As we drive through the lush countryside, we are stunned that this island cannot feed itself. But the perversions of Soviet-style agriculture have left their legacy. To trade for Russian oil, Castro converted much of Cuba's arable land to sugar. A government bureaucrat sighs as he tells the potato story. During the cold weather in Russia, Cuba would grow potatoes and ship them all to Moscow. Then six months later, when the Russian harvest came in, Moscow would send a year's worth of potatoes back to Cuba, where they would have to be stored in huge refrigerated warehouses. Now the warehouses stand empty and useless.

Many people doubt the latest changes in agricultural policy will make much difference. Noel Prado, 37, farms 98 acres in Vegas, southeast of Havana, on which he must produce his government allotment of sugarcane. He seems content with Castro's policies. "Food is not a problem here," he says, patting his big stomach. He can sell some of his surplus peanuts, sweet potatoes, coffee, sheep and pigs. City friends travel 25 miles from the capital to barter for his vegetables and meat, but since he has no fertilizer, no pesticides and no electricity to pump water for irrigation, his production will not increase soon. He hopes private ownership will encourage other farmers to grow more, but he is dubious. "Cubans are used to receiving everything from the state," he says.

The mine workers in the mountain town of El Cobre, west of Santiago de Cuba in Oriente province, where the revolution was born, are afraid of the dreamers in Havana. Oh, yes, Cuba needs to change, says a 57-year-old welder we'll call Alberto. "But we need something for everybody, not just for a few." He does not want his real name used, and he keeps looking nervously over his shoulder. "If they see me talking to you, tomorrow I will have trouble with the police," he says.

But the *clara*, the rough-brewed beer the state sells on Sunday in the town plaza, has loosened his tongue. For 30 years his life was good, he says, until dollars were allowed. "I worked, I earned my pay, my family could live just like my neighbors." But he has no family in the U.S. to send money, no relatives working in tourism to collect tips. "Some people can have dollars; I only earn pesos," says Alberto. "The people with dollars can buy a pair of shoes, and I cannot. Why should my neighbor have more than me?"

The advent of the dollar has brought dismay even to the party faithful. Riding in an aging Lada to the countryside to buy food, a loyal government employee gripes, "We felt betrayed. Legalizing the dollar favors people who kept ties to

their families in Miami, people who were not dedicated to the revolution, people who tried to kill us."

Octavio lives better by betraying the system. We stop in front of his pristine white bungalow in the Havana suburb of Miramar. A knock on the door brings a discreet peek from behind freshly painted shutters. A voice murmurs to come around into the garden. Suddenly, we could be in Miami. American rock plays softly; red and blue lights color a trimly clipped lawn. Our host offers a hamburger, steak, perhaps a lobster? Red or white wine? A rum collins?

He runs one of Havana's new speakeasies. Home restaurants are legal, but as a university-trained engineer, Octavio is barred from private enterprise. His official job earns him 300 pesos a month, a good salary in Cuba, but that equals a mere $2.50, the cost of a pork sandwich and a bottle of Labatt's beer on his patio. "I have kids, and they need to eat. They want ice cream, things in the stores," says Octavio, "so I do this. I have to have dollars."

He sold some family antiques to foreigners—also illegal—to stock his giant freezer with pork, chicken and beef bought at the new dollar stores. Saturday nights his tables are full of "friends of friends" who can pay dollars for food they cannot find elsewhere. If his neighbors snitch, the government will confiscate everything. Wearing a white polo shirt, gold Seiko watch and Italian shoes, Octavio shrugs at the danger. "I will do what I must for my family," he says, "no matter what Fidel [he makes the beard gesture with his fingers] says."

He feels no remorse about cheating a government that he believes has failed him by its lies and mistakes. "First you have to guarantee food, then you guarantee health and education," says Octavio. "Their priorities are backward. They spend on sports! You can't eat sports." Yet this son of a family that was well off before the revolution is not keen about the capitalist changes. "I think it's an error to give purchasing power to the dollar," he says. "My family lost financially from the revolution, but we gained spiritually, we gained morally."

Varadero Beach, where rich gringos used to cavort in the days of the Batista dictatorship, is once again a clean, green ghetto for foreigners. Tourism is supposed to be the country's short-term salvation, but it also accentuates the difference between those with dollars

and those without. Everyone wants to work at Varadero: hotel maids earn more in tips than peso-poor engineers; teachers and Angola veterans drive cabs; and psychologists make plane reservations. The expertise of the Cubans who work for Eamonn Donnelly, the Irish manager of two German-owned hotels, runs from agronomy to piloting MiG fighters.

Now they just have to master Econ 101. Lawyer Julio González, who oversees Donnelly's busy Tuxpan Hotel, did not grasp some basic concepts at first. Put in charge of personnel, he let profits plummet as the staff, heavily padded with relatives and friends, ballooned. Once faced with the capitalist notion of being fired if he failed to meet his budget, Julio straightened out. "No one had ever been fired for anything before," says Donnelly. "Now Julio is a devil of a capitalist."

González pats the computer printout on his desk showing a 92% occupancy rate at the Tuxpan and lights up an imported Kool Filter. He plans someday to be manager, even owner of a hotel chain. Does he believe in capitalism now? He grins: "I think like Jesus Christ that the bread has to be divided. Was Christ a communist or a capitalist?"

For many other Cubans, tourism is a pact with the devil. They remember how they felt exploited by rich foreigners before 1959. At the Tuxpan disco, the only Cubans allowed in are pubescent girls dressed in scanty Lycra minis who have bartered their company to rum-swilling tourists for a meal. It makes Julio González angry even as he takes their money.

"Tourism is a sort of chemotherapy," says historian Juan Antonio Blanco, director of a new private think tank. "You have cancer and it's the only possible cure, but it might kill you before the cancer does." The inequality, the privileges derived from separating the foreigner from his dollar, he says, "could prove more socially disruptive than the bad shape of the economy."

We wonder why we cannot find more signs of brewing revolt. Cubans have a genius for adapting, we are told. Cubans are law abiding and have no taste for civil disobedience. Cubans are happy "if they have one plate of food and a bottle of rum," says restaurateur Octavio. Cubans don't believe in any ism but paternalism. "The state has provided for 30 years," says Blanco. "That's not the case anymore, but half the population has not adapted to reality."

Exiles who dream of a revolution from below would despair. Many of the Cubans we meet show no interest in politics, nor do they talk about a political solution to their country's problems. But not because this is a nation of devout communists: "Most people became revolutionary not from reading Karl Marx," says Blanco, "but because they saw suffering in the streets." Even in the privacy of a dissident's house, there is no eager call for multiparty democracy. Most Cubans do not seem to care what kind of political system they have as long as they have an economy that works.

"A vast majority of the population," says a Western diplomat, "is sitting and waiting until the situation is resolved for them." In the streets of Havana there is little proto-capitalist bustle. The government says 86,000 people out of Cuba's 11 million have applied for the required license, but it is not easy to find the new mom-and-pop enterprises. Canadian mining executive Bill McGuinty thinks his Cuban co-workers are eager to learn capitalist ways—up to a point. They are shocked by his attempts to bypass bureaucracy and befuddled by the quid pro quos of networking. "It will take a while for the mentality to change," he says. "They have gone from 34 years of working together to every man for himself."

How much of the lethargy is fear? Cuba's detachment from the Soviet orbit has not lessened the state's powerful instruments of political control. The security apparatus is omnipresent. Driving through Palma Soriano in the mountains above Santiago, we stop in a tiny café and strike up a conversation with a customer. In less than five minutes, a car screeches to a halt outside and four hard-eyed men stride in. Everyone falls silent as they shake hands all around, staring intently into each face. We get up to leave, and the leader smugly inquires, "Going already?" Marked on the outside of the car is the logo of the local party watch committee.

The government has been very effective at crushing opposition. The most ardent anti-Castro groups are in exile. Those remaining have been reduced to small, timid groups, and human-rights organizations report that the number of arrests of even moderate dissidents has risen sharply. Very few people, says Félix de la Uz, "are willing to do something to make the system fall."

Friends of De la Uz call him a Dr. Zhivago. He fought underground with Castro's 26th of July movement and in his early 20s went to the Communist Party school in Moscow for grooming. But by 1968 he had lost his zeal and wrote a stinging critique of the party for being undemocratic. He was banished to a railway shop, where he labored in silence until now.

"Marxism is a very coherent ideology," he says, lighting a harsh Populares cigarette in his small, dim living room. "It seemed to have all the answers." He laughs at the idea as he fingers his worn ration book. The modest economic steps the government has taken "won't solve anything," he says. "I think it's more to save the government's face. We're making some changes to look good to the outside world." He explains how each new decree will still leave the state in charge. "They don't want to take these measures, or any measures," he says. "The man with the beard knows very well that these steps signify that the power he has is being lost."

Arranging an interview with a human-rights activist entails maps drawn on shreds of paper and mysterious phone numbers passed along by hand. When we finally catch up with Elizardo Sánchez, he tells us to leave our taxi a block away. Sánchez has been outspoken enough to land in prison for eight of the past 12 years. "People don't understand what a regimented state we have," he says. "The proof is that here, unlike Eastern Europe, the government is *not* changing, even though we have far worse economic pressures."

Control is implanted in every crevice of the system, from the individual dossiers to the vigilante block committees. "We have the largest number of police per capita in the world," says Sánchez, and he claims that nearly 1% of the population is in jail. In the past few months, he says, 5,000 to 10,000 citizens have been imprisoned for illegal economic activities, sentenced to eight to 10 years for slaughtering a state-owned cow or stealing state property. He warns, "The government is pushing the country to the edge of violence."

No visitor can miss the real hatred Cubans express for their countrymen in Miami—despised for fleeing, feared for their threats to take back their property, blamed for the U.S. embargo that prevents Cuba from seeking assistance from friendlier Western nations. "We will never accept a government dictated by Miami," says Sánchez.

The U.S. embargo, in place for 32 years, comes across to Cubans as an attempt to starve them into bringing Castro down. As the rigors of the "special period" worsen, Fidel has appealed to Cuba's fierce nationalism and its image of itself as a David fighting Goliath. He has made Uncle Sam the scapegoat for the country's economic disaster. Sophisticated citizens may not buy the argument, but at a visceral level it has helped reinforce Cubans' siege mentality. Congress's decision last year to toughen the embargo by barring foreign subsidiaries of U.S. companies from trading with the island embitters and puzzles many. "You deal with China, Syria, why not Fidel Castro?" asks Sánchez. "The view in Miami, believed in Washington, that he is going to go away is a huge error. If Washington had a truly pragmatic vision, it would renounce its anti-Castro policy and help us reform."

Travel around the island for two weeks and the lasting impression is the same: Cuba may be falling apart, but Fidel is not falling with it. Through a combination of charisma, national pride and repression, he still holds the island's fate in his hands.

To an astonishing degree, people have separated their discontent with the way things are from the man in charge. Fidel can continue to count on a deep reserve of support from a populace proud that he freed the island from the foreigners who once owned the casinos and the sugar fields and the rich who exploited the poor. "He is like the godfather who will always look after you," says historian Blanco. Things may be hard now, say three elderly ladies in a party-run senior citizens' center in El Cobre, but thanks to Fidel, *somos feliz*. We are happy."

Cubans take as fierce a pride in their revolutionary heroes as Americans do in the men of 1776: they are the nation's embodiments of freedom and independence. Che Guevara is their Lafayette, Fidel their George Washington. "He has a place in people's hearts that goes far beyond the Communist Party or government structure," observes mining executive McGuinty.

Bone-thin after four years of declining rations, Mario Caballero, a 52-year-old school administrator in Santiago de Cuba, is one of the older generation whose faith in Fidel is well-nigh religious. If his rhetoric recalls communist dogma of the '50s, it still reflects sentiments deeply etched in the Cuban soul. "Before, our best land was Yankee. The sugar was Yankee. The electric system was Yankee. The phones were Yankee." Never mind that the sugar crop is failing for the second year, that electricity and phones rarely work. "We may be living through a special period," he says, "but at least all the property is Cuban."

His friend Albert Memo, a retired electronics technician, remains content to entrust the future to Fidel. "We have a government we like," he says. Cubans know capitalism, "and we don't want it." But if Castro says Cubans have to do things differently, Memo will go along. He leans back and reminisces: "I am exactly the same age as Fidel, 67. When you meet him, he is so impressive. When he talks, you really trust him, you would follow whatever he decides to do. I love him. Everyone loves him."

Those who do not love Fidel have few options: wait until he dies, or flee. Ricardo and Raúl are scheming to escape by sea, when they are not drunk on bootleg rum. Quaffing cocktails and beer at Ernest Hemingway's old haunt, La Bodeguita del Medio in Old Havana, they rail against the system, unconcerned that they might be overheard. At 21, Ricardo is just out of prison after serving a nine-month term: he got drunk and spat on a statue of independence hero José Martí. Now he is officially a nonperson and unable to find a job. "How am I supposed to live?" he asks bitterly. He earns his keep by "inventing," selling his jeans for 200 pesos, which fetched 40 lbs. of rice that he resold at quadruple the price.

Raúl, 28, cadges meals from his mother when he is not selling goods a friend steals from a state factory. Although he speaks three languages, he cannot find work either, because his history of alcoholism is duly noted in his dossier.

With Ricardo and two others, Raúl is arranging to buy a motorized boat to sail to Miami, where a brother recently landed on a raft. The youths have paid out half the 30,000-peso price, but have no idea how they'll get the rest. "I want to be free!" shouts Raúl. "I want to go to a hotel for a vacation. I want to take a car and drive into the countryside. We are Negroes in our own country; we are slaves." His voice rises close to hysteria as waiters in the restaurant pretend not to hear. "I won't stay here! I hate this country."

We leave not knowing whether Cuba can safely make the journey back from a failed communist state, but the country is already on that road, like it or not. "People say we are a dinosaur," says Juan Antonio Blanco. "But look at the map. Cuba is shaped like a crocodile. And like the crocodile, the Cubans have learned to adapt. That's why we're still around."

Article 24　　　　　　　　　　　　　　　　　　　　　*Vanity Fair*, February 1994

A Place Called Fear

Haiti continues to be the thorniest foreign-policy crisis of the Clinton administration. As exiled president Jean-Bertrand Aristide calls for tighter sanctions, his country is at the mercy of those who ousted him: the defiant Lieutenant General Raoul Cédras and the sinister chief of police, Lieutenant Colonel Michel François. In Port-au-Prince and in Washington, D.C., Bella Stumbo gained rare access to the men who are leading a dying country —perhaps into the grave.

He deposed Haiti's democratically elected president, drove the United Nations envoy out of the country, embarrassed the president of the United States, and thumbed his nose at an international embargo designed to beat him into submission. As such, Lieutenant General Raoul Cédras has become one of the world's ranking Bad Guys, right up there with Somalia's Mohammed Farah Aidid and Serbia's Slobodan Milošević. Now the Western world routinely calls him a murderer, assassin, dictator, Fascist, probable drug lord, liar, and, in some circles, even a clandestine C.I.A. puppet.

But in person Cédras is so mildly pleasant and tediously thoughtful that he's more reminiscent of a droning Haitian history teacher than democracy's newest demon, the military villain who overthrew President Jean-Bertrand Aristide in a bloody coup on September 30, 1991, pitching this tiny Caribbean nation into its darkest, most desperate days since the brutal Duvalier dictatorship. Now, more than two years later, Cédras controls Haiti while Aristide still sits in exile in Washington, D.C., demanding the General's resignation as a condition of his return.

Physically, Cédras is slender and gaunt-faced, a bland blur of beige from his khaki uniform to his complexion. Sitting at a long conference table in his military headquarters, just across from the gleaming, now vacant National Palace in downtown Port-au-Prince, he is flanked this November evening by a staff translator and his protocol officer, a wealthy, elegant matron in a designer dress who interrupts whenever she doesn't approve of the translator's French, which is often.

The presence of both is of course absurd, since Cédras speaks English well enough to laugh at jokes before they are translated. He even admits coyly that the tiresome four-way conversation "gives me more time to think, and besides, I can then blame the translator for any quotes I don't like." The General is equally coy about his age. Vain as any fading beauty queen, he first asks how old he appears, then dismisses the question entirely "because I just don't want to say." Not that it really matters, but the man who now defies the world is 44.

A servant enters, bearing coffee and tiny floral demitasse cups. The General takes two sugars. The matron pours. Lighting up a Benson & Hedges, the General jokes that it's "a crazy world" when he finds himself smoking a weaker brand than the women present (Winston).

It's a crazy world all right, not to say surreal—especially when you consider that the General needs only to open his office door to glimpse a U.S. warship idling on the distant horizon of his empty bay. "Oh," he says pleasantly, he's not worried about that. The Marines won't land. "If that was their solution, they would have done it a long time ago."

Cédras rarely gives personal interviews, but today he has a lot on his mind. He wants to set the record straight. First, he didn't seize power "just for the sake of power." He did it for the good of Haiti, and especially to protect the military. Although Aristide had handpicked Cédras as his commander in chief, the two clashed repeatedly over the president's attempts to purge the army brass. "Mr. Aristide's actions were unconstitutional and incorrect," says the General, who adds that Aristide even threatened him. "He warned me that the crowds could do to me what they had done to others."

Even so, Cédras would like some credit for saving Aristide's life. In the final, chaotic hours of the coup, two soldiers marched Aristide across the plaza from the palace to military headquarters. "One clearly planned to shoot him," recalls Cédras. "But I shouted down orders to stop, to bring him upstairs instead." Aristide was so frightened that, by later accounts, he wept, vomited, and lost control of his bowels. "He humiliated himself," says Cédras delicately. "Mr. Aristide was in an extremely difficult situation at that time, and I think it was very humiliating to him to be witnessed. . . . I think he can never forgive me for being present at that sad scene."

Only three days earlier, Cédras says, Aristide had precipitated the coup by delivering a speech that threatened violence, particularly against the vestiges of the fearsome Duvalier militia, the Tonton Macoutes. The rebellion "started from the soldiers at the bottom of the army," says Cédras, and spread like wildfire. As word reached Aristide supporters, a counterrebellion broke out. The square below Cédras's balcony at headquarters was soon "filled with growing crowds sharpening their machetes, carrying guns and gas cans and their famous Père Lebrun necklaces [rubber tires set ablaze around the necks of victims]. At that time they had also burned some soldiers at Cité Soleil. . . . I felt like a prisoner. The place was surrounded."

Cédras says he called Aristide at home and begged him to go on national radio to calm the crowds. "But he said no, that the people in the streets knew what they had to do." That, says Cédras, "was the breaking point. The military decided to go into the streets and bring order."

The General claims he also offered to send soldiers to Aristide's home to take him to the palace for greater security. Aristide refused—only to go there later in a death-defying drive with the French ambassador. "And 30 minutes later, Aristide was a prisoner . . . and I am thinking to myself, How long can I control the crowd pressure? And I made the decision that the safest way to save Aristide's life was to get him out of the country."

But instead of thanking Cédras, Aristide "has not spoken to me since." Not even at Governors Island in New York City, where the two finally signed an accord providing for Aristide's return to power on October 30, 1993, and Cédras's "early retirement."

The deal soon collapsed, partly over the terms of amnesty, but also because Aristide later decided that he wanted several other military leaders to resign as well. "I said I would resign," says Cédras, flashing anger for the first time, "*but nobody else*. I knew his ideas were quite fixed. But I thought that he would have the decency to respect what he had signed."

"Although [Aristide] came to power by elections, he thought he came to power by revolution."

Now that all bets are off, Raoul Cédras is at liberty to speak his mind. And he warms to the subject. He never thought the election of Aristide was truly democratic, but was marked instead "by enormous fraud," ranging from polls that never opened to uncounted ballots. What's more, he always despised Aristide's style. "There were only two presidents who could have changed the face of Haiti through their popularity, Aristide and François ["Papa Doc"] Duvalier. But Aristide lost his chance to bring everybody together. . . . Although he came to power by elections, he thought he came to power by revolution. He was violating the Constitution from his first day in office [by purging the military]."

Had Aristide remained in power, says Cédras, he would probably have eviscerated government institutions and "the end result would have probably been another Haitian regime, like Duvalier's, that lasted 30 years."

Cédras likes to compare himself to Boris Yeltsin. Both kicked out corruption—but while Yeltsin got international support, the General won only "the wrath of the whole world . . . Aristide is seen as the little priest who can do no wrong. It's so subjective." Even now, the General complains, the international community denies Haitians the right of choice. "Every time they say they are against Aristide, they are subject to sanctions by the Americans as friends of the military. Nobody can freely be against him."

Not that Raoul Cédras is any flaming democrat himself. He doesn't even bother to make the right rhetorical sounds anymore. He flatly states, for example, that he doesn't think Haiti, the poorest nation in the hemisphere, is ready for democracy yet. "Democracy is a process of evolution, education. It is not something that you can impose . . . and we cannot start at the end. Democracy is an organization of institutions, rules, and disciplinary measures which must be taken first."

In truth, the General thinks Haiti can function just fine without any elected government whatsoever. For example, when Prime Minister Marc Bazin resigned last June, "the country kept on functioning from then until September 3, with no president, no prime minister. This is indication enough that this isn't a political problem. We need some *order* in this country first, so that people can work and feed themselves. Then we can put together some institutions working toward democracy."

As for the multiple killings that have swept the island since the coup, Cédras is sanguine. Like any other country, he says, Haiti has its violence—but a lot of the deaths are due to "delinquency, poverty, and drug dealing. The difference is the media turns everything in Haiti into a political crime."

Nor does he seem much concerned by the embargo. The first one, imposed by President Bush after the coup, "had no adverse effects—the population was very indifferent." And the latest one? "It's just another day of the week," he says with a shrug.

One lasting effect of the embargo, however, is the resurrection of the right wing. "All the Duvalierists, who had to hide or be burned [during Aristide's reign]—now we see there is some comeback." Mildly, Cédras denounces "the extremists," although he adds in the next breath that he doesn't think Macoutes are any more extremist than members of Aristide's Lavalas movement. "Both are a state of mind, of intolerance." Nor can Duvalierists be expelled from Haitian society. The General now also supports FRAPH (Front for the Advancement and Progress of Haiti), the three-month-old, supposedly civilian political party which many see as just another form of Macoutism.

And what of new elections? Cédras actually looks startled. Elections? "What will that solve if there is no consensus? No, I don't foresee elections. No. No time soon."

It is but a short walk across the plaza from the pretty, white military headquarters with its pastel-yellow shutters, a converted two-story French mansion filled with men in khaki, to the ugly, low-slung police station, painted a dismal shade of brownish yellow, where everyone is clad in crisp police blue.

But the gulf may be far wider, judging from all the sleuths who skitter furtively back and forth between the two buildings, thriving for their own personal reasons on the subterfuge of impending coups and mindless gossip: Is George a Lavalas spy? Is John making a fortune on drugs? Some days, it's a comedy too bizarre to be believed.

Consider, for example, Lynn Garrison, the only white foreigner who hangs about military headquarters regularly. What he does precisely isn't certain, only that he is often inside the tiny, crowded antechamber of General Cédras. Garrison delights in the media attention devoted to him. Recently, *Time* magazine billed him as a major shadow figure in Cédras's inner councils.

Trim, silvery-haired, and Canadian, Garrison refuses to explain his presence in any meaningful terms. One day, grinning slyly, he says he is "just a scholar, writing a history of Haiti." The next day, he confides that it was he who helped found the new FRAPH party, who first raided Aristide's home after the coup (scavenging everything from his personal papers to the contents of his medicine chest). Sometimes, Garrison also adds vaguely that he is a "military consultant." He also says he has a Haitian-art gallery in Los Angeles.

There is dark humor here, too. After someone spots an off-duty Marine from the U.S. Embassy wearing a T-shirt that reads, WE'RE BACK AND WE'RE BAD! a Haitian army officer growls, " . . . them. We're gonna get one that says, WE'RE HERE AND WE'RE HOT!

"I'm so sick of this crap," he continues, "25 months of it! I just wanna put on my khakis and go kick ass and take names. Furthermore, I'm sick of all this talk about democracy. I don't *care* if 67 percent voted for Aristide. What about the other 33 percent? *We're* the producers of the country, and I'm not about to let them tell me a crazy man should run my country. I'm not a democrat, I'm a republican!"

"I've never heard him talk this way," apologizes his wife. Wives hang around headquarters a lot. "Just the other day I had to make him stop on the road to pick up a pregnant woman who couldn't get to the hospital. This embargo is making us all inhuman."

So here is Haiti today, a country dominated by a general who comes across as a genial wimp; his reception room is more like an informal coffee klatch than a political command center. Soldiers snore at their posts, buzzed by flies, or play dominoes, rifles at their feet. Wives and girlfriends in spike heels come and go, fanning their damp hairdos beneath the lazy ceiling fans and painting their faces, mirrored in framed pictures of generals 100 years dead.

So where is the heavy here? Every coup has one. Where lies the heart of this madness?

Across the plaza, at police barracks, is where. Lieutenant Colonel Joseph Michel François is his name, and although military, he is the de facto police chief of Port-au-Prince. Since the coup, he has become nearly as infamous abroad as Cédras himself, thanks largely to Aristide's demand that, along with Cédras, François also resign or, better yet, leave Haiti altogether.

Few Haitians blame Aristide for his insistence. To many, Cédras is just a basically mellow fellow incapable of ordering any serious violence without prompting from more passionate, dangerous forces—namely, Michel François. "They may buy Cédras off with a villa in France," says one military observer, "but François is not afraid to die. He's the real firepower, the mastermind of the coup."

Certainly, François is the most interesting, charismatic character in this little cast, unto Cédras as a leopard is to a tabby cat. At 36, François has constructed a careful mystique: seldom interviewed, almost never photographed, he is always on the streets with his men, forever wearing his signature summer helmet. By reputation, he is anything from the most murderous man in Haiti to the friendliest cop in town.

We first meet at a police party at the 22nd Division, now known to some terrified Haitians as the new Fort Dimanche, Papa Doc's prison of torture and terror, which was turned into a museum of mourning by Aristide during his first week in office. I get in thanks to Emmanuel Constant, one of the leaders of FRAPH. The room is dim, filled with men in civilian clothes, all staring at me suspiciously, all armed with Uzis, M16s, and semi-automatic handguns. Sitting in the corner is a very dark, round-faced Haitian in cheap polyester pants and a black T-shirt.

"That's Michel," Constant announces, proud as a hunter who has just bagged a white Siberian tiger. Impossible. Not this harmless-looking young man lounging casually against a wall with a plate of rice and pork.

I sit down and ask Michel François the obvious: How does it feel to be one of the world's ranking Bad Guys? He laughs, obviously enjoying the notoriety. Above the blare of the Creole music, the most I can learn is that he has only dropped by to say hello to his troops. He is no socializer. "I don't drink, EVER," he thunders, beaming radiantly, "because I have to have my wits about me AT ALL TIMES!"

And why does he dislike Aristide? His face changes. His brown eyes harden as he leans forward, his whole muscular body tensed. "Because," he hisses, "HE TRIED TO KILL ME."

With that, he has to go. As he rises, half a dozen personal bodyguards do too, clicking off their safety catches, and, within seconds, they have disappeared into the night.

The air conditioner is turned up so high that it's cold in his office. The fuel embargo obviously hasn't yet affected Michel François's personal comfort. The room is otherwise ordinary, unadorned and orderly—except for a dozen FRAPHers who also file in to await their turn with the police chief.

"No cameras!" he commands, his body bristling with energy, his eyes sparkling with something between defiance and amusement. "No tape recorders! Not now. For security!" Furthermore, he declares with a chortle, glancing at the dozen FRAPHers, "no smoking! I am NOT polite!" They all sit down obediently at a long mahogany conference table.

François, in a frisky mood, slaps on his trademark helmet—"I am François!"—and does a little jig around his desk, then, just as suddenly, takes it off and sits down on a long white corner couch. He is now ready to talk.

So how did Aristide try to kill him?

He loves the question. It happened, he says, after the day in August '91 when Parliament tried to cast a vote of no confidence against Aristide's prime minister, a former baker named René Préval. "At the time, Aristide doesn't even *know* me. But he had made arrangements to burn some of [the parliamentarians]. And I was responsible for the security, so," François says, smashing his palm into his hand, "I STOP IT."

From then on, he continues, Aristide hated him. The president ordered Cédras to transfer François, but Cédras refused. "Then," says François, whacking his knees, "he tried another way! He had the S.S.P. [Aristide's private security force], so they arranged a team to kill me. They wanted to roast me. But my soldiers were aware of that . . . and they provided me with security for my life."

Finally, in September 1991, before Aristide flew to New York to deliver a speech to the U.N., François says, the president gave orders "to kill me and General Cédras, because he didn't want to come back to Haiti and see us." But—François grins delightedly—he foiled them again. When the assassins came to his house, he was gone, thanks to tips from his men. "And," he finishes, again whacking his palm, "THAT WAS IT. THEY MISSED ME AGAIN!" Across the room, the table of FRAPHers sit bright-eyed with admiration.

But what about the possibility of U.S. intervention? Would the Marines miss him, too?

François actually giggles. He won't comment "because right now the whole world knows Michel François, and when you talk too much you may be weak, because they're going to see your position and know how to attack."

And what of all the violent deaths? Where was his police force?

He sobers, eyes darkening. Of course Port-au-Prince, with only 1,000 officers, cannot be protected as well as American cities. "We do not have the means.... But *still*," he explodes, "WE DO THE JOB!" Besides, "when you see people dying in the streets, they can be dead from starving, from a vehicle accident, and so on. Sometimes, the robbers—*zenglendu*—are responsible. But everyone now takes all this together to say it is repression, the police, FRAPH."

So, despite his president's demands, he doesn't intend to resign?

His big face moves close again, eyes gleaming, his voice husky, low, and full of menace. "Nooooooooo waaaaaaaaaaay—and I *mean* it, too."

Can Aristide ever return then?

François rises. The interview is over. Moving toward the table of FRAPHers, he glances over his shoulder and offers only a single, laughing line: "What do *you* guess?"

Nothing has ever been worse in Haiti, where conditions have always been horrible. How many ways can you say that people have always been starving 600 miles from U.S. shores, just as in Somalia? How to convey the fact that, thanks to the world embargo, conditions are now infinitely worse? How to describe the emaciated young mother living in the city cemetery—itself desecrated by desperate Haitians smashing crypts in search of gold teeth and watches—hopelessly trying to feed her half-dead baby from a breast as shriveled as a prune? How to express the futility of taking her to a hospital, where it costs 20 cents just to get in line, where a wearied nurse only shrugs and says, "She obviously has tuberculosis. The baby probably does too. Both of them will die."

How to convey the anguish of volunteer workers who can no longer find the fuel to run the generators that keep their patients alive, or even potable water to serve them as they lay dying? "Even worse, the people can't get to the hospital anymore because there is no gas for

transportation," says a French doctor. "Now they only get there in time to die." It's not uncommon to see an ambulance being pushed toward emergency wards by the loved ones of those within.

Feeding stations can no longer provide poor Haitians with their only solid meal of the day—a biscuit and a glass of milk—because bakers have no fuel. For the first time in my 15-year experience with Haiti, beggars now line up at the hotels to ask for food as often as money. One night a Dutch reporter, not a woman easily shaken, returned to her hotel paled because, she said, "I have just seen Haitians fighting with dogs over bones." She had been eating at a cheap patio café, and when she finished her chicken, a crowd of small children snatched the empty plate from a passing waiter. It dropped to the ground. Two starving dogs fell upon it, along with the children. "I will never again eat outside of this hotel," she said, nearly in tears.

And then there was my own old friend, a hardworking taxi driver. He has no work because he has no gas. He is also, at age 53, going blind. He has cataracts, and Haiti of course has nothing even remotely resembling a public-welfare program. "My life is done," he tells me without self-pity. "I will get a gun and shoot myself because I am too old to become a blind beggar."

Now bewildered Haitians can only wonder why they are denied the means to even get to their three-dollar-per-day factory jobs. And why is their exiled president calling upon the world to increase their suffering with tighter sanctions at the same time he makes toasts at the weddings of the Kennedys? Why must they survive on herbs and leaves when, they are told, he is dining on catered meals in Georgetown? Some are openly angry, others only confused. And from those willing to pay the price if it means Aristide's return, there is only frightened silence. Because now the military is in command. And, realistically, not even the poorest, most ignorant Haitian expects Aristide to come back to Haiti, short of a landing by the U.S. Marines.

Above all else, there is the unending, unfocused fear. Every night, sporadic gunfire can be heard throughout Port-au-Prince. Where it's coming from, nobody knows—FRAPHers, "attachés" (plainclothes police), the military, common criminals. Or, as some insist, from a handful of stray Lavalas—guerrillas loyal to Aristide—committing murders that will inevitably be ascribed to the military. "Whether it's a money changer or a drug dealer who gets shot in a deal gone bad, or a dog run over by a car, the army gets the blame," says one officer bitterly. "Well, I've got the solution. If we are all the murderous thugs, the immoral killers, the international press describes, then let the entire army resign tomorrow! Then the world will see what total anarchy is."

"I've never seen anything like it," says a prominent doctor, who, like nearly everyone else in Haiti, wants anonymity for fear of retribution. He works with an extensive network of hospitals, including one in Cité Soleil, Port-au-Prince's largest, most stunning slum, a place where people bathe in fetid sewers and where there are only three running water taps for a population of 180,000. It is also a hotbed of Lavalas sentiment, where dozens, if not hundreds, were shot in their hovels by plainclothes goons and soldiers in the days surrounding the coup. "Before, people only looked resigned. Now there's a panic in their eyes that I've never seen before, because they don't know where the attack is coming from. Every night, the people of Cité Soleil go to bed afraid they will be shot before dawn."

"We find on average at least one body a day. Who killed them and why, I don't know."

From the poorest to the richest, Haitians today, past masters of adaptation and survival, know better than ever just how cheap life is. By the most modest accounts, at least 3,000 have been killed since the '91 coup; one U.N. human-rights observer pushes the figure as high as 25,000, counting those who have died because of the nutritional and medical deprivations of the embargo. According to a human-rights worker in La Saline, another sprawling slum, "We find on an average at least one body a day. Who killed them and why, I don't know. But some have even been shot with their hands tied."

So now the streets of once teeming Port-au-Prince are deserted by nightfall, homes shuttered and blackened, residents hiding within. No transistor draws attention with Creole music; no candles flicker. The effect is eerie, reminiscent of a W.W. II movie of London during the blackouts. "My wife is going to be sick with worry," says a teacher, sitting on the terrace of the Hotel Oloffson at nine P.M., listening to sporadic gunfire nearby. "Here only fools are out at night."

Not all of the shooting is deadly, however. Some of it comes from the Haitian elite—glibly dubbed the MREs by the media (Morally Repugnant Elite), a group that has come to include almost everybody who lives in the hills above the worst squalor of Port-au-Prince. "A lot of it is *us* shooting into the air, to warn off attackers," says an MRE late at night, sitting on his pretty hillside terrace, gunfire crackling not far away as a security guard with an M16 patrols his compound. "It's a form of ballistic therapy. And it works. These guys only shoot defenseless people."

It's very important to get the facts straight," says U.S. ambassador William Swing, a nice man with a distinguished foreign-service career, mostly in Africa, who is now in the untenable position of defending the embargo. "The *military* is starving the Haitians," he insists—not the U.N. Certainly, the embargo will exacerbate common misery "in the short to medium term," but only sanctions will force the military and the elite "to understand that the country is not going anywhere without democracy." How many Haitians must die first? Swing evades the question.

In the hills above the city, at a luxury hotel, U.N. spokesman Eric Falt is more impassioned. In fact, Falt, a young man who last served in Cambodia, is outraged at the bleeding-heart press. Just this day *The New York Times* has reported a Harvard University study saying that as many as 1,000 children a month are dying because of the embargo. "You die from disease or a violent death," Falt snaps, "but you *don't* die from an embargo. That's ridiculous and irresponsible that scientists would say that!" And that the media would report it. But journalists "are avid beasts. They *want* starving children and blood." Besides, he adds, Haitians have always been poor. "How do you go from nothing to nothing? People who are dying would have died anyway!"

Meanwhile, he finishes, nobody respects the dangers faced by those trying to restore democracy to Haiti. This thing could turn into a siege, he says. pointing dramatically toward a closet crammed with stores of canned tuna and biscuits. "They could cut us off from the outside anytime, you know."

Only former prime minister Robert Malval, the wealthy mulatto businessman who ran the remnants of Haiti's government out of his heavily guarded suburban home for three months this fall, refuses to endorse the embargo, except in the mildest way. It is there to impress upon the military the seriousness of world intent to restore Aristide, he says quietly. A big, doleful-eyed man with a slight stutter, Malval looks miserable at his lot. Twice already he has tried to resign only to be talked out of it. (Not until December 15 did he officially quit, though even then he agreed to stay on as caretaker.) After all, he says, the idea that Haiti has any government at all anymore is a joke. "This country is a functional anarchy. I think I'm the only man in the world who knows the burden of powerlessness.... I'm just here to avoid a constitutional vacuum, but I'm aware that I'm not running anything. They have the force with no power; I have the power with no force."

Nothing that has happened surprises Malval. He tried to talk Aristide out of running in the first place. "Because I knew the country wasn't ready for him," Malval says, "and Aristide wasn't ready for power. I told him to go to the Senate instead . . . that otherwise he would be overthrown after six months. I missed by a month."

Even now, Malval doesn't defend his boss. "It was by far the most democratic government we've had in 200 years," but "Aristide had no political program of his own . . . he ran by anti-bourgeoisie slogans alone. The approach was wrong. You can negotiate with the adversary . . . but using the microphone is wrong. And I told him to stop attacking the army as a whole . . . only 5 to 10 percent of them are involved in wrongdoings. Ninety percent just want a decent life; many are very professional. These guys are not in favor of human-rights violations—they don't go after the people."

Malval also thinks Aristide is wrong to single out François for removal. "François is right. He is a military commander, not the police chief . . . and the agreement calls only for a new police chief." Nor does he think François is the heavy behind the coup. "He has the firepower but not the brainpower," says Malval. As for Cédras, he only laughs. "He's just the front man for the others."

It is perhaps just another measure of the chaotic state of Haiti that the prime minister himself wonders if, in fact, the elusive army chief of staff named Philippe Biamby "is really the strongman behind the coup."

Haiti has always been a throwaway nation, ever since its uppity slaves rebelled against the mighty Napoleon Bonaparte some 200 years ago to become the world's first independent black republic—only to be punished by a world trade embargo for the next 70 years. Then, in 1915, fearing the Germans might try to establish a Caribbean beachhead during World War I, the U.S. invaded and remained for the next 19 years. It was a racist, Jim Crow occupation that no elderly Haitian has forgotten. "Dear me, just *think* of it—niggers speaking French!" William Jennings Bryan once remarked, summing up the times.

Nearly six more decades of benign neglect followed, including 30 murderous years under "Papa Doc" and his son, Jean-Claude ("Baby Doc") Duvalier, before Haiti commanded world attention again.

Lavalas. In 1990, it meant hope—"the flood" or "the avalanche" in Creole. It was the grassroots movement that swept Jean-Bertrand Aristide into power in the closest thing to a truly direct, democratic election Haiti has ever had. He won by a landslide—67 percent of the vote, most cast by slum-dwelling illiterates who knew only that marking their X by the symbol of the brilliantly feathered fighting cock meant a vote for Father Aristide,

or Titid, as they called him. Little Aristide. The fiery, radical priest with the chipped front tooth and drooping left eyelid who had spent years denouncing the American capitalists, the Haitian elite, and the military alike for two centuries of repression; Titid, the former Salesian priest who escaped at least three assassination attempts and so challenged the Vatican itself with his liberation theology that he was finally expelled from his order. Titid. He was one of them, a son of the slums. Like François Duvalier, he appealed to the poorest, blackest Haitians. Now Titid promised true justice at last.

From his first day in office, he started to raise revenues and reduce the deficit. But he also began a humiliating public purge of the military leadership that antagonized the most influential segments of Haitian society: not only the army but also the handful of millionaires, whom he denounced for not sharing their wealth, as well as the small middle class of veteran civil-service employees, fired wholesale in an impatient bid to cleanse the bureaucracy of corruption.

Not least, Aristide frightened even some of his supporters with what seemed to be veiled references to Père Lebrun, the burning-tire trick Haitian mobs apparently learned from South Africans. In a rampage, following a 1991 coup attempt, dozens of Macoutes were incinerated, some of them eaten as well. And Aristide did nothing to control them. To the contrary, he often hinted that he would again unleash "the power of the people" to ensure "justice" against his enemies. One form of mob justice simply replaced another.

On September 27, 1991, Aristide delivered his most incendiary speech. "If you catch a thief," he said, "if you catch a sticky-fingered slob, if you catch a false Lavalas, if you catch one who does not deserve to be there, don't hesitate to give him what he deserves. . . . Your tool is in hand, your instrument in hand. . . . What a beautiful tool. What a beautiful instrument. . . . It's beautiful, yes, it's beautiful. It's pretty. It's elegant. . . . It has a good smell. Wherever you go, you want to inhale it. Since the law of the country says Macoute isn't in the game, whatever happens to him he deserves—he came looking for trouble."

Aristide's defenders later insisted he was referring only to the Constitution. Nevertheless, a few soldiers were necklaced, along with former presidential candidate Sylvio Claude. On September 29, a failed Macoute coup leader, Roger Lafontant, was shot in his jail cell—on direct orders of Aristide, according to Lafontant's widow (a charge Aristide denies). Hours later, Aristide was deposed—seven months into his five-year term.

Soon after, President Bush, with typical fire in the belly concerning foreign affairs, declared that the coup "could not stand" and imposed a partial embargo on oil and military supplies, which dragged on, ineffectively, for two years. In the meantime, during his presidential campaign, Bill Clinton vowed to reverse the cruel, blatantly racist U.S. policy of returning Haitian boat people to their country, where many face certain death (while at the same time accepting almost any Cuban who manages to make it to American shores). After his election, in a shameless turnabout, Clinton continued to either send back Haitian refugees or confine them in a semi-concentration camp at Guantánamo Bay, Cuba. Suddenly they presented "a national-security problem."

But Clinton couldn't escape the nagging problem of Aristide, who now lives right under his nose, in tony Georgetown, and whose high-priced lobbyists include attorney Michael Barnes, a well-connected former Maryland congressman who charges $55,000 a month—not to mention a vocal group of Congressional Black Caucus members. Republican opposition to Aristide and American involvement in Haiti was equally vociferous. Following a C.I.A. briefing, Senator Jesse Helms called Aristide "a psychopath," "a demonstrable killer," a lithium-soaked manic-depressive, and worse. Although Aristide hotly denied ever being treated or medicated for any mental disorder, other Republican leaders insisted that, regardless, Haiti wasn't worth one American life.

Caught in the middle, Clinton settled for tighter sanctions, which led to the July 3 Governors Island Accord, providing for Aristide's return to power on October 30. But about the only major provision of the accord that was honored was Aristide's selection of a new prime minister, Robert Malval.

Who is at fault for the breakdown of the agreement will remain a matter of debate for decades to come. Chief among the deal breakers was the ambiguous language granting amnesty to the coup leaders. Aristide issued an amnesty decree, but Cédras insisted on a law, which could not be undone by Aristide once he was back in the palace.

Then came the matter of separating Haiti's historically intertwined army and police. Enter Lieutenant Colonel Michel François, who functions as the police chief although he is actually a military officer. Aristide later insisted that François must also go, even though his name is not mentioned in the accord. François's reply was blunt: he is a career military officer whose resignation should be subject to the rules of the army.

In the most dramatic evidence that the Governors Island agreement was going nowhere, the Haitian military refused to provide protection for a transition team aboard the U.S.S. *Harlan County* when it tried to dock in Port-au-Prince. The military claimed that the crew was in violation of the accord because it arrived with automatic weapons. Diplomats should never forget Haitian sensitivity, even after 60 years, to anything smacking of occupation.

As the pact crumbled, terror set in. On September 11, Aristide's close friend millionaire businessman Antoine Izmery was taken from a church by armed men and shot in the head. A month later, Justice Minister Guy Malary was gunned down in broad daylight on a city street. The military denied responsibility despite eyewitnesses who claimed they saw plainclothes police watching idly nearby.

So October 30 came and went with no Aristide. In a final touch, while Haiti swarmed with international press anticipating high drama—perhaps even a U.S. invasion—Cédras defiantly boycotted a meeting called by U.N. special envoy Dante Caputo, explaining in a letter that he was displeased, among other reasons, with the insulting security arrangements, which included no Haitian personnel. Again, Haitian pride should never be forgotten.

TV cameras happily filmed the large foursquare table, lined on three sides with dark-suited ambassadors and legislators—with one long row of empty chairs on the fourth side. The next day, Caputo left Haiti for consultations in New York and has yet to return. Haiti had truly become the Mouse That Roared.

The U.N. reimposed oil sanctions, and, in a show of added force, warships were dispatched to inspect all Haitian-bound cargo vessels. Some days, from the highest balconies in Pétionville, you can see the U.S.S. *Gettysburg*, armed with cruise missiles, lolling in the empty bay. "Jesus Christ, talk about overkill," says one Haitian. "It's like shooting an ant with a .357 magnum. If the U.S. wants these guys out, then why don't they *get them out?* It would take the Marines about three hours."

"I *still* can't believe we succeeded," marvels FRAPH leader Emmanuel Constant as he sits in his middle-class home, stroking his little white terrier. He's describing the day when, in a televised spectacle to shame Americans from Manhattan to Topeka, a group of maybe 100 pistol-wielding FRAPHers and attachés ran the mighty U.S.S. *Harlan County* out of Haiti's port, mainly by kicking a few cars, waving a couple of guinea hens, and scattering baking soda all about in a voodoo ritual.

"We were all so scared," Constant remembers. "My people kept wanting to run away. But I took the gamble and urged them to stay. Then the Americans pulled out! We were astonished. That was the day FRAPH was actually born. Before, everyone said we were crazy, suicidal, that we would all be burned if Aristide returned. But now," he finishes with a giggle, "we know he is *never* going to return."

Constant ("Toto" to his friends), the 37-year-old son of an army commander under Papa Doc, is now an avowed presidential candidate. Tall and skinny with bad teeth, Constant doesn't look especially presidential. But thanks to years of education and work in Canada and New York, he speaks perfect English, and is both quick-witted and personable. His initially raw, naïve political rap also improves by the day. Now Toto publicly weeps for the poor, threatens tax hikes on the Haitian elite, and, along with his standard suit and tie, has even begun to wear socks with his loafers at his mobbed press conferences, where he boasts that FRAPH already has at least 300,000 card-carrying members. All that remains is for him to abandon his tendency to show off his Uzi for photographers.

"I feel like somebody who just won the lottery," Toto says of his overnight change in status. Just last week, he boasts, he gave 84 interviews to the international press. Best of all, Aristide himself is playing into FRAPH's hands by calling for a stricter embargo. "Even after the coup, he was still very popular," says Constant gleefully. "But now he's destroying his own support! If he was smart, he would be begging the world to send rice to Haitians, not starve them."

The co-founder of FRAPH is Jodel Chamblain ("Jojo"), a small, cherub-faced former Tonton Macoute who says his pregnant wife was murdered and mutilated by a rampaging pro-Aristide mob in 1991. Chamblain speaks no English, but it's clear in this Mutt-and-Jeff duo where the guiding fury lies. If Toto is FRAPH's friendly, ambitious public face, Jojo is the searing fire at his backside.

Today we are setting out for a FRAPH rally in Gonaïves, two hours north of Port-au-Prince, in a four-car caravan armed with enough M16s and Uzis to give Rambo pause. A crowd of about 1,000 waits in the town square, dominated by a statue of the revolutionary-war hero Jean-Jacques Dessalines. Since FRAPH is a grassroots movement carefully aimed at the masses, its ceremonies always begin with voodoo rites, the primary religion of most Haitians. As the crowd cheers, Toto and Jojo solemnly smash a couple of bottles of Haitian rum across Dessalines's bronzed feet. "Rum is from the earth," Constant explains, looking transparently amused at his own rhetoric. "It is a voodoo ceremony to protect the people from harm. The spirits are everywhere—on the ground, in the air. You have to share *everything* with them."

Bodyguards now leap forward, looking as fierce as any of Papa Doc's Macoutes in their mirrored silver sunglasses, as the crowd swarms toward the vans, yearning to touch the Leaders, to hold on to something promising in a world where nothing seems real anymore. "FRAPH! FRAPH!" they chant as the bodyguards roam about, searching for some lone, crazy Lavalas kamikaze. But of course there is none, for Lavalas is vanished, its leaders either fled into exile or in hiding underground.

"*À bas* Caputo!" the crowd cries. Down with United Nations envoy Dante Caputo. "*À bas* U.N.! *À bas* Aris-tide! *À bas* Malval! *À bas* embargo!" Down with everything. Except FRAPH.

Haiti's affluent elite has of course always despised the ugly little black man who took over their country. "And then Aristide turned out to be primitive too," says one Haitian aristocrat. "We all know what can happen when the lower classes take power—I did so want us to have someone we could present—but, still, I thought, He's a priest. I expected decency. But we didn't know he was *insane*. With my own eyes, I saw his mob on television with their tires and gas, and some of them were waving bones—the tibias, the ribs—of those they had already burned. I was ashamed to be Haitian. And he did nothing to disapprove, to disperse them. And now that tacky little man has traded his cassock for tailored suits and—and excuse me for being vulgar—up there in Washington, where I believe he is—how do you say?—licking their behinds."

Some are even more savage. "Not only is Aristide imbalanced, but you do know that he was also involved in a secret voodoo sect?" asks one of the richest, best-educated men in Haiti today. He is serious too. In fact, his story gets even more fantastic. He claims that after the coup he visited Aristide's home, where he saw "a secret, circular room beneath for human sacrifices. So far, we *know* that he sacrificed at least seven children in one of his ceremonies." He even draws a map of the house.

Other wealthy Haitians are concerned less with Aristide's personal problems than with inconveniences caused by his ouster. "My God, the prices!" complains one. "These black marketeers are making a fortune! Just the other day, a large bag of dog food, which used to cost $7, was marked up to $57. And the price of chlorine pellets for my pool has gone up 10 times!"

"It's all just too depressing to bear," says one Haitian socialite after descending from her hillside home on a day FRAPH ordered a citywide strike. "It's like death down there. I was so depressed I went to my beach house for the weekend and looked at my herb garden and chatted with the peasants. But it didn't help. I've decided to go to Paris until it's over."

There are other, less self-absorbed voices in the mix. "It's a world gone mad," sighs Gérard Bissainthe, a retired university professor and longtime opponent of the Duvaliers who is now also a thoughtful leader of the anti-Aristide movement. "The embargo is genocide, it's completely immoral. It's like child abuse—it should be prohibited in a civilized world.

"I was never against Aristide," he says. "I was for social justice. I had only one problem with him—Père Lebrun, that's all. And he never had a social program. From the day he started, it was just an obsession with revenge. Frankly, I think he now hates Haitians. He thought they should all die for him after the coup, and now he wants to punish them. He has the same mentality as Jim Jones—everyone must go with him."

Then there are the democrats. "He may be a crazy little bastard," says a wealthy Haitian architect. "But he must return if Haiti is ever to start on the road to democracy. And we must open the new government up to them all—even the Macoutes in their bandannas and shades. Only a fool would keep out the Duvalierists. My God, half the people in this country worked for them."

And, finally, the Americans living in Haiti. "I'm going broke," moans Tony Shindler, owner of a beach club, "and I've never seen conditions here so bad in 35 years. If Jean-Claude ["Baby Doc" Duvalier] were here today he'd probably be re-elected. At least then there was stability and you knew where the threat was coming from."

Not surprisingly, none of the Haitian elite says much about the military beyond the fact that, as far as they can tell, Raoul Cédras is no killer. "If he were," chortles one industrialist, "we wouldn't have this mess. Aristide would be dead."

So where have Titid's people all gone? Despite their campaign to discredit him, and despite his own mistakes, neither the military nor FRAPH is stupid enough to believe that, in all the masses of sweaty, tired faces, Jean-Bertrand Aristide is dead. And, occasionally, some brave Haitian will say as much. "Aristide will *never* die," says Kareem Abdul Martin, a young Haitian Muslim. "Even if it takes 50 years! Even some FRAPH are Aristide. People wake up Aristide, they drink Aristide, they eat Aristide. Aristide is their hope, their future. Without him, they become nonexistent."

At the same time, Martin doesn't think Aristide will ever return. "But it doesn't matter. There will be another Aristide. *Inshallah.*"

But perhaps there is no better measure of Haitian sentiment than the music they choose—and for the last several weeks a song by a decidedly political, pro-democracy voodoo rock band called Ram, led by Richard Morse, the American proprietor of the Hotel Oloffson, has been No. 1 on independent radio stations throughout Haiti. Although the beautiful, haunting words lose much in translation from Creole to English, the lyrics say:

I'm a leaf, I'm sitting on my branch
A bad storm came and knocked me down
The day I fall is not the day I die
When they need me, where are they going to
    find me?
Oh my good Lord, oh Saint Nicholas, I only have
    one son
They made him leave the country and he
    went away.

For all he's been through—the many threats on his life, being marched out of Haiti at gunpoint, the two years of waiting, the vicious personal attacks, not to mention the frustrations of dealing with a world which increasingly seems only halfway committed to its pledges to him—Jean-Bertrand Aristide today is still far more relaxed than he was during his inaugural week in 1991. His English is better, he laughs more easily, and he doesn't waste so much time picking precise, statesman-like words.

"The embargo," says Aristide, "is just a weapon for Cédras and François."

Contrary to rumor, he does not live in a mansion. His one-bedroom home is instead in one of Washington, D.C.'s comfortable furnished apartment buildings, where the tenants are mainly transient politicians, journalists, and other visitors. Nor is he attended by an entourage of servants—only a few staff members, plus half a dozen Secret Service agents ensconced in an adjacent apartment. He chuckles good-naturedly at a joking remark that his navy suit looks more like J. C. Penney than the extravagant Armanis the Haitian military swears he wears.

But the anger and frustration are still there. The little priest has not yet lost all his fire—now directed at "the international community, which was supposed to be there, but is not. They promised the restoration of democracy 11 months ago. It is *time.*" He laughs sardonically. What a joke it all is. "Today they can make a difference by just doing what they say. They have to move faster, not slower!"

And, yes, he wants a tighter embargo. "I want it to be over. I don't want the poor to suffer anymore while the coup leaders are still killing and getting rich on drug traffic. A *real* embargo would not be the problem, it would be the *end* of it. We cannot continue to have this genocide while the world watches. So do it quickly! Because the current embargo is just a weapon for Cédras and François."

So, "we have to raise some ethical questions." But this he says without spirit. Ethical questions concerning Haiti have little or no weight in the world, especially in the United States, as Aristide well knows. Take the Clinton administration's policy of returning boat people. "It is so wrong," he says simply.

Equally wrong are those who say that he violated the Governors Island Accord. "We did *everything* we were supposed to do," he says heatedly. "Cédras and François are professional liars and murderers. According to [the agreement], I had to grant an amnesty, and I did. If Parliament wants a law, they can do it, but the coup leaders don't want Parliament to meet to satisfy that. They want to have a false issue so they can go on, in control."

But he refuses to give up hope, even though many of his supporters have. "I will go back! I *will* go back," he exclaims, grinning spontaneously. "I will *never* give up."

And to the poor, to the taxi drivers without gas, to those without food, what does he say?

"I tell them not to give up. I say just do what you can. Cry if you can cry. Get together if you can. . . . And never forget." Lavalas.

Credits

REGIONAL ARTICLES

Page 140 Article 1. © 1993 by The Economist, Ltd. Distributed by The New York Times/Special Features.

Page 147 Article 2. Reprinted with permission from *Foreign Policy* #92 (Fall 1993). © 1993 by the Carnegie Endowment for International Peace.

Page 153 Article 3. "Latin America Transformed: An Accounting," Albert Fishlow, *New Perspectives Quarterly,* Fall 1993, pp. 19–26.

Page 160 Article 4. "Privatization Is Not Democratization," Guillermo O'Donnell and Mario Vargas Llosa, *New Perspectives Quarterly,* Fall 1993, pp. 50–55.

MEXICO

Page 164 Article 5. Reprinted by permission of *Foreign Affairs,* September/October 1993. © 1993 by the Council on Foreign Relations, Inc.

Page 170 Article 6. © 1994 by The Economist, Ltd. Distributed by The New York Times/Special Features.

Page 173 Article 7. "A New Chapter in Mexican Politics?" Lorenzo Meyer, *Excélsior* (Mexico City). Reprinted with permission from *World Press Review,* January 1994.

Page 175 Article 8. Reprinted with permission from *Current History* magazine, February 1993. © 1993 by Current History, Inc.

CENTRAL AMERICA

Page 180 Article 9. © 1993 by the *Washington Post.* Reprinted with permission.

Page 183 Article 10. © 1994 by the Society for the Advancement of Education.

Page 187 Article 11. "Central America's Latest War," Yazmím Ross, *Pensamiento Propio* (Managaua). Reprinted with permission from *World Press Review,* May 1993.

Page 189 Article 12. © 1993 by the *Washington Post.* Reprinted with permission.

Page 193 Article 13. ©1993 by The Economist, Ltd. Distributed by The New York Times/Special Features.

Page 195 Article 14. © 1994 by the Society for the Advancement of Education.

Page 196 Article 15. Courtesy of *The UNESCO Courier.*

SOUTH AMERICA

Page 199 Article 16. By Manuel Long from *Latinamerica Press.*

Page 200 Article 17. From *Parade* magazine, April 12, 1992. © 1992 by Hank Whittemore.

Page 204 Article 18. Reprinted by permission of *Forbes* magazine. © 1993 by Forbes, Inc.

Page 207 Article 19. Reprinted from *Américas,* a bimonthly magazine published by the General Secretariat of the Organization of American States in English and Spanish.

Page 210 Article 20. Reprinted by permission from the *Christian Science Monitor.* © 1993 by The Christian Science Publishing Society. All rights reserved.

Page 212 Article 21. "Kicking the Habit," Steve Xydas, *Harvard International Review,* Summer 1993.

THE CARIBBEAN

Page 215 Article 22. Reprinted with permission from *Current History* magazine, March 1991. © 1991 by Current History, Inc.

Page 220 Article 23. © 1993 by The Time Magazine Company. Reprinted by permission.

Page 224 Article 24. From *Vanity Fair,* February 1994. © 1994 by Bella Stumbo.

Sources for Statistical Reports

U.S. State Department, *Background Notes* (1990–1993).

The World Factbook (1993).

World Statistics in Brief (1993).

World Almanac (1994).

The Statesman's Yearbook (1993–1994).

Demographic Yearbook (1992).

Statistical Yearbook (1993).

World Bank, World Development Report (1993).

Ayers Directory of Publications (1993).

Glossary of Terms and Abbreviations

Agrarian   Relating to the land; the cultivation and ownership of land.

Amerindian   The general term for any Indian from America.

Andean Pact (Cartagena Agreement)   Established on October 16, 1969, to end trade barriers among member nations and to create a common market. Members: Bolivia, Colombia, Ecuador, Peru, and Venezuela.

Antilles   A geographical region in the Caribbean made up of the Greater Antilles: Cuba, Hispaniola (Haiti and the Dominican Republic), Jamaica, the Cayman Islands, Puerto Rico, and the Virgin Islands; and the Lesser Antilles: Antigua and Barbuda, Dominica, St. Lucia, St. Vincent and the Grenadines, St. Kitts-Nevis, as well as various French departments and Dutch territories.

Araucanians   An Indian people of south-central Chile and adjacent areas of Argentina.

Arawak   An Indian people originally found on certain Caribbean islands, who now live chiefly along the coast of Guyana. Also, their language.

Aymara   An Indian people and language of Bolivia and Peru.

Bicameral   A government made up of two legislative branches.

Bipolar World   The division of the world into two opposite parts. The term has come to mean the political division of democracy (the West) and communism (Russia, Eurasian Republics, and the East).

CACM (Central American Common Market)   Established on June 3, 1961, to form a common market in Central America. Members: Costa Rica, El Salvador, Guatemala, and Nicaragua.

Campesino   A Spanish word meaning "peasant."

Caudillo   Literally, "a man on horseback." A term that has come to mean "leader."

Carib   An Indian people and their language native to several islands in the Caribbean and some countries in Central America and South America.

CARICOM (Caribbean Community and Common Market)   Established on August 1, 1973, to coordinate economic and foreign policies.

CDB (Caribbean Development Bank)   Established on October 18, 1969, to promote economic growth and development of member countries in the Caribbean.

The Commonwealth   (Originally the British Commonwealth of Nations) An association of nations and dependencies loosely joined by the common tie of having been part of the British Empire.

Compadrazgo   The Mexican word meaning "cogodparenthood" or "sponsorship."

Compadres   Literally, "friends"; but in Mexico, the term includes neighbors, relatives, fellow migrants, coworkers, or employers.

Contadora Process   A Latin American intiative developed by Venezuela, Colombia, Panama, and Mexico to search for a negotiated solution that would secure borders and reduce the foreign military presence in Central America.

Contras   A guerrilla army opposed to the Sandinista government of Nicaragua. They were armed and supplied by the United States.

Costeños   Coast dwellers in Central America.

Creole   The term has several meanings: a native-born person of European descent or a person of mixed French and black or Spanish and black descent speaking a dialect of French or Spanish.

ECCA (Eastern Caribbean Currency Authority)   A regional organization that monitors the integrity of the monetary unit for the area and sets policies for revaluation and devaluation.

ECLA (Economic Commission for Latin America)   Established on February 28, 1948, to develop and strengthen economic relations among Latin American countries.

FAO (Food and Agricultural Organization of the United Nations)   Established on October 16, 1945, to oversee good nutrition and agricultural development.

FSLN (Frente Sandinista de Liberación Nacionál)   Organized in the early 1960s with the object of ousting the Somoza family from its control of Nicaragua. After 1979 it assumed control of the government. The election of Violeta Chamorro in 1990 marked the end of the FSLN.

Fuegians   An Indian people of the most southern area of Argentina (Tierra del Fuego).

GATT (General Agreement on Tariffs and Trade)   Established on January 1, 1948, to provide international trade and tariff standards.

GDP (Gross Domestic Product)   The value of production attributable to the factors of production in a given country, regardless of their ownership. GDP equals GNP minus the product of a country's residents originating in the rest of the world.

GNP (Gross National Product)   The sum of the values of all goods and services produced by a country's residents in any given year.

Group of 77   Established in 1964 by 77 developing countries. It functions as a caucus on economic matters for the developing countries.

Guerrilla   Any member of a small force of "irregular" soldiers. Generally, guerrilla forces are made up of volunteers who make surprise raids against the incumbent military or political force.

IADB (Inter-American Defense Board)   Established in 1942 at Rio de Janeiro to coordinate the efforts of all American countries in World War II. It is now an advisory defense committee on problems of military cooperation for the OAS.

IADB (Inter-American Development Bank) Established in 1959 to help accelerate economic and social development in Latin America.

IBA (International Bauxite Association) Established in 1974 to promote orderly and rational development of the bauxite industry. Membership is worldwide, with a number of Latin American members.

IBRD (International Bank for Reconstruction and Development) Established on December 27, 1945, to make loans to governments at conventional rates of interest for high-priority productive projects. There are many Latin American members.

ICAO (International Civil Aviation Organization) Established on December 7, 1944, to develop techniques of international air navigation and to ensure safe and orderly growth of international civil aviation. Membership is worldwide, with many Latin American members.

ICO (International Coffee Organization) Established in August 1963 to maintain cooperation between coffee producers and to control the world market prices. Membership is worldwide, with a number of Latin American members.

IDA (International Development Association) Established on September 24, 1960, to promote better and more flexible financing arrangements; it supplements the World Bank's activities.

ILO (International Labor Organization) Established on April 11, 1919, to improve labor conditions and living standards through international action.

IMCO (Inter-Governmental Maritime Consultative Organization) Established in 1948 to provide cooperation among governments on technical matters of international merchant shipping as well as to set safety standards. Membership is worldwide, with more than a dozen Latin American members.

IMF (International Monetary Fund) Established on December 27, 1945 to promote international monetary cooperation.

IPU (Inter-Parliamentary Union) Established on June 30, 1889, as a forum for personal contacts between members of the world parliamentary governments. Membership is worldwide, with the following Latin American members: Argentina, Brazil, Colombia, Costa Rica, Haiti, Mexico, Nicaragua, Paraguay, and Venezuela.

ISO (International Sugar Organization) Establishedon January 1, 1969, to administer the international sugar agreement and to compile data on the industry. Membership is worldwide, with the following Latin American members: Argentina, Brazil, Colombia, Cuba, Ecuador, Mexico, Uruguay, and Venezuela.

ITU (International Telecommunications Union) Established on May 17, 1895, to develop international regulations for telegraph, telephone, and radio services.

Junta A Spanish word meaning "assembly" or "council"; the legislative body of a country.

Ladino A Westernized Spanish-speaking Latin American, often of mixed Spanish and Indian blood.

LAFTA (Latin American Free Trade Association) Established on June 2, 1961, with headquarters in Montevideo, Uruguay.

Machismo The male sense of honor; connotes the showy power of a "knight in shining armor."

Marianismo The feminine counterpart of machismo; the sense of strength that comes from controlling the family and the male.

Mennonite A strict Protestant denomination that derived from a sixteenth-century religious movement.

Mestizo The offspring of a Spaniard or Portuguese and an American Indian.

Mulatto A person of mixed Caucasian and black ancestry.

Nahuatl The language of an Amerindian people of southern Mexico and Central America who are descended from the Aztec.

NAM (Non-Aligned Movement) A group of nations that chose not to be politically or militarily associated with either the West or the former Communist Bloc.

OAS (Organization of American States) (Formerly the Pan American Union) Established on December 31, 1951, with headquarters in Washington, DC.

ODECA (Central American Defense Organization) Established on October 14, 1951, to strengthen bonds among the Central American countries and to promote their economic, social, and cultural development through cooperation. Members: Costa Rica, El Salvador, Guatemala, Honduras, and Nicaragua.

OECS (Organization of Eastern Caribbean States) A Caribbean organization established on June 18, 1981, and headquartered in Castries, St. Lucia.

PAHO (Pan American Health Organization) Established in 1902 to promote and coordinate Western Hemisphere efforts to combat disease. All Latin American countries are members.

Patois A dialect other than the standard or literary dialect, such as some of the languages used in the Caribbean that are offshoots of French.

Peon Historically, a person forced to work off a debt or to perform penal servitude. It has come to mean a member of the working class.

PRI (Institutional Revolutionary Party) The dominant political party in Mexico.

Quechua The language of the Inca. It is still widely spoken in Peru.

Rastafarian   A religious sect in the West Indies whose members believe in the deity of Haile Selassie, the deposed emperor of Ethiopia who died in 1975.

Rio Pact (Inter-American Treaty of Reciprocal Assistance)   Established in 1947 at the Rio Conference to set up a policy of joint defense of Western Hemisphere countries. In case of aggression against any American state, all member countries will come to its aid.

Sandinistas   The popular name for the government of Nicaragua from 1979 to 1990, following the ouster of President Anastasio Somoza. The name derives from César Augusto Sandino, a Nicaraguan guerrilla fighter of the 1920s.

SELA (Latin American Economic System)   Established on October 18, 1975, as an economic forum for all Latin American countries.

Suffrage   The right to vote in political matters.

UN (United Nations)   Established on June 26, 1945, through official approval of the charter by delegates of 50 nations at an international conference in San Francisco. The charter went into effect on October 24, 1945.

UNESCO (United Nations Educational, Scientific, and Cultural Organization)   Established on November 4, 1946, to promote international collaboration in education, science, and culture.

Unicameral   A political structure with a single legislative branch.

UPU (Universal Postal Union)   Established on July 1, 1875, to promote cooperation in international postal services.

World Bank   A closely integrated group of international institutions providing financial and technical assistance to developing countries.

Bibliography

GENERAL WORKS

Mark A. Burkholder and Lyman L. Johnson, *Colonial Latin America,* 2nd ed. (New York: Oxford University Press, 1994).

E. Bradford Burns, *Latin America: A Concise Interpretive History*, 6th ed. (New Brunswick: Prentice-Hall, 1994).

David Bushnell and Neill Macaulay, *The Emergence of Latin America in the Nineteenth Century,* 2nd ed. (New York: Oxford University Press, 1994).

Thomas E. Skidmore and Peter Smith, *Modern Latin America*, 3rd ed. (New York: Oxford University Press, 1992).

Claudio Veliz, *The Centralist Tradition of Latin America* (Princeton: Princeton University Press, 1980).

NATIONAL HISTORIES

The following studies provide keen insights into the particular characteristics of individual Latin American nations.

Argentina

Leslie Bethell, *Argentina Since Independence* (New York: Cambridge University Press, 1994).

Nicholas Shumway, *The Invention of Argentina* (Berkeley: University of California Press, 1991).

Bolivia

Herbert S. Klein, *Bolivia: The Evolution of a Multi-Ethnic Society,* 2nd ed. (New York: Oxford University Press, 1992).

Brazil

E. Bradford Burns, *A History of Brazil,* 3rd ed. (New York: Columbia University Press, 1993).

Caribbean Nations

Franklin W. Knight, *The Caribbean: The Genesis of a Fragmented Nationalism*, 2nd ed. (New York: Oxford University Press, 1990).

David Lowenthal, *West Indian Societies* (New York: Oxford University Press, 1972).

Louis A. Perez, Jr., *Cuba: Between Reform and Revolution* (New York: Oxford University Press, 1988).

Central America

Ralph Lee Woodward, Jr., *Central America: A Nation Divided*, 2nd ed. (New York: Oxford University Press, 1985).

Chile

Brian Loveman, *Chile: The Legacy of Hispanic Capitalism,* 2nd ed. (New York: Oxford University Press, 1988).

Mexico

Michael C. Meyer and William L. Sherman, *The Course of Mexican History*, 4th ed. (New York: Oxford University Press, 1991).

Eric Wolf, *Sons of the Shaking Earth: The Peoples of Mexico and Guatemala; Their Land, History, and Culture* (Chicago: University of Chicago Press, 1970).

Ricardo Pozas Arciniega, *Juan Chamula: An Ethnolographical Recreation of the Life of a Mexican Indian* (Berkeley: University of California Press, 1962).

Peru

Henry F. Dobyns and Paul L. Doughty, *Peru: A Cultural History* (New York: Oxford University Press, 1976).

José Carlos Mariategui, *Seven Interpretive Essays on Peruvian Reality* (Austin: University of Texas Press, 1974).

Venezuela

John V. Lombardi, *Venezuela: The Search for Order, The Dream of Progress* (New York: Oxford University Press, 1982).

NOVELS IN TRANSLATION

The Latin American novel is perhaps one of the best windows on the cultures of Latin America. The following are just a few of many highly recommended novels.

Jorge Amado, *Clove and Cinnamon* (New York: Avon, 1988).

Manlio Argueta, *One Day of Life* (New York: Vintage, 1990).

Miguel Ángel Asturias, *El Señor Presidenté* (Macmillan, 1975).

Mariano Azuela, *The Underdogs* (Buccaneer Books, 1986).

Alejo Carpentier, *Reasons of State* (Writers & Readers, 1981).

Carlos Fuentes, *The Death of Artemio Cruz* (FS&G, 1964).

Jorge Icaza, *Huasipungo: The Villagers* (Arcturus Books, 1973).

Gabriel García Márquez, *One Hundred Years of Solitude* (Penguin, 1971).

Mario Vargas Llosa, *The Green House* (FS&G, 1985).

Victor Montejo, *Testimony: Death of a Guatemalan Village* (Willimantic: Curbstone Press, 1987).

Rachel de Queiroz, *The Three Marias* (Austin: University of Texas Press, 1991).

Graham Greene's novels about Latin America, such as *The Comedians* (New York: 1966), and V. S. Naipaul's study of Trinidad, *The Loss of El Dorado: A History* (New York: 1969), also offer profound insights into Latin America and the Caribbean.

CURRENT EVENTS

To keep up to date on the unfolding drama of Latin American events, the following are especially useful.

Current History: A World Affairs Journal
The Latin American issue usually appears in February.

Latin America Press (Lima)
A newsletter (48 issues per year) that focuses on human rights and the role of the Catholic Church in Latin America. Also available in Spanish as *Noticias Aliadas*.

Latin America Weekly Report (London)
An excellent weekly review of economic and political developments in Latin America.

Latin American and Caribbean Contemporary Record (annual)
Includes essays on current issues, country reviews, documents, and economic, social, and political data. The most recent volume (VI) covers 1986–1987.

Latin American Regional Report (London)
The Regional Reports are published monthly on Brazil, Mexico and Central America, the Caribbean, the Andean Group, and the Southern Cone.

Times of the Americas (Washington, D.C.)
Competent coverage of politics, culture, and current events.

Update Latin America
This bimonthly news analysis, published by the Washington Office on Latin America, pays particular attention to human rights problems in Latin America.

PERIODICALS

Americas
Organization of American States
17 and Constitution Avenues, NW, Washington, D.C. 20006
This periodical by the OAS is published 10 times per year in English, Spanish, and Portuguese.

The Christian Science Monitor
One Norway Street, Boston, MA 02115
This newspaper is published 5 days per week, with news coverage, articles, and specific features on world events.

Commonweal
Commonweal Publishing Co., Inc.
232 Madison Avenue, New York, NY 10016
This biweekly publication reviews literature, current events, religion, and the arts.

Dollars and Sense
Economics Affairs Bureau, Inc.
38 Union Square, Room 14, Somerville, MA 02143
Published monthly (except June and August), this magazine offers interpretations of current economic events from the perspective of social change.

The Economist
25 St. James's St., London, England
This periodical presents world events from a British perspective.

Multinational Monitor
Ralph Nader's Corporate Accountability Research Group
1346 Connecticut Avenue, NW, Washington, D.C. 20006
This monthly periodical offers editorials and articles on world events and current issues.

The Nation
Nation Enterprises/Nation Associates, Inc.
72 Fifth Avenue, New York, NY 10011
Published 47 times during the year, this magazine presents editorials and articles dealing with areas of public interest—with special attention given to American politics and foreign policy, social problems, and education. Also covers literature and the arts.

The New Republic
The New Republic, Inc.
1220 19th Street, NW, Suite 200, Washington, D.C. 20036
Weekly coverage of politics, literature, and world events.

The New York Times
The New York Times Co.
229 West 43rd Street, New York, NY 10036
A daily newspaper that covers world news through articles and editorials. ,

Science News
Science Service
1719 N Street, NW, Washington, D.C. 20036
For those interested in science, this weekly publication gives an overview of worldwide scientific developments.

UNESCO Courier
7 Place de Fontenoy, Paris, France
Published by the UN, the magazine presents extensive treatment of world events by devoting each monthly issue to a specific topic.

The Wall Street Journal
Dow Jones Books
Box 300, Princeton, NJ 08540
Presents broad daily coverage of world news through articles and editorials.

World Press Review
The Stanley Foundation
230 Park Avenue, New York, NY 10169
Each month this publication presents foreign magazine and newspaper stories on political, social, and economic affairs.

Index